C000091762

WHAT THE REVIEWERS HAVE SAID ...

'Naim Attallah is a good interviewer. He is curious about other people; he is modest enough to let them say their piece without feeling the need to put his oar in; he is obviously a good listener.'

Lynn Barber, *Independent on Sunday*

'Part of Attallah's skill as an interviewer is that nothing shocks him. He greets each damaging admission with cries of delight and encouragement.'

Auberon Waugh, *Sunday Telegraph*

'Men are curiously eager to talk about their childhoods ... Attallah is very conscious of that Englishman's fear of self-knowledge and the Englishman's hatred ... of laying himself open to embarrassment.'

Fiona MacCarthy, *Observer*

'Attallah's book ... reveals what hilarious rot most men talk about on the subject of the opposite sex ... When Attallah asks about feminism, many of his interviewees react to the very mention of the word by screeching and flapping like demented fruit-bats.'

Francis Wheen, *Spectator*

'The overall effect is rather like being at a gentleman's club as the port is passed around. Witty, indiscreet but sometimes incoherent.'

Polly Samson, *Daily Mail*

'The one thing that must sweeten the bitter pill of old age for the Great and the Good is the prospect of Naim Attallah coming to interview them. Who could ask for a more thoughtful recorder of a lifetime's achievement?'

Catholic Herald

'[Naim Attallah] is courteous, diffident and, above all, curious; he genuinely wants to listen rather than sit in judgement. Polite but not sycophantic, his gentle coaxing puts several prickly customers at their ease ... He is not shy of venturing into forbidden zones, but he does so with cat-like stealth.'

Times Literary Supplement

NO LONGER WITH US

Encounters with Naim Attallah

With an introduction by
Richard Ingrams

To
Maya
the lovely
Maya with much
love. xx
Nam
28-11-18

QUARTET BOOKS

First published in 2018 by Quartet Books Limited
A member of the Namara Group
27 Goodge Street, London, W1T 2LD

Copyright © Naim Attallah 2018

The moral right of the author has been asserted by him in accordance with the
Copyright, Designs and Patents Act, 1988

All rights reserved

The publishers wish to thank Silvy Pilkington for her epic
work in preparing these interviews for publication

No part of this publication may be reproduced, stored in a retrieval system, or
transmitted in any form or by any means, without the prior permission in writing of
the publisher, nor be otherwise circulated in any form of binding or cover other than
that in which it is published and without a similar condition including this condition
being imposed on the subsequent purchaser

Reasonable efforts have been made to find the copyright holders of third party
copyright material. An appropriate acknowledgement can be inserted by the
publisher in any subsequent printing or edition

A catalogue record for this book is available from the British Library

ISBN 9780704374560

Typeset by Tetragon, London
Printed and bound in Great Britain by
TJ International Ltd, Padstow, Cornwall

To my beloved granddaughter Maria,
whose charm is limitless

Contents

APPENDIX

Introduction

'YOU WILL HAVE TO DEAL WITH THE CULTURAL ISOLATION OF THE OLD,' Bill Deedes, the legendary editor of the *Daily Telegraph*, advised me when we launched *The Oldie* in 1992. It was appropriate that Bill was Naim Attallah's first interviewee in the long series which played such an important role in establishing the magazine as a permanent fixture.

I remember very well lunching with Naim along with Alexander Chancellor and Stephen Glover (one of the three founders of *The Independent*) in the hope of persuading him to finance the new magazine, which at that stage was only a nice idea.

It was during the discussion that I had the bright idea of suggesting to Naim that as well as backing *The Oldie* he could do interviews with famous oldies with my guarantee that they would be 'in depth', covering four or five pages.

I wasn't talking off the top of my head – two years previously Naim, fresh from the success of his best-selling book *Women*, had turned his attention to the male sex and I had been the first to volunteer to be interviewed, later persuading some of my friends, including Auberon Waugh and Willie Rushton, to follow suit (Willie was to do a memorable cover for the book, *Singular Encounters*, which followed).

It was an offer that Naim could not refuse and he agreed to back the venture, even providing me with an office in Poland Street and a beautiful assistant, Lucy Blackburn.

In order to survive, a new magazine has to be different from the other magazines, which tend to consist of the same sort of articles for the same sort of people. What made *The Oldie* a bit different were the number of cartoons (eventually about twenty-five per issue) and the high proportion of unsolicited material. Naim's interviews were an essential ingredient, as they were quite unlike the kind of interviews then in vogue, in which the interviewer was given equal prominence to the interviewee and encouraged to voice his or her views and probe for personal disclosures of intimate and hopefully sexual secrets.

The drawback of such an approach was to make the interviewee clam up or, if familiar with the interviewer's reputation, refuse to do the interview in the first place. Naim was well aware of the risks. His questions ranged over a wide field and almost always embraced the two areas that tend to be most revealing – parentage and religion, a topic generally considered irrelevant. This is not to say that his questions were bland and Naim had his fair share of set-to's, as when he told Prince William's godfather Sir Laurens van der Post that some people regarded him as a charlatan – a judgement since upheld by his biographer J. D. F. Jones.*

The republication of forty-nine of Naim's interviews will preserve the memory of a group of remarkable individuals and prove to be an invaluable assistance to the historians of our troubled times.

For myself, I will always be grateful to him for backing a project which gave me over twenty years of employment and an enormous amount of entertainment.

RICHARD INGRAMS

* *Storyteller* (John Murray, 2002)

SIR HAROLD ACTON

Harold Acton was born in 1904 and educated at Eton and Christ Church, Oxford. He enjoyed a long friendship with Evelyn Waugh and was a fond admirer of Edith Sitwell and Gertrude Stein. He spent seven years in Peking, where he lectured in English at the University of Peking and became a devotee of Chinese classical theatre. He served in the RAF during the Second World War, chiefly in the Far East, where he worked in Intelligence. He was a prolific author, writing some twenty-eight books, believing his best to be history books, in particular *The Bourbons of Naples* (1956). He was awarded the CBE in 1965 and knighted in 1974. He lived for many years in La Pietra, a magnificent Renaissance villa in Tuscany, which he left to New York University to become a cultural centre, after his death in 1994.

On the subject of beauty, you have written that those who philosophise most loudly and persistently about it seldom have intrinsic taste. Is beauty purely subjective?

I fear it is. In my case I've been privileged: born in Florence and surrounded by beautiful things with a father who was a painter and collector and whose friends were art historians, art critics. I think of Offner, whose centenary will be celebrated very soon, and Berenson, and Herbert Horne, who bequeathed his collection to Florence – his place is now a museum – and Stibbert, another Englishman who lived not far from where I do. All these men were collectors and I imbibed something of that atmosphere when I was young. There were many beautiful villas, all full of treasures.

The British community was then predominant, though it's been ebbing now for some time, ever since just before the last war. People gave up their houses and went back to live in England. I suppose that really they were scared away by fascism. Life was made very unpleasant for them by the young blackshirts, you know, so they started to retreat, to leave their lovely houses in the Italian countryside. One or two, like Lord Lambton, have in more recent times bought properties here in beautiful situations near Siena, Signa, Pistoia, all around here. In fact, some parts of Tuscany are today quite Anglicised, you might say. Young English historians and art critics like John Fleming and Hugh Honour live near Lucca and write well on Italian painting, and those are the few who remain. Formerly every other Englishman here was an art historian or collector or painter. It was like a kitchen of the arts.

You have said that your most valued experiences have been aesthetic. Could you elaborate?

A single visit to Florence can answer that question, though Florence is suffering from new horrors. There is an appalling lack of architectural taste today. It's rather sad, this degradation of architecture in Italy which I don't think applies in the same way in England. Incidentally, where England is concerned, I do think Prince Charles is very enlightened. Aren't we lucky to have a prince who takes an interest in architecture. It's unique. After all, architecture in England has always been very important, but lately people have closed their eyes to the horrors that have arisen in London. Prince Charles is absolutely right to point it out. Of course, good architects do exist, but Prince Charles is in revolt against the vulgarisation of everything. He's a man of taste. I don't think the Duke of Edinburgh cares two hoots. As for the Queen, she has other things to think of.

Are there any objective, or at least non-subjective, criteria for beauty?

Yes, I think there are. The French, after all, have Versailles, and they have so many marvellous buildings which are perfectly proportioned in every sort of style. They have the classical tradition of remarkable taste but, unfortunately, as soon as the *petite bourgeoisie* takes over, then it becomes grotesque. French taste has gone down the drain. Even their painting is now very poor. Only think what they used to be in the eighteenth century.

The whole question of taste is very difficult because taste is so personal, so private a thing, but I think that a person who has a certain classical education is entitled to some say in matters of taste. Classical education is the background. I'm afraid there is also natural bad taste, and bad taste is more general than good taste. When I see the garish, the obvious, the bright, the sexy, all of that appals, alas.

In your memoirs you say: 'In spirit I remain a nomad, a restless and nostalgic ex-pat.' Is this still true?

The older I get the more true it seems. With age I feel that I am more devoted to travel in search of art, of international art, not limited to English or Italian. I've always been drawn, for instance, to Chinese art. I also like their drama, which I have translated with L. C. Arlington, and I have translated popular Chinese plays, which are immensely artistic and beautiful in performance. Unfortunately, China today is too different from the China I knew in the seven happy years I lived in Peking. I have no particular yearning to return under the present regime, but all the same I'm haunted by the happy years I lived there just before the war.

All the accounts that friends bring me of China today are rather depressing, but I love the country and I like the people. Wherever I went, whether in the north, to Honan and Hoonan, or all the way south to Hong Kong, I always got on well with the Chinese. I feel homesick sometimes for China, but I know it's been transformed under Mao Tse-tung. How could it be otherwise? When I was there, there were still the remains of the Imperial Manchu dynasty. I met several who were talented painters, Prince P'u Ju P'u Hsin-yu, for instance, a cousin of the ex-emperor, who was a very talented poet and painter and who I think eventually fled to Japan. I don't expect he's alive now, but I knew him well and his place was not far from where I had a house in Kung Hsien Hutung. He painted a portrait of me, which I haven't got because I left everything behind in Peking, expecting to go back after the war, but of course the revolution changed all those expectations. Instead I returned to Italy where I was born, and here I have remained: all my eggs in one basket.

You wrote about your early years: 'I cannot remember thinking of myself as a child, for I was as embarrassed by children then as I am now and whined when I was referred to as one of their species.'

I've always been uncomfortable with children and they're uncomfortable with me. I don't know why, but I never felt at ease with children, and, of course, if you're surrounded by works of art then you're always terrified that they're going to break them; and those children that I know will immediately go towards a little statue and *crash!*, within a moment the statue is down and in smithereens on the floor. Children are very destructive, particularly English children, though I don't think I was ever destructive as a child. I was always rather careful. I had a natural instinctive love of art and so was always extremely careful of everything in this house. I never played with the statues or the paintings I admired. Quite early in life I became attached to Italian art. I used to go to the galleries, which children would not normally do nowadays, and would feast in the Pitti and the Uffizi and the different churches of Florence.

I don't know that I could say I had a very happy nature. I enjoyed Florence, I enjoyed Italy, so when I was at school in England I was very homesick for Italy. I never settled happily in the English atmosphere. Not when I was a child, at any rate. Oxford was another matter. Those days in England were very exciting.

There were the three Sitwells, for instance, all of them publishing, and reciting their poems to music composed by William Walton. They, too, had a place here in

Florence at Montegufoni, a huge palatial structure about fifteen miles on the way to Siena. It was bought by Sir George Sitwell, the father, and there they stayed for many years. Sir Osbert Sitwell lived there after Sir George's death, and continued to write, and I think his work, which is detailed and beautifully written, will be more appreciated in the future for the history of our time and the figures he knew in the arts. Sacheverell Sitwell, too, woke people up to appreciate the baroque and his book on Italian Baroque is still excellent. Of course, baroque has now come to be generally understood and appreciated, but the Sitwells were voices crying a little in advance of the present success.

Of all the literary people you knew during your Oxford days, you speak with special fondness of Edith Sitwell and Gertrude Stein.

Both of them in their ways were poets. Edith Sitwell is probably underestimated as a poet today, but she brought new life, new colour into the English language with *Façade*, set to music so beautifully by Walton. Gertrude Stein was playing pranks with the English language, but as recited by her, her portraits of human beings sounded rather imposing. Anybody who reads them, and reads them in her slow American voice, will see how they were very sharp portrayals of artists and people she knew. She was in Florence at a time when Mabel Dodge lived at the Villa Curonia here, and she did a portrait that doesn't make sense from a logical point of view but which is somehow a creative abstract portrait of Mabel Dodge. I think it is quite extraordinary how she managed it. In terms of abstract language, her portraits of people are really rather good. Nobody else has done it; she's unique. Her first book, *Three Lives*, is still a rather remarkable work, not especially exciting but successful as a literary experiment.

You once said, 'Most novels are confessions in disguise; most "confessions", like Rousseau's, are novels in disguise.' Where did your poetry fit into such a scheme of things? Did you see your early poetry as confessional or were you aware that others might view it as such?

I think all poetry is confessional. It seems to me that the poet unburdens himself of his dreams, of his subconscious, and I'm sure that my poems, which I never look at nowadays, were really subconscious confessions that had to come out in one way or another. Though I'm a Roman Catholic, I don't think they ever came out in the confessional. They had to come out in more elaborate ways and they came out in verse.

You said of writing that you wanted to pour honey from your hive, but what people wanted was gall and wormwood. Were you ever tempted to compromise?

I was never so tempted. All the poets around me, such as Auden, Spender and others whose names I forget, were left-wingers producing poems of protest. There will always be poems of protest, but poetry should take other forms, should not be limited. Poems of protest have existed since Dante, you might say, but I'm not at all politically minded, and I take the view that politics and poetry do not combine. I suppose Byron with his love of Greece was politically minded, but it is not something you find very often at the heart of the English tradition. Among Italian poets – Leopardi and Carducci – you do, but in English poetry I don't think it's ever that important. With the English, in poetry as in painting, it is nature that is all-important. My poetry was just colour and rhythm, and it was joyful, but as I now realise, it had no depth. It was no more than the exuberance of youth, and every young man has a poetic mood. I was just trying to express my *joie de vivre*, which is nothing to be ashamed of. The older I grow the more I admire the quality in other people.

You once called Cyril Connolly a treacherous Irishman on the grounds that he was a hundred per cent homosexual at school, slept with everyone, then turned against those who remained so.

Well, Connolly was personally *antipatico* to me. He laid down the law, a little dictator surrounded by yes-sayers, all of whom agreed with him, though it also has to be said that he did a good job editing the magazine *Horizon*. When we were contemporaries at Eton I used to get very irritated with his dictatorial manner. He was rather a bully, and he was entirely homosexual, then he changed over to the women and never stopped. He discovered the girls rather late in life, and then it was one after another. A treacherous Irishman is what he was, and I didn't care much for him.

You sometimes make Eton sound like one of the 'cities of the plain'.

Oh, no. It was the most innocent place. No cities of the plain there. In fact, a sharp eye was kept on the morals of the Etonians by the housemasters, so they could not stray, though I suppose subconsciously there was a good deal of homosexuality.

Your friendship with Evelyn Waugh spanned many years. Did you admire him as a man and writer equally?

I admired his writing far more than I admired his character, but he was a delightful, warm-hearted, hot-tempered personality such as you rarely find today. He was a man of extreme views and a convert to Catholicism, and a passionate convert at that, which is also rather rare nowadays. He was a deeply religious person, but his gifts were not really in the most serious vein. His gifts were humorous and I think his best novels are the least serious. For instance, *Decline and Fall,* dedicated to myself, is still I think one of the most brilliant of English light novels. He got a little more serious towards the end, and he lost somehow the light touch, so rare in English literature. Not many people have that light touch. Evelyn Waugh was a master of prose as well; he wrote very good English. That's another thing that is rare nowadays: good, sound, logical English.

I wouldn't say Waugh was depressing as a person. He was rather more depressed than depressing because he saw the way the world was going and it didn't appeal to him at all. But he had a heart of gold and I was really very fond of him. I was best man at his first wedding, a marriage which went badly, alas. I'm afraid he married a rather superficial lady who flirted with others and he couldn't stand it. He was very old-fashioned, expected his wife to be loyal and faithful to him. He couldn't stand the strain of her going off on her own. He was a proud man and he was very loyal as a friend. We stayed friends till the day he died and he's one of the few friends I've never quarrelled with. I'm also a friend of his son Bron.

Towards the end of his life, Evelyn became a kind of recluse, except that he loved his family, and loved to be in the company of his devoted wife, surrounded by his children. He didn't care to join literary societies, but liked to stand on his own. He was independent. There's too much nowadays of congregating in these literary societies, of people blowing their own trumpets, but Evelyn was dignified about all of that.

It has been said that characters in Brideshead Revisited *are based on your own character. Do you find the idea flattering or provoking?*

I think it is very flattering, but I don't recognise any character in *Brideshead* connected with myself. He's taken little traits from me in one of the characters, certain physical traits so that people confuse me sometimes with that particular character, but I don't think it was in his mind. A novelist has to take everything in his experience and use it. That's why we respond. If we felt a novelist's work was false, we wouldn't admire it, unless his fiction were absolutely farcical and fantastic, and Evelyn's is only farcical up to a certain degree. There is seriousness underlining all his fiction.

Max Beerbohm and Somerset Maugham seem to have belonged in quite separate worlds, but you knew them both. Were they at all alike?

They were not very alike, except that they belonged to the same period in a sense, Beerbohm being very much a figure of the 1890s, a sort of dandy of that era who survived into the present century. Maugham, too, had all the mannerisms of a man of the nineteenth century: very formal and living in the South of France in sumptuous splendour. He was not a modern; he didn't really change with the century. He had this stutter, poor man, which only vanished on certain occasions. When he had to speak in public he stopped stammering, but in private life it was embarrassing because he took a long time to come out with any sentence. Pathetic. He used to stay here next to us before he went to the South of France.

As for being an admirer of his writing, I would have to answer yes and no. I don't think he's a first-rate novelist. *Of Human Bondage* is a book that will last, and there are a lot of things he wrote that exactly struck the mood of the moment.

Is there any foundation in the rumour of a rift between you and Gore Vidal?

It's a fabrication. He's not exactly one of my heroes, far from it, but he is in a way a very amiable young man, though very naïve. He thinks himself sophisticated, but he's really very simple. If there's any disagreement, it's entirely on his side not mine. I live, as you see, in a totally different atmosphere. He was in Rome, I think, for a time, used to turn up here occasionally, but I have very little in common with him. He's not an aesthete, not by any means. The arts don't mean much to him. He's an embryo politician and all his ambitions are towards the Senate in the United States. He's a fish out of water here in Florence. We have never quarrelled on my side. On his, I do believe he bears me ill will. I'm very sorry for it because to me he is just like an American sophomore. I can't say I take him seriously as a writer.

You have dismissed most English novelists as preachers who mistake their vocation.

Lately they have tended to preach less. I don't think, for instance, that Somerset Maugham was much of a preacher and the Bloomsbury writers, Virginia Woolf – or even Aldous Huxley – did not preach much. But the Victorians were eminently preachers. If you pick out any Victorian novelist, you find they have a tendency to speak from a pulpit, to address an imaginary public.

If I were to have my reading confined to one English novelist I should say Dickens because I think he was a man of overall breadth of view and knowledge of society. Though his language is very dated, it is very vital English. As you read him you are still living in a sort of Victorian present. Thackeray is also remarkable, but I feel he is more of the past. I don't feel he is as alive as Dickens is today.

As for the English being a literary nation, I find the claim exaggerated. I fear they're not literary. They do not buy literary works, they want something different.

Nowadays it's sex, sex and lively fashion magazines. The stress of modern life drives them to the frivolous by contrast, it seems to me.

On the subject of religion, you write that the Protestant faith has much misery to answer for. Why single out the Protestant faith?

I think it could be said of many religions, but as a Roman Catholic I remain firm in seeing all around me in this country how religion lives among the people and how it is the inspiration, the joy and the philosophy of the Italians that has kept them going for centuries. I feel a stronger Catholic here than anywhere else, though it is always a delight, a joy to me when I go to England to find that Westminster Cathedral is full. I can't say I'm deeply religious, but I believe religion is essential to us and that without it we lose our bearings. It is extremely important for us to have a faith if we're fortunate enough. I cannot imagine being without faith, I cannot imagine the purpose of life in that case.

After a good long life, my faith is stronger than ever. My belief is in the Church and in our wonderful Pope. I have the greatest admiration for him. He is a heroic man. I'm very happy to have been with a Polish squadron during the war. They were all deeply religious: heroic boys, but deeply pious. If you went to Mass in Blackpool it was all Poles at that time. They sang beautifully, and in their voices you could hear their faith ringing out. It was quite splendid, an inspiration, and wherever I've been – even in India – the Catholics were always far more vocal than the Protestants. I wouldn't want to make any sort of comparison, but it was a great inspiration. There's only one faith for me. It's in the Church of Rome.

Of course the Pope is a traditionalist. The Church is traditional, it has to be. We can't revolutionise what Our Lord has preached in the past, we can't change his words. I freely admit, though, that I was saddened by the abandonment of the Tridentine rite. The strength of the Church is in the old Tridentine.

Do you believe in sin?

I believe rather in weakness than in sin, though certain politicians make me believe seriously in sin. If one turns to politics, one has to admit that there are evil people about.

Can you think of any really honest and straightforward politicians?

I remember at Oxford how the young men who were going in for politics and the Union were very shallow, very superficial. They were only ambitious for themselves. I stayed aloof from all those brilliant geniuses who were passing all their exams with top marks, double firsts and all that, then disappearing into the House of Commons. We've heard nothing from them since. Those with the biggest reputations at that time have vanished. Roger Hollis is still known, perhaps, though he was a scandalous fellow, a traitor. I also met Guy Burgess, but I prefer to forget him. A boorish sort of fellow, not an intellectual. He was nothing. I don't know why people talked about him. He had a talent for making noise, that's all.

Speaking of politicians, I did admire Churchill. He was an outstanding person who also wrote well. He was enlightened, the sort of universal man who can be admired anywhere in the world. He was a great draughtsman and he could also paint. Some of his earlier work will endure, I'm sure, but then he became experimental. The desire always to be young, always to experiment, always just to beget children has been, in my view, a great loss in art. Instead of clinging to his own natural talent for beautiful draughtsmanship and colour, Churchill turned his back on his talent, and, like several other painters today, though they don't realise it, was led astray by the critics. I think the wish to be modern at all costs, to alarm, to shock, to startle is the trouble, whereas great painters in the past were not thinking about startling anybody, they were just devoted to their vision and to trying to interpret it in a way others could share. I don't believe anybody can share the vision of Picasso, or even Matisse.

The political animal is something very foreign to me, though, because I have lived in a world of aesthetics, of love of the arts, which it seems to me is natural to anybody born in Europe. Although a good many Englishmen born here were not as interested in the arts as you might expect, generally speaking all the English who were here had one foot in the art world.

Did you ever live in Italy under fascism?

The atmosphere was too unpleasant for me, so that was when I went off to China. But whenever I came back in those years I could feel this rather unpleasant atmosphere of coercion, and many of my English friends sympathised with fascism, thinking it very splendid and dramatic. It's hard to believe now, but they were taken in by the show, by the theatrical element. My parents were here under fascism. I paid them a visit and found the atmosphere very bellicose at that time. It wasn't something that could be said of the Italians in general, because they were peace-loving and didn't want war at all, but the people one met – journalists, writers – were all very bellicose and attracted to Nazism. The Germans had tremendous influence. My parents were both in prison for a short time before getting away to Switzerland.

Eventually I felt I couldn't sit there in Peking any longer, enjoying life while Britain was at war. I had to do my duty in some way and so went back to England

and joined the RAF. I didn't fly because my vision and my age were against me – I was already in my thirties. They took me because of my knowledge of Chinese and things Oriental after living in China for seven years. The war was also by then being fought in the Far East, and so I was sent off there after a period at various air stations to pick up the methods. I was in Intelligence, so called. The people I met were all very brilliant, but I never give those years a thought today. Now that I'm eighty-five years old, it's strange to think of how I was once restricted to air stations in England as an interrogating Intelligence officer, listening to the crews who had been bombing Germany when they arrived back absolutely worn out from their sorties.

Have you ever been a romantic?

I've been an admirer of Schiller, of the romantics, and so on. I think we've all gone through a romantic phase, particularly in youth.

Did you ever fall in love?

Oh, yes, I think we all did, but I suppose I haven't got the depth of character to fall desperately in love, like so many of my friends. No, I never had that. I suppose I must be a cold-blooded fish, really – more mental than physical.

Certainly it occurred to me to marry. I was proposed to many times, but I lived in China then and it would have been very inconvenient. I liked to be an independent bachelor in Peking, having my choice of friends and of girlfriends. I preferred my freedom. I'm happy now. I'm an old bachelor, but I don't suffer from solitude. I sometimes regret that I never chose such and such a person, but I have many particularly good friends here.

I spent a long time with a Chinese woman, which was a very happy time, except when I had to leave, of course, but you couldn't continue for ever. It was a rewarding relationship. The Chinese have such an exquisite old civilisation and Chinese women have a wonderful instinct for affection. They're warm-hearted, and I love everything about their figures: very graceful and unhairy. I don't like a lot of hair, so they appealed to me. If I had married I would have married a Chinese. So I was living with a Chinese girl for many years, and happily because I was never disturbed; no scenes, no jealousy, nothing of that sort. They had another tempo. With an Italian woman it would be a series of scenes and life would become impossible. I know, because I have so many Italian friends.

I never felt any regret at the lack of an heir. I'm leaving everything to the New York University. I don't think Oxford would look after it properly and, anyway, they haven't got the money. I offered it all to Oxford first, but was met with such little response that I changed my mind. So everything goes to New York University and they will take the villa over and use it as a centre for Italian studies. My father didn't like the idea at all. I discussed it with him before he died and he, of course, would have preferred me to marry and have children, but I never had that desire. I never had a feeling for children and family. Even my mother didn't have much of a feeling of that kind, and I think she agreed with me fundamentally. She always preferred the place to be lived in by people who appreciated the arts.

Do you feel you had to forsake the pleasures of the flesh for the sake of art, or can the two go together?

They can go together, of course, but the pleasures of the flesh were very small in my case. They are an important part of life, but they didn't dominate me in the way they dominate so many people. Talking of Maughan, he was always in the hands of some dreadful creature. Gerald Hackston, for instance, who dominated him, or his wife, whom he hated. In my case I have nothing of that sort, thank God. No hatreds. I feel I have chosen wisely to be my own master and to leave everything to a university that can enjoy and use it. After all, Florence will continue to be the capital of the arts. It's bound to be. It always has been since the Medici.

Have you ever been attracted to erotic art?

As a juvenile I was rather interested in certain Beardsley drawings and others appealed to me. I still think Beardsley is a very good draughtsman, but on the whole I think that art should rise above the erotic.

How do you see the relationship between art and morality? Presumably the two can never be separated.

Many artists have been considered deeply immoral. Art is to me beyond morality. If you start moralising then art disappears. It becomes a sort of preaching.

Throughout your memoirs you display an irritation with and contempt for critics, especially for art critics.

I think that many art critics are would-be painters. They are disappointed and frustrated and consequently their frustration is brought out in their criticism of others. That's my opinion, particularly in England where many of the critics I have known personally have been painters on the sly who have had no success and no chance of success and consequently have been bitter about others. I am afraid it is a weakness of human nature to be like that, but it is a sad thing that most of the critics are failed painters.

Literary critics are larger, broader. I'm not capable of judging, for instance, modern poetry, because I'm rather indifferent to what I see in the way of poetry today, but on the whole I consider that our literary critics are excellent. I read *The Spectator* every week with pleasure for its admirable, clear, well-written criticism. It's an excellent journal, and the *New Statesman* and others of high quality compare well with any publication of the past. The late-Victorian publications seem rather heavy going now if we try to look through them, but still they contain very good criticism.

Are scholarly works and critical explanations the most helpful ways of making art available?

No. I don't think people pay much attention to the critics. The critics don't possess much weight any longer. In the days of Ruskin, of course, it was quite different.

What about Bernard Shaw?

He was a very loud, able and brilliant critic, but I think he was sometimes deeply inhuman. I met him once at a public meeting. He had a most beautiful voice and great charm of manner, there's no doubt about it, but I think he was fundamentally a eunuch. I don't think he had any sex. That's my own private view. He was married, of course, but I don't think he was a marrying man. He was all brain and, in spite of the beard, I don't think he was very virile. At least, that was my own personal impression.

Why inhuman? Well, I think that of people entirely given to politics and the stage and boosting themselves. He was a tremendous egocentric, the best propagandist for himself that ever was.

You say of Charles Loeser: 'He would question every object d'art until it vouchsafed an answer.' What sort of an answer, and in what way does one question an objet d'art? You go on to speak of the way Loeser would interpret a great master's drawing. What is it to interpret a drawing?

Oh dear, very difficult. Loeser had an impeccable eye. He was one of the first people to collect Cezanne and he used to tell his servants or his ignorant cook to come in, and he would ask them, 'Do you feel that is a landscape?' And they'd say, '*Si, si.*' 'My cook knows more about it than I do,' he would say. 'She has the eye, she is unspoilt, untutored. I am, unfortunately, a Harvard graduate with too much education to be able to see properly.' Of course, he was exaggerating, but still, there was a certain amount of truth in it. He was a very original man.

At the beginning of your memoirs you write: 'Peace and goodwill towards men will only be brought about by individuals like myself.' Can you elaborate?

It's a very conceited statement. I'm rather shocked that I ever wrote it. But I think that people like us, who are only interested in culture and history, do perhaps a little more for the general public than is recognised and yet we are dismissed by journalists as decorative people on the fringe. In fact, we influence people far more than they're ready to admit. That's my opinion.

It sometimes seems that high art must necessarily be a restricted pleasure. Do you think the taste of the connoisseur can ever really coincide with the larger, more democratic, taste, if you like?

It can't coincide, but it's a guide. The connoisseur must guide taste and most people pay attention to the connoisseur when they know he's genuine. They may laugh at him to begin with, but they follow. They laughed at Whistler, but his 'Ten O'Clock Lecture' is a wonderful piece of prose, quite apart from the fact that the message had a great influence.

What do you think an aesthetic emotion is? Is it really distinguishable from other sorts of feelings?

Oh, yes. It's the most difficult thing to put into words. Aesthetic emotions require a Walter Pater, who wrote his book on the Renaissance with great difficulty over many years. It was a product of careful thought, and we cannot suddenly express that in a few words. Think of the aesthetic philosophers in Germany and in Italy. They are rather long-winded and obscure, and it's very difficult to tone that down to the level of popular understanding. Very difficult – though I think that the average person confronted with a great statue can tell the difference between that and, say, the sort of abstract stuff that is supposed to be a statue now. I think the average man or woman in England can respond immediately to a genuine work of art, a fine Niobe or an Apollo and Marsyas. I think it is extraordinary that the public tolerates the sort of thing that I see very often being put up in London. In my day we'd have tarred and feathered those statues, but they've even spread to Italy. It's a blight.

Some literary artists like Oscar Wilde and T. S. Eliot have seemed to allow art to border on the trivial by saying that all art is useless, as Wilde did, or by calling it a superior entertainment, as Eliot did. What are your feelings about this?

I think they're both very mistaken. I think art is an essential to civilised life, to our private existence. I cannot conceive of an existence without art. But alas, in many places, in industrial cities in the North of England, people manage to live without it very well, but still it's a severe loss to them. If they had beautiful things to look at, it would inspire them to do even better work. But art in England has always been a small group of people, wealthy, old families with an interest in painting or architecture. It's never been open to the masses, unfortunately, and we have suffered accordingly.

You quote Andrew Marvell's lines, 'My love is of a birth so rare / As 'tis for object strange and high, / It was begotten by Despair / Upon Impossibility.' Why did these lines seem to you to explain the otherwise inexplicable?

Marvell was a man of profound vision and of deep spirituality which is rare in the poetry of that period. But it seems to me that these lines are modern and can convey that twilight of the consciousness which is so seldom expressed nowadays.

Over the centuries many hundreds of men and women have devoted their lives to music or painting or dance. Does such a devotion in itself give value to their art?

Certainly. It must give value to their art, if they are devoted in the real, true sense of the word. Pavlova, until she was quite old, was still dancing. I remember seeing her when she was about to retire. She was still the most graceful sylph-like figure one could possibly dream of. She was exquisite, and that's a triumph of art.

You record in your memoirs the fate of works of art at the hands of the Germans in Florence. You describe, for example, an 'Adoration of the Magi' being used as a tablecloth and stabbed with a knife. At the same time you praise the Germans and say that in courage and fortitude they were certainly our peers. Why did they behave so badly, do you think?

Well, unfortunately, that's a sort of racial thing that they have inherited: the rough, primitive instincts which have been glorified by certain great geniuses like Wagner. Wagner glorifies the coarsest instincts in the *Ring*. It's a sign of strength they feel, this great love of their own strength, their own power. It's quite a good thing in a way from the point of view of art, because that is the way good art is produced, but also, alas, bad art.

Why do you think that art seems not to affect people's behaviour as one might hope? Both the Germans and the Japanese seem to have been capable of terrible savagery concurrently with an appreciation of the subtlest effects of art.

That's a very strange point, yes. The Japanese can certainly be split personalities. I've never quite understood their Buddhism; it's not like the Buddhism of the Indians, not contemplative. Everything that they do has got to be active in a hysterical sort of way. They are very peculiar, the Japanese, very peculiar people. The women in Japan, I should say, are superior to the men. They are people of very refined taste: the way they dress, the way they paint, the poems they write. Many of the best novels written in Japan are written by women, such as *The Tale of Genji*. The Japanese are full of surprises, because the women are so refined and elegant and the men fundamentally so crude and rough. They believe strongly in virility, of course, and virility is mixed up with militarism. They occupied Peking when I was there and behaved appallingly. I have no great love of the Japanese male.

It's very difficult to say anything definite about Germans because they are so different from each other. Germany's a land of individualists. People think that they are all together, all followers of Bismarck, Hitler or whatever it is, but they're not. Germans are strongly individual characters. You can see that in their music, in their philosophy, in their works of art.

The journey to your home in Tuscany has become a kind of pilgrimage for many. Are you happy to end your days in Florence, or do you ever feel like coming home?

I was born here, so my home is here. I feel Florentine and I'm an honorary citizen of Florence, and all my lifelong friends, my closest associations are with Florentines. I left for China because of *fascismo* and China was my next love but, of course, in view of what's happened there, it's worse even than *fascismo* was here. So I could never think of going back or living as I did in Peking in a private house, surrounded by Chinese.

What was it that drew you into China initially? You say you felt strangely at home there.

I always loved Chinese art. The Chinese written character is in itself a very beautiful thing, a work of art, and their cooking is a very important element in civilisation. I think people who feed well are on the side of the angels. It's very important that people should eat decent food, properly cooked, and the Chinese do. It's strongly in their favour. And their poetry is sung. When I was there, they would sing their poems. The effect was so very striking. Unlike our poets. We can hardly say that they sing.

I understand that the Chinese do not distinguish between an original work of art and an exact copy. Is that the best approach?

Their tradition is so strong that they go on painting in the same style as they did in the fifteenth century. Landscape artists, for instance, continue to paint in the style of the fifteenth-century Ming Dynasty. It may be a sort of limitation to talent. I don't think that always remaining so traditional is such a good thing. The great artists have always broken with tradition. Turner, for instance, with his billowing seas and all that, broke with the tradition of the eighteenth-century landscape in his landscapes. That's the way art should be: alive. Start with the tradition, but then break it; rules have got to be broken.

How can we really enter into the appropriate frame of reference to allow us to respond properly to work in an alien tradition, like that of China?

I feel there's too much emphasis on the word alien. I think it's exaggerated. A Chinese artist can appreciate a drawing by Michelangelo and Michelangelo would appreciate a good landscape by some eighteenth-century Chinese. Art is a republic, not a monarchy.

Writing about China, you say: 'Behind the broad main streets were networks of alleys, rather slummy, with their mounds of refuse and mongrel dogs.' Did you not find this public indifference distressing?

The back streets were full of families all living together, crowded, but not really squalid, because they had a certain dignity. The Chinese lived in a very agreeable way. I wouldn't have minded joining one of those households.

You also record that in the average year, 29,000 corpses, the bodies of over-worked young mill-workers, were gathered on the streets. Didn't your knowledge of this interfere with your admiration of China?

I think all countries have something of that kind, you know. It's not publicised, but I think it's not so extraordinary. It happens everywhere.

Do you think there is anything left in Communist China of what originally drew you to the country?

The landscape remains, and they have protected a good many of their old monuments, I imagine, and from what I hear the Forbidden City in Peking remains the same. But the spirit perhaps has gone, as people are unified by Marxism. I can't believe that that suits the Chinese, not the Chinese I knew, who were very independent and individual. But I never think of China now. I try not to think of it because I was extremely happy there and saw it *couleur de rose*.

What is it like to smoke opium?

I never became an addict, but I occasionally joined a Chinese friend and smoked a pipe and very much enjoyed it. It seemed to clear my mind and allowed me to forget about the tiresome irritations of life. I found it soothing. And I think that the danger of opium is grossly exaggerated. I have known many people who have smoked it for years who are now old, and yet in spite of their age are flourishing.

You give an account of a visit to an astrologer in Calcutta. Do you, or did you, believe in such things?

Oh, yes. I believe in these things. I don't begin to understand it, but that it exists and that it has existed for centuries and is very strong in India there is no doubt at all. I feel that the Indians have got another sense for astrology which we lack here. Our lives are so different from theirs in that way. We can't keep pace with that strange other-worldliness.

You wrote that a book of memoirs should concentrate on all that is vital and attempt to recapture the moments of exultation and delight. Is there no place for a recollection of sadder times?

I don't think that sadness adds to other people's vitality, and I'm all in favour of vitality. The sad, the gloomy, the depressing are life-diminishing, and I'm for the life-enhancing. So much is life-diminishing nowadays that we must return to the National Gallery and the Louvre to refresh ourselves. In all our lives we have had sad, not to say tragic, times, especially during the world wars. One is surrounded by tragedy, but man is helpless against that sort of tragedy.

I would say I have been fortunate in my own life. I've been privileged to live here in Florence in a fifteenth-century villa with a garden surrounded by statues by well-known sculptors. If I were unhappy it would be a crime. But I do have a horror of death, an absolute horror of it. I enjoy life so much that I would really not welcome death at all. So many friends of mine commit suicide or threaten it. I just don't understand. Life is so wonderful, there's so much more to discover. We're given these blessings, and living here in Florence I'd be mad to wish to die.

I don't consider my work to be of much importance, but I don't think I have done yet what I have it in me to do, which is to write a good short story. But if I were to live my life again, I think I would do the same things again. I would write, I would edit magazines at Oxford. I don't think I could have chosen another path. My only regret is that I didn't write better, that I haven't done more with a flow of imagination. But you can't force that. It is something you are born with. Otherwise I have nothing but thankfulness for the life I have enjoyed.

What fortifies you nowadays against life's disappointments?

It's a very difficult question, but with age I enjoy the beauty of landscapes, scenery and architecture more perhaps than ever, and that keeps me alert and optimistic in my outlook, but otherwise I'm afraid I don't really enjoy the present moment. It's only through art that I exist: through my love of the arts. I have no belief of any kind in my genius. No, that is a part of youth. In youth we're all geniuses. When one is young one has a spirit, but it grows rather feeble as the years pass. Now I find myself rather disappointed with life. I suppose that is a part of creeping age, of getting feebler with the years and becoming mentally not quite so alert. I don't really feel so buoyant as I used to. I used to be very active, particularly when I was at Oxford, editing *Oxford Poetry* and surrounded by very talented poets like Peter Quennell and Robert Graves, and a great many distinguished dons like Beazley, the greatest authority on Greek vases in the world, and Gow on the plough, famous also as a Greek scholar. It seemed like a Renaissance when I was at Oxford, but the Renaissance didn't last.

LORD ALEXANDER QC

Born in 1936, Robert Alexander was educated at Brighton College and King's College, Cambridge. He was called to the Bar (Middle Temple) in 1961 and became a Queen's Counsel in 1973. His briefs included Ken Livingstone's bid to maintain fair fares on London transport, Mrs Thatcher's ban on trade unions at GCHQ and Jeffrey Archer's libel action against *The Star* newspaper. He was created a life peer in 1988 and relinquished his position on the Takeover Panel in October 1989 when he was appointed chairman of the National Westminster Bank. He was chairman of the Royal Shakespeare Company from 2000 until ill health forced him to retire in 2004. He was married three times, had two sons and a daughter, and died from a stroke, aged sixty-nine.

Your origins were relatively humble, your parents had to make sacrifices for your schooling and education. Were you conscious at the time of there being different social classes, hence different opportunities?

I was well aware that the opportunities that were given me were opportunities which were hard earned by my parents. They actually did go without things so I could be educated. I was equally well aware in the area in which we initially lived, Stoke-on-Trent, and to a lesser extent when we moved south, that these opportunities weren't available to many people. But at that time there were also the grammar schools, and many parents who weren't able to send children to schools such as the one I went to could send their bright children to grammar schools. I might easily have gone to a grammar school, and I'm sure I would have received a very good education.

Both my parents were immensely supportive. My father, who himself left school at fourteen or fifteen, was dedicated to my receiving the best education possible and becoming a member of a profession. He had been very well served by a solicitor at one stage of his life when he was establishing his filling station, and, unlike many sections of the population, he had a high regard for lawyers as a group. So when I decided to turn to law, he encouraged me. My mother was also an intelligent person, perhaps without the same single-minded drive towards education for her sons that my father had, but giving considerable and generous backing to it.

Would you say your upbringing and parental influence stood you in good stead for what you were to make of your life, or did you feel set apart from your family?

I felt a great affection for my parents. I knew they wanted me to succeed, to make something of my life, to have high educational standards and good values. Indeed, my father showed his concern for that in stressing the importance of dressing correctly and neatly, making certain that shoes were clean, making sure everything about one was as he would like to see – worthy of respect. Inevitably, however, the education they gave me was one they'd not had themselves, and therefore they couldn't share it. They could not appreciate what I read in history, what I read in literature, so although there was affection and gratitude it wasn't easy to have shared interests as I grew older. But they remained immensely enthusiastic about and proud of my progress. They were very understanding.

When you were at Cambridge, you apparently felt diffident about speaking in union debates. Yet public speaking was to be pivotal to your chosen profession. When did your talent for public speaking emerge?

Certainly not at university. I had done some public speaking at school, in a small group, in debates, in preparing essays to be spoken; and I had won poetry-reading prizes. But in the larger arena of Cambridge, as someone who was conscious of being very tall, thin and rather angular, not particularly socially accomplished and feeling that others around were much more sophisticated with perhaps a dazzling ability, I didn't feel able to walk into the spotlight of that large stage. I never spoke in the Union then, and I would have found it almost impossible to get to my feet with an audience of that size. I decided to become a lawyer at the end of my second year at university. I was reading English, but didn't feel I had the talent to be a dramatist, nor the inclination to be a journalist, and I knew I didn't want to be a schoolteacher. I liked what I'd heard of the disciplined approach of the law. I enjoyed English literary criticism where it appeared to be particularly logical in its analysis, and was attracted by the way in which Dr Leavis wrote, even though he was not particularly well regarded in my own college, King's.

When I changed over to the law, I did so with a view to becoming a solicitor, but at the back of my mind somewhere was the nagging interest in the Bar. I read the biographies of all the great advocates of the past – Marshall Hall, Isaacs, Birkenhead, Birkett, Hastings, Carson – and I became fascinated by their careers, the challenges and particularly perhaps their early careers when they were breaking through to become successful. That decided me to attempt the Bar myself. I was encouraged by my Cambridge tutor, Kenneth Polack, who was a law tutor at King's College. He was the first law tutor they'd had for many generations and had himself just done a pupillage at the Bar. He encouraged me to believe that the Bar was changing in the sense that it was perhaps becoming open to people without private money. So I decided to make an attempt at the Bar without having any clear view in my own mind whether I would be good at that form of public speaking.

From the first time I stood up in court, it seemed to go reasonably well. I didn't feel overawed by arguing a case prepared from a brief where the court was the forum, where the purpose was representing the client, where there was something clear to say which was the argument of the case. At that stage it went well in that I enjoyed the speaking element and seemed able to marshal and present the arguments reasonably. That was the only form of public speaking I did for many years, and for a long time I felt very diffident about anything approaching, for example, an after-dinner speech.

Your style as a barrister was not flamboyant, not thundering, not at all like the image of Rumpole. What exactly was it that attracted you to the Bar?

I liked the challenge of representing a client in a case which would often be difficult. The satisfaction that clearly came from doing it to your best ability, and winning, was immense. I was fascinated by the advocacy, for example, of Isaacs and Birkett, and, of course, by the standards of their time some of those were not flamboyant. They would seem flamboyant by our standards, but Isaacs, for example, set a quite different approach to advocacy from Carson or Marshall Hall – much quieter, much more logical in terms of presentation, and perhaps a forerunner of the modern manner. I got the greatest satisfaction in cases which were not obviously jury cases, but civil cases or appeal cases, where the critical part of the case would be the court's questions. In a real sense, this would be the central idea. You would have done the preparatory work, have laid it out before the court; you would have got into the details of the argument. But then the argument had to be tested by what classicists would call the Socratic dialogue, and it was that area where I found I could react well to the questions, could put forward the answers in a way that seemed reasonably convincing. In other words, I had some facility for thinking on my feet.

Our legal system has always been adversarial, so doesn't that make for certain difficulties, such as that the truth will not necessarily prevail because victory is a function of successful rhetoric?

I don't accept that the adversarial system is contrary to truth and makes success dependent on rhetoric. I've never been able to work out in my own mind what percentage of cases would have the same result whatever the advocacy, and what percentage is either won or lost by advocacy, but I suspect the latter occasions are comparatively few. I also believe that the adversarial system evolved as a very effective way of seeking to get at the truth of issues raised before the court. There are obviously limitations. In a criminal case the judge and jury only look at the issues which the prosecution and defence put before them. They don't have any roving commission of their own. My own main concern about the adversarial system is that, although it may lead to a just result, it's a very slow and expensive way of getting to a result. This is a concern that I had at the Bar, and still have now I have left the Bar. The problems of delay and cost are central. The wheels of God grind slowly, but they grind sure; the same can be said of the legal system, but that isn't too much of a consolation to those for whom the delay is unacceptable or who can't afford to ride in the carriage. For those reasons I would particularly like to see a situation where the system was altered in four ways.

First, I would like to see a greater balance between written and oral work. They've carried it too far in the United States where, in much appellate work, there is very little oral advocacy and not enough time for questioning; but they have not carried it far enough in this country where there ought to be a considerable amount of the case put before the judge in writing. He should then be granted proper time to read it as part of his working day. I found when I was arguing a case that the most tedious part would be introducing the court to the documents – the affidavits or written evidence. It seemed absurd that all this process had to be done orally. Sometimes it was said that it was important it should all be done in open court so that justice could be seen to be done. Sometimes it was said that you couldn't necessarily trust the judges to read the material unless it was read out to them aloud. But overall our system has to develop, and of course it is to some extent already developing towards a greater balance between written and oral argument. This evolution has farther to go.

The second feature that I think is very important is that there should be a greater interplay between the judge and those presenting the case right from the outset; that from the moment a case is started it should become part of a particular judge's list; that he should have the computerised facilities to monitor its progress, and should be able to inquire whether it was not coming forward speedily. This actually happened for a time when Sir John Donaldson was chairman of the Industrial Relations Court during the short-lived 1971 Trade Union and Labour Relations Act. The judge should be able, at these early stages, to look at the issues which have been raised by the parties and should be able to say that a particular issue looks a rather barren one, and hear brief argument on it and guide the advocates for the parties towards what really matters. The advocates should make certain that they get to grips with the real issues, that there are not unnecessary documents put before the court, nor unnecessary witnesses called. I think that the Bar is very good at advising people when it's sensible to settle a case before going to court. What I don't think it's always as good at is pruning the issues that actually go before the court when the case is contested. A bit of a lead has to come from the judiciary.

The third area – and this is much more controversial, and it may be that it's theoretical and fanciful – is that I wonder, as we approach the twenty-first century, if people are going to expect a different form of duty to be discharged by a lawyer. At the moment the lawyer has a duty to represent his client to the best of his ability. That meant that if his client, for some reason, isn't in a hurry to have the case tried, then the lawyer has no obligation to put pressure on his client. I think that possibly the function of the lawyer is increasingly going to move towards being a reconciler, a problem-solver, and that the more we can get away from what is the adversarial conflict, the more we will ultimately meet society's expectations as they develop. The gladiatorial element will then be minimised. But, of course, it would need a great deal of working out, it will only come to pass gradually and it will require changing attitudes from society. Nor, in saying this, am I being critical of the approach currently adopted by the legal profession. It is societal expectations which must shape their future role.

The fourth area where I think our system has to develop is informal dispute resolution. We must find a way of offering people an alternative system whereby they can have their dispute brought speedily before an arbitrator who is in a position to do his or her best: to look at the material, hear some evidence and say, I think the result should be this. Otherwise you may get a denial of justice. You may get a denial where a defendant does not respond to a demand for payment and puts forward an arguable defence, gains time, and the plaintiff suffers very much in the meantime. I've heard of one situation in the present economic turndown where a constructor has gone into a receivership undoubtedly owing money, and can't continue trading until the litigation is concluded. You may also get a denial of justice where someone does not pursue their rights because the process is unaffordable. The importance of being able to find a quick and fair solution in this situation is very great. The Americans are working on alternative dispute resolution. I hope we will do more in this country.

I think those four areas are very much more important than what is coming out of all the populist conflict about the legal profession that the government has initiated over the past year. It's been applauded by the public and the media because they believe that what's being suggested will reduce delay and reduce cost. In fact, the principal changes to the structure of the legal profession will not reduce delay, will not reduce cost.

Why do you think people are suspicious of members of the legal profession?

It's difficult this, isn't it? Whichever group you're in in society, you frequently see that the public perception of it is not particularly high. I don't think the public perception of politicians is particularly high, nor the public perception of journalists, which is influenced by invasion of privacy and unnecessary trivialisation. I don't believe that the public perception of bankers, which is my new occupation, is uniformly high either. As a lawyer, it's important not to think that yours is the only section of society which is under attack. But throughout history lawyers have not been a popular group. Chaucer made fun of his lawyer, who was rather busy, rather pompous, very keen on the fees and had a bustling image, pretending he was busier than he actually was. Shakespeare didn't have a wonderfully kind view of lawyers either. What causes it?

First, I don't think people like being involved with the law. There's rarely any particular profit in it; it's solving a dispute at a cost. If, for example, you are involved in a criminal case and are acquitted, you will then consider that that's no more than your due. If you're convicted, that's probably because of the unfriendliness of the judge and the incompetence of your advocate. The same applies in a civil case. A plaintiff who wins considers justice is done. A defendant who loses considers injustice is done. Thus, within the whole nature of the legal process there is obvious scope for potential resentment. No one wants to be involved with the law anyway. No one wants to pay lawyers.

In saying this, I don't want to exonerate the lawyers entirely. Sometimes our profession has been seen as formal, as remote; sometimes as self-satisfied, sometimes even as pompous. Obviously, a perception of that kind, in an area of life that people don't want to be involved with anyway, is not good for the reputation of lawyers. It may, of course, be a perception that is unjust to a majority of lawyers, but I grant that it undoubtedly exists. The fact that the profession is becoming more informal and more widely based socially is very important and ought to help its future development. Improved communications with clients, avoiding jargon and pedantic language, will also help.

The legal profession in recent years seems to have been in some turmoil, with one group trying to preserve its privileges, the other to trespass on them. It's difficult for outsiders to see which principles are involved.

The principle involved is essentially whether you want specialist advocacy, and if you do, what ought to be the rules that govern the work of advocates. The view taken by many people at the Bar and by the judges is that, to have good independent advocacy, there ought to be certain qualities an advocate accepts and strives towards. The first is that they dedicate their whole work to advocacy or litigation so that they constantly keep their talents well honed. The second is independence: independence of large administrative burdens and independence of financial reliance on partners so that the essential pressure of the need to secure 'billable hours', which is a driving force of the corporate law firms, ought to be absent, and yet leave people the opportunity to make a reasonably good living. The third is that, in important cases, the solicitor prepares the case and the barrister presents it in court. This lessens any danger of the barrister being other than scrupulous in his presentation. He or she does not get close to the client, as they might do if they were involved with every aspect of the case. It is, moreover, extremely helpful and valuable to have skilled preparation done separately from the presentation. If the barrister is using the skills of an advocate as the principal skills, he should not be dissipating those skills by spending a great deal of time preparing cases.

I, for example, once had a United States lawyer come into my room, sit down in an armchair – he was the leading advocate for a particular case – and say, 'I've worked on nothing but this case for twelve years.' Now that is not good. He could not be gaining wide advocacy experience. Our principles involve acceptance on the part of the Bar of certain restrictions and obligations. First, as a self-denying ordinance, barristers don't have direct contact with lay clients. Secondly, the Bar takes on cases popular and unpopular and should not refuse cases because they're legally aided.

The argument some solicitors have raised is that they should be entitled to take cases in court without subscribing to these principles. Clearly that would have major implications, because if solicitors were able to have all the advantages of following the profession of advocacy without accepting the rules by which advocates have been governed, then they would have an economic advantage. Let me illustrate in this way: if a barrister goes into chambers, he is briefed by a solicitor, so there is a filter of confidence he has to go through; but a solicitor who joins a firm could, if able to argue cases in the highest courts, simply argue for the clients of that firm without having to have his ability to do so vetted or proved by a solicitor instructing him. Those are some of the fears, and those are some of the concerns.

It is regrettable that there's been this argument. A legal profession should not be squabbling within itself. It has a duty to serve the public, and there are many more important issues. I think that part of the problem is in any event being solved, because more cases are now to be heard in the Country Court, where any lawyer can argue cases. Hence the smaller cases are going that route, and there was in any event clearly a reasonable argument for widening the rights of audience of solicitors in the Crown Courts. But I feel it is regrettable that it's become a public profile argument over a period of years, because the legal profession should be seeking to work together on the much more important problems that it has to tackle if it is to give a full service to society. Equally I don't know how far those solicitors who were pressing for rights of audience were representative of solicitors generally. In my experience, many solicitors were content with the existing structure, but the public undoubtedly saw it as an argument about who should be entitled to a particular slice of cake. It was a demarcation dispute and so seemed unattractive.

Would it bring costs down if solicitors were able to plead?

We shall discover. The answer is thought by many to be no. There was a Royal Commission report ten years ago which researched costs in detail. The government, incidentally, did not research costs at all before bringing their current reforms. The research ten years ago showed that, in very small cases, the costs might come down, but in the majority of cases they wouldn't, and some might go up. If a large corporate law firm, for example, was both preparing a case and arguing it in court, as opposed to preparing a case and instructing barristers to argue it in court, I don't believe that costs would in any way go down. Equally, where you get a good provincial law firm instructing a barrister, the costs may be considerably below what they would be if you were having to go to one of the large corporate law firms to get a competent barrister. In other words, having a pool of independent advocates available to all solicitors is an important factor in ensuring that costs do not go up.

Isn't the argument that, because barristers are rather few, they can charge a lot, whereas if solicitors were allowed to plead, there would be more competition and costs would go down?

But, generally speaking, the Bar has expanded to meet demand. When I became a barrister in 1961, there were fewer than 2,000. At the last tally I think there were almost 6,000, and the numbers may now have gone even higher. Broadly speaking, the Bar has expanded to meet demand. There have been some areas where there's a shortage of specialists, but if the Bar were to erode or wither, there would probably be far fewer really competent advocates in particular fields, and they would all be tied to a particular large firm and not available to the bulk of solicitors. If the Bar were to be destroyed, then you would undoubtedly have less accessibility to good advocates. That, of course, would have implications not only in terms of price but also in terms of getting the representation you want in court; and the ability to get that representation is really a keystone of our system of justice.

Won't something have to be done eventually about legal costs? We seem to have reached a position where justice in a number of areas – libel, maladministration, even divorce – depends for all practical purposes on what money you have. You can't exactly buy justice in a free market yet, but many believe it can be denied to those who lack resources.

I don't believe you can buy justice by having money, but I think you can be denied justice by not having it. How do you deal with this? First, you must have a proper system of legal aid for the more disadvantaged. Within the past decade, the eligibility for legal aid has declined, and that is not healthy. Secondly, we must have simpler trial procedures. Thirdly, I don't think that contingency fees will necessarily help. If the contingency fee level is set high enough to be an incentive to the lawyer, it may be a source of abuse, and if it's not set high enough to be an incentive, then it will not make a substantial difference. Fourthly, I think we do have great potential for development in the concept of legal expenses insurance. This exists, for example, in your household policy: you may be able to recover costs for a claim for negligence or nuisance arising in certain activities. It exists for trade unionists whose trade union dues give them legal insurance to enable them to pursue a proper claim if they're injured at work. But there's a whole area where legal expenses insurance has not been significantly developed in this country. I believe it's more developed in Western Germany, though I don't know too much about the details, but this may be one area in which our system can develop in regard to costs.

In your dispute with Lord Hailsham over increased legal aid for barristers, you fought the barristers' corner fiercely. You also decided to breach normal Bar practices and go public in the sense that you gave radio and TV interviews. Why did you do that?

I certainly took the view that, if a profession serves the public, the public is entitled to know what its practices and problems are. So it seemed logical that we should be willing to discuss any issue that anyone wanted to raise with us. I also thought that our case on legal aid fees was very good, and a case to get across to the public. We did get it across in a pretty good way. One large meeting was open to the press, and the press up to then had had an image of barristers as too elitist; withdrawn and too conscious of their supposed dignity to speak to the public. Now they were suddenly at a meeting where people were talking plain language about the problems of fees. I remember one member of the Bar saying, 'How do I keep myself in spite of legal aid fees? Answer: I work as a waiter in a Chinese restaurant in the evenings.' We had a number of these, and people from different ethnic groups and both sexes, and the press realised there were a lot of human beings at the Bar in just the same way that there were outside.

What sort of legal aid sums would be appropriate in your view?

Figures change. The way I would look at it is that someone who is doing full-time legal aid work should be able to earn enough to be on a parallel with lawyers in government service or local authority service, but bearing in mind that barristers also have to pay their expenses and make their own pension contributions. It is a straight comparison between one area of public legal service and another.

But if I may pursue this a little further, large numbers of barristers are pretty well dependent on fees provided out of public funds for legal aid. How would you determine what level of remuneration is appropriate? Might the time come when there has to be a distinction between those depending on public funds and those who command private fees?

That distinction exists anyway. That's why it's so important for all those who command private fees to be willing to do some legal aid cases. I believe it's a very important factor in a responsible legal profession, but the level of remuneration must be such that qualified lawyers can say, 'This is a reasonable career.' If legal aid fees were to be significantly below what those lawyers could earn anywhere else, even in other areas of the public legal service, it would become more and more difficult to attract competent people to do the work. The same is, incidentally, just as true for solicitors who do legal aid work.

You described Lord Mackay's Green Paper on legal reform as 'superficial, unsupported by research, unaided by consultation'. Others, like Lord Hailsham, thought the independence of the judiciary itself was under threat. Was this not a bit of an over-reaction?

I don't believe so. May I take our Lord Chief Justice, Lord Lane, who, as someone very highly respected within the legal profession, reacted strongly against the document. Lord Rees-Mogg also described the failure of the government's arguments as total, and he is not a lawyer. It was, I thought, a serious mistake and an ill-informed document. May I take just a few examples from memory?

What the proposals suggested was that the way in which the rules for the profession were made should be brought under the control of the Lord Chancellor, this being a matter too important to be left by the government to the profession itself. Now, imagine if that statement had been made by the government of South Africa, namely, that the government should take control of the very profession whose duty it is to represent the citizen against the government. Lord Hailsham and a lot of others found it virtually unbelievable that a government committed to democracy should feel able to introduce such a suggestion.

On advocacy, the suggestion was that advocates should be certificated by professional bodies but in accordance with rules laid down by the government. What would have been the criteria, and who was to determine the criteria? Again, it was to be the government. I don't believe that those who said that liberties are lost, not in one great stride, but by small and accumulating steps, were being over-dramatic. This was a very clear encroachment on the independence of the profession. It was seen that way throughout the Commonwealth, and seen that way in the United States.

One of the most remarkable features was that, four years beforehand, the government accepted the report of the Royal Commission chaired by Lord Benson. Yet the Green Paper never once referred to the existence of that report, never dealt with its arguments nor suggested why the government had suddenly decided to do a complete U-turn. The proposals as put forward would inevitably have benefited the large firms of corporate lawyers to the detriment of an independent Bar and to the detriment of the smaller firms of solicitors. We found it very surprising that there was no serious recognition of this danger. It is remarkable that the judges, who very rarely speak publicly, should have spoken out so strongly. It reflects a deep concern that the proposals were dangerous.

The question everyone wants to ask an advocate is do you need to believe your client? Would you defend a client you knew to be lying on the grounds that even such a client has a right to representation?

The basic position was explained beautifully years ago by Lord Birkett. If you believe your client to be guilty, but he is asserting he is not, then it is not for you but the Court to decide the issue. You are part of the process of leading to that judgement. If, however, the client told you he was guilty, then you would not be entitled to suggest he was innocent because, as opposed to simply having a shrewd idea, you would actually know he was guilty. If he said, 'I am guilty but I want to plead not guilty,' your duty would then be to say to him, 'I cannot represent you in that case, and if you wish to plead not guilty and have an advocate representing you, then you must not tell that advocate you are guilty'. It's essential to remember that the advocate's role is as a part of the administration of justice, and that the advocate is not the judge. The advocate's role is to present one side of the case to the best of his or her ability.

You are said to believe that advocacy is a pure science in that it can be applied with equal effectiveness to any case.

I don't know where that comes from. I'm not conscious of having said it, and I'm not conscious of believing it. I know there are some cases I can argue a great deal better than others. If, for example, I believed that my client was guilty and I had to put forward an explanation I thought was nonsense, I think I would feel uncomfortable because I would feel sure that someone would see through it. So I don't see advocacy as a science, but more as an art. I think there are very much advocates for particular cases. There are those who appeal beautifully to the emotions, those who are strong in cross-examination, those who are subtly probing. There are those who are brilliant at arguing a subtle civil suit who would be hopeless at arguing a criminal case and the other way round. So I actually think advocacy at its best is an art, a matter of flair rather than a matter of science.

What would you say was your strength as a QC?

It's very hard to judge your own strength. The starting point was that I liked to manage the case in the sense that, although the solicitor was involved in the preparation, I liked to be involved in considering the way forward from a very early stage. I believe that, in a complex case, good management before you ever get to the court is of the absolute essence – deciding which points should be argued, how strongly one can be pursued, whether one argument fits well with another or whether an argument might be so unattractive as to detract from another. In terms of personal strength, it's very hard to judge. I gained some experience of cross-examination when I went on circuit as a young advocate, doing criminal cases for four years, in court every day, cross-examining, thinking during the course of the case, adapting in the light of answers. I found that was of priceless value in my later civil work. I also, I suppose, tried to think what arguments would appeal to me if I was a judge, because I didn't much enjoy putting forward arguments that I did not personally find reasonably appealing. If I was cross-examining, I wrote out every question in advance, and sometimes, where there were two possible answers, I would write out at the next question: if yes, go one route; if no, go another. In the same way I made very full notes for written argument, even if I didn't use the argument in the order of those notes.

You did your homework well.

There's absolutely no substitute for it. When I was in silk, I felt it was right to delegate certain areas of research to good juniors, that being part of the teamwork; but in terms of the critical court work, there is no delegation to be done. I always went into court with a very full note indeed of the issues.

Some of your more celebrated cases seem to suggest that you did approach them in a scientific way. For example, in the GLC for fair fares, you were apparently defending the cause of socialism, but in representing the government in its ban on trades unions at GCHQ, some suggested you were defending the cause of authoritarianism against basic civil liberties.

The cases were about four years apart, so it wasn't brought quite into the focus you suggest. The way I saw the GLC case was that I actually felt that Ken Livingstone and the GLC had been elected and had, as part of their election policy, said they were going to attract people back to the Underground by a low-fares policy and subsidised fares. I felt deeply disappointed by the result of that case because, only a few years beforehand, in a case about education, the House of Lords had actually given weight to the fact that a Conservative local authority had been elected with a particular view on education and schooling, and this was a relevant factor in that authority deciding how it should exercise its discretion. I myself felt that the judgement in the GLC case was not the best judgement in the House of Lords in my lifetime. I still feel it should have been decided the other way. The GLC should have been allowed to implement their policy and see how it worked.

As for the GCHQ case, when it came to the House of Lords, which was when I became involved, it was an issue of whether the government should have engaged in consultation before banning trade union activists. The Government said they feared that, if they engaged in consultation, there would have been trade union dislocation before they imposed the ban and the court accepted that evidence. It was my task to invite them to accept the government's view as part of the process of evaluating the rival arguments. It was not my task to form a political judgement. I think the legal judgement in that case was absolutely right. If I had to form a political judgement, I'm not convinced that the government went about it sensitively. But can I emphasise that my views on the legal case have nothing to do with my political views. Each case has to do with legal rights and the limits upon power which are placed by administrative law. I didn't particularly agree with Ken Livingstone's policy, but I did take the view that he should be allowed to give it a crack, because they had been elected on that policy.

If I may press this a little further, you said of the GCHQ case that you don't have to believe a point is right, you just have to believe it is reasonable. Isn't it better to believe something is reasonable and right at the same time?

If we carried that too far we'd get a situation where advocates only argued cases they thought were right. What would happen if there was a case that nobody thought was right? We are a cog in the machine of justice. The system of the administration of justice is a central element in a democracy. Without a democracy you can't have an independent system of justice. Without an independent system of justice, you can't have a democracy. The advocate is but one element in that system. His job is to ensure that a case is properly presented, which is a fundamental right. I have no sympathy with people who say they won't take a particular case because they're a Conservative and this seems a socialist cause. To adopt that approach is contrary to the duty of an advocate.

Did you ever take a case you considered absolutely hopeless?

Yes. In a career of twenty-eight years one's bound to have had some hopeless cases. In hopeless cases I would generally advise my client to settle, to compromise, or not to fight particular issues. If, in the end, they didn't take that advice, that was their right. I didn't enjoy arguing hopeless cases, and I'm glad to say I don't think I argued too many of them, because clients were prepared in general to make the best of it in that situation either by settling a civil case or pleading guilty and mitigating sentence in a criminal case.

Were there ever any cases you wanted to win for their own sake, rather than for the sake of legal argument?

I can think of one example. It was in the late 1960s or early 1970s, at the height of what is now called the Permissive society. A doctor had told the parents of a fifteen-year-old girl that the daughter had asked to be put on the Pill, and had been. He was the family doctor, liked the family and was gravely concerned about the situation, but it was suggested he had breached confidence by telling the parents. I represented him before the General Medical Council, and we established that the breach of confidence was not improper because, in all the circumstances, it was a reasonable judgment on his part that the parents should be told. I felt that was overall a very proper outcome.

There were other cases I was glad to win, such as the cricket case, brought by Kerry Packer and others against the Test and County Cricket Board. It wasn't because I approved of their particular brand of cricket, or disapproved of the MCC. I've loved cricket all my life, and I could see the disruption that action was bringing to cricket, but it produced a tremendous degree of unfair public revulsion against Packer. It sparked a tremendous degree of righteous indignation, when he was only doing something he was fully entitled to do – which was to set up a rival outfit. I cared very much about the result of that case, as a matter of basic fairness. In the same way, I thought Jeffrey Archer had been badly treated by the press over the allegation of paying money to a prostitute, and felt it would have been most unfair for him, and indeed for his family, had he not won. I was very glad and relieved when he did.

What is your view about the size of damages awarded in libel cases these days? Has the time come for some more rational system to be devised? For a man accused of dealing with a prostitute to be awarded many times more than a brain-damaged child hardly seems rational.

I believe that now a brain-damaged child would get more than Jeffrey Archer did in his libel action, if that is the example you have in mind. What we have to remember about that case is that the newspaper article cost him a position in life that he valued as much as any he had. Although he was a successful author, he had to resign his deputy chairmanship of the Conservative party, and Jeffrey Archer is passionately committed to politics. The paper did not apologise, and it put him through a severe trial which made the front page for a fortnight. Therefore, it really sold its newspaper for a fortnight on the back of the trial. Now I don't believe, once you take all those facts together, that the award of damages of half a million pounds was unreasonable. The newspaper did not appeal either.

It's difficult to correlate awards for libel with awards for personal injury, but I would agree that in general there's obviously something haphazard about libel awards. It's very strange that they should be decided by a jury which does not have a figure mentioned to it and has probably never before sat on a libel case. I would say the provision the Lord Chancellor introduced into the Courts and Legal Services Bill, under which the Court of Appeal can review damages and substitute its own figure if it thinks the damages awarded by a jury too high, should perhaps be very helpful in enabling a more balanced and logical tariff to be presented.

In the famous Spycatcher *case, you had essentially to marshal the battered remains of a principle against the fact that anyone who actually wanted to know the substance of Wright's allegations could know them, and there was nothing anyone could do to stop it. Many onlookers found the absurdity of the government's position quite staggering, not to mention the vast cost to the public purse. Looking back, wasn't it all a bit of a nightmare?*

It wasn't a nightmare. The government was in a dilemma. The principle it wanted to enforce, that the secret service should keep confidence, was a good and sound principle. The difficulty lay in the fact that jurisdiction is territorial and therefore it couldn't enforce that principle in other countries. That meant, inevitably, that it couldn't prevent the book being circulated.

In fact, if Mrs Thatcher hadn't taken legal action against Spycatcher, *they would hardly have sold 5,000 copies.*

Absolutely right in the individual case. The action benefited Wright's sales figures. But supposing the government hadn't taken action. Would it then have been said that anyone who wants to write a book about the security service can go abroad with impunity and write and publish it? She had a very difficult dilemma and there was no easy choice. Wright might have become a millionaire, but I don't think that necessarily makes the case a total disaster. It must have been made plain to others that the government would do its best to enforce confidentiality. The courts unequivocally endorsed the principle that the security service should keep quiet about this work. Equally, we're looking at the outcome with the priceless benefit of hindsight. It can't have been obvious to the government when it started that it would lose in the Australian courts. The judgement of the Australian High Court has not been highly regarded as a matter of law by many lawyers. It's easy to say now that the government lost and Wright became a millionaire. It wasn't necessarily so easy for people at the beginning to know that the government were going to lose before ever they'd argued their case.

Are there ever occasions when it may become necessary to flout the law? I have in mind what is sometimes called the tyranny of the majority: such areas as religious observances, or abortion, where people feel that the law clashes with moral necessity or natural justice?

I would in general draw the line between, on the one hand, peaceful and prominent public demonstrations and, on the other, defiance of the law. Any individual is entitled to defy the law, or certain laws, on grounds of conscience, and go to prison for that cause. A journalist, for example, who decides he will go to prison rather than disclose his confidential sources, is, I think, fully entitled to take that view as a matter of conscience. But I don't believe that in general people should defy the law in a democracy. They should use all democratic means to get the law changed.

It's highly unusual for a barrister to step outside his profession, especially when a glittering career could presumably have led to an appointment to the bench. Why this change of direction?

It's hard to know the motivation in one's own life. I have an immensely high respect for judges and the judicial function. The results of the cases I've done all my life have depended on the quality of the judges and the way they conducted them. But I have never had an ambition to become a judge. It's hard to identify a single reason. I think the assumption that, because you are an advocate, you will necessarily enjoy becoming a judge, is not correct for everyone. I didn't feel I would enjoy the role nearly as much as I had enjoyed the advocacy. So when I got opportunities to do other tasks that I thought equally valuable, I took them.

Shortly after being chairman of the Bar Council, I was approached to become part-time chairman of the Takeover Panel. The panel is a valuable institution because, where people are striving to win a battle, an organisation that sets the rules and sees fairness for shareholders is vital. I got a lot of satisfaction from it, and I suppose it was because I'd had that partial involvement in the City that I was then approached to become chairman of NatWest. I hesitated over that for quite some time. To begin with, it involved severing my links with practice at the Bar, in contrast with the Takeover Panel. That job had been part-time and I'd continued practising. Secondly, I'd never had experience as a banker and was concerned about going into the unknown. I consulted a number of people who were encouraging enough to suggest I could do the job and emphasised that it was very important. Since I believe that large national banks are in a sense essential to the community and are national assets, I didn't in the end feel I should decline the challenge. I felt fortunate to be offered the opportunity to join in the work of the bank. I am really enjoying the work.

The profession of barrister has often been compared to that of actor, the court being like a stage where the performance is all and the adrenalin flows. Do you not miss that platform, that excitement?

No. I've never been sure how perfect the theatrical comparison was in civil cases. In criminal cases, yes. Gerald Gardiner, a wonderful advocate, had, of course, been an amateur actor and thought of going on the stage. I can see the element of acting, but in modern civil cases it's relatively small. But you're right that the adrenalin can flow, and that when the adrenalin flows and you do it really well, you get a feeling of elation. Obviously, I will not get that particular feeling of elation again. On the other hand, advocacy is a very exacting, stressful process, a lonely process, both in the preparation and in arguing before the court. You and you alone are answering questions which may affect the outcome of an issue that is immensely important to your client, and so you are in a continuously exposed position.

Having been a part-time chairman of the Takeover Panel, do you think the law adequate in its present form to ensure that the merchant banks give sufficiently accurate information on behalf of clients to any legal entity or government department?

In general, yes, because of the responsibility placed on the merchant banks. The present position is that it is an offence to give false information during the course of a takeover and anyone who gives misleading information during that stage could be liable to prosecution. In addition, the merchant bank has a duty to the Takeover Panel to be responsible for the accuracy of the statements it makes.

If it fails in that, it is open to disciplinary action at the hands of its regulators. I therefore feel that the machinery exists for ensuring fair information is given to shareholders.

The official enquiry into share-rigging at NatWest in the County affair concluded that a highly unsatisfactory state of affairs had existed. Did this give you any reservations about joining the bank?

I joined them during the course of the inquiry and I was told of the problem. I had no reservation about joining because, although mistakes were made at that time, I was absolutely satisfied that NatWest is committed to the highest ethical standards and the mistakes made within the merchant bank were not typical of the organisation. Dealing with that unfortunate incident was part of the challenge. That revelation affected everyone deeply. If you have, as NatWest has, a pride in your own ability and integrity, then you're much more affected by something going wrong than if you're a buccaneer who does not have that pride. It was inevitably wounding to a fine bank to have something like that happening.

Blue Arrow was a major setback to try to recover from. How did you approach the challenge?

We all approached it together. We appointed new management in County NatWest, which was given the task of ensuring that systems were in place to make certain that all dealings were conducted with total propriety in future. We had independent accountants advise us as to every area in which we needed proper controls. We submitted these to our City regulators, and they approved them. In addition, we have directors of high quality from the parent bank on the board of the investment bank. If you have a misfortune like this, you must learn lessons and make certain that you emerge stronger. Everyone is determined to do this.

I want to ask one last question about that. Your predecessor, Lord Boardman, a politician rather than a banker, was obviously unaware of what was going on at County NatWest and it was suggested at the time that his lack of sophistication in investment banking affairs was partly responsible for matters developing as they did. Isn't there a danger in a chairman of a bank lacking banking expertise?

There must be a danger, but none of us can have all the expertise. I work closely with a very able chief executive, Tom Frost, who has been a banker all his life. I think our different backgrounds bring strengths to the partnership.

Now that you have been at the bank for some time, you must have a pronounced interest in whether Britain joins the EMS. Why is the present government so reluctant to do so when the rest of Europe thinks it such a good idea?

I don't believe that this country has ever been as involved in Europe as those countries which are part of continental Europe. Let me give one illustration from personal observation. Last year we were in France, which we love, at the time of the European elections. An election poster there had a photograph of President Mitterrand and Chancellor Kohl walking hand in hand into the future of Europe, but the interesting thing was that it was a back view of each of them. I don't believe that a back view of Chancellor Kohl would have been recognised by very many people in this country. Continental states have been more deeply involved with each other for a long time in a way that this country, with its island history, has been outside. It's no accident that the founding fathers of the European Community came from countries that had been the victims of invasion by each other and who recognised that the whole of the future lay in setting aside those aspects of nationalism which bred conflict.

Industry and business clearly recognise increasingly that we're part of a single market of 320 million people which will probably be expanded significantly by the addition of the EFTA countries and the people of East Germany. They see the opportunities. I think that our government, given our history, is understandably reluctant to surrender sovereignty and the freedom of independent action. I think that reluctance is made all the harder because, when we do subscribe to a European policy, we do implement it. Our government has a very good record of implementing directives, so it does tend to look at the commitment on the basis that it is a real and genuine commitment. That may explain why the government is being slow to surrender freedom of action – the freedom which has been part of our history – but it doesn't mean that we can stand apart from the process.

We are now part of Europe. It is absolutely critical that we should be involved in the shaping of the future of Europe, and we can't be involved unless we are, as a first stage, part of the exchange rate mechanism. Equally, our economic record does not suggest that there is any advantage in staying out. One of the depressing features is that after ten years of one of the strongest, most courageous and successful governments of any adult lifetime, we have double-digit interest rates, which look to be continuing for a long time, and we're close to double-digit inflation. The countries of continental Europe which have accepted the discipline of the exchange rate mechanism are now in a better position. France, for example, which began the 1980s worse off, is entering the 1990s considerably better off and with a higher GNP per head of population. Italy, whom we once looked at with pity, has achieved considerable economic success in the past decade. The exchange rate mechanism is not a simple panacea for all ills. It will be uncomfortable when we join because it will put upon us the discipline of disinflation, but it's absolutely critical if we're to benefit from Europe.

Do you consider yourself a European?

Increasingly so. I don't consider myself equally at home in all the European capitals. I suspect that in another European country people will probably be able to look at me and my clothes and guess my nationality, but I feel very committed to the importance of Europe as a whole becoming a successful organisation because it is important for all of us economically and politically and in terms of human tolerances.

So our future lies less with the United States and more with Europe?

Our future must lie with Europe, there's no doubt about it. It doesn't follow that there will not be a close and good relationship between the United States and Europe. It's important that there should be one, but the danger must be there that a United States somewhat weakened economically will turn in on itself. The Pax American has lasted a remarkably short time overall.

Yet many politicians in this country still believe that there is a special relationship between Great Britain and the United States.

There was clearly the great Churchill / Roosevelt combination in the war. Their exchange was one of the great co-operations in human history and must rank as an alliance without parallel. After the war there was the United States' involvement in Europe, then the nadir of Suez, which didn't do great credit to the government of this country and in some ways to certain members of the US government. Since then I think the special relationship was rather doubtful until it was re-created by Mrs Thatcher and President Reagan. It depended on the ability on the part of Mrs Thatcher, a brilliantly intelligent woman, to form a relationship with a man who had some good instincts and a genius for presentation but was not very clever or well informed. That was kept going for seven or eight years to the advantage of this country. Now I think that we're settling into a more professional administration of political relationships where the current administration in Washington recognises that Germany is the focal point in Europe and, within that context, is anxious not to have too special a relationship with Britain. But, that said, the individual relationship between Britain and the United States, if not a so-called special one, will remain of some value.

How has it come about that Britain has exposed itself to legal proceedings in the European Parliament over its failure to comply with EEC regulations to protect the environment and establish, among other things, a healthy standard for drinking water. Should we not be in the forefront of nations giving a good example?

Yes, I believe that we should be active in seeking to achieve the standards. Sometimes you start from a position where you're somewhere behind and you need to play for time a little if you're to reach the appropriate standards. Equally, I don't think we should single out this country as one that doesn't comply with European directives. You can look at all the countries and see that they are having to take some time to adjust to European standards in particular areas. I don't believe we have a bad record in complying with directives of the European Commission, or indeed in complying with the European Convention on Human Rights. Water is clearly an issue, and the duty of the privatised water companies should be to improve standards, but as with so many areas, you can't always achieve your aim overnight. It's right that the issue should go on being highlighted.

I want to talk to you a bit about banking. What is the rationale behind banks lending vast sums of money to people who basically speculate on a particular market, whether it be land, property, commodities or even grandiose schemes that are extremely vulnerable to market conditions?

The banks have lending as a major aspect of their business. Their task is to lend to the creditworthy; to be a willing but responsible lender. They would not wish to be seen to be lending to those who will end up by not being able to repay, but they wouldn't generally wish to pass judgement on the commercial purpose of the regular customer who seeks to borrow money if that regular customer is willing and able to make repayments. So the banks have to evaluate proposals to form a judgement as to whether a loan makes some commercial sense.

Now, that's what takes me into my next question. My own banking experience leads me to believe that the honest individual, struggling to make it on his own, is given a hard time by the banks as far as collateral is concerned when he tries to borrow money. It seems that much stricter conditions apply to the small borrower. Is that true, and if so, why? When the property market collapsed, banks lost hundreds of millions of pounds. If they had applied the same rules they apply to a small borrower, it wouldn't have happened.

Banks do seek very substantial collateral, but when they lose money to that extent, it may indicate that the market has turned even more substantially than anyone thought possible. Because of the 1974–5 property crash, many banks are more cautious in lending money to the construction and property sector.

To the mind untrained in the complexities of banking, it seems inconceivable that banks should lose hundreds of millions of pounds in property transactions and in overseas lending if they were to apply the same strict rationale as they do to the small borrower. It is perhaps a case of waiving the rules to accommodate the mighty?

No, it's not a question of that. It may be that they make misjudgements because the sovereign countries or large companies appear to have the ability to repay. In terms of sovereign lending to the Third World countries, it was certainly thought that the governments would not default. But there's no question of the bank saying consciously, we will accept a lesser risk because these people are 'mighty'. The one thing banks hate are bad debts. Commercial discipline applies equally when dealing with the large organisations as when dealing with the small borrower.

A previous barrister chairman of NatWest was Robin Leigh Pemberton, now governor of the Bank of England. Would you be pleased to follow in his footsteps one day?

I'm fully content to have undertaken an extremely large job with a very major bank, and in none of the jobs I have done have I ever given a thought to the future. I believe that Robert Leigh Pemberton has proved to be an extremely impressive governor in the way in which he has increasingly stated an independent line on the part of the bank. I believe that what he's doing to establish the bank as an effective spokesman in Europe for the appropriate policy for this country is very valuable indeed. The interest of the job of the governor of the Bank of England must be very much linked to the extent to which the bank is free to fulfil its essential role, which must be to secure sound money.

It surprises me that you have never been tempted into politics. Have you never been attracted?

Not enormously. In my late twenties or early thirties I thought it was something I might be attracted to a little later, but to make the commitment you have to make to the hours, to the loyalty to one political view, to the uncertainties of the future, and to some extent to the financial sacrifice, you have to have a certain dedication. I've obviously never had anything approaching that level of involvement or interest.

The economic policy of this government is to beat inflation at all costs. They are doing this by maintaining a high interest rate which is itself inflationary. It discourages spending up to a point, but over a period it negates the very thing it aspired to achieve. High interest rates cripple small business, have an adverse effect on industrial expansion, make us less competitive in world markets, and above all divide the classes, since they widen the gap between rich and poor. What are your views?

High interest rates are obviously unattractive. But they would not now be necessary without rising inflation. High inflation has always operated in a way that presses down upon those who are disadvantaged, pensioners being an obvious example. So high inflation is obviously an evil. You then ask how you can reduce high inflation without high interest rates. Inflation was not initially made high by high interest rates. On the contrary, inflation grew again from 1988 in what might be described with hindsight as an over-lax monetary regime. The consequences were that the only way to bring it down was to raise interest rates. That way, as you say, has a degree of imperfection about it because it inevitably leads to distress in the personal business sector and to some distress for those who have taken on high mortgage commitments – and it clearly makes investment for industry more costly. No one welcomes high interest rates, but how would you seek to bring inflation down without high interest rates? What other mechanism could you bring to bear on it?

But we used to criticise the Labour government for having high interest rates, and now we have a Conservative government very much to the right and the highest interest rates ever.

I don't want to debate whether any one party's criticisms of another party's policy are right or wrong. I'd rather look at it in terms of what action has to be taken for the economy as a whole. In a sense it may be regrettable that one can't find a weapon other than high interest rates for bearing down on inflation, but I think it's generally accepted that it is, if not the only weapon you can use, a very important one in trying to reduce inflation.

The present government also pursues policies which basically encourage initiative through financial rewards. While there is nothing wrong with that, what I find disconcerting is the lack of compassion this government seems to project. Is that an inevitable result, do you think, of the prime minister's own character and personality – the Iron Lady image?

I don't believe it's an inevitable result of the prime minister's own character and personality. It is in very large part the prime minister's courage and clarity of thought that have achieved a considerable measure of recovery for this country from the position it was in in 1979. I remember 1979 as a time when not only were prices controlled, when union pay claims bore no real relation to the productivity of the company they were involved with, when there was a dereliction in the industrial

North and Midlands, and when there was no serious hope that this country could achieve an economic recovery. It's perhaps easy in a time when we've reverted to some economic difficulty to forget the steps that have been taken during this decade. But I've recently seen, going to Midlands' towns such as Nottingham or Stoke-on-Trent, where I was born, the extent to which there has been a substantial increase in business or industrial activities and prosperity in those areas over that period. That hasn't come about by accident. It came from a very depressed base and a state of apparently irreversible decline.

Now it may be, and I can't really speculate about this, that the prime minister herself privately realises that there is still an immense amount to be done to make her achievements permanent, and believes that if we relax too much we won't achieve it. It may be that this leads to a message being put across which does not sometimes appear to be a compassionate one. Undoubtedly there are administrative steps that have been taken, such as the alteration of the basis on which people sought social security benefits, which have not made life easy for the disadvantaged. The homelessness that's developed in the past decade is a reproach and concern to all of us, but I think it's difficult to be critical of the person who's been primarily responsible for what success we have achieved. Striking the balance is immensely hard. I suspect it will be struck in a different way in the 1990s, but that may be because of what was achieved in the early and mid-1980s.

How do you view the poll tax?

The poll tax at present is clearly socially divisive. There were many criticisms of the rates that were justified, but I don't think you can introduce a new tax which causes dramatic increases in the tax burdens on some individuals and reduces the burden on others. Especially when the better off gain and the worse off lose. It clearly is too crude in its entire application. If it was to be introduced at all, it would have been desirable to have had it banded. You can't attempt to reduce taxation for the lower paid and then suddenly impose a high new tax upon them. But I do support the attempt to secure the proper accountability of local government.

Parliament has recently been considering legislation so that any remaining Nazi war criminals in the UK may still be brought to justice. In view of the time lapse since the war, would it not revive hatreds best forgotten and would it not be extremely difficult to conduct proper justice when witnesses are perhaps too old to give accurate testimony?

The proposal is deplorable. When it was debated in the Lords, the majority was heavily against it. It will revive incidents which are historically as separate from today as the Napoleonic Wars from the battles in the Crimea, a fifty-year interlude. It creates a new offence in territorial terms – it makes past actions outside our jurisdiction into a crime in this country retrospectively. It calls for a near impossibility of accurate reflection and makes the presentation of a suitable defence almost impossible. It's a very retrograde step, and I hope very much that circumstances will never arise in which the Attorney-General gives his consent to a prosecution.

There are people who dedicate their lives to issues when they feel some injustice has been perpetrated on a minority or in some cases on a whole nation. Are there any issues for which you would fight on strictly moral and humanitarian grounds?

That's a very difficult question. There are many moral issues that inevitably involve one's time, commitment, and energies, and there are a number of issues that keenly engage one's sympathies. I'm involved in quite a number of them. I mentioned the problem of homelessness just now, and it is a slur that, in a capital city, people are sleeping on the streets. I also feel that there are certain central elements in our society that are very precious. We've spoken about the importance of democracy. I would say that anything that is an attack on democracy, which for all its imperfections is the best and fairest system of government you can have, would engage me strongly. Equally, I feel passionately about anything that attacks the fundamentals of the system of justice. You asked me earlier about my reaction and that of others to the government's Green Papers. I have not been able to think about some of the proposals in these Green Papers without deep concern, deep distaste and I wonder that a democratically elected government could have introduced them. If they had gone through as proposed, they would have put under government control the very profession which exists to represent the citizen against the government. And that explains the part that I and some others have sought to play in the debate. Although they have been amended, the original proposals were utterly deplorable.

Do you think religion is a force for good in our society, if so, does it have any drawbacks?

Religion is a force for good, a powerful impetus for human good, because it encourages imperfect human beings towards a better course of conduct. I don't think it's necessary to be religious to seek to lead a good life or to be fully committed. The forces of humanism can be very strong in that particular area. Indeed, there are clearly drawbacks and have been drawbacks to religion throughout history. It was the force of civilisation, the force of education, but was also sometimes the supposed justification for wars of immense brutality. That has been the paradox of religion through the ages. But ultimately it enhances humanity.

What would you say are your greatest qualities, and what your vices?

I feel disqualified really to answer either question. I suppose I work reasonably hard at whatever I'm doing. I hope I'm reasonably sensitive to the views of others on the issues involved. I don't have limitless self-confidence, so a good result is something which I tend to need to sustain me. As to faults, there are plenty others could tell you about!

But human frailties?

Oh, human frailties … I can get cross, although it evaporates. I can very easily come to think I'm being overworked. I sometimes assume that my own contribution matters more than it does. Whether you call it vanity or what I don't know.

Isn't it always difficult to ignore the public acclaim and remain unaffected?

I've always been somewhat surprised by any public acclaim. I was surprised that you wanted to do this interview. I think in terms of achievements that my own are reasonably modest. I've a long way to travel before I could say that I had made a real contribution to life. The Bar is a very critical profession that keeps you down to earth. All its members are proud of their achievements, so no barrister will go into a room and be regarded as a star by all his colleagues.

What are the primary causes of marital breakdown in our society today, do you think?

It's very hard to generalise. I think it can be a combination of circumstances and issues. It also reflects the fact that society does not expect people to live together in situations which have become intolerable for them. In the past there were far fewer divorces, and people were in situations of considerable misery. The reasons are complex.

Lord Goodman said on television recently, that the absence of a wife added eight hours to his working day. Have you found that marriage adds to or relieves constraints on a working life?

I think that if anyone's unhappily married for a period, then they may take refuge from that in working even harder. If you're happily married, then you get to tug both ways. First, you can feel that your work can be very effective and therefore you want to do it, but on the other hand you can feel you want to spend more time away from the work with your partner.

If I could ask you to look into the future, what sort of country and indeed what sort of European continent do you foresee?

I believe that something more homogeneous will emerge. I hope that isn't just because I want to believe it, but I think it's extremely important. We come towards the end of this century with the developments in Eastern Europe bringing back a map of Europe that would not be dissimilar to the one that existed before the First World War, if it were not for the European Community. I believe that the forces of nationalism are not the purest of human forces. It's immensely important that we should try as a Community to transcend this and seek ever larger groupings of people to live in harmony and co-operation. I think and hope that the European Community provides the focus for those aspirations as far as Europe is concerned.

Have you any ambition left?

Yes. On different levels. I took up tennis late. I'd like to be a better tennis player. I like history and am conscious of my ignorance – I'd like to be much more knowledgeable about English and European history. I would like to be a successful chairman of my bank in my very new occupation. I have no other really definite ambition except that I would like not to lose my links with the law. I'm glad to have become chairman of Justice, the all-party group of lawyers. I'm privileged to have the opportunity to take part in debate on law reform in the House of Lords. So I hope that, having moved into banking, I will still preserve in a very tangible way my links with the law and try to make a contribution to the development of the legal system and the substantive law. I am immensely fortunate in the range of activities in which I can take part.

Is it ever conceivable that you might return to the Bar?

I think not. I don't believe I would want to. I was a barrister for twenty-eight years. Barristers can go over the hill and fashions can change. I wouldn't like to go back to the Bar on a declining path.

The last question: If you were to live your life again, would you live it differently?

I would certainly go to the Bar, although I'm very conscious that the Bar is a demanding profession and would mean that, for twenty years probably, I would have to focus on it almost exclusively. The only thing I'm doubtful about is whether I focused too long on just arguing cases to the exclusion of other interests. The last six years, since I became chairman of the Bar and involved in public issues, have been the most interesting and personally satisfying of my life. So, looking back on it, I wish I'd got involved in certain aspects of public affairs and started to make a contribution there quite a lot earlier.

Lord Amery

Julian Amery was born in 1919 and educated at Eton and Balliol College, Oxford. He was a war correspondent in Spain during the last part of the Spanish Civil War. He joined the RAF and served as sergeant 1940 to 1941, after which he transferred to the army and fought in the Middle East, Malta and Yugoslavia. In 1941 he organised the first military missions to the Yugoslavian Resistance Movement and in 1944 was wounded in Albania when leading a force of escaped Russian prisoners. His brother John, who made pro-Hitler broadcasts from Berlin, was later tried for high treason and hanged in London in 1945. In 1950, Julian Amery married Catherine, daughter of a future prime minister, Harold Macmillan, and in the same year he was elected MP for Preston North. He was defeated in 1966 but was elected for Brighton at a by-election in 1969, a seat he would hold until 1992 when he was created a life peer. As minister of aviation, he was responsible for signing the agreement with the French government on the Concorde project. He died in 1996.

You grew up in a family which was as much a part of the Establishment as any could be. Has that ever worked to your disadvantage, do you think?

It worked both ways, though I don't agree that my family was so very much part of the Establishment. My father was a fellow of All Souls, but he didn't have money or any particular family connections. He got on to *The Times* and later became a leader writer and a supporter of Joseph Chamberlain in the tariff reform campaign, but that hardly puts him in the Establishment class. Perhaps at the end of it all he had graduated into it.

But you went to Eton, did you not?

Yes, of course. That was not a difficult thing to do, however, and it hardly makes me part of the Establishment.

Was your father the most influential figure in your life?

Certainly. He always treated me as an adult and would talk to me about economics when I could hardly understand it. I grew up imbibing the atmosphere of politics and I met Churchill and other leading figures when I was seventeen or eighteen. It was part of the air I breathed. And later in the early part of the war when I was catapulted into the whole morass of Balkan intrigue, we had the shared experience of political interest in that part of the world. This made a great difference and established a partnership between us which otherwise might have been difficult to achieve.

Most children seem to have a period of rebellion, quite often when they are students. They become Marxists for a while or hopelessly idealistic about the world. Did you ever waver from the Tory traditions in which you were reared?

Yes, indeed. My youthful political career was not exactly straightforward, and not all that Tory. When I was eleven years old my father took me to the House of Commons where I met Lloyd George who asked me what I wanted to do when I grew up. I told him I wanted to go into the navy. 'Why the navy?' he asked. 'There are much greater storms in politics, you know. If you really want the broadsides, walking the plank and blood on the deck, this is the place.' The scales fell from my eyes, and his comparison of modern parliamentary life to *Treasure Island* made me opt for politics. My father was of course delighted, but I kept in touch with Lloyd George, and whenever we had mock elections in my school I was always a liberal candidate. Then I examined communism and fascism and it was only when I went to Oxford that I opted for the Conservative Party, though I also joined the Labour and the Liberal clubs so as to be able to go to their meetings.

Some people have suggested that the driving force of your ambition may have been a determination to honour a well-loved father's memory. Do you see it that way?

I certainly inherited my father's views on the Commonwealth and the importance of Britain as the centre of the Commonwealth and a leading power in Europe, and all my life I was greatly influenced by his thinking. The year after he died I fought what I thought was the last great battle of the Commonwealth, the battle over Suez. When we gave in at Suez it was really the end of the Middle Eastern and African empire which Britain had built up over many decades. I was very sad at that, and it seemed to me then that our only chance of playing an important role in history was within Europe; and so while I did my best to defend what was left of the imperial position, in Cyprus, in Aden and elsewhere, Europe has become increasingly the important area for British influence to exert itself. I see no other.

At the Oxford Union you spoke in favour of conscription, which reversed the notorious 'We will not fight for King and Country' motion of some years previously. Did your conviction spring from the mood of the time or was it ingrained in your background?

It had been ingrained. My colleague in the debate was Randolph Churchill, who had by that time become a friend. It was the first of several campaigns that we fought together. When I left the debate, I went at once and joined the Royal Air Force reserve.

You had what people would call a good war, risking your life many times in undercover operations. How do you look back on these years ... with pride, nostalgia, perhaps with incredulity?

I have to confess, with enjoyment. There were of course moments of danger, moments of discomfort, but if you look at the whole spectrum of that sort of life it was pretty agreeable. Sometimes there were three or four days without anything to eat at all, then there would be a roast sheep. And then there were the times when we were sitting around in Cairo waiting for the next assignment, where all the delights of the flesh were available. Denis Healey once said I was nostalgic for the life of Richard Hannay in the Buchan novels. I don't think that's true, but I did enjoy those days.

Didn't you work for the Secret Service?

There were always two secret services, intelligence and operations. I was in operations. My role was always to do things, to blow up trains or bridges, or to shoot convoys. One of our more dramatic coups was when the Bulgarian government wanted to arrest, and perhaps to kill, the leader of the peasant party. I supervised the arrangements which brought him out of Bulgaria in a diplomatic bag. He was transported to Istanbul where we unpacked him and released him for his future activities.

Were you ever a spy?

The word is of course derogatory, and a spy is someone who learns or acquires information. If the spying side involves itself in operations it loses its security.

Apparently, you made the suggestion to Churchill that he visit his weary troops in the desert, and as a result you are sometimes dubbed 'The Victor of Alamein'. Do you think that visit had a significant impact on the outcome of war?

Who shall ever say? What happened was this: I was flown back from Cairo to London to report on our plans, and when I came to my father's house, I found him lunching with Harold Macmillan, then a junior minister. They asked me what the mood of the troops was and I told them I thought the Eighth Army was rather demoralised. When they asked what could be done, I told them that it would be difficult to change the balance of forces, but the balance of morale could conceivably be altered by Churchill visiting the troops himself. I then went on to the SOE headquarters where I received a telephone call summoning me to Downing Street. When I arrived, there was the prime minister in a boiler suit with a rather weak whisky and soda in front of him. Alanbrooke, the Chief of the Imperial General Staff, was also there, and the PM asked me to tell my story. Of course the field marshal didn't like the idea of a junior captain, not even in a regiment, criticising the morale of the army and he kept trying to interrupt, but Churchill said, 'Let him talk.' I told him if he went out and talked to the troops it would have a dynamic effect on morale. When I left Churchill thanked me, but I heard nothing for a while. Later of course he did go, and it was his private secretary, John Martin, who said to me afterwards that my talk had inspired Churchill with the idea, so to that extent I could claim to have won the Battle of Alamein.

You were a war correspondent during the Spanish Civil War. Did you have any sympathy with the Republicans?

I went three times to Franco's Spain. The first time was in the spring of 1937, and I came away rather pro-Franco. I went again in the summer of the same year when I met Philby, who was then the *Times'* correspondent, and very pro-Franco, rather more than I was myself. Then in a hotel bar I ran into a German colonel of my acquaintance who was fighting on Franco's side. We had a drink together and, referring to the Munich agreement, he said, 'I think we've got the better of you this time.' That was the moment I understood that the Germans and the Italians were about to fight against us, and this changed my whole attitude. The Germans and the Italians were using Spain to advance their control of Europe at our expense, and once I realised that, there followed a kind of Pauline conversion. I came back to England determined to see what I could do to oppose it.

You mentioned Philby. Did it ever occur to you that he could be a Communist spy?

No, I met him once during the war and once after the war, and he appeared on both occasions to be a rather right-wing Conservative.

In 1950 you married Harold Macmillan's daughter. In political terms I imagine this was a mixed blessing in that there were the inevitable cries of nepotism and an element of resentment that you had a direct line to the prime minister. Was that difficult to deal with?

I would want to get the story in perspective. Macmillan was then not even in office, and when he did get into office it was as minister of housing, so he wasn't at all a senior figure. I'd also known him before because his son Maurice was one of my closest friends at school, and I had often been to their house. But there were many steps between him and the premiership. I liked Harold but my affection for his daughter was entirely personal.

Macmillan aroused very different opinions, both as a man and as a politician. Some people thought him devious, a charlatan and ultimately a very cold man. In so far as you could stand back from family ties, how did you view him?

Every prime minister has to be to some extent devious and cold; he has to sacrifice people. If you're at No. 10 Downing Street you have to keep the party together, the Cabinet together, you have to drive through the policies to which you're committed. And Macmillan served all these well. He was enthusiastic for Europe, though it took him a long time to get the Cabinet and House of Commons to accept his proposal to join Europe, and then he was defeated by De Gaulle. He was always determined to maintain Britain as a nuclear power which now everybody accepts, even the Labour Party; but it wasn't accepted in those days, and he fought a good battle. As Chancellor of the Exchequer he gave in too soon to American pressure over Suez – I don't want to say he lost his nerve, but he became frightened by the run on sterling. He then made it his first objective to repair relations with the Americans, which he did. And we have to remember that inflation in his time never topped three per cent.

And yet people call him the father of inflation.

There's a lot of nonsense talked now about the Macmillan government and its effect on the economy, but in the light of the circumstances of the time he was doing just about the right thing.

But how would you rate him as a prime minister?

I wouldn't put him in the Churchill or perhaps even the Disraeli class, but I think he held his party together, he held the country together and he was vindicated at successive elections. He was a very remarkable political operator.

When I interviewed Mollie Butler there was no doubt in her mind that Macmillan was determined from the first day of his leadership to the last never to be succeeded by Butler, even though Butler was the obvious candidate. Do you think that's true?

Yes. He thought of Butler as an extremely able, intelligent political leader, but he didn't regard him as a commander-in-chief. I don't think it was jealousy – in fact he had very good personal relations with Butler.

Most people believe that Macmillan rigged the results of the investigation into whom the party wanted as his successor, and Enoch Powell even wrote an article entitled 'How Macmillan Lied to the Queen'. What view did you take at the time and what view do you take now?

I don't think he rigged the election. What happened was fairly simple: The Lord Chancellor and Chief Whip consulted members of the party as to whom they would like as leader. There was a strong vote for Quintin Hailsham and a strong vote for Butler. We were all asked, myself included, whom we would choose if we couldn't get the candidate we favoured, and there was a very large vote in favour of Alec Home. The prime minister had no choice but to tell the Queen that the party was divided between Hailsham and Butler, but there would be a consensus for Sir Alec Home; and so Home got it. I don't call that rigging it.

Why do you think Enoch Powell in particular opposed Alec Home?

The official reason was that he didn't think a fourteenth earl had the right image for the modern Tory Party, but I think it was really that he wanted Butler to succeed. He thought that if the leadership of the party refused to accept Alec Home then Butler would have it, but when the time came Butler wasn't prepared to throw his hat in the ring.

That Butler was prepared to serve under Home was commendable in itself, was it not?

It was a matter of political morals.

What did you think of Enoch Powell at the time? I believe you have described him as something of a werewolf.

He was always a friend of mine, I always liked him, but he does have some of the characteristics of a strange creature.

Butler is often referred to as the greatest prime minister we never had and indeed people often say you are the greatest Foreign Secretary we never had. Do you think these labels are ones which emerge only when we have events in some kind of historical perspective, or is it the case that you felt at the time you were being passed over?

Let's take Rab Butler first. I think if elected he would have been a great prime minister; what I'm not sure about is whether he could ever have been elected by the people. Of course he was an able man, but he lacked charisma and I don't think he was a natural leader, though he was a great chief-of-staff. In my own case, the only comment I would make is that there is a difference, not always appreciated, between diplomacy and foreign policy. Diplomacy is the art of negotiation; foreign policy is determining where the interests of your country lie. Looking back on the years between the wars I had a clearer view of where the interests of our country lay and would have fought for those rather than attempted negotiation. Anthony Eden, who was perhaps the greatest negotiator we ever had, fought very hard over Vietnam, where there was no great British interest, yet he surrendered in what I thought was an area of vital interest, in the Suez Canal Zone in 1954. This effectively meant the end of the Commonwealth as a world force, and a major defeat for Europe, and for British influence in Europe. Later on there was the Rhodesian crisis where again Lord Carrington achieved a great success in producing agreement between the different sides, but in my view at the expense of vital British interests in South Africa. So I have sometimes said that we have to be careful not to let diplomacy triumph over foreign policy; I would have put the latter ahead of the former.

Don't you think the loss of the Commonwealth, or the loss of the empire, was only a matter of time?

Not necessarily. It might well have survived. The resilience of the old Commonwealth was quite remarkable – in 1931 when we went off gold, in 1940 when we went into the war, in 1945 when we came out of the war – and with a little encouragement we could have kept the system going for quite a long time, perhaps indefinitely.

Would it be fair to say that your views are right-wing as opposed to middle-of-the-road?

I never know what people mean by right-wing. My views on domestic policy have been rather centre, some might say slightly wet. Where foreign policy is concerned I've always taken the Churchillian view that you first of all identify the enemy, and having made up your mind where lies the threat, who is the enemy, you must stand up against them and take whatever precautions are needed to counter them. I've always thought it right to defend British interests and to take a fairly long-term view of what they are.

When Alec Douglas Home became prime minister, your position became increasingly difficult and there was a move to oust you from government. Do you look back on that period as being particularly difficult?

Unpleasant ... but these things happen. I was perceived as an extravagant minister, with Concorde, TSR2 and space projects, and people were beginning to say we must cut back on public expenditure.

Do you think they were justified in trying to remove you?

No, I think I was right. Concorde has been a great technological success. It may not have been a money-spinner but it's been our little space programme and it hasn't lost any more money than space has lost to the Americans and Russians. And the TSR2 and the P1154 would have been remarkable aircraft – they haven't found anything better twenty years later.

I suppose you came close to becoming Foreign Secretary when Lord Carrington resigned over the Falklands. Were you disappointed not to have been chosen?

I don't think politicians should be disappointed. But it was perfectly true, there was a strong movement from the Tory backbenches to make me Foreign Secretary at the time, and I would have enjoyed the opportunity.

Your career was badly damaged during your time at the Ministry of Aviation in the last days of the Tory government – I'm thinking of the Ferranti business. How serious was the damage in your view?

Not very serious. I think I overcame that. The Ferranti family were prepared to cough up the money which we thought they had unduly gained. They repaid the debt, perhaps even more than they should have done.

Before 1962 your career was extremely promising, and you were tipped as a possible minister of defence. Are you philosophical about the volatility of political life?

You have to be, otherwise you couldn't go on in politics. I've never been very keen on securing a particular job; it's been much more important to achieve certain policies and objectives. There's no point in being embittered.

You were aviation minister when Profumo ran the War Office. What view did you take of the Profumo Scandal?

I supported him as far as I could. He was a friend, he's remained a friend, and I thought he was not really as important as the media made out.

The official reason why Profumo had to go was that he lied to the House of Commons, but of course the real reason was his involvement with a prostitute. Isn't that the ultimate in British hypocrisy?

I think they could have tolerated the involvement with the prostitute; the real reason was that he was led into a situation where he told a lie to the House, and this was an indefensible position to be in. Had he not lied to the House, and had simply admitted to the affair, he might still have had to resign but would have remained in the House of Commons, and continued to claim the viscountcy which was the right of any Secretary of State in those days.

The number of scandals involving MPs has increased over the years, or at least the diligence with which the media expose the scandals has increased. Do you think the private lives of MPs are a legitimate area of public interest?

In principle no, but of course if an MP or a minister gets himself into a flagrant position it's bound to be discussed.

Discussed is one thing, but hounded out of office is another.

Where do you draw the line between the two? None of this is new ... it went on in the last century, and it goes on today. I think the public will accept a good deal, and any incidental action on the part of a politician does not necessarily render him incompetent; on the other hand, a man who gives a lead in not only political but moral affairs, obviously can become a little ridiculous if he's caught in the wrong situation. Before the Second World War, the rule was that if the wife didn't complain the press had no right to complain, but in those days a divorce was a clear block to continuing in political life. That convention has now disappeared; indeed, it's sometimes said that you can't get into the Cabinet unless you're divorced. But the balance has not changed very much; things go on very much now as they did before.

Thirty years ago, you signed the Concorde deal with the French. Was that your proudest moment?

No. I suppose my proudest moment was when Nasser proved me right about the Suez Canal, and I was able to say in the House of Commons, much more politely than I'm saying it now, 'I told you so.'

You seem always to have had a thinly disguised suspicion of America and the Americans. Even in the 1960s when the cold war with Russia was at its height, you said you were more alarmed by the Americans than the Russians ... what was the origin of this alarm and suspicion?

Objective historians recognise that it was the aim of American foreign policy to destroy the British, French and Dutch empires. I myself became aware of this during the Second World War when I was attached to Chiang Kai Shek's headquarters in China. It became quite clear that although American policy was well aligned with our own in Europe and the Middle East, it was quite plainly anti-British, anti-French and anti-Dutch in the Far East. And Suez was the touchstone, Suez was the *coup de grâce*.

So you don't believe in the so-called 'special relationship' between Britain and America?

On the contrary, but it doesn't alter the fact that there was an American policy to destroy the British Empire; and it succeeded.

Do you have difficulty in accepting the view that without the Americans we would not have won the Second World War?

I don't see how we could have won without the Americans. I remember a curious occasion – January '41 I think it was – when I was invited to a little dinner party where Churchill and Harriman were the principal guests and the talk came round to how the British were going to win the war. There were still oranges on the table, though they became rarer as the war went on, and Churchill picked one up and said, 'If I were a worm wanting to get into this orange I would crawl round it until I found a rotten spot.' He then turned to Harriman and said, 'But you've got to keep the worm alive until it finds the rotten spot.' Without the Americans I don't think we could have won the war, but we'd already got to the point where we weren't going to lose the war.

Did you yourself ever have any doubts about that?

At the time when Rommel came to Alamein, I think my heart never doubted, but my head may have wondered a bit.

Your own patriotism during the war must have made your brother's behaviour all the harder to bear. I wonder how you think it was possible for two brothers born of the same parents and brought up in the same environment to have turned out so differently. You must have asked yourself this a million times – what is the answer?

Although you talk about the same environment, he had in fact lived on the Continent for several years, and that made all the difference. He'd been involved in the Spanish War, and then came very much under the influence of Doriot in France. He was convinced the Germans were going to lose the war and that the Communists would sweep over the whole of Europe. This was a view that became increasingly prominent in the occupied countries. Of course it was not for him to intervene, and he was able to do so only because of my father's standing. He should have kept him mouth shut, but he felt he had to say something. It was regrettable but understandable.

It is difficult to imagine the depths of disappointment, the shame, the anger which must have been wrought on the family at the time, feelings which must have been made worse by the heightened tension of the war. How did you all cope? Did you talk about it, or was it suppressed?

It wasn't suppressed. My father offered his resignation and I offered mine; we were both quite clear that it was the right thing to do, but we were both refused.

Did your father ever manage to come to terms with what happened?

Yes. He came with me to say goodbye to my brother in prison and indeed he wrote a short verse in the taxi which took us there, and I think it sums up his feelings: 'At end of wayward days / You found a cause / If not your country's. / Who shall say whether that betrayal of our ancient laws / Was treason or foreknowledge? / He rests well.'

In the course of my research I was struck by the fact that although you said you might have killed your brother with your bare hands if you had met him during the war, after you saw him in prison your feelings changed. Compassion took the place of anger, blood was thicker than water perhaps?

I think that is about true. Also, if I had seen him during fighting he would have been with Hitler and I would have been fighting against Hitler, but when I saw him in prison the war was over and the Russians were dominating half of Europe.

Did your brother's plea of guilty come as a shock especially after all your efforts on his behalf?

No, I think it was a logical act.

Albert Pierrepoint, the famous hangman, said that of all the people he executed your brother was by far the bravest. Did that make the pain all the harder to bear?

No, I think it was appropriate. He was an Amery.

As an MP you have consistently voted against capital punishment. Is that shaped directly from your personal experience?

It has been influenced by it. Within our legal system when someone is charged for a potentially capital offence there is a considerable delay while the lawyers prepare their case, then there's the trial, the appeal, and even when that is rejected there is the appeal for mercy. All this takes a long time and it exacts its toll on all concerned, especially the family, quite apart from the person charged.

You were a vociferous opponent of the Official Secrets Act and were against the lifelong confidentiality imposed on former members of security and intelligence services. Why was that?

There used to be a very flexible arrangement under which former secret agents could publish their memoirs if they had first of all submitted them to the proper authorities. This was a very good system and it should be allowed to continue, because it is right that people who spend their whole lives in the Secret Service should be able to explain to their family and friends what they've been doing, provided it doesn't endanger future operations. It is wrong to have a blanket veto on anybody writing anything, even about what they saw of butterflies in Anatolia. I produced what I thought was a rather good amendment which was accepted by the Home Secretary of the day. But he then went back on it – orders from No. 10.

Do you think Mrs Thatcher made herself and her government look foolish over the Peter Wright memoirs?

Yes. She was his best publicist.

In a BBC interview with Robin Day in 1979, just after the Commons debate on Anthony Blunt, you remarked that there were a dozen traitors in the House of Commons, a remark which you later – under pressure – unreservedly withdrew. Why did you make that remark in the first place, and why did you then feel bound to withdraw it?

I was not in a position to prove that the members concerned had been bought by the enemy; I could only have attempted to prove that objectively they were siding with the enemy. Mr Speaker asked me to withdraw my remark, otherwise there would have been a long and complicated debate. And so I withdrew.

You had great doubts about American foreign policy, especially in South East Asia and in the Middle East. Did you therefore have doubts about the Iraqi war and the reasons, largely dominated by America, for going to war?

I had no doubt about the American decision to go into the war. I still have the greatest doubts about their decision to stop. In Churchill's famous words: 'I don't know whether I would have dared to start; I would never have dared to stop.'

You once said of Mrs Thatcher: 'Her aims have usually been defensible, but her methods deplorable.' What did you mean by that?

I don't remember ever saying that, though I remember seeing it in print. I've always had great respect and considerable admiration for her. We didn't always agree about Europe, but she made a great prime minister.

You have crossed swords with Ted Heath in the past over oil sanctions and he sacked you from the opposition front bench, and yet on other matters you have been closely aligned. Am I right in thinking you have high regard for Ted Heath?

We've known each other since student days at Balliol. I've always liked him, and I am a strong supporter of the European Union, though I think he goes sometimes too far in that regard. I thought he was wrong about Rhodesia, and wrong about the Suez Crisis when he was Chief Whip, but we have a good relationship.

And was he wrong about Mrs Thatcher?

Well, that was his opinion.

You're very diplomatic. It has often been said that personal loyalty is one of your best attributes. Do you regard loyalty as a necessary political virtue?

Personal relations play a much greater part in politics than is generally understood, and loyalty to friends at home and abroad is of great importance. Sometimes necessity makes you change friends, but if you have to change friends you should always take steps to ensure that it is done with proper decency and decorum.

The Tories at the moment seem riven with disloyalty … but isn't that ultimately a more honest approach than the normal closing of ranks in political parties?

I'm not a great believer in open government, and I confess I'm rather shocked by the speed with which friends of mine publish their memoirs. They bare all sorts of secrets which would have been thought very indecent until quite recently.

Politics can sometimes be a dirty business. Have you ever felt a distaste or at least an ambivalence towards the political life?

No. If you go into the business you should be prepared to get your hands dirty.

As a politician you concentrated your energies on the wider issues of national importance – some said at the expense of your own constituency and the local interests of your own people. Do you think that is a valid criticism?

Not really. I managed to retain the wholehearted support of both my constituencies, in Lancashire and in Brighton. But I've always thought that the fate of more people is determined by what goes on abroad than by what goes on at home. Whether with the old imperial connection or the modern European connection, or issues of peace and war, or issues of export and import, the British people are terribly dependent on what goes on in the world.

What would you describe as your greatest failing?

Perhaps it was to take up positions that were not popular at the time – I'm thinking of my support for Britain's imperial and Commonwealth role when it was unfashionable (though probably right), and my tendency to make realistic judgements in foreign affairs when these were thought rather reactionary. I've usually been a little out of phase with the mood of the time.

If you were to relive your political life, would you do it differently?

I don't think so, I might have made greater efforts to soften some of the things I said, and I might have tried to sell my views rather more plausibly to audiences who didn't want to hear the truth; but I would still have taken the same line.

Do you think you will be vindicated by history in all the causes you have chosen to champion?

All is saying a lot, but I've already been vindicated to a very large extent in many of them. The chaos that has overtaken Africa as a result of a premature decolonisation speaks for itself; the successive Arab-Israeli wars came about directly as a result of Britain's withdrawal from the Suez Canal Zone; and the anxieties I expressed about Soviet domination of Eastern Europe, alas, were proved to be well-founded.

You were an advisor to BCCI. Wasn't that a major embarrassment to you in view of what happened?

No, because I was merely a consultant. I was only ever asked for my judgement on the political climate, the validity of investing in Africa or Europe. I was never involved in the banking or the finance, nor would I have been capable of helping in that way; they simply wanted political advice, which I was happy to give them at the invitation of the Sheikh of Abu Dhabi, who was a good friend of this country and a friend of mine.

But you didn't suspect anything at all? Weren't you taken in?

I was never anywhere near their books. I had no idea what they were doing. I certainly don't think I was taken in.

You began life with many advantages: financial independence, public schooling, intellect, powerful connections. You still live in the house in Eton Square in which you were born. Do you ever think that these factors have effectively removed you from the lives of the vast majority of people in this country?

No. Don't forget I was for eighteen years Member of Parliament for Preston in Lancashire, a very marginal constituency, and in order to keep the seat I had to see very much how everybody else lived. I never felt out of touch.

How did you cope with the death of your wife, your companion for forty years?

Of course it was a terrible blow, I can't conceal that, though up to a point I was prepared because she had been ill for a couple of years.

Do you ever think you might see her again in another life?

I don't know. These are mysteries which are not unveiled to me.

Were women very important in your life?

The whole problem is this: Which is more difficult? To have to do with women or to do without them?

And what is your answer?

It is a dilemma. Further disclosures will await my memoirs.

Though you have had a very distinguished career in politics, many have remarked that it is so much less than you should have had. You give no outward sign of being disappointed. Does that reflect your inner feelings also?

What is the use of being disappointed? In life one learns that the prizes don't always go to the ablest or to the ones who were right; they go to people who are better connected, or have the ear of the powers that be. It's stupid to be disappointed.

SIR HARDY AMIES

Hardy Amies was born in London in 1909. After studying languages in France and Germany he trained as a weighing-machine salesman in Birmingham before entering the world of design. In the 1930s he rose to become one of Britain's leading couturiers. During the war he served as an intelligence officer in the SOE, and in 1946 he founded his own fashion house. His salon was one of the few in Britain to rival the great dress houses of Paris. He was dressmaker by appointment to Queen Elizabeth and was knighted in 1989. Stanley Kubrick asked him to design the costumes of *2001: A Space Odyssey*, and he held the Royal Warrant for thirty-five years. He retired in 2001 after selling his business to the Luxury Brands Group. His books, *The Englishman's Suit* (1994) and *ABC of Men's Fashion* (1964), remain classics in their field. He died in 2003.

In your autobiography you record that there was no marked display of affection in your childhood. Was that something you were aware of at the time or did it occur to you only on mature reflection?

I was never aware of it. I have the feeling of having had loving parents who were not demonstrative; I have no feeling of ever having been deprived of affection.

Were they ambitious for you?

Yes, my mother particularly so – and fortunately she lived just long enough to see the glimmering of the first successes.

Yet in your book you make a point of avoiding discussing the relationship with your mother. Why is that?

I don't know. I actually got on better with her than I did with my father, though he was a most affectionate man, and we didn't get on badly by any means, but in the long run he wasn't very bright, and she was brighter. My mother had what is laughingly called taste – of course it was restricted to suburban taste, her life being very circumscribed. She was a village girl, but because of the years that she'd spent in a court dressmaker's she could recognise a real lady, and how she behaved, and she respected that.

Your brother who was Down's Syndrome 'coloured your childhood' as you put it. Did you resent the amount of attention and care he required?

Not in any way whatsoever. It's only looking back that I realise that it must have been a tremendous strain on my mother and on the resources of my father. But I wasn't conscious of that at the time, and I never had any feelings of disappointment. We loved him – Down's Syndrome children are always loveable – and later I inherited responsibility for him when my parents died, but by that time he had been in a home for several years.

You left the family circle at the first opportunity, and though you insist there was nothing 'unpleasant' about your upbringing, one has the impression that yours was not a very happy childhood …

I was certainly pursued by lack of money, but although that imposed huge restrictions, we were not on the poverty line. Overall, I think we were happy.

Your mother's death seems to have been a terrible blow. What are your memories of that time?

She had been ill with cancer for so long that there was an element of relief; it was only afterwards that I was moved.

Your father remarried within a short time, and both you and your sister seem to have disapproved of his second wife. Why was that?

Although she was a goodhearted woman she was socially very inferior to our standards, which is an awfully snobbish thing to say, but it's true. As in most families the daughter is closer to the father, and so my sister minded more than I did. She was at first jealous of this really hideous woman. She was so ugly apart from anything else.

Then why did he marry her?

I wouldn't care to go into the details. I now realise that my father was a very sexy man, and obviously she had certain tricks which satisfied him.

You are very close to your sister Rosemary … is she the most important person in your life?

Yes. I'm six years older than she is, rather bossy and, frankly, much cleverer than she is, something she has always admitted herself. There are strains which are difficult to articulate. I am very conscious of my responsibility towards her, but one of the difficulties is that she is, I think, sexless, in the sense of not really being interested in sex, although she has had sentimental attachments to women. Consequently, she's never really understood my life, which perplexes her still. It's difficult for her to accept that I have male friends, though there are some who have always been in my life and with them she has made friends, I'm happy to say.

She hates it when people call you effeminate.

Yes. I am able to laugh at it, because I'm not really effeminate at all. In fact, I would loathe to be a woman. Another difficulty is that she accuses me of not liking women; and that is true to an extent. I like them as artistic figures, as a sculptor likes his clay, but on the whole I despise their minds.

So you feel more comfortable in the presence of men.

Yes. It's not that I don't want women in my life – I'm very happy to have them around. But we're in danger of getting on to sex, which I said we weren't going to talk about.

In the early 1930s when you were in Germany you were a great enthusiast for Hitler – like, of course, a great many other people then, before the direction of his interests became clear. Were you very disillusioned?

The disillusionment came gradually. The family with whom I stayed welcomed Hitler as a saviour of the middle classes and the aristocracy, and I simply went along with them and didn't question their judgement. A much greater influence in my life at that time was the manager of the local factory, a north German, an extremely orderly man, who, I now realise, was very attracted to me. He was an intelligent, politically clear-thinking man, who favoured the Nazis to begin with, but changed in the course of events, and by the time I left he was very disillusioned.

Have you ever taken a serious interest in politics since then? Have you ever joined a political party?

No. I'm only interested from the outside. Our local MP is Douglas Hurd, and I go to his meetings out of politeness to him. Also, before the last election I couldn't bear the thought of the socialists winning, so I wanted to give him all the help I could.

I doubt whether it's generally known that you were part of the special forces during the last war. That would seem improbable to those with stereotypical ideas of a dress designer. Did you enjoy that period of your life?

Not really. I considered myself lucky to have spent the major part of the war in a branch of the War Office in London. Unless I was on duty, which was about once a month, I had every Sunday and half of Saturday free and was generally home by six o'clock. This enabled me to keep my hand in the dressmaking world. I still suffer from a bad conscience from that time, however, since I think I ought to have resigned because I didn't believe in what I was doing. I didn't think the idea of dropping parachutists into occupied countries was working; I suspected always that we were so infiltrated that we dropped people straight into enemy hands. I considered the whole operation tremendously amateurish and I started to feel quite cynical about things.

Did you always want to be a dressmaker?

No, I never thought about it. It always seemed something so remote from our lives, in spite of my mother. And in those days there were no designers in England; clothes were bought in Paris. It wasn't until I had an offer from the husband of my mother's boss that I suddenly thought, my God, this of course is what I want to do.

I imagine that a lot of people not in the business regard dress design as a frivolous affair. Does that bother you?

No. I am not aware that people regard it in that way. On the contrary, they are always amazed to hear about how much I earn for the country. At the time I joined the profession it was becoming socially acceptable, so I profited from that development.

How on earth did you manage to set up any sort of business, let alone a fashion house, at a time of such terrible austerity?

The war was a long time starting and it was a long time finishing. Churchill wanted unconditional surrender, which horrified me in view of my German connections. But during the time it dragged on I had the chance to lay down plans. I felt no guilt, since I didn't take any hours off, just my full allowance of free time. Then my darling stepmother gave me a thousand pounds, which was quite a lot of money in those days. I had ten thousand pounds when I started, and we made ten thousand pounds profit during the first year. There was actually no feeling of austerity; everybody wanted new clothes. The Americans were the ones who really encouraged us, because they were on my doorstep before we even had the clothes – in fact they bought them from paper patterns. I opened on 1 February 1946, and by April I was in America at their expense.

In an interview with Richard Rosenfeld you used terms like 'smarty pants' with some affection and talked about the 'gentry'. Did you feel very conscious of social divisions when you began? You appeared to adore the smart set.

Yes, I knew that I had to get on. Looking back, I learned the language of the English upper class just as I'd learned German and French. The London upper class is like a club and I am always amazed when I am admitted as a member. And I'm so very pleased, because one meets much more interesting people. Sometimes I see others in the same business and I think, how naff you are. I'm not naff, but I easily could have been.

You describe yourself as a self-confessed snob. Have you no qualms about that at all?

No. I am a staunch supporter of the class system. I uphold it out of conviction; it's the best of England, no question about it.

Don't you have a commercial incentive to say that?

Of course, the commercial side suits me very well, but there are two more important reasons. Firstly, I have a happier life for being a snob because I have a wide circle of friends, and the top people are far more interesting than the bottom people. Secondly, I'm very keen on English history and have an above average knowledge of it, certainly above average for a dressmaker. I have also lived in Germany, and I am perfectly at home in France, and I know how much both these countries would love to have a queen. The French and German aristocracies are clubs within themselves; they are self-supporting, but there's no top.

So you're a great supporter of the monarchy?

I would die for it. I really would take out a gun and go and shoot people if they ever threatened it. It's one of our most precious assets. To destroy it would be the most wicked thing. I say this not just because I admire the present queen. I would still support the monarchy even if we had a bad queen, heaven forfend that we did. It's the idea I defend; primogeniture is order – it's God.

You design dresses for the Queen. How important is that to you?

I'm really a supplier, a *fournisseur,* a furnisher of clothing to her. She accepts my advice if it suits her to do so. Her guiding principle in ordering clothes is that they shall be appropriate to the occasion for which she wants them. Not that she has explained all that to me – it's something I sense. She has supremely good manners.

You clearly have great admiration for her.

Enormous, and for many reasons – her politeness, the order of her mind, the way the palace is run, the way she has never failed to keep an appointment.

I suppose there is a sense in which the fashion business depends on a certain sort of snobbery, on the urge to be differently and better dressed than others.

I don't think there's an urge of any consequence. Our customers simply want to be comfortable and correctly dressed for the occasion. There is sometimes a competitive element, most evident when mothers are choosing a dress for their daughter, and want it to be better than the one they saw on their friend's daughter. But the competitiveness is not so strong in their ordinary buying; in many cases they don't want to stand out, they just want to be comfortably acceptable.

You have promoted an 'English style'. What do you think are its characteristics?

The main characteristics of the English style is that it has to have something to do with the country. A well-dressed, well-bred Englishwoman is at her best when she looks as though she has either just come up from the country or is just going back there. Urban clothes are better made by the French. Another feature is a certain nonchalance – a word invented in my studio. We abhor the dressed-up look, and we're not good at what is called dead chic – *mort chic* – that's not our line of country. There also has to be a curious timelessness about English clothes, because it's not good style to wear a new dress. My favourite duchess gave a very important private ball for which she wore a twenty-five-year-old dress. She had a new dress made by me for the servants' ball which took place the day before so the servants could not say that her grace was wearing an old dress. But for her own proper ball she wore an old dress and she looked marvellous. That is English style at its best.

Do you think of your designs as artworks? After all, they are clearly works of the imagination …

Absolutely not. I look on them as the work of an artisan. I don't like going to museums where they have collections of garments which have usually been designed for one particular occasion, then put away. My clothes are worn out and do not appear in museums.

I suppose dress designing is so personal a service that you become closely acquainted with some of your customers, a bit like a portrait painter …

That's not quite true. I have seen very few of my customers over forty years. Don't forget the structure of the house which dictates that clients are seen by a *vendeuse*, who does more than just sell; she serves the customer and waits on her and guides her through all the fittings, and very often becomes her friend. I like to retire and leave it to her. It is also a question of using up time and energy; I love to see my customers, but if my business were based on their always having to see me, I'd have been dead years ago. I don't even see the Queen anymore.

I have always wondered quite how it is that fashions change in the way they do. It never seems to be the case that things are suddenly and radically different. Do you think there is some sort of revolutionary law which governs it?

Fashion changes much less than you think. The idea of it changing is one promoted by newspapers which find it a very good way of filling a page. The women I know, not only my own customers but in my life generally, change the length of their skirts by perhaps one inch per season. Good expensive clothes for ladies don't actually date. I recently went to a very high-class wedding in Scotland and saw five different women wearing coats which were ten years old. I felt proud of that.

And they looked smart?

They looked correct. There is a difference. It's a difference the Queen understands; she knows being too smart implies something hard. The Duchess of Windsor on the other hand is dressed too smartly.

You said once that you can always tell when a lady's got style – 'You have only to see her in her underclothes to appreciate that.' Perhaps you've been luckier than I have, but how else can you tell … I mean, what constitutes style?

I think the word is insouciance. You must never show that you are impressed by your own clothes, or have that 'Don't I look wonderful?' expression. You must never be conquered by your clothes; style is to be the master of your clothes. When you see women in their underwear they must be immaculate. I take a rather old-fashioned view since most ladies of great style nowadays wear Marks and Spencer underwear, but I prefer the undergarment to be of beautiful quality, superbly handmade, and extremely plain. Frilly underclothes constitute extremely bad style.

There are now design schools and indeed art schools with sections devoted to clothes design. Do you think it is actually possible for the industry to sustain the current numbers of designers?

No. A very wise question. Firstly, I deplore the fact that there are design departments in art schools; it gives them quite the wrong idea, because clothes design is not art, it's craftsmanship. They even give degrees now which is totally idiotic. In my view a dress is not a dress until it has been sold; before that it's just a rough sketch, a suggestion. There must be the desire for a woman to possess it, to pay money for it, and that philosophy is sadly lacking in the art schools. Secondly, there has definitely been a decline in the teaching of craft. There should be more prizes for craftsmanship rather than design. What we lack are trained craftsmen and craftswomen, not designers. There are too many designers.

Fashion will, I suppose, become more and more international, especially with the advent of the Common Market at the end of this year. Will there be room for distinctive national differences? Indeed, is it possible now to see that a particular dress is French or Italian?

If it looks vulgar it has a good chance of being Italian as distinct from French. But that is an unattractive remark.

You have been outspoken, if not scathing, about women in design. Why is it that there are so few well-known women designers? One would have thought that they were the obvious source for ideas and yet many of the more famous designers seem to be men.

Men are objective, women are not – about clothes, or indeed anything else. The one outstanding exception was Chanel, and it is extraordinary how her influence is still felt today. But she had a man's mind and was very disciplined in her designs. Also, a designer of high-class expensive clothes cannot exist alone; he has to have a team with him, and this is what is forgotten by most people, and certainly not appreciated by the press. I am here today at the age of eighty-three because I have support, and in three years' time my house will have been fifty years in existence. I am the boss, and men make better bosses than women do. Because we're more intelligent.

Twenty years ago you were saying that the couture business was really finished; it was too labour intensive to make any money. But it still seems to be going. How long do you think such businesses might continue?

Well, we lose money at the moment, but if we are clever enough to earn in other fields, in licensing fees, in design labels, and in using our studio intelligently, then I think we will win through.

Have you ever designed clothes to be provocative?

Not consciously. They are sometimes seductive, but not provocative. If a dress is too sexy it's a bad dress, I've always said.

At one point you sold a considerable share in your business to Debenhams only to buy it back again later on. Why did you feel it was necessary to do that? Did they try to control your creative output?

No, they didn't do that. The disadvantage was essentially in having new bosses, in fact in having bosses at all, since I'd always been totally independent. When they bought us they promised to do two things: one was to help launch a women's ready-to-wear business which would have had the marvellous platform of Debenhams's sixty shops; secondly, they were going to launch a proper scent business – but they did neither. And in addition, we had the aggravation of being bossed by them. There was blatant jealousy towards me, and it was also quite clear to them that they couldn't control me. Though I had no shares in the business most of the contracts were in my name – Japan, for example, would never have given contract to Debenhams, they would only give it to Hardy Amies. This irked them, but in the end it always comes down to personalities, and the personalities at Debenhams were inferior. When it all came to a head and they wanted me to do something which I wouldn't do, they said – and the words still ring in my ears – 'If you don't do this, Hardy, we'll cut you up into little pieces,' meaning they would destroy me. I thought it was time to part company, so a favourable price was arranged and I bought myself back.

The recession continues to bite despite all the government talks. I imagine that the fashion business must feel the force of that very early ...

When there is a recession people buy wisely. If a woman is prepared to spend £2,500 on a suit, she knows she is buying the best possible value. So, the recession hits shoddier merchandise more than ours. We suffer a little bit, but my retail figures for the last year are down only ten per cent, which is not too bad, and the overseas revenue is up.

You never married. Was that a conscious decision or was it just that the right circumstances never occurred?

It never occurred to me that I would marry. I did once get engaged to a girl, but I cannot think why; it certainly wasn't because I wanted to go to bed with her. I thought perhaps she would make a good wife to me, but she was sensible enough to say no. I have been quite content and self-contained in the way I have lived, and I've never felt lonely for one minute. I have my sister, and I love having friends around. Ken Fleetwood who has been with me for forty-two years and is now the design director of my business comes to my country house fifty weekends out of fifty-two. We are not lovers, but he is like a son to me in the broadest sense.

About three years ago I interviewed Harold Acton who is a confirmed bachelor, but when I asked him if he had ever desired a woman, he said that he had, and indeed had a penchant for oriental women. Have you ever desired a woman?

No. I'm tremendously physical but I can't say I have ever desired a woman. I love flesh, I'm very tactile, very 'MTF' – Must Touch Flesh. I actually love touching women for the pleasure of it, to hold their hands, to stroke their arms, and I love beautiful women. It gives me immense pleasure to dress a woman to perfection. You can't do it to a man because he just looks a prat, a bloody fool. So curiously enough whilst I am obviously attracted to men more than I am to women, I still think it is idiotic to dress a man. I've always said a man should order his clothes with intelligence, put them on with care and then forget all about them.

You have, I believe, made arrangements to leave your fashion house to your employees. Certainly, a very generous gesture, but I wonder if you have ever regretted not having had children to come after you?

It never crossed my mind. In fact, I'm very grateful I haven't got children. The children of men in the dress business all seem to want to be lawyers or bankers, they never want to follow their fathers. When I see the trouble and responsibilities that children bring, I don't regret not having had children for one moment.

How would you sum up your recipe for success?

I've worked hard, not desperately hard, but I've always done my duty and I have a conscience about not doing the right thing. I have also had an amazing amount of luck. Perhaps the most significant factor was my three years on the road as a salesman selling weighing machines; it was not a very happy existence, but I did it and created an aura of orderliness and of dutifulness which somehow stood me in good stead. If I hadn't done my duty with this rotten job I would never have got the good one.

I understand Molyneux was your god, why is that?

Firstly because he was an Englishman, secondly he had extremely good taste in clothes. He believed in simplicity, as I do. All good clothes are totally unfussy. The first dress I ever saw of his was the simplest possible garment that just buttoned up the front, but it was absolutely impeccably made in beige linen with black buttons. And I learned that lesson and I follow it to this day. Although I can't draw, I have a gift of being able to see a garment from a piece of cloth. There are glib designers, little boys who can draw, make a little sketch, but they never seriously think of it, as I do. When I'm working on an article I think about it all the time, and then it takes me ten minutes to write it, because it's already written in my head. Although I don't want to compare myself with a genius, this is exactly what Mozart did. On the way to Prague he was thinking about what he was going to write when he got there, and then he sat down and wrote the overture to *Don Giovanni* in ten minutes.

How important is a beautiful face for the success of a dress?

A beautiful face helps tremendously, but the real challenge for the designer is to give a woman grace; it's what I call honouring cloth – you mustn't foul it up. No seam is ever attractive, so you must have a minimum of seams, then you have to achieve a certain skill of disguise. A woman of a certain age does not have an attractive bosom, and anyway to show the bosom too markedly is common; to disguise it is very important. Then you indicate the waist by the position of the buttons, rather than by nipping it in – the cloth must not be fucked up.

At the age of eighty-three you seem very fit. What is your secret?

Homeopathy is very important in my life. I'm not fanatical about it but I will use a homeopathic remedy if I possibly can. I haven't taken an aspirin for fifty years.

And tennis is a very good cosmetic. I play an hour's tennis on Saturday and Sunday, and for the rest of the week people tell me how well I look.

I read somewhere that you're not in the least afraid of death.

No. You're just going into nothing, so why should you be frightened of nothing? I don't believe in an afterlife. I believe in the existence of God, but it could have been any other name – nature, for example, or order. I think there's something that was put into our minds, and the question is, why the fuck are we here? I don't know the answer, but there is something we want to order, but the order is gone when you're dead, totally gone. And I don't mind it. I was meant to have a life, not a death.

A lot of people who are not religious in their youth, tend to become more religious with advancing years.

I don't have that feeling at all. My sister, being six years younger, thinks I'm going to die before her, and she would like to have a funeral for me. I quite agree, because I don't know of any other way of doing it. These non-denominational affairs are too awful for words. I'd rather have the whole thing, incense and choir, the lot. But this is nothing to do with fear, nothing to do with getting on the right side of God, not remotely.

And nothing to do with conviction?

No. It's *toujours la politesse*. It's good manners.

You were knighted in 1989. After the long association with the royal family did you not think this was a somewhat belated honour?

No. It never crossed my mind. I still think it's the biggest stroke of luck. Queen Victoria founded the Royal Victorian Order for services to the sovereign. I don't think she ever intended it for dressmakers.

You've had two books published now. Has that been a rewarding experience?

Publishers have one serious fault and that is that they never read anything. [Laughs.] You just know they haven't read the bloody book. George Weidenfeld is quite an inspiring man to help you make a book, but I don't think he's terribly interested. In any case I think my books are pretty dull in the end because they've got so many tactful omissions. Men should never have women editors because they don't understand how men's minds work. Diana Mosley was so funny when she said apropos of publishers that they all keep a troupe of Nigerians in their cupboards and when they edit a book they bring one out of the cupboard and give her a stub pencil. Women always bring in irrelevances. They're illogical creatures. Even Mrs Thatcher is a typical example, quite illogical, doesn't follow it through. She also imitates an upper-class voice which is the biggest grating thing that anybody can do. The voice is the key to the class system in England; once a man or woman opens his or her mouth you know what his or her class is. True Scots accents, or Lancashire, or Manchester, they're lovely; what is awful is the whine, the Walthamstow whine.

You're a very emotional man. Have you ever fallen madly in love?

Oh yes ... every week, mostly with the milkman. [Laughs.]

How would you like to be remembered?

I would like people to say, oh we miss him, he was such fun. I like laughing with people more than anything in the world. Life is a joke, a big joke.

SYBILLE BEDFORD

Sybille Bedford had a long and distinguished career in writing and journalism. She was born in Berlin in 1911 and educated privately in Italy, England and France. She wrote her first novel when she was nineteen and around that time she became friends with Aldous Huxley, whose two-volume biography she published in 1973–4. As a reporter she covered the Auschwitz trial in Frankfurt and the *Lady Chatterley* trial at the Old Bailey. Her books include *A Favourite of the Gods* (1963) and its sequel *A Compass Error* (1968). Her autobiographical novel, *Jigsaw*, appeared in 1989 and was shortlisted for the Booker Prize. Novelist, biographer, essayist and journalist, she was elected a Companion of Literature in 1994 and died in London in 2006.

In an epigraph to one of your novels, A Compass Error, *you quote Victor Hugo: 'Le passé s tune partie de nous-mêmes, la plus essentielle peut-être.' Is that something you believe yourself?*

Very much. All my writing has always been about *le passé*. I can't write about what happened yesterday, I have to write about events of fifty years ago. It's a big drawback.

There appears to be something of a contradiction in your character: on the one hand you want to shroud your life in mystery, to muddy the waters of your own biography; on the other hand, your novels are full of detail and events from your own life. Does it seem much safer to you if such things are confined to the pages of a book?

It's not a question of safety. I write as I must, and when I do, a great deal comes out which I normally don't talk about. Most novelists use the experience of their own lives, and I am no exception. I am a very private person, but there is a compulsion to writing.

You left Germany at the age of nine and did not return to till long after the war. You have described that early period as being 'suspended in amber' till you came to write about it much later, in 1956. Do you think you were in some way scarred by your early experiences in Germany?

Not at all because I was a small child. The book you refer to sprang from a great distaste and dislike for Prussia, and I've always had an antipathy towards the German side, but I had no difficult experiences in my early childhood. It's not quite correct that I never went to Germany till after the war because, in fact, when I was twenty-one I visited Germany with Aldous Huxley. I was absolutely appalled to see the Hitler Youth march about. I was, of course, half Jewish – two thirds Jewish, in fact – but one never talked about such things then.

In view of later events – Hitler and the rise of National Socialism – did you ever come to feel ashamed of having associations with Germany?

I had no associations with it.

But you were born there.

Yes, but I was born in Charlottenburg, which was a suburb of Berlin, and I was always very keen to put Charlottenburg rather than Berlin on my passport to make it sound a little bit more respectable. I had an early introduction to fascism because my mother married an Italian when I was a child. I went to live in Italy with her and her husband, and in their own very small way they resisted fascism.

Your father was German, wasn't he?

Yes, but he belonged to the south German aristocracy who married into Italians and into the Tyrolese. He lived most of his life in Paris or in Spain or in Corsica because he loathed Germany and was very cosmopolitan minded.

Do you think you have drawn strength from the richness of your background or has there been a problem of national identity?

The richness of background was very good, except I never felt I had the German identity, the Germanic mind. I feel I'm a complete outsider, but the fact that I had any connections with this terrible country became a curse of guilt, and for some time I tried desperately to anglicise myself entirely.

I suppose your childhood was not very unusual for its time, although it would be considered extraordinary and even traumatic nowadays. Your father died when you were nine; *you joined your mother in Italy, but you were sent off to England to be educated by tutors; your mother had a drug addiction problem – and so on. Did it seem difficult to you at the time?*

I think I was perfectly happy until I was about five, when my parents got divorced. My mother was always having great love affairs, and she deserted my father, which hurt his pride very much. My father was much older than my mother, but a very good-looking man. He was a great womaniser in his time – the Parisian *demi-monde*, and so on. My mother was his second wife, but she only married him because she couldn't marry her great love. All this was told to me as a child, and they certainly didn't want me. I was a terrible disaster. My mother had just decided to leave my father when she discovered she was pregnant. They were living in Spain at the time, which my father adored, but Spain was too primitive for a baby. When they divorced he got custody of me. That was a very difficult time because I felt very alone, and when my mother left there was nothing – no money whatsoever because he had none. I was wretched because my father was almost sixty, and although I think he loved me very much, I never had any maternal love. My mother was not interested in children, not at all. She once said to me: 'You were very sweet as a baby, but you're going to be very, very dull for a very long time, perhaps ten or fifteen years … we'll speak then when you've made yourself a mind.' Of course, I thought that was quite normal.

Did you ever regret not having a more formal education?

Very much. I longed to go to university, I longed to learn, but I never had a proper education at all. Tutors never came, there was never any money.

Your novel Jigsaw *described the cruelty of the emotional and physical neglect of a child by her parents. I know you are sensitive to there being too much extrapolation to your own childhood, but the similarities are obvious. Did you find it difficult to forgive your parents?*

Not at all. I used to wonder if my parents would forgive me. I actually behaved unforgivably to my father because I didn't love him and I couldn't show him affection. I was acutely aware of his loneliness, but I was like an ungrateful child. I grieved him awfully. As for my mother, I had a lot to be grateful for because she taught me everything about literature and art and world affairs. She was very well educated and she instilled into me the idea that it was a very grand thing to be a writer. She was a great influence on my intellectual life. I suppose I always had a passion for writing, but being brought up to talk about Dostoevsky at breakfast was a great advantage. I owe her an enormous amount.

Did you love her?

No. I was frightened of her as a child. She had a terrible temper. I began to love her when she started taking drugs and became unhappy in love and lived a lonely life. It was all much worse than in my novel because it went on longer.

A Legacy was reviewed favourably by Evelyn Waugh in The Spectator. *He said: 'We know nothing of the author's age, nationality or religion, but we gratefully salute a new artist.' I imagine these words gave you a tremendous thrill …*

Still do … still do. It's the one thing I hang on to sometimes when I start to wonder what I have done with my life. It's much the best thing that ever happened to me.

When you were eighteen or nineteen and living in Provence, you met a number of writers, including Thomas Mann and Bertolt Brecht … do you think that was a significant turning point in your own aspirations?

Not at all. We were living in a small seaside resort when all the refugees arrived, and although one was of course very much aware of their plight, they all called themselves princes or poets. They had enormous pretensions, and people like Brecht and Furtwängler and the Manns, they were very grand. They were not all poor exiles, and we thought how extraordinarily badly they behaved. They were more figures of fun in our milieu.

It was at that time that you also met Aldous Huxley, who was to be very influential in your life. You became close friends with him … were you also in awe of him?

I was absolutely awestruck because I had read him when I was fifteen and admired him enormously as a writer. I thought that one day, in ten or twenty years' time when I became a writer myself, I could perhaps be like him. At first the Huxleys were friends of my mother's, and I was just a young person sitting at the lower end of the table, but after all the terrible things happened they befriended me, and my moral education was really due to them.

Was Huxley's wife influential?

Enormously … she was one of the best human beings I've ever known. It was she who made his life possible. She was a near saint.

Was there perhaps a part of you that was in love with Aldous Huxley?

No. I loved him enormously, but I was not in love with him, no.

Isaiah Berlin said of Huxley that he had helped liberate a generation by shedding light in dark places ... do you go along with that?

I think he did, and he continued to do so with a later generation when he became religious and then a mystic. He liberated a great many English people who had been entirely bound by Victorian morality. He did not do it for me, of course, because in my milieu and with my parents' history we lived sexually emancipated lives.

Huxley was very concerned with moral anarchy in a scientific age and he made a number of sinister prophecies. Do you think at the end of the twentieth century that his pessimism was perhaps justified?

It was completely justified, but I think he was far less pessimistic than I am about it now. In his later life he thought that mankind could be saved by goodwill and at the very end of his life, when he was asked what was the most important thing, he said that we should all try to be a little kinder to each other. That was the measure of a man.

In another life you might have been a barrister and when you were young you used to go to the law courts. Your book The Faces of Justice *is a study of legal and judicial methods in different countries. Do you think that what happens in a country's law courts sheds light on other aspects of national identity?*

To my mind it does to a large extent. I must admit that I was infinitely surprised when I went to Germany by the quality of fairness in their law courts. It reflected the new spirit of the Germans. By contrast I was horrified by what I saw in French courts. The French are so civilised and yet their courts are so corrupt and so encrusted with neurotic issues. English law is fair as one might expect it to be, but then it's not so very good at finding out the truth. What struck me so much about the continental system was that at least the trials tried to bring out what actually happened.

You covered the so-called Auschwitz trial for The Observer. *Were you able to treat that as a professional assignment or were your emotions involved to some degree?*

My emotions were entirely involved but you learn as a writer to control those. When I was asked to do it I thought, I can't do it, I don't want to do it, but because

I had felt so much about it all my life, I thought it was my duty. Everything one heard was so appalling.

The judge was anxious that the trial should not be a short trial or a foregone conclusion but there should be a genuine effort to get at the truth. Do you think the truth was uncovered?

Yes ... the truth was there for everyone to see. It was a very fair trial indeed.

The trial lasted for nearly two years. You describe how Doctor Hofmeyer, the judge who had kept calm throughout the proceedings, broke down at the end because of the emotional strain ... what were your own feelings at the time?

I can't really remember my own feelings, I just knew there was great pressure at the end of the last afternoon and my piece had to be telephoned to England next morning from Frankfurt. I had no time to think about my own emotions. I became simply a machine which received information.

You also covered the obscenity case against the publishers of Lady Chatterley's Lover. *Did you as a writer have a sense of incredulity that this case was actually being brought, that the Establishment could believe that there was a serious risk of the nation's morals being corrupted, and so on ... was there not a fantastic element to the whole proceedings?*

Oh, it was grotesque. I sat in court with like-minded people. I shared the special correspondents' bench with Ken Tynan and we were nearly thrown out of court because we had to laugh, which wasn't allowed of course. Yes, it was utterly fantastic. It sounds absurd now that it was all taken seriously.

What is it that makes you write do you think? Iris Murdoch describes it as an attempt to bring order out of chaos ... how would you describe it?

I like to shape in words what I have received. It's a strange urge, and I don't know where it comes from. I have no confidence in my own writing, and I find it very difficult, but in writing one pays back the life that one has had.

In talking about your novel, A Legacy, V. S. Pritchett mentioned your 'passion for justice, for moral courage, the truth of the heart'. Do you recognise that in yourself?

Passion for justice, yes, though perhaps not moral courage. I admire moral behaviour, by which I mean forgiveness, gentleness, and the fight against all the things

I've had to contend with in myself, like bad temper, jealousy, unkindness, acts of selfishness.

Were you jealous in love? Did you have a weakness where men were concerned?

Not a weakness, no. I was very fond of some men; I had a few liaisons, a few affairs, but I didn't ever fall in love with men. One never fell in love with men.

Not even the ones you had liaisons with?

Oh no, there would be friends whom I admired or father figures, or very intelligent men perhaps.

V. S. Pritchett also detects two other emotions in your novels – pity and a sense of indignation. Do you agree?

Yes. I'd forgotten that. One mustn't be too indignant, because it quickly turns into self-righteousness. I've been trying for the last twenty years, not very successfully, to reform myself ...

In A Favourite of the Gods *which was published in 1963, you examine the nature of love. Would you say that your fictional treatment of love has come from your own experience and observation, or is it purely imaginative?*

It comes from my own observation and experience, yes. I wish I'd written more books and spent less time being in love. It's very difficult doing both at the same time.

In that novel the character Anna displays a certain ineptness for love. Do you think people in real life are either suited or unsuited to love?

Yes. In Anna I was thinking very much of Lady Byron, or of my own maternal grandmother. They all had a horror of the sexual love life, which is to my mind a curse. Some people are born like that, and it's very unfortunate.

Which would better describe your own disposition ... suited or unsuited?

Suited, most definitely. It was immensely important. I have had the great fortune of having received and given a great deal of love. Some of it has been unrequited love and I have suffered as a result of love, but on the whole I've been very fortunate.

You married Walter Bedford in 1935 but the marriage was short-lived. Was that a very painful time for you?

No, not at all. It was a very dangerous time, but not painful. It was an arranged marriage, set up by the Huxleys, because I needed British nationality. He was a homosexual and Aldous Huxley gave him twenty pounds to take me out to the Criterion and then to a musical. The marriage was never consummated; it was a complete fraud and a rather comic interlude, but because the Home Office stepped in and tried to prevent it, it was very frightening.

In A Compass Error, *published in 1968, you describe a love affair between two women. Would you have written about this kind of love earlier if it had not been such a risky topic?*

Oddly enough I did not consider it a risky topic. In any case it was quite delicately done. Nowadays, God knows what they do.

But do you see love between women as an extension of friendship?

Not as an extension of friendship. It can be fulfilled and complete sexual love, as fulfilling as heterosexual love.

How do you know?

Because I've experienced it in sexual love. One knows when love is love.

Doris Lessing spoke of the shrill voice of feminism. Is that also how you have found it?

Oh, I can't bear the feminists. I think they are appalling.

Have the feminists ever tried to claim you as one of their own?

Virago once wanted to put my name on their masthead but I wrote to them declining. Apparently, my letter was so awful they hung it up in their lavatory for years. Nobody's ever asked me again.

In most of your novels there is a sense of the transience of love, the impermanence of things. Is that something you have accepted easily?

No, it is a source of great sadness. Times change, places change; I've lived in places which I loved, the South of France between the wars, and then the five years in

Rome, but everything came to an end. I've lost so many very dear and important friends, particularly in the last two years and that of course leaves an appalling age gap. One misses them terribly, and one misses the stimulus.

You were brought up as a Roman Catholic, weren't you?

Yes. But nobody practised, although when we were living in the country at Baden my father went to mass on Sunday. I turned against the church very early and for childish reasons, because the village people told me my parents would go to hell since they had divorced. I couldn't accept that, so I decided that religion couldn't be true. But one doesn't lose it that easily, and I used to be quite frightened sometimes that Hell might exist. But now I've lost it more, and I dislike the Catholic Church very much, the Church of England even more.

Jigsaw ends with a sense of forgiveness and of hope. So these feelings come from a religious sense, would you say?

No. I believe in forgiveness and hope for their own sake. Looking back on my life, there are certain acts of selfishness and meanness which I would like not to have committed. But what I can say is that all the people I've loved, I loved till the end. I mean, not only to the end of one's living with them and one's affair with them, but as long as they lived. That is a very rare thing.

Tony Benn

Tony Benn was born in 1925, the son of Viscount Stansgate. He was educated at Westminster School and New College, Oxford, and served as an
RAF pilot from 1943 to 1945. Between 1950 and 1960 he was Labour MP
for Bristol, before being compelled to leave the House of Commons on
inheriting his father's title. He fought successfully to renounce the peerage,
and in 1963 he was re-elected to Parliament. He served on the Labour
Party's National Executive and failed to be elected its leader though he
held a number of ministerial posts in the Wilson government, including
Postmaster General (1964–6) and Minister of Technology (1966–70). His
publications include *Arguments for Socialism* (1979), *Writings on the Wall*
(1984) and several volumes of *Diaries*. He did not fight the 2001 election
but had the Speaker's permission to still use the House of Commons
Library and its refreshment facilities. He was a leading activist against
the Iraq and Afghanistan wars, appearing at rallies and on television and
radio programmes defending his cause. He took a roadshow, *An Evening
with Tony Benn*, around the country. He died in 2014. 'The Red Flag' was
sung at the conclusion of his funeral service in St Margaret's Church,
Westminster.

*There are many routes into politics but yours seem almost to have been predetermined
genetically. Have you ever regarded your political orientation as an accident of birth in
the way people often regard religion?*

Both my grandfathers were Members of Parliament; John Benn was elected a
hundred years ago for East London, and my mother's father in 1911 for Govan. My
own father was elected in 1906, so I was brought up in a very political household,
and my political memories go back to the time when I was three or four. In 1928 I
went to the house of Oswald Mosley, who was then a Labour MP, and I remember
the 1929 election when I was four, and visiting No. 10 Downing Street when I was
five. I met Ramsay MacDonald and in 1931. I met Mr Gandhi when he came to
London. I only ever wanted to be in political life, not so much from ambition, but
because this was an area of great interest where you could contribute something.

I wouldn't call it genetic, I would simply say this was what my life was like, and just as a doctor's son might want to be a doctor, or a miner's son might want to be a miner, I wanted to go into politics. I was very lucky, and I entered Parliament when I was twenty-five.

The twin pillars of religion and politics are a feature of your family history as far back as it can be traced. Did you ever feel a pull in the other direction, to the Church?

Not really. My brother Michael who was killed in the war wanted to be a Christian minister, but as far as I'm concerned, my own interest is confined to the social ethics of religion, the teachings about humanity and community rather than the mystery of life. The work of a local Member of Parliament, however, is very much like that of a conscientious minister. People come and seek my advice and tell me their problems, and I find that the most satisfying part of my job.

According to your brother, you both had a very good political upbringing but a very poor cultural upbringing. Is that something you felt to be a handicap in later life?

It's true that we never went to museums or art galleries and my father wasn't very musical. I suppose if you concentrate on one particular part of life you are deprived in other areas. You can't be competent and interested in everything, and I sense that a bit in my life. My children are very musical, and my wife is a great opera lover, but my horizons may be a little narrower than they should be.

You were greatly influenced by your father's politics and ideas. On a personal level, were you very conscious of the age gap which could have made him a rather remote Victorian figure?

He was born in 1877, and when I was born he was forty-eight, which is quite old for a father. But he had a very young mind and in terms of his behaviour and his vitality he never quite grew up. He was a mature and wise person but there was no sense of remoteness, no sense of his being a Victorian grandfather whom you had to look up to.

Your mother gave to you, in your brother's words, 'the precious gift of religion'. How important has that been in your life?

Very important. My mother's grandfather was a very strict Scottish protestant. He was a member of the Irvine Brethren, much the same as the Plymouth Brethren in England. This drove my mother's father to atheism, and the atheism drove my mother back to religion. It was like the shunting of coaches on a train. She came to religion, not because of any belief in the mystery of it, but because she believed there must be a good spirit behind the creation of the universe. It was never the idea of the sacred nature of Jesus, but she saw that his life embodied the spiritual community which she believed existed, and at the end of her life she became the head of the Congregational Federation. Independence of mind, both in religion and politics, contributed very strongly to my upbringing. Since my wife is of Huguenot stock from France via America, that same quality has been fed in through my marriage, and gives me a rock on which to stand when things are very difficult.

You were devastated by your brother Michael's early death in 1944. Was the family's grief more easily borne, do you think, because of faith in God?

As far as my mother was concerned, yes, but my father was absolutely shattered by it. My mother had a stronger personal religious faith, and she survived it. I myself was terribly distressed. I was in Rhodesia at the time learning to fly, and I had just turned up for a lecture one morning when somebody gave me a telegram which announced he was dead. I had to sit there for an hour in the class pretending to listen, overcome by sadness. I was very fond of my brother. He and I had a lot of correspondence together during the war, and when I look back on it it's not only his strength of character that comes through but also what it was that young people were thinking about, even during the destruction of war; what the post-war world would be like. His letters were full of hope, the very opposite of the pessimism and cynicism of today. That is an important element to keep in mind; fear drives you into yourself and encourages fascism, but when you have confidence and hope you can look at the world straight in the eye and not be frightened by it.

Your mother was a lifelong campaigner within the Church and notably for the ordination of women. Do you support the idea of women priests?

Oh absolutely. I can't think of many central beliefs of my parents that I have repudiated. She was a member of an organisation committed to the ordination of women called the League of the Church Militant and she was summoned to Lambeth Place in 1925 and rebuked by the Archbishop of Canterbury, Randall Davidson. She left the Church of England in 1948 because they would not move on the question of ordination of women, and became a member of the Congregationalist Church where there have always been women ministers. I feel very sorry that she died a few months before the Synod agreed to women priests but she knew it was coming and the appointment in America of Bishop Barbara Harris, the first black woman bishop, gave her such pleasure.

Although you describe Westminster as your local school, it nevertheless had all the trappings and rituals and customs of the famous public schools. Did that make you feel at all uneasy?

I didn't like the politics of it. In 1938 there was quite a strong political strain developing and the headmaster was very right-wing. I can't say I cared for it very much and I never felt that it gave me anything of real value in my subsequent life. My children all went to the local comprehensive school and even if they had won the pools you couldn't have induced them to go to a public school. Westminster was a part of my childhood but I can't say it really influenced my thinking, except perhaps to make me more determined to be independent. I can't say I was very happy there but in the end you make your own life wherever you are. They always say that public schoolboys can cope with prison because they are familiar with the circumstances of prison life, and I can understand that.

At a school debate you denounced the English public-school system as 'the breeding ground of snobbery'. Did you experience discomfort at being part of that system?

Yes and No. There were no comprehensive schools at the time and my parents sent me there as a sort of normal thing to do if you were middle-class parents. I can't say I felt very much at home there but I've always been an easy-going person, and wherever I am I try to fit myself in.

Would you accept that but for your schooling at Westminster and your father's eminence, entry to Oxford might have been more difficult?

There was a kind of automaticity about it; I'd been to Westminster so I was admitted to New College. But you must remember that it was quite a different period of history. I was there for six months in 1943 and then I joined the Air Force. When I came back at the end of the war, university life was quite different; it was serious and informal and modest in lifestyle, so it is misleading to think of that period of university life as having much to do with the Oxford you may visit now or the Oxford that existed in the 1930s. The luxury and splendour one associates with Oxford was not a feature of my time there; it was just like serving in an Air Force camp in Egypt, except there was enough to eat.

By the age of sixteen you had drawn up a list of things to achieve – to become an RAF pilot, to become an MP, to marry and have a family. All of these were realised within ten years. That suggests an extraordinary degree of self-knowledge and self-confidence.

I don't know whether it was self-knowledge or planning of a kind that has characterised my life from then till now, but I still look ahead. I have a diary that goes up to my hundredth birthday. If I live to be a hundred I have another thirty-one years to fill, and I find it a very good way of focusing my mind. For example, in 2025 I've marked in my 100th birthday on 3 April; my wife will be ninety-nine that year, and my older son will be seventy-eight. It is a way of developing your capacity to use every moment of the day.

You have often achieved a goal by means of what you call the stiletto principle – i.e. putting all your weight on one point. Has the principle ever let you down?

I've certainly made lots of mistakes. The only difference between other political people and myself is that I publish my mistakes in my diaries, whereas other people in their memoirs forget theirs. But it is true that if you really do press very hard on something you can win, just as a woman with a high-heeled shoe can go through a parquet floor.

You were the first man in history who, by Act of Parliament, was allowed to forgo a hereditary peerage. Your long battle was essentially to enable you to continue to serve in the House of Commons, but there was surely an underlying ideological battle of Benn versus the Establishment.

Yes, but it wasn't, as people think, an ambition to be prime minister. I deeply resented being expelled, having been in Parliament for ten years and elected many times by Bristol. My father, who was a very radically minded man, took a peerage in 1942 when he was sixty-five because Attlee wanted some Labour peers. There were no life peerages at the time; all peers were hereditary. He consulted my brother who wanted to become a Christian minister and didn't care if he became a peer, but he didn't consult me and I was very angry with him that he didn't. When my brother was killed my father was full of guilt, and he said 'I've landed you with this – you'll have to try and change it.' It took me ten years to change the constitution, and I learned a great deal in the process. Resentment of the idea that privilege should take precedence over democracy was the principle of it. Other people saw it as a human-interest story of the 'man bites dog' variety, but it was a long and very worrying period. It worked out all right in the end and I learned the most important political lesson in my life: never rely on judges, cabinets or parliaments to give you justice; if you've got a case take it to the people and get public support. I've never forgotten that and I've applied it many times to other issues.

Before you achieved your victory, most people thought you could not possibly win. Did that make success especially sweet?

It had been a long battle, but it was about the winning of it, so success was sweet in that sense. After the by-election in 1963 I went to the House one day when it was empty and I just sat there and thought of what a struggle it had been. It didn't make me bitter in any way, but it made me very strong against the privileged people who thought they ran the world. They didn't and they don't.

But would you consider that single act as your greatest achievement?

Not at all. It was a very inconsequential thing politically, and I would be very sorry if when I die that were the only thing in my obituaries. I would like to be remembered for totally different things.

It was the same Renunciation Act that allowed Alec Douglas Home to become prime minister. Was that a bitter irony for you?

It was a bit of a disappointment on the day, but on the other hand it was the same act that made Harold Wilson prime minister, because if it had been Iain MacLeod rather than Home, Harold Wilson wouldn't have won. I made it possible for the Tories to pick a leader so weak that Labour could win.

From as far back as the 1970s you argued that the principles of socialism were being betrayed by Labour leaders. This was a view that did considerable damage to the party you loved. Is it still a view you adhere to?

It depends on how you define socialism. For me socialism has a moral basis going back to the book of Genesis and to the New Testament: 'Am I my brother's keeper?' and 'Love thy neighbour as thyself.' Politics are based on moral judgement of what is right and wrong, and not on what is profitable and what is loss-making. No one wants to run a business that is loss-making, and everybody wants to get a return for their labour, but to run a society where the main criterion is profit and loss is criminal in my opinion. Homeless people don't get houses because it's not profitable; Canary Wharf which nobody wants was built by the government because they thought it would be profitable. The permanent critique of any society – capitalist, communist, fascist – is right and wrong in a moral sense. The second thing about socialism is that it is about democracy. If we are brothers and sisters under God then we have equal rights to govern ourselves and to enjoy a full life. The democratic argument is also very threatening to communism, fascism and capitalism, because none of those systems really believes that ordinary people have rights, save to be put down, kept down, brainwashed, manipulated, told what to, told to bow and scrape. The third thing about socialism is that because it analyses why things happen and tells you there is a conflict between those who create the wealth and those who own the wealth, it helps you to understand what's happening in the world. And the fourth thing is that it tells you that if you band together and you don't depend on a benevolent prime minister or leader or landlord to help you, you can do it yourselves. When you look at all that, the idea that the Labour Party could win by deliberately and explicitly repudiating its history and tradition – particularly at a time when the slump is worse, injustice is worse, the gap between rich and poor is worse, the world is in a mess – is very foolish. The only time we have ever won an election is when, as in 1945, it was fought on principle; 1964 and 1974 were also quite strong on principle; every other time we've put forward this milk-and-water liberalism, and we've lost. So I don't see any conflict between taking a strong position and winning support. After all, to look at the other side, Mrs Thatcher wasn't exactly a compromiser; people knew where they stood with her. But with the Labour Party you don't know where you stand; Dr Gallup writes our manifesto, so people don't believe us.

I'm intrigued that you mention Mrs Thatcher … if you could detach yourself politically, how would you asses her?

She was a strong, principled woman who defended her class with absolute commitment, and was determined to crush trade unionism, local government and democracy itself. I regard her policies as absolutely evil and destructive, but at least you knew where you were with her. By contrast Labour Party policy is like a bit of cloud blowing up – you don't know where it is, what it's covering up and where it's going next. I'll tell you an interesting thing. When Eric Heffer died, there was a memorial service in St Margaret's Westminster at which I gave the address. The Labour Party didn't send anybody, but Mrs Thatcher was there, standing just behind me. As I get older what matters to me is not so much whether I agree with people but whether I respect them, and I can respect people with whom I profoundly disagree if I think they mean what they say and say what they mean.

Your biographer Jad Adams acknowledged that you wanted to be leader, but not at any price. He writes: 'He would be leader if they acquiesced in his judgement, but he would not bend his principles to them.' And in that respect he suggests you are more of a Coriolanus than a Macbeth. Is that how you see it yourself?

There's not much point in leading a party that elects you without knowing what you stand for. People used to say to me regularly that if I just kept quiet about this or that I would become leader, but the idea of getting there by stealth, slithering up by concealing my real intentions is false, and it would have destroyed my self-respect. Leadership must be based on integrity and some understanding and acceptance of what you're saying, and that was the principle I worked on. I fought four elections, two for the deputy leadership and two for the leadership, and I didn't win any of them, but ideas were planted then and are beginning to grow now. As far as I'm concerned I'm a teacher, not a would-be managing director, so I judge my electoral campaigns in quite a different way from the way the political correspondents do, where everything is judged in terms of how far you have climbed up the slippery pole.

But had you been elected, do you think you would have made a good leader?

I don't know, but I would certainly have regarded the leadership as having a very different sort of function. My view, particularly as I've become older, is that the real political role is as a student and a teacher. I do hundreds and hundreds of meetings around the country, and everywhere I go I learn something, and I also try to teach something. That is very different from the modern view of political leadership which is that if you haven't got a policy you buy a new suit, you engage a new advisor, and you smile more. But you cannot build a political movement on sand. The Labour Party doesn't believe in public meetings anymore; they believe in soundbites and photo opportunities. We're witnessing the destruction of democracy, not by communists or Trotskyists, but by a conspiracy between the political leaders and the political correspondents that there will be no discussion allowed. However, you stir me too much ...

Most politicians would prefer to be compared to Coriolanus rather than to Macbeth, but the tragedy of Coriolanus was that he believed a statesman could act alone without bowing to others, and in the end his obstinate pride and lack of self-control got the better of his nobility and heroic virtue. Do you see anything of yourself in Coriolanus?

I'm not sure I know enough about Coriolanus to answer your question, but this theory that I'm isolated is without foundation. I've been on the National Executive longer than anyone in the history of the Labour Party, so if I'm an isolated figure, why do the constituencies still put me there? I've been elected without having to make the concessions that you're supposed to make in order to get to power. The idea that I have hovered on the margins out of obstinate pride is simply not true. The truth is I've been much influenced by what I've seen and I've had some influence in persuading other people. Where are the great figures who fitted all the patterns you describe, where are they, what footprints have they left in the sands of time?

Peter Riddell observed of you: 'For all his energy and affability, Tony Benn's inability to trust his fellow politicians means he has never really understood what politics is about.' Do you accept this inability to trust has been a weakness?

No. Peter Riddell's idea of politics is that you say anything to get personal power. That's not the politics I'm interested in, not the politics of any durability. The trouble with political correspondents is that they are interested in politicians' careers, which have very little to do with politics. The most influential people in the history of humanity have been Galileo, Marx, Freud, Darwin, and so on, but who are the people who have held political office? They simply disappear. My mother taught me, and I never forgot, that the Old Testament story was a conflict between the kings who had power and the prophets who preached righteousness, and if you ever think that power without righteousness is satisfying, then you disappear. Peter Riddell is a courtier of the governing class; he hovers round hoping for titbits from somebody who can tell him what happened in the Cabinet. In any court in medieval Europe there would have been a Peter Riddell. I don't mean to be personal, but the cynicism of the political correspondents, of the disillusioned liberals who hover in the lobby, of these people who were once progressive and now can't bear to think that anybody can have legitimate reason for hope, the cynicism that destroys democracy. If democracy goes it will be due to that view of politics, not the militant tendency. Peter Riddell's review of my book was the most revealing I ever read; it told me so much about Peter Riddell and very little about myself.

Political observers have often drawn a comparison between you and Enoch Powell, pointing out that you are both great debaters, both brilliant, evangelical and romantic. Does the comparison strike you as absurd, or even offensive perhaps?

I've known Enoch for years, and I respect him the way I respect Mrs Thatcher. He made one terrible mistake in the speech about rivers of blood, but he is a thoughtful academic, and I'm not intellectual in the way he is at all. People compare me to Enoch in order to make me seem extremist, but the difference between Enoch and myself is that he has never been elected to any position in the Conservative Party, while I have been elected for thirty-odd years to the National Executive. Enoch is worth listening to; you can disagree with him but at least he is motivated by a desire to illuminate. There are three ways in which politicians can operate: they can oversimplify like the demagogues, they can mystify like the people who say you can't discuss unemployment unless you have a PhD in economics, or they can clarify. Enoch is a clarifier. I also try to be a clarifier, and I like him very much.

Enoch Powell's 'rivers of blood' speech and your own riposte in which you evoked images of Dachau and Belsen came to be regarded as suicidal in political terms. Was it not one of the great political ironies of all times, i.e., that in attacking what you saw as the great evil of radicalism, you should have done yourself untold damage?

Radical questions are so explosive that political leaders have a conspiracy of silence about them. When Enoch made that speech, I did not think the issue could be allowed to rest, so I made the speech about the flag of Dachau. I wonder whether I was right to make it personal to Powell, but the argument itself was absolutely right. Wilson was furious with me because he and Heath had agreed that race would not be an election issue, but Enoch was right to open up such a big question. He opened it up as a white nationalist, while I opened it up as an anti-racist. On these matters you do have to take a stand, and looking back on it I'm glad I did.

You felt uneasy about having made the remark so personal, but you claimed that it was a statement which 'came out of my stomach'. Do you think the political arena would benefit from more remarks from the stomach and fewer from the collective party brain, so to speak?

I don't know that there is a collective party brain, more a collective party public relations officer. If I thought a great brain was working at the top I might be more at ease with myself. You have to say what you think. I don't want a peerage, I don't want cash, I don't want office; all I can do is use my experience to convey my convictions, and if I'm wrong I'll be criticised, if I'm right I'll persuade. When I look back I wish I'd done more of that. You compared me to Coriolanus, but I was rather slow in many respects to say what had to be said. The one principle I've always tried to work on is 'Don't make it personal', because if you do you reduce the issue to the yah-boo of politics, which is an absolute switch off; the public hate it, and it doesn't influence anybody.

Michael Foot, in one of the most troubled denunciations of our time, argued that after 1970 you underwent a radical change and in the eyes of the political associates and cabinet colleagues you became 'someone not to be trusted'. Can you see how that impression, however erroneous, might have arisen?

Michael began as a left-winger and ended up as a right-wing leader whereas I have radicalised with the years. It was actually in 1968 that I decided, having been a minister for four years, it was time to come out with a lot of serious political thought, and I made a series of speeches, long before we were defeated, about the referendum, the party, socialism, the media, and so on. Michael, who was not a member but a critic of that government, though it was only after we were defeated that I spoke out, which wasn't true at all. I was saying it all when I was in office and being attacked for it too. Michael's own position, however, has changed on everything: he's no longer a unilateralist, he supported the Falklands War, and so on. That of course is his right, he can do what he likes, but I don't accept this idea that trust must require you to move to the right as you get older.

Would you say that Foot's attitude was based more on rivalry than substance?

I don't think so. He became leader of the party by following the principles you describe. What's interesting about both Foot and Kinnock's election is that the party picked people with left-wing credentials to destroy the left. Michael's function as leader was to secure victory over the left on behalf of the right, and Neil's function was to do the same. Clearly, I had a different approach.

Your biographer's comment on Michael Foot's list of recriminations against you is: 'Indeed there are no friends at the top.' Have you felt the acute loneliness of political life?

It is a very cynical phrase, but it is true that alliances move, and only very good friendships can survive differences of opinion. Clearly my personal relations, though courteous, lack warmth if I have been engaged in a real argument with somebody; that is true, I must confess.

It has nevertheless been a common criticism of you that you have regarded your reputation and ideas as more important than the party you have served. How would you defend yourself against that charge?

I don't honestly feel I have to defend myself against any charge; I'm not a criminal coming up for trial. All I can say is that I've tried to speak my mind and I've been elected. It's not a charge ever made against David Owen, Roy Jenkins, George Brown, Hartley Shawcross, Dick Marsh or Reg Prentice; but only against me. I've seen other people who have been carried to the top on the shoulders of the Labour movement, people who have kicked away the ladder and yet are still treated as men of principle. For example, David Owen has been in six parties, yet he's now 'a man of principle'. Just exactly what is it about his political life that makes it in some way more uniquely principled and trustworthy than mine? It's a charge motivated by political disagreement, and without substance.

Perhaps another way of putting it is that you have been loyal to principles and ideals rather than people, something which has led you to argue with all the leaders of the Labour

Party in your time, Wilson, Callaghan, Foot and Kinnock … have you ever regretted that particular price of principle?

I have good relations with them all. I was out of Parliament when Wilson was elected but I voted for Wilson when he first stood against Gaitskell in 1960, just before I was thrown out of Parliament on the grounds of my peerage. Wilson made me a minister, and I was very close to him. Though we had our arguments, I regarded him as a prime minister with a capacity to keep the party on the road. I didn't vote for Callaghan, but I liked him very much, and preferred him in many ways to the latter-day Wilson because he was straightforward. After Callaghan came Foot, and I voted for him. Healey didn't vote for Foot, Silkin didn't vote for Foot, Shore didn't vote for Foot, but I voted for Foot. Kinnock I've known over a long period; he supported me when we had the so-called left-wing-dominated National Executive, and then when he was elected I wasn't in Parliament, so wasn't able to vote for anybody. I stood against Kinnock in 1988 because I thought his policies would lead to defeat, and they did. But it was a principled thing, nothing personal about it, so this idea that I've fought with everybody is just an illusion. You put me in a position where I appear to be defending myself; I'm not interested in defending myself, only in putting the record straight. The theory you suggest is put about because people disagree with me, which they are quite entitled to do; but they don't have to cook up imaginary arguments.

Harold Wilson is probably the least respected or talked about former prime minister. Why do you think this is?

Harold is not very well, but when his life comes to be assessed, he will be remembered for three things. First of all, for getting Labour elected four times, a formidable achievement after many years in opposition. Secondly, he reminded the public that without careful planning the technological revolution could destroy communities, as it has done. The third thing he will be remembered for is the Open University, and any man who founds a university is a man whom history will honour and praise for all time. He was also very committed to third-world matters, but of course he was always hated by the right. When he resigned with Bevan in 1951, he was treated with contempt by the right wing of the party. They loathed him and called him Nye's little dog, but he came through it all with considerable dignity, became leader, won us the election of '64 and carried through '66, '70, '74, then retired. At the end of his political life he was a bit of a spent force and I had many arguments with him about policy because I thought he was a bit technocratic and centralised, not democratic and open enough. I'm bound to say, however, that his was a successful life, more successful than Callaghan's or

Kinnock's or Foot's, more successful than that of Gaitskell who fought an election and lost it. So the man will be remembered in a rather different way from that in which the scornful Peter Riddells dismiss him.

A common complaint is that you are out of touch with the electorate and even your own party. Bill Deedes in an article in The Telegraph *a few years ago wrote: 'Tony Benn, though a highly sensitive man, is not sensitive to what's going on around him if it is not what he wishes to see. He lacks political feel because his mind is dominated by the kind of society he desires to bring about.' How do you go about countering that rather deep-rooted idea of you?*

It's very simple. I've been elected to Parliament sixteen times which is a record in the House of Commons, and every year for all those years I've been elected to the National Executive. I receive 15,000 letters a year, a thousand people come to my surgeries for advice – I couldn't be more in contact with the life and opinions of people except if I were a priest perhaps, but then it would be very much personal and rather less political. The test of my credentials is straightforward: if the local party wants me I am nominated as a candidate, if the electorate wants me I am elected. These arguments you put forward are just a way of trying to undermine the position I hold; I don't mind at all, they don't worry me, but if I'm asked then I'm bound to give the answer. I like Bill Deedes very much but all he is saying is, 'Mr Benn is not in touch with what is happening at the Carlton Club', and I confess that is correct; I'm not.

Bill Deedes in the same article wrote: 'There has been a marked petulance about his behaviour in recent years, when his main achievement has been to raise the standard of the wild miscellany of extremists who have done the public life of this country no good at all.' You will perhaps say that this is standard Telegraph *fare, but isn't it a perception which goes beyond the columns of the Tory press?*

The wildest extremist I've ever come across in my life was Mrs Thatcher. She destroyed trade unionism, she destroyed local government, democracy, she took us into the Common Market and the single European Act without a referendum … so it depends on how you define extremism. I've argued a case which would only succeed if I win a majority. Bill Deedes probably represents his class very well; I try to do the same.

Your last volume of diaries 1980–1990 was called The End of an Era. *Presumably the era referred to is the Bennite era?*

No. It was the end of Thatcher, and the end of Communism. It wasn't the end of my era – in fact, there's probably more public support for my ideas now than there's been at any time in the last ten years. People have rejected Thatcherism, they've rejected selfishness, they see our industry being destroyed, they see homeless people, unemployment, and much of what I have argued for has now won support. People wrongly thought it was the last volume of diaries, but I'm working now on 1942–1962, and the one after that will be 1990–2000 and the final one will take me up to my 100th birthday.

How would you like to celebrate your 100th birthday?

I'd like to be re-elected to Parliament on that day for the first five years of my second century.

In the volume 1980–1990 Neil Kinnock is vilified again and again as someone shallow, ambitious and a traitor to the left of the party. Wouldn't you allow that there is a good chance that history will come to judge him as the man who reformed the party for its own good, something which had to be done to avert disaster?

I don't know how many times you have to be defeated to prove you're unelectable. To be candid, nobody believed a word that was said. Election policies were made on the hoof, but I've never blamed Neil for this; I've only commented on his contribution. The people who accepted Neil were the National Executive, the Shadow Cabinet, the parliamentary party and what interested me about the recent conferences of the party was that the delegates were cheering because they thought Kinnock was going to win, and the media people were cheering because they knew he was killing socialism. What neither realised was that he would not kill socialism because it's alive, and that he would not win.

But did you think he would win the election?

I obviously hoped that we would win, but I had grave doubts about our capacity to win because it was very difficult to know what we stood for. For the first time in my life I voted against the manifesto along with Dennis Skinner. It never came out since they didn't want it to be known that there was a disagreement within the party on the manifesto, but I put up my own posters in Chesterfield and told the voters what I believed in, and my vote increased. I did not think it made sense in the middle of a slump and with the Cold War over to give high priority to nuclear weapons, to abandon commitment to a democratic economy and go over to Maastricht. It was a terrible manifesto which had no credibility. It was not laying the foundation for victory; it was laying the foundation for a fourth defeat. But I can't blame the leader because he was supported by everybody.

Would it be fair or accurate to say that the extremely gifted and talented tend not to enter politics nowadays, and that consequentially our lives are governed by rather mediocre people on the whole?

No, I don't think so. Clever people can be very stupid and I have known some very clever fools in politics and also some very simple people who are wise. Eric Heffer, who was entirely self-educated, was one of the most intellectual men I knew; his library and his knowledge were phenomenal. Then there are people with top degrees who haven't a single thought since they left college. Politics has always attracted ambitious and shallow people, also very good and gifted people. In the end the public have to choose; they get the government they want or deserve, whichever way you look at it.

I have the impression that you see yourself as being on the side of the angels. Does this stem from your radical Christian upbringing, do you think?

I don't think that's true at all. I'm an ordinary human being who has had a lot of experience, doesn't want anything and speaks his mind. I'm sure that Neil Kinnock thought he was on the side of the angels, but the angels in his case were all newspaper proprietors. I think I'm a hard-nosed realist who's confronting the harsh reality that Britain is rapidly declining and becoming a third-world country, losing its democracy, its morale, its self-confidence, and its hope. The dream that somehow you can get into power by joining with the liberals, having proportional representation, keeping the bomb ... I would call that romanticism of a foolish character. It depends entirely on how you use language.

'In the end,' as Rab Butler famously remarked, 'politics has to be the art of the possible.' Is that a maxim which you have tried to keep in mind?

Of course. I've never been able to do anything without consent. I've said things that were unpopular, I've been defeated sometimes, and other times I've won, but everything that's ever been achieved has been by consent. It's terribly interesting being interviewed by you because you produce all the language of the right, and when it's examined it's found to have no substance. I didn't become the leader of the Labour Party, but the elected leader, although he had the support of the party, failed to persuade the public. What I try to do is to get people to see a different point of view, a different perspective.

You have been described as a compulsive optimist, a natural leader always rallying the troops. Do you see despair as the worst enemy?

I see it as very dangerous because when people are despairing, they look for a Hitler or a Mussolini. You can't be foolishly optimistic, but hope is the great fuel of social change, hope keeps you going, the idea that we will reach the promised land, we will get there one day. 'I have a dream,' said Martin Luther King, and that is what makes people work. Cynical journalists try to eliminate hope and there's a great deal of anger directed against anyone who tries to spread hope. For years *The Guardian* has attacked anyone who has anything constructive to say, and when they've cleared the board of anything hopeful, then they say there's no vision. It is *la trahison des clercs*, a defect of the chattering classes.

In 1983 you were devastated to lose your seat in the General Election. How did you come to terms with this defeat and find the strength to fight another day?

I decided to be defeated in 1983. When my constituency was abolished I had six invitations to go to safe Labour seats and I refused on the grounds that I had been a member for Bristol for thirty-three years and I owed the people of Bristol everything. I chose to stay and be defeated, and I'm pleased that I did. I couldn't have walked away from the city that had supported me through the whole peerage case and just leave them to their fate; and it was the best decision I ever made. But you mustn't misunderstand me; to be defeated in the city I'd represented longer than anyone in the whole history of Bristol was a terrible bereavement.

How much have you relied on your wife and family for support during difficult times?

Oh enormously. My wife is an intellectual of formidable proportions and her understanding and academic capacity are far greater than mine, but she and my children have been very supportive. They've all paid a price for living in a house with someone who has been engaged in lifelong controversy, but as far as I'm concerned it would be quite impossible without the help of my family – parents, children and grandchildren. My little grandson came to Chesterfield on May Day and said afterwards, 'You weren't half as boring as you were last year.' Now when your grandchild tells you that, you know you've got a valuable adviser, and I take more notice of him than of Peter Riddell or *Guardian* leading articles.

Divorce seems to be an occupational hazard in political life. To what do you attribute the success of your own very long and happy marriage?

It's been a very good partnership and friendship, and I'm very fortunate in it. I met Caroline in Oxford and proposed to her after nine days, and from then on it's just been a very happy life together. We are very lucky.

You once advocated that instead of making divorce easier, marriage might be made more difficult, and that there might be compulsory education for the engaged couple. Was that a serious workable proposal in your view?

You must have done a lot of research into my writings. I remember writing that somewhere, but nowadays marriage is really more optional; it's partnerships that are developing now. In the end everything hinges not upon the formalities but upon the confidence of the relationship and the safeguarding of the children. So it is not now a question of making marriage more difficult because nowadays you don't have to marry at all.

Do you approve of that?

Oh yes. Marriage in one sense has been an enslavement of women, and I have been much influenced by having feminist arguments brought to bear in my own family. When my daughter was sixteen I remember she put up notices all over the house saying: 'End sexism in the Benn family.' That altered my attitude quite substantially.

As someone who has suffered from relentless press intrusion into your own private left and that of your family, what view do you take of the proposed reforms of the press?

I've had a very hard time, which I don't generally speak about. To give just one example, my rubbish was once collected in a fast car every day. My son made a bell so that when they lifted the sack the bell rang, we looked out and saw the Rover taking it away. They also rented a flat opposite, and they harassed my children. It was worse for my family than it was for myself. It has been a terrible burden on the children, and I dare say there have been ill effects, though not in terms of breaking up the closeness of the family. I would never take libel action, because all the money goes to lawyers, and anyway, if you win, what does it amount to? You have to recognise that a press intrusion is designed to intimidate you, and you just have to survive it though it is very unpleasant. I'm not in favour of any state control of the media at all because I think it would be used against the left. The government wanted to stop the Peter Wright book being published and to stop Gerry Adams talking on the radio, so I'm never going to believe the government is an instrument of freedom.

You have always been sensitive to comments about private wealth and trust funds for your family, and so on. Is that because these things sit so uneasily with left-wing politicians?

My father had a pension of £500 a year from a publishing house and my wife's father was a lawyer in Cincinnati, but otherwise most of what was published was completely untrue. I just have to live with that lie. I mustn't pretend I've ever been short of cash, but this sort of millionaire stuff that has been put about is just part of the lie. The newspapers have five lines about me: he's mad, he's dangerous, he's a hypocrite, he's incompetent, he's ill, and they have run them all, and when they get very excited they run them all at once. I've got to know them now.

Khrushchev once said: 'Politicians are the same the world over – they promise to build a bridge even when there's no river.' Would you agree?

[Laughs] I've come to the conclusion that you should not make promises of what you will do for people; rather you should invite them to join you in doing things together. If I knock at a door and say, 'Vote for me and I'll solve your problem,' people don't believe it and neither do I. I favour a manifesto which asks people to help, not a manifesto of promises. It's a different approach to the political process.

Despite your energy, your vision, your tireless campaigning for social justice, it's difficult not to sense that your story is marked by disappointment. Are you ever in the still watches of the night overcome by feelings of failure or self-doubt?

The one thing I do conceal are moments of despair, because if you spread your anxieties then other people won't make the effort. I don't think of personal failure; my life has been rewarded beyond any reasonable dreams, and I've had the most marvellous family and political career. At the moment I'm very optimistic because I think the whole tide is turning politically. I am sustained by letters of support and what people say to me in ordinary daily life – that's worth a million articles by Bill Deedes or Peter Riddell. But of course I am human and yes there are moments of terrible despair. I find the National Executive of the Labour Party the most painful thing in my monthly calendar; I dread going, I feel unhappy when I'm there, and I come away and lie down afterwards. The best discussions I attend are the ones in the Chesterfield constituency party; they are brilliant, clear, principled and knowledgeable, but the National Executive I find terribly distressing.

How has it been possible in the dirty business of politics to avoid bitterness and cynicism?

Cynicism is a very destructive thing. I would say I have been guided by certain things I was taught by my parents. They used to say, 'Never let the sun go down on your wrath' and 'Dare to be a Daniel, dare to stand alone', and so on. All these little sayings lodge, and when you get older you realise the whole of human wisdom is summed up in seven little phrases. I am genuinely not a bitter man, and I am not cynical because cynicism would destroy me.

Jad Adams writes at the conclusion of your biography: 'He was always true to himself and no sacrifice made a stone of his heart.' Would you be happy to have that as your eventual epitaph?

It was very generous of him to write that. I've made a million mistakes, many of which are published in my diaries, and there are many things I wish I had done differently, but I have been blessed with lovely parents, and a marvellous wife, children and grandchildren. I have been so richly endowed that it's impossible to express the gratitude I feel.

Sir Douglas Black

Douglas Black was one of Britain's most respected medical figures. Born in Scotland in 1913, he rose to become professor of medicine at Manchester University, a post he held for nearly twenty years. In the early 1970s he was chief scientist at the Department of Health and Social Security, and from 1977 to 1980 he chaired the Research Working Group on Inequalities in Health, which resulted in the publication of the controversial Black Report. He published extensively in medical journals and was president of the Royal College of Physicians from 1977 to 1983. Black chaired the UK government investigation into childhood leukaemia around the nuclear reprocessing plant at Sellafield, in Cumbria. He died in 2002.

You were a son of the manse and grew up in Scotland. How far did these two factors influence and shape the man you became?

Being brought up in Scotland gave me the accent you can hear, and being a son of the manse gave me the twin advantages of poverty and culture. My father's salary peaked at £300 a year, but we had plenty of books. There was no television, thank heaven, and we didn't even have a radio, so I was able to read and think.

Did you ever think of following your father into the church?

Not really. This was not from any aversion to the church at all, but just that my father was rather keen for me to become a doctor and I had a fairly strong scientific streak. Being Scots, I had C. P. Snow's two cultures embedded in me – my subjects in the higher school certificate were English, Latin, physics and chemistry.

I assume your family were Church of Scotland … did the Presbyterian ethic stay with you throughout your life, would you say?

Very much so. I'm firmly adherent to the so-called Protestant work ethic, but I'm very ecumenical in my outlook. I mean, anyone who's seen patients and mixed in the world could hardly be a narrow-minded adherent of one particular sect, but

I still think that religion means something. Like anyone else in this day and age I'm puzzled by the conflicts between cosmology as revealed by science and 'truth' as revealed in the Judaeo-Christian scriptures – or the Koran, if it comes to that.

When you qualified as a doctor, the National Health Service was not yet in place. What are your chief memories of medical practice at the time?

I qualified in 1936 and so I had twelve years before the NHS came in. Four of these years were spent in the Royal Army Medical Corps as a biochemist – not that I knew much about biochemistry, but that's where I was put, and I went where I was told. What I remember about general practice was – to put it dramatically – you could have young people coming in with lobar pneumonia, and one in five would die. Nowadays you would expect one hundred per cent of them to walk out of hospital, but before antibiotic medicine it was a different story. Some people talk about complete conquest of infection, but that of course is nonsense. At the moment we are bedevilled by at least two infections – BSE, to give the topical one, and the terrible AIDS business. Bacteria and viruses often just jump ahead. The other striking difference between then and now was access. In the old days only rich people could buy good treatment, not always as good as they thought they were buying, but they could still buy it. Poor people could go to the voluntary hospitals as they then were, and again get pretty reasonable treatment, but the poor middle class was greatly disadvantaged because they could not afford specialist fees, and stubborn pride – certainly in Scotland – kept them from soliciting charity.

Were you a young idealist then? Did you want very much to make your mark and improve conditions?

Very much so, both medically and socially. I wanted to practise good medicine, and also to investigate the leading edge of medicine. My own research field was body fluid, because someone told me when I was a medical student that the body was 60 per cent fluid, so I thought, well, that's for me. I'm an opportunist and a pragmatist.

Since you started out the medical world must have changed beyond all recognition. Have all the changes been improvements, would you say?

The improvements far outbalance the non-improvements. The National Health Service was a tremendous success for the first twenty-five years and shrewd people celebrated its twenty-fifth birthday not knowing what was going to happen thereafter. The incursion of market values has made very big changes. Whilst market values are tremendously important in other areas, for example in publishing, I think in medicine it's a shade different. I'm not being idealistic or starry-eyed here, but I would say that health is so important to people that there shouldn't be an additional financial barrier placed on top of the disability of illness.

Would you say there is a need nowadays to remind ourselves of the founding principles and values of the National Health Service? Do you think we have perhaps moved too far away from the original concept?

Yes. The NHS has been reorganised four or five times since 1973 and no service can stand up to that. It's so disruptive. What has happened is that a somewhat artificial system of contracts has been introduced to govern all transactions which used to be quite informal. And doctors have been made to think very much more about finance. While it's good that doctors should know what they're costing the public, it's bad if they have to think of money first.

Doctors traditionally maintain a professional detachment from political and social issues. In your own case, did you feel a responsibility, a duty perhaps, to go beyond the mere medical issues involved, or is it more the case that you think medicine cannot be isolated from other social issues?

My favourite answer to almost any question is both. I've got a built-in social interest, not a strongly political one, but one which just makes me *feel* for the poor. That's part of being Scots, I think. My spontaneous interest was strongly reinforced when I worked in the Department of Health for a short period as chief scientist, and I was asked to get a working party together to study the relationship between social class and health. I found that social class is really not a particularly good indicator of poverty because there are those in social class 1 who are struggling quite hard, and conversely in social class 5 you can get people who are unskilled but who have the Midas touch. That made me take a much more structured interest in these problems.

You are perhaps best known for the Black Report into inequalities in health care, which had considerable political impact in 1980. You established beyond doubt the links between social deprivation and ill health. Were you surprised by your own findings, or had you always expected as much?

What we discovered was not particularly surprising, since we have records going back to the last century showing that poor people have shorter expectation of life and experience more ill health than people who are substantially better off. That's of course something that anyone could see just by looking, but it was in the middle of last century that it was put on a quantitative basis by a man called Chadwick. Our particular contribution was to produce such a mass of statistics that it's now an unassailable fact that poverty and ill health are linked. That doesn't actually mean that poverty inevitably causes ill health, though it can do, just as ill health can lead to poverty. But we were able to argue quite strongly that there was evidence of poverty causing ill health, and the simplest evidence for that was that often the children of working-class people, manual labourers in particular, experience illness that accompanies them throughout their lives. It's unlikely to be due to their being weaklings, forcing themselves to be poor; it's more likely the other way round, though it's contentious.

Is it true that Mrs Thatcher tried to suppress your report and would not accept your recommendations on the grounds that they were too expensive to implement?

The formal evidence we have is that Patrick Jenkin, then Secretary of State for Health, wrote a foreword to the report in which he admitted just that. It's then conjecture whether Mrs Thatcher herself had anything to do with it, bearing in mind that it is unlikely that any secretary of state in her government would come out with such a potentially contentious statement without first having secured her complete backing. There may even have been dirty tricks, because our report came out in a dull cover in a pretty tatty condition. My friend Peter Townsend later brought out a shorter version in Penguin which had tremendous sales throughout the world. Some years later the Health Education Council brought out a further report called 'The Health Divide', and quite remarkable events attended its appearance. A press conference which had been arranged was cancelled by the Director General. There were strong denials that ministers had in any way tried to influence the abandonment of the press conference, but it seemed to me that the very strength of the denials implied they were untrue.

No one really disputes the association between poor health and poverty, but what exactly constitutes poverty in your view? Is there a minimum standard above which the term poverty no longer applies?

In this country there is of course no poverty approaching the extremes of third world poverty, which is accompanied by extreme morbidity and mortality. In Britain you get some people who are pretty destitute and others who are pretty affluent, so there is a graduation. A definition of poverty is rather elusive, partly because there's a tendency to think that if someone has a television set, he is not experiencing extreme poverty. The official definition is actually when someone has resources of less than half the average wage.

But poverty is such a relative term. I mean, there must be a difference between what we now call poverty and what you yourself observed growing up in Scotland in the 1920s …

That's right. As a working doctor in Scotland I saw people at the outpatient clinic in bare feet and woollen long johns which they wore because their houses were so cold. But to some extent these conditions are coming back, as you can see from the number of people sleeping in doorways.

Would you also allow that there are some people who sleep rough through choice? They're healthy enough, but they perhaps don't want to work, or are not disciplined enough to work.

I think that's true. It's difficult to know to what extent they are prey to circumstances and to what extent they lack motivation.

Did you distinguish between poverty and deprivation in your report? Which is more closely associated with poor health?

In a way deprivation is easier to define than poverty, because it's not purely economic, it's also cultural – lack of education and lifestyle factors which are linked with poverty, but are not of course a necessary part of it. For instance, it's paradoxical that people in social class 5 on the whole smoke more than people in social classes 1 and 2, but it may be their only consolation, their way of escape.

Doesn't the question of what can or should be done about inequalities in health remain an ideological one which can only be decided by politicians?

It has ideological components, that's for sure. I mean, the degree to which people want to do something about inequality depends on their political set of mind. But it's a blurred picture. For example, it's not the case that all socialists have nightmares about poverty and all conservatives never give it a thought; it's much more complex than that. May people in the Conservative Party are deeply unhappy about the relationship between poverty and health and the extent to which poverty has been recreated.

You have been critical of both Labour and Tory administrations of the health service. Although Labour were sympathetic to the principles of the NHS they were guilty of what you call 'doctrine socialism' with regard to private practice. Under the Tories you suggested in 1988 that the National Health Service was threatened by 'monetarist and managerial dogma'. Where are we as regards political approaches to the NHS today?

A lot of this is about power and who makes decisions. To me there have been two shifts of power which are a direct result of reforms. One shift has been from the professionals – doctors, nurses, biochemists – to the managers. Of course the health service needs management just like any other comparable enterprise, and I'm totally in favour of strengthening management wherever that can be well done. The second very considerable shift of power has been from a service centred on hospitals to a service centred on family doctors and other people. There are strong elements of good in that because, after all, more people see their family doctor than are ever going to need to go into hospital. But where it's not so much of a good thing is that general practitioners, instead of producing clinical arguments in favour of their patients being admitted to hospital, now have a financial stick with which to belabour the hospitals, and I've seen some very bad consequences of this. Sometimes hospitals literally run out of money with only a month or so to go, and conversely there is sometimes a budgetary surplus which leads to all sorts of unnecessary expenditure for its own sake. The annual budget has big problems.

How do you view the National Health Service today?

It's not as good as it was ten years ago. I don't think it's as bad as the reforms might have made it, because we've still got the people who are reasonably dedicated to the original objectives of the health service. My major worry is that if the market forces continue and increase, then recruitment to the health service will bring in a different kind of person.

In an article in the British Medical Journal *three years ago you wrote that the recurrence of monetarism over the last dozen years has revived evils that should have been relegated to history. What are the evils you were thinking of?*

I can be just as rhetorical as any politician when I'm writing a rather popular article, but the sort of evils I had in mind were unequal access to health care and an increase in the disadvantages of poverty and unemployment, two of the huge changes in the past twenty years.

In the same article for the BMJ *you quoted John Ruskin who said: 'Above all a nation cannot last as a money-making mob; it cannot with impunity go despising literature, despising science, despising art, despising nature, despising compassion, and concentrating its soul on Pence.' This is quite strong stuff. Do you really believe our priorities are quite wrong, that we have lost our souls to money-making?*

That's a rhetorical statement in a rhetorical article followed by a rhetorical question. No, we haven't lost our soul, though I think we've damaged it.

There appears to be a class factor in the use of tobacco and the quality of diet, and the amount of exercise taken. Isn't the answer – in part at least – better education leading to prevention? Or is that a pie-in-the-sky approach?

It's a very important approach, but it's certainly not one that ranks tremendously high in efficiency. To give a very concrete example, the Royal College of Physicians has produced four reports on smoking in general, and a further one on smoking among young people. But there are more young women smoking than ever, and also more young children. So education is not the only answer.

Where do you stand on the question of medical treatment for those who refuse to help themselves – by continuing to smoke, for example?

We should treat them as well as we possibly can to the limit of our resources. I'm against any kind of moral sanction on so-called self-induced illness. One sometimes feels the temptation, but it's one to be resisted. No, we're not there as judges, and we're not there as padres; we're there as doctors, and our job is to do the best we can for an individual. Of course by doing the best for the individual, we may be acting unfairly to the rest of society. But when I was in clinical practice, the basic principle was just take the case in front of you and not to worry too much about the hinterland ... very reprehensible.

Do you think we are moving in the general direction of making medical treatment conditional upon responsible behaviour in the patient?

I doubt it. I think that some of my fellow puritans would want to do that, but I'm not so convinced of the veracity of my own attitudes that I would want to impose them on anyone else, either by implication or exhortation.

You regard yourself as a puritan, rather than a liberal?

I'm not against liberalism as such, but I think it has to be balanced by responsibility. There has to be a balance between liberty and libertarianism, between rights and duties. Nowadays rights have been elevated to such a huge extent, and duties have become rather neglected. For example, when you enter marriage you are not only entering a career of great enjoyment and promise, you're also undertaking some obligations. I think the emphasis has to some extent fallen away from the obligations.

As a doctor – setting aside any moral principles you might have – are you in favour of the current relaxed attitudes towards sex … I'm talking about safe sex, of course.

I'm afraid I'm a dyed-in-the-wool puritan. I can't justify puritanism, but I just can't help thinking that on balance extra-marital sex does more harm than good. Sex is a good thing, I agree with that all right, but I also think it has to be controlled to some extent.

Are there any moral absolutes in the practice of medicine?

If you think about it, there are none at all – even if you consider something like 'Thou shalt not kill'. If I had someone with a disseminated cancer and he got a lobal pneumonia, I'd be only too happy to let him die from the pneumonia. Philosophers say that that's no different at all from taking a syringe of potassium and pushing it into a vein and killing in that way … I can only say that it feels very different. I myself have never actually given a lethal injection, but I have some sympathy with people who do it in cases of intractable pain that they can't otherwise relieve, even though I think it's a very slippery slope that doctors shouldn't go down.

When I interviewed Baroness Warnock she said that she did not believe in the sanctity of life at all costs, and that compassion was the single moral absolute. Would you agree?

No, I wouldn't agree. I'm not a believer in absolute moral dogmas at all. When I have to formalise it, I'm a situation ethicist; in other words, I believe that the facts of a given situation are so preponderant over moral principles that one shouldn't have absolute moral principles. In the case of the man with pneumonia who's riddled with cancer and in unbearable pain, I'd let him go. I think that's compassion, but I don't make that an absolute, otherwise I wouldn't be inclined to condemn lethal injection.

Would you agree that developments in medical science are now so rapid that they happen before our moral thinking is ready for them?

Yes, and it's almost inevitable, because as soon as some apparently worthwhile medical discovery is made, everyone wants to apply it that week. Science runs and ethics comes plodding along behind it, and that's probably not how it should be in an ideal world.

Since it is undoubtedly true that things which people scarcely entertained as possibilities are now actualities, and assuming this trend continues, isn't it going to challenge the whole moral fabric of our society?

Yes, of course it is, but I think that the challenge should be directed at the scientists and doctors themselves.

What sort of ethical restraints, if any, should be placed on doctors?

Most important is the judgement of their peers in a moral climate. It's very difficult for outside people to know what doctors are doing, let alone come to a judgement of whether it's right or wrong. Obviously, the extreme case is easy; it's the marginal case that's always the difficult one.

On the question earlier this year of whether or not a woman should be able to use her dead husband's sperm, you wrote to The Times *supporting her case. You said amongst other things that the woman was a victim of 'corporate tyranny' and that 'people banded together are capable of follies and excesses beyond what the same people acting as individuals would perpetrate on other individuals'. This was a reference to the Human Fertilisation and Embryological Authority. First of all, what in your view is the alternative to such an authority, which is there to safeguard standards and to see that the rules are implemented?*

It so happened that I was on the original committee which was the Voluntary Licensing Association. My experience of the work of the VLA made me very watchful for the future of the statutory licensing authority. It seemed to me they were applying general principles too rigidly to particular situations. That's really the germ of my idea that there might be such a thing as corporate tyranny.

Well, how can this corporate tyranny be avoided? What would you replace it with?

I'm not generally an advocate of centralisation, but I think I would feel happier with a central committee on ethics which would have a general surveying function, and which as specific cases arose could call in the appropriate experts to acquaint them in depth with the medical aspects. That would be a better long-term solution than a whole lot of ad hoc committees, each of which might become too narrowly focused on its own neck of the woods.

As regards the woman in question and the issues arising from her case, do you think that women have a right to have children, come what may, provided medical science can provide them with the means?

It's not a universal right – I wouldn't go as far as that – but unless there are strong contradictory circumstances, I think the woman is the best judge as to whether she should have a child or not.

You obviously believed in the case of Diane Blood that the authority in their decision had caused her undue stress and hardship. But haven't we also a duty to consider the implications for a child born in these circumstances? Can we be absolutely sure that it is morally right for the child to be brought into the world in this way – not only fatherless, but using the sperm of its dead father?

It is difficult to exclude remote possibilities, but if we come to the evidence in this particular case she said that the husband wanted a child, and it's not an unreasonable thing for a husband to want. What is the disadvantage to a wanted child of having lost one parent? Pretty small I would say.

But I'm talking about the psychological effect of being born from the sperm of a dead father ...

Well, it might worry many people, but it certainly wouldn't worry me. Maybe I should explain why I wrote the letter. There was perhaps a reasonable case to prohibit the use in this country, but when the authority then became so determined in their opposition as to preventing her going abroad, I regarded that as a step too far in pursuing an attitude about which I feel they shouldn't have been 100 per cent certain. But I have learned something since that worries me, and that is that the sperm was taken by rectal stimulation. That strikes me as being distasteful. It doesn't mean that it's necessarily immoral or wrong, but it is distasteful.

But aren't you also morally offended, if only by the very unnaturalness of it?

No. I'm a kind doctor, and it seems to me that the advantages to Mrs Blood of having a baby outweigh a hypothetical psychological disadvantage based on imagination – this business of the dead father. I mean, it is an aesthetic worry, not a moral worry. I've always tried to distinguish between things that are aesthetically wrong, morally wrong and illegal, because they are each different. They can be the same in so far as a lot of illegal things are also immoral and distasteful. But there are things which are distasteful which are perfectly legal.

Coming from someone with your views, there is surely a contradiction there ...

Yes, I'm a contradictory chap.

Well does the time factor play any part here? Would you feel happy if the same woman wanted to use her dead husband's sperm after, say, ten years? Would there be a stage where it would be viewed as a morbid obsession with the past unlikely to benefit the resultant child?

That question could only be properly answered by meeting Mrs Blood and having a talk with her and coming to some kind of a view about her psychology.

There is much talk at present of genetic engineering and cloning. With such possibilities, do you ever get a sense that Huxley's Brave New World *is closer than we think?*

It depends how close you think it is. Huxley's *Brave New World* involved the universal use of drugs to make people feel better, and something like that is not too far beyond the horizon. But I don't think there ever will be human clones because prohibition by government will prove to be sufficient.

People in general react very passionately to such issues, whereas doctors are renowned for their dispassionate approach to medical ethics. Is it mainly a question of knowledge and ignorance here, that is to say that the vast majority of lay people are deeply ignorant of the facts?

No, I think it goes far beyond ignorance. It's the doctor's real dilemma in a way. You have to maintain your professional detachment, otherwise you get so emotionally involved that you can't really provide the kind of help the patient needs. The patient introduces all the emotion that is required, and if any were lacking, the relatives would introduce still more. So I think one has to keep one's professional cool. That doesn't mean that one mustn't feel for the patient. You're no sort of doctor if you fail to do that, and appreciate what an illness is doing to a person – that's a necessary component of medicine, but you mustn't get so carried away by total sympathy for patient and relatives that you don't give them the best medical advice possible. Old-fashioned paternalism is out, even though I'm something of an old-fashioned paternalist myself. It is very difficult to be detached. Many patients have caused me great sorrow and I've taken actions that I have had cause to regret, but it wouldn't really have helped the situation very much if I had, you know, gone mad.

You were president of the Royal College of Physicians from 1977 to 1983. What were your responsibilities there, and did holding that office enable you to achieve certain goals?

I have a hedonistic approach: if you're enjoying a job, it's at least possible you may be doing well, whereas if you don't enjoy what you're doing, it's almost certain you're doing it badly. I tremendously enjoyed my six years at the college. My main responsibility was to supervise professional standards in the interests of patients, a very worthwhile objective.

Where do you stand on the question of attitude of mind being able to influence health and illness? And are you a believer in alternative medicine?

There's inevitably an interaction between body, mind and soul, and psychosomatic conditions are certainly rife. There's no doubt that attitude of mind plays a big part. To answer the second part of your question, one really has to approve of anything that's going to help patients, and undoubtedly many patients are greatly benefitted by alternative medicine in all its various forms. I have a twofold difficulty with it: first, that the burden of scientific proof is often difficult to obtain, and secondly, nature itself is a very good doctor, so a lot of the good things which happen may not necessarily be due to the alternative medicine but rather the healing power of nature. There are some areas where getting an actual operation done is terribly important, acute appendix being the most straightforward example, so I would say that people should obtain an informal medical opinion before they go off to alternative medicine if they feel really ill. Apart from that, it's not for me to condemn it.

Do you think that in our more secular society we are increasingly less able to come to terms with the fact of our own death? In the old days people felt themselves to be in God's hands ...

I'm certainly against prolonging life that's past its purpose, as it were. I've had to think about this a lot in the last year or two because I've been chairing college committees on brain stem death and also on the persistent vegetative state. I certainly think that there are some states of life that are worse than death. The decline of religion may have made people stick more to this terrestrial life, but like so much else, it's a mixed non-blessing.

How do you feel about your own mortality?

Not much in the way of fear, though when I wake up in the morning I recognise that as a blessing. I once gave a lecture in which the opening paragraph recalled Joseph Addison's essay about a crowd of people crossing a bridge which ends in a series of broken arches and is also perforated by trapdoors through which some of them fall into the flood below. Some of them clamber precariously from one arch to another, but in the end they all fall. That's very much the sort of picture you get of life as a doctor. There's a tendency in my profession to think that illness is something that happens to other people, but when you get to my age you have to recognise it's going to happen to you.

If you look back over your own lifetime, do you think society is more chaotic now, in the sense that the old certainties have been eroded, and material improvements in our standard of living, for example, have perhaps led to a corresponding decline in other areas?

Yes, I do. I once wrote a paper called 'Dead Sea Fruit', and I think perhaps we've experienced some of that. So many of the things that blossom brightly with promise have turned to ashes. In the 1960s we were promised universal happiness, but it hasn't quite worked out that way.

LORD BLAKE

Robert Blake was a historian and the biographer of Haig, Bonar Law and Disraeli. He also wrote the classic history of his political party, *The Conservative Party from Peel to Churchill* (1970). He was born in 1916 and educated at King Edward VI Grammar School in Norwich and Magdalen College, Oxford. During the war he served with the Royal Artillery and was taken prisoner in Italy in 1942. He escaped in 1944 and was mentioned in despatches. From 1947 to 1968 he was tutor in Politics at Christ Church, Oxford. He then became Provost of Queen's College, Oxford, and from 1971 to 1987 he was pro-vice-chancellor of the university. From 1980 to 1990 he was joint editor of the *Dictionary of National Biography*. He was made a life peer in 1971. He was a director of Channel 4 Television, had three daughters and died in 2003.

Do you believe there is such a thing as historical truth, or is it all a matter of interpretation?

I think there is historical truth in the sense of there being some facts which are certain. For example, one can't deny that William the Conqueror came over in 1066. But, of course, there is a great deal of interpretation involved within a framework of fact.

Let me ask the question differently. Is there such a thing as the correct *perspective in history?*

I doubt if there is, since the perspective is always changing as time goes by. One particularly notices this if one is dealing with very recent history, which I happen to be doing at the moment. I'm trying to update my history of the Conservative Party from 1983, where it ended before, to 1995, but I'm sure that whatever I write, although it may be useful for the time being, may look quite a distortion in ten years' time.

Gibbon said that history is little other than the register of the crimes, follies and misfortunes of mankind. Would you agree?

I think he was being unduly gloomy about that. Some good things have also happened in history. Gibbon did have a rather sombre and pessimistic view, but one needn't regard history quite like that. I don't anyway.

Historians very often say that a knowledge and appreciation of history is essential to an understanding of the present, and yet the empirical evidence would seem to suggest that in fact we learn very little from history. What is your view?

I think we do learn something from history. I don't believe history repeats itself; particular situations may look alike but there's usually a difference. There are certain lessons one can learn, however, and certain things which cannot be understood without historical knowledge. All the current arguments about the monarchy, for example, are pretty difficult to understand without some knowledge of how the British monarchy has developed.

Is there perhaps a case for saying that we learn from the historian *rather than from history itself? After all, the past has gone, we can't really know it, and historians are creative people like novelists, making things up, reflecting on the present, but in the context of the past. Is there anything in that?*

I think there is. Historians reflecting on the past can certainly help us to understand the present. What I'm against is claiming too much for historians. Although I've been a historian most of my life, I find some of them overpitch their claims. There is an inherent interest in understanding the past; that's all I say.

Do you think history and biography are sisters under the skin ... in other words, the greatness of a person's life is directly related to the response that he makes to the times in which he lives?

I would agree with that, although I wouldn't go so far as Disraeli who said, 'Read no history, only biography.' You cannot understand or assess an important political character in the past without knowing something about the surroundings and atmosphere in which he operated.

You are distinguished biographer of Haig, Bonar Law and Disraeli. I read recently that Edmund White, himself a biographer of the writer Genet, believed that biography is a way which allows little men to take revenge on giants. Is there any truth in that, do you think?

I hope not in my case. There are biographers who are simply in the business of debunking, finding out something discreditable, making the person concerned have feet of clay, and so on. I deplore that kind of biography and it's certainly not one which I've ever engaged in myself. And, of course, you can go to the opposite extreme. There are biographers – many of the famous Victorian biographers were cases in point – who can see no wrong at all in their subject and they start erecting a marble tomb almost. It is possible, however, to have a balanced biography, even of detestable figures in modern history. Alan Bullock, for example, wrote a very good book about Hitler. He gives a rounded picture, while in no way diminishing the odiousness and horror of most of the things that Hitler did.

Your biography of Disraeli is an acknowledged classic. Is that the publication which has brought you most satisfaction?

Yes. I spend eight years on it altogether, and greatly enjoyed doing it because although Disraeli had many defects he was a fascinating figure, and at the time I was writing, between 1958 and 1965 roughly, there really was room for a new biography which would put Disraeli in his proper political context. I think I could say I did achieve that to some extent, and without boasting unduly, I don't think subsequent biographies of Disraeli, of which there have been quite a number, have really added very much to what I did.

Why do you think that today we have no politicians of the stature of Disraeli?

That's not at all an easy thing to answer, though I think the fact is true. On the other hand, there are people of immense stature. Margaret Thatcher was very remarkable indeed, and a proper biography of her, which can only be done after she's no longer with us, could be a very interesting work.

Do you think history and historians will be kinder to Margaret Thatcher than they are to her today?

Yes. They'll have to recognise a lot of things she achieved, and virtues she had. Hers is one of the most remarkable prime ministerial careers in the twentieth century actually, and historians will look at her in a more rounded and fairer way, while recognising of course that she did have many defects.

It has sometimes been said that you allow your own political views to colour your writing ... does this not detract from the historian's objectivity?

It does if he allows it to happen, but I don't think I have actually. I am known to be a Conservative in politics and I've never pretended to be otherwise, but I don't think that made me necessarily unfair to Gladstone, for example. Indeed, the Gladstone family were very pleased with my depiction of him and invited me to give an important Gladstone memorial lecture on one occasion. So I think I am reasonably detached in that way.

How much was your own choice of career due to your family background and to the fact that your father was a schoolmaster? Do you feel you owe him a great deal?

I do feel I owe my father a great deal. He was a senior history master at the school I went to, so he actually taught me. My original intention, however, was not to be a historian at all, but to go to the Bar. But then the war came and I was in the army for six years, and somehow I had a different perspective after that. Rather out of the blue I was offered the post of politics tutor at Christ Church, and I thought I'd take it on. I've never regretted it. I might have made a lot more money if I'd been at the Bar, but I've got enough.

Did you get on well with your father?

Yes, he was always a very interesting man, with a great sense of humour, and he was always a devotee of history and a very good teacher. Everybody who was taught by him in those years would give testimony to that fact. My mother too – although not an influence to the extent that my father was – was a very affectionate and kind person. She also had a great sense of humour and was fun to talk to. I feel lucky to have had a very happy upbringing.

Do you feel you have influenced your children to the same extent as you yourself were influenced?

You'd have to ask them that, but I like to think I've had some influence on them. I have three daughters who are independent and pursue their own courses, and they are, if I may say so, extremely nice and pleasant girls, and very affectionate towards me.

Your academic life has been a great success. Has it been equally important to be successful as a family man?

I've never thought of comparing them, but I think it is important to be successful as a family man. I'm probably not the most impartial person on this, but I would say I have been reasonably successful. Of course, I was enormously helped by my wife, who died a year ago; she was really the one who had most influence on my daughters.

Disraeli said that a university should be a place of light and liberty and learning. Does that definition reflect the state of the modern university?

I wish it did. I agree with Disraeli's definition, but the universities are becoming almost factories for turning out graduates for a future career. The old idea, which

I certainly adhere to, of learning for its own sake, because of the inherent interest in it, does seem to be diminishing at the moment, and this is partly because the universities are so underfunded. The university world is not a happy one now at all, and in many ways I'm quite glad I'm no longer in it.

There are many who would say that our standards of education have fallen far below those of our European counterparts. Would you agree?

I would, but I agree simply because I'm told this is so. I'm not very knowledgeable about French, German or Italian education systems, but it seems to me widely accepted that the introduction of comprehensive school in Britain has been damaging to the standards of education, substituting a dull mediocrity for bringing out the best in the cleverest and ablest people. There are many signs that the Labour Party, New Labour, is recognising this for the first time, and it may be that we shall have a bit of reaction against that type of mediocre teaching which was dictated in part by the trendy notions of the 1960s.

Putting it another way, do you think a young student graduating in PPE from Oxford today is likely to be as well educated as you and your fellow students graduating before the war?

Probably yes, because the people who get to Oxford even now are not mediocre boys and girls; they are the cream of the schools. The teaching, at Oxford and Cambridge at any rate, has not gone down. The standards are pretty good, and I would have thought the students to be fairly near to being of the same calibre as we were. It all sounds rather condescending …

During the war you were a prisoner in Italy and made a daring escape when the Germans took over the camp. Does all of that now seem to have happened a lifetime ago, or was that experience so significant that It goes on shaping your life today?

I've certainly never forgotten it. It was a very vivid and exciting experience, and I and my two companions who escaped with me were very lucky not to be injured or hurt in any way. We got through to the British outposts of the Eighth Army in Italy in January 1944, and it's something I shall never forget. But I wouldn't say it continues to shape my life, since my life as it is today and as it has been for quite a long while would probably not be very different if I'd never escaped at all.

When I interviewed Diana Mosley, she told me that the experience of being interned during the war taught her to hate discomfort above all else …

I would agree with her on the whole, but it's fair to say that being a prisoner of war of the Italians was not remotely as distressing and grim as being a prisoner of the Japanese. That was not just discomfort, that was extremely painful and unpleasant. My main memory of being a prisoner of war in Italy was boredom and never really having quite enough to eat. But there were books in the camp, and I read the whole of Gibbon and all Shakespeare's plays, and I read the Bible from beginning to end. I don't think I'd have done any of those things if I hadn't been a prisoner of war, so there were possibly some countervailing advantages.

Your war service was completed at MI6 where you worked under Kim Philby ... presumably you suspected nothing?

Absolutely nothing. I knew him quite well, liked him, he was charming to talk to, with a rather engaging stutter, very amusing, good company. Very few suspected anything at all.

When you discovered that Philby was a secret agent, did that make you think that the basis for recruiting people in those days was seriously flawed? Didn't it tend to be done on the strength of 'there's this chap I know ... '?

I think one should recognise that Philby was a very exceptional case, but the method of recruitment was pretty uncertain to say the least. Too many people were recruited at the bar of Whites. It was very haphazard.

You once contemplated a safe seat in the House of Commons but claimed you were too lazy. Have you ever regretted the decision not to become an MP?

No, and considering what goes on now in the House of Commons, I regret it even less. It's been a very agreeable consolation prize, which I never expected, to be a member of the House of Lords. It is a much more enjoyable place than the House of Commons.

What does it mean to be a Conservative nowadays?

I would define it by negatives. One of the things that made me firmly a Conservative was that I disliked a great deal about Labour. I still believe the Conservatives are a preferable alternative to Labour.

Given that the Labour Party has changed its leadership and Blair looks very different from the others – even Margaret Thatcher seems to think he's all right – has that altered your view?

Blair has given a very remarkable performance, and he has made a lot of people feel that a change wouldn't be so dangerous for their values as it would have been when Labour was dominated by a very left-wing clique. I would never have believed that Labour could change to the extent it has. But it remains to be seen how far it really has changed. But he has achieved a great deal, and ironically he has fulfilled Margaret Thatcher's objective. She always said, 'My purpose is to destroy socialism', and the new Labour Party has certainly taken over a great many of the things which the Conservatives were propagating and maintaining in the 1980s. Having said all that, I would never desert the Conservative party. New Labour is an improvement, but I would still prefer to stay where I am, and I should say at once that I'm a great admirer of John Major. He is a remarkable and tenacious prime minister and he's much more formidable than people recognise. His chances of winning the next election are pretty slim, but I wouldn't rule it out altogether. A great deal can happen in politics in a very short time.

But you're almost a lonely voice in that respect. I mean, John Major does lack charisma …

He lacks charisma, yes, but that isn't necessarily fatal. I always think of Bonar Law who was a very successful leader of the Conservative party, and he had no charisma whatsoever. But he was respected and trusted, and he was intelligent and quick in his mind. Another man I would compare John Major with even more closely is Stanley Baldwin; and he didn't have much charisma either.

The problem with that argument is that in those days politicians were not exposed on television, or even in the newspapers to the same extent. You do need charisma today to win elections.

That is the big difference, I agree, and undoubtedly this is a difficulty which John Major faces. But it may not be insuperable.

As a Conservative you are presumably naturally sympathetic to authority and institutions. When authority and institutions are shown to be negligent, does that also undermine conservatism?

I think it does to some degree. The Scott Report has been damaging to the Conservative party. I say this without having read it, but I read the debates in both Houses of Parliament, and although I think the enquiry was flawed in many ways, the general impression that Whitehall was not working as it should has got out, and this is undoubtedly damaging to the Conservatives. It has given a general impression of incompetence and cover up.

But nobody paid the price for it.

That is perfectly true, nobody did. I think it was more incompetence than plotting, but they got away with it. My own view, if one was going into detail, is that William Waldegrave didn't do anything outrageous, but the Attorney-General actually ought to have resigned.

Where do you stand on the question of the monarchy? There now seems to be a real feeling in the country at large that it is an expensive and undignified anachronism …

I don't take that view myself, and how far the country at large really does take that view, I don't know either. There's no doubt that the activities of the Royal Family have been damaging to the monarchy, but one has to remember that the monarchy really comes down to the Queen, and nobody has anything against the Queen. She has behaved impeccably, and her constitutional role has never been criticised. For that reason, I believe the monarchy is not in any immediate danger. I also believe that Prince Charles will succeed to the throne. I don't agree with the theories that he may abdicate or be pushed out in favour of his elder son. His whole life has been built on the assumption that he would eventuality succeed as king, and I think he will succeed as king, and I don't myself believe there's republican feeling of any strength in Britain. There have been many periods in the past when the monarchy has been pretty unpopular. For example, it was only right at the end of Queen Victoria's reign, after her Golden and Diamond Jubilees, that she gained any degree of popularity. The monarchy doesn't depend on temporary popularity and opinion polls; it would take real revolutionary sentiment to convert Britain from a monarchy into a republic. Historically when monarchies have disappeared it's nearly always been through defeat in war, or an actual revolution like the French Revolution; they have very seldom just petered out.

As a member of the House of Lords, do you find the principle of an unelected body of legislators difficult to defend?

On grounds of logic it is very difficult to defend and nobody beginning from scratch would create a body like the House of Lords, a large number of whom are there by virtue of descent and not inheritance. The hereditary system is difficult to defend except on the argument that there are a lot of hereditary peers who are very able and sensible and make good speeches. My own feeling is that it would be better to leave the House of Lords as it stands, because its powers are very limited; if it had a lot of power, that would be a different matter, but it's really essential an amending chamber and hardly ever throws out legislation. It would certainly not be a good situation to have the House of Lords as a giant quango, consisting solely of life peers like myself.

There is still a climate of secrecy in government. Is this something you support?

I think I do. I may be prejudiced having worked in MI6, but I am very conscious that there are some things which governments simply cannot reveal. You cannot conduct diplomacy or foreign policy or trade policy in a goldfish bowl; it can't be done. This isn't to say that we couldn't go a bit more in the direction of open government than we have – I think we should – but government can never be completely open. It will never be as open as the opposition will invariably want it to be at any one time, but that's true with governments all over the world. The Americans, in spite of the freedom of information act, are very secretive about some things, particularly trade policy.

After the heavy Conservative defeat in 1966 you advised your party to sit tight and avoid damaging divisions within the ranks. What would be your advice to them today, if they are to avoid defeat at the next election?

I would give the same advice to a large extent. I'd put it like this: The Conservative party has been defeated even when it's been united on occasions, but if it is disunited, it is always defeated. This is perhaps true of political parties generally, but it is especially true of the Conservative party. The great danger for them is Europe. I can see a split coming in the party almost as bad as the one that occurred in the days of Balfour and led to a tremendous Liberal victory. Whether unity is achievable given the attitudes of the party at present I don't know, but that certainly would be my main advice.

When you look at the member of the cabinet today, can you honestly say that they have the statesmanlike qualities of those in the past, even a generation or two ago?

No, I think the quality of politicians has declined. I'm not all clear why it has, or what we can do to remedy the situation, but I've lived long enough to see that although, of course, there have been plenty of mediocre cabinet ministers in the past, the general standard was much higher. The same people don't go into politics nowadays; there are a lot of other avenues they can go into to fulfil their ambitions. There is a noticeable shortage of good lawyers in politics, and the reason for that is that you can't combine a career at the Bar and a career in Parliament at all easily, whereas you could in the days of F. E. Smith and Carson. Also they ought to be paid more. I have never shared the view, based on envy, that we shouldn't pay politicians more because there are plenty of people ready to do the job for the current pay. I think they should be paid about double what they get, about sixty or seventy thousand a year.

You said back in 1966 that the great Conservative victories have usually occurred because the radicals, whether Liberals or Labour, have made a hash of things. 'Historically, what is encouraging about the matter is that they very often do make a hash of things', you said. Would you extend the charge of 'making a hash of things' to your own party perhaps?

I fear I would. At the moment that is just what may happen. New Labour, at least ostensibly, appears united, and the Conservatives, while they haven't exactly made a terrible hash, have given a general impression of hanging on too long.

Over twenty years ago in an article in The Guardian *you suggested that pulling troops out of Northern Ireland and ceasing to defend the union was not an absolute impossibility. You said, 'The Conservative party must be extremely careful not to get into the situation where it is the only party defending the principle of British troops in Ulster because of traditional views about the union.' What is your view now?*

To withdraw troops from Ulster now would be courting disaster. I would be against that. There would be a major backbench revolt in Parliament apart from anything else, and Labour wouldn't back withdrawal either. My feeling is that things have moved a lot since 1966 as far as Ireland is concerned, so I would to some extent eat my words.

Do you think the peace process is unlikely to succeed?

I hope very much it will succeed, and I'm absolutely convinced that John Major is quite right to try. But if you're in parliamentary democracy where the ordinary rules of freedom and liberty apply, it is very difficult to combat a small group of fanatical terrorists who are prepared to murder and kill innocent people for the sake of a cause which they will never achieve.

Is there anything in life you would like still to achieve?

I have reached the age of seventy-nine, so I've got to do it fairly quickly. What I would like to do is to write a sensible book about the British monarchy, a subject on which an awful lot of nonsense is written. Although I am pro-monarchist, I'm not a starry-eyed adulator of monarchs; I am very well aware of the defects and errors. Oxford University Press wants me to do a history of the British monarchy from the accession of Queen Victoria to the present day. That will be enough to be going on with.

Disraeli said: 'Youth is a blunder, Manhood a struggle, Old Age a regret … ' Have you found it thus?

I'm not sure that I agree about youth being a blunder. I don't think I made any very good blunders when I was young. I've had to struggle a bit in manhood. Old age a regret? No, I've had a happy old age.

WILLIAM F. BUCKLEY JR.

William F. Buckley Jr. was the editor of the *National Review* for thirty-five years. He was born in New York City in 1925 into a staunch Roman Catholic family and was educated in Europe, Mexico and at Yale, where he took a BA in 1950. At the age of nineteen he joined the United States Army, leaving two years later with the rank of lieutenant. He married when he was twenty-five and the following year wrote his seminal work against the liberal establishment, *God and Man at Yale*. He was a syndicated columnist, and in 1966 he began hosting the popular and influential weekly chat show *Firing Line*. In 1981 he received a Creative Leadership Award from New York University and his many books included *American Conservative Thought in the Twentieth Century* (1970) and his controversial novel about the Queen of England, *Saving the Queen* (1976). He conducted an infamous feud with Gore Vidal over many years and was given the Presidential Medal of Freedom from President George H. W. Bush in 1991, publishing his memoir, *Miles Gone By*, a few months later. He died in 2008.

Who has been the primary influence on your life, apart from Edmund Burke?

My father, whom I found entirely admirable and in many senses unique. He was well educated but he was a self-made man. His father was a sheriff in Texas, which was a pretty high position after the Civil War. But there was no wealth in the South, none whatsoever, so he worked his way through university, and when his father died, put the entire family through university too. He went to Texas, started a business, married at the age of thirty-six, had ten children, educated them all, and we grew up a happy and well-informed family. He was an intellectual by inclination, a successful businessman, a wonderful father and husband. That's pretty unusual. The responsibility of ten children when you are in the oil business and knowing the great fluctuations of fortune is something I've never had to go through, thank God.

William F. Buckley Jr.

What is it exactly that an American conservative seeks to conserve?

American conservatives are guided by the notion that there are some stable insights in the idea of America which are not subject to essential change. They might change in respect of modality, of emphasis, but not otherwise. In that sense we take the word conservative and use it a little bit differently from the way it might be used, say, in Russia, where they speak of the conservatives who want to restore Stalinism. What we want to retain is understandings having to do with the division of power politically, and other understandings having to do with the recognition of two cities – the city of God and the city of man – as coexisting in modern society and each commanding a loyalty.

Many might regard your conservatism as a natural consequence of being rich. Is there any reason why a poor man should be a conservative?

I should think so. The value of conservative arrangements to a rich man is *pari passu* valuable also to a poor man. A poor man suffers much more than a rich man from inflation, for instance, and a poor man has a much greater chance to change his own status in a society with the upward mobility the conservatives emphasise. Nineteen per cent of the people in the lowest quintals in America moved to different quintals during the 1980s, which is a significant achievement. We're talking about a society in which, by current standards of poverty, 90 per cent of the American people were poor in 1900, a figure that has reduced to somewhere between 13 and 14 per cent. That shows a tremendous upward mobility, which obviously caused a broad prosperity to a lot of people who didn't have it. But just as you can go up, so you obviously have a chance to go down. Now, if you say that rich people are better off than poor people, I'd say that's so obvious it's hardly worth commenting on. But if I may say so, there seems to be more interest in genuine upward mobility in America than there is in Britain.

But do the rich become richer and the poor poorer?

No, it's not true. I had an interesting argument on this point with Kenneth Galbraith's son, who said that, in nineteenth-century England, the disparity between the most and the least rich was greater even than in America today. The answer to your question is that more people are getting richer, but there is a compensating elevation in the lowest quintal. What you really have is a structure to be compared with a mobile, a string to which various things attach. The whole string goes up. There is no other way to account for a reduction from 90 percent to 13 per cent in the poor over a period of ninety years, and that 13 percent reduces to 10 percent when you take into account the market value of perquisites or necessities handed over by the state. The static analysis from which liberals tend to suffer is the assumption that, every time you earn one dollar, somebody else loses one dollar. It doesn't work that way. If you can earn one dollar, it's likely that somebody else is also going to earn a dollar.

Milton Friedman says he's no longer willing to say that there's no such thing as a free lunch, this being the aphorism most associated with Miltonic economics. The reason he's not now willing to say it is that, if I give you a sweater in exchange for a shoe, we're both better off. Applying that dynamic analysis as distinct from the static analysis, you find a general elevation of standards. Obviously, there are lacunae, but these don't affect the secular drifts.

You and Galbraith are friends, yet the public perception is that you are miles apart politically.

The common ground is civility, geniality. The public perception that we're miles apart is exactly correct; he would be the first to emphasise it and I would be the next. If Kenneth's views had prevailed in American policy during the past forty-five years, first, we'd be broke, and secondly, we'd be a Soviet satellite. But he happens to be a wonderful writer, a wonderful friend, wonderfully genial, very gifted, and has a nice sense of humour, therefore I delight in his company.

It seems you have made only one attempt to enter active politics, when you stood for mayor of New York.

I stood for mayor only to make pedagogical points. I was never a candidate in any serious sense. In fact, I predicted that my vote would be one per cent or less the day I announced my candidacy, but it was an opening to ventilate points of view that I had been ventilating for a number of years through other media. If, from time to time, through direct political exposure, you can get free access to media to put forward points of view, it doesn't make sense to turn it down. It can't happen frequently. For that reason I ran, but I considered it then, and still do, to be an act of criticism rather than an act of political candidacy. In Britain someone can be simultaneously a critic and a politician, but not here. Here we have no safe seats.

Is the impression accurate that the very talented tend not to enter politics and that conse-quently our lives are ruled and shaped by the best of the mediocre?

I think it is, but I'm not entirely certain that this is upsetting. If one makes the general commitment to democracy that most of us are prepared to make, one has to recognise the virtue of temporising. The intellectual and the very gifted man tends in the direction of hubris, total self-absorption and the conviction of his own correctness. For that reason he is probably a little less flexible than a democratic politician ought to be. I know that I always have to guard in *National Review* against judging a politician against the pragmatic measure, because the tendency is to insist that the paradigm is the correct way to judge him, and if you do that, you are engaged in the politics of evangelism, and that isn't very productive. You do get extraordinary figures that come in, but they tend to be extraordinary with reference to criteria other than those which singled out a Churchill or a Lincoln. Nixon is an extraordinary man. Reagan is an extraordinary man. Yet they are extraordinary in a strictly political context. They wouldn't be extraordinary in an academic context, or in most other secular contexts. So you do find among your so-called mediocrities remarkable men.

It sometimes seems that the politician able to give the best performance on television is the one who wins the day.

There is no question that a lack of success on television can be critical. One doesn't necessarily have to be telegenic, but if one repels on television, then that puts a quietus on a political career, even as it would in Hollywood. Most American voters get their news from television. You may have seen the recently published report that fifty per cent of voters did not know the name of the vice-presidential candidate on a democratic ticket. Pretty disappointing. So the capacity of television to influence public opinion is a thousand times as high as any preceding competitor, and that works, I think, mostly against the common weal. Demagogy tends to attract more attention than statesmanship. Therefore, I would guess that, given the rapidity with which the public can be influenced, it can more easily be influenced in a negative than a positive direction.

Has there been a degradation? The philosophical and political argument here tends to centre on the constitutional amendment that changed the composition of the Senate. After 1912, the responsibility devolved from the legislators to the people. Ken Galbraith is very insistent that the quality of the Senate is improved. I tend to resist that, making, however, a concession for the fifty years after the end of the Civil War when senators were very much the creatures of big-business bullies who were buying up legislators. But if I were to take that period between 1800 and 1850 and the period between 1900 and 1950, I would certainly prefer the quality of the first to the second. My reason is that the sense of security that came with being selected by the legislators – allowing you to have a name for yourself and be less dependent on whim – encouraged people of a certain character to think of themselves in the Roman sense as having a patriarchal responsibility to discharge. Remember that, in those days, people didn't think of politics as a full-time career. There were a few like Clay and Calhoun Webster who did, but it was a little bit infra dig. As a matter of fact, when Lincoln wondered whether he would go back to Congress, he actually consulted his friends about whether it would ruin his reputation to look so greedy as to want to go to Congress for a second term. A single term was considered about right, but certainly not three or four terms. Now it's a vocation.

In what important respects does American conservatism differ from the conservatism of the British Conservative government?

Conservatives in the British government are much more influenced by class than we are. In America we conservatives tend to welcome changes which would cause a little alarm in Britain. Here, if we find out, let's say, that sixty-five percent of the upper quintal have arisen from the third quintal or the second quintal in the past generation, we would feel that is terrific. No corresponding sense of pleasure communicates itself to me from reading the British press. That's one reason why Thatcher is not really all that popular with the old-time Conservatives in Great Britain, who think of themselves as guardians of a perpetual caste into which only a certain rash of newcomers is welcome.

How do you evaluate Mrs Thatcher?

I'm very much in favour of Mrs Thatcher. I was an early enthusiast. It's true of her, as it is of anybody who is around that long, that they develop, and what was once a rather amusing mannerism becomes a horrible affectation. So certain of her traits – and I'm talking now not only about personality but about her traits as a leader – rasp in a sense that they didn't five years ago. But she has been a clear and positive leader, her priorities have been acceptable, and she has moved with uneven but general success in their direction. Inflation and unemployment are now going down a little bit, so I think history will think of her as somebody who did a lot to revitalise an economy that had lost a lot of faith in itself.

Many would say that the problem with Mrs Thatcher is that she doesn't appear to have compassion.

They're right. She doesn't. Interestingly enough, the same charge has been made against Ronald Reagan, even though he is an effective populist speaker in a way she is not. I have found it extremely difficult, in my personal experience, to know the extent to which somebody is compassionate generally from their public behaviour.

I know men and women who seem icy cold but they are very philanthropic, but she doesn't give an impression of being one of those.

She had a very good working relationship with Reagan. The same chemistry doesn't seem to operate with Bush.

That's probably because Thatcher and Reagan thought of themselves as compelled by an ideological appetite to reorient their countries in a direction they thought correct. They were missionaries. George Bush is not a missionary, he is a consolidator. Thatcher and Reagan said that their countries had been going in the wrong direction for a number of years and they'd got to do something real fast to turn them around. That created an affinity of purpose compounded by what turned out to be a rather unexpected affinity of temperament, for they're very different people, she so precise and meticulous, he sort of sprawly and communicative almost by osmosis sometimes. Yet I know from conversations that there was a genuine sense of I like her and I think she likes me. That was absolutely genuine. It was not put up for public display.

As to which of them was dominant, Reagan's a very subtle creature in that he tends to agree as a matter of manners but two weeks later will simply take his own course. The notion that Reagan was a creature of other people's thinking is historically incorrect. I'm not saying that he wasn't influenced in the general sense in which everybody's influenced, but he genuinely made up his own mind. Once, when he was briefing the congressional leaders at six o'clock while American parachutists were in the air, Mrs Thatcher came on the line and said, 'Ronald, I've done a lot of thinking about the situation in Granada, and we must do nothing for at least three months.' He said, 'You're quite right, Margaret,' but he was moved exclusively by the possibility that the Cubans were listening in to the conversation. He wasn't going to have American paratroopers shot down by Cuban fighter planes. Her feelings were hurt on that occasion. She was rumpled. However, that would be an example of his giving her the general impression that she was the dominant figure in any action, when in fact he was perfectly prepared to act.

Is the 'special relationship' fact or myth today?

I think it's a fragile fact. It's a fact that we speak the same language, that we haven't warred against each other for 150 years, and the slight geographical isolation of Great Britain gives it just that little detachment from continental imbroglios that makes for an affinity with our much more general geographical isolation. It is fragile in the sense that we are the great superpower and Britain is one no longer, yet Britain considers itself in almost every respect brighter than America: more stable, more mature, more at home with democratic institutions, and more at home with the stability of the caste or semi-caste system; which causes a certain amount of friction. Now the Brits are prepared to make certain broad concessions. For instance, in the new introduction to the OED they concede that all the important work of a lexicographical character is being carried on by Americans and recognise the great resources of America. But with that recognition goes a very considerable contempt for what are considered distinctively American manners, vulgarities, excesses, violence, so that the admiration that makes for the special relationship with America is a detached admiration and one that is really condescending. Still, it's useful and practicable and is to be encouraged. It occasionally figures very strongly, as, for instance, during the high point of the Macmillan-Kennedy association.

Is the British Conservative party right to resist the level of freedom of information you now have in America?

Yes, it is. I oppose the idea that an extension of democratic government presupposes instant familiarity with details of government which are not crucial to the general understanding. Your fifty-year rule strikes me as much more sensible than our overnight rule. Our overnight rule, of course, has limitations, but we have been permitted, for example, to read conversations by Richard Nixon which are useful to the Trollopes of this world but I wouldn't say were useful in enhancing a kind of alarmed and democratic society in which, while acknowledging that certain things go on, some measure of satisfaction should be taken in the fact that the knowledge is not documented every day. To read fifty of thirty years after Churchill's death about some of his unattractive vanities is, I think, a satisfaction to which I'm entitled as someone who is historically curious, but I do not feel that democracy functions better by having a freedom of information that could have told me about Churchill's private conversations while he was still living and contending for office. So privacy has a public usefulness which is, I would say, better guarded in your country than mine.

The practice as opposed to the theory of conservative values in Britain seems to have entailed poverty at the level of living in cardboard boxes and beggars in the street. How is that to be avoided in a conservative scheme of things?

My information is different from yours. My information is that in Great Britain the thinking political class recognises that England is subsidising on a perpetual basis an indolent non-working class and chooses to do so rather than stoke up economic energy. We had that attitude here and there, towards Appalachia, for instance. I once wrote, thirty years ago, that John F. Kennedy went to West Virginia and guaranteed the coalminers that they could continue to not make coal for a living – which was what it amounted to. I see that happening on a much larger scale in Britain. It brings about a certain tranquillity: we'll have ten percent unemployed and we'll just bear the burden. Now I may be completely misinformed, but if so, so are some of my English friends who have told me that this is pretty well the way it's going. I happen to think it's wrong for psychological reasons, and it's obviously wrong for economic reasons because somebody who is unproductive is not adding to the common pool. I tend to be enough of a puritan to believe that people really aren't satisfied unless they're producing something. It can be an intangible, like mother love, they're producing, but it has to be something. And the answer, of course, is that to get movement going in that direction, you've got to put the people on the assembly line towards productivity.

They've got to find this out in East Germany very soon, because that engine is going to be pushing right at them in a way it's not going to push in Romania or Poland, which both have a more lackadaisical habit. In East Germany, with $125 billion invested in the equalisation of the mark, people are going to find out that a working day is much closer to eight hours than three. *Mutatis mutandis.* Applying that to Great Britain, you would certainly simply not tolerate the perpetual dole without some effort to cause people to seek out work where work's available. By American standards the British are lazy. Not by Indian standards, or Eastern European standards, but then even the Japanese are lazy by American standards.

Has your Catholicism had a significant effect on your political thinking?

I hope so. Catholicism, somebody once said, has everything to say about some things and something to say about everything. I don't think that's true. I don't think it has much to say about peanut butter. But I think that a believing Christian always has a second perspective. I'm going to write a book the year after next on why I'm still a Catholic, and by my standards, I will spend a fair amount of time on it. It's a faith that I have never attempted to conceal. I think it's simply incorrect to wed that faith to particularities of political positions. For instance, the notion that we should stand up under all circumstances against the Soviet Union is highly rooted in my belief in Christianity, and I quarrelled very openly with the bishops who argued against a nuclear deterrent, and quarrelled with the Pope on that silly speech he gave on capitalism in Mexico. But on the big issues – the incorrectness of a political society attempting to occupy the place of God – I think that's a very liberating concept.

Have I ever been disillusioned with Catholicism? I've often been disillusioned about what the Catholic Church has done or not done, but if you mean have I ever felt a weakening of faith, well, I lie down until I get over it. Christians call it grace. And grace is not earned, it's adventitious.

In your new introduction to God and Man at Yale, *you suggest that the interests of the state and those of civilisation were sometimes at odds. What brought you to this conclusion?*

I think it was the indecision of prominent American universities to act in the way that Swiss universities had acted during the crisis of 1948 over Czechoslovakia, or as they did subsequently in Hungary. There were affirmations by the faculties denouncing this new act of Soviet oppression and servitude, whereas we were bound by the protocols of academic freedom against that kind of action. I remember the president of Yale never spoke to me again after that. He was a classicist, became a baseball commissioner, and died tragically of a heart attack a couple of years ago. He declined to permit the Yale University Glee Club to sing in a one-hour ceremony celebrating the birthday of Solidarity, on the grounds that it would commit the university to a political cause. I thought that so flatulent and silly that I was provoked to write that book, which amusingly enough is referred to as my novel in the current *Spectator*. You can see how serious that interviewer's research was. The offence I took that provoked this book was a John Stuart Millsian notion that, as long as one believed in a position, one could not consider that position as having been fatally condemned. It would mean presumably that if one person believed the genocide against the Jews in Germany was excusable, one must consider that an open position. I thought that nihilistic.

The notion that a student going to Yale oughtn't to be helped in the direction of civilised thought but is told there is no distinction between the Declaration of Independence and the *Communist Manifesto* as to which is the more virtuous, the more enlightened instrument, I find more of a pose than a serious and thoughtful position. They took the view that any position taken by a faculty was not of anyone's concern. That may be true in graduate school, when you're hiring a researcher, but an undergraduate school should undertake to teach some of those values which were learned by a civilisation after very hard work and to assume that a society doesn't have an interest in projecting what it has developed over two millennia is simply dereliction of duty.

How does one apply in the political arena principles derived from faith?

Well, you don't. It is not a simple exercise. If there are certain things you shouldn't do, you've got to ask yourself why should you not do them and who said not. Kant can plead his autonomous idea of ethics, but overwhelmingly we are taught these are religious prescriptions, whether under the Koran, the Talmud, the Old Testament or the New Testament. Certain kinds of behaviour are not tolerated. You have to refine the question a long way to decide whether you have crossed that line, but to be preoccupied with that exercise is the important thing.

What do you feel about the aftermath of the Vatican II?

I think it was a terrible mistake. Having said that, I accept Vatican II as probably divinely instituted, but the lengths to which Vatican II has been taken are not the responsibility of Vatican II. For instance, there is nothing in Vatican II that says you should forsake the mass in Latin. There's quite a lot in Vatican II which says you ought not to forsake the mass in Latin. In fact, it has been almost universally forsaken. That was the doing of bishops. There's nothing in Vatican II that says the suspension against eating meat on Friday shall end, but it did end. There seemed to be no constitutional resistance built up in the clergy to these huge changes in the liturgy, and that surprised a great many people. Certainly, the notion that the vernacularisation of religious language would breed more Catholics is simply wrong – wrong judged against any criterion. The loss of vocations, the laicisations, the diminishing number of people in church stabilised at about sixty per cent of the level of 1963.

What is the chance of unification in the Christian Churches?

Slight, in part because faith has been highly diluted. Paradoxically, I think the unification of the Christian Churches is a development that would more likely come about after a maximisation rather than a minimisation of faith. To the extent that you become a fervent Methodist, you become a little bit more anti-Catholic than you were before. If you become more pro-Harvard, you become a little bit more anti-Yale. That's true through a certain stage, but if you then reach beyond that stage, your common concern is for the teaching of Christ more than for the denomination differences that divide. We certainly haven't reached that latter stage, and we're not far advanced into the second stage. There still are denominational enthusiasts. Southern Baptists in America are one example. The Mormons would be another.

Does the new religious fundamentalism in America and what might be called the church of the extreme right worry you?

It doesn't worry me at all. In the first place, the so-called extreme-right fundamentalism was the workaday understanding of America throughout most of my life. I had the big deal in the moral majority on my programme, begging to find out what it is that I could be furious with him about. Did he believe in persecuting homosexuals? No; but he didn't believe a homosexual should teach in a situation in which peer pressure was an aspect. Well, I agree with that. Pretty soon I found myself thinking, what is it these people want that Americans think of as extreme? It suddenly occurred to me. What they think of as extreme is what we totally accepted up until I was about forty-five or fifty years old – you know, people had a right to teach religion in schools, if it was acceptable to the community; pornography was not available at the local kiosk; commercial establishments were closed on Sunday. All that stuff considered absolutely preposterous was absolutely routine and acceptable right up until 1955, 1965, so I'm not in the least worried about it.

A lot of people regard sex as the motivating force in their lives, whereas the Catholic Church regards it as a means of procreation, not to be used for gratification?

What you say is not so in the Catholic Church. The church has no ban against sexual congress during pregnancy. To say that procreation's a primary objective of the sexual act is no different from saying that the primary purpose of eating is to stay alive. It is, but that isn't mostly why you and I eat. We have to do that to stay alive, but that doesn't dictate in the least our appetite for cuisine. I would say it's rather healthy of the Church to the extent that it indirectly attempts to diminish the sex act as the principle Freudian compulsion in one's life. Individuals are often moved primarily by the sexual drive, but (a) it doesn't mean they ought to be, (b) it doesn't mean they can't be persuaded from being so. After all, there are celibate orders that are very successful, and it by no means suggests that subordinating the sexual drive is to deprive it of importance or that there isn't great joy and gratification to be got from it.

But isn't it a fact that the Church appears to begrudge sexual gratification?

On the surface it gives that impression, especially, for instance, in the *Humani Vitae* encyclical where it suggests that, if you're not willing to run the risk of pregnancy, you ought not to have sex. In that respect it certainly does. But it's simply not practised, even by Catholics who have no reluctance about going to communion.

At one point you were part of the CIA, which has had a bad press over the years in connection with such events as the murder of Allende in Chile.

Criticism of the CIA should restrict itself to things it didn't do well, but I don't think it ought to be criticised for anything it may have sought to do. In my judgement, the historical records are very clear that the assassination of Allende had nothing to do with the CIA. I've written nine novels about the CIA, and if I had to summarise in a sentence what I sought to say in them, it would be that, in an apocalyptic world, the nature and mandate of counter-intelligence is a moral need which can't be quantified. I mean by that that certain challenges arise which require and indicate the advisability of a certain action being taken which cannot discreetly be applauded. An assassination, for instance. Supposing you have Idi Amin, who's got hold of an atom bomb, and the CIA in the field finds out that at midnight he's going to dispatch a bomber with instructions to drop it over Jerusalem. The CIA man says he's got a man there with a sniper rifle. Does he pull the trigger and abort the mission? If I were the US president, I would tell him to go ahead and do so, but under no circumstances would I, as a theorist, ask you to come up with a set of conditions under which it is OK to order a private assassination, because there are too many imponderables to make it possible to quantify such a thing satisfactorily. For that reason, I think counter-intelligence is an art form and has to be judged more pragmatically than aprioristically.

There are people all over the world who are astonished by an American government committed to democracy at home yet seemingly eager to league itself with the most repressive dictatorships.

There's absolutely no question that the containment policy of the United States invited abuse. There are even jokes about it: the president of Venezuela in 1956 is told that he doesn't qualify for more US aid than he is getting because he isn't enough of a communist problem, so he goes out and imports communists. At a more serious level, I've always found very liberating a distinction drawn by Senator Fulbright, and he was speaking from the other side of the political fence from my own when he said it. He said that the American government has no proper quarrel against the practices of any government in the world, however odious, unless it is a government trying to export its policies. I apply that, for instance, to the landing of the marines in the Dominican Republic in 1965 on the orders of Lyndon Johnson. Lyndon Johnson was convinced that Juan Bosch was going to make the Dominican Republic another Cuba. So the marines landed there, cleaned that situation up, but ignored entirely the western half of Hispaniola where Papa Doc was torturing people to death every night. We don't have the power to follow the Wilsonian mandate of making all the world safe for democracy. The logical distinction is to contain aggressive hideosities, such as the Soviet Union has been foremost in committing during the past forty years, and that seems a clean division on the relevant responsibilities of the state.

What about the moral dimension, especially where one is preaching morality in one's own country?

I'm glad you use the word preaching. The American people have very definite moral responsibility. John Quincey Adams said the American people are friends of liberty everywhere but custodians only of their own. He said that in 1828, so he was reminding us that we are for good people everywhere, but can't and don't have the power to take responsibility for them. For instance, I'm very sympathetic to the idea of any American who refuses to buy any product from South Africa. It may be mistaken as a matter of policy, but I'm sympathetic with the idea. I'm totally unsympathetic with the American government attempting to boycott South Africa. There they are violating the Fulbright distinction in a way that is impractical and wrong. So the moral impulse to preach, inveigh and hector is and ought to be exactly that: a moral backed by whatever economic power an individual has, expressed usually through boycotts.

Yet it sometimes seems to the outside world that no degree of violence or repression is enough to cut off American aid.

It happens in part, I suppose, because of a notion that we recognise de facto power. If Peron is in charge of Argentina, we do business with Argentina. This is in part because that's the way nations work. It's also in part because there are mutual interests. We want to import certain Argentinian things; they want to import certain American things; so the question becomes, is the United States going to stand in the way of this exchange? In fact, we're required under law to pass judgement once a year against individual countries as to whether they are or are not free. If a country is not free, the president must suspend all aid to that country unless, in the exercise of his judgement, it is strategically necessary to override this recommendation. They can go farther and have what they call state-specific prohibitions, which are levied against South Africa, against Vietnam, against Korea – countries with which even the president doesn't have the power to authorise trade. This strikes me as a not ill-considered way of doing things, as long as the president does retain the power in ambiguous cases to continue to do business. For instance, our handling of Pinochet's situation in Chile, however long his reign, was I think sensible. Chile regraduated into a democratic situation. There was damage done, but in historical terms, not huge. It was a comparable state to Franco's Spain. It would have been very wrong to have attempted to slow down the economic rejuvenation of Chile, which made its return to democracy likelier.

Have the lessons of Vietnam been adequately learned by America?

I don't think they have. I wrote a piece recently in which I said that President Bush, in going slowly on Lithuania, is probably correct in saying he is reflecting the will of the American people. I think he is making a mistake, strategic and moral, but he is undoubtedly influenced by Vietnam: that is, if the American people aren't a hundred percent behind you, don't do it. The lesson of Vietnam is incompletely learned in part because it became so complicated along the line. The relevant school of thought was, if you want to win the war you can do it, but be tough. The second school of thought was that there was no way to win the war because it was a war that pitted you against indigenous forces. And the third was, it's a war you should never have gotten into in the first place. A little bit of each of these lingers in the American mind. They haven't sorted it out, nor are they likely to, given the recent retrenchment of the communist empire.

At the time of Vietnam, I felt we should get on with it, and I felt it important for two reasons. No. 1, strategic, and no. 2, that our commitment to Vietnam, having been made by three presidents in such unmistakeable accents, meant that the credibility of America's guarantees everywhere in the world was very much at risk. Every guarantee that we made in NATO could in the future be held to be of no account, given our failure to make good our guarantees to Vietnam. What we tried to do, in effect, was blame it on Vietnam: they were the ones that collapsed, we didn't desert them. In fact we did desert them.

Oh, yes, I do believe it was a war we could have won. And I believe it all the more now. It is increasingly documented that the war against Vietnam was against an invading force. The notion that it was a war against an indigenous force is simply incorrect. It became increasingly a war against an indigenous force as communist pressures against the peasants began to work. If you start executing everybody who doesn't cooperate with you, you get a lot of cooperation. There were a lot of Lidice operations that took place in South Vietnam, but the time to move would have been very early, in 1965, 1966. After that it became progressively difficult. But the great risk was China. We now know that China would have welcomed an American victory, but, of course, neither Lyndon Johnson or Nixon was willing to bank on that, and therefore we exercised certain restraints we would not have exercised otherwise.

What led you to the imaginative work of writing fiction?

What led me specifically was an offer of a contract by a publisher. I had no reason whatsoever to suppose I could do it successfully, but I didn't want to do it on a gamble of which I was the only creditor. Therefore, they gave me an advance on the following terms: I would send them the first 100 pages. If they liked what they read, they would guarantee the full advance. If they didn't, I'd keep one third. They did like it and it was a bestseller. That was *Saving the Queen*.

One reviewer spoke of Saving the Queen *as a 'hotchpotch of snobbery and twaddle'. Are you wounded by such criticism?*

Criticism like that would not wound me, because it's utterly incorrect. If it was subtle criticism and I thought it correct, that would very much arrest me. But I'm utterly unaffected by criticism that I think is motivated either by ignorance or malice. I pay no attention at all.

Your book Overdrive *was attacked by critics and readers, not on literary grounds but more for the personality that came across. Even friends like John Leonard called it a piece of self-indulgence. You seemed unaware of the offence such a book might cause. Was it a miscalculation? Did you regret it? Were you chastened by the experience?*

No to all of those. It was self-indulgent in the sense that is was easy to write in terms of research required, but it was bought by the *New Yorker*, where it was thought to be an interesting book. I had a tremendous amount of mail, all of which was very gratifying.

As one of the top journalists in the United States, your column is syndicated to over 300 publications. Journalists often see themselves as opinion makers, but can they form opinions in any real sense?

I don't think you can form opinion, but what you can do is open doors. I'll give you a recent example: how to handle drug policy. When I wrote *The Unmaking of a Mayor*, I was resolute that drugs should be proscribed. In the past eight to ten years I've come to the conclusion that it wouldn't work. Now, this is very different from coming to a position saying I had no right to proscribe them. I continue to reserve the right to proscribe, but empirically I'm instructed this doesn't work, so I have been talking in the last few years about examining the possibility of legalising drugs under certain circumstances. What I have done is not so much form opinion as open a door to ventilate the alternative to people who might not otherwise examine it.

Have you reached a stage in life where, because people expect you to say something contro-versial, you do it for effect?

No, I haven't reached that stage, because I have a *Weltanschauung* and certainly won't spend any part of my life trying to make an awkward fit. If I take a position simply to be mischievous and am forever asked to integrate that opinion in that *Weltanschauung*, it would cause me much more pain than the momentary satisfaction I got from it the day before. So I just don't do it.

William F. Buckley Jr.

A lot of Jewish voters in the United States identify the right with anti-Semitism. Was that a factor when you ran for mayor in New York?

That's an interesting question. It's certainly a factor that, in 1965, the Jewish vote was very anti-conservative. I think three per cent of Jews voted for me – a very small percentage. I would guess that the automatic assumption in the Jewish community that the right was anti-Semitic had begun to attenuate around the late 1950s. We had something to do with that in *National Review*. By 1965, I don't think it was by any means the universal conviction. In 1965 maybe a third or a half of the Jews thought there was a lurking anti-Semitism in the American right, but no more.

But there was an anti-Semitism in the American right?

I would say yes, among older people. You see, the cultural anti-Semitism, which was almost universal, was killed among middle-aged and younger people by Hitler, but preserved among those in their seventies. My father, for instance, was a cultural anti-Semite, and so, I hate to say, was just about everybody. But that, I think, was simply turned around by the experience of 1942–5 among people in whom it was not so deeply set.

Are you at all optimistic about peace in the Middle East?

I'm not an optimist. It seems to me that we aren't really any closer to a natural solution than we were three years ago, and the unsettled state of Israeli politics makes a movement there extremely problematical. I predict at least another four to five years of stalemate. After that I can see one of two things happening: either Israel, through a sheer sense of fatigue, attempts to come to a solution, or the Arab states in effect abandon the whole Palestinian cause on the grounds that it costs them too much time and effort, and the Palestinians become a nomadic people. The existing animosity is extremely expensive and time-consuming, and if there's no sense of progress, it might simply go in a different direction. Now obviously there are factors that are weighing in on the scene. The great Israeli nightmare has been that the Arabs would simply exceed them in population, which is the source of Rabbi Kahane's party. That seems to be temporarily relieved by the present prospect of 500,000 Jews coming in from the Soviet Union, which should greatly help redress that balance within Israel. But it's not going to bring about the kind of comity people want. A lot depends too on the attitude of the younger generation.

Are you sympathetic to the Palestinian's plight?

Totally. A people as well defined culturally, historically and ethnically as they are is entitled to a homeland. Israel is by no means uniquely to blame for them not having one. I think Hussein's most to blame for not having acted between 1948 and 1967. My impression is that most Jews agree with the Palestinians having a homeland, but they want to make absolutely certain that homeland doesn't become a threat to their own survival.

Your proposal in the New York Times *that, to stop the spread of Aids, victims should be tattooed on the upper forearm and buttocks, produced a predictable outcry, but your biographer suggests you delighted in the resultant tempest.*

Not at all. This is one of the thousand instances in which dear John Judis didn't exercise elementary perspective. In the first place, it came from an open conversation between me and Alan Dershowitz, a professor of law from Harvard. The question was how do you protect people who are uncontaminated from people who are contaminated and know they are? He said, well, the way, of course, was to prosecute them, make it a felony for anybody to have sex or exchange blood, exchange needles, share needles if they knew they were contaminated. I said that's hardly going to help the uncontaminated community because, by the time you prosecute, those people are going to be dead anyway. I went on to say that presumably you've got to have some way of warning the uncontaminated person that this other person has this communicable disease. In the old days there was a sort of smallpox mark that made it easy for nurses or doctors to know you had had a smallpox vaccination, so I suggested you might, for instance, have tiny tattoo marks. This was interpreted as wanting to tattoo people who had the disease for purposes of exhibitionism. My only motive was to give them a mark which could be inspected in private by somebody who might then be spared. But after I saw the fuss, I said, OK, I withdraw it, because people who can't distinguish between the use of barbed wire in Auschwitz and barbed wire to keep cows away from bulls can't distinguish between the use of a tattoo to damn somebody and the use of it to save somebody. I wonder how many people would be alive today who are now dead because my idea wasn't accepted.

In 1971 you pretended you had a further set of Pentagon Papers. Why did you indulge in a game like that when in it was something you couldn't sustain for more than a few days?

It was to make a particular point. Reading the Pentagon Papers, we were convinced that there were other papers that were not exhibited, and the idea came to me, let's forge these papers, simply make them up. I couldn't have believed they would be so successful. I had six papers, for instance, ostensibly addressed or written to Admiral Radford, and when he read them he said, 'I don't remember these in particular, but I can't say they're not true.' In that sense it was almost dangerously successful. Whereas I had thought it would last about six hours, it lasted five days before I finally had a press conference. But I perhaps overproved my case, because attention turned to the scandal rather than to the pedagogical point we were attempting to make.

Were you shocked when the truth about Nixon became apparent?

By the time the truth became apparent I was not surprised at all. I thought the accumulation of evidence, showing he was implicated, had become overwhelming. I came out in favour of his resignation five months before the so-called burning tape. George Bush, then head of the Republican party, and I made a gentlemanly bet: George Bush said that Nixon would still be in office at the end of the year, I that he would not. Gerald Ford swore on my programme that Nixon was innocent nine days before he became president, so that was the part of the loyalist wing of the Republican party that, in my opinion, refused to see the evidence.

We spoke about your admiration for Ronald Reagan, but your biographer, John B. Judis, writes: 'Privately Buckley despaired over Reagan and the last years of his term', and goes on to suggest that you thought the Iran-Contra scandal 'incapacitated' Reagan. Was this a temporary crisis of faith or did your view of Reagan change radically?

I thought the Iran-Contra mess a terrible lapse in Reagan's own record. Irrespective of his not having had personal knowledge of the details, that it should have happened in his administration was definitely a blight on his record. But I don't remember ever saying that this caused a revision in my general attitude towards Reagan. I think he was incapacitated from November 1986 until the general pick-up in his popularity began about twelve months later. On account of that, 1987 was a lost year for Reagan.

You are regarded as an opponent of so-called woman's liberation. Why?

The part of the feminist movement that upsets me is a part which urges indiscrimination that is *extra natura*. To suggest that men and women are in every sense equal is in my judgement correct before the law and in terms of opportunity, but it's absolutely incorrect to suggest they are organically equal. Men and women are just different. It has nothing to do with equality. Under the circumstances, a certain attitude towards women is logical and appropriate, and that includes a disposition to agree that certain occupations aren't appropriate to women. I don't think women in trenches is a civilised idea. And, as an aesthetic matter, I hate the approach towards genderless nouns such as 'chairperson'. The disappearance of the masculine as doing double gender duty is an aesthetic affront against literature.

Many American men, as compared with European men, seem dominated by their wives. What is the principle reason?

I think what you say is right if you compare it to Europe. I'm not sure it's all that right compared to England. At least, my impression is that there are henpecked men in England as there are here. American women tend to be more strident in marriage. Americans are more outspoken at every level, and there's no reason why that shouldn't be so among American women. But the nature of marriage imposes more natural commitments on the man than on the women. It's a very stupid man who doesn't take fully into account what his wife wants to do, but a marriage tends to be unsuccessful when the sense of authority is so disputed that there isn't a natural dominance by the woman over certain aspects of the marriage, or by the man over certain other aspects of the marriage.

Isn't the movement for the renewal of the idea of family unity doomed to fail in a modern context?

No. It's having a hard time, but marriage as an institution has been rediscovered in America. In the last two or three years, liaisons that would otherwise have tended to be simply that, have ended in marriage; so there continues to be in civil and religious marriage some sense of satisfaction that apparently couples don't get from cohabitation. There are a lot of civil accretions around cohabitation that may have something to do with influencing matters in one direction or another, but by and large the idea of marriage continues to exercise a certain romance and a certain sense of security.

What do you see as the basic cultural differences between America and Europe?

The basic cultural difference is a completely different historical tradition. The memory of the European is much longer than the memory of the American. America is far more transient in its habits. I read somewhere that, on the anniversary of the liberation of France, somebody asked a farmer what life had been like under the Nazis. He said, 'Very bad, very bad,' then paused and added, 'but nothing like what it was under the Swedes in the seventeenth century. That was terrible.' That kind of thing is amusing to an American. We couldn't remember conditions fifty years ago, let alone three hundred years ago. The distillation of tradition in Europe is responsible for attitudes, loyalties and hostilities that tend to wash out more in America.

In 1984 you met Neil Kinnock, whose views on nuclear disarmament you found naïve. Have your own views changed in the light of Mr Gorbachev's initiative on disarmament?

Not at all. They've been reinforced. If Mr Kinnock had had his way and other countries had imitated him, there's no reason at all to suppose that Gorbachev would have released Eastern Europe. He would have had every enticement to do the contrary and to renew the passionate goal to subjugate Europe. And Kinnock would not repeat today the arguments he used then, because he knows, among other things, that they lost him an election.

Might the trend towards disarmament in the Soviet Union reinforce the perception of those who see America as the greater threat to world peace?

It's so Orwellian in its stupidity to suppose that we are a threat to Europe that it's hard to answer on a rational level people who make the charge. God knows, a lot of them do. I simply have to believe there are Europeans – I've not met them – who think the United States has a dark design to subjugate Europe or start a war because wars are such fun. They must exist, but they can't occupy me intellectually because the idea is so perverse. When we called the Reagan administration's contemplation of an arms agreement with the Soviet Union a 'suicide pact', we were much concerned about getting talked into a situation in which a credible nuclear deterrent no longer existed. That threat has not disappeared. As Richard Perle has said, the Russians are angling to get a situation in Europe from this total *détente* which they haven't succeeded in getting in forty years: the absence of the nuclear deterrent commanded by NATO.

With the prospect of German unification, the collapse of the Iron Curtain and the emergence of Japan as an economic superpower, do you see American influence waning the world?

Yes, I do. After the war we were consuming fifty per cent of international production. That's already cut in half. *The Economist* reminds us that we are still the most productive nation. It takes the American thirty-one minutes to make what it takes the Japanese an hour to make. So we've got a lot of resources, but it's true that we're very self-indulgent and the young generation is not being taught to work hard enough or to learn industriously. You can't be all that optimistic about the per capita competitive situation between a country whose schoolchildren work three hours a week on homework and a country whose schoolchildren work thirty hours a week.

You are said to have a long-running feud with Gore Vidal, who characterised you as 'the Marie Antoinette of politics'.

It's not really a long-running feud since I haven't mentioned his name in twenty years, nor he mine that I know of. The reference is to an exchange we had on television in 1968, followed by a law suit. His case was thrown out of court; mine was sustained. I then accepted damages and an apology from *Esquire* magazine for publishing his piece, but I wrote a long essay on that whole episode, published it in 1969 and said I wouldn't speak any more about it.

I have seen it suggested that you are most disliked, not for your views, but for the figure you cut; for applying conservatism 'with the fastidious grace of a Regency man against a mantelpiece'.

I don't give much time to that because I am as I am. Judis talked to a lot of people who knew me when I was ten years old, and none of them charge that between ten and thirty I tried to ape anybody or anything. I had a cosmopolitan education, for which I had no responsibility. I too have read this business about me, as being a conservative, casting a sort of non-proletariat figure. I don't know how I capitalised on it, except by here and there writing autobiographical essays acknowledging how I live. If you drive around in a limousine, there's no way of disguising it.

Why do you so vigorously oppose the idea of Utopia as an ideal to strive towards?

The idea obviously is to live commendably in the eyes of the Lord. Utopia is not of this world, in my judgement, and I think that we are all going to be judged with some reference to how hard we tried and how honestly we behaved. Given the human predicament, none of us is going to do too well on that, but certainly the struggle ought to be to do as well as you reasonably can.

You've sailed the Atlantic, been down to the Titanic, *have even played the harpsichord in the concert hall. What drives you to do these extraordinary things?*

I've sailed the Atlantic twice and the Pacific once, and will sail it again in November. That's a combination of adventure plus something that I can write a book about. I've sailed all my life. Going down to the *Titanic* was an invitation few people have had, so I didn't think twice about it. Playing the harpsichord is a great strain, because I don't have the time or the natural talent to learn quickly and I'm struggling now with a chromatic fantasy, which is rough. I've played all my life, but only sort of episodically, yet the dream of playing something tolerably well in an exigent situation is a challenge.

Would I be right in thinking that underneath the polemical controversial exterior there is a less self-confident and more mellow William Buckley waiting to get out?

Well, I don't think those are contradictions. A lot of people have observed that my public persona is different from my private persona. All I can say is that, when I appear in public, I try hard not to be demagogic; and a failure to be demagogic may suggest that you don't care about what people think, though obviously I do care. That's why I'm in the business to begin with. Inevitably people are a little bit different in private from the way they are in public. All I can say is that this is not intentional.

Have you any regrets in your life?

No. I can't imagine having elected any other profession. Somebody once said, 'if you had worked hard in this other direction, might you not have become president of the United States?' The answer is that the chances of it happening are so infinitely small that I really can't take seriously people who plan to be president. That's simply a star falling in a particular direction. And I don't think I'm temperamentally suited to have been one. I'd like to have been one in the sense that I have confidence in my own judgement, so that would have been good. If you feel you know the correct approach, it gives you a lot of confidence. On the other hand, you might feel that in a democracy the correct approach would be politically unpalatable. In the event you'll be frustrated, so you go back to your little typewriter and think, at least I feel I want to be here.

Quentin Crewe

Quentin Crewe was a writer, journalist, restaurateur and inveterate traveller. He was born in 1926 and educated at Eton and Trinity College, Cambridge. He joined the *Evening Standard* in 1953 and subsequently worked for *Queen*, *Vogue*, the *Daily Mail* and the *Sunday Mirror* before going freelance. His muscular dystrophy was diagnosed when he was six and he was confined to a wheelchair for most of his life. Despite his disability he became the fourth Westerner to cross the Empty Quarter of Saudi Arabia. He also toured South America and made a 25,000-mile journey throughout the Sahara. He was married three times: to Martha Sharp in 1956; to Angela Huth in 1961; and to Susan Cavendish in 1970. There are five children from the marriages. His books included *In Search of the Sahara*, *The Last Maharaja*, *In the Realms of Gold* and *Touch the Happy Isles*, which was shortlisted for the 1987 Thomas Cook Travel Book Award. He was asked on two occasions to be the subject of Desert Island Discs, a rare distinction, and died in 1998, despite a prediction that he would not live past sixteen.

You had a conventional aristocratic upbringing, yet seem to have always wanted to break out of the mould: sacked from Eton, later sent down from Cambridge. What went wrong; why didn't you conform?

I don't know that things went wrong so much as that I just didn't get on with or fit in with my parents. They were very much older than usual in that my mother was forty-five when I was born, my father forty-six. By the time one is growing up, that makes a terrible gap. There isn't any memory left for the parents of what it's like to be a child. My upbringing wasn't altogether conventional, in that my father was in the Consular Service, though in one sense it was a Victorian upbringing: one was brought down from the nursery at six o'clock and sent up again at seven. My mother was a very distant woman in a way hard to describe. My father was much more conventional. I grew up for the first five years in Sicily, until my father was moved to the South of France as Consul General for the Riviera. Then I went to live with my sister, and was brought up by her from the age of five. She was a much older half-sister, and had children older than me.

Again, funnily enough, I didn't fit in. It was a very hearty sort of background. My sister was married to a brewer who was keen on sports – shooting and hunting. But children are amazingly accepting of circumstances, whatever they may be. I accepted mine and I didn't necessarily feel unhappy. This is true of all human beings. If you go to Calcutta and you see how people live, you think they must be the most wretched and miserable people on earth. Not at all. They're laughing and joking, because that's what human beings do. Unhappiness is something you think of afterwards. I don't think I was unhappy in any day-to-day sense; it was more an overall feeling of not fitting in.

How did you manage to reconcile yourself to your disability?

That was very easy really, though one isn't ever reconciled in a sense. I was taken to a doctor when I was six at the insistence of my sister, who could see that I didn't walk or run properly, though my mother hadn't particularly noticed. The doctor said to my mother that I had muscular dystrophy and would die before I was sixteen, but to me he said I would be all right when I reached the age of sixteen. That was the last time the subject was mentioned with my parents until I was eighteen. I never went to another doctor in my childhood, and I was treated absolutely as if I were normal. I was expected to get on with it. No question of, oh, what shall we do about Quentin? Will he be able to manage? I was sent off to perfectly ordinary boarding schools, and that was fine, because it made me not think about it. My mother was generally unsympathetic, and annoyed by a suggestion that it had possibly come hereditarily from her. She wasn't having that, and said it must be my father. What they didn't realise in those days was that these things tend to happen more when the parents are so much older than usual. The imperfections in children from mothers over forty are now well known, and in fact my brother, just older than myself, had a cleft palate.

Quite early on I decided that I was not going to be sorry for myself. I remember overhearing an old cousin saying, he's so brave, and then he gave me a fiver, so in a way I'm grateful to my mother for her ruthlessness. My father used to make me walk across ploughed fields with a gun to shoot partridges. I used to fall down, and it was awful, but he made no concessions. I think an awful lot of my resourcefulness was, fortunately, born in me. I'm not subject to depressions, and I'm very bad at dealing with people who do have them.

I was, however, very lazy as a child, and always most dissatisfied with rules and conventions. I thought my prep school perfectly dreadful. I couldn't understand why the people there behaved as they did. The schoolmasters were bullying, the boys were bullying. All of this was foreign to me. Eton was much much better, but I was unlucky in being there during the war, when the younger masters had all gone off to fight. Our masters had all been hauled out of retirement and were a very eccentric lot. The absurdity of the rules was intolerable. If you wore an overcoat, you must never put the collar down. You had to carry your umbrella unrolled, so you carried the thing beside you, flapping like a dead bird. And so on. The sacking from Eton was for going up to London one day. I had a copy of the fire-door key made, and although I got back late, nobody knew I had been absent. But, of course, it was found out afterwards, and that was that.

I wanted to get into normal life, or what I thought was normal as early as possible. Although I found Cambridge very stimulating, it somehow didn't make me do any work. I studied law, but unfortunately Roman law was what you had to start on, and that seemed to me both boring and idiotic. I didn't see why one needed to know about the manumission of slaves two thousand years ago. That aside, Cambridge was pure indolence. It was absolutely wonderful from the point of view of liberty and freedom, and suddenly I was into a whole new world and way of thinking. I was there at the end of the war, with great changes on the way, including a Labour government coming in, and that was all a great shock to my family, and so therefore to me; because one does in a way accept what one's parents tell one. Even so, Cambridge was an extraordinary release. There were so many things to unlearn in my life: all the things that had been dinned into me as a child. Anti-Semitism, for example, was a perfectly normal topic of everyday conversation; people would say, 'Oh, she's Jewish,' and that meant somehow that she was a little bit foreign. One had to unlearn all that.

How did the war years affect you?

Two of my three half-brothers were killed and the third was wounded, while my full brother was taken prisoner. In that sense it did impinge on me, and I was very aware of it. In another sense, some of it was fun. The bombs were nice and frightening, and there was something exciting about being frightened. I remember being in a swimming pool and watching a V-1 come over while I was swimming. It stopped in the way that they did, and I wondered where it was going to land, not minding because it was so exciting. But that sort of exhilaration had to be set against the distress of members of one's family being killed.

Did you go into journalism straight away after Cambridge?

No. I did lots of small jobs. My first was working in a bookshop called Sutherland's in Sackville Street. I loved it. It was very Dickensian and I well remember the comedy of getting one's £4 a week. The accountant was downstairs in the basement, and when it came to the Friday morning, you didn't go down and say,

'Where are my wages?' You went down and hovered about near the accountant's office until suddenly he'd look up and say, 'Oh, Mr Crewe, there you are. Would you step this way a minute?' In you would go, and he'd give you an envelope, beautifully inscribed, your name in copperplate on the outside. It would have been very indelicate to open it there and then to see what was inside it, so you took it off to the loo, and there was your £4.

After that I went to work for something called the Art Exhibitions Bureau, an office that acted as secretary to various societies, such as the Royal Society of Portrait Painters. We used to hang exhibitions in various galleries; and it was interesting because it meant I met a lot of artists. But, again, it paid very badly, and I didn't really get on with the owner, the organisation was so fuddy-duddy. Then I worked a short time in a factory, then in a shipping line. The latter came about because I had a girlfriend who said she would leave me unless I got a job. I went out to an agency and picked up the first job going, which was as a ticket clerk in the French Line.

I was still able to walk a certain amount at that time, but was almost at the end of it, and was having a lot of trouble with falling over. In the end the doctors said I had better not keep struggling to work, and I was perfectly delighted to be told this, being, as I say, lazy by nature. So I stopped working and went to live in Italy, reading to a blind man – the scholar and historian, Percy Lubbock. I spent a year reading aloud to him for anything up to ten hours a day. It was good for my education and a pleasant place to live, and I also got to know Bernard Berenson and Harold Acton and all the people who lived in Florence in those days. Then I came home for a holiday, intending to go back and continue reading to Percy Lubbock, but a lunch with Lord Boothby intervened. John Junor was also present, having then, in 1953, just been made deputy editor of the *Evening Standard*. He offered me what then seemed the princely sum of £15 a week, and I couldn't resist it.

By all accounts, you got on well with Beaverbrook, though he was a notoriously difficult character.

Beaverbrook was able to enthuse people. You felt he was a man of action. At the time Burgess and Maclean disappeared, I said I would like to go to search for them. I had an idea of how to get into Czechoslovakia, which was where some people thought they'd run to. My editor refused me permission, but I went to Beaverbrook, who overruled the editor. It was his enthusiasm that was the attractive thing about him, and he had some very winning ways.

At a later stage I was doing some hard writing about art for the *Evening Standard* at the time when there was some unhappiness over how the Tate Gallery was being run by Sir John Robbins. Sir John did a great deal for the Tate, but he was also doing some rather funny things with funds that had been left to buy British pictures. He would actually buy something different and cook the labels on the pictures. I wrote rather a lot about this, and the deputy director of the Tate at that time, a South African called Larue Smith Larue, was sacked. Beaverbrook asked me if he ought to take him on as an adviser to help him buy pictures, and I said he should. Some nine months later, Beaverbrook called me to see him and said, 'You advised me to take on Larue Smith Larue. Now look at this picture. What sort of a picture do you think that is?' I told him it looked like a very nice Constable. 'That's what your friend Larue Smith Larue told me,' he said, 'and I paid £30,000 for that picture, which is worth only £30.' But what was rather touching was that he continued to regard the fake Constable as his favourite picture. In that way he could be very winning.'

But he did do one thing to me which was inexcusable, and led to one of the acts I'm most ashamed of in my life. I was working at the *Evening Standard* late one evening when the telephone rang and Beaverbrook said, 'I've got a great story for you.' The story was that a man called Albert Crowther, who had been in gaol for receiving a stolen mantelpiece, had died there. The funeral had been that afternoon, and Beaverbrook wanted me to go and see Mrs Crowther and write a warm human story. I told him I couldn't possibly interview her the same day as she'd buried her husband. 'Oh,' he said, 'I thought you had a great future in journalism' – implying he was going to sack me, in that case. I'm ashamed to say that, instead of saying, 'All right, but I'm still not going to do the story,' I went to see Mrs Crowther, and it was awful. I waited for her until eleven o'clock that night when she came home with her family. I went up to one of the men escorting her and said, 'Look, I'm terribly sorry. I come from the *Evening Standard* and Lord Beaverbrook is particularly anxious that I should do a story. Could I just talk to Mrs Crowther for a minute or two?' He said he would ask her. Eventually he came out and said, 'Yes, she says she'll see you, but I think you're shit.'

I remember Harold Macmillan telling me how he was able once or twice to contradict Beaverbrook when he was minister of aircraft production at the beginning of the war. He did it by saying to Beaverbrook, 'If you do this, you will fry in hell.' Beaverbrook was terrified of hellfire. He was a son of the manse, his father a Presbyterian minister, so he was brought up in true Calvinist terror of God and could never really throw it off.

Weren't you romantically involved with Macmillan's daughter Sarah at one point? What did you make of Macmillan?

He was such a complex character. He was an extremely generous man, but had such a miserable family life that this coloured much of his nature and he spent a lot of time covering up his unhappiness. He was horrified by the betrayal of the people after the First World War; he genuinely minded it and wanted to fight for a better world. Perhaps he was a bit too world weary by the time he became prime minister, but I'm absolutely certain he would never have been party to brutality. If he could have avoided sending back the Cossacks, he would have avoided it. I'm certain it was not in any way a cynical act, and that he was not as deeply implicated as Tolstoy maintains; it simply wasn't in his character. He was extremely kind, and Sarah, incidentally, was not his daughter but Boothby's daughter, and what he did for her was amazing. I remember when she was ill, and indeed had become an alcoholic, that he flew out quite anonymously to Switzerland where she was in a clinic. People recognised him at the airport and asked why he was there, and he replied that he was going to visit a friend. He took the trouble to go and see her, although she might have been regarded as an embarrassment to him. He was a good man in that sense.

Did Boothby care about her?

Boothby was more inclined to care about himself. He enjoyed the situation, enjoyed patronising Sarah and giving her presents and so on, but he wasn't a proper father to her. He was a very shallow man, Boothby – clever but shallow. Macmillan occasionally gave an impression of shallowness, but that was part of his act.

During your time as 'Charles Greville' on the Daily Mail *gossip column, you proscribed stories about royalty, divorces and adultery. As a lover of gossip why did you do that?*

The gossip columns had become so squalid at that point. One of worst examples occurred when Selwyn Lloyd was getting divorced and a journalist pretended to be the godfather of Selwyn Lloyd's child. He went with a present to Carlton House and followed the nanny to find out where Mrs Selwyn Lloyd was. I considered that sort of behaviour intolerable. So far as royalty went, I didn't want a lot of royal family tittle-tattle in my column, and I certainly didn't want to have anybody's divorce or even anything about whether they were having babies. Of course, almost anything is legitimate gossip in ordinary conversation unless somebody's told you something in strict privacy, but in the context of a newspaper, I don't think it necessarily is legitimate gossip. If the foreign secretary's getting divorced, then of course you write that the foreign secretary's getting divorced, but you don't hound his family.

As for the right to privacy and whether it's in the public interest to reveal indiscretions, I wouldn't say it matters if it's just somebody having an affair with someone else and it isn't going to affect anything. I know plenty of MPs who have affairs, and although journalists know about these affairs, they don't write about them. But I rather wonder when it comes to someone in Kennedy's position, for instance. It might be different if a man's judgement were affected by, shall we say, libertine behaviour or excessive womanising. Kennedy was an example of a man who really did want to sleep with every woman he met. Whether this is a sign of immaturity, I'm not sure, but it might be relevant to whether or not a man should be running a country, particularly when it's the United States – rather a big country. On the other hand, this is such a difficult area. You might also say there is something odd about a man who never sleeps with a woman.

You resigned from Queen *magazine because of a proposed supplement on South Africa. What are the liberal political causes you feel most strongly about?*

South Africa has always been top of the list, but about any tyranny, I think – and poverty. But how cynical we are in choosing places. For example, what is going on in Burma seems to me far worse than anything that is happening to Lithuania. What are we doing about Burma; what do we care about it? The Burmese are just left to rot. Nobody's standing up, shouting, screaming and saying the sort of things they're saying about the situation in Lithuania. We're terribly selective.

I do applaud the courage of people like Mary Benson who made the decision that what was going on in South Africa was wrong. Those people could lead perfectly comfortable lives in their own country, but chose to stand up for what they believed was right. It raises one of the big questions. Would one have joined the Hitler Youth Movement if one had been born a German child? Of course one would. Or supposing fascism had come to Britain, would one have stood up against it or would one have been as feeble as people were in Italy and in Germany? That's the kind of courage I most admire, and I just hope to God I would have had it, though I don't know if I would. To know that something is right is one thing. Whether you can live up to it is another.

The liberalism of your views on sexual codes is widely shared nowadays, but where would you draw the line about sex now?

Interfering with children. Anyone under sixteen. Otherwise I don't mind. Gross perversions are just very unhappy for the people who feel them necessary, but in general people make too much fuss about ordinary sex.

Don't you feel that the fundamental cement of society – the formalised partnership of man and woman – ought to be one of society's greatest priorities, even today?

When I was in Sri Lanka, I visited a man and his wife. His mother lived with them, and this was absolutely natural, a normal course of events. He expected to have his mother living there. And this is a terrible loss in our lives: the fact that we've cut down to these nuclear families of a husband, wife, children and maybe a granny flat. The whole thing is lost. I don't see that we're ever going to get it back. I don't see how we can or how we could make it a priority. You can't dictate to people how to live. You can't abolish the idea that women's lives have changed. Yet I also think this is good in a way. I've always been a feminist in the sense that I can't bear it when women are just sat on and used.

You have a legendary reputation for seducing women in general and beautiful young women in particular. Most men who know you well are envious. What is your secret?

I've often wondered. I may tell you, it gets less easy, but I think they're intrigued by something different – that is to say, somebody in a wheelchair. The only explanation I can think of is that those women who have seduced me wanted to discover what it was like to go to bed with somebody disabled. Or there is always the other possibility, that one is less frightening to them, that one isn't a great beast who's going to leap on top of them and beat them. Whatever it is, I've been very lucky.

Extremely lucky.

Well, I don't think I'm able to shed any light on it.

Could it be because you are such a great raconteur?

I think, really, that what I said to you once about Lord Weidenfield is the answer: if you take a real interest in women, they respond amazingly. Concentrating on them at a dinner party, you talk just to one woman, exclusively to her, and brush everybody else aside. They find that very attractive.

So you don't have to work hard at it.

I don't work very hard at it.

It comes naturally?

I don't know, Naim. What difficult questions you ask. I think it's fading.

Your disability means that you need a male companion to help you, and some have been young, good looking and intelligent. Does the physical dependence ever develop into a physical attachment in the sense that you get a crush on someone?

Not necessarily. Young men can be attractive physically, but I don't think I get a crush. They've mostly been good healthy normal lads. I don't like ugly people. Of course, one has some ugly friends, but I find it much easier to like good-looking people.

You are also said to be a Professor Higgins type in that you become a mentor to your women or wives and thus able to exercise a power over them.

I don't think I've exercised power over them. I may have taught Angela a certain amount about writing, and I certainly introduced the others to various ideas that influenced their lives, but to call it power is going too far.

Is it a source of regret that your marital history has been so tempestuous?

Regrets are not very much a part of my life. Naturally I could wish that my marriages had turned out better, but on the other hand, for years they were a success. They were all good for a period.

What of the rumours that your first wife tried to kill you, your second left yet was willing to remarry you, and the third became so exasperated that she used to hit you? How did you come to generate such stormy emotional responses?

I really don't know. I'm nomadic, so that's perhaps one difficulty. Secondly, it's not at all easy to live with someone who's disabled. That's a particularly important point, and I certainly wouldn't ever reproach any of my wives for having found it difficult. It's better that a marriage came to an end than that they struggled on out of guilt, so maybe that had a lot to do with it. I always think I'm very calm, so perhaps I just picked tempestuous ladies.

One of your former wives said it was a great privilege to have been married to you. What is it about you that makes a former wife pay such a loyal tribute?

It must be partly her sweetness of character. Once she gives her devotion to somebody, it's for good. The fact that she didn't feel able to go on being married didn't interfere with the relationship, if you see what I mean. I don't think we ever at any point had any feelings of dislike for each other -just an inability to live together. I don't know whether the other two would say anything similar, but she is very nice.

Have you regretted any of your marriages?

This is too difficult an area to cover. The answer must be no. There was so much that was agreeable about all of them that they can't be considered disasters, and I have five wonderful children as a result. I don't think I would ever marry again. The point of getting married is if you're going to have children, and I'm not going to have any more.

How would you advise your own children about marriage and relationships?

It's something you can only learn by experience. I'd never advise anybody about marriage. The only time I've ever done it was with somebody who then married the person I was advising them very strongly not to marry and who has had a perfectly happy married life ever since, so you can't predict. Look at the funny people who are married to one another and who get on, and then look at the seemingly compatible people who get married and don't stay together longer than ten minutes. It's all most peculiar. I don't think anybody can understand marriage at all till they've been married. It's very hard for young people nowadays because girls have changed and have become as independent as the boys used to be, and then they find it hard to give up that freedom.

Your daughter Candida called you great as a friend but hopeless as a father. How did you feel about that judgement?

It's probably true as far as my children are concerned. There's evidently something that I don't do that my children think I ought to do, because I don't seem able to get over to them my feelings for them. If one fails to convince them that one is a good father, one obviously isn't a good father.

You wrote in The Sunday Times *that you never felt responsible for your children. Many people might be shocked by such an idea.*

Of course I'm responsible for them in the sense that, if they're in trouble, I must get them out of it. But I don't feel responsible for their achievement and I don't think that, if one of them became a murderer, I would feel responsible for that either.

You also spoke with some derision about people who 'moulder on about what their parents have done to destroy or make them', but what greater influence can there be on a child than its parents?

Its own innate character. If you take twin babies in a cot, a few days old, their mother will tell you that there is something different about this one from that one. It's precisely that which I think is the interesting thing about human beings. Of course there are influences: school and environment, whether you're brought up in Yorkshire or Zimbabwe. But ultimately a child is itself, to my mind.

Do you think the fact that you have unavoidably spent so much time separated from your children may have coloured your view of parental influence?

No, I don't think so. I spent a great deal of time shaking off the parental influence that I had on me. Of course, bits go deep, but we can get rid of a lot of it.

Do you believe that children must fend for themselves to some extent?

Looking at my very rich friends who had given their children a lot of money early, it's nearly always been a disaster. Everybody in life needs to forge their way a bit. When things are too easy for them, it's corrupting. Strawberries from Kenya don't taste like good strawberries from the harsher climates. It's the same with wine. It's the northern wine that's best – Bordeaux and Champagne. The southern French wine is nothing like so good. The same thing applies to people. They've got to have some sort of struggle.

When explaining your unwillingness to instil any sort of sexual moral code, you said that doubtless you would have something to say if a daughter of yours became a 'courtesan'. Why choose that rather romantic word instead of 'prostitute'?

Well, to become a prostitute is unthinkable. I mean, none of them would become prostitutes. A courtesan is a possibility, I suppose. One could entertain the idea. But I would have something to say, merely because I think it would not make them very happy. There is a difference between the two words. A prostitute is somebody who's doing it straightforwardly for money, and a courtesan is probably sticking to one person at a time for a way of life rather than for straight cash. She might have a nice flat or house and a cash allowance, but not £200 for a night or whatever. But I'd never disown my children whatever they did. If they did something absolutely dreadful, I would feel very upset, but I would still think it was my duty to help them. It seems to me that love for somebody is complete, that it must encompass whatever their faults may be. You may get angry with them, you may get fed up with the child who's done something tiresome or annoying, but you can't ever abandon them. Love is constant, to my mind, and permanent. I don't feel for my daughters that they ought not to go to bed with somebody. That idea doesn't worry me.

People who were or still are close to you have mentioned the down side to your character, saying you can be hurtful, cruel and selfish, and can publicly humiliate those you love.

It's true except for the last bit. I suspect my children are putting forward this view. I am much too sharp-tongued, which comes from impatience with what I see as stupidity. As for being selfish, I don't know whether I'm more selfish than others. And I don't think I humiliate anyone. There's no malice in me.

Angela Huth told me that your daughter Candida has all your best qualities.

Obviously there has to be something in genetic influence. I'm not sure whether I'd set more store by environmental influence. In my own case, I was lucky to be brought up from the age of thirteen in a house full of books. There were 20,000 volumes at least, and marvellous paintings, beautiful furniture. All this had its influence too, but then there are lots of people who are brought up in circumstances of that sort who don't even notice there is a book or a painting there. We don't know the answer to this, and I don't think even psychiatrists do. As far as Candida is concerned, I would reverse the comment and say she has Angela's best qualities.

What did you mean exactly when you described your daughter Candida's books as done in good taste?

Her first romantic novel was done in an unvulgar way, but the second one wasn't quite so good. I regard a lot of romantic novels as being straightforwardly vulgar, and her first was not. But I felt the publishers then leant on her to put more sex into the second. She was hopelessly bad at writing about it, and it was obviously against her instincts. I daresay she could write about sex extremely well, but what she was trying to do was something somebody else was imposing on her, and it was hopeless.

You always give the impression of treating your disability lightly and inviting others to do the same, but beneath the composure must lie years of anguish, frustration and pain.

I didn't used to suffer much pain. Latterly I have, but if I started giving in to the idea of being unfortunate and allowed myself to think I'm unlucky, I would feel very depressed. It sounds trite, but one just has to count one's blessings. I sometimes ask myself if I would like to swap places with some very stupid athletic man, and the answer is that I wouldn't. I'd rather be me and I'd always rather be me.

Has your view of life changed with your disability?

Not really. I suppose I suppress the fact of it to some extent. In a way, I don't think of myself as disabled. It may sound stupid, but it's true: I think of myself as somebody who doesn't ski and who can't run, but then I look at someone else in a wheelchair and think, oh, poor them they're in a wheelchair. It's bizarre, perhaps, but perhaps the only way of dealing with it.

Might you never have become such an intrepid traveller without the challenge of being confined to a wheelchair?

I often wonder that myself. Was I driven by some urge? I don't think so. I am by nature a nomad. I really want to wander. I'm never so happy as when I'm on the move. Bruce Chatwin was a friend of mine, and this was something we had in common.

What do you consider to be most important in your life?

Oh, my family, obviously. I think that is the thing everybody must consider of prime importance in life. I feel very strongly about my children, that I owe everything to them but they owe nothing to me. I don't think it's right to be proud of one's children. You can be pleased for them, but I don't consider that something my son does goes down to my credit. I mind passionately that my children should be thought of as being themselves. My daughter Candida writes extremely well, works unbelievably hard, but that's her, and it's nothing to do with me. Very little else matters to me desperately, except I think unkindness. I like good manners very much, though God knows I don't always write all the thank-you letters I should, but I do feel manners make the world so much easier to live in.

Looking back on a career embracing journalism, the restaurant business, travelling and writing, which has been most difficult and which has given you most satisfaction?

You missed out farming. Farming – which gave me enormous satisfaction, but was a total disaster. It's really writing that gives me more and more satisfaction as I find what I want to write, or, rather, how I want to write. I've enjoyed journalism, but my visit to South Africa was the only thing I would ever claim as something worthwhile, something that actually mattered. Writing has something else to it than journalism. I hate writing so far as the physical act of sitting there and trying to achieve something is concerned. That's absolute hell. But it does give one much more satisfaction in the end.

Have you ever been tempted to seek comfort in religion, or have your circumstances had the opposite effect?

They haven't had any effect on that at all. I certainly don't sit about swearing and asking why God inflicted this upon me, because I don't think He did. Religion does become more interesting to people as they get older, because they're nearing the end, but I'm not very frightened of death. I can't help but be impressed by the Eastern religions in countries like Sri Lanka, Thailand and so on, and of course in the Arab countries. I find the everyday quality of Islam very impressive. When you're travelling in the desert, you see people praying five times a day and it's absolutely natural to them. Religion ought to be an everyday affair. The Christian religion is much too shut away in its churches. It gives far too much power to bishops and priests. They are too dictatorial, whereas in Islam it's easily accessible, and in Buddhism there is the feeling that God is within you. I find that very attractive and possibly something which I will continue to read more and more about.

My research reveals your philosophy of life to be that nothing matters very much and very little matters at all. Is this anything more than a self-preserving maxim?

Of course not, and it's a joke to some extent. People make too much fuss about too many things, like all the food fads, for example. One of my complaints about the younger generation is that they're so absorbed; they think all the time about what's good for you and what's not. And all this health kick is really because they haven't got anything else to think about. I see no evidence that they are healthier as a result. People take themselves too seriously. We're all rather absurd in that way.

QUENTIN CRISP

Quentin Crisp was born Denis Charles Pratt in Surrey in 1908. He worked as an artist's model until the 1970s, when his book *The Naked Civil Servant* was dramatised for television to great acclaim. He wrote several books including a second volume of autobiography, *How to Become a Virgin* (1981), and a book of film criticism, *How to Go to the Movies* (1989). In 1993 he played the role of Elizabeth I in the film version of *Orlando*. In 1981 he left England for New York where he lived in a single room on the Lower East Side. His experiences in the US were captured in *Resident Alien – The New York Diaries*, published in 1996. In December 1998 he celebrated his ninetieth birthday by performing the opening night of his one-man show, *An Evening with Quentin Crisp*, at a theatre on 42nd Street in New York. He died in Manchester in November 1999 on the eve of the UK revival of his one-man show.

From an early age you were aware of what you call your predicament. Do you think your predicament was largely genetic or do you think there were other factors involved?

There must have been something genetic because so many people have such absolutely conventional upbringings and they still are peculiar in some way or another, including sexually peculiar. But there may have been other factors involved. For example, you could say that I lacked anyone to tell me how to be a grown person. My mother alternately protected me from the world and threatened me with it; my father took absolutely no notice of any of us, he hardly ever spoke to us.

You obviously had a very difficult relationship with your father. How much do you think this was a symptom, how much a cause of your own problems?

I never tried to talk to my father about anything, certainly never about anything serious, so I think that was a cause. The more appalling I was, the less he talked to me.

You said that in later years you found ways to fuel the furnaces of his hatred. That sounds like a deliberate attempt to do battle.

In some ways, yes. I became more frivolous and more deliberately helpless. I knew I was a hopeless case, and I paraded my hopelessness before my father.

Money always seems to have been a bit of a problem. Yet the impression is of a middle-class upbringing with domestic servants and so on ... would you say that was the case?

We did have a middle-class suburban upbringing, and there were servants with black dresses and starched aprons, but I now know we had no money. My father was permanently in debt, and there were bailiffs in the house regularly.

In your autobiography, your three siblings are given hardly a mention. Did you always feel apart from them, and they from you?

Yes, I think I was apart from them, and they felt glad that I was apart from them. My sister, who died only about ten years ago, once said long after all the trouble was over, that I had been a terrible child. My brother next to me in age was horrified by having to be associated with me. The brother after that was so much older that he didn't really bother.

As a child, your unhappiness, or sense of being different, manifested itself in all kinds of attention-seeking behaviour. Were you aware of what you were doing at the time, was it a means to an end, or did you become aware of what it was only retrospectively?

I certainly did draw attention to myself, and I think I knew that I did, but I would have denied it, I imagine.

Do you look back on that period when you were wetting your trousers and soiling yourself with a kind of revulsion?

Well, I suppose I should. I really don't look back on it at all, but certainly I was a disgusting child, there is no doubt about it. But I don't remember being ashamed.

Boarding school seems to have been a terrible time. You were half-starved, half-frozen and humiliated in a number of ways. Did you never appeal to your parents to take you away?

I didn't. I never tried to get them to take me away. It never occurred to me to challenge my destiny.

You hated boarding school, but you describe it as a dress rehearsal for the treatment you were soon to receive in the streets of London. Would you say in that sense it was a good preparation?

Yes. I think if I had left straight from home and gone out into the world, it would have been like falling over a cliff. I had a doll's-house view of the world when I was at public school. I had to learn that everybody was my enemy, and that I would have to find ways of dealing with this if I was going to go on living.

You were so unpopular at boarding school that you say that you came to regard your unpopularity as a gift, and what was originally something you tried to avoid, you later came to cultivate. Deep down didn't you still crave friendship and approval?

I think I must have wanted friendship – it seems so unlikely that I wanted none. I didn't want approval enough to alter myself in order to get any. On some days I would think, I can't bear this anymore, I will try and behave like a normal schoolboy, and then I would think, I'm doing this so badly, it's too humiliating, and I would go back to being my horrible self.

Although there was a great deal of homosexual coupling at your school, you said in your autobiography that effeminate homosexuals did not indulge very much in sex with other boys. Why was that exactly?

Effeminate homosexuals tend to want love at the beginning, but they will not find it. It wouldn't have meant anything to me just to go behind a hedge with a boy and do it, and come away again. I wanted the world to care about me, and that included anybody that I met.

So you weren't driven at the time by a sexual urge?

I've never really been driven by a sexual urge, certainly not deeply. Of course I very quickly realised that love was out of the question, that any contact I made with people would have to be sexual, and I tried to give myself up to this, not at school, but later on. I thought at one time that sex would take me away from all this, without knowing where it would take me. I thought that if I could find someone who would cherish me, everything would be all right, but this never happened.

You also wrote of that period: 'What I wanted most of all was to use sex as a weapon to allure, subjugate, and if possible to destroy the personality of others.' That seems a remarkably well-formulated analysis for a boy of fourteen or fifteen. Did you actually think of it in that way at the time?

I think I did. I thought I could meet someone who would be sufficiently interested in me to do as I told him, but of course no such person existed. At the age of about eighteen, that would have been in 1927, I was much influenced by what I saw in the movies. Gloria Swanson, Greta Garbo and Marlene Dietrich were all icons of power, and the great German films were all about vamps – the word has all but disappeared from the language. The women were vamps, and they destroyed men. In one film Miss Helm, the most beautiful woman who ever lived, sits in a tent while the men struggle across the desert, their lips blistered with thirst. She orders some champagne, drinks it, then breaks the glass on the edge of her throne and cuts the throat of one of the men for no reason whatsoever.

When your father died, you say you felt only irritation at having to return for his funeral. Did you ever come to revise those feelings?

No, I didn't really. I had no feelings about his death. I ought to have been pleased he was dead, but actually I had already left home, so I felt nothing. It was just an event. Even now that I can, if I wish, think of my father as a character in fiction, it's still impossible to like him. Why did he saddle my mother with four children when he had no money? When he died, she had to go and live with my sister, there was nothing else she could do.

What was it like when your mother died? Were you more attached to her?

We were all relieved, because she had had such a terrible life. She didn't die until she was eighty-six and by that time she had to be lifted out of the bed into a wheelchair and at night had to be lifted back into bed. I don't seem to be able to be deeply attached to anybody. It's hard to tell how much people mean when they talk about such things. I don't know how different I am from other people, but I certainly do feel I have fewer of what would be called proper sentiments in regard to other people.

At some point in your youth, you managed to shift homosexuality from being a burden to being a cause. Presumably in some ways, far from making your life easier, it must have been made more difficult … ?

Of course, I know now that it was nonsense to think of it as a cause, but at the time I spent my life in cafés where I sat with other gay boys, most of whom were on the game, and we pooled our tears. They were miserable and for no justifiable reason, and I therefore decided that somebody had to live the homosexual life – it was no good writing books about it, because they would be read only by homo-sexuals. The important thing was to live it so that people would get used to the idea. The great weapon in the hands of integration is boredom. When you say to somebody, I'm gay, and they say, and then? – you're in the clear. It's while you have to explain yourself and justify yourself, and they try to be tolerant of you, that the problem still exists.

Did you ever dabble in prostitution?

Yes, but I was so bad at it. The reason why men go with boys is usually in the spirit of hilarious research. They want someone who's no bother, someone who doesn't try to weave an emotion into it. I didn't so much want to have sex as to be admired, and of course that was no good. So I gave it up the moment I got any real work to do.

Was the wearing of make-up a kind of acceptance of your own sexuality, a statement to society that this was you, and they had better get used to the idea?

Yes. First of all, I wore very little make-up, but exhibitionism is like a drug – after a while you can take a dose of it that would kill anyone who is just starting out. When you don't get noticed, you think, I must do more. You start to expect to cause a stare, and you're frightened when you can't do without it.

You describe the homosexuals you befriended in those days as 'pseudo-women in search of pseudo-men'. Did that mean it was a disappointment when they had encounters with similarly effeminate men?

Yes, that's right, it worried them. They would express to me their disappointment, their indignation at finding out that someone who they thought was going to turn out to be a man was just as effeminate secretly as they were. Nowadays the homosexual world is a world apart, and they don't really want to bother with real people, but in those days we all thought we would reinforce our idea of ourselves by gaining the attention of real men. Of course, it led to disaster over and over again.

At what point did you realise that it was pointless to expect people to be tolerant or under-standing towards you?

Very early on. By the time I was thirty I didn't really expect anything.

Your early working life was precarious to say the least, spells of unsuitable jobs interspersed with dole money. You must have lived in a state of permanent anxiety ...

Yes, and I was always hungry. The dole was fourteen shillings a week. I had one meal a day and lived in a room which cost six shillings a week. The room was long enough to lie down in one way, not quite long enough to lie down the other way, and not quite high enough to stand up in. It was a very difficult period.

You turned your hand to writing – poems, libretti, stories – but you describe the problem as being one of having a genius but no talent. What did you mean by that exactly?

My genius is for the smiling and nodding racket which I can now practically live on. If you can get by on peanuts and champagne in America you need never buy food again, but in England you can't do that; you need to be able to do something and do it well, and possibly even study it. I've never studied anything in my life.

At one point in The Naked Civil Servant *you liken homosexuality to an illness. That implies that it cannot be helped but in some cases it might be cured. Was that your view?*

I suppose it still is my view. I don't remember what I thought at the time, but I have known homosexuals who have got married because they thought it might help. I didn't ever say, 'Help whom?' and indeed, since they remain married and they have children, it obviously did help. The idea that people are either heterosexual or homosexual is nonsense; they will sometimes drift backwards and forwards for an hour or for a week or for years, it depends. The more the gay people now insist on their rights, the greater the distance becomes between the gay world and the straight world, and this is such a pity. I suppose I have to be careful about calling it an illness, but homosexuals seem to me to be people standing on the bank watching other people swim. In some way it takes you away from real life, away from the main stream, so if it isn't an illness, it's certainly like having an illness.

Did you ever sleep with a woman?

Never. I don't think it could have worked. Sexually I have no interest in women at all. I don't shun them, I simply have no interest in them.

You say at one point in the book that you regarded all heterosexuals, however low, as superior to all homosexuals, however noble. What did you mean by that?

The world belongs to straight people, and they must be regarded as superior. The superiority of numbers, of power, of know-how, of worldliness is all with straight people – that's the sense in which they are superior.

Do you have a secret admiration for heterosexuals?

I suppose I do, yes. Especially the ones who seem so totally at ease with themselves.

During the 1930s you began to meet a greater number and variety of homosexuals, but because you did not conform to their rules you were ostracised by them too. It must surely have been much harder to bear the hostility of homosexuals.

Yes, I was very disappointed when I first found that the homosexual community distrusted, disliked, even despised me. I got used to it and I suppose in England most of my friends were straight women, because they expected nothing of me, and in any case these were women in happier times, before they decided they had to be people. When women were women, one of the things they liked to do was chatter, and I'm a born chatterer, so I could sit with them, and entertain them and they could be nice to me. I didn't really ever get on with men because they only ever speak to me about money and politics and sport, about which I know nothing.

It seems that because you publicised homosexuality and flaunted your own, you angered a great many homosexuals who preferred to remain incognito. Did you not sympathise with their position?

I understood their position but I don't really believe that my being obvious made any difference to them. Everything is so changed now. Nowadays if two men take an apartment in any big city in the western world, it is assumed they are gay. In a time gone by, people would have assumed they were sharing a place and halving the rent. Friendship is disappearing altogether and sex has taken its place.

From where did you derive the courage to display all the trappings of homosexuality at a time when it was firmly in the closet?

I couldn't do otherwise. I was hopeless at being a real person, and even when on occasions I was not wearing make-up, it made no difference. People still stared at me.

When the war broke out you were turned down by the medical board on grounds of sexual perversion. Did you receive that as an accolade or were you humiliated by it?

I wasn't humiliated. People had told me I would never get into the forces, but I hadn't believed them. I had no money, I couldn't get a job, and I imagined it would solve all my problems.

What were your feelings about the war?

It was very nice when it came. First of all, there was a whole year in which you never saw any war whatsoever, and you could only read about it in the papers. But then the war came to London and the sky was pink with doom, the ground shook with the anti-aircraft fire, and you could hear the shrapnel falling. And that was very exciting. I decided I wouldn't accommodate the war at all, so if I was invited out I went out, whether there had been the air-raid warning or not – it was all a lottery in any case.

The war seems scarcely to have impinged on you – at least it hardly figures in your account of those years. How did you manage to avoid thinking about it, worrying about it?

I just didn't alter my life, I went on exactly as though there was no war. The only wonderful aspect of the war was the American soldiers. Americans listen to what you say; Englishmen never do. It felt like you were being courted to some extent.

When you found unfurnished accommodation, you discovered that squalor was your 'natural setting', as you called it. Was this primarily a reaction against your mother's domestic orderliness?

I don't think so. It was just natural laziness. I didn't want to clean everything, and so I thought, I won't, and we'll see what happens. Then I formulated the idea that after the first four years the dirt doesn't get any worse.

Is that what you truly believe, or was it something you said primarily to shock people or to amuse them?

I never say what I don't mean. And I'm not the only person to think that way. There was once a woman called Nancy Spain who went on to *Woman's Hour* and said that only a fool would make the bed every day. It shook England, but in fact it was a message of hope. I once watched a woman dust the rails under the chairs, and I told her there was no need to do that. She said, 'I know there isn't, but if I don't do it they haunt me.' And that is the way women feel. Women in England are all in a blind rage by half-past ten in the morning, because they've had to skirmish round the house, and dust everything, and put everything right, wash everything. But there's no need.

You criticise the advertising industry for spreading the idea, against all evidence to the contrary, that sex leads to happiness. Would you at least concede that it leads to pleasure, perhaps the greatest pleasure of all?

It leads to pleasure, but with penalties. Homosexual intercourse is often actually painful, sometimes uncomfortable, sometimes nasty, so you have to think, do I really want this? There was once a programme about hepatitis, and a woman interviewed a young man and asked how many times on average he had sexual relations. He replied, 'Six', and she said, 'Six times a week?' He replied, 'No, six times a night.' Now at that rate, it can't go on being a pleasure – it must simply be a score. I think it's a form of pleasure which some people cannot do without, but I don't believe it is a form of happiness.

Could you yourself do without it?

I can do without it now, and I have done for the last twenty years or so. In the past if I felt sexual urges I usually masturbated, which is less trouble. And so much cheaper.

Why is the homosexual generally more promiscuous than the heterosexual?

I secretly think – though I have been shouted down on this – that it is because it is not very satisfactory. Just as if you eat food that doesn't nourish you, you eat more food, so people who indulge in unsatisfactory sex are often extraordinarily promiscuous.

You seem very cynical about sex, calling it 'the last refuge of the miserable'. Was this some sort of defence mechanism operating?

I don't think so. It's just that I don't set much store by sex, and I have had less sexual experience than most people. But certainly, it is a refuge of the miserable in so far as people who are not content with their lives have to go out to look for sex. And that applies to the heterosexual man as well.

Have you ever had a happy sexual relationship?

I've had pleasant sexual relationships. I couldn't say I ever met anyone who fulfilled my dream which was to be admired for sexual and other reasons. I suppose the truth is, I do not deserve it, but you don't realise that in the beginning.

Your relationship with the American G.I. seemed to be one of the most satisfactory but even then there was no love. Was there affection?

There was affection, and he was friendly, which is rare in homosexual relationships.

But you never really fell in love ...

I don't think I quite know what that phrase means. I understand that you can fancy somebody, or wish them well, or you can enjoy their company, but I don't know anything beyond that.

Towards the end of the war you became a model and posed for art students. I imagine that had greater appeal than your other jobs ...

It did. In the beginning I really liked it in spite of the terrible suffering involved in sitting. There was hardly any limit to the discomfort I could endure, but you can only get better at it for the first two or three years. When you begin, you think I wonder if I'm going to faint, but after a bit there's nothing you can't do. I did it on and off for thirty-five years and in the end I was half asleep half the time. But yes, I liked it in the beginning.

One imagines that you might have lived a rather promiscuous life, but this seems not to have been the case in the early days. For many years you were able to live without sexual encounters at all. Was this primarily lack of opportunity or lack of desire?

I never really desired much sex. I don't ever remember thinking, 'I've got to get a man from somewhere.' If it presented itself to me, fine, if it didn't, I went without it. Now I haven't had any sex for at least twenty years and this doesn't worry me in the least. My appetites are in general much weaker than other people's – I've never been drunk, I never overeat, I have never done anything to excess. Even at my worst I was never as promiscuous as most homosexual men are.

After the war you took to the movies and watched anything as long as it wasn't English. Was this a kind of escapism or was it a genuine passion?

It is a genuine passion. Nothing ever happens in English movies, which is why I dislike them, and, in any case, I've always been American in my heart. When I was a child my mother took me to the movies in the spirit of ostentatious condescension; the cinema was for servant girls, and people with taste went to the theatre. She told me America was nothing like how it looked in the movies, but she was wrong. Everybody who comes from England to America agrees it's more like the movies than you'd ever dream.

Are you lonely ever?

I like solitude, but of course I've never been put to the test because I've always lived in big cities. If I spent a whole week in my room doing nothing, I would reconstruct myself, go out, walk from where I live up to 14th street and back again and I would be really surprised not to meet somebody with whom I could have a cup of coffee and discuss the secret of the universe. I've never lived in a village and I hope I never shall.

Your first major writing success was The Naked Civil Servant *which was soon made into a TV movie. Was that the first real flush of success for you?*

Yes, but it was only a mini-success. It did not lead to any work, I wasn't invited to review other people's books and say they were worse than mine, and no one asked me to write anything else. It wasn't until it was made into a television play that my whole life changed. That was in 1975, and the book came out in 1968, so there were seven long, dark years in between.

John Hart's portrayal of you was so widely acclaimed. Were you yourself happy with it?

I was indeed. It was a marvellous reproduction of my voice for one thing. He was slightly more defiant than I ever was, but only minimally. He's born to play victims. After he played me he went on to play Claudius, which is really only me in a sheet, and then he was the Elephant Man. People sometimes ask me if I feel like an elephant man, and I do, I do.

One success led to another, and you soon had your own one-man show at the Duke of York's. Did your life change as a result?

I felt my way of speaking, my way of expressing myself, had started to pay off, yes, but my life didn't change much. I didn't branch out, I didn't spend a lot of money. I went on living in one room, and I still live in one room.

Your success in England was readily exported to America. You say you have always felt your natural milieu to be American. It must have seemed like a dream come true ...

To come here was quite quite wonderful. Happiness rains down from the sky in America. I agree with Millicent Martin who is now an American by marriage. She said the difference between America and England is that in America everyone is always in favour of whatever you propose to do, and this is absolutely true. If you stand up in a bar and announce that you're getting up a cabaret act, everybody will ask, where are you gonna appear? What are you gonna wear? In England if you told your friends you were getting up a cabaret act, they would say, for God's sake, don't make a fool of yourself. Everything is a warning in England. I didn't know there was any happiness in the world, till I got here.

You say the English have etiquette and the Americans have manners. How would you explain the difference?

Etiquette is a process of exclusion. The English have rules, and if you don't know how to eat an artichoke then you're not one of us; if you call a table napkin a serviette, you will not to be invited again. In America you have manners, which are a process of inclusion. When you're with Americans they want you to feel you can do no wrong; that's the difference.

Your performance in Orlando, *as Elizabeth the First, has been widely praised. Was that something you enjoyed?*

It was absolute hell, but being in a movie is always absolute hell. I wore two rolls of fabric round my middle tied with tapes, and then a hooped skirt tied with tape, and then a quilted petticoat and then an ordinary petticoat and then a dress, and I had a bodice so tight that it blistered my stomach. No wonder Queen Elizabeth was always chopping off people's heads – she must have been in a permanent rage from having to wear those clothes.

Presumably now, with your writing and lecturing and TV and film appearances, you are better off in your eighties than you have ever been. Do you feel there is an irony there?

I suppose there is. I am better off, but not very much better off. People assume that if you're famous you're rich, which of course is not necessarily so, but provided I die in the next two or three years, I'm in the clear. In America everybody is your friend, but the system is ruthless. Once you're unproductive you will end up living in a cardboard box on the street corner. So you have to get into your grave fairly quickly.

In your autobiographical writing you seem much concerned with the notion of happiness and what it consists in … for example, you think money is a prerequisite, and to look forward to the future spells the death of happiness. How would you describe the state of happiness, and have you achieved it in your life?

I've achieved a little of it. Happiness, I would say, is to live in the present, not to think about the past, not to think about the future, but to be here and to be now, to be aware, to live inside your body. I think happiness is a physical thing.

Most people would define happiness in terms of loving and being loved. Does that strike you as being completely alien?

It's alien to me. My happiness is a relationship between me and myself, not between me and someone else, which is always full of uncertainty.

You have described yourself as doing deliberately what you used to do by mistake, a way of getting the joke on your own terms. Have you arrived at a kind of contentment now, would you say?

Yes. Now I can behave in a way that is perfectly natural for me, and other people accept it, or appear to accept it. Perhaps it's all an illusion, because in America if they don't like you, they don't say so, whereas if they do like you, they tell you. It's completely the other way round in England – there you feel terribly disliked, but here in America it's easy to get the impression that everybody adores you. But I would say that I'm happier than I ever expected to be.

You were a martyr, weren't you, but your martyrdom was partly self-inflicted. You got used to living in a world which scorned and hated you. Did you become a willing martyr in the end?

I suppose I expected the world in general not to accept me, not to like me, and to throw things at me and shout at me, so yes, I suppose I was the willing kind.

Would you have had the sex-change operation if it had been available at the time?

If it had been available when I was in my late teens, and I had had the money, I would certainly have had the operation. Then I could have gone away to a provincial town and run a knitting-wool shop, and nobody would ever have known my terrible secret. I would have been free.

You have been much preoccupied with the business of death, and have been predicting your own for some time now. Do you look forward to it?

Yes, it's the next big event in my life. Like most people, I imagine, what one is concerned with is behaving nicely when you're dying. A lot of people think it terrible to die alone, but if you die in the presence of other people you have to be polite while you die, which must be very difficult. So that is one of my chief preoccupations: how to behave nicely when I'm dying.

What is your attitude to religion ... has it changed at all over the years?

No, I think it's always been the same. I don't want to say anything that might give offence, but I can't believe in a God susceptible to prayer. If God is the universe that encloses the universe, or if God is the cell inside the cell, or if God is the cause behind the cause, this I can accept. But I think it is actually wrong to teach children to bargain with whatever they think is God – for example, if you don't eat sweets in Lent, He will give you a bicycle with ten speeds. This is undignified. If there is a force that keeps the spheres moving in the heavens, why would it be preoccupied with us, and why would it be endowed with such wretched human characteristics? Why is it angry, why is it jealous, why is it forgiving? No, I don't believe in that sort of God.

But do you expect any life after death?

I can't afford to. What little I can do, say and be is complete, so it would be very dreary to have to come back. I can't really imagine what life after death would entail; I can only imagine more of the life that I've already led, and that has been long enough.

Your life has been extraordinary by any standards, but it strikes the outside observer as having been a tragic one in some measure. Would you agree?

Yes. I don't know how it could have been changed to make it less tragic. Other people grow up with their brothers and sisters, and they get on fine for the most part with them, and then they go to school and make friends, and then they go out into the world and acquire workmates. None of that happened to me. I was alone, and I had to invent happiness.

Your autobiography ends with the words: 'I stumble towards my grave confused and hurt and hungry ... ' Would you use the same words today?

No. Today I am less confused, my hurts have been mostly healed, and I am well fed.

Sir Julian Critchley

Julian Critchley was born in 1930 and educated at Shrewsbury and Pembroke College, Oxford. Until he retired in 1997, he was a Conservative MP for over thirty years, winning his first seat in 1959. From 1979 to 1987 he chaired the Conservative Party Defence Committee, and he wrote extensively on the subject of defence and nuclear weapons. He was an acute observer of political life and enjoyed a successful career as a writer, broadcaster and journalist. His publications included *Westminster Blues*, *Palace of Varieties* and a biography of Michael Heseltine. His autobiography, *A Bag of Boiled Sweets*, appeared in 1994. He was expelled from the Tory Party for backing a splinter pro-Euro Conservative group in the 1999 European Parliament election and died, a year later, from cancer, aged sixty-nine.

Is there life after the House of Commons, would you say? Or is it a slow and painful decline from the world of politics?

I'm afraid it is a slow and painful decline. I was unlucky enough to fall ill in 1991, and although I remained an MP, I missed most of the last Parliament and could not stand at the last election because of ill health. Had I been fit enough to stand, I would have held the seat and would now still be a Tory member of parliament. Of course, I love living in Ludlow, and because I come from this part of the world, I've always wanted to retire here. But I was obliged to retire much too early. So much is happening in politics in general and with the Conservative Party in particular that I feel utterly frustrated that I have no part to play anymore. There is nothing as ex as an ex-MP, and as I make what living I can out of freelance journalism, mainly political, it becomes increasingly difficult to do so with the passing of time.

In your autobiography, A Bag of Boiled Sweets, *you seem obsessed with your own fail-ure or lack of achievement. There is a slight sense that you protest your failure too much. Would you agree?*

That is not an unreasonable criticism. If I do protest my failure too greatly it is for two reasons. First, I was always brought up to admire the intellectual capacity of my father, and my mother always used to say that I was nothing like as clever as he was. Secondly, politics is such a transparent profession; at any given time it is possible to judge the progress of a member of parliament within his own party, and it is very tiresome to observe the soles of the feet of people climbing above you up the ladder of politics – particularly when you regard them as not particularly bright. As a consequence of my relative failure, I became an observer of politics as opposed to a participant. The more I observed, the more enemies I made, and my greatest mistake was to confuse political journalism with politics, and you can't ride both horses. I had no money of my own, and since I was not a businessman or a lawyer or a company director, the only way I could earn money was to scribble. In the early days, as a very young man in the House, I did not appreciate the extent to which the old things in the Tory party were upset by the fact that I wrote about them in my *Spectator* column. People didn't do things like that then. The main person who destroyed my political career – if it can be described as such – was Francis Pym, Ted Heath's chief whip. Pym told a friend of mine in the whips' office that he did not consider me a Conservative, and that opinion was passed on to Ted. So Pym was – to use the politically incorrect phrase – the nigger in the woodpile. Promotion was also blocked by Margaret Thatcher, but with good reason, since I was very hostile to her. All I could do after that was be my own man. I believe I pursued that course honestly enough, though that is of course a matter of opinion.

Jeremy Paxman called your memoirs the most entertaining to have been published for years and said they were free of the mendacity, distortion and self-importance which characterise most political memoirs. Was that the highest form of praise as far as you were concerned?

Yes, I was delighted with that, because I think what he said was broadly true. And Paxman is a pretty formidable character, not given to flattery.

In your book you quote Graham Greene's view that fear is the dominant emotion of childhood, but you relate it to your move from prep school to Shrewsbury. In the context of your early family life, would you say that you had a happy childhood?

How nice to be asked some intelligent questions for a change instead of being interrogated by some silly girl who doesn't know her arse from her elbow. Well, my mother and father are dead so I can tell the truth. I was happy at home, but unhappy for a great deal of time at school. My father was a distant, clever man who suffered from the English disease of not being able to touch. He never showed affection, never kissed me – it would have been inconceivable. My mother and he did not get on, but this didn't dawn on me until I was an adult – it's curious how blind children can be to the unfortunate nature of their parents' relationship. When I said that fear was the dominant emotion, I was referring to my experience at Brockhurst when I was ten, when the very formidable and unpleasant headmaster, knowing that I was terrified of water, threw me into the deep end in public in order to 'make a man of me'. I was also thinking of my time at Shrewsbury, which in 1945 had not really changed from Arnold's Rugby. One was either frightened of being beaten by older boys, cold because the central heating was minimal, or hungry because it was the height of the rationing period. But I don't want to give the wrong impression on this; fortunately, I was powerfully built, and my uncle, whom I adored, taught me how to box, with the result that nobody took me on idly. In the public-school system your first two years are hell, your third year becomes marginally better, and in your fourth year you come into your own and begin to do what the others have done to you. However, since I was a bit of a rebel, my housemaster told me at the end of my third year that however long I stayed at Shrewsbury he would never make me a monitor. In effect he deprived me of a fourth year, cheated my father out of his money and me out of my education. The truth is I was a sensitive, difficult child, nervous and neurotic, and it did not help to be sent to the wrong sort of schools.

Where do you think the neurosis came from?

I guess it was a genetic inheritance from my father. As a small boy in Bristol, where he lived, he was so neurotic that he could tell how long it would take him to get to a public lavatory from whatever position in Bristol he happened to be in, even if he was on a bus. I have not shared the same neurosis, but there were others. I don't know whether you read my father's obituary notices – he died in October – but he was much cleverer than I am. Indeed, Jonathan Miller once described him as the greatest medical philosopher since Locke. I therefore always had a sense of inferiority, of not living up to his standard – an idea reinforced by my mother.

In your autobiography, you describe your mother in warm, human terms: a chain smoker, a gin drinker, an amusing companion; but your father is a remote figure, emotionally shy, and your brother scarcely emerges as a person. From the reader's point of view, there is a definite imbalance ... was it conscious on your part?

No. I've always got on well with my brother, but he was five years younger and the gap meant that he didn't loom very largely in my life. We went to different schools and universities. My mother was indeed all of those things you describe until she became a sick woman towards the end of the war. She drank a great deal, and she never recovered from a series of illnesses and died a miserable death. Father had tremendous wit and elegance and verve, but only for other people; when he came home he switched off. Like an actor, he went out to perform and came home to rest.

It is often said that you inherited your wit from your mother. What qualities has your father passed on to you, would you say?

A degree of intellectual curiosity, and also a generalised interest in subjects which he knew a great deal about – for instance, nineteenth-century French history and Oscar Wilde.

You and your father had little to say to each other until his old age. Did you try to make up for all the silent years?

Yes, I did. My mother died in 1974 and father married a woman who was approximately my age. He retired to Somerset where I used to go every summer to stay in my cousin's house, and it was then that I attempted to make up for lost ground by taking father and his wife out to lunch. There were terrible problems, however, when I sent him the draft of *A Bag of Boiled Sweets*. It was a great mistake, for he took intense objection to various comments I made about him. They were frivolous and marginal, but by then he was old, and since he was always vain and had a Victorian idea of privacy, he hated the idea of appearing in what might be described as a frivolous book. For example, I told the story of my mother overhearing a couple in the grocer's saying: 'That's Mrs Critchley – she and her husband are the sort of people who drink wine with their meals.' I wrote in my book that while this was certainly true, it was mainly Algerian wine. Father wrote me a very stiff letter saying that he had never drunk Algerian wine in his life, and for the next four and a half years we had no contact except to exchange increasingly irritable letters. When I got my knighthood, he didn't even write to congratulate me. Last September his wife and my brother arranged that we should meet for a sort of reconciliation, and I think Father then must have known that death was near – he was ninety-seven after all. We had the meeting; there was no emotional scene – which might have been the case had we been French or Italian – we shook hands, and within four days he was dead. So that was good news, because I could go to his funeral without the awful feeling that there was unfinished business and that the unfinished business itself had been so trivial.

Your unwillingness to be confirmed at Shrewsbury, lest it led to further compulsory church attendance, was part of a nonconformity established at school and continued as a Tory MP. But you confess it was partly a pose, and that while you played poacher, you wanted to be gamekeeper, and would have welcomed promotion in both spheres. Have you consciously encouraged the pose?

Yes, I think I have. There is certainly a thread of nonconformity running through my life. I disliked intensely what was called the house spirit at school. I did not want to watch on a compulsory basis the house playing football on a wet afternoon; I would rather have read or done anything else. My nonconformity was carried on almost instinctively throughout my life, and certainly held me back within the Conservative Party. I've often wondered whether I made the wrong choice of party. I think I would have been happier as a Liberal, but as Liberals did not get elected in those days unless they were extraordinarily fortunate, the only choice was between Labour and Conservative, and since the whole of my background was professional middle class, thanks to my father's brains, it had to be Conservative. I remember Michael Heseltine and I – we were great mates at Oxford – talking about politics, and deciding there was only really one party we could join. But that was not an intellectual decision; it was a social decision, forced upon us by the attitudes and outlook of our families. We had almost identical backgrounds.

Could your father's record of outstanding achievement – subconsciously perhaps – have anything to do with what looks more like a failure of will than lack of ability?

There is perhaps a failure of will. The fact that I only got a fourth at Oxford was due not to a lack of intelligence, but to two other factors, namely, that it took me a long time to learn to work on my own and also the fact that I contracted polio. The latter certainly was traumatic in its effect on me and, sadly, it has come back to haunt me after forty years. 1949–51 were the years of the great polio epidemics and, as a neurologist, my father must have seen half a dozen polio patients a day. He would come back in the evening with tales of the iron lung. As a nervous, neurotic youth, I was convinced that I was going to get it and, by God, I did.

Did it affect you psychologically as well as physically?

Indeed, it did. I became very depressed. But it's an ill wind, as they say, and instead of going to the Rifle Brigade, which would have had me buried on some hillside in Korea, I went instead to Paris where I met and fell in love with Prue. That was the immediate consolation for polio, but when you are a young man in your prime, good looking as I was then, vigorous and athletic, it is a terrible business suddenly to become a cripple, unable to run for a bus, unable to walk at more than a steady pace, always anxious lest you find yourself in a situation in which you are walked off your feet by someone else. All this added up to a feeling of negotiation, and for a time blunted my ambition. In 1991 the paralysis spread down my leg, so that now I can barely walk at all, and I can't stand for any length of time. Over the last five years, I suppose I've been without pain for only about four days. I have to suck opiates most of the time.

You describe your life at Shrewsbury as consisting of cold baths, freezing dormitories and filthy food. You speak rather disparagingly about the 'sensitive' and 'misunderstood' souls who write about the horrors of public-school life, and you refuse to be numbered among them. Why?

I don't think I deliberately denied the connection, but it's a simple matter of fact that the happy schoolboy upon whose tomb is the epitaph HE WAS HEAD OF SCHOOL does not put pen to paper about his education. You could not find a more able and successful man than Michael Heseltine, worth about seventy-four million, and yet he was utterly neglected at Shrewsbury, and treated with a sort of contempt because he was not athletic. He felt exactly as I did, that it was a pretty appalling place. And so it was. Shrewsbury in the 1950s and 1960s was full of iconoclasts, but the Richard Ingrams and the Willie Rushtons were the next generation to the Heseltines and Critchleys. They were kicking an open door, but we were kicking at a bolted and barred door, and the sanctions for us were much more severe than for those who came after us.

On a visit to Shrewsbury from Oxford, Michael Heseltine proposed a motion, seconded by you, in a debate on the future of public schools, in which he castigated them as 'breeding grounds of class privilege, intellectually narrow and conformist and a gross encouragement to homosexual practices'. Did either of you believe any of what was said, or was it all in fun?

Oh, we believed it. All the younger boys voted for us, while the older ones were dragooned into voting against us, the villain of the piece being a housemaster who went on to become headmaster of Eton. He had the unpleasant habit of beating boys on their bare bottoms and then kissing them on the same bare bottoms. He was a sadist without a shadow of a doubt, and we absolutely went for him. I can see his face to this day. He was absolutely humiliated and made furious by it. I rang up the Press Association and told them that a great public school had voted to dissolve itself and was then accused by the school authorities of selling the story. In fact, I was so green, I didn't know you *could* sell a story to a newspaper, but of course the headmaster was rung up at 6 o'clock in the morning and the *Daily Mirror* had it all over the front page. The authorities looked into whether or not they could expel us both from the Old Salopian Society, only to find that neither of us had joined in the first place. It was all very childish but extremely satisfying revenge for my three miserable years.

Did you feel any qualms about sending your own children away from home?

My two daughters from my first marriage were sent to Dartington over my dead body. I couldn't prevent it. My first wife's mother had a lot of money and that is why they went there. When I visited Dartington I would be greeted by my daughters and a long line of other children, all with a Woodbine at the corner of their mouths. The school was a disgrace, though it was very fashionable before the war as a progressive place. The girls were always having affairs with the masters, there was a degree of drug-taking, the richer pupils arrived by helicopter and, in the end, the headmaster's wife appeared in the centrefold of *Playboy* – and that was the end of Dartington. There is the old story about Dartington which Shaw uses in one of his plays. A mother visits the school and knocks on the door, which is opened by a small girl, stark naked. The mother is horrified and takes a step back, saying 'My God!' – to which the small girl replies, 'There is no God,' and slams the door in her face. My other two children by my second wife, Melissa and Joshua, were rather different. Melissa went to a Catholic convent at Farnborough, on the basis that this was the middle class's best educational buy. She hated it, though I don't think she was bitterly unhappy. Nothing would have persuaded me to send Joshua to Shrewsbury, and in fact he was a day boy at the Royal Grammar School, Guildford, and he did very well.

You went through Oxford with Michael Heseltine and became close to him. Have you been wounded by the withering of your friendship with him?

Yes, I have. We were very close indeed for a long time – we hunted together, so to speak. I was his best man and he was mine. I'm a year or two older than Michael and initially I made rather faster progress than he did in the Oxford Tories, but he overtook me pretty quickly. I've never known anyone with such overweening ambition and such high horsepower. He is not an intellectual, he may not even be a particularly clever man, but he makes up for that by having a twelve-cylinder engine, the looks of a Greek god and a stamina which I could never match. We fell out over my editorship of *Town* magazine and the fact that I couldn't make a success of it. Incidentally the magazine lasted only a fortnight after I left and had never made money in its six years of existence.

He sacked you, didn't he?

Yes; but what hurt me more than anything else was that we were both living in the same house and, as an old friend, he should have taken me to one side and told me that the magazine was losing money and perhaps given me three months' notice and time to find another job. But instead he got his henchman to make life unpleasant for me, and that I disliked intensely. We were driven out of our flat as well as my job, and it took me a long time to forgive him. There is definitely a ruthless side to Michael. He chooses his friends for what they can contribute to him, and when they can no longer make a contribution, they are expendable.

But that's not true friendship …

No, of course it isn't, but this is how he's developed. However, I don't want to be bitter and twisted about this, and to give him his due he is almost certainly responsible for my knighthood. He came to visit me here when I was out of action, and as he left, he said that he was determined to get me my K. And in 1990 I supported Michael throughout that very intensive election campaign; I was never off the telly or the radio, being nice about him and backing him up, with the consequence that the local Tories wanted to de-select me. They failed, but it was a very unpleasant experience. Michael thanked me for risking my career on his behalf, and since then we've been good acquaintances, but never close friends in the way that we were.

Matthew Parris said that loyalty to your friends was one of the nice qualities which have been your downfall. Would you agree?

I'd like to think I'm loyal to my friends, and the other side of the picture is that I'm certainly loyal to my enemies. I think I'm a bad enemy and a good friend. Whether it's the cause of my downfall, I don't really know. As I indicated, the essential reason for my lack of progress was a suspicion, not altogether unjustified, that I was not really a natural Conservative at all. People detected that pretty quickly.

Would you go as far as E. M. Forster and put loyalty to a friend before loyalty to your country? For example, would you have voted for Heseltine as leader even though you thought someone else would have made a better prime minister?

No, I don't agree with falsehood. And I think one's country is more important that one's party, and my loyalty would always lie there, so I would never fall for what is a very seductive Forsterian idea. I voted for Michael because I thought he would make the best leader of the party and very probably the best prime minister. Don't forget, we never knew each other properly at Shrewsbury because we were in different houses and although we were friendly at Oxford, Michael got married in 1966, and I don't think his wife Anne liked me. Wives are always a little suspicious about close male friends of their husband's, not because there was ever anything sexual between myself and Michael – that's unthinkable nonsense – but because of so much shared experience in which they cannot participate. And Heather, who was my wife at that time, couldn't bear Anne, so it didn't make for a happy relationship.

You say in your memoir that you were never either converted or convinced by Conservatism and you entered politics with no sense of social obligation. This strikes me as the most astonishingly honest statement any politician has ever made …

It's absolutely true. I entered politics because I thought it was an honourable trade and also immensely exciting. There was no intellectual experience which turned me into a High Tory, Low Tory or Conservative. Trollope says that the greatest honour for an Englishman is to have the initials MP after his name; I'm sure that was true in the nineteenth century, but it also appeared to me to be true in the early 1950s. The party system was a necessary evil and since no independent candidates ever got elected, one was obliged to join a party. I thought that the Tory party was a broader church than the Labour Party in those days.

The problem as you described it is that you have never believed strongly enough in any-thing … have you regarded that as a handicap or not?

I have believed strongly in European unity – I'm an idealist in that sense. I would look forward to a United States of Europe and I hurriedly concede that the common currency is a political and not an economic matter. Another passionately held belief was collective security as a means of avoiding nuclear war. But I could never really get worked up very much about internal politics. I was also very hostile to Margaret Thatcher, on the grounds that I didn't like her and I didn't like her policies. I never considered her a Conservative in any meaningful sense at all. She was also a very unpleasant woman to work for, or rather to work with.

There is no attempt to set yourself up as champion of the poor, or as a solver of problems other than your own. Is this a false impression? Do you have a social conscience under the veneer of bon viveur and satirist?

Not much. Of course, I had my constituency surgeries and correspondence which I worked on assiduously, but in general I am vulnerable to your charge. I don't have a particularly strong social conscience.

As a specialist in defence you consistently criticised the government's nuclear policies, spoke out against apartheid, and supported 'the wind of change' in South Africa, and you were always pro-Europe. It seems you were a liberal in fact, but to join the Liberals would have meant political wilderness. Did you never suffer from political wilderness in your own party?

I did indeed. It wasn't so apparent perhaps, but clearly I was not regarded as officer material. I had two heroes in politics: Macmillan and Roy Jenkins. Macmillan, because he controlled to a very great extent Britain's decline in power and was responsible for our adjustment in straitened circumstances – something he managed despite a party of fools. My admiration for Roy Jenkins was based on the fact that as a young Labour MP he would advocate the cause of Europe in cross-party meetings, and he advocated brilliantly.

Why then did you say that joining the Labour Party would have been unthinkable? Can you explain 'unthinkable'?

In that context it might have been slightly careless writing, but what I meant was this: having, as it were, made no progress within the Conservative party, but having become none the less much better known as a public figure than most of the ministers who were not yet cabinet ministers, I had carved out a comfortable niche for myself. And writing a lot enabled me to make quite a bit of money – in my terms, that is, since I've never been rich. Had I gone over to Labour, I would have had to start all over again and I probably would have found myself kicking against the pricks in the Labour party just as vigorously as I'd been kicking against the pricks in the Tory party. I thought I might as well remain a minor celebrity …

The early career of Tony Blair has something in common with yours – his father also made the leap into the professional middle class, which enabled his son to have a public-school and Oxford education. Do you admire him and his social conscience?

Yes, I can't help but admire Tony Blair. He has dragged the Labour Party kicking and screaming into the last part of the twentieth century, or perhaps into the twenty-first, and that is no mean achievement. He has helped to destroy Marxist socialism, which of course was the bane of Labour, and he appears to have helped shore up the monarchy when it was in danger. To be honest, I think Blair's a very good thing, and if I were forced to choose between Blair and Hague, I would choose Blair. Instead of Ken Clarke, we were foolish enough to choose an entirely untried thirty-six-year-old whose frivolity is self-evident. Propriety is suffering from a collective nervous breakdown. I think if I were coming down from Oxford today I would be a member of the Labour Party.

In your book Palace of Varieties *you describe the worst aspects of the Tory party as jingoism, anti-Semitism, obscurantism and self-righteousness –*

No wonder I wasn't promoted …

– are these elements still alive and well in the Tory party?

They, my dear friend, are flourishing. The party shows every sign of becoming a right-wing rump, obscurantist and nationalist. They aren't necessarily anti-Semitic, simply because it's not a big issue, but if you scratch them you'll find that many of them *are* anti-Semitic; they're certainly anti-black. By and large, most of them are so unattractive I wonder that I stayed with them as long as I did.

In the 1975 leadership election you voted for Mrs Thatcher who, you suggest, won comfortably for no better reason than she was not Ted Heath. Was that a sufficient reason to elect her, and did you ever regret voting for her?

I did regret voting for her, very much indeed. Ian Gilmour writes in one of his books that, given the circumstances of the time, it was not surprising that many left-wing Conservatives, despairing of Ted Heath, voted for Margaret. But we had a rude awakening. I remember in 1977 lunching with Reggie Maudling, then her opposition-front-bench foreign-affairs spokesman, and he said to me, 'What on earth are we going to do with this dreadful woman? I cannot make her see sense and she will drag us into war unless we are very careful. She is intolerant and intolerable.' So it didn't take long before I realised the extent of my error, but I was not the only left-winger to have decided that since Ted had lost three out of four elections, he was never going to hold the support of the bulk of the Conservative Party. He was also, like so many of us, his own worst enemy; he would pass you in the corridor without so much as a nod in your direction, and he treated a lot of the Tory backbenchers with contempt. I don't blame him, I would have done the same myself, but I wasn't standing as leader of the party.

In 1980 you wrote an unsigned article for The Observer *attacking Mrs Thatcher comprehensively and bringing yourself instant notoriety when you confessed to authorship. As I understand it, you regretted not signing it in the first place, but you did not regret the contents, is that right?*

That's true. I was foolish. I was prepared to lie to the press, but I was rung up by the most prominent Conservative supporter in Aldershot, a personal friend and a man whom I admired. He asked if it was me, and I felt I had to say yes, and then of course it became public. Curiously enough, some years later I ran into David English who said, 'You should have kept your bloody mouth shut and gone on denying it.' But as in the Spanish proverb, the blow that does not kill you, makes you, and I moved from being a minor player in the political field to being a kind of celebrity, a focus of anti-Thatcher Conservatism. The short answer to your question, however, is yes, it would have been more sensible to sign it.

I was interested in your comments on class, something which features a great deal in A Bag of Boiled Sweets. *You have been called a snob, a term which you refute. Yet behind the emphasis on the humble origins of your family on both sides, and the jokes about 'passing for white' among Tories because of your public-school and Oxford education, is there not some truth in the charge?*

I will confess to being an intellectual snob and if it were not the case that I find class differences in England hilariously funny, I would be guilty of being a snob. A snob is a person who finds class differences in speech usage, in what people wear, in what they eat. A snob is a person who takes these particular distinctions seriously, and I don't. If you can talk about it in an amusing way and laugh with it and at it, I think you're not a snob. What gave rise to the charge of snobbery was my teasing of the Thatcherites. This was fun because there were a lot of them, they were very obstreperous, and you could make fun of them on the grounds that they were the sort of people who ate peas off their knives. It was quite deliberate satire which I used against certain people – for example, Tebbit, whom I dislike intensely. In my view, he is a savage man who is full of hatred. One of the ways of pricking the bubble of Thatcherism, and by God, she had enough sycophants around her one way or another, was to pretend that they were all as common as muck. This would annoy them intensely, and that got me the reputation of being a snob.

You write about prejudice, and in particular anti-Semitism, which you deplore and which you say was quite common among your fellow Tories. It puzzles me that you felt it necessary to identify Jewishness in your writing. For example, Keith Joseph at Oxford is described as 'a charming Jew', while Leo Amery, born in India, is described as 'of Levantine origin', which struck me as a phrase straight out of the novels and prejudices of John Buchan. Is this something you've thought about?

I was wrong about Leo Amery. I was told by John Rogers, a mischievous old boy, that the Amerys were of Levantine extraction, and I didn't bother to check it. But I don't think it is a sign of anti-Semitism to mention the fact that Keith Joseph is a Jew; in fact, the reverse. It's people who are afraid of being thought anti-Semitic who don't use what is a perfectly accurate term. My mother was bitterly anti-Semitic in a sort of Shropshire working-class way, and what hurt me even more was that my father, whose brains I respected, had also caught from his lower-middle-class, upper-working-class background a similar anti-Semitism, and they were both so beastly about my fiancée, who was a Jew, that I felt driven into marriage with the poor girl. It turned out to be a terrible mistake.

As a young man you fell in love with Prue and you describe a romantic time in Paris, a passionate affair conducted without sex. Do you think you were unusual in exercising such restraint?

No. This was the tragedy of people of my generation and class and upbringing. Prue and I were both well-brought-up middle-class children, passionately in love, who could do practically anything except sexual intercourse. In a sense, my mother was responsible, because whenever I left the house to meet pretty girls at the Hampstead Young Conservatives, she used to shout, so loud it could be heard down Harvard Road, 'Don't you get those girls in the family way!' I would have loved to have got those girls in the family way, but I knew jolly well that they were not the sort of girls who would permit you to get them in the family way. This was 1951, not 1991. Prue and I would book into a hotel, go to bed but not undress entirely, and we would lie there doing something called necking. None of my children know what necking is, but necking was the substitute for sexual intercourse in those days.

You have been what is sometimes known as 'a serial monogamist' – that is, you have loved and been loved by three beautiful women in turn. You insist you have not been promiscuous. Is that a point of honour, or part of your nature?

Part of my nature really. When I fell in love with Prue and she gave me the push in 1952, that broke my heart. Both my wives discovered, tucked away in drawers, pictures of Prue which they promptly tore up. For a variety of reasons the first marriage didn't work, and the second didn't either, although it went on a long time. Falling in love again with Prue and coming to live with her here in 1992 has closed my emotional circle; despite my illness, I have never been happier in my life.

When your early love affair with Prue came to an end you suffered all the anguish of unrequited love and resolved never again to be the injured party in any love affair. Did you manage to keep your resolve?

That resolve was perhaps not to my credit, but I was determined not to be bro-ken-hearted again. Once was enough.

You say you are happier than you have ever been … would you, if given the chance, have chosen the promise of domestic happiness over the hope of high office? Mill Street, Ludlow, rather than No. 10 Downing Street?

It's not really a fair choice. I would have preferred to have been fit in the last six years, to have lived with Prue, to have remained a member of parliament, and to have participated with her in political life. She would have had my constituency eating out of our hands within twenty minutes, and we would have been a very successful duo without any doubt. But it hasn't worked out like that.

What did you make of the so-called Tory sleaze? Was it all hysteria whipped up by the media?

First of all, you have to define sleaze. If sleaze is asking questions for financial reward, then I would disapprove very strongly of that. Fortunately, the Ian Greers of this world never approached me – because of my political reputation there was no door I could open for them. But if sleaze means sexual misconduct, that doesn't worry me particularly. Although I am a journalist, I hate the British press, the tabloid press in particular. I think the press can be remarkably cruel. Prue and I were very lucky; we escaped with the minimum of public attention and that was because I invited Lynda Lee-Potter, of blessed memory, to come and interview us and talk to us about our affair. She did it sympathetically, so sympathetically that it made us cringe, but none the less she did it. And this put a stop to all the speculation in other papers. Prue and I just behaved like thousands of other people behave; it's sad, but also joyful.

You do not mention if any of the women in your life had an independent career. Would it have worried you to have a wife earning more than you and deemed to be more successful?

It wouldn't have worried me had she earned more than I did, providing our relationship was good. If she had become more important than me, that would have been more difficult to deal with.

In your memoir you do not – as you put it – 'do an Osborne' and write unkindly about your wives. Most people cannot resist the urge to claim that they behaved well in marital breakdowns while their partners behaved badly. Have you found it hard to resist that urge?

I think I was right to write that, since that is very much what I believe, but I must be very careful here because in the case of wife no. 1, there is an injunction out against me, so I can't mention her name. What I do begrudge is that after thirty-five years of separation I'm still paying her over a thousand pounds a month. I don't want to get into legal trouble, but she was no angel, and yet she has a meal ticket for life. That makes me bitter when I think about it. I have to work hard all the time in order to find the money, and it is becoming more difficult for me now as an ex-MP to earn the sort of money that I did two or three years ago. That is the great anxiety of my life. I wish I had had enough money to pay her off, but I never did, so she's been an albatross for forty years. She has more money than I have, and yet the law of this country means that I have to go on paying through the nose. It's very unfair, but then life is unfair.

How would you describe your personal code, the principles and values by which you have lived?

You flatter me to imagine that I have ever worked out a pattern of behaviour to which I've adhered. I think I was 'well brought up', and that has lasted, save for my marital difficulties. I am honest financially, and although I might be accused of marital dishonesty, I still have a sense of honour. I would like to think that I have behaved well.

Do your children blame you for the breakdown of your marriages?

No, not at all. They know what both the women were like.

Your record of criticising your own party, although carried off with great wit and style, nevertheless deprived you of ministerial office. Has the price of freedom to speak your mind been worth it, would you say?

I would be dishonest if I didn't say that I would have liked to become a cabinet minister, or more particularly to have had a junior ministry in defence or foreign affairs, particularly in the 1970s. I would have accepted that with alacrity. But I also know my own limitations. I lack stamina and I have not got my father's brains, and I don't think I would have made a cabinet minister. Alan Clark, even as a junior minister in a rather inconvenient ministry, found it was absolute hell. Your first appointment was at half past eight in the morning, your last appointment was at 9 o'clock at night, and then you had to go into the House of Commons with everyone else and stay there till 3 a.m. I couldn't have stood that.

You say that a religious temperament – that is, faith without scrutiny – is the principal quality required for success in politics, and it was a quality you lacked. Is religious faith in the conventional sense a feature of your life?

No. I sometimes wish it were. I'm not afraid of death itself, but I am afraid of dying, and as I have prostate cancer I am anxious about how it will develop. I'm afraid of a painful death, and I think that euthanasia is a justifiable concept.

Have you been changed by illness? Has it put a different perspective on things?

Yes. My cancer was diagnosed four years ago, and every three months I have an injection which castrates me. The fact that I am impotent has not in any way upset my relationship with Prue, thank God, and we had a marvellous four years before that. But there are times in the middle of the night when one becomes very frightened.

Are you ever tempted to acquire faith, so to speak, in order to deal with the fear?

Not really. I think we all face annihilation, and we live only for as long as people who remember us live, and after that we're forgotten. I know that religion is a comfort for people in my position, but I would regard it as something like cheating to go to a priest at this stage. For the whole of my life I have looked on Christianity as useful for keeping the social order, but have certainly not believed in the mysteries of religion. If there were a God, I don't think he would appreciate so late a conversion. No, it's a bit late in the day to start asking for favours, and I am stuck with my agnosticism.

LORD DACRE

Hugh Trevor-Roper was born in 1914 and educated at Charterhouse and Christ Church, Oxford. In 1947 he won international recognition for his book *The Last Days of Hitler*, a reconstruction based on research on behalf of British forces in occupied Germany. He was Regius Professor of Modern History and fellow of Oriel College, Oxford (1957–80) and Master of Peterhouse, Cambridge (1980–87). He published on a wide range of topics, including medieval Christendom, European witch-hunting, the Kennedy assassination, the Kim Philby affair and the Scottish Enlightenment. In 1983, in a rare misjudgement, he authenticated the so-called Hitler diaries but was unable to prevent their publication when their fraudulence was revealed. He was a director of Times Newspapers between 1974 and 1988 and he was made a life peer in 1979. He continued writing for the remainder of his life, despite failing eyesight and other ailments, borne, according to his stepson 'stoically and without complaint'. He died in 2003, aged eighty-nine.

Why exactly did you choose the title Dacre? I gather it upset the wife of William Douglas-Home who already had the title Lady Dacre and is a baroness in her own right.

That is right. I chose it after consulting the Garter King of Arms. It was a title which had been in my family, so Garter considered it was reasonable for me to take it, provided it was differentiated by being *of* something. And so it became Lord Dacre of Glanton.

Did you predict that you would upset Lady Dacre by choosing that title?

No. Time was short but I rang her up and asked her if she had any objections. She said she had none, so I went ahead. Parliament was going into recess and it therefore had to go through at once, so once she had agreed I told the Garter, and it was duly registered. By the time she expressed second thoughts it was too late. When I reminded her that she had had no objection, she said that she had been suffering from mussel poisoning at the time and hadn't really been herself. We had a correspondence afterwards which was at times animated, but in the end she wrote me a very charming letter and peace was restored.

You have spent most of your life in the universities. There is quite a lot of talk at present about grading universities in such a way that only some of them do research. To an outsider the whole idea of research in, say, Greek noun phrases or the negative in Middle English seems a strange one. What is it for in your view?

Knowledge does not advance on any front without research. A university without a research side is like a hospital which has no teaching branch to it; it tends to stay put. You make a legitimate point in that some subjects are not worth researching into; research can become a fetish and like all professional subjects it is in danger of over-professionalisation, with academics writing for other academics on smaller and smaller topics. That is an inherent danger in any research unless it is carefully controlled. People build empires out of research and sometimes the conquests are not worth making. But research is the basis of a university; otherwise it is simply a school.

What sort of duties did you undertake during the war? I know that you were with the security service, but what did that entail?

You must know I'm subject to the new official secrets act. However, I can say that I came to be in the security service by accident, that is to say I came to work on the activities of the German secret service, which was not what was intended for me. My superior officer and I discovered and identified the radio communications of the German secret service which created a great convulsion in the intelligence world. We were then moved into the secret service proper, and from then on we became an essential part of the business of reading and working out the organisation of the German intelligence services.

Among your colleagues in the security service was Kim Philby. It rather undermines one's confidence to discover that our security service not only catches spies but recruits them. How were people recruited in those days? To an outsider it all has the air of 'there's this chap I know', and so many turned out to be duds.

I think it is true that at the beginning of the war and before, the secret intelligence service, MI6, was recruited on a personal basis by people of rather limited experience. They couldn't advertise of course, and the people chosen were not always ideal. Accidents happened.

In your own case, how were you recruited?

I was recruited because of the work which we had already done. The secret service judged it essential to keep control of this work which had been done outside the secret service, and therefore I was moved as part of an organisational change. I was not chosen personally.

But how did this work start in the first place?

Accidentally. I was drafted at first and had a territorial commission. We were given a task which had nothing whatever to do with intelligence but by chance we made a huge discovery. To begin with no one would take it seriously, and consequently my superior officer and I worked on it in the evenings privately in our flat which we shared, and we deciphered the messages. It was a very simple cipher and I'm not claiming any great achievement, but once it was realised that we had discovered the operations of the German secret service, there was quite a storm. We were severely rebuked for making the discovery, and even more so for having deciphered it.

How do you think people ought to be recruited for such services? Is there, do you think, any way of ensuring loyalty, or at any rate of limiting the damage of disloyalty?

I don't know of any infallible test which would exclude the wrong people. I myself was astonished when Philby joined SIS. I was already there and was surprised to hear people talk with great enthusiasm about his appointment. I knew that Philby had been a communist.

You knew then?

Yes, but I was as wrong as everybody else, only in a different way. Lots of people, my friends included, had been communists at university, but it was not taken seriously. It was a passing phase, and it all evaporated at the time of the Russo-German pact. I considered that our superior officers in the security service were often unreasonable, seeing reds under the bed all the time, and turning down clever people on the grounds that they had left-wing views. When Philby joined I was rather glad someone had got through the net. It never occurred to me that he was a communist still, even less that he would be a communist spy. So we were all mistaken on this. Recruiting policy, however, was not the only thing that kept able people out. It wasn't a job in the usual sense, in that you couldn't talk about your work, not even to your wife, it was not well paid because the budget was small, you disappeared in the morning, came back in the afternoon, and it led nowhere. It was not a very glamorous job unless you lived in a world of fantasy, in the Bulldog Drummond, Philip Oppenheim kind of world, which of course some of them did. People were therefore chosen out of a rather limited pool; they generally had some money of their own and they often lacked normal ambition. I was pretty censorious about them at the time, though I came to perceive the difficulties inherent in the situation. Nowadays of course recruitment is on a different basis; it's no longer done in clubs.

If money was not the motivating factor, did people join for a sense of adventure?

I suppose it was adventure of a kind, at least for people who joined in peacetime. In wartime we didn't so much join as end up there. I made a distinction between the amateurs and the professionals. The amateurs thought, and were blamed for thinking, in short terms; we wanted to win the war and we had no long-term aims, but the grandees of the service tended to regard the war as an inconvenient interruption and were determined not to allow the amateurs to burst the system. Philby was obviously determined to stay a professional, and he played the professional game. We made nuisances of ourselves since we didn't care if we were kicked out, but Philby didn't cause trouble; he was ingratiating and very competent. I don't think he did us any harm during the war. He did afterwards, but if he did pass information to the Russians during the war, they either had it anyway, or they didn't use it. I doubt if he actually did anything dangerous or contrary to British policy or aims during the war.

Setting aside the war, how much harm do you think Philby, Blunt and company actually did?

It's difficult to be sure in concrete terms. One can of course say that they gave a bad name to their service, they spread distrust and suspicion and did a great deal of harm within their own world, the society to which they belonged. They certainly damaged the aims and interests of the British government and the West as they were at that time. It is possible, for example, that Albania would not have fallen so completely into the communist grip if it hadn't been for Philby revealing the operations of the SIS or the CIA. Equally, you can look back on it and say, well, perhaps it wasn't decisive after all, perhaps the CIA and SIS operations were rather madcap. Some people were killed, but then Philby would have said that the secret service involves everybody taking risks, and it's the luck of the game. Another thing Philby did quite early on was to prevent the exposure of the Russian espionage system in Britain. There was a Russian defector to Istanbul called Ivanov who offered to provide the British government with the names of the Russian agents operating in the British intelligence world. If that information had reached the right people it would have exposed Blunt, Philby, Burgess and Maclean at an early date, but Philby had got himself into the position of being able to take charge of the matter. He obviously informed the Russians, who kidnapped Ivanov and he's never been heard of since. There's no doubt that he was shot. In this way Philby protected himself and the others from exposure.

When you reflected on why it should have been Cambridge rather than Oxford that produced communist spies in the 1930s you blamed a certain puritan high-mindedness, but in itself that is surely no bad thing. What was it that narrowed that outlook to the point of treason?

I don't know. Supposing there had been a high-powered Russian recruiter operating in Oxford, can I be sure that he wouldn't have found Philbys there? I honestly can't answer that. That puritanism, however, that extraordinary self-satisfaction which I do ascribe to Cambridge is lacking in Oxford. People don't take themselves so seriously at Oxford. Cambridge people issue writs against each other inside the university, which I find laughable. There is a world in Cambridge which takes itself extremely seriously, and if you do that, it's a stage nearer deciding that your conscience is more imperative than convention, humanity and loyalty to the government. It's that kind of high-mindedness which I ascribe to Cambridge.

The present government's determination to maintain secrecy at every level appears to many people to be perverse. Do you think it right that the defence of national interests should be barred in that anyone who has gone through 'the proper channels' with suspicions about Philby or Maclean or Blunt would have got nowhere?

Many people have found their way round these restrictions; sometimes they do it by going through the proper channels and sometimes they do it by knowing how to create interest in the right quarters. For all I know it may sometimes be done with official encouragement. I hold the view that most secrets are in print if you know where to look for them, and half the time the secrecy rules are merely a means of preventing the public knowing what is already known to the foreign governments from which ostensibly it is being concealed. For instance, during the war, and indeed until recently, one couldn't even name the head of the British secret service, nor could people say that anyone was in it, yet the entire professional staff of the secret service was known by name in Germany and had been publicised in the German press in October 1939. I have seen it for myself and they were all named.

Were they accurate?

Absolutely accurate, and I know exactly how they came by the names. Right at the beginning of the war agents from the German secret service lured two British secret-service officers in the Netherlands to the frontier under the pretence of being the representatives of an anti-Hitler group. They then kidnapped them by force and carried them off to Berlin. The British officers were kept prisoner throughout the war, and under interrogation they revealed all the facts. When I was in Berlin in 1945 I found in the ruins of the Gestapo headquarters a secret document which set out the structure of the British intelligence services and ascribed its knowledge, some of which was coloured by German fantasy, to these two men. But MI6 knew perfectly well that all their names had been blown because Himmler, after the seizure of these two officers, had made a public speech about information received, and this was then reported in the German press.

Of course, I can see that one doesn't want to encourage too much curiosity into the operations of the secret service which, whatever one says about it, does have its useful functions – we live in a world of terrorism after all – but I do think it's carried too far and that the secret services tend to breed within themselves a separation from reality. I've known several cases of people who have simply become *fantasists*, and Peter Wright of course is an instance. A kind of mania can develop, a paranoia, a sort of mini-McCarthyism which feeds on itself.

Why do you think the government went to such lengths to ban Wright's book?

I cannot say. I think it was mad, but I don't know where the move came from. I suppose it grew gradually and was probably a question of pride. They started by thinking they could stop it at a lower level without any fuss, and then when that failed, they had to stop it at a slightly higher level. But it was absurd, because he lived outside the jurisdiction and he could publish outside the jurisdiction.

Do you think fascism has really been put behind us? The neo-Nazi movement seems to be gaining ground in an alarming way now.

People are misled by words. What is meant by fascism? Fascism and Nazism were quite different, although fascism was taken prisoner by Nazism in the course of the war. Mussolini's regime was not anti-Semitic until it fell under German control, yet anti-Semitism was absolutely central to German Nazism. They are different movements with different origins, and yet we call them both fascism. Since I'm something of a pedant, I like words to be used so that one can argue on the basis of them, and therefore they must be used accurately. I believe that the movements we knew in the 1930s which reached their head in the war are dead, because they were inseparable from a particular political conjuncture which is now over and which will never be repeated in the same form. If by fascism we mean the Italian fascism of Mussolini, and if by Nazism we mean the German Nazism of Hitler with its total philosophy and aims, they cannot happen again. But if we use the terms in a vulgar way, meaning thuggery, right-wing xenophobia, brutality, stamping on the lower classes and so on, that is a far more generalised thing, and is liable to break out at any time.

At present there are some historians, such as David Irving, suggesting that Nazi atrocities were either the result of Allied propaganda or were grossly exaggerated. Will it ever be possible, do you think, to rewrite history, given the pressures for European unity?

Assuming that Europe, whether united or disunited, remains liberal, and that we have free press and free exchange of information, I don't think that historical revisionism of that kind is possible. History is always being revised, but it's revised from within rational norms; when we have more evidence, and different documents are produced, we see things from a slightly different point of view, but assuming a certain honesty in the historical profession, that is not a sign of perversity, it's just a sign of what is always happening.

But isn't history largely a matter of interpretation?

Yes, but what historians call historical revision is reinterpretation of agreed objective evidence, whereas what people like David Irving are trying to do is to rewrite history in defiance of the evidence. They thereby exploit legitimate revisionism in order to argue a political thesis, which in my opinion is unarguable. Their interpretations are scandalous, not honest.

Do you think the atrocities perpetrated by the Nazis during the war could have been exaggerated?

In the First World War there had been atrocity-mongering which afterwards was proved to have been false, and therefore there were people during the Second World War who did not believe all the talk of atrocities which they fully expected to be disproved afterwards. But one of the advantages of the Nuremberg trials was that it put the evidence on the record in a way in which it couldn't be contested. After the First World War the victorious allies didn't occupy Germany, they didn't change the government of Germany, they didn't confiscate or even have access to German secret documents, and therefore the Germans were able to build up the theory of the stab in the back, the myths on which Nazism afterwards fed. In 1945 it was different: Germany was totally defeated and occupied, documents were seized and trials were held, and whatever one may say about the trials, the fact is that all the documents that were produced were put to the court and could be ruled illegitimate or irrelevant. The defence had lawyers whose business it was to disprove allegations if they could, and no German historian has suggested that the documents used at Nuremberg were not valid documents. The evidence is public and has been agreed and cannot be contested, and that is the great difference between the post-1945 position in relation to history and the post-1918 position. So I don't think that revisionism which exploits the mood of incredulity or the desire for European unity, or the wish to forget the past to the extent of negating well-established and undeniable facts, I don't think that is a possibility now.

I gather you read Mein Kampf *in the original when you worked for intelligence. What sort of impression did it make on you at the time?*

That's not quite true. I read *Mein Kampf* in German in 1938 as a consequence of an article by Ensor, a very able historian, who had been prophesying that there would be a major international crisis resolved either by European war or by a climbdown by the West in the autumn of 1938. One thing he said was that the beginning of wisdom in international affairs was to read *Mein Kampf*, and that it had to be read in German because it was not fully translated. People at that time tended to regard Hitler as a mere froth-blowing demagogue, nasty, but slightly comic, whereas Ensor was claiming he was very dangerous. That article decided me to read *Mein Kampf* in the original. I could see it was the work of a man with a powerful mind who had already achieved much of what he had threatened to achieve and showed no signs of weakness of any kind. It was a coherent ideology, a horrible one but nevertheless coherent, and I decided that it was serious. And I became rather serious myself in consequence; I'd led rather a frivolous life up to that time, but I reckoned then that we were in for a war. I did not believe as many others did that Hitler was a clown, a mere adventurer. He was a gangster, though not only a gangster; he was a dangerous and effective political force.

How do you view someone like Lady Diana Mosley who admired Hitler and believes that many of the atrocities attributed to him are not possible?

She is one of those people who think that because somebody is polite and considerate to her personally, he can't possibly be a criminal. The world is full of people who are conned by confidence tricksters, ladies who listen to honeyed words and can't imagine such a nice person having another side to him. I once wrote a review of an article about Goebbels, and she wrote a letter of protest, saying how monstrously I had misrepresented Goebbels. She said she had often dined with Goebbels and his wife who were such kind hosts and conversation was so agreeable and they lived in quite modest style. It was the same with Hitler. I'm afraid she's just a gull, as was her sister Unity.

Do you think the last war was the inevitable outcome of the Versailles Treaty?

The Treaty of Versailles provided the excuse. The real reason was that the Germans did not believe that they were defeated. They were of course defeated, but there's a difference between defeat and recognising defeat. The ruling classes maintained that they have been deprived of victory; and in the spring of 1918, just as in 1940, they considered they had won the war, and couldn't understand why everyone didn't then surrender. And then suddenly at the end of 1918, they were totally defeated, which came as a great shock. The entire organisation of propaganda, the doctoring of documents, even before Hitler, shows that they were determined that this be rectified. They needn't have done it by war; they could have tried to build up German power and negotiate from strength. But Hitler wanted war; he was an all-or-nothing man, and he was determined that it could be done only in his lifetime. It was the same argument used in 1914, that Russia was going to be too powerful and that the social basis of Germany had to be changed. This is where anti-Semitism comes in. Hitler's complaint in *Mein Kampf* is that the Kaiser's Germany was a Byzantine Judaised aristocratically-run incompetent Germany; it had all the German virtues of racial and military strength, if only it had been properly led. In order to be sure of victory this useless aristocracy had to be eliminated and replaced by an organisation based on blood. He really believed in race and blood, and elimination of the Jews. According to Hitler the social structure had to be changed in order to liberate the full energies of Germany and then, led by him, they could win. That was the real cause of the war, in my opinion.

What do you consider the origin of anti-Semitism to be? Is there a definitive historical explanation, or is it specifically religious and cultural?

I've thought a good deal about this, and I'm sure that it is not religious. In the Middle Ages there was anti-Semitism in Germany and in Spain, and it was religiously based. The Jews were the people who had crucified Christ and had refused to accept Christianity, and were consequently public enemy no. 1. But in the eighteenth century this sectarian attitude dissolved with the weakening of religion and religious persecution; and yet anti-Semitism didn't disappear. In the nineteenth century it revived with vengeance and adapted to an industrial society, this time not for religious reasons at all, but on the basis of blood. This was equally irrational, because there is no such thing as Jewish blood. The only way you can define a Jew is by religion. Hitler had no interest in religion, Jewish or Christian. His problem was how to identify Jews among German lawyers or German police, or indeed Germans in general. It was simple when Jews had come in from Poland, for example, and were called Moses or Abraham, but among Germans how could you distinguish who was a Jew and who wasn't? The only way to distinguish them was by religion; and in this way we have the phenomenon that anti-Semitism survives its particular explanations. Different rationalisations are produced at different times, but one has to ask, what is the real basis of it? My own theory is that it is the determination inherent in the human race to find a scapegoat for one's misfortunes, particularly in an unassimilable group in society. They may be religious dissenters, they may be as in the witch craze of the sixteenth and seventeenth centuries, people who just don't mix, who don't fit in, who make their neighbours uncomfortable, who seem to belong to a different world. Any minority group is liable to persecution, even genocide. Often the unassimilable group is relatively prosperous, like the Armenians, or Parsees in India, or the Ismailis in East Africa, or even the Quakers in England; they're shut in on themselves, perhaps they don't even try to become assimilated, so they concentrate on business and they become rich, and in turn they become envied. The Jews single themselves out, and they fit into all these categories, and that is my explanation.

I believe you covered the Eichmann trial for the Sunday Times. *Did you undertake the work as a historian, or was it primarily a journalistic assignment?*

I was asked to go by the *Sunday Times* and was glad to do so for my own education. (I had attended the Nuremberg Trials, and I afterwards attended the Auschwitz Trials in Frankfurt.) I was interested both in the revelations in the evidence, and in the procedure. I had been in Israel before and was interested to see the way in which the Israelis would handle the trial.

Your historical researches have covered a number of periods. Which has given you the most satisfaction?

Although I have studied and written about Nazi Germany, it does not give me satisfaction. I find it in some ways a repulsive subject and I have not allowed myself to be tied to it. If I'm an expert in anything I suppose it is sixteenth-and seventeenth-century history, but I don't really think in 'periods'. I came to the conclusion at one time that political history is really rather small beer; seeing people digging deeper and deeper into a petty cabinet crisis in eighteenth-century English politics – I found that poor stuff. Humanity does not live for this, I thought, and I gradually found myself more drawn to intellectual history. So rather than being interested in a particular period, I'm interested in a particular side of history, the intellect of man rather than the politics. I consider that intellectual history is not separable from its context in practical history; that is to say, ideas do not develop out of previous ideas. This is falsely maintained by professional intellectual historians who, as it were, follow an idea from one generation to another as if people read the books of their predecessors but didn't live in the context of the present. I'm Marxist to the extent that I would allow that ideas are conditioned by the context, which means that one is going to understand the intellectual views of this century, and the same is true of any other century.

I understand that your political antennae were developed in the thirties but gradually your imagination was captured more by academic rather than political intrigue. How did this come about?

I find this a rather offensive question. It implies that I am only interested in 'intrigue' and merely changed direction within that constant. I am not interested in intrigue. If I have occasionally found myself in controversy it has always been open – perhaps too open for my own good (but that, in my opinion, is because I am a victim of the media!) My answer to the substantive question – how did I come to prefer academic to political *life* (*not* intrigue) is quite simple. I was an undergraduate at a very political college – several of my friends and several of the dons went into politics – and I did at one time think of a political career. Munich made politics very actual to me. But then came the war; and during the war I decided that my real interest was in literature and the study of history. I also valued my independence, or perhaps my ease. The thought of constituents, 'surgeries', public meetings, party conferences, whips (not to say scorpions) repelled me. I also loved country life and shrank from smoke-filled rooms in London. I'm afraid I was rather indolent in those days.

You are a distinguished historian, so I ask this question rather diffidently. Why does history matter? I can see that chemistry, physics, medicine, computer technology, agriculture, even perhaps psychology, have real consequences, but history seems to fall into a different category. By the time we meditate on the past it's all over. The study of literature may make us aware of the way language is used to manipulate, but it sometimes seems as if the clashing opinions of historians only catalogue possible past mistakes ...

I agree with Gibbon who says that history is little else than the register of the crimes, follies and misfortunes of mankind. I nevertheless think that it is worth studying because I think that nations are conditioned even though they may not recognise this by their history. If one cuts oneself off from one's history, one is losing a capacity to understand the present, or indeed perhaps the future, not that anyone can understand the future but at least you can speculate. I also think that the study of history enriches the study of thought and art and literature. If somebody totally ignorant of his history goes round a picture gallery, let us say, and relies entirely on his aesthetic sense, his appreciation is entirely different. I'm not saying that paintings should be studied solely as historical documents, because obviously they have an aesthetic quality which transcends that context, but I do think that appreciation is deepened and made intelligent and articulate by an understanding of history.

Historians are constrained by facts, but even in the selection of which facts to highlight, there is a degree of interpretation involved. Since interpretation is necessarily subjective, do you think there can be such a thing as a correct perspective in history?

No, and indeed I don't want there to be. Interest in history really depends to a large extent on the problems which it raises, and the idea that it can be reduced to a science as people thought about 1900 (and the Marxists continue to maintain) is very perverse in my opinion. The attempts to reduce it to a science have all failed and now look very ridiculous. History is made up of continued pressures and options and mistakes. At every point in history there are decisions to be made; decisions can be wrong in a technical sense, I will allow this, if they are simply impossible in the context of the times, but one cannot say that there are no alternatives, that there is a course specifically plotted, because there is no such course. And indeed that is the interest of it; that is what makes it a living subject, not a dead subject.

What is your view of the relationship between history and biography. Are they very different animals, or can they be 'cross bred'?

I think they can be cross bred. A biography reduced to mere biography would be a very jejune affair. Of course I can envisage a biography of some unimportant shoemaker in Nottingham simply describing his life in shoemaking, but that's not of great moment. He may be a very worthy person but it's not of very much interest. But the greatness of an intellectual or artistic figure depends on his response to his times. You can't detach the biography altogether from the context.

There has been rather disturbing work done in France in recent years which seems to undermine the legitimacy of history. I'm thinking of the views of men like Jacques Derrida and Foucault. Is there any answer to the charge that we make history in our own image?

I think this is a defeatist view. We write history in a more social way than that, we test our arguments against other people's arguments, whether in books or in discussion. Obviously there are subjective interpretations, but honest historians try to discover an objectivity. I'm afraid I'm not in love with Derrida and Foucault.

It would not be too far from the truth to say that you are anti-clerical. Is it that you think priests hypocrites or fools?

I'd have you know that I am a doctor of divinity. I don't think I'm particularly anti-clerical, but I've long ago given up thinking what I am. People say that I'm so many different things that I've decided to let them say it. It's true I don't like folly combined with persecution, and I can't take theological doctrine very seriously. I regard it as at best legitimate myth to which one pays lip service but one doesn't engage one's mind with it. I find it rather absurd when the clergy involve themselves with abstruse doctrines, when they give themselves airs and try to dictate to us or to persecute us or to persecute each other; then I'm anti-clerical I daresay, but I don't feel anti-clerical.

Are you a believer?

I think the answer is no. If you mean, do I believe the content of the Athanasian Creed, no I certainly don't. Do I believe in the Virgin Birth, certainly not.

Do you believe in God?

I'm a sort of eighteenth-century deist really. I would adopt the position of Voltaire and Gibbon.

My research would seem to indicate you are anti-Catholic ... and that you reserve a particular dislike for converts to Catholicism.

The great Lord Halifax, George Savile, said at the end of the seventeenth century that the impudence of a bawd is modesty compared with that of a convert. I often think of this when I meet certain converts. They also tend to revile the church from which they have been converted, which is a form of intolerance I dislike. I was fairly anti-Catholic at the time when the Catholic Church was ruled by Pope Pius XI, whom I regarded as one of the more disastrous figures of this century. The Papacy was responsible for the dictatorship of both Mussolini and Hitler. I know that is a very serious charge, but it is one I can document. If it hadn't been for the activity of Pope Pius XI in suddenly forbidding priests to take part in politics, thereby wrecking the Christian Democrat Party, Mussolini would not have been able to take power in Italy. And if it hadn't been for his persuading the Centre Party in Germany to vote for the Enabling Act which gave Hitler his dictatorial powers, he could not have become a legitimate dictator. The Papacy wanted to get a concordat with Italy and Germany which it would never have achieved if it had

had to operate through a liberal government dependent on a parliament containing agnostics, protestants and so on; but it could do a bargain with a dictator. Of course Hitler and Mussolini both broke the concordats, but the Papacy was silly in making them; it should have realised it was dealing with crooks.

But do you see a role for the church in politics nowadays?

I think the church's intervention in day-to-day politics is generally disastrous. I sometimes listen in the House of Lords to bishops making speeches on subjects about which they seem to me to know very little. I draw a veil over that; there's quite enough for the church to do outside politics.

They should be saving souls, you mean …

Precisely, though saving souls is a metaphor. I don't mean that they should be forcing their particular doctrines on people.

There have surely been good men and women who drew their strength from their faith. Why do you think so many people turn to religion? The Soviet Union tried to suppress it for seventy years without success.

People come to the conclusion, which is a legitimate one, that the purpose of life is not political orthodoxy, not even political success, that politics and public life contain a great deal of ambition and hypocrisy, and that if we have a purpose in life it should be rather higher. We have at times to think of what are vulgarly called higher things, and religion is a kind of distillation of one's loftier aspirations; the trouble is that it is distilled into such an extraordinary crystallised form that it is difficult to take, or it becomes sectarianism, or a sort of conventional sanctimonious church-going. To put it bluntly, I think that one needs an awareness of a metaphysical dimension in order not to be absorbed in what may be at best dreary and at worst dishonourable courses.

Do you think that your attitudes towards religion ever put you at a disadvantage professionally? I am thinking of occasions such as attendance at conferences like the proposed one at the Vatican on Eastern Europe.

It has never occurred to me that my views on religion were objectionable or even eccentric. I am not irreligious. I do not believe, with Freud, that religion is an 'illusion' which can be 'ended' by psychoanalysis. Rather, I regard psychoanalysis as a superstitious illusion. I consider that a sense of religion is necessary to a complete man: it is a framework giving metaphysical coherence to the natural and mortal world, the primitive myths which it retains having been converted into metaphor. Of course I do not believe these myths – who does? – but I am happy to accept them as metaphors representing the mysteries of nature and the human condition, insoluble as intellectual problems. I regard theology – the attempt to create a system out of these myths – as absurd: an absolute historical curiosity; but I get on perfectly well with (sensible) clergy, whom I regard with respect as a useful body of men – provided they don't pontificate or persecute.

You're a conservative, but of what sort? Are you an old Macmillan conservative with what one might call a sense of obligation, or one of the newer Thatcherite type?

I can't quite answer that. I approve of Mrs Thatcher in as much as I think she saw that a moment had come when consensus had been turned into a continuing slide of appeasement; it was no longer a consensus from a position of rationality and strength. I was therefore in favour of her strong measures. On the other hand, I think there is an unacceptable side of Thatcherism, a kind of ruthlessness which I find unattractive.

So you're more of a Macmillan conservative?

I am, but Harold Macmillan did sell the pass in a way. He believed, or behaved as if he believed, that one could always go on yielding a bit more for the sake of consensus, but consensus is a game at which two have to play, otherwise it loses its reality. If the trade unions on one side believe in pursuit of power at the expense of consensus, then it's got to stop. I was a director of *The Times* when it was losing millions and faced ruin. The unions were totally unappeasable, and what were described euphemistically as 'old Spanish practises' were rife – people drawing salaries under false names for no work, and so on. They thought they had the management in their hands and that somehow this gravy train would go on for ever, on the grounds that the Thomson Organisation which was then in charge was so rich from its other activities that it would go on paying this Danegeld for ever. Rupert Murdoch turned that round by being as rough to the unions as the unions had been rough to the Thomson Organisation. I think a consensus has to depend on a willingness of both sides to consent, and that had been sacrificed in the Macmillan period.

You have a reputation for being something of a dandy ...

Oh really? My wife would be very surprised to hear me described as a dandy. I did read somewhere that I gave a tutorial in hunting clothes, but it is a complete myth.

Is it fair to say you are a social climber?

I don't think so. I like intelligent people really. I have moved in bits of the *beau monde*, that I admit.

Would you consider yourself a snob?

Yes, I am in a way. Except that I don't take it seriously. I think snobbism is a harmless affectation. To say that somebody is a snob *tout court* is not an offensive thing; it's rather like saying that somebody is interested in going to race meetings. I'm interested in the diversity of humankind, but yes, I quite like sophisticated parties.

Well, that's no sin. In 1957 when you gave your inaugural lecture as Regius Professor of History, I understand that a notice appeared on the board to the effect that your lecture was cancelled and that A. J. P. Taylor was lecturing in your place. This was presumably symptomatic of the animosity and rivalry between you … what was the origin of those feelings?

First of all, it isn't true. It was entirely invented by the press, and Alan Taylor objected to it as much as I did. We were always friends and we differed only on the thesis of his book *The Origins of the Second World War*. The book became a *succès de scandale* and because I'd reviewed it critically I had to appear on television with him and the whole thing was blown up by the press. Alan and I both got very bored by it. There was an issue about which we dissented, as scholars are entitled to dissent from each other, but the rest is a myth.

But was he expected to be appointed at the time instead of you?

Well, yes. It is true that Alan was tipped, and, being a vain man, he believed he was really entitled to it. This was what surprised me about Alan: generally speaking he adopted a tolerant attitude towards history, he accepted that everything is chance, anything can happen, there is no directing purpose in it, that things always turn out differently from what is expected – this was really his basic, rather nihilistic philosophy. But the one point where he failed to apply it was to his own history. Deducing from his general historical attitudes I would have expected Alan to say, well I expected to be made Regius Professor, but the right person is never appointed, things never turn out as we expect, well, that's how things go … but he never applied this attitude to himself. He considered that he was entitled to the chair, that he was the most distinguished person in the running and that it was a miscarriage of justice. But he never blamed me for this; he blamed Harold Macmillan. Later he said he would not have accepted it from this hand stained with the blood of Suez.

Talking of Harold Macmillan, what prompted you to promote him as candidate for the chancellorship of Oxford in opposition to Lord Franks? Did you not feel that it would be interpreted as a quid pro quo? *After all he had appointed you.*

I don't really care about what people say, but I certainly didn't like the way Maurice Bowra had pushed through the nomination of Franks (whom I respect). After Lord Halifax died, the vice chancellor took ill, and Maurice became acting vice chancellor. Maurice was a bully, quite an agreeable bully, but a bully nevertheless, and he always fought to win. He summoned a meeting of the heads of houses who were all very feeble, and he simply railroaded Franks through. I wasn't there, of course, but I had full accounts, and Maurice was so determined to get his candidate appointed that he simply vetoed other names in his brutal way. When Lord Salisbury was mentioned, for example, Maurice said, 'He's no friend to this university,' and moved on to the next man. Harold Macmillan, who after all was prime minister, a distinguished man and a scholar, a man of intellectual interests who would have been very suitable, was never even mentioned. I thought that this was improper. I had means of communicating with Harold who was in South Africa at the time, and I asked him if he would be willing to stand. He sent back a message to me, saying, 'Nothing would give me greater pleasure. I shall not shrink from the contest.' Those were his very words. It was a very enjoyable contest.

Was it a real battle?

It was rather a good battle because Harold won, yet it was not humiliating for Franks. And Maurice Bowra was furious. There was no nonsense about a secret ballot, and he sat there receiving the votes, examining each one, and either scowling or beaming.

Do you ever regret going to Peterhouse?

That's a difficult question. On the whole I value experience by what I learn from it. I learned something at Peterhouse, and I made many friends there, especially among the scientists, but I'd rather not say too much about Peterhouse.

Peterhouse is well known for reaffirming the importance of high politics and intellectual movement against the fashionable concentration on the grass roots and the masses. Is this something you applaud?

No. I think it's a perfectly reasonable point of view, but in Peterhouse it was combined with politics so reactionary that I found them both ridiculous and rather offensive.

People have said of you that in the background of your life and career there lurks a book, the magnum opus that you didn't write. Is that something that worries you?

Not greatly. I would like to have written a great work … who wouldn't … but when I consider historical writing I see that it very quickly perishes and if it's any good it is boiled down into an article. Students of history have not read the books that they talk about; they've only read concentrations of the argument.

You were, I believe, the author of the wonderfully funny series in The Spectator *under the pseudonym Mercurious Oxoniensis.*

I know nothing about Mercurious.

You weren't involved in it at all?

I've heard people suggest I was involved, but I've never acknowledged it.

But you were the author?

Well, you've said so. I haven't. I don't contest whatever people say about me.

Do you deny that you are the author of it?

[Laughs.] Yes.

Is that a half-hearted denial?

No. *Toto animo.*

You are of course a member of the House of Lords. Do you think it proper in the late twentieth century that there should be an unelected body of legislators, however distinguished, in parliament?

I see nothing wrong in an unelected body. The hereditary principle I admit is very difficult to defend. But it's irreformable in a way, and any replacement would, of course, be liable to different objections. The House of Lords carries some fat, if one may use the phrase, but then so does the House of Commons. The Lords is much more of a real debating chamber than the Commons, because there's not so much of a party side to it.

Do you think it will ever be possible to forge a real federal state in Europe out of the animosities of the last thousand years?

Neither possible nor desirable. I am very much a pluralist and I consider that the pluralism of Europe is what has been the essential feature, if not cause, of its superiority. The various states have distinct identities, irreconcilable attitudes, which compete against each other and these have been the main factors in Europe's effervescence and efflorescence, and I don't wish to see it all homogenised. I support the idea of a free trade area in order that Europe may pull its weight in the world, but that does not mean that it should be ruled by an unelected bureaucracy in Brussels, establishing identical norms everywhere.

You must sometimes reflect ironically on the forged Hitler diaries when you recall your own work on Backhaus. In the appendix of your book you list 'three learned forgers'. Is that something which made matters worse for you?

No, I didn't think about it. What was traumatic was my inability to prevent extracts being published, which was due to complicated muddles at *The Times*. I couldn't stop the process which was forced by a series of episodes outside my control. When the business blew up I decided the only honourable thing to do was to state publicly that I had made a mistake, although I had tried to remedy the mistake and had been prevented from doing so. The mistake wasn't the one I was accused of making, but still, I said I had made a mistake, and I thought naïvely that the other people whose responsibility had been far greater than mine would admit their part in it. But not at all; they all turned on me and kept completely silent about their own involvement, and regarded me as a sort of expendable scapegoat. All the media persecution was concentrated on me, and the rest sat smugly behind their barriers. That was a shock. It lowered my opinion of human behaviour. One likes to feel that people are honourable, and it's painful to find that they aren't.

Your enemies of course delighted in your mistake. You have always maintained that other people's opinions of you were of little importance. Is that really the case, or have you put a brave front on it?

No. Long before that episode I decided that other people's opinions, within limits, are not of interest to me. I'm afraid it's a rather arrogant thing to say, but I don't really respect the opinions of people whom I don't know. I think it's as simple as that. If a trusted friend were to say harsh things about me, that would upset me, but if a journalist whom I've never met makes statements about me I'm quite indifferent to it. I have a kind of proud stoic attitude in this; I just say a man is himself, not what strangers say of him. To thine own self be true, that's my philosophy.

What was your feeling when you learned that a TV series was to be made of the Hitler diaries saga?

I paid no attention at all. I neither saw the film nor read the book. And I declined to write to the papers about it. I simply treated it as non-existent.

A. J. Ayer once said of you: 'Some may think him lacking in charity', and it is true that over the years you have joined battle with a number of enemies, often distinguished people, such as Lawrence Stone, Evelyn Waugh and Arthur Toynbee. The last of these you demolished in an article in Encounter. *Some people, while admiring the scholarship of that article, detected a streak of cruelty. Is that something you are conscious of?*

No. I may say it was Evelyn Waugh who declared war on me, not I on him. Lawrence Stone also asked for it. He borrowed transcripts which I had made from documents in the Records Office, and that was the basis of this half-baked article which he wrote and which I criticised. He behaved very badly. I don't think I've ever severely criticised any young scholar; it's when people give themselves great airs and are taken seriously, that's what arouses me.

I have always heard it said that in your eagerness to win battles you do not shrink from making personal attacks on colleagues. Do you accept that charge?

I am not aware of having made personal attacks on colleagues. If I have engaged in controversy, it has always been because I thought at the time that a serious issue was at stake. I wonder what colleague I am said to have attacked personally?

Richard Cobb has spoken of your love of combat, your readiness to jump into the fray over public issues. Is this something you have ever had cause to regret?

I don't think I love combat: it's true I enjoyed the election for chancellorship of Oxford, but it was a genial, good-tempered affair, and there was a serious issue involved. Maurice Bowra, by bouncing a single gathering of heads of houses, had effectively disfranchised the university. This was widely felt (hence the strong support I received). Of course, once the battle was on, Maurice was determined to win, and so was I. Have I ever regretted controversy? I regret them all in so far as they were extended (largely by the media) beyond their original terms. I regret having been involved with Evelyn Waugh, whose writing I admired. But he opened fire on me in 1947, both publicly (in the *Tablet*) and privately (in an abusive letter to me), and continued the one-sided vendetta for nine years before I finally took notice of him in the article which provoked his onslaught on my historical scholarship; to which I felt I had to reply.

The controversy whose extension I most regretted was with A. J. P. Taylor. I criticised his book *The Origins of the Second World War* because I thought his thesis wrong, indeed irresponsible. But then the press took over; and from then on I was always represented as the constant adversary of A. J. P. Taylor. In fact, I never criticised any other work of his. I minded this, as did he. In 1979 he wrote, in the *London Review of Books*: 'I often read that Trevor-Roper and I are rivals or even antagonists. On my side, and I can confidently say on Hugh's, this is totally untrue. We have always been good friends and no cross word has ever been passed between us.' And he wrote to me in 1983: 'I can assure you that my feelings towards you have always been those of friendly affection.' It was the repeated (and successful) attempts of the press to persuade the world that Taylor and I were permanent adversaries that bred in me that distaste for the media which, I'm afraid is now ingrained in me. (Of course, the affair of the Hitler diaries strengthened it.)

Another controversy was my critique of Toynbee. I admit that I was nauseated by the pretensions and sanctimonious *humbug* of Toynbee, and (especially) his message which was defeatist and obscurantist; disgusted too by the idiot sycophancy towards him of the American academia and media. But effectively all I did was to quote his own words, which none of his sycophants had read – they had only read Somervell's potted one-volume abridgement of his first six volumes, whereas the real revelation of his purpose, and his vanity, was in volumes seven to ten, published later. I do *not* regret this episode! Toynbee's recent biographer, William McNeill, says that Toynbee's reputation never recovered from my essay. That *pleases* me!

But neither here nor in any other controversy was I drawn in merely by 'love of combat'; there was always a real issue on which, at the time, I felt strongly: Stone's total misrepresentation of historical documents which he pretended he had discovered (when in fact he had borrowed my transcripts and had not tried to understand them); Bowra's contempt for the Oxford electorate and its rights; Taylor's special pleading for Hitler; Toynbee's hatred of reason and the Enlightenment ... As I don't think I was wrong, intellectually, in any of these encounters (or in my critique of E. H. Carr), I don't regret them – only the personalisation of them, or some of them. Perhaps it is all the fault of my style: not enough emollient, shock-absorbing pulp, sawdust, stuffing, etc ...

LORD DEEDES

William Deedes was born in 1913 and educated at Harrow before becoming a journalist with the *Morning Post* (1931–7). During the war he served with the Queen's Westminsters and from 1950 until 1974 he was Conservative MP for Ashford. Between 1962 and 1964 he was Minister without Portfolio. He was long associated with the *Daily Telegraph*, which he edited from 1974 to 1986. He was made a life peer in 1986. He became an ambassador for UNICEF in 1998, having previously worked with Diana, Princess of Wales in a high-profile campaign against landmines. He published a memoir in 2005, and continued to write for the *Telegraph*, publishing his final article on Darfur two weeks before his death in 2007, aged ninety-four.

How do you recall your childhood ... was it a happy time for you?

Not altogether because when I was six my father, who was living peacefully on £900 a year with five servants, suddenly inherited a large shattered castle. From then on life became exiguous and if you're young, even if you're only six or seven, you feel the anxieties of your parents. Living as we were on a tumbledown estate after the First World War, when farming was bringing in nothing, many acres had to be sold off to make ends meet. Therefore, I remember my childhood as being privately happy, because I had the land to roam over, but anxious also because I sensed that the foundations of life were shaky as a result of Father's predicament in taking on for family reasons more than he could cope with.

Yours was quite a large family ... five children, I believe. Did you see that as an advantage at the time?

Yes, because I think there is a lot to be said for boys being bullied by sisters. I'm the only boy and I owe a great deal to my sisters, who prodded me at certain times when I needed it. I have always felt that my sisters had more ambition for me than I had for myself. People nowadays who go in for much smaller families lose an ingredient which bigger families enjoyed. It's difficult to define, but you build up a certain inner relationship which lasts all your life. It's not an essential dimension, but it's a useful one. I'm grateful for it anyway.

I wonder which of your parents now seems to you to have been most influential in your life? Perhaps that kind of question seems too overtly psychological. Do you think parents really have the strong influence that is always attributed to them?

I was aware of tension between my parents because my mother, who was Protestant Irish, born in Dublin and conservative in her outlook, greatly desired that I should go to Winchester and follow her brothers there, which I proved too stupid to do. My father, on the other hand, had a great many newfangled ideas which he alternated rather rapidly with his political views. He had had a curious background. He had gone to the Boer War at the age of seventeen, which did his health no good and he was really an invalid most of his life. He was ostensibly a landowner, but he was also a socialist. In fact he was greatly attached to the Labour Party in those days and stood for parliament once as a labour candidate, then as an independent candidate. About that time – it was around the birth of the Labour Party – he shared a feeling that society was unequal and there was too big a gap between the well-to-do and the rest. He had what you might call the Edwardian, old Etonian conscience, and I look back on him as a very respected Christian socialist. He was left of centre for what might be described as inner reasons rather than ideology. There was one period, for example, when he bought every book he could lay his hands on about Mussolini. There was an endearing enthusiasm about my father's political beliefs and in the early stages he even thought Hitler might do Germany a bit of good. My mother, however, was a staunch conservative and found all this rather difficult. So as a child I remember my mind being pulled between my mother's innate conservativeness and my father's rather dashing radicalism; but this may have done me no harm at all. I didn't follow one or the other, I just realised there was a difference. As it happened, however, I did follow my mother eventually.

Do you think your relationship with your own son was very different from your father's with you?

No. I'm ashamed to this day by the fact that my relationship with my son, who was born during the last war, was more like my father's with me. In other words, I was almost the last of that generation of men who did not feel that a great intimacy with his children was part of a father's duty. Today I find that my own children share the lives of their children in a way that never occurred to me. If my children enjoy modest success now I am always the first to attribute this to my wife because my own contribution was minimal. Frankly I was neglectful and I treated my children as my father treated me. And, of course, there were nurses and governesses to look after them.

I suppose there will be people to whom your life will seem to have been remarkably privileged: a childhood household with five servants, school-days at Harrow, your own son sent to Eton. Has it been as enviable as it seems?

Not a bit. I actually left Harrow a year early. My housemaster sent for me one day and said: 'I've very sorry … we had a letter from your father to say that he has been seriously affected by the Wall Street Crash.' Everyone was very sympathetic; the housemaster even gave me a couple of quid to pay my fare home. But I suppose there was a bit of privilege in my getting my first job on the *Morning Post* since the paper's managing editor had just got a gun in Uncle Wyndham's shoot in Hampshire and as a *quid pro quo* I got a job on the paper, but I still had to work my way.

You are obviously a very political animal. Was that interest the result of family background or was it something that developed out of your career as a journalist?

It was more family background. I think the Deedes family have had a member of parliament in every century since 1600. A year as a lobby correspondent in 1936–7 certainly gave me a taste for politics and so when an opening arose after the war I wasn't unfamiliar with what the work would entail, but I suspect it's mainly heredity.

You have been both a cabinet minister and a distinguished journalist. Which do you think is the most influential position in the end? What I had in mind is that while a cabinet minister has a good deal of authority he must be constrained by government policy, so I wonder just how much room there is for manoeuvre?

There's never been any doubt about this. A politician is by far the stronger figure for this reason; he is a decision-making figure. Journalists can advocate, campaign, attack, and though they can make themselves immensely influential, they can't make decisions. Only a member of parliament, and even more so a minister, can actually do that, and therefore the two are not really comparable. In terms of power the politician has always got it over the journalist. The journalist might look at times to be more powerful, particularly if you have a figure like Northcliffe or Maxwell or Murdoch, who decides to attack politicians and possibly appears even to change a government; in reality, however, the politician always has the stronger position.

No Longer with Us

Was Beaverbrook powerful because he was a journalist baron or because he was a politician?

Beaverbrook had another value altogether. Beaverbrook was a major contributor to the social revolution in Britain. I remember my pre-war *Daily Express* very well, and that newspaper was revolutionary in saying to the reader: 'You're as good as any other man.' Beaverbrook was a great believer in making his readers feel the equal of royalty, plutocracy or the aristocracy. He did more to make the reader feel that he was on the up and up than any other proprietor I've ever known. His huge empire and all his political convictions appeared to be very strong and influential but the real revolution he brought about – though he may not have known what he was doing – was to tell his readers that their daughters would look as good at Ascot as anybody else's. It was immensely influential journalism. I didn't like him, but he had a great instinct.

You spent your entire career as a journalist on a right-wing paper, or one which is certainly thought to be so. Have you ever had any doubts about that political allegiance?

I think I can truthfully say no. I would be regarded in Mrs Thatcher's terms as a wet, and I *am* wet, though I'm dry on a number of subjects, South Africa, for example. I'm more of a wet on social issues – possibly I owe something to my father and my uncle, both of whom were in the other camp. I've shifted here and there, I've had minor changes of opinion, but I've never regretted being on the right or having to write for a right-wing newspaper.

In the hard times in the 1930s there was, it is always said, some sense of community, but now in the 1990s even that is disappearing; a political philosophy has emerged which seems content to place more emphasis on the individual. Do you think this is a healthy trend?

I used to go to the distressed areas as a reporter before the war, and one of the things that struck me was that even in places like South Wales, Newcastle upon Tyne or West Cumberland, where there was real poverty and a shortage of food, there was a definite social empathy; they clung together. If one week you literally couldn't afford a loaf of bread you relied upon your neighbour to give you half a loaf of bread. It was a very different social pattern from what we have now when neighbours are almost strangers one to another. I don't understand the reasons. All I know is that there is a great contrast between (shall we say) the society I found in Newcastle when I went up there in the thirties and the society that has just been uncorked by recent events and reported in the press. Society has become more self-contained, much more cellular. I use that word because modern living is like a beehive in which everybody is in a cell rather than in human association. The other day I went to Moscow and I was very struck by how much more socially interdependent the Russians are. I rather envied them. I talked to countless people on the streets, and I saw almost a throwback to the years before we had home entertainments and distractions which kept us apart. The Russians are very dependent on human association, and it's something that we have – I won't say sacrificed – but it's something we've let slip.

Do you ever have a feeling that politicians have misjudged the degree to which rhetoric can be substituted for reality? I have in mind the way figures, for example, can be manipulated; even if bad they are presented as reasonably good. Doesn't that sort of thing damage the trust needed between government and governed?

That is a difficult question. There is far less direct connection between the people and those who govern them than there was in the past. When I began in politics, public meetings were *de rigeur*; they're very rare today. In my view there is no better recording of where the shoe pinches than at a public meeting of not more than say eighty to a hundred people; even thirty to forty will do. I don't know any better way of discovering what lies inside people's minds and hearts. I am astonished at what you get out of people if you give yourself the time to talk to them for more than ten minutes. It's something that's irreplaceable; it's not something you can read in the papers, or something you can guess. In the great public meetings of the past, politicians did have the advantage of learning from people directly what hurt them. Indeed, in very distant days this is what the sovereign did until the whole thing became too burdensome. This is something missing now in our modern democracy and it may in the end prove to be its undoing. One form of redress is for ministers to appear at public meetings where public feeling will make itself felt. I have been to meetings that have been broken up and the minister left in doubt as to what people thought. There were times in the 1920s when Lloyd George's 'Land Fit for Heroes' produced massive demonstrations. Today, unless you get some extravagant demonstration by young people in Newcastle, there is no outlet for public feeling, no forum. It's no good telling me that *Any Questions* or *Question Time* or any rubbish on Thursday night is going to replace that, because it doesn't. It may be good entertainment but it doesn't get the *vox pop*.

You were once minister of information. That must have been an ironic situation for a journalist. Wasn't there a danger in that position of suppressing exactly the information that as a journalist you would have been trying to reveal?

Absolutely. As a journalist I have always supposed that the cabinet had countless secrets which I've never been lucky enough to find out. As a minister without portfolio, I could not think of anything the cabinet had decided which the press had not already got hold of. From the outside you appear to be attacking a fortress when you're a journalist. From the inside you appear to be in a mud castle, the walls of which are rapidly being eroded. In other words, you've got no protection. The cabinet ministers for their own reasons talk to their cronies in the press over lunch and then the ministry of information becomes redundant. I'm bound to say towards the end of my two years in that job a sense of superfluity overwhelmed me [laughter]. I was most grateful for the experience, but for future prime ministers, it's not a job that ought ever to be included in any cabinet of sensible men.

Why is there such distaste among British politicians for allowing the people who elect and pay them to have information about the way they are to be governed? The Americans are infinitely less secretive but their government remains intact.

I'm not a great subscriber to this school of thought. First of all, I think that countries fundamentally have differences and it's a mistake to think that the system in one country is going to work in another. I understand the American freedom of information; I understand their First Amendment, I also look without much envy at their libel laws. I have been in America and seen public figures completely destroyed by the freedom with which the Americans are allowed to attack or investigate and expose, and I am therefore not starry-eyed about their system. Nor am I absolutely convinced that the so-called blanket of secrecy which the press feel is kept over everything here really exists. Having seen it from both ends, I can assure the press that far less is covered over with secrecy than they believe. I don't believe you can run any business, let alone government, without a degree of confidentiality. Good government does depend to a certain extent on trusting that colleagues will not, for their own purposes, blow government business to the press or to the public. Of course, the public have a right to know what is being done in their name, but there's a balance to be struck. I was on the Franks Official Secrets Committee. With Oliver Franks, probably the best chairman I've ever served under in my life, we spent fifteen months going through this whole problem of what should be said to the public and what should not. In the end, as you know, we fenced off defence, some fiscal treasury matters and certain foreign affairs matters. I am powerfully persuaded that good government has a right to a degree of secrecy. What that degree is will never be agreed between the press and government. I'll accept your point that we are more secretive here than we need to be; I don't accept that the American system would be the better one.

But would you support a kind of freedom of information – not the same as the Americans', but one which would enable the public to get more information? The present state of affairs is surely not very satisfactory.

Experience shows that in Canada and in America where there is a right of the public to discover certain information, they don't always look for what you think they would look for. They look for your income tax return; they look for detail which is frankly not relevant to the public weal. All right, there may well be a case, if it increases public confidence, for giving more access to what government is doing, but don't be disappointed if having granted them access, you find it's not used to a very high purpose.

There is now, and has been for some time, pressure for an act guaranteeing a right to privacy. Do you think that it is a sensible thing or are the private lives of public figures of legitimate public interest?

I've thought about this a lot. I have to say that I think the lives of public figures are of public interest and legitimate areas for press enquiry. I regret the fact that we should find it interesting that a cabinet minister has a liaison with a woman other than his wife, and I think we should not confuse public interest and prurience. There's a distinction between the two, but we shall never agree on what the distinction is. And so I accept that the private affairs of a public man may become a matter of public interest. However, I draw the line where children are concerned. Very few people in the press ever calculate the effect upon a child at school of an accusation (on possibly not very solid grounds) against its father or it may be the mother. Of course if it is proved that a man has indulged in criminal activity, then too bad if the child suffers, but I've seen tittle tattle about public figures which has made children at school terribly miserable. When there was a brief interest in my own private life, the only newspapers I really despised were those who encouraged my children to talk on the telephone. That is not a form of journalism that I think is acceptable; but I'm liberal and I have to accept that if you go into public life your private misdemeanours become public property. In a democracy you must go along with the public mood and people today are very sensitive about any affection of superiority. The most potent word in the English language today is 'inferior' and any politician who may have delivered a homily on the subject of one-parent families and is then found to have a mistress in Rome, Paris and Vancouver should be exposed. The public are entitled to know and to draw their conclusions.

You were minister without portfolio in 1963 when the Profumo scandal broke which eventually led to Macmillan's downfall. Did you see that as inevitable at the time? Would it be different now?

In retrospect I think there were a number of errors made in addition to the original error, that is to say I think there was a certain amount of press hype, and I'm not speaking now as one who was a minister at the time. The whole tale became almost a satire of the British in their moral suit of clothes. This is reinforced with hindsight by the fact that Jack, with whom I was at school and have known all my life and am still very fond of, has in the intervening twenty-five years reclaimed his status and his right to be regarded as a good man in a way which none of us can emulate. I regard this as a very interesting moral tale. Those who would be the first to condemn Jack and would still be saying, 'Oh, but didn't he tell a lie to the House of Commons and so on ... ', very few of them can hold a candle to what he has done since in Toynbee Hall. I have a secret respect for people who have a tumble and recover, and this includes Jack, it includes Nixon, and it even includes Bob Maxwell. I respect the people I've known who have taken a big fall and recovered. I doubt my own capacity to do so.

But would you condemn Profumo for his sexual morality, or for telling a lie to parliament? Which was the more serious?

The falsehood to parliament was the serious aspect of the case, no question about that, but the circumstances in which he was induced to make that unwise statement have always mitigated what he did in my view.

When I interviewed leading women in France for my book, it was suggested to me that indiscretions were considered to be among the perks of being a politician. Do you think the British are simply more hypocritical or is it rather a matter of competition between newspapers, the need to sell?

I think we must respect national differences which have historical backgrounds. The French have a view about sex, the British have a view about sex, and that is just one problem we're going to run into when we start a federal Europe. I am not prepared to make invidious comparisons, but I do think that we have developed a class of newspaper in this country now which knows that the published peccadilloes of public figures sell like hot cakes. I think possibly we sell more hot cakes in this country than the French do in theirs. Indiscretions in Paris would simply not produce the fuss they produce here. I've never found a word to describe the British attitude towards sex. It's still really schoolboys' lavatory-wall stuff and this is what the newspapers cash in on. I'm not devoted to the French, I don't find myself naturally attracted to them, but I do deeply admire their more adult and mature attitude towards sex, and the more I look at what our tabloids breakfast on, the more I envy the French. It's going to take a very long time to get this silliness out of the British system.

When Lord Lambton left politics he remarked that there was a world of difference between doing a thing and being found out. That remark was seen by some as being a sophisticated response, by others as cynical indifference. How do you see it?

Lambton was a minister at the time, and I do think that ministers have a certain duty to keep their private affairs from exciting the *News of the World*. Lambton was making a philosopher's point, but the fact is that he was a disgraced minister and I do not think that any amount of satire or humour can really rationalise what he did. I'm quite consistent about this. If you're in public office, you have a duty to your colleagues and to your government to live in the context of your times. It's no good saying, 'If I were in Paris nobody would take any notice of my going to bed with a black woman and a white woman.' The fact is if you're in the UK and you have the *News of the World* looking over your shoulder, then you must take that into account.

Do you ever think that journalism is bound to be constantly concerned with the trivial because of its ephemeral nature? There's nothing quite so dead as yesterday's newspaper. Perhaps the serious papers are just entertaining a different set of people from the tabloids. Or would you argue that there is a difference?

The answer to that is to make a comparison between today's newspapers and the newspapers of the thirties or even the fifties. I've just had to look through the newspapers of the fifties and I am mildly alarmed, as a professional journalist, to discover the extent to which, especially in popular newspapers, the content of serious news has gone down and the amount of trivia has gone up. Assuming that newspapers are guided by men who know where public taste lies, this is a disturbing commentary on public education. I don't want to be too tendentious, but when people abuse *The Star* or *The Sun* or the *News of the World*, I ask myself whether they're picking the right target. Let's take the old *Daily Mirror* of Cudlip's day, or the old *Daily Herald* of Southwood's. I look back on them and, alas, I fear public tastes are not what they were at one time. The appetite for serious news has virtually vanished. I think the attention span is much shorter than it was ... television has something to do with this ... and there are many children now who find it almost impossible to read through a whole book. But this is something outside the realm of journalism.

Journalists often like to present themselves as opinion makers. They certainly give opinions but do you think they actually change minds or do they rather bolster prejudices?

The irony here is that in the old days when they knew what was news and what was opinion, and the editorial columns of the papers were strictly confined to the opinion, then I think they did influence people. I'm thinking of something like the *Times'* editorial which recommended that Czechoslovakia should yield to Hitler and save Europe a grave embarrassment; or of some of the leading articles even in the *Daily Mail* during the First World War about the shell scandal, the shortage of shells on the Western Front. Now the irony is this: the newspapers have rather self-indulgently enlarged the realm of opinion, and they no longer separate news from editorial. Most news is presented in a way to persuade you of this or that. For example, news about Mr Kinnock in the right-wing newspapers is designed to persuade you that he's in a mess. Nowadays you have far more columnists than before, opinionated fellows (like myself, I suppose I have to add) who write weekly or daily columns and who are expressing views all the time. It follows that the influence of newspapers has greatly diminished because their spread of rather subjective material is such that the public has become almost inoculated against it. People are very careful today about accepting what any newspaper says, so the newspapers have defeated themselves.

Before the war the unemployed were, I suppose, relatively unaware of what one might call the context of their poverty. There was a social cordon sanitaire *around them, but the situation is now very different. Put bluntly, they can see what they are missing. Is that not bound to produce great social unrest and a see-saw of repression and resistance?*

I think about this. Before the war, the problem for many people was literally getting enough to eat. Today it's rather different. Poverty today relates to what other people have in relation to what you yourself have. We're dealing with comparative standards of living. You're asking me if I think that this is more inflammatory than the old hunger standard, and I'm not sure. There are manifestations amongst young people that they are prepared to show their discontent in a way which the old poor were not – car nicking, and so on. In theory a different standard of life shouldn't lead to a revolution, yet in a way I think it does. I've just been in the Sudan where people are almost at the end of their tether through lack of food, but there is no mood of revolution there, no rising up against the government. You have to remind yourself that when people are denied the necessities of life they go very quiet, but when they're denied the so-called good things of life which they see widely advertised in our consumer society, there is probably a more inflammatory situation.

I recall you writing about Tyneside and drawing attention among other things to the prevalence of one-parent families there. What do you think can be done about that? Is it a sign of social disintegration?

We've learned recently that about a third of the children in this country are born out of wedlock. I do not doubt that there are many lone mothers devoted to their children, but there is no question that more children are in some way handicapped, and therefore the state has to concern itself. It's not a matter of morality, it's a matter of public welfare. Furthermore, a degree of public cost is involved in this. If you look at the figures you will discover that the number of children born outside wedlock creates quite a heavy bill for a government. My philosophy about this is really lamentable because I am a great believer in a self-correcting mechanism. I do not ever think that politicians can alter human behaviour.

If the government feels it a duty to make sure that the parents of those children suffer in no way at all and are treated through public funds, then in my view you will delay the working of a self-correcting mechanism which I deeply believe in. One generation learns from the previous generation. If the government neglects the problem and allows the public to see that a one-parent family suffers in a way which is unacceptable in our sort of democracy, then it is my belief that the self-correcting mechanism would work sooner. But we have to compromise; we have to do the minimum to prevent the children being handicapped and at the same time be aware as politicians that our powers are limited – we cannot correct the situation.

Very soon now we shall be in Europe ... how do you think it will develop? Is it going to be a federal organisation in the end?

On certain terms we can as readily share the culture, history and economy of Europe as any other nation. My principal anxiety is this: that if the architects of Europe with every good intention move too fast, become too enthusiastic, work towards a federal Europe too quickly, they will sow the seeds of conflict. If they overstress conformity then they could produce a reaction against the whole concept of Europe and defeat their own best endeavours. That is the centre of my European belief. I am pro-European as anyone who can remember both world wars has to be. Even Mr Delors is preferable to Marshal Foch. However, you must have proportion, historical proportion. I do not want to see Europe defeated and undermined by excessive zeal, and I think that could happen. There's a limit to the notion whereby European cultures, beliefs, civilisation and peoples can be pulled into what some imaginatively regard as being akin to the United States of America, which had totally different origins.

Do you think that Mrs Thatcher is right in her views on Europe?

I think she's right in her views, and wrong on how she expressed them. Her instinct was that there would be a public revulsion against a demand for excessive conformity. It's an instinct I share. She was perhaps clumsy, perhaps over-forceful in the way in which she expressed her opposition to all this, but I know and you know that many in Europe were secretly rather grateful for the things she was saying. She lacked finesse, she could have harnessed people's anxieties, but instead she antagonised them. That was her mistake.

You have served as a cabinet minister so I suppose you must approve of the centrality of 'market forces', but won't an attempt to emulate America in that way produce the same large underclass with all its attendant problems? There are already riots in the streets of Cardiff and in Oxford for whatever reason …

In Russia the underclass is incomparably larger than the underclass in the United States or in the UK. If you go to the food markets you discover that at one end the poor relations are scrabbling for food at government prices and at the other end there is Californian food for those who can afford it. I've never seen a country with greater distinctions between the poor and the privileged. So before we say that the market economy leads to impoverishment as indeed it does for a proportion of the population, let's say that we've got something built in here which is difficult to avoid. To some extent a degree of human poverty is unavoidable in almost any society. I can't think of a formula by which you can avoid a certain number of people going to the wall. But ours is better than anything they've got in Africa, or Latin America, or the Soviet Union. What I think the wealthier societies have to do is to find a means, without crippling themselves, of tempering the wind of the shorn lamb. I'm a great believer in Keith Joseph's philosophy – that the real advantage of a market economy is that you can afford to do more for the impoverished people than by any other means. That is the only solution to what you're postulating.

From time to time you have complained in the context of the newspaper world of the way accountants now rule the roost. Is that not the inevitable outcome of the political faith you have espoused?

I do think that newspapers are at risk of becoming too prone to the advice of the marketing man, and I have seen in my time a very big shift from the authority of an editor to the authority of those who have to sell the newspaper. Editors are now more and more persuaded by marketing people to cater for a certain class of public that they say is necessary for the health of the newspaper. The irony about newspapers today is that we're now employing some of the best minds that come out of the universities. I've never known a period in which we've recruited abler people to journalism, incomparably abler than the people we had a generation ago or in my early days, yet this is not reflected in the quality of the newspaper. Journalists are now much better qualified; they can actually write English and do joined-up writing, yet we have on the whole a more trivialised, a brasher, perhaps less informative set of newspapers. I've only ever had one view about the press: it is there to offer people the basis for making their decisions. And that function has not actually improved under all the better minds from Oxbridge and other universities. That is one of the sadnesses.

With the demise of communism and the triumph of capitalism, are we not going to have a world which simply dances to the tunes played by the United States?

We're between acts at the moment, the curtain is down, and I'm not sure what's going to happen next. But I'm quite sure of this: that the human race, being born to trouble as the sparks fly upwards, has problems that are not going to be cured by the death of communism. I don't know that we're going to live a tranquil and easy-going life and I am doubtful whether in the end we're going to see this rather simplistic solution of the United States prevailing over all. One of the things I worry about with the United States is whether behind all the wealth and the dollars, it is actually a nation in decline. My impression of Eastern European countries, by contrast, is that they are going to evolve some compromises between the failure of Marxism and the falsehood of capitalism, and I think we may find some new formulas developing which will be of great interest. A country like Hungary, for example, may well produce something which is better than anything we've yet attained.

You have spoken of 'capitalism in the service of humanity', but that is surely a utopian idea. Most liberals would disagree and argue that in the first instance capitalism is necessarily at the service of capitalists. Isn't it the 'overflow' which serves the rest?

We're talking about the most efficient way of dealing with human resources which must in the end provide more of the means which every nation has to find for dealing with the unfortunate section of the population which has to be – to put it bluntly – subsidised. Communism did not work, though many had high hopes of it, nor did fascism, so we have this imperfect mechanism, the market economy. It may be a very bad system, but we're now learning that nobody yet has produced anything better. In so far as it can provide enough to enable a country to look after those below the line, then it is a good system. What else can we do? If you say to me that you doubt whether capitalists ever wished to help, and that most of them are out for what they can get for themselves, then I say that is where government has a role to play. It is for government to decide what capitalists should keep to themselves and what governments should lay their hands on for the benefit of the unfortunates.

You sent your own son to Eton. If those who can afford private education do that, does it not dilute the pool of talent available to teach the vast majority of our children?

When I was in the army I was sharing a room with a man who was going to have a house at Eton. We agreed that we ought to put faith in the future – it was just before D-Day – and my son had just been born. My friend said, 'There are preferential terms for penitent old Harrovians, so would you like to put your son's name in my book?' and so I did. We both survived and so my son went to Eton. That's the story there. I accept that the English private education system is now becoming exorbitantly expensive, and I think it's just possible for this reason that there is a limited future for it. I also accept that we are internationally almost singular in our public schools. But I have never believed that their existence damages the national system. The national system is not in a very healthy state, but that does not in my view relate to the public schools. I don't accept the theory that if parents of children who go the private sector were required to use the state schools they would exert enormous influence. I don't see any harm in the public schools continuing. They are enjoyed by labour supporters as well as conservative supporters, so let's have no humbug about that. I myself set a very high value on them. There is a great inclination to reduce standards in education generally, to make exams easier, to reduce the rigours of the academic world. And it seems to me absolutely imperative, however noxious or class conscious it might appear, to keep a sort of yardstick against which you can measure quality. I know this is a very aggressive thing to say, but I feel this very strongly. I do think state education has gone through a very bad patch, that it is on the slide, but if you abolish the only comparative standard you've got, not only in terms of academic results, but in terms of discipline and what you turn out, then I don't think you're doing society any good.

But aren't you maintaining the class system? That's the danger that I see.

I think the class system in this country, compared with the twenties and thirties, has altered far more than anybody can believe. The speed at which we have reduced the enormous differences in class since the First World War is barely recognised today. I would wish in many ways that we had rather more of a pyramid, that all the old grammar schools were still there, rather than this uneven structure of public schools, one or two grant-aided schools and the rest comprehensives.

The distinctions are too great. But I don't think there's any need for public-school masters to beat their breasts with guilt and say (as they often do) that they barely have the right to exist. I think the class thing can be exaggerated. It's unimportant compared to standards, which are immensely important.

I imagine you were an admirer of Mrs Thatcher.

Yes.

What was your feeling when she was obliged to resign?

I felt very worried about the way in which it was done, and wrongly thought that it would have a very bad effect on the Conservative Party. I underrated its resilience and the ability of Tories to gloss over what I regarded as a rather doubtful episode historically. The sacking of a conservative leader on a ballot is an unusual occurrence, and it's not in my view in the tradition of the Conservative Party. I never approved of the Humphrey Berkeley rules in the first place. My initial feelings lasted for about three months and then to my surprise I realised I was wrong. Judging from the most recent meetings I've conducted, the conservative public have accepted the outcome with far less bitterness than I expected. Some credit for this is due to John Major who has conducted himself well for a man who had very little chance to think out what he was going to do before he had to do it. Some credit is also due to Mrs Thatcher who, notwithstanding the efforts of the press to involve her in bitterness, has in fact, like her husband, stepped outside any sort of controversy. The Conservative Party constantly surprises me.

Had Mrs Thatcher remained would we have fared better?

The action was unfortunate, but I think that it was ultimately for the benefit of the Conservative Party. I'm not revealing anything I shouldn't, but I have a feeling that retirement had been uppermost in her mind for some time and but for the recession all this might have come about in another way. The most difficult decision any prime minister has to make is not when to call a general election, but when to go. For historical reasons no prime minister wants to go on a low, and I think Mrs Thatcher of her own nature might have called it a day a little bit sooner had it not been for the fact that the recession left her with a sense of 'I'd better see this through.' As it was she was not allowed to make her own decision and was forced out through a concatenation of circumstances – the Rome summit, the Howe speech, the Heseltine challenge and then the denouement. I'll sum it up by saying that the Tory Party has had rather more luck than it deserves.

I can readily understand that as the editor of a national newspaper you must have been extremely frustrated by the practices and demands of the print unions, but what view do you take of the idea of trade unions, do you think they are necessary to ensure that employees are not exploited?

The fact of the matter is that those print unions so overplayed their hands as to make life unsupportable, and in so doing they did their fellows a bad turn. One of the great ironies of modern times is that the dockers behaved in such a way as to empty the docks of London, and the printers of Fleet Street who came from much the same background behaved in such a way as to make Fleet Street untenable. Now the newspapers have moved into the vacancies in the docks left by the dockers. It's true, there's a lot of management today which needs superintendence by vigilant trade unions, I've no doubt about that. As part of our meritocracy, there is a standard of modern management which looks awfully like the steel masters and the iron masters and the cotton masters who rose in Victorian times and who treated their work forces very badly. I am totally convinced of the need for a vigilant trade union to keep management from exploitation, but it's unfortunate that excessive zeal by the printers and some other unions have led to this state of affairs. I don't think Mrs Thatcher emasculated the unions, but there is a balance to be struck between leaving trade unions to fulfil their role, and at the same time not enabling them to cripple the economy for reasons which are irrelevant.

Who made the deepest impression on you in your role as a politician?

Though he was dead before I became an active politician, the man I've always followed more closely than anybody else was Stanley Baldwin. I have all his speeches, I constantly refer to him, and I've always regarded him as a thoroughly underrated member of the Conservative Party for several reasons. Firstly he understood the doctrine of one society. We talk about a classless society, but look up some of Baldwin's speeches and you will see that he was the first man to realise that if this country was going to get anywhere we would have to get there together. The General Strike conflicted with Baldwin's philosophy, but with all the criticism that is levelled at him, it has to be said that against all predictions through the thirties he got us into the Second World War more or less as one people; this is not a thing that I underrate at all. Similarly, I've thought often that Alec Home represented something which is missing in British politics now, namely the figure who has better things to do but goes in out of a sense of something which is not ambition, not a desire to better himself, not a desire to win. There is an element of public service about Alec Home which is an essential ingredient of English public life. Think of the way in which when he surrendered the premiership he was perfectly happy to continue as foreign secretary. There was a degree of selflessness about that which I think the modern Tory Party, which has become rather self-regarding, would do well to take up.

You served under several prime ministers. How did you asses them?

I've always had a theory that every prime minister has one special historical function in his time. In Winston's case it was obviously the war. With Alec it was rather different. Just when the Tory party was becoming very inward looking and material Alec reminded us of other values; he set a certain example. Macmillan's primary function was to speed up the process of independence for the colonies. He knew that after India there was no alternative but to dismantle. The wind of change was essentially his business. Eden was really too short-lived to have any particular function except to remind us perhaps through Suez that – as Kipling called it – our dominion over palm and pine had diminished, had in fact finished. Eden was a historical reminder that we were not where we thought we were (I'm thinking of Suez).

What about Thatcher?

The most important thing about her was that in an age in which women sought equality her example was of greater value than all the equal opportunities acts put together. She came at a critical moment for women and was a huge encouragement to them. I'm pro-woman and anti-feminist in a funny way, if you know what I mean. I think it's stupid not to make more use of the abundant talents of so many women, but I'm not in favour of all these artificial arrangements to make certain that every woman has a position she doesn't necessarily want. And Thatcher embodied all that. She also broke down a whole lot of adhesions in the Tory Party which had become a slightly clublike organisation. As a Tory MP for twenty-five years I knew there were certain understandings, but she would have none of it. She had her own idea of how to go about things and she changed the whole way of thinking in the party. She never felt herself handicapped by anybody who looked down on her; she never felt handicapped by any minister who opposed her.

When the war came, do you think you were more aware than other people of fascism and what it meant because of your background as a journalist?

I wish I had been. It's one of my laments that although the politicians of the 1930s have been roundly abused for failure to know what Nazi Germany was doing, a great amount of unapportioned blame lies with the journalists of those years. As journalists in the thirties we failed lamentably to produce as we should have done a loud enough warning note of what was happening in Germany. There were reasons for this. Proprietors and editors were too much in the pocket of those in the Foreign Office who wanted to give Hitler the benefit of the doubt. The great thing was not to rock the boat, not to write something that was going to infuriate Hitler. There was a certain element of responsibility attached to this but it was fatally misconceived. As a result, the British up to 1938 did not get the warning that they should have had from the free press.

At present there is a bill going through parliament designed to provide people with the right to reply to incorrect information. I know you feel it is an awkward way to deal with the problem and that it would be exploited. But is it not a problem which has to be tackled? How would you do it?

It ought to be done by the editor and if the editor fails to give the reader a right of reply, then I am quite clear in my mind that we have to go to a statutory right of reply which will land us in a most unholy mess. We shall have to entertain not only a right of reply on fact, but on opinion, and once you've started to do that it will run and run and there will never be an end to it. I only hope every editor understands what the penalty will be. Mind you, I'm very sceptical, more sceptical than Lord MacGregor, about any parliamentary move against the press. I know my political parties on this score. No party before, or even after a general election is willingly going to antagonise the newspapers by taking a step such as the statutory right of reply. It is a perfectly reasonable sword of Damocles for people like Lord MacGregor to hold over editors' heads but my political instinct tells me that there is not the slightest possible prospect of either a conservative or even a government under Mr Kinnock doing it. Politicians know which side their bread is buttered.

Is there any effective way of reconciling the freedom of the press with the protection of the individual, or for that matter of minorities? There are already restrictions about inciting racial hatred, for example. On the face of it, it seems very proper, but all governments love to restrict the press – think of the D notices …

I don't myself regard the press as unduly threatened by the Official Secrets Act or by D notices. I worked as an editor for nine years before I even had to refer to a D notice, and I think the newspapers for their own reasons tend to exaggerate the extent to which their ability to tell the public what they ought to know is impeded by D notices or fear of official secrets, or, to go wider, fear of defamation or libel. I think the balance in this country is just about right. Every now and again we get huge libel damages and people say the law is an ass. I think we went through a rather exceptional period in which juries lacked guidance from the judge, but that probably will be corrected. In terms of the Temple Court, I'm rather old fashioned; I think that newspapers should not be free to ridicule judges and to attack them in public and say that their sentences lead one to suppose they ought to be in lunatic asylums. Furthermore, the prejudicing of a trial of an individual by pre-press trial as happens in America is, to my mind, obnoxious. To hell with the First Amendment on that score. Let's not have the illusion of loosening the law of secrecy which is simply going to lead to a raising of the levels at which documents are marked confidential or secret. You can take the horse to water but you've got to make the horse drink, and no system with which the civil service will not cooperate is workable or of any value at all, whatever politicians say. If the civil service considers that the law of secrecy is not inimical to the public good then the law will remain what it was, regardless of what parliament says. So I don't want to get into that situation. For the moment we've got something which everybody cooperates with. I can't remember in twelve years of editing the *Daily Telegraph* feeling impeded about telling my readers something they should know; other editors may have different experiences, but I'm afraid I'm individual, I'm odd man out on this.

Would you ever have prevented publication of something on moral grounds, as it were, or because you yourself held strong views on a particular subject?

No. I'm entirely beholden to the tradition of the paper. As you well know the *Daily Telegraph* carries a page 3 which is the envy of some of the tabloids. As the old *News of the World* used to say, all human life is there on our page 3. There are very few known sins that aren't at some point recounted on the *Daily Telegraph's* page 3, and I would regard it as obnoxious if on subjective grounds I prevented something from being printed. If it is within the tradition of the paper, my personal views on the matter are irrelevant.

Do you believe in censorship at any level?

Don't let's mix up censorship and editorial judgement. The latter, whether it is in broadcasting, in television or in newspapers, has to be exercised. I absolutely hold to that. But that is not censorship. A lot of modern authors regard any failure to publish what they've done as an act of censorship, but it is not, though it is sometimes an act of editorial judgement.

When you decided to stand for parliament, did you have an ambition to reach high office or to implement some particular scheme? What was it that prompted you to take up so different a career?

There were about eight members of my family who had been in parliament before me and they had all chugged along quite cheerfully. There's a wonderful passage in Henri Leroi's *Life of Disraeli* in which there is described an encounter in the Carlton Club during the fall of the coalition. Somebody rushes in and says to the chief whip: 'There's no need for the coalition to fall. There are good men waiting … such as Deedes, Snoops and Swift' … to which the chief whip replies, 'These are not names that I can lay before the Queen.' I don't think any of my relatives held high office; they just felt quite content, as I did, to represent a constituency. So I entered parliament with the idea that I was perfectly happy to follow in the footsteps of my ancestors and if anything came of it, it came. But I wasn't very keen, truth to tell, because all my life the *Daily Telegraph* has been a very generous host to my small talents and I didn't particularly want my connections with the paper to be interrupted by politics. I could work for the *Daily Telegraph* as a member of parliament but it would have been difficult as a minister. So I can honestly say that I went in hoping to chug along happily as a backbencher.

Working as a politician must have been very different from being a newspaper man or a soldier. Did you find it a congenial environment?

Absolutely not. It's as different as you can imagine. A journalist has to live on his initiative; if he gets an idea, he can pursue it. Provided he gets his bosses' countenance he can get on with it. In Whitehall it's a totally different world because everything you do is subject to scrutiny. You're part of an enormous chain, and the process through which your bright idea has to travel are unimaginably sick, and so you get rather discouraged, unless you're a very powerful figure which I never pretended to be. It was the contrast between journalism and ministerial life that made me think that I preferred journalism.

As an MP you were once concerned with the drug problem. Some people such as Judge Pickles take the radical view that their use should be legalised. Taking drugs might then become a habit like social drinking and they could be taxed. What view did you take?

I worked chiefly in this field with people like Barbra Wootton who took a more radical view than I did. I swotted up the subject and was helped by doctors, and I must first of all say that it is not a moral position I hold on this. But I do take the view that there are enough health hazards – and other hazards – strewn about the feet of young people today without adding one more. I know that it may be said that if you legalise cannabis or even harder drugs you avoid damage to the law which is being made a mockery of at the moment by people, often well-connected people, who smoke cannabis around the clock. All right, that is a fact. But the higher priority in my view is not to add to hazards that already exist in the way of alcohol, and so on. I've also had it argued to me that fewer young people would smoke cannabis if it was legalised, since it's the illegality which appeals. This is all very beguiling but I simply don't accept it.

Which side were you on in the great poll-tax debate? Is it true, do you think, that its demise represented the triumph of political expediency over principle – its fairness was much trumpeted by government ministers at the time?

I've always accepted that a mistake was made here. What threw ministers off their balance was the misconduct of a minority of councils who proved extremely difficult to bring to account; they were overspending, and they were doing it in such a way that there was no chance of their electorate throwing them out. The government was driven to the poll tax by a desire to produce the mechanism which would make a small minority of councils more accountable. Now, if you produce a large law fundamentally to deal with a minority problem you embark on a very dangerous course. The result was of course that they trapped both the good and the bad; everybody got it wrong. It was a brilliant idea on paper, but they failed to apply to it that acid test of practicality. If a law is not enforceable it is a bad law.

You were for many years part of the Peterborough column – really a high-class gossip column. Do you think you could have been a gossip columnist in the mould of Nigel Dempster, for example?

I'm an admirer certainly. It really consists of knowing a tremendous number of people, and what is more it satisfies a tremendous human want. Provided it's not malicious or libellous, there's no great harm in tittle-tattle about people; it's a service to journalism. I'm not prepared to be tendentious about Nigel Dempster or any of the other columns. I would be ill suited to them, partly because I prefer writing about things rather than people, and it's not quite my cup of tea. But I wouldn't be ashamed to do it.

Five years ago, you accepted a peerage. There is some disquiet about the honours system in this country: so often such things seem rewards for political loyalty. Do you think this is fair in a democracy such as ours?

I've had doubts about all prefixes in honours, that is to say anything that goes in front of somebody's name. I think that suffixes, however, are rather different. I also believe that this country with a social revolution which has travelled much faster than most of us appreciate, is growing out of the honours system. The system as it's now constructed has a limited life, but I would prefer to see the country grow out of it than have a swift termination. I find certain difficulties about the House of Lords because, for reasons I can only surmise, the temperature of the House of Lords is kept at the level of an intensive-care ward, and I find it very hard to concentrate my mind when I'm there. The heating arrangements are excessive, but that's a purely personal problem.

I recall that you wrote somewhere that politics kept you apart from your son when he was young, and indeed he explained that he has avoided politics as a career partly because of the effect it might have on his own family. Have you ever regretted this side of things?

I have in a way. Had I not had an admirable wife my children would have suffered. A great many children suffer through the excessive zeal of their families in public life, so I would think more carefully about it given my time again. In reality, and far beyond my deserts, my children do not seem to have been adversely affected by my preoccupation with public affairs. As for my son, he has made a considerably greater success of his life in journalism than I ever did and in fact is now in a position of responsibility in which politics are ruled out anyway.

Laurence Marks in a profile of you spoke of your 'determination to keep The Telegraph *independent of the Tory government it supports'. What does it mean to be independent in that context?*

Not to find yourself in the pocket of any minister, including the prime minister, of whom I was personally very fond but whose company I avoided in relation to anything to do with the *Daily Telegraph*. If I learned one thing before the war, apropos of the relationship between the foreign secretary and *The Times* at the time of Munich and relations between proprietors and ministers in the thirties, it was that there were great dangers in editors getting themselves too close to people in office. Once you are made a repository of a confidence, an invisible mechanism starts to work; you play it the way he would like to see it played and not the way you should play it. So I found as an editor it was imperative to be perfectly friendly with all ministers, to accept invitations, to go and talk to them, to be briefed by them, but it was important to keep a certain distance; that seemed to me as an editor to be the most important thing. I'm sure my successor, Max Hastings, does exactly the same thing so that editorial judgements are totally independent. It doesn't matter what arises, you have made no commitment; you have no agreement, and you have no understanding with any minister, and you are therefore free to say 'this is rubbish'.

Every decade had its own conflict. The sixties saw the evolution of so-called free love and student power – in England we had Tariq Ali and in France we had Daniel Cohn-Bendit; the seventies saw the emergence of feminism; the eighties saw Thatcherism at full throttle. The nineties bear witness to the beginning of the end of communism ... where do you see the next conflict?

Just when we think that the communist world has ended and the threat to our existence is diminished, we begin to worry ourselves – and rightly so – about certain faults and crevices which are beginning to appear in Western civilisation. The big issue for us in the next decade is how to tackle very rapid and not altogether beneficial changes in our society. It's almost impossible for ministers to interfere with certain courses which society takes, and in the ethical and moral field, I wonder how far we can depend on what Reginald Maudling when he was home secretary called the self-correcting mechanism. The really important political issue in the West is going to be to what extent government has a responsibility to interfere, and to what extent we are prepared to wait and see how far learning from our own mistakes will work. I put full confidence in the second, not much confidence in the ministers.

In my interview with Prime Minister Edith Cresson, which was published recently in The Observer, *she caused a bit of a stir by suggesting that a large proportion of Anglo-Saxons are homosexuals. Although her claims are not based on any scientific research, would you not say it's true that most Englishmen are not comfortable in the presence of women?*

Well, a proportion are certainly not. I can perhaps best answer by relating an experience when I was chairman of our home affairs committee. Mr Butler who was then shadow home secretary said to me: 'Bill, I hope that you will be able to persuade our party to oppose the Abse bill' (the legalising of homosexuality). I think it's the only time in my life I was perhaps right and Mr Butler, who has a magnificent intellect, wrong. I said, 'Rab, bear in mind that altering the law will not be enough. People being what they are, this will be followed by a long and continuous campaign of self-justification.' To be told that you are legal is not enough; you must also feel that you are socially acceptable. And indeed I think I have been proved right in this, for you will observe that the law as it stands is not enough and pressure is going to be put on the prime minister to alter it yet again. People are not content with finding themselves within the law, they are insistent upon a form of social equality. The homosexual today desires and indeed insists not only on equality in employment but in all departments, that he should be regarded as – in Mrs Thatcher's well-known phrase – one of us.

But why do you think it is that many Englishmen are not very comfortable in the presence of women?

In this country there has always been a sort of shyness between the two sexes. When I went to my first deb dances in London, there was always a certain reserve, but I don't relate this to homosexuality about which my views are complex. I was in San Francisco not long ago and watched one of these gigantic marches of homosexuals protesting about the failure of the government to deal with their problems. It is jolly difficult at my age to avoid drawing any conclusions from certain phenomena. I fight against this very hard. If you are going to remain in active journalism, you don't want to regard every symptom that you don't like as a process of degeneration, but I do find this new phenomenon gives me pause, and I think that a world in which virtually everything has become socially acceptable is a world in which standards, frankly, have slipped. There is far more freedom for people to indulge in habits which twenty or thirty or forty years ago would have been regarded as socially unacceptable. The degree of tolerance which has entered our society is too high. There is a great struggle among the liberals in Hampstead as to the misuse of part of the Health by homosexuals, and the liberal camp is divided. One set say they have every entitlement to do what they wish to do, another set of liberals say that they are interfering with the freedom of families who want to walk round with their children. I find that a very interesting conflict. But I do believe there is a lack of restraint in public behaviour today, and I'm not absolutely certain that this is an advance in a civilised nation.

Most people hate to grow old, yet old age brings maturity and often peace of mind ... what are your own feelings on this?

I count myself jolly lucky at my age to be kept actively working five days a week, because I've come to the conclusion that as you get older, you have to look at your mind, very much as when you're young you attend to the fitness of your body. The great risk of old age, unless you exercise your mind, is that you become a tremendous bore to other people. There is a great tendency for your mind to close in on itself, and then all you really do is go on about the past. The great virtue of journalism is that it keeps your mind concentrated. People ask why I don't write my memoirs. The practical reason, apart from the fact that I rather object to the idea anyway, is that I cannot possibly devote my mind to thinking of what's going to happen tomorrow, which is, for journalistic purposes, essential, while half my mind is occupied with digging out what happened yesterday. And tomorrow on the whole keeps me fitter.

What weakness, if any, would you attribute to yourself?

I really admire people who have a bit more dash about them. I'm cautious, over cautious. I do too much thinking before I leap. If I'm pushed into it I will take initiatives, but I suffer from a certain passivity. It sounds a rather odd thing to say, but every now and again I get mildly alarmed at the extent to which someone of my rather limited intellectual capacities has succeeded in doing certain things. I've done a certain amount of self-education but not nearly enough, and therefore my capacities are more limited than you might suppose and occasionally it looks to me as if I'm like one of these children who are accused of getting very easy A levels and that is how I've slipped through my life.

NIGEL DEMPSTER

Nigel Dempster was born in 1941 in India, where he spent his first six years. He was educated at Sherborne and became a broker for Lloyd's of London. He entered journalism in 1960, first with the *Daily Express*, then in 1963 as a columnist on the *Daily Mail*, where in 1973 he was appointed editorial executive and editor of 'Mail Diary'. Between 1969 and 1985 he was a columnist on *Private Eye* magazine ('Grovel'), leaving the magazine on bad terms when the new editor, Ian Hislop, was appointed. His first marriage in 1971, to Emma de Bendern, was dissolved in 1974. In 1978 he married Lady Camilla Osborne; they had one daughter. He worked for ABC (USA) and CBC (Canada) and was under contract to the short-lived TV-am. His books included *HRH The Princess Margaret – A Life Unfulfilled* (1981) and *Christina: The Last Onassis*. His last years were troubled by illness and he converted to Roman Catholicism in 2004 and died in 2007.

You were born in India, but left when you were six. Do you remember anything of that life?

I remember everything because it's almost as if it were yesterday. There was sunshine and jungles and the sorts of things you can't believe a child had: elephants and tigers in the garden, pythons and boa constrictors. We literally lived in the jungle, 133 miles south-west of Calcutta. I know the distance, because when you buy a ticket in India it tells you exactly how long the train journey is. I've got a very clear memory from the age of two. I can say that because we had a dog that I remember dying when I was two. The whole joy of being born in India was that there were no guidelines. You never felt that you had to do anything; you never felt you had to get up in the morning. I had no form of discipline. I learned Hindustani since that was the only language my *ayah* spoke, and it never occurred to me that there was any world outside. My *ayah* would sleep at the end of my bed, guarding me from the world.

My father was managing director of the Indian Copper Corporation, and we lived where we did because the mine was nearby – about the third largest copper mine in what used to be the Commonwealth. He employed something like 12,000 miners and was a tremendously hard-working man with no interests in life except mining. His whole joy was his work. He certainly had no interest in women or children, but would work seven days a week, fourteen hours a day, and all his people remembered him for that. When he married my mother he told her, 'All right, you can have children, but don't expect me to have anything to do with them.' A great treat for me was, he thought, to take me down the mine, so instead of being taken out to the zoo or to a film, as would have happened in England, my entertainment was to be taken down the mine. I can remember at the very early age of about four, descending 4,000 feet into the bowels of the earth and seeing all the miners. It's an extraordinary memory I have of watching people knocking things out of rock deep underground.

My memory of India is one of total joy. We never wore shoes, we had a swimming pool, a tennis court and a staff of about fifteen. We even had what was called a sepoy, who, rather like the guards at Buckingham Palace, stood in a guard-box at the entrance to the house to make sure no one came in who shouldn't. There was no one who wanted to come in, so it was quite ridiculous. But it was an idyllic childhood, and so privileged, though everyone lived like that as far as I was concerned. I was born when the war was on, not that I knew about it. The only thing to occur to me as strange was having two airfields within about ten miles, one a US airbase and the other RAF. The officers used our swimming pool and tennis court, and I charged them gum in the case of the Americans and I can't remember what in the case of the British – whatever was going probably. It was a wonderful life, without responsibility, without care.

In later years, I went back several times. At thirteen it was difficult, because although I had only been away six years, everyone was speaking to me in Hindustani and I couldn't understand. I was there for the summer holidays for two months, and was glad to be back, but by then I'd become English, having been at an English boarding school in the meantime.

When the time came for me to leave for England in 1947, it never occurred to me that anything different was going to happen because my mother had explained that this was where I'd have to go to school, even though my father came from Australia. My father was forty-seven years older than me, and his father fifty-seven years older than him, so the Australian connection had vanished and my parents looked towards Britain as a place to educate their children. I saw nothing wrong with it, but what happened was a tremendous shock because I couldn't read or write and was coming up to my sixth birthday. The reason why I couldn't read or write was that I hadn't wanted to. In India I had spent most of my time in the servants' quarters, learning wonderful folklore and hearing stories of their lives.

The first thing that sticks in my mind about England was the cold from the beginning of the winter of 1947, which was the coldest winter until 1963. My clothes were totally inadequate. I'd never known such numbing, freezing cold, and in those days, of course, schools didn't have central heating. Also, I had never had to live in a disciplined society, but had always done exactly what I wanted. If I didn't want to eat, I didn't eat; if I didn't like the food, I used to throw it about. The only discipline had been provided by my father, who sometimes used to beat the hell out of me with his belt, but that was fair enough.

The next thing about England was the austerity, because in India we had everything: milk, butter, animals we could kill. One of the great delights of my childhood in India was the cook's compound, where I watched him behead chickens. In England, where there was very little food, the fact came as a jolt, and certainly food has been something uppermost in my mind ever since. I wake up every day looking forward to meals, and I'm sure that's something to do with that period of my life. My prep school was very small. There were thirty boarders, and I was the youngest by far. It was an extraordinary life, and I almost forgot the previous life in India, because I realised that you had to adapt, and if you didn't adapt you were dead. You knew, if you didn't get on, awful things were going to happen to you – you would be put in Coventry, people wouldn't speak to you. You could literally not be spoken to because you had body odour. I remember boys at school and how awful calamitous things which they had nothing to do with haunted them for the rest of their lives.

But the first person who influenced my life was the English master there – a man called Michael Gardiner, who was a bachelor, I suspect an eternal bachelor. He was enormously interested in the English language and made me interested too. He was also a Catholic, and I remember our having a spirited discussion about Jimmy Goldsmith, of all people. I must have been twelve at the time, and the news was that Jimmy Goldsmith's wife, Isobel, had died in childbirth producing a daughter, also called Isobel. I started discussing this because the papers, which were rather blurred in those days, made it look as if Goldsmith had said, 'Save the daughter but let my wife die.' In fact, if you read up the story, you discover that what happened was that his wife had a brain haemorrhage that virtually killed her, then the child was born, and after that his wife died. Michael Gardiner told me that the Catholic ethic was that you save the child rather than the mother, and over that we had a tremendously spirited discussion. It's curious that it should have been about Jimmy Goldsmith, who now lives a couple of hundred yards from me.

After prep school I went on to public school.

Would you send a child of your own to Sherborne?

The extraordinary thing about Sherborne is that it's become a much better school than when I was there. The only reason why I went there was that my mother, who came from the Dartmoor area, remembered it as the best school in the West

Country, the West Country starting, I suppose, somewhere near Salisbury and running through to Cornwall. When I went there in April 1955, it was a good, modest, second-rank public school. It goes back a thousand years, and Sherborne Abbey apparently has the remains of Alfred the Great who was said to have been educated there. It's a beautiful part of the world, and my mother was entranced by its beauty. It's a much better school today; it's got tremendous endowments. If I had a son, which I never will, and he wanted to go to boarding school, I can't actually think of a better one. It's academically very sound, its sporting record is tremendous and it produces rather nice boys. Having said that, there are only about five of my contemporaries whom I still see out of, I suppose, a thousand boys I knew in my day.

Why do you say you'll never have a son?

Well, unless I marry again. Certainly, my wife doesn't want to have another child. We had a daughter in 1979, and that seems to be it. I also feel that people have children for all the wrong reasons. We had a child for the right reason. We wanted a child and we got a daughter, whom I dote on, adore. I think people who go on having children till they have a son do it for all the wrong reasons. Many do it for reasons of inheritance, and it's a crazy motive. Why not just stop when you've got what you want; why buck fate? Anyone is lucky to have children that are normal, happy and healthy. One in ten children in Britain is born with some abnormality. I know enough people, like Jocelyn Stephens, who have suffered that way.

When you left school at sixteen, did you have any idea at all what you were going to do in life?

In those days, the whole public-school careers system wanted to put you into the established trades, and in 1958, when I left, that meant the City, which meant stockbroking, Lloyd's of London, merchant not commercial banking, or chartered accountancy. There were other professions which you positively did not enter, journalism being one. You could just about go into advertising, which was a coming thing in those days, a fledgling industry. But everyone who left Sherborne went into either the industries, which people thought would give them a leg up into the future, or into the army, the navy or the air force.

I had absolutely no idea what I wanted to do, and leaving was a terrible shock to me, because I hadn't meant to leave so early. But I had been at boarding school ten years, and it was far too long. I had become rebellious and achieved a certain notoriety at the school. Everything that went wrong was blamed on me. I'd started people drinking, smoking and talking to girls, which was not allowed. You actually used to get beaten at Sherborne if you talked to a girl. In the summer of 1958, I was booked to go to Davies's, a tutorial establishment in Addison Road, Holland

Park, but the first thing I did when I came to London was to get a job as a porter at the Westminster Hospital. The money was good – something like £8 or £9 a week – and if you worked the night shift you had to wheel bodies out and put them in the mortuary. I discovered more in those two months than I would ever have known otherwise. I saw bodies having their heads cut off at post mortems; I had to put stiffs into fridges at three in the morning. It was a quick growing-up process.

Then I did go to Davies's, the reason being that at Sherborne I was top of the class in English and history, for which I would win prizes, but bottom of the class in my other six subjects. The other people who were trying to get their exams were Etonians thrown out of Eton, Harrovians thrown out of Harrow. We all realised that the last thing we wanted to do was pass exams, so we'd go and have lunch in different places. Suddenly we learned that there was another life, and no one I met at Davies's ever achieved what they went there for. I realised I must have a new life, and one of the people at Davies's, whose father was a broker, said, 'Go and see my father,' and so I got a job as a broker at Lloyd's, literally on my seventeenth birthday, and entered a new world. Suddenly in Lloyd's there were people from Eton, Winchester and Harrow, and I discovered the extraordinary life of debutante parties in the late 1950s, at the time when Harold Macmillan was telling us we'd never had it so good.

You could go about London and be wined and dined for nothing, though there wasn't much sex around in those days. In the late 1950s, perhaps 5 per cent of the girls went to bed with men; in the late 1960s, perhaps 5 per cent didn't. It never occurred to the people whose parties I went to that I was any different from those who introduced me. I got into that stream and stayed there simply by being amusing, charming and nice to the girls and their parents. There was an enormous amount of snobbishness. I'm sure you'll find hundreds of people out in the shires, thirty years on from the deb season of 1959, who will say, 'What a filthy little yob Nigel Dempster was. I always knew he was a parvenu. He gate-crashed my sister's party' – that sort of thing. So what? It doesn't worry me.

I don't think they gave a thought to me being Australian. They might even have thought it slightly romantic. All people really cared about in those days was that you didn't sleep with their daughter, and very few did. The deb parties were proliferating. In 1959, every day from the beginning of May till the end of July, there were at least two cocktail parties, and each weekend there were at least three dances. You could choose which county you wanted to go to dance in. All it required was a white tie and tails. My first weekly pay check was £6, plus 2s. 6d. (12½p) a day in luncheon vouchers. I also got an allowance of £200 a year from my father, and on that one could live very well. I shared a flat in Lennox Gardens, which cost £2 10s. (£2.50) a week and was a good address. The rest was free, except for the cleaning of your clothes.

I don't think money made much difference. Girls liked men because they liked men. A girl who liked a man with a car was a girl who had a different view on life. But in those days we were all children. We fumbled each other occasionally; we made love if we were lucky. Very few girls were overtly after men with money, and I think it went on personality. I was still only seventeen, and it was amazing, because I was younger than the girls, and at seventeen or eighteen girls are much more mature than boys the same age. I simply don't know how I did it. It must have been with gritted teeth and perseverance, because I was very much a baby, though I had been seduced very young. In Devon, my home was with my grandparents, and about three miles up the road in Budleigh Salterton I had a friend with a large house who used to give parties in the basement. We'd fumble around with girls and, without knowing what we were doing, used to get laid. That would have been when I was fourteen or fifteen. It wasn't a satisfactory experience, but it wasn't terribly unsatisfactory either.

What sort of qualities do you need for work as a gossip writer?

First, a phenomenal memory. Secondly, an acquaintanceship with a wide section of society. No one could have invented a better gossip columnist than me because, by a quirk of fate – my upbringing – and luck I managed to meet an awful lot of people. I remember having dinner at No. 11 Downing Street, because Reggie Maudling's daughter was there and there you were, right in the midst of government. From seventeen onwards I met all the children and grandchildren of the people who were Establishment Britain. That's why, to this day, they can say, 'God, that creep, that bastard,' but we knew each other, and because I had an innate interest in other people, I'm able to remember how, where and why I met them, what their ages were and who they were with. I have that sort of encyclopaedic memory and can recall things you can't get in cuttings. It's having a vast log-jam of past memories – that's the gossip columnist's art. By some fluke I managed to acquire it.

It never occurred to me that I'd become a journalist. In those years being a journalist was a very grubby profession; journalists were grammar school boys who wore dirty macs, behaved badly and worked in an appalling part of London called Fleet Street, which was somewhere you never went. Those of us in the City used to look west towards Fleet Street as if it was a sort of nuclear rubbish tip.

How do you check the information that comes your way? There must surely be a lot of people who try to exploit your column for their own interests?

None whatsoever. If people were to ring up saying, 'Would you write about me?' you'd make them look so ridiculous. It's rather like a man asking a woman, 'Would you make love to me?' He fears rejection. Similarly, no first-person attempt to infiltrate is ever made because people fear being humiliated. My view has always been that if you don't want to get into a column then, like the Aga Khan, you surely will. I've been in gossip columns now for twenty-seven years, and I've never known anyone get a story beneficial to themselves into the columns I've worked on.

As for checking information, the information these days comes first hand. Part of the deal has to be that informants get paid for what they tell. Every part of the newspaper, from front page to back, is marked up every morning for payment. Sometimes we have seven or eight items a day. Sometimes our bill for payment to informants is as little as £50, sometimes as much as £500.

Everyone believes that gossip column stories are about marriage break-ups. It's absolutely untrue. The number of stories about marriage break-ups come to perhaps one every two or three weeks, and when they happen they are of historical importance. It needs to be noted that the Duke of X has left his wife because it's something to go into a book, a part of history. The idea of Fleet Street gossip columns being grubby little areas where we expose the seamy side of people's lives is wrong. Most of the stories are about money, privilege and power, and the other area is basically the historical aspect of Britain – births, marriages and deaths, with divorces obviously included.

A gossip column has got to be scandalous in terms of raising an eyebrow because you can't have a column which simply massages the back. There are two sides to every great person: the public side – the approbation of the masses – and the private side. That's life. If you get into some sort of dialogue with a journalist, as people in public life want to do, then the journalist enters into a pact with them. They get publicity for what they're doing, but as soon as things go wrong in their life, it would be foolish to have these rich, powerful and privileged people believing they can pull the shutters down and say, 'Look, don't write about me anymore.' They've incited the public's interest, and I'm afraid they've got to realise that once you're started on the treadmill, you keep going.

What sort of editorial freedom do you have?

When I went to the *Daily Mail* in August 1971, the paper had just merged with the *Daily Sketch* and something like 300 people had lost their jobs. Paul Callan and I were the first two signings to the new *Mail* to start columns, and I can honestly say that, from that day to this, I have never suffered any form of interference from anyone. I can only assume that is a sign of great success, because you only interfere with something that's going wrong. I've never been asked by the editor or the proprietor to put in a story. I've never been asked to take one out. The measure of Lord Rothermere's urbanity is that, when I came back from the United States in 1973 and went to work on the Diary, my very first story on 8 October was that Lady Annabel Birley, who was married to Mark Birley and after whom Annabel's in Berkeley Square was named, was having another baby. She'd already had three, and this was her fourth, and the story went that Mark Birley was not the father but Jimmy Goldsmith was.

I rang up Jimmy, whom I knew even in those days, and said, 'There's a story that you're the father of the baby Lady Annabel Birley is expecting in January 1974,' and he laughed and joked but I wrote the story just the same. It appeared on the Monday, and on Monday evening Lord and Lady Rothermere went into Annabel's to be met by Mark Birley in a high fury. I think Lady Rothermere was allowed to stay, but Lord Rothermere was thrown out, and the measure of my esteem for Lord Rothermere was that I never heard a whisper about the story at the time. Five or six years later, someone asked did I know that after my very first column as Nigel Dempster on the Diary my proprietor was thrown out of Annabel's? My response came close to worship. Anyone else would have had me fired, but I never even heard about it.

If the trade of the gossip columnist is trivial, I think that all of life is trivial. Kierkegaard said all life will be gossip, and I suspect that my trade gives a far greater insight into the workings of those people who are above us in terms of power and privilege, position and money. People aren't that interested in the pronouncements from the pulpit or what's happening in the House of Commons, because the British are a very cynical race. No one cares what politicians say. We know they're all liars, cheats and fools. What we want to know is what's going on in their backgrounds, why they're saying whatever, why a certain minister does this, a politician that. The answer invariably lies in their personal life, and this is why the gossip columnist is as invaluable now as he was two hundred years ago, for the only way the British public knew King George III was mad was through gossip. The reason why the serfs, the ordinary working people of Britain, realised things were going wrong was through gossip, because there weren't any newspapers in their time.

What we do today is an advanced, streamlined version of village gossip, and we provide a fantastic service. People want to know if those who are rich, powerful and privileged are having a better life than they are. They're having a better life materially maybe, but things are going horrifically wrong for them too. Cecil Parkinson's daughter is a drug addict; the Duke of Marlborough's heir is as drug addict; the Marquis of Bristol, with 4,000 acres and £20 million, is a drug addict who has been in prison. It gives people a sort of comfort.

Investigative journalism can be defended as part of a free society. If a minister, for example, has a liaison with a foreign embassy official, or shares a prostitute with one, it might well

*be in the public interest to reveal it. But if someone's husband or wife leaves, or takes to
adultery, doesn't broadcasting it merely compound the misery?*

Gossip columnists only print stories long after they've happened. Rarely do you
write in the middle of a story. What you're doing is dotting the i's and crossing
the t's. People go off with other people, people have hiccups in their marriages.
By the time it gets into a gossip column, it's history. The people involved have
explained it all to their children, they've moved out, moved into other houses,
and it comes as something of a merciful release to see it written in a decent
newspaper like the *Daily Mail* because then they don't need to answer any questions any more.

The profession can't be called intrusive because the people who are written
about on the whole welcome journalistic attention. In this day and age, it's not
enough to exist. You have to be seen to exist. People enjoy publicity and realise that
if you are in the spotlight for whatever reason – birth or ancestry, accumulation
of wealth, inheritance – it's a two-edged sword.

If you ask me whether we need a right to privacy in this country, I say absolutely not. The only reason anyone wants a right to privacy is if they've got to
hide something. The privacy bill in France was introduced by a libidinous premier
with a saucy wife. Pompidou didn't want the French papers writing about him
or his saucy wife. Pompidou's personal life was a sorry mess, and so he passed an
Invasion of Privacy Act, which means that in France you cannot write about any
aspect of the private life of a public person. It also means that there are all known
forms of chicanery going on. The French public have no idea whether their peers
are murderers, rapists, finaglers, thieves or liars, and that's very sad.

Over the years there has been a call for a privacy bill here, but it's always come
from members of parliament who have been exposed. In the 1970s, I exposed
Maureen Colquhoun, who was Labour MP for Northampton and a lesbian. Many
of the voters in Northampton may well not have known about her lesbian tendencies, but they certainly did when she and her girlfriend, Babs Todd, sent out
change-of-address cards with a Sappho motif. I got hold of one of the cards and
exposed her in the *Daily Mail* as a lesbian. All I was doing was bringing to a wider
public what she herself had advertised, but all hell broke loose. I was reported to
the Press Council. I was this and that and all the rest of it. Meanwhile Maureen
Colquhoun's leftist friends in Parliament – including one Arnold Latham, who
was MP for Paddington, I think, and a particularly unattractive little man – tried
to bring in a privacy bill.

Every time you hit the raw nerve of an MP – and the most recent is this one
called John Browne, the MP for Winchester, who has caused his ex-wife great
financial hardship – they start a rumble for a privacy bill. I never see the decent MPs

who have their lives rent asunder, like Cecil Parkinson or Roy Hattersley, calling for privacy legislation, because they understand the rules of the game. And the rules are very simple: if you behave yourself, you won't be written about, and if you don't it's no good hiding behind a cloak of privacy.

I started off in this business with an enormous number of friends and ended up with very few, but the few I've ended up with are the same friends I've had for thirty years. All the people I've known for a long time understand that, if they do something horrible or heinous, it's going to end up in a column, and they'd rather have it in my column. They know it's a decent newspaper it's going into, and they know I'm not going to twist the quotes. The whole point about being British is that you realise that, if you've done wrong, you put your hands up and say, 'Got me!'

As far as outside pressures go, people realise that they'll get nowhere trying to put pressure on a journalist, at least one of my standing. Therefore, the pressure comes in lesser ways, such as, 'What do you want to know? Can we do a deal? Could you perhaps say this rather than that?' People know that they can only put pressure on someone if they've got a lever, and no one has a lever on me. I don't need the money, I don't lead a salacious private life, so I can't be blackmailed on either count. No one can say, 'Look here, you've committed adultery with my sister, how dare you write that story.' I'm not saying I lead an unblemished life, but I am saying there are no areas of my life about which I can be pressured. The only pressure is internal pressure. If I write something, how is it going to affect my future?

I'm also helped by not leading a social life myself, which is a great joy. I belong to the most egalitarian club in the world, the RAC, which is full of very middle-class people, and our common delight is playing squash and running. I run marathons, the most egalitarian form sport on earth. People who stop being friends with me I don't regard as friends anyway, because they can't expect a journalist to behave other than the way he does. You can't give a party at which something extraordinary happens and not expect a journalist who is there to write about it. Certainly, people like Peregrine Worsthorne can't resist it. For example, we were all invited to a party at Jimmy Goldsmith's on what happened to be a General Election night, and Jimmy had said to everyone that they could either come and not write about it or write about it but not come. So I said, all right, I'd come but wouldn't write about it. Then I was furious the next morning to find that Peregrine Worsthorne, who had been there, had gone and written about it.

The thing that makes me angry is that journalists should be viewed in this curious way. I don't know whether Jimmy will ever invite Worsthorne again, but the point for me was that I stood by my word. Nevertheless, journalists are journalists and people must realise that occasionally they break every rule because the urge to tell overcomes the need for discretion.

Finding myself the occasional butt of other gossip columnists has, in fact, only reinforced my views about accuracy, because what I've discovered in ninety-nine per cent of items written about me is their inaccuracy – dates and places wrong, names and people wrong. All that has done is convince me to tighten guidelines to staff even further, so we check everything not once, not twice, but three times. We make the most ludicrous checks. Sometimes we spend two days ringing up to make sure 'Susie' is not spelt 'Suzy', because once you get one thing wrong, people doubt the veracity of the rest. I was brought up in the Fleet Street of the old days. I joined the *Daily Express* in 1953, when Lord Beaverbrook was at the helm and you used to get sacked if you spelt a name incorrectly or got someone's age wrong. Nowadays journalism is so sloppy. There's no form to it. I despair. The last redoubt of accurate journalism is in the gossip column.

Have you ever had information which you did not print for non-journalistic reasons?

I've always printed everything I've ever known, because, for a start, I work on the assumption that, if I don't print it, someone else will; and if someone else will print it, then I should have printed it in the first place. I must qualify that, on the other hand, by saying that I don't write homosexual stories. The *Daily Express* column has gone markedly downhill over the past eight or nine years, simply because of its preponderance of homosexual stories. They seem to find homosexuals intriguing. Why, I don't know. Certainly, the editors have never been homosexual. Homosexual stories have never been part of my diet, and the reason I wouldn't print them is simply because I find them tasteless and not because they impinge on my relationships with other people.

Once you said in defence of your profession: 'It is not the exposure of an indiscretion but rather the indiscretion itself that causes hurt.' Isn't that special pleading?

No. I know a lot of people who are privileged, who have ancient titles, a lot of people who have money and who are never written about. I could name you two or three dozen who live in houses filled with Reubens paintings and Chippendale furniture, Louis Seize this and Louis Quinze that, but these people are never written about because they've never done anything. They've led blameless lives, quiet, happy existences. Their children live likewise and the public and gossip columnists are unaware of their existence. If everyone lived that sort of life, then gossip columnists would obviously not have subjects for gossip.

You can very much lead your own life and avoid the press and public censure by leading a blameless, boring life. As soon as you start mixing it, you're going to be caught out, especially in this day and age. And once you're caught out, you've got to come to a decision. I don't lead a stainless life. I gamble, I drink a lot. But what I do doesn't affect my ability to write and comment. Once you lose that ability, then you've had it.

The kind of thing you're looking for in a gossip column has got to be financial or sexual or anything aberrant to the mind of the normal person who lives in Bootle or Chipping Norton, Budleigh Salterton or Bideford – people who lead Christian lives and have decent relations with their neighbours. Where I come into it is that I'm very much middle class, middle Britain. My background is not the rarified ionosphere of social life. I take a middle-class view, much like that of the *Daily Mail* itself. And I'm shocked by what people do and how they behave, and the stories that appear in my column are very much there because of my shock at what goes on. Richard Ingrams is the same, another middle-class moralist. We're helped by the fact that we lead fairly humdrum lives. I'm not an adulterer, not an alcoholic, not a thief, not a finagler, and anyone who is any of those things tends to jar on me, because I think that this is not how one was brought up to behave. Basically, the gossip column is a pulpit from which you're saying, 'You shouldn't be doing all this, but you've done it and now you're paying for it.' In the old days, they would have been put in the stocks and had eggs thrown at them.

I don't think we can ever be accused of causing hurt for the simple reason that any hurt and harm have already been occasioned by the people themselves. All we do is report what's happened. If you murder your wife, you end up in court and it's going to be written about. If you do something of an unworthy nature and you're a great, powerful or privileged person, one day it will come out. All we do is follow the age-old journalistic practice of producing for the public stories of interest about the people in positions of power and privilege. I don't incite people to leave their wives or to leave their husbands. I don't incite them to become heroin addicts. I can't see how I can be blamed for the original act.

Which stories have you been most proud of?

I think there are very few stories in our world in the last twenty years that I haven't started. The best story of the last half century, the one story that got away, that I was never offered, was that madman Fagin sitting on the Queen's bed in Buckingham Palace. But apart from that, just about all the stories that have enlivened gossip life in the past twenty years have started in the *Daily Mail* diary. It's been a fantastic achievement, but one that was only realisable because it had at the heart of it the *Daily Mail*, a very good newspaper with a highly regarded patrician chairman, Lord Rothermere, and the best editor in the business, David English.

I have always had a very clear idea of my position. I work extremely hard six days a week. I'm the only journalist in the history of Fleet Street to have a column on both a daily newspaper and a Sunday newspaper, and on top of that I have various other outside interests. I'm contracted to TV-am to appear fifty-two times a year, to ABC in the States and so on. My reward for hard work is that I shouldn't be criticised. When I've been subjected to criticism in the past, I've always felt that if I'm going to be criticised, I'm not appreciated, and if I'm not appreciated, I'm going to leave. It's as simple as that. I'm awfully confident of my ability to find another role in the market place, and I've always felt that the best way of doing anything is to do it in public, which is what I exhort the people I write about to do. I've always had very public rows with editors and with my proprietor, and he with me. And it's always helped to clear the air. It's never been for financial gain, but entirely to preserve my professional integrity. The fact that I could run my column from Mars if I wanted, and no one would interfere, shows I've taken the right track.

You have regularly condemned the way some of the royal family are harassed by reporters and photographers, but where do you draw the line where they are concerned? Couldn't it be said that you simply want them to be harassed to the point that suits your own purposes?

By great fortune I've never needed to harass the royal family. Contrary to speculation, I rarely see the royal family. It just so happens that last night I went to a cocktail party which Prince Charles also attended, but that is another matter. What we have is confrontational journalism, a form of journalism usually exercised by photographers who harass not just the royal family but film stars and whoever – pushing up against them, knocking them to the pavement and then photographing them; and there you have the story the next day – members of the royal family or Robert Redford jostled to the pavement, shouting and screaming, 'You fucking photographers!' That's not my thing. Our stories about the royal family are done at a remove. We don't get within miles of them. They never see us, we never see them. Our stories come from friends and, if I dare say so, even relations. I've never harassed any member of the royal family. I've never had a conversation with any of them, except at dinner. Our stories of the royal family are intimate stories about their personal lives, and I say personal rather than private because I don't think they have a private life. Obviously, they do have personal lives, and the royal family, like anyone else, could have a private life simply by being private.

But weren't you once very critical of certain members of the royal family on a chat show in the United States, calling Princess Diana a 'fiend' and a 'little monster' and saying that Princess Margaret was 'obsessed with bisexuals'?

I never regretted that because all that I said was true. I told the American television show about Princess Diana's behaviour towards Charles, and it wasn't I who invented the words 'fiend' and 'monster'. They came from a high-up member of the staff, not just a butler, valet or chauffeur. The Anthony Holden book on Charles and Diana totally vindicates what I said, which was that the marriage was going through a very bad period and she was behaving as she did because she was furious with Charles for neglecting her. A wife who is neglected behaves like a fiend and a monster, that is to say, she was being what Charles thought of as selfish. In fact, I saw my remarks as a fine piece of journalism because they showed I was in the middle of a family row, and what better gossip can you have than that?

I was hardly the first person to draw attention to the fact that Princess Margaret liked bisexuals. In my own book on Princess Margaret, I pointed out that the man who became her escort for almost eight years, Roddy Llewellyn, had previously shared a double bed with Nicky Haslam, an interior decorator, and lived with him for at least six months. However, I never said what they did in that double bed. Every time I've been asked to go on television to explain something during the last sixteen or seventeen years, everything I've said has been borne out later in a book or a biography.

For the future, I cannot see the royal family lasting beyond the death of the Queen. The Queen is sixty-four this April, the Queen Mother ninety this August. The Queen, I would have thought, has a life expectancy of at least another twenty-five years, by which time Prince Charles will be sixty-six. I do not believe that the forces Mrs Thatcher has unleashed – the yobs, the lager louts, the young who don't really have any feeling of history – will be royalists. You can only be a royalist if you have a knowledge of history, if you understand what the royal family's contribution to this country has been over the last thousand years. The lager louts of today are the parents of tomorrow, and I do not believe that their children will feel any empathy towards the royal family or think that Prince Charles is a good egg. The people who think Prince Charles a good egg are those around at the moment, and the only reason why the royal family is in favour is because Princess Diana is a pin-up, a jolly good pin-up too. In twenty-five years' time this country will have grown out of the idea of kings or queens, and when Charles ascends the throne, as he will as soon as the Queen dies, I think the gig is up. There will be a referendum at some stage after that, and the referendum will say, 'Thanks, but no thanks.'

It was an aristocrat who said to me that Dempster had done more than anyone to maintain class divisions in this country.

Others have said I'm a communist because, by constantly delving into the unsavoury elements of the aristocracy, like revealing that Lord Blandford, the Duke of Marlborough's heir, and Lord Bristol were drug addicts, I was undermining the class system. I think myself that, by writing about them in the way I have, by making it amusing and immediate, I have helped to keep the class system afloat. People want to belong to a class system which is admired, and we're never going to be without a class system in this country as long as there are titles and a royal family, and there are always going to be people who want to join.

Mrs Thatcher has changed British society during the past decade. Is that change for the better or for the worse?

She has changed it in such a way that she's made a new class of spiv. Now, whether the spiv would have risen without Mrs Thatcher I don't know, but she has given the green light to spivvery. All round Britain, but especially in London, you see illiterate yobs driving £60,000 cars and you're bloody sure they're not paying taxes. Mrs Thatcher has allowed these people to proliferate and profit, and it's the by-product of her greater design, the entrepreneurial society. Against that she has got to be praised for bringing down taxes. When I married my wife she was paying 98 per cent on unearned income, and I was paying something like 82 per cent on earned income. Those draconian measures to tax one out of existence were crazy, so that's the good part, but I deprecate what she has unleashed upon us.

What exactly happened to cause your rift with Private Eye?

There was only one reason. I went to work for *Private Eye* because I liked Richard Ingrams enormously and had known Auberon Waugh since my schooldays. I never got paid because I didn't want money and didn't ask for it. During their problems with Goldsmith I never took any salary, yet raised, I think, about £9,000 for their appeal, from among my friends. So I was working for *Private Eye* out of a sense of mischief and a sense of love for Richard and Auberon Waugh and Patrick Marnham. Clearly I was a very great selling point, and the acceptable face of *Private Eye* throughout all those struggles. People used to look on *Private Eye* as a rabble who poked fun at their betters, and tee-hee. I was the only person who had any position in society. 'Grovel' of *Private Eye* worked on a decent newspaper; his wife was a duke's daughter; he appeared on television and was a public person.

During the Goldsmith case, I was the centre-forward, very much taking on Goldsmith and his gang because I was on the same level as them, so to speak. That all passed, and in the early 1980s Ingrams was introduced to Ian Hislop, who I thought then, as I do now, was talented in the way of being able to write jokes, but no journalist. The fact that he was appallingly unattractive didn't help him. He was a runtish figure who looked like a sort of bat you see at London Zoo, and was always oiling up to Ingrams and no one else. I'm not saying he should have oiled up to me, for I wouldn't have given him the time of day. But then it became apparent that Ingrams was going to have to leave *Private Eye*, which, one must remember, was practically his only form of income. Although he did the occasional radio show, *Private Eye* was his whole life, whereas it was a very minor part of mine: maybe 5 per cent, and certainly less than 1 per cent of my income. I therefore became rather disquieted at Richard Ingram's absences and the fact that, during his absences, a totally unpredictable man was in charge of what I was doing.

I don't know that I ever spoke to Hislop at that time. I certainly can't remember having a conversation with him. I would go and do 'Grovel' and that would be the end of it. Then came what I most feared: a disgraceful act. I was playing squash in the RAC when Liz Elliott rang me up at about half-past eleven on the Friday and said, 'Look, we haven't got a "Grovel" column.' I said, 'Aah, I don't want to do one.' She said, 'You've got to do it, we're relying on it. We've got a blank page.' So I left the squash court, went to *Private Eye*, sat down at a typewriter and wrote the thing, the main item being that Sir Geoffrey Stirling, head of P & O, had had an illegitimate daughter. This was yet another *blah blah blah*, because he was one of Mrs Thatcher's blue-eyed boys and one of her unpaid political advisers. Underneath it I inserted a story which was in the 'Grovel' folder about Cecil Parkinson and his new secretary and there were various other items.

I handed the 'Grovel' copy over, and for the first time in my life Hislop was there. I said, 'Look, these stories I can vouch for, but this one about Parkinson I know nothing about.' Now, what normally happened on a Friday or a Monday at *Private Eye* was that the lawyer would ring me and say, 'Look this story … ' and I'd say, 'Don't worry, it comes from a friend.' That Friday the lawyer didn't ring, so I assumed Hislop had either had it passed by the lawyer or taken the story out. It was nothing to do with me anymore. Then someone, in *Private Eye* perhaps, leaked the story to Parkinson. He issued an injunction for libel and had the issue scrapped. The first thing I read was that Ian Hislop, who was meant to be the editor of *Private Eye* in the absence of Richard Ingrams, had done what I feared, which was to tell the world that I wrote the story.

That was wrong on two counts. First, as an editor he should have protected his sources; secondly, I hadn't written the story in the first place. I walked in and screamed at Hislop, 'You know nothing about journalism. You're a little shit. I never want to have anything to do with you again. This has just gone to prove everything I've said to Ingrams about you. You have no knowledge of journalism whatsoever and I'm not going to put my reputation on the line for you.' And that was the end of it. My reward for having worked mostly without pay, certainly without any form of proper recompense, was that for the next three or four years I was written about, sometimes three or four times in the same issue, invariably in an unpleasant manner. They even said I was being paid by Peter Cadbury to write about him in a flattering way, or worse, being paid not to write about him. So I sued and won and got, I think, £8,000 plus costs. Cadbury also sued and won, so that vindictive little paragraph cost them about £25,000.

There were no other reasons for ending my *Private Eye* connection. I'm a professional Fleet Street journalist of some standing, and I helped out in what I believed to be a good cause, which *Private Eye* was originally. Then suddenly it became a commercial venture; they tried to make money. The reason I left was because I didn't see why I should have my career threatened by a man like Ian Hislop, who couldn't understand that the first thing an editor does is protect his sources. The reason why *Private Eye* has never had a decent story since dates from that time, because everyone in Fleet Street saw that Hislop didn't understand the basic tenets of journalistic behaviour.

I wouldn't say there's a bitterness on my part, because that's a negative emotion. I just think *Private Eye* is now a rather pathetic magazine of very little interest. There is no information in it as there used to be in the old days and you'd golly or wow. Now I know more than they do, week in, week out.

I haven't spoken to Ingrams for a very long time. I've rung him once in the last two years. I feel that originally when Richard was involved in *Private Eye*, it was an excellent publication because it took on the Goliaths and, win or lose, went on taking them on. Then it became a tool for abuse. You don't use a publication to bash your enemies. You simply don't do it.

It is often noted that men with macho images are given a high profile in your column, suggesting you have a secret admiration for men who make a name for themselves by seducing women.

The only reason they get it into the column is because, if you've got mistresses, you're an interesting person. Jimmy Goldsmith denies he ever said, after his marriage to Lady Annabel Birley, 'When you marry your mistress you create a job vacancy.' I told him he should stop denying it and go down in history as the author of one of the immortal remarks of our time. The point is that if you have a lot of women, then you are attractive and my readers find you attractive. The fact that you're a womaniser, like Dai Llewellyn, who was engaged to three attractive girls at the same time, is something readers enjoy, even though these people all come to grief in the end.

Jimmy Goldsmith hasn't come to grief yet.

He's come to grief emotionally. He's got problems ahead with the present mistress, I imagine. But I don't write about such people because I respect or admire their macho side. It's simply one of the crazy vagaries of life that people behave in this way – like sultans or potentates – and others love to read about it.

Lord Longford said of you, 'I like Nigel Dempster, but I can't bring myself to approve of him.' And the Mail *art critic, Paul Johnson, called your trade a loathsome business.*

I get on very well with Lord Longford and his wife, and I was a great friend of his late daughter Catherine. As for Paul Johnson, if he finds my business so loathsome, why is he collecting money by writing for my newspaper so frequently? I find him loathsome. I find him humbug. As someone once said about Paul Johnson in his leftie days, he eats more oysters than a duke. He is a terrible snob, the sort of person who'd be oiling up to my wife's father if he were alive. He'd have loved to have met the Duke of Leeds.

It has sometimes been said that you make an intransigent foe. Is this balanced, would you say, by your loyalty as a friend?

I don't think I've ever been intransigent and I don't think I've ever been a foe. I haven't got it in me to hate anyone. I don't hate Ian Hislop, for instance. I just think he's a twerp. People who are loyal to me are friends. We've always been friends and obviously I help them and they help me. I never conducted a campaign against anyone, because if you were to do that as a gossip columnist, you'd lose your job. You're not employed to conduct personal campaigns but to write about the people out there who interest your public.

It doesn't happen that I walk into a parlour of my enemies and I'd be a damned fool to do so. I only go to places where I want to go. Anyway, who are these enemies? I've outgrown all my childhood enemies from when I was in my twenties to thirties. I'm bigger and better than they are. I work hard and I'm appreciated. The only people who are enemies now are those who have suffered by my exposing them, and I'm very happy to have such people as enemies because they should be exposed. There are a lot of unpleasant people around.

You married twice into the aristocracy. Is that a world where you feel entirely at home?

Ever since I went to deb dances in 1959, I've known a world which is populated by people who, if not aristocratic, are related to the aristocracy, simply because that is the tribe. When you mix at a certain level, it becomes almost impossible not to marry someone who isn't related to the aristocracy. It's just coincidence that, of the two women I've fallen in love with, one had a mother who was titled and the other had a title of her own.

You're not an Englishman, but most Englishmen, even those who are heterosexual, prefer the company of other men. What's your feeling about that?

If you've gone to an English public school and been brought up in a sporting ethic, you like to spend your leisure hours doing sporting things. You can't play squash with a woman, or golf with a woman, or tennis with a woman, because women are not very good at it. British men who have been to public schools tend to stick together because their pastimes are male-orientated. I take women out to lunch, not because I'm trying to have affairs but because whatever they do interests me, but the major part of your leisure hours must be spent with men.

Do you have ambitions outside the world of newspapers? For example, you breed horses.

I don't think I would be happy to leave that world, but obviously it's going to happen in the not too distant future. My whole life has been spent working ten to sixteen hours a day, six days week. I wouldn't know what to do if I didn't work those sort of hours. My wife says I'm the only person among my friends who works, but I wouldn't know what to do if I didn't. Breeding a horse is a two-minute job. In fact, horses ejaculate so quickly it's about a thirty-second job. It just wouldn't be enough.

THE DUKE OF DEVONSHIRE

Andrew Cavendish was born in 1920, son of the 10th Duke of Devonshire and Lady Mary Cecil. He was educated at Eton and Trinity College, Cambridge, and was then commissioned in the Coldstream Guards. He was awarded the Military Cross for gallantry on the Italian front in 1944, and the same year became heir to the dukedom when his brother was killed in action. He married Deborah Mitford in 1941 and they had one son and two daughters. After his father's sudden death in 1950 he devoted himself to securing the future of Chatsworth, the family estate in Derbyshire. From 1962 to 1964 he was Minister of State at the Commonwealth Relations Office and from 1965 to 1986 he was chancellor at Manchester University. He was vice president of the London Library from 1993 until his death in 2004.

Your family can be traced back to feudal times, to the famous Bess of Hardwick ... has the sense of your own history affected your outlook on life very much?

Yes. I'm proud of my forebears. Bess was a very remarkable woman who married four men of property; fortunately, she only had children by her Cavendish husband, so we inherited that lot. She was the first lady who put us on the way to fortune.

Have you felt an immense responsibility as a member of one of the important aristocratic families of England?

My years as head of my family have coincided with the decline of the influence of the aristocracy. Nowadays they have no power and virtually no influence.

Do you regret that decline?

No, it's right. Mr Major is a man for his times, but I sometimes wonder whether it is just coincidence that the decline of Britain as a world power has also coincided with the decline of the power and influence of the aristocracy.

You were born just after the First World War. During your childhood were you aware of the huge legacy of grief and horror which resulted from that war, or were you completely sheltered from it?

Two things brought it home to me as a child: one was the vast crowds that used to walk on the pavements on either side of military bands, no doubt largely composed of ex-servicemen; and the other was that we lived in Belgravia and used to walk to Hyde Park to see the construction of those great memorials, particularly the Royal Artillery one at Hyde Park Corner. And I remember my mother saying that all her dancing partners had been killed.

How do you look back on your schooldays at Eton?

I enjoyed being there, but I was a horrible boy, and I'm not being falsely modest about this. I was dirty, I was lazy, and I have lived long enough to regret deeply my wasted opportunities. I could have had a marvellous education and yet I did so little.

Did you ever question your privileged status in those days, or did you regard education at Eton as part of your birthright?

I wouldn't have used the word birthright, but I did accept it. And, of course, although my mother and father took great care in our schooldays not to differentiate in any way between my elder brother and myself, I was becoming aware of the principle of primogeniture. My father would talk to me about it, making clear that it would ensure the survival of the estate. He knew it was unfair but he said, 'I accept the unfairness, and you must also accept the unfairness.'

Those who were sent away as children to boarding school often say that it distanced them in every way from their parents and family. Did you experience anything of that?

Yes. I didn't like it when I went back to school, but it's right, and it's got to be done sooner or later. When I had the honour and privilege of being chancellor of Manchester University, I saw undergraduates in their late teens or early twenties away from home for the first time, and many of them found it very difficult to cope. It's a brutal system but you've got be thrown in at the deep end, and it works.

Did you send your children to public school?

I did indeed. One of the worst things I've ever experienced was the first time I deposited my son at his private school; it was dreadful. I felt pain, and so did he.

How did you meet Deborah Mitford … was it love at first sight?

I first saw her at Eton, when she was fifteen or sixteen and strikingly beautiful. Then we met at a dinner party in 1938, and if it wasn't love at first sight it was certainly attraction at first sight.

The Mitford girls were a legend in their own time. How did you feel about becoming a part of that legend?

I was mildly jealous at being an addendum to the Mitford sisters.

Debo was involved in helping Unity travel back from Germany after she had shot herself … do you remember that time and the emotion it aroused?

I remember it vividly. My wife was very courageous during what was a dreadful and searing experience for her, and I had great admiration for Unity also in what she did. Rightly or wrongly she had a deep feeling for Nazi Germany, and when it came to war, she couldn't face the clash of loyalties between the two countries. One shouldn't condone suicide or attempted suicide, but, it was, I thought, a heroic gesture.

You were married in London in 1941 as the bombs fell. Did the fact of war lend a heightened sense of emotion to the occasion?

Yes, I suppose it did. The Blitz was very exciting – I loved it. I was in the army, stationed in London, and there was a terrible raid the night before we got married, but we went to the wedding as if nothing was happening.

You were commissioned in the Coldstream Guards and your first child was born in 1943. Did you ever think that normal family life would be impossible because of the war, or did you always manage to keep the faith?

I think we managed to keep the faith … you see, it never crossed our minds that we were going to lose the war; it just never occurred to people of my generation. The war was just something that had to be got through.

Your brother was killed in action shortly after D-Day. You must have been shattered by his death …

Yes, I was. I felt terribly inadequate because I wasn't there – I was in Italy. Of course, it was awful for my father and mother. And my brother had only just married

Kathleen Kennedy who might well have been expecting his child, and it was perhaps only human to be curious to know.

Your father was a minister in Churchill's government. Was Churchill supportive, compassionate at that time?

My father was only a junior minister, and he and my mother were friends of Sir Winston's, but not very close friends. I'm sure Sir Winston would have been supportive, but he wouldn't have played a role in my family's grief.

Did you ever meet Churchill?

Not as a child, but when I was in the army in this country we did guard duty at Chequers and Sir Winston used to ask me up to dinner sometimes. He was very kind; he thought we never had enough to eat in the army, and pressed me with food. I was at Chequers the night the *Bismarck* was sunk. Churchill was getting all the radio messages, and it was one of the most thrilling nights of my life.

Your brother only had a few weeks of marriage before his death. That must surely have made you and Debo very aware of the fragility of family life …

It was worse, much worse for Debo. I actually enjoyed the war in Italy. I liked my fellow men, the camaraderie, and we were doing something: but for the wives here it must have been terrible.

Later in the same year you were decorated for gallantry on the Italian front. Did your brother's death make you all the more determined to defeat the enemy?

Yes, it did. I hated the Germans – I think I still do. Yes, it brought a sense of personal resentment.

Your brother's wife, Kathleen Kennedy, died in an air crash in 1948, one of a succession of tragedies in the Kennedy family. Were you closely involved with the Kennedys?

Yes, we kept up the connection, and still do, and when they come to England, they nearly always visit Chatsworth. My sister-in-law was one of the most delightful ladies I've ever met. She wasn't exactly beautiful but she had great vitality. We all loved her. And Jack Kennedy was the most marvellous man. My wife and I went to his inauguration which was very exciting and thrilling. I went to his funeral also, which was terrible.

Both your families were touched by the terrible effects of war. Debo's brother Tom and also Unity were casualties of the war. Did you feel at the time that you had been signed out for a particularly harsh treatment, or was there a kind of universal loss and grief?

It was very sad that Tom was killed so late in the war. He could have had a distinguished career in politics if he'd wanted to. But we all lost a lot of our close friends and family, and though it wasn't anything like the First World War, it wasn't a scythe right through society, it was universal. But Tom's death in Burma when the war was really over was particularly hard.

Your brother's death altered the course of your life in that you became successor to your father, the Duke. Were you a reluctant heir?

My brother had been killed in action so it wasn't right, was it? It wasn't my fault, but it certainly made me uneasy.

Apropos your father's sudden death in 1950, your wife has written, 'Not only did Andrew lose his father; he also lost his friend and wise counsellor.' Does that describe how you felt?

Exactly. He was marvellous. My father wasn't a mean man, but he spent very little money on himself, whereas I've always been extravagant, and my father vicariously enjoyed these extravagances. He didn't like horse-racing at all, but he was only too delighted to find the funds for me to buy horses, nearly always bad ones.

In addition to the title, you inherited enormous problems in the form of death duties which it took over twenty years to clear. How did you face up to this colossal task?

There again I was singularly lucky. First of all, at thirty I was young and resilient. Secondly and more importantly, I had the most brilliant financial and legal adviser, a man called W. D. Macpherson, now dead. If we'd panicked, I wouldn't be sitting here now. We had to pay eighty per cent of everything but thanks to the way it was handled, a great deal survived on the art side which was perhaps what mattered most to me. We had to lose the ten best things we had, and they went – perhaps rightly – to our national institutions, the V&A, the National Gallery and so on. I had to take the decision whether to lose the very best and keep the bulk of the contents of Chatsworth, or to sell a tremendous lot and keep the very best. Rightly or wrongly I settled for the very best to go, but we've got a very nice collection.

But do you feel any bitterness about it?

No. The Lord gives and the Lord takes away. I'm one of the luckiest men in the world, and most people would give the eyes in their head for what's in Chatsworth. I'm philosophical about it, though I do sometimes think that but for that German sniper's bullet none of Chatsworth would have been lost.

You must surely at times have felt defeated by the enormity of the problem. What was it that kept you going?

My wife, my relative youth and my advisers.

It must have given you great satisfaction to secure the future of Chatsworth and moreover to make it completely self-financing.

I've achieved virtually nothing in life, but that is certainly what I am most proud of. It was due to my advisors more than to me, and my wife has been a pillar, but to keep Chatsworth going is my overwhelming ambition, as it was my father's; and I would guess it will be my son's.

Do you get on well with your son?

I get on very well with my son. I'm proud of him, and I put him very high on my list of good fortune. He also gets on well with his mother and stands up to her too, more than I do.

She is a strong character?

That would be an understatement.

During the 1960s you held various political posts which you say yourself you would never have held but for Harold Macmillan's nepotism. Is that false modesty or something you genuinely believe?

Oh, it's true. It was gross nepotism. I had made a few speeches about the reorganisation of betting in this country, but I hadn't been very active in the House of Lords, so there was no justification. But Harold obviously thought I could do it. I imagine he thought, 'I can risk him, he won't make too much of an ass of himself.'

Harold Macmillan is a very controversial figure; the historians disagree about him. What was your view?

To begin with, unlike many politicians, he was a clever man. He was also an extremely astute politician – 'wily' is an apt description. My judgement of him is biased because he was so good to me that I can never repay the debt I owe him. Not only did he give me a job which I enjoyed very much, but it led to other things. For example, I became chancellor of Manchester University which was one of the great experiences of my life. He also had the best manners of any man I ever met.

But was he trustworthy?

I was too junior in government to have political dealings with him so I never had any reason not to trust him. It would be presumptuous of me to sit in judgement on him.

You say that you left the Conservative Party and joined the Social Democrats 'largely for sentimental reasons'. What exactly did you mean by that?

We were Whigs and then we were Liberals, and we left the Liberal Party over Home Rule for Ireland. We were wrong about Home Rule for Ireland, wrong for good reasons. We thought that the Irish would suffer materially from independence, and indeed they have, but I'm a fervent believer in the political nostrum: 'It is better to govern yourself badly than to be well governed by others.' I like to think I am still a good Whig.

You have an impressive record of public service. Is that area of your life as important as sitting on the cross benches in the Lords?

Sitting on the cross benches in the Lords is not important. You've been kind about my record of public service which is very modest, and what I'm going to say now sounds extremely priggish. I'm aware of how lucky I am, and if I can help people or do anything in the way of charitable work, well, God knows, that's the least I can do. Also, I really like people, and if I come away from meeting someone and I've been bored, I regard that as my failure.

Some time ago you hosted at Chatsworth a gathering to promote peace in the Middle East. Is that a special area of interest for you?

Yes, it is one of my great interests. Through my father I've always had a great affinity with the Jewish community. My father was a friend of Weizmann and I can remember the excitement in our house in London when he was coming to lunch. My father much regretted that he himself had no Jewish blood, and occasionally after dinner he could be seen looking through the *Peerage* and when asked what he was doing, he would say, 'Surely somewhere there must be some Jewish blood ... ' There is a large Jewish community in Manchester and when I became chancellor to Manchester University, that's where I strengthened my links. I've been to Israel six times now.

You were formerly president of the Conservative Friends of Israel, but now you support the neutral Next Century Foundation. Why did you change?

I ceased to be a Tory so I couldn't go on being president of the Friends of Israel, and the Next Century Foundation is trying to build bridges between Palestinian and Jewish communities.

Are you optimistic that eventually a solution will be found?

I cannot say I am, and I regret that very much. I used to endorse the Jewish cause without question, but last April I went to the West Bank, and I was horrified by what I saw; the army was everywhere. Israel's got a lot to answer for, but of course there are a great many people in that part of the world who want to see Israel in the sea, so I think it is not quite fair to judge them by ordinary standards. Nevertheless, however simplistic it may sound, if the Jewish people are justified in having their own state, are not the Palestinians? Forgive me for talking vulgarly, but what is sauce for the goose is sauce for the gander.

I sense in you a certain discomfort with your aristocratic status. Would you have preferred to live your life in comparative obscurity perhaps?

No, I can't say that. It has great advantages, but there are also disadvantages. I dislike being called 'Your Grace', for example, and ninety-nine per cent of the population of this country think dukes are freaks, and they may well be right. People will not accept that you can have perfectly ordinary interests – for example, I really care about professional football, it interests me a great deal, but when I talk about it most people think I'm putting it on.

You once said that the trouble with being a duke was that people thought you were a blithering idiot. Do you care very much about what other people think?

Too much. It is an attractive quality not to give a damn what people think of you, but I haven't got it.

Debo once said of the late Duke of Beaufort that he was the most pointless man she had ever met.

I'm very sorry to hear that.

Do you think that in the late twentieth century pointlessness is a sad feature of much of the aristocracy?

I suppose we've only got ourselves to blame, but our power's been taken away. The caravan moves on, the days of the aristocracy are over. I wouldn't exactly use the word pointless, but we've had our day. We have had a good long run.

Would you be upset if a future government were to disband the House of Lords?

I should be very sorry if there weren't a second chamber, although I wouldn't in the least mind losing my title and being called Andrew Cavendish, but all the newspapers would add to it 'formerly the Duke of Devonshire', so it wouldn't make much difference. I'd mind very much if my wealth and possessions were taken away, but my title, no.

Do you think the House of Lords makes a valuable contribution to the political system?

Yes, I do. The standard of debate is extremely high and I think the House of Commons has got a great deal to learn from it. One of the problems in this country is our over-adversarial attitude in the Commons, as exemplified by Prime Minister's Question Time; I can only describe it as extreme disagreeableness which sets a bad example to the rest of the country.

Your image was rather tarnished a few years ago when in the Old Bailey witness box you revealed what many people would consider the rather disreputable side of your private life at the time. Was that a difficult period for you?

Very. It was very disagreeable. Being in the witness box and speaking on oath is a salutary experience, and it was very painful for my family. The only consolation was that I didn't attempt to lie. My private life isn't all it might be, but it would only make it worse to lie about it.

Do you resent the way that dukes and duchesses are public property in the sense that they are thought to be accountable to the nation – in much the same way as the royal family are under constant scrutiny?

I don't know that we are; we don't count any more. As I say, we're regarded as freaks, and we're totally marginalised now.

Infidelity has been the breaking point of a great many marriages and yet yours seems so very stable and solid. To what do you owe its success, do you think?

I'm not sure that's a fair question. You're going too deeply into my private life. The essential ingredient of marriage is tolerance, but I really can't go any further than that.

Do you believe that men are not naturally monogamous and that perhaps too much significance is given to one or other partner straying from the path?

Those marriages where neither partner has been unfaithful are relatively few and astonishingly lucky.

I think it would be fair to say that the Cavendish line has had something of a reputation of philandering, right back to the first duke in the seventeenth century. Is this something you would prefer not to be the case, or is it more a badge of honour?

It is certainly not a badge of honour. Philandering is nothing to be proud of; it's a weakness.

Have you yourself repented?

I find repentance very difficult, particularly if you are aware that you may do the same thing again … one has to be very careful of repentance.

Do you think the Establishment is under serious threat and if so, are you dismayed by that?

I don't know what the Establishment is, but I'm certainly not part of it. I don't think it exists any more. In this country the civil service has much more power than the politicians. I was never more than a middle-ranking minister but it was enough to know just how powerful the civil servants are. I long for someone to define to me what the Establishment is. Is there a group of people in this country who can fix things? I don't know.

Do you think that politicians today are less powerful than they once were?

The economic conditions prevailing in the country limit the power of the politicians. If the Labour Party had got in at the last election, and it is a great pity they didn't,

Black Wednesday would have happened just the same. I have my own views on political matters but the downside of privilege is that there are great constraints on what you may speak about. If I were to express my views on the Welfare State, for example, people would say, 'How dare he?' and they'd be quite right to say that. When I was on the opposition front bench I was number two to Peter Carrington and foreign affairs, and after about eighteen months I was moved to transport which was rather absurd because I must have been the only member of the House of Lords who couldn't drive. But transport was the only thing which a duke could speak about. Privilege prohibits you from commenting on a vast swathe of national issues.

Are you a religious man?

I can't make up my mind. I can't believe in another world, although I shall certainly go to hell if there is one. The Sermon on the Mount is absolutely right, as are Christian values; I have no doubt about that; but I envy those with real faith.

Would you consider yourself to have been a good man?

No, I'm afraid not. Even with money I'm not really a generous man. I only give to charity what I can afford, and not enough to affect my standard of living. The truly generous man gives a sacrifice of himself. I've never done that.

Does death worry you?

No. I don't look forward to it. Wonderful things have happened to me in my life; I've had too much good fortune. It's time my son had his turn. When I was young I used to like casinos, fast women and God knows what; now my idea of heaven, apart from being at Chatsworth, is to sit in the hall of Brooke's having China tea. I can't think of a greater pleasure than that ... that's what comes of being old.

Lord Donaldson QC

John Donaldson was born in 1920 and educated at Charterhouse and Trinity College, Cambridge. After being commissioned in the Royal Signals, he was called to the Bar in 1946, becoming a QC in 1961. From 1966 to 1979 he was a judge of the High Court, and from 1971 to 1974 he was president of the National Industrial Relations Court, often upsetting the trade unions. He was the presiding judge in several high-profile cases, including the Maguires, the Guildford Four and the Bridgewater Three. In 1982 he became Master of the Rolls, an office which he held for ten years. He was made a life peer in 1988, the year he refused to prevent newspapers from publishing the controversial *Spycatcher* memoir, in direct opposition to the government, who wanted the book banned. He died in 2005.

The typical caricature of a judge is of a rather pompous and unapproachable character. You obviously don't fit into that category ... have you felt rather set apart from most of your colleagues in that regard?

It's a complete myth that judges are like that. I'm not saying that there isn't the odd judge of whom that might be said, but in general it certainly isn't true. And in so far as I'm not pompous, I don't feel set apart.

Your education and background – Charterhouse and Trinity, Cambridge – are, however, rather typical for a High Court judge. Is it a good thing, do you think, that you were in the traditional mould?

You have to go back to that period when most of the jobs, not only in the law but elsewhere, were held by people who came from public schools and Oxbridge. It wasn't that there was anything special about the judiciary. Today it is very different; it would be quite wrong to think that the current judiciary comes from public schools and Oxbridge. This has to do with an evolving society in which there are much wider opportunities than existed in pre-war times.

In 1984 you said that one thing lawyers are trained to do is to know their prejudices and their preconceptions and to isolate themselves from them. How would you identify your own prejudices and preconceptions?

[Laughter.] I don't actually keep a check list of prejudices and preconceptions. The context is everything. Suppose, for example, you believe that in the shipping world there are certain nationalities which are more suspect than others, you still have to approach each individual from that nation on the basis that he is honest until the contrary is proved.

Do you think you have succeeded in standing back from these prejudices in your own professional life?

The answer to that must be yes, but if I hadn't succeeded I'm not sure I would be conscious of the fact. As a barrister, however, you are trained to be objective, it's in the interest of your client that you should be objective, and when you go on to the bench you're merely continuing the objectivity. As a barrister you sometimes have to act for someone whom you regard as a most objectionable character, but you just have to ignore your dislike. When you are a judge it's the same thing – you just put it on one side.

You once said that you have always regarded the law as a benevolent force in our complex society. Have you ever had reason to take the opposite view – also a common perception – that the law is an ass?

Individual laws perhaps, but the law as a whole, no. It's much misunderstood, notably by the media, but I don't regard it as an ass at all. There are of course people who litigate in circumstances where the costs grossly exceed what's at stake. One of the things that most irritates me is when litigants tell me that there is a point of principle involved. I've only ever known one man who litigated as a matter of principle and that was one of the McWhirter twins. He himself probably had only a marginal personal interest but he thought that the point was of general importance, and significantly he was proved right.

You first rose to fame – or perhaps notoriety – at the time of the ill-fated National Industrial Relations Court [1972–4]. Rightly or wrongly you were seen as a political appointment, and a number of Labour MPs signed a motion calling for your dismissal on grounds of political bias. How did you cope with being in the firing line?

The fact that I was irremovable made the whole thing so much easier. The pressures from various segments of society were absolutely enormous, but it would all have been much more difficult if I could have been removed. If somebody is standing on the edge of a cliff and there is a gale blowing, his difficulty is knowing to what extent he can lean forward into the gale without falling over the edge. If you know that you are planted firmly you don't have to bother. Of course, I'd rather not have had those numbers of people objecting, particularly when it was on entirely false grounds. You must remember that I was well aware at the time that much of the comment being made about the way I was carrying on the job had nothing to do with how I was performing; it was a political campaign. One irritation which I suffered was a story which ran and ran that I had been a Conservative parliamentary candidate. It was totally untrue. I believe the originator of the story was somebody who should have known better, namely Lord Jenkins of Putney. What he was actually referring to was an election for the Croydon Burgh Council in which I was a ratepayer candidate. I agree that ratepayers were Conservatives, but in those days they called themselves ratepayers because they were purely local politicians and didn't wish to have anything to do with national politics.

You took the unusual step of defending yourself against the charge of political bias at the time ... were you absolutely confident that you could be free of such bias?

I can't remember doing so ... but if you tell me I did I suppose I must have done. There was certainly no question of political bias; what we were there to do was to try and smooth the course of industrial relations, and in many ways we were quite successful actually. It was an interesting world in which nothing was as it appeared to the public at all. We had excellent relations with the unions, subject to the proviso that we never revealed that we were talking to the unions. The unions, while perfectly reasonable in talking to us, remained free to be totally unreasonable in public. It has been a feature of trade-union life – certainly in my experience – that they operate on two levels. People may regard that as dishonest or reprehensible; I actually don't, because unions have been brought up to do this and that's fine by me. As long as you understand the system then it works perfectly well.

In 1972 you spoke to the High Court Journalists' Association and made a most colourful remark in defence of the charge of political bias which has followed you around ever since. You said: 'My attitude towards political life is much the same as that of a monk towards sex – nostalgic memories of youthful indiscretion, a frank acknowledgement of its attractions, and an unshakeable conviction that I could do better than those engaged in it.' What puzzles me is this: granted that we allow the monk a bit of sexual experience, albeit in the past, it is surely not unreasonable to assume that during his sexually active period he might have developed certain preferences for one thing rather than another, and that these might remain with him, even if at a purely imaginative and notional level. In other words, your own politically active life, albeit in the past, might continue to influence you later opinions and judgements …

What the remark was really meant to reflect was that during the 1930s I was an active Conservative politician, not in the sense of being a member of the House of Commons, but in my capacity as chairman of the Federation of University Conservative and Unionist Associations. I was secretary of the Cambridge Union and if I had been asked at that stage about my future career I would have said I wanted to be to be a Conservative politician and then prime minister. It was partly with that in mind that I became a member of the Croydon County Burgh Council, but it became perfectly apparent to me as time went on that as a junior barrister it was impossible to have a political career. It was like sitting on a three-legged stool, one leg being family, another politics and another the Bar, and it was quite clear that one leg was going to give way. So beyond being active in the Inns of Court Conservative Association and similar organisations I did nothing about it. By the time I took silk I had become a good deal less enchanted with the political life. I once heard a member of the Commons, a Conservative politician, talking complete rubbish in Croydon, and that made me question whether the career was a sensible one. It certainly mitigated my enthusiasm. When it became quite apparent that as a silk I couldn't do it, I became more and more non-political. My philosophy at that time would certainly have been much more on the Conservative or Liberal wing of the spectrum than on the Socialist wing, and I think that is probably still true, except that New Labour seems to have caught up. But it never occurs to me now to be party political; I'm a cross-bench peer and that's not out of loyalty to my past profession – it's my actual philosophy.

Would you agree, however, with the public perception that most judges are conservative in both senses … to what extent is it reasonable to expect them to overcome their natural leanings in court?

It's probably true to say that most judges are conservative with a small c, but one thing which is not sufficiently appreciated is that when the heads of divisions and the Lord Chancellor meet to discuss what name should be put forward to the Queen, the political views of the judge are never discussed.

The law, or the complex workings of the law, is often perceived to be remote from ordinary people and sometimes unavailable to them. Is this something which worries you?

Yes, indeed. The remoteness takes two forms. First of all there's limited access, and secondly there's the fact that the law has its technicalities, for most of which there's a good reason. It's very difficult to get rid of these technicalities or explain them in terms which would make sense to the general public. To say it's a public-relations problem is perhaps misleading, but it is an education problem. There's also the business of costs which are absolutely formidable. I don't think that in general it is the fault of the lawyers, since it has become vastly more expensive to run a practice nowadays. If you decreed that no solicitor was allowed to make a profit, I don't believe that costs would come down all that much because such a very high proportion of solicitor's fees represents pure expense. What we've really got to do is to try and find systems which render the skills of a lawyer unnecessary. We also have to see if we can't develop systems for dealing with disputes which are simpler and are perhaps taken outside the ordinary mainstream of the courts.

On the question of legal costs, it's surely the case that some illustrious QCs today demand fees like film stars ... do you think that's justifiable?

Well, it's a market, isn't it? I also wonder just how much they do actually earn. For example, I remember once when the question was raised about having subscriptions to the Bar Council put on a voluntary basis, I thought it would be a very good idea to ask members of the Bar to declare what their incomes were and to pay one pound per thousand. I thought the Bar would make a large sum of money because everybody would be very happy to exaggerate their income, but that wasn't the case at all.

You were one of England's youngest high-court judges at the age of forty-five. Did you feel that as an awesome responsibility?

Not on grounds of age. I don't think that people are conscious of the age of judges, and in any case I'd had an army career, I'd been a junior barrister, I'd been a QC – it was a natural progression. I was lucky in that a vacancy occurred which I was thought suitable to fill, but it didn't bother me at all that I was young.

In 1974, after a Labour victory, you spent some years in the wilderness until Mrs Thatcher sent you to the Court of Appeal in 1979. Three years later she appointed you Master of the Rolls. Setting aside the merits of your own case, do you think it is actually healthy that these appointments should be political? Doesn't that make them open to abuse, or at least to the charge of abuse?

Obviously, they are open to the charge of abuse. I've no idea whether or not my appointment to the Court of Appeal was on political grounds – I'm not privy to that. We'll have to wait until you and I are both dead before any documentation emerges about that. I do know there's a popular belief that that was the case. As I said to you, however, in the discussions to which I was privy, politics just didn't enter into it at all; they were as irrelevant as the colour of the judge's hair. Yet the charge persists. There are some who think that it would be a good idea to have a judicial appointments commission in order to get rid of the charge. One of the troubles is that a judicial appointments commission is also open to the charge of being political. And there are real difficulties if you start revealing the considerations which go towards appointments.

You succeeded Lord Denning as Master of the Rolls ... was that a particularly hard act to follow?

Yes, quite impossible. One of the first things I had to do was to make it clear that I wasn't Lord Denning, the second thing was to make clear that I was not Lord Denning mark II.

When you took up the appointment you immediately introduced changes to speed up the hearing of cases. In fact, your ability to dispose of cases became quite legendary. This led some clients and barristers to believe they were getting a less than fair hearing. How would you respond to that?

That was never the case. The plain fact is that in many cases when you first read the papers you can form a pretty accurate view as to what the answer is. The one vital thing is that you must always be prepared to change your mind, and I was. I once said, with only slight exaggeration that the art of being a presiding judge in the Court of Appeal was to ensure that you never heard arguments from more than one side; the trick was to know which side.

You seem to be defending yourself against criticism by saying that as long as the right answer is arrived at, there is no harm in taking short cuts. But surely the point is that by speeding up the process and cutting short the argument, the right answer may not be arrived at.

Obviously, that's a risk you've got to guard against. It's true I have always been conscious of the fact that in trial work you get a barrister who bangs on and on and eventually you tell him that he's made that point three times already, and suddenly, perhaps because he slightly alters the way he puts it, you become aware that he has in fact got a point. That has always worried me a little bit, because if I had succeeded in shutting him up I wouldn't have understood it. The answer is, you're not infallible.

When English law comes under attack, the normal defence is that even if it doesn't always establish the truth, it tries to be fair. But over the years we have discovered that the big trials of the 1970s and 1980s were not fair. Surely this is a serious indictment of the system.

I don't want to talk about the 1970s trial, because I was the presiding judge at two of them. It would be quite wrong for me to discuss them. What I would say is this: in every one of these cases the problem was one of evidence which has subsequently been found to be not what it appeared to be at the time. That is certainly not an indictment of the judges, and I don't think it's an indictment of the juries either. A case has to be tried on the basis of the evidence as it is presented to the court. The crown counsel in a criminal case is not there to get a conviction, he's there to present the prosecution case, and if anything comes to his knowledge which casts doubt on the prosecution case, he's under a duty to either bring it out himself or hand it over to the defence. The defence on the other hand is there to get the man off within professional limits which are well known. There is a major difference between the two roles.

But shouldn't we be much more tough on police evidence than we've been before?

Who is it who has to be more tough on police evidence? It is the jury that decides under our system, and a judge would be stepping outside his role if he said to the jury, look, you ought not to believe the superintendent. All that a judge can and should do is to advise them to weigh up the evidence. I've certainly said on many occasions to juries that the accused goes into the witness box in exactly the same position as a police officer: either may be telling the truth or not be telling the truth. It's a great mistake to think that judges have suddenly woken up to the fact that there are bent policemen; we've known this for years.

Let me put it this way, shouldn't the public prosecutor be more vigilant about police evidence?

Obviously, it's desirable that he should be as vigilant as possible. But when you suggest to me that he should be more vigilant I honestly don't know to what extent he is vigilant at the moment, so it would not be fair for me to suggest that he should be more vigilant.

In the tricky area of miscarriages of justices your own record is rather worrying, because in 1976 you were responsible for sentencing the Guildford Four and the MacGuires. Do these cases still haunt you?

Not in the least.

Why is that? It was surely wrong to sentence them?

I said I didn't want to discuss those cases. It would be quite wrong of me.

All right, we won't discuss them, but they were innocent men, were they not?

Well, this is where we get into difficulties. The plain fact is that the courts are not in the business of deciding whether people are innocent; they're in the business of deciding whether people are guilty. These are not two sides of a single coin. If you had something like a swingometer where the vertical position is the truth, you're going to be to one side of vertical or the other in a significant number of cases, human fallibility being what it is. What the courts have done traditionally for a couple of centuries is – rather than to aim at the truth – to aim in favour of acquittal to a degree where we are reasonably satisfied that no innocent man will be convicted, bar the exceptional case. Now it follows from this that if on appeal a man is found not guilty it means that the needle hasn't gone far enough towards the truth point to justify convicting him. The media always say that when somebody is acquitted, or if a conviction is quashed, that a man's innocence has been established. Well, that just simply isn't true. There are exceptional cases where that could be said, where, for example, a man put forward an alibi defence which wasn't accepted by the jury and at a subsequent stage it was shown by unimpeachable evidence to be a watertight alibi. Then it could be said that he was innocent of the charge against him, but that is a very rare event.

If I might just take this a little further ... Sir John May who enquired into the trial of the MacGuires in 1990 suggested that you seriously misunderstood and mishandled critical evidence during the trial. He said, 'The conduct of the trial can be validly challenged on at least two counts.' How do you respond to that?

There are two responses. One is that I don't think that such a comment was within his terms of reference. Secondly, I don't agree with it. He's entitled to his view, but I think he's wrong.

You declined to give evidence to Sir John May's enquiry ... why was that?

My recollection is that I didn't decline to give evidence; what I said was that I thought that it was wrong for a trial judge to say anything other than that which was contained in the transcripts. One of the features of a criminal trial is that only communication between the judge and the jury is in open court. It is the jury who convict, and find the man guilty, and it would be wrong for the trial judge to say anything afterwards other than that which he said at the time.

Are you saying that a judge does not have much influence over a jury?

I think he has influence to secure an acquittal; I don't think he has influence to secure a conviction. As I've said it is extremely important that the innocent shall be acquitted, even if some of the guilty are acquitted as well. I have done a very considerable body of criminal work, and never in that time was anybody ever convicted whom I wouldn't have been quite happy to convict. There were also a very large number of cases in which I was totally satisfied that the accused was guilty and yet the jury acquitted. The whole thing is stacked, and rightly stacked, in favour of the accused.

Robert Kee said of you: 'He does his best to be dispassionate, but he cannot see his unconscious prejudice in favour of prosecution.' How do you respond to that?

If I cannot see my unconscious prejudice, it's difficult to know how I can comment on it. He's entitled to his view. I'm very glad he thinks I do my best.

But what is puzzling, and really rather worrying, is that in your case you have something of a reputation for not leaning towards the establishment, for not necessarily going for the obvious solution, and yet terrible mistakes happen ...

What terrible mistakes?

For example, when people are sent to prison and after about eighteen years they're suddenly released ...

Well, mistakes will happen, it's a fallible system. You're obviously talking about the Bridgewater case, and as I've said, neither judges nor juries can do other than try cases on the evidence presented to them. Of what I've heard of the Bridgewater case, that's precisely what happened. What worries me is that members of the juries who convicted in these so-called miscarriages of justice cases may feel that they have a responsibility for what happened. I don't think they do, because they did their job, and they did it to the best of their ability. They have nothing to blame themselves for.

Shouldn't the prosecutors bear a heavy responsibility for the number of wrongful prosecutions? I mean, either evidence was improperly obtained or faked, as in the case of the late Patrick Malloy, the fourth Bridgewater man, or details which might have helped the defence were withheld ... Shouldn't the prosecutors be accountable as they would be in any other profession?

Accountable to whom? The plain fact is that if individuals don't do their job properly they don't get employed again. It's different with judges and barristers, but they are immune for a very good reason. If they could be challenged there would never be any finality in litigation. The losing party would probably start an action against his or her counsel and enthusiastic litigants would make sure that the process went on for ever.

Is there perhaps a more general problem built into our legal system? Since we have an adversarial system, have you ever been worried that in some cases the truth will not necessarily prevail because victory is sometimes merely a function of successful argument?

I think I've only once or twice thought an advocate so good that I really had to be a bit careful about accepting his arguments. But in general, adversarial justice is probably the best possible system.

But would you accept that there may be a small percentage of cases won or lost through advocacy, rather than the prevailing of truth?

There are perhaps one or two cases that are lost through bad advocacy, but I'm not sure that cases are won by good advocacy. The theory is much exaggerated if it's true at all.

After the appeal of the Birmingham Six, Lord Denning said on television that public confidence in the law was more important than one or two people being wrongfully convicted ... what was your reaction to that remark?

It was an unfortunate remark.

Lord Denning also said that Chris Mullin had done a great disservice to British justice. Many people believe that Lord Denning ought to have been publicly condemned and brought to account for that remark. Do you?

I don't know about the remark, but I do think there is a problem with programmes like *Rough Justice* and their newspaper equivalents, because they only present one side, and the great British public assumes that there is no other side. I don't criticise journalists for not going into it objectively – they don't have the facilities to do it – but what that means is that you then get two systems of justice, trial by media and trial by the courts; and that is bad for the courts. I really would be much happier if investigative journalists would reach their conclusions and then pass them on to the appropriate authorities rather than making them public. That would serve the interests of justice, just as much as what they're doing at the moment. Of course, it wouldn't serve the interests of newspapers, and that's the problem.

Is that why you intervened when the Daily Mail *accused the five men of the murder of Stephen Lawrence?*

Yes. There could be nothing more directly designed to destroy confidence in our legal system than for the *Daily Mail* to denounce the five men as murderers and suggest that therefore the system of justice had failed. In truth, of course, the *Daily Mail* may or may not have been right that they were responsible for the killing of the Lawrence boy, but as I said, the system is designed not to establish that fact but to establish whether we were all so sure that they could be properly convicted. The fact was that on the available evidence, the court was not satisfied. It's not then the business of the *Daily Mail* to say that they were satisfied that the men were murderers. They could have done no greater disservice to our system of justice, but the public at large don't understand this.

Some years ago, I interviewed Hugh Callaghan, one of the Birmingham Six, and that put the enormity of miscarriages of justice in a very human context. It's difficult not to feel a sense of shame and humility in the face of an innocent man's life having being largely destroyed. Aren't we all demeaned by such a tragedy?

No, certainly not demeaned. Human justice is fallible. We have in every case to examine what went wrong and the degree to which it went wrong, and then we have to try and see how the system can be improved.

How do you view people like Robert Kee, Ludovic Kennedy and Chris Mullin and more recently Paul Foot? Have they been thorns in the flesh of the legal system?

They are not thorns in the flesh. They are pursuing campaigns; whether they are as objective as one would like is a matter for argument. I suppose it can be said that they do good when where eventually convictions are quashed, but some things they say go a good deal further than are fully justified.

But if it does some good in the end …

But it's also doing harm in the sense that it is destroying confidence in the system. The assumption the public make is that if people complain enough then they must be right, and that isn't true. If the system rejects the claims, then the public feel that there are innocent people in jail, which may also not be true.

Looking back on your career, do you have any regrets about anything – things you might have done differently?

We will always make mistakes, and I will give you an example of a case where I certainly got it wrong. In the Industrial Relations Court with the Midlands coldstore dockers, they were defying the court and it seemed to me to be perfectly clear that if we imposed a small fine they would go round to the pub and have a whip round and laugh all the way to court to pay their fine. If we imposed a large fine which would seem disproportionate if they were individuals (which of course they weren't because there was an enormous organisation behind them) they would all claim that they were being oppressed by the size of the fine. Since I thought this was all perfectly obvious to everybody, I decided the only answer was to imprison them. That turned out to be an error of judgement. What I should have done was to impose a small fine, let them have their laugh at the incompetence of the judge, and then put them inside because the public would have understood. It was really an error of presentation, not of justice.

You have had a long and happy marriage, ahead of its time perhaps in the sense that your wife had her own independent professional life, and you were sometimes in the Denis Thatcher role. Did you mind that?

Not in the least, though I think it would have been more difficult if I hadn't had my own role in life. Of course Denis Thatcher had his role but it wasn't a public role. We never felt competitive because we were operating in totally different fields. My wife would certainly have been very unhappy not to have had an independent role once the children were of an age where they could be left. Of course in the early days of their growing up she devoted herself full time to them. We both think there are enormous stresses and strains in families where the children are young and both partners are working full time. It may be necessary, but it certainly is not an ideal situation.

Are you a religious man?

I don't know if that really has much to do with my professional career. The public does not have a legitimate interest in one's personal beliefs.

I just wondered if you think it necessary or desirable for our judges to be religious, to be seen to live a good life?

Well, they're two quite different things. You can live a good life without being religious ... as it happens I'm not actually religious, but I believe in the values of Christianity.

SIR KENNETH DOVER

Kenneth Dover was one of the foremost classical scholars of his generation. He was born in 1920 and educated at St Paul's School and Balliol College, Oxford. During the Second World War he served with the Royal Artillery and was mentioned in despatches. From 1948 to 1955 he was a fellow and tutor at Balliol College and from 1955 to 1976 he was Professor of Greek at the University of St Andrews. From 1976 to 1986 he was president of Corpus Christi College, Oxford. His many publications include *Greek Homosexuality* (1978) and *The Greeks* (1980), which led to the BBC TV series of the same name. From 1978 to 1981 he was president of the British Academy, and from 1981 to 2005 he was chancellor of the University of St Andrews. His controversial autobiography, *Marginal Comment*, was published in 1994. He died in 2010.

You suggest in your autobiography that your choice of Greek offered you an escape from the tensions and frustrations of life at home and at school. What was it about classics – as opposed to any other discipline – which you felt could offer you this security?

There is an element of chance in it being classics. If one is unhappy at home, any kind of activity that fully engages one's mind is a self-rewarding escape. I happened to be precocious in the sense of being able to read very early in life and having a strong appetite for learning, but my first line of escape was into the study of insects, and until the age of twelve I hoped to be an entomologist. Then I started Greek and got hooked on language, but even then my interest was much more what you might call scientific, essentially *wissenschaftlich*, rather than any kind of aesthetic response, which came only later. My school rather pushed me away from science and in the direction of classics, simply because my natural talents, such as they were, seemed to lie in language. By the time I went to university, I would have hoped to have a degree in linguistics, but this option was not open to me. Looking back on it now I am very glad because I've had such immense enjoyment out of studying the ancient world. And if I were asked now what my field really is, I'd be tempted to say Greek behaviour – social, moral, sexual and political – and I would count language and literature as an area of human behaviour.

Most people fail to recognise the relevance of classics to the modern world. Do you feel absolutely confident about defending its abiding significance?

I'd hate to defend it with some of the arguments which are used in its defence. For example, it is sometimes put out that learning Latin and Greek makes one think logically; in fact, what one acquires through the study of language is not logic, but sensitive antennae – a very different matter. And if one is looking for the sort of advantages to be obtained from solving the problem of translating from one language to another, then I suspect that more might be gained from studying Chinese or Japanese than by studying Latin and Greek. My own attraction is to the culture of the Greeks, because I so enormously admire their literary skill. And I've no doubt whatever about the utility of studying another culture; it shakes one's own presuppositions, and this is immensely valuable.

In an address to the Classical Association in 1976 you said: 'Language engages me intellec-tually more than any other kind of human interaction. And this more than anything else is what stands between the classicist and the general public.' Have you had any interest in engaging the attention of the general public, or is the study of classics too elitist an activity?

I'm never worried about elitism, or indeed any word ending in –ism. It's true that the general temper of the age is rather hostile to linguistic difficulty. There are all kinds of reasons for that and I suspect the main one is that by now there is such an enormous range of interesting and rewarding activities which depend not on natural language but on artificial language; by which I mean mathematical and scientific symbols and the operation of those symbols. And this tends to make people rather impatient with the study of natural language.

Your father was by your account a difficult man. Looking back now, do you understand him better than you did?

Yes, but of course understanding doesn't necessarily make one like something better. One famous saying that I don't actually believe to be true is *tout compren-dre, c'est tout pardonner*, because it sometimes happens that when you understand something better you are less inclined to forgive it.

Do you feel either the need or obligation to forgive him?

I'm not really worried about commendation or forgiveness, because I never wanted revenge on my father or to hurt him; I just wanted him not to be there, because it made life so tense and uncomfortable. Besides, it wouldn't actually mean anything now to say yes, I still condemn him, or no, I now forgive him. It wouldn't make me remember the unpleasant things about my childhood any differently.

Since you could not change your parents or your circumstances, you embarked on the deliberate business of changing yourself, and indeed you claim some success in the matter. Are you convinced that this is a feasible exercise and available to most people?

I've no idea about its availability to other people, and my feeling for many years that I had deliberately changed myself was probably exaggerated, in the sense that one changes at that age quite a bit anyway. What I believed to be a large element of deliberate planning was possibly much more caused by external things. But people do rather tend to feel that whatever goes wrong with them is externally caused and that they can't very well sit down and plan how they're going to react to things; but to a certain extent they can.

You have been very frank about what you regarded as a physical deformity, your funnel chest, and how it distressed you as a youngster. Was it something that continued to weigh on your mind? And did it affect the course of your life, do you think?

Yes, because I've never lost the sense of inferiority. Of course, I'm talking about a feeling, rather than a rational thought, and if I were looking back on a process of rational thinking, then of course it might be possible for me to say, yes, I was mistaken. But if I'm looking back on the feeling caused by this awareness of deformity, I'm not at all surprised that I felt as I did. For I have never shed that sense of basic inferiority in shape to other people, and to this day I don't take off my shirt in public. I don't go swimming in the sea unless it's a deserted beach.

Your autobiography seems remarkable for the degree of reliance you place on intellect and intellection. Do you think there is any place for human feeling, for tradition, for instinct?

Well, there's any amount of room for feeling. One reaction to my book which rather surprised me was that of one of my former colleagues in Corpus. He described me as an evil man, because I was cold and calculating. I can laugh that one off easily enough because calculation is an ingredient of all purposeful action, and without calculation one gets things wrong, except by remarkable good luck. After all, what is the alternative to calculation? Impulsiveness, thoughtlessness what should one call it? A lot of the time, I would certainly regard calculation as equivalent to rational thinking, but then to say that I don't have feelings, I don't have emotions, seems to me quite absurd. I have strong feelings, strong emotions, and I think about what the consequences would be in acting upon them; that's a different activity. Calculation, reasoning, intellect – these things are to do with means, not ends; the choice of ends, this does seem to me an emotional matter.

You say that you prefer 'nasty truths to silly lies', and to that end you have aimed at complete candour in your book. Have you had any cause since publication to doubt this approach?

No. Undoubtedly I have upset some people, but not many compared to the much larger number who have expressed very strong approval of my inclination to tell nasty truths. There are only two people whom I like and respect and whom I would have liked to please, who disapproved of the book, I'm sorry to find myself on the other side from them, but overwhelmingly the line I've taken seems to be approved of by the people whose approval I would have wanted.

The problem with candour is surely that it affects and sometimes distresses other people. Are you not persuaded that there is a place for reticence in an autobiography?

I have been very careful not to say things which would have an adverse effect on anyone who is still alive. And there are a very great number of things, amusing sometimes, interesting sometimes, which I could have said about living people, but which I have refrained from saying. When it comes to people who are dead, it may be distressing for those who liked them or perhaps loved them, to learn things they'd rather not have known. But there the harsh duty of the historians comes in; and I so feel a strong compulsion to tell the truth about the dead, who will not after all themselves be hurt or disadvantaged by what I say. There are a couple of cases in the book where I have refrained from saying things about people who are now dead out of consideration for their surviving family, but only two. On the whole, in cases of doubt, I have preferred to tell the truth.

Do you ever feel that others might be tempted to regard it less as truth-telling than revenge?

God, no. Oddly enough, there are remarkably few people I've ever disliked. I've had some enemies, but they decided to make themselves my enemies; I have not made enemies of them, and I've never wanted revenge. I don't think any-body has hurt me badly enough for me to want to hurt them in return, or to feel that I would enjoy hurting them in return, but perhaps I've just been very lucky. This doesn't apply to things one hears or reads of, where some totally innocent person has been grotesquely harmed. On their behalf, naturally, I would very much like to harm the harmer; but I haven't been in the position of victim myself.

But what about those people who are no longer in a position to dispute your version of events?

This is true of all historical characters. Alexander the Great or Cromwell or Queen Victoria are not in a position to dispute anything we say about them. Once somebody's dead, whether it is yesterday or a thousand years ago, it makes no difference. If one were to refrain from writing about a person because he's not in a position to defend himself, this would rule out history entirely. Of course, when one is writing about one's feelings or intentions or thoughts, the reader can have no control at all over whether one is telling the truth or not. There's simply no way of knowing, but this is true of all autobiographies, and something one has to accept from the start.

Your TV series on the Greeks seems to have been a great personal disappointment, and fell far short of what you had hoped for. Was it principally because you failed to spread the word of the Greeks to a popular audience, or was it more complex than that?

It was a lot more complex, and looking back now it is arguable that the whole concept was a mistake, because I'm not an art historian, I'm not an archaeologist, and it was a hell of a problem right from the start to get across the kind of thing I wanted to get across via popular use of the visual media. I also disagreed with the producer's approach as to how it should be done, and it certainly was a considerable disappointment to me when it appeared. It was also a shattering disappointment to Alasdair Milne, and the book I wrote to go with it didn't sell at all well. I had rather hoped that the programmes would serve the purpose of interesting a wide public in the Greek world, and create a favourable climate of opinion so that people wouldn't say to their children who were wondering what to do at university: 'Oh, don't bother about that, classics is dull.' But there it is ...

Both your parents were irreconcilably hostile to your religion – your father called Christianity 'God-slobber'. You say that your own position on religion was arrived at separately, but it is difficult to imagine that your parents had no influence in this ...

They were very different sorts of influence. My mother had a poor opinion of any kind of ritual ceremonial, and she took a pretty distant attitude to church services, and never went to church for that reason. But I myself came very much under the influence of evangelical friends at school and that lasted about seven years, and then I switched to being irreligious, or even anti-religious. Then I had a bit of a tacking back towards religion in my late thirties, until I had what I called a mystical experience in reverse, a sort of voice from the sky saying, 'You don't need a god' – which is just the same as happened to A. J. P. Taylor at a much earlier age. Since then I've never been tempted to be religious. I'm enormously interested in religion, and I look upon it as a way in which a lot of people express things that matter to them very much. I also find the history of religion absorbing, but I just don't actually believe it's true; which is a different matter.

But do you think, for example, that if you had been born into a Roman Catholic household and steeped in the creed and dogma of the church, you would still have arrived at an anti-clerical position?

Well, to judge by many of my friends who have had exactly that life, yes. I know many ex-Catholics, people brought up from birth as Catholics, who have now become very anti-religious. So it could perfectly well have happened to me.

But what exactly is the nature of your objection? After all, even if believers are wrong, most of them will mean well. So what is the problem … is it an intellectual objection or a moral one?

Mainly intellectual, in the sense that belief is something that happens to me when the evidence or the reasons for belief reach a certain critical point, so to speak. In the case of religious propositions, there aren't any in my experience which have pushed me into belief; I simply do not think that I have adequate reasons for believing. I'm not an atheist; I don't consider that it is reasonable to say there is no God, but I don't think it is reasonable to say that there is a God either. I am a genuine agnostic. And if I can have recourse to the Greeks at this point, there's a peculiarly interesting work by Protagoras, a contemporary of Socrates, of which – alas – only the first sentence survives. The work is entitled *On the Gods*, and he started off by saying, 'I don't know whether there are gods or not, or if there are, what they are like; the problem is too difficult and life is too short.' How he went on, we don't know, but that is a fifth-century-BC statement of the position with which I have some sympathy.

Is there nothing whatsoever to be said for what are called the comforts of religion? What alternative is there other than a brutal stoicism?

I have no doubt whatever that religion brings enormous comfort to a great many people, but to compare the consequences of a belief with the truth of a belief does seem to me a major confusion. You can derive any degree of assurance, confidence, comfort, call it what you like, from holding a totally untrue belief and how firmly you hold it; whether it's true or not doesn't come into it. I don't go around trying to stop people being comforted by their religion. I merely say, if they ask me, that I don't share the belief, and therefore I don't derive comfort.

This mystical experience you had in which you described the heavens opening and a voice declaring you had no need of a god ... I understand the difficulty in communicating such an experience to others, but what gives it precedence over those experiences of others which point, as it were, in a different direction, i.e. to the existence of God?

There is an important difference between Alan Taylor's experience of a voice saying, there is no God, and my own saying, I had no need of a god. It is possible to have theology without being religious. Epicurus was a case in point. He did not deny the existence of gods, indeed he believed they existed. But he argued there was nothing we could conceivably do or say or think which would affect or influence them, and they had no part whatever in intervening in human life. So there you have a belief in the existence of gods coupled with a strong assertion that they don't need us and we don't need them. I did not, however, have Epicurus in mind when I had that experience.

But do you have any attitudes or principles which are in some sense a philosophical alternative to religion? I mean something sustaining and convincing which would seem to you an adequate background to life's vicissitudes?

I have a very strong sense of being an individual in a social species. We are in an interesting predicament since every one of us is simultaneously a competing individual and a social unit with a need for love and acceptance and so on, but of course no two of us are quite alike in our needs. If you take a graph of a human population and at one end you put the most selfish, aggressive, hostile, psychopathic people, and at the other end the most compassionate, generous, affectionate and caring people, it will be a normal graph, since most of us are somewhere round the middle. The important point in morality is to start off by recognising our need for acceptance and love, and if this is going to be meaningless to a few people, then too bad. It's going to be constantly overwhelmingly meaningful to a few others, and that's the way it is. I have no difficulty whatever in imagining, and indeed in making a minute contribution towards creating, the kind of human society that I want to exist, the kind of society where we can rely on one another.

You are obviously a man who is much moved by nature and the beauty of the countryside. And yet in your response to beautiful places, such as Wester Ross, there is nothing which remotely approaches pantheism, nothing of the Wordsworth idea of 'a sense sublime / Of something far more deeply interfused'. Why is that, do you think?

I think it's almost hopeless to try to explain why one likes what one likes. This is true not only in terms of the natural world, but also in the arts. I mean, how can one explain preferences for particular works of art or particular poems? One just has to start off by recognising what it is that one responds to and accepting that.

You describe an occasion in 1944 when you were so struck by the beauty on the top of a hill south of Mignano, that you sat down on a log and masturbated, something which you described as 'the appropriate response'. Would you say it was principally an aesthetic response, or was it more biological, or what?

Goodness knows, goodness knows. All I know now is that it wasn't unique, because since my book appeared I've heard of other people having very similar experiences. It seemed to strike one reviewer as something very odd indeed, but it is not as odd as all that.

You are remarkably frank in your discussion of sex, which has obviously played an extremely important and happy part in your married life. You describe the orgasm as 'the purest and the most powerful of all the good emotional experiences available to mankind'. In another context, the context of religious experiences, you say that feelings of conviction tell us much about the person who experiences them but nothing about their truth-value. Would you agree it is difficult to assess the truth-value of your statement on the orgasm?

Oh yes, quite impossible. What I've said there about the orgasm was meant to be slightly jocular, and I was talking more about adolescence. It's not a considered opinion on a scale of values in 1995.

Is there anything about sex that might shock you?

Yes. False promises. Or deception. I mean, a man claiming he is wearing a condom when he's not – things like that. Perhaps I should have said rape before I said deception, but I was rather taking rape for granted. One must distinguish between aesthetic distaste and moral repugnance; they're not the same thing at all. There are quite a number of possible sexual goings-on which I find aesthetically surprising, and sometimes repugnant. I recall a novel by William Boyd in which a couple use honey as a genital lubricant, which sounds just incredibly messy; things like that are aesthetically repugnant but not necessarily morally so. To have moral significance they have to come into a category of actions which would also be morally objectionable even if they were not sexual; and that's why I include force, violence, deception, false promises, because those are ways of behaving which cover the non-sexual as well as the sexual; but it's in the sexual sphere that they are particularly brutal.

During a brief spell of impotence your thoughts turned to suicide. Looking back, does this not seem to have been an overreaction?

Well, perhaps it was. But so what? I mean, that's how I felt, and I told the truth about how I felt. It was of course the product of ignorance because I thought once one started being impotent, that was it.

But supposing that it had been permanent. I mean, is impotence such a terrible thing as to warrant suicide?

How does one decide whether something is such a terrible thing or not? I described the feeling I had, and I felt it made life not worth living. There's nothing to be said for old age, absolutely nothing. One becomes weaker, one's eyesight deteriorates, one's hearing deteriorates, one can't walk as far as one did, one becomes impotent and so on. What is there to be said for old age?

A kind of serenity, some might say ...

No, no, I don't think so. I'm serene only as long as I'm physically in good shape. I'm still waiting to be told by somebody of my age or older in what way it is better to be old than to be young.

Going back to suicide, it is something you have contemplated more than once, as did your father before you. Is it possible to make up a sound intellectual case for taking one's life, or is one always emotionally driven?

So far as I know, one is emotionally driven. Plainly there are cases where one could take an intellectual decision; suppose, for example, that I knew for sure that I was getting Alzheimer's disease, or that I was at the start of some kind of condition which would impose nothing but distress on my family, I think that would be a good sound reason, a product of thinking. Otherwise contemplating suicide is perhaps almost invariably an overemotional reaction.

What was the principal constraint on a suicide attempt? Was it lack of courage, or the thought of your wife or children, or what?

All those things enter into it, but I suppose it was not so much lack of courage as lack of conviction, by which I mean just not feeling strongly enough that there was no other way out. After all, it's the one decision you can't reverse, and although I was telling the truth when I said there had been occasions when I had seriously thought about it, quite obviously the conviction that it was the only escape had not been anything like strong enough.

You say in your book that you have never experienced what could properly be called grief at anybody's death. This might be regarded as almost an emotional failing or impairment. Do you see it like that, or do you regard it as a strength?

I don't know if it's either really. One thing I should say is that I do regret making the remark in 1994 because it hadn't been true for some years. The first time I felt something like grief on the death of a friend was in 1984. But it is generally true that although I react very strongly to other people's suffering, for some reason or other I don't react in the same way to death. I can't be sorry for somebody who's dead, because they're not there any longer and they're not suffering. I can be tortured by people suffering, but not in any comparable degree grieved by their death.

Were you disappointed that your autobiography was rejected for publication by Oxford University Press, especially in view of your long association with Oxford?

I had never taken it for granted that they would necessarily want to publish it. The reason I submitted it to them is that years ago I had promised them first refusal, and I was just keeping a promise.

Why do you think they rejected it?

That's for them to say, but I think one thing that must have entered into it was the feeling that I was quite wrong in my chapter about Oxford and my chapter about Trevor Aston, and also wrong to reveal what were generally regarded as confidential matters from inside college. I gathered third or fourth hand that there was a feeling that it gave an unfavourable picture of Oxford. I don't agree. In fact I don't think I've been uncomplimentary about Oxford in any unreasonable way in the book at all. And I'm not altogether in sympathy with OUP's attitude to confidentiality which, after all, is not something which is laid down by God or by nature. A thing is confidential if somebody has decided to make it so, and I think excessive confidentiality, and secrecy do far more harm than good. The one principle I observed, both in the chapter on the university and in the chapter on Trevor Aston, was not to reveal anything derogatory that could be attributed to a living individual.

You seem rather surprised by the fact that response to your book concentrated on what you called 'the Aston affair', and your confession to having had murderous thoughts towards your colleague at Corpus Christi College. Do you think you were perhaps naïve in not anticipating this response?

Even if I was I couldn't have acted differently. The Aston business mattered so much to me in the ten years I was at Corpus, and any historian has to pick on the things which in his view really made the difference. The reason I was surprised by the fuss was that a number of people had read the typescript and had written to me about various points of interest in it. Not one of them had picked on the Aston chapter as objectionable, and it was only after the fuss was started in *The Guardian* that it all blew up. The one place where I may have made a mistake, though I'm not totally convinced of it, was the actual wording I used when I said something like 'the practical problem was how to kill him without getting into trouble'. Brian Harrison in Corpus, who was very helpful in reading part of the typescript, thought it was expressed in too brutal a way. My daughter also rather took against it, not because she was shocked at my wanting Aston to die, but because she thought the way I put it was self-indulgent. She knows that I'm fairly guarded in my expression of emotion, and she thought this went over the top. So I can't say I wasn't warned, but on the other hand, I can't help feeling that whatever one contemplates doing, one should translate into real terms and face the consequences. If I was saying to myself in effect, as indeed I was, can I possibly create a situation in which there is no more Trevor Aston, then I ought to say it outright. How could I bring about a situation in which he was dead is a very long-winded way of saying, how could I kill him? That was why I kept the words.

Yes, but those words will have shocked and appalled a great many people …

I also know a number of people who were not shocked or appalled, particularly people who were, or had been, responsible for colleges, universities, departments, institutions and the like.

In defending your position vis-à-vis Aston, you rather appealed to the Greeks who would always have been more concerned about the harm or benefit to the community in general than the individual. Would you allow that there are dangers in applying Socratic law in the twentieth century, even if it is confined to the cloisters of an Oxford college?

I'm in a difficult position here because if I'm going to defend myself against some of the criticisms to which I've been subjected, it becomes terribly long-winded and I don't want to get into the position of saying, ah, but you see … What I've said in the chapter about my dealings with Aston is only a sample. The real catalogue would be a great deal longer. One of my critics wrote to *The Times* saying that if

Aston had been given the support he needed by his colleagues, this tragic outcome could have been avoided. I pointed out in reply that Aston had had any amount of support from his colleagues for over twenty years and for eight of those years he's had a great deal of help and support from me, and indeed he told me that he always felt better after talking with me. But there came a point eventually when it obviously wasn't doing any good, and that was when I felt my responsibilities for the wellbeing of the college were looming rather large.

Dr Thomas Charles-Edwards, tutor in modern history at Corpus, disputed your account of Aston and said: 'Dover was the sort of person to derive intellectual interest from ana-lysing Aston's predicament. It doesn't surprise me that he consulted a lawyer to judge the consequences of any action. Dover seemed to have no need for emotions and little time for those who did.' How do you react to that kind of criticism?

I don't understand how he can say that I had no room for emotion when I had an overriding emotional need to serve the interests of the college.

James Howard-Johnston, another fellow at Corpus, wrote: 'I found the moral stance of the author quite abhorrent. The welfare of the institution should not be prized above life.' Did this sort of reaction give you pause?

No, because I went on being patient and tolerant and supportive for eight years, but there comes a point when you have to write somebody off. That's my feeling, and to say that you can't prize the wellbeing of an institution above an individual life is just not true as far as I'm concerned. Certainly, one has to go on trying for years to reconcile the two interests, but when it becomes clear that it's not going to work, at that point I will sacrifice the individual. The extraordinary thing is that it was my emotional commitment to the wellbeing of the college which made me act as I did. If I had been all that calculating I wouldn't have bothered about it, because I knew I was retiring in ten months' time. The fact was, I wanted to hand over a good college to my successor.

But your behaviour was surely open to misunderstanding. I mean, there seems to be an almost clinical detachment in your account of the Aston affair and particularly your reaction to Aston's suicide. You write, 'I got up from a long sound sleep, I can't say for sure if the sun was shining, but I certainly felt it was.' That degree of disengagement is quite chilling …

The *Times'* leader used the word gloating. Now that seemed to me an extraordinary word to use of the feeling one has when one is relieved of a heavy burden. It was the lifting of a weight that had been there for years; that's what I felt, and I can't believe that I was wrong to feel that. If it had been a matter of revenge or vindictiveness, then gloating would have been an appropriate word; but that's precisely what it wasn't. The other thing is that people like Thomas Charles-Edwards and James Howard-Johnston honestly believed they knew Trevor better than I knew him, and I think they were wrong. Not only was I a friend of Trevor's for eight years but I was also in many respects his confidant. He told me a lot about himself that I don't think they knew, and for them to talk as if they really knew his virtues and I didn't was not accurate. I think I knew him better.

Although you conceded afterwards that you were not claiming the right to execute Aston, you said that you do not have reverence for human life per se *in this instance. What is the force of* per se *in this instance?*

At all costs. I was contrasting my own feelings as a non-pacifist with the belief of pacifists that it is always wrong deliberately to cause somebody's death in any circumstances. I don't have this feeling of reverence for life as such – perhaps I should have said 'as such' rather than *per se*. I don't have a feeling it is always necessarily the worst thing one can do to cause somebody to die. I plainly didn't have a 'right' to cause his death – and I wouldn't for a moment claim that – partly because I don't actually think one has rights other than those which one is specifically given. I have rights under the law, but the law does not give me the right to cause the death of a colleague, I'm absolutely sure about that. But then there are occasions when one does things without having the right to do them because one decides it is a good thing to do.

You were president of the British Academy when Anthony Blunt's treachery was revealed. Would it be fair to say that your writing to Blunt was instrumental in bringing about his resignation?

It was instrumental in the sense that it must have had some cause and effect, but I didn't exactly demand his resignation. There were people – the late E. H. Carr was one of them – who thought I had pushed Blunt into resigning, and Carr wanted me to circulate to fellows of the Academy a copy of our correspondence. I couldn't in fact do that because I had written to Blunt in longhand and I hadn't kept a copy, but I told Carr if he wanted to see it, he could ask Blunt and I had no objection whatever. What mattered more was that after I had written to Blunt and asked him if he would consider the possibility of healing the wound in the Academy by resigning, we had a telephone conversation in which I emphasised to him that there was no way I could put pressure on him, that a president of the Academy cannot tell someone to resign; his danger had passed, he'd not been expelled, so he was absolutely free to decide whether to resign or not. We discussed this in a perfectly amicable way, but there was no transcript of that telephone conversation which I could send to Carr or to anyone else; yet to me it was that which mattered much more than the letter.

A. J. P. Taylor resigned in protest at what he called a 'witch hunt'. He felt that the BA should not concern itself with matters other than academic. Did you have any sympathy with this view?

As a matter of fact I did. Although my first reaction to the news of Blunt's treachery was very hostile, the more I looked at the legal side of it in terms of the charter of the British Academy, the more difficult it seemed to be to justify expelling Blunt. And if we had simply reacted with horror and said we won't have this man around, we'll expel him, that would have been lynching and not law. By the time it came to the discussion at the AGM, if I had been put in the awful predicament of giving a casting vote, I would have cast against expulsion simply on legal grounds. But there was of course another line that could be taken, which was that Blunt had damaged the whole international community by serving the interests of a totalitarian government under which historical and scientific work was not free. The extraordinary thing was that at the two meetings of the council of the Academy at which the Blunt case was exhaustively discussed, that point was not raised. I agonised over whether I should raise it from the chair, but I was very anxious not to lean on anyone as chairman. Indeed, this crucial point was not made until after Blunt had resigned and the whole fuss had subsided, where a piece in *Encounter* put the issue of Blunt having served the interests of a totalitarian government hostile to the study of history. But until then even Blunt's most ferocious enemies had not raised the matter.

What sort of man was he? Did you like him?

He wasn't a terribly easy man to know, I must say. There was something guarded about him, which I think was probably accounted for by his homosexuality and the fact that he'd belonged to a generation which had treated homosexuality as an enemy. But I got on with him well. I never had any reason to dislike him.

At around the same time there were various stresses and strains in your life, notably the dilemma of whether or not to embark on adulterous affairs. Have you ever regretted not allowing yourself that indulgence?

No, no. Oh no, I was right to pass it over.

Once again, when talking about the possibility of infidelity, the case for and against it is argued in the cold light of reason. I would have thought that this was precisely an area in which reason played very little part, and that to pretend otherwise is to be disingenuous.

But one has to make a decision. I mean, is one going to go ahead or not? How does one make the choice? If it's not reason, what is it?

If there had been no risk of being found out, would you perhaps have gone ahead?

That's getting into an unreal world, to imagine that one can embark on any course of action which one can conceal forever. I wouldn't even contemplate that because I don't believe it's particularly sensible to do anything that one wouldn't want revealed. Supposing it had been certain that nobody would ever find out about it ... that to me is an imaginary world, and I tend to stick to the real world. It's also a moral issue, not in the sense that I believe fornication is necessarily wrong, but I wasn't willing to hurt my wife, and that makes it a moral issue.

Do you think that your own moral sense has been shaped in any measure by the Greeks and the study of classics?

It may have been shaped in certain ways, possibly more than I know, but more probably it is the other way around; that I'm particularly attracted to Greek culture and civilisation because they echo inclinations of my own. For example, this business of not having a reverence for human life – that's certainly true of the Greeks because they were tremendous users of capital punishment and they executed people for all kinds of things. If you served on a jury and took a bribe, then you were for the chop, because they regarded the integrity of the jury system as vitally important to the life of the community.

Your book on Greek homosexuality was punished in 1978 to general acclaim. Do you think it is possible to have a perfect understanding of homosexuality, Greek or otherwise, without being a homosexual oneself?

Possibly not, Greek homosexuality fascinated me because it was such an immensely important ingredient of Greek culture. I also thought that virtually everything that had been said about it or written on the subject was nonsense. There was a complete failure to understand how in the Greek culture the attitude towards the active and the passive partner can be radically contradictory, even irreconcilable. It was common to find people writing about Greeks as perverts, using nouns for which there was no Greek equivalent, when in point of fact the essential division in Greek society was between the adult male penetrator and the female or imma-ture male who are grouped together as the object of penetration. This is really what got me interested in it. Curiously enough I'm not wildly in sympathy with homosexuals on a purely emotional level. Aesthetically I feel a certain revulsion at the idea of kissing a man, but I don't think that marred my historical investigation of the phenomenon.

During your time as professor of Greek at St Andrews, you were a great defender of aca-demic standards and there was a suggestion that after you left in 1976 those standards rather declined. What view do you take now? Is the battle lost?

You're probably thinking of courses in classical civilisation and culture, of which I was a very strong advocate at first-year level. What worries me really is the con-tinuation of that way of studying things beyond the first year, even perhaps up to honours level which does happen in some universities. Although it undoubtedly brings good people in, whose primary interest perhaps is medieval history, art history, English literature and so on, my own feeling is that if you are studying another culture at a level which is called honours in a university, it doesn't deserve the name honours unless it includes a knowledge of the language of that culture. It's as simple as that.

You have been chancellor at St Andrews since 1981. And you are the first chancellor of St Andrews who is not a duke, a peer or an archbishop. Is that a source of pride?

Yes, it is, but I'm not the first in Scotland of course, because Alec Cairncross at Glasgow is a former professor, as I am, and Kenneth Alexander at Aberdeen is another one since me. So it's become comparatively fashionable now.

At the age of fifteen you coined the dictum: 'Instinct is the force that makes us repeat our mistakes.' Have you tried to resist your instincts throughout your life?

I've never trusted them, but I've been interested to observe them. I accept my instincts as a fact, but I don't attach value to something because it is an instinct. I'm sceptical of instincts in the same way I'm sceptical of the beneficence of nature. Civilisation consists in combating nature, and I take the view that what we inherit in the way of instinctive or genetically determined responses is not to be worshipped just because it's natural; it needs to be scrutinised rather carefully.

You say that in recent years you have been repeatedly struck by the wisdom of some of Plato's observations on society, notably that devotion to justice can be truly assessed only by one's behaviour towards those who are weaker than oneself and in one's power. You suggest that this is equally applicable to politics and sex. Looking round modern society, do you think there is any evidence that this principle is alive and well?

I'm not sure that any good principles are alive and well at any stage in human history, but fortunately they do survive from one generation to another.

You say that you have searched for aspects of old age which might compensate for its ills but have found none. Is there no sense of a job well done or a life well lived?

I have a great deal to be pleased about, but I think that at any given stage in life I have adequate reason to feel that. I don't necessarily feel it more now looking back over a longer period than I would have felt it, let us say, at forty-five or fifty looking back over a shorter period.

Your doctor once assured you that one can never with any degree of confidence say, 'That was my last fuck.' Has this at least given you continuing and abiding grounds for optimism and happiness?

One can't of course be wildly optimistic. I remember seeing a very amusing graph which showed there are a number of men who are still sexually active at eighty-five, but it's a very small number indeed.

You have compared death to the returning of a book to the stack. Are you completely unsentimental in contemplation of your own death?

I think so, yes. I regret it in the sense that I'm always writing something and I want to finish it, and I feel aggrieved at the idea that it is going to be cut short by my dying at some point. But I don't fear death. Hell may be real; I'd be very surprised if it were, but all the same, one doesn't know. But then one's not knowing, indeed the impossibility of knowing, I feel to be so complete, that it's not worth worrying about.

SIR DENIS FORMAN

Denis Forman was born in Scotland in 1917 and educated at Loretto and Pembroke College, Cambridge. During the war he served with the Argyll and Sutherland Highlanders, being wounded at Cassino in 1944. His war experiences were recounted in *To Reason Why*, which appeared in 1991. After the war he began producing films for the Central Office of Information and in 1948 he became a director of the British Film Institute. He was the inspiration behind the establishment of the National Film Theatre before joining Granada Television in 1964. His book, *Persona Granada* (1997), charts the history of Granada Television, of which he was chairman from 1974 to 1987. His interest in music culminated in his deputy chairmanship of the Royal Opera House and in his books, *Mozart's Piano Concertos* (1971), *The Good Opera Guide* (1994) and *The Good Wagner Guide* (2000). He died in 2013.

In your reminiscences you describe how two people inhabited the one person. One was perplexed and often unhappy, the other was extrovert and charming. Do these two people still coexist?

Over the years they've become familiar with each other and although they haven't moulded into one person, they are much less dissimilar than they used to be in the early days.

You grew up in a prosperous Scottish family with all the trappings of the upper class – nannies, under-nurses, afternoon tea, servant halls, and so on, yet you never really felt comfortable ...

No, I was not happy with the upstairs life. The top part of the house in which I grew up was the nursery, and there were eight children, six brothers and sisters and two adopted, and they made up one community, one culture. On the ground floors were the grown-ups, people who were remote and a bit pompous, people we didn't really know very well, and below that were the servants. These three cultures coexisted, but my favourite culture was the servants; I preferred them to the noisy nursery and the posh middle floor.

Did that remain the case as you grew older?

I've always had a strong prejudice against well-bred, aristocratic people. It takes a lot for me to get over the fact that a man's been to Eton. I really have to struggle to like a man who has been to Eton. That has stayed with me all my life, and the upper-class accent is something that sets my teeth on edge, and when I hear the royals speak I have to close my ears.

Do you think you were born with an innate sense of independence, as it were? The struc-tures of your upbringing were so firm it's difficult to see how you could have questioned them and rejected them so completely without a strong freedom of spirit …

It was more that I refused to accept any convention, any received wisdom, or indeed any view if I had not convinced myself that it was sane and sensible. This came about by reading. My father, who had been a clerk in holy orders, had a huge library of theology and amongst this was an encyclopaedia of ethics. I found in my reading that most of the Christian ethics were actually remnants of tribal beliefs which had been going on for thousands and thousands of years. If the tribal beliefs were no longer thought to be valid, I couldn't see why the hell Christianity should still be thought to be valid, and I was very firm on this from an early age, from about twelve or thirteen. I found that the Christian religion was unacceptable.

Did this apply to all religions?

It was particularly the self-confident religions, including the whole of Islam, which I found unacceptable. And because I grew up with Christianity, and people were always praying or talking about God or giving you a lecture, Christianity was on the doorstep all the time, and that made it worse. Hinduism and Buddhism seemed more tolerant, more agreeable, and I loved the Greek myths. I thought they had the right way to treat gods – that was the proper place for them.

Looking back, do you feel grateful that you had something to rebel against?

I suppose it served a purpose. It made me self-reliant and you also have to have a great deal of stamina and courage, if you're going to rebel and stick to it, because you make yourself exceedingly unpopular. Nobody likes a rebel who contradicts their deepest and most dearly held beliefs. I mean, I loved my mother and father, I loved my brothers and sisters, and to offend them so deeply was not easy, but it seemed to me I had to do it.

Were you the only rebellious member of the family?

I was the first, but one by one they dropped off the perch. By the time they were mature people there was perhaps only one out of the eight who still believed in God. It wasn't particularly my influence – they were sensible people and they came to their own conclusions.

In many ways you rebelled against the things you also loved best. Was it painful to you that you couldn't enjoy the circumstances of your childhood – the countryside, the privileges – without the evocation of class which they entailed?

Actually, I had a great capacity for enjoyment, especially with the servants and my brothers and sisters. My deep disquiet with the upper class didn't in any way inhibit me from having a happy childhood. I just cut myself off from the nonsense that was going on upstairs.

So did you in fact enjoy the privileges of your upbringing?

I took them for granted; all children do. I knew there were poor people, but I absolutely never questioned the fact that we had a lot of cars and ponies and servants. That was just the life we led.

It struck me when reading your memoirs that many people would have given anything to have the advantages of your childhood, not just in material terms but in the sense of it not being banal. At least your parents discussed the nature of sin, the problem of evil ... in other words, it can't have been dull. Have you thought of it in that way?

Yes. One of the great advantages of being brought up in our household was the constant debate on every topic – music, poetry, literature. My grandmother in particular was a great taster of new novels. She read all the brilliant new novels that came out, although every now and then she would reject one because the characters were too disreputable. Music was always a subject which was very close to everyone's interest, and of course religion was always being debated. I didn't care for that so much, but the debate itself was good fun. All my life I have enjoyed debate, even though I'm very often arguing a case I don't really feel very strongly.

Your feeling of being different from those in the outside world was developed fairly early on. Has this sense of being different from others continued throughout your life?

There are of course different ways of being different. The fact that I am a Scotsman born and bred has given me a particular view of the English whom I still see as a foreign race. I have worked with Jews a lot in my life, and I see them as a race for whom I have more affection and with whom I have more affinity than the English. I have never been able to tolerate the top-class English very easily. During my upbringing I formed a very close association with working people, and I still feel that they are the basic human ingredient in life, those people who worked on the farm in Dumfriesshire. Subconsciously, I think I measure important people, rich people, clever people, against that inbred feeling that the farm workers really were the guys I liked.

You say you sometimes felt ashamed for not liking your father better, especially when everyone else thought him such a decent chap. Why did he disappoint you so much?

That is a very fundamental question about fathers and sons. He was a decent chap, but he was also unconscious of the fact that he was treating his wife as if she were a second-class person. He behaved towards his family as if he were the major general and they were all private soldiers, and he treated the outside world very often as would a public relations man. He was extremely good at ingratiating himself with certain kinds of visitors, churchmen, for example, and within his own orbit he was very well thought of. In my home town even today, they speak of my father with great affection. But there was a very firm code of conduct which you could not break.

What sort of father would you have chosen for yourself?

I think I would have chosen a more open-minded and better educated father. I would have liked a father who was prepared to discuss and debate on equal terms with me, not simply hand down received wisdom and tell me it was true. There was no interplay, only commands from on high. One of the awful things, of course, is sending children to boarding school, a terrible thing to do. It emphasises the fact that father and mother are home, but you have to leave and get educated. I don't like that.

You described attendance at the United Free Church as the greatest penance of the week. Why do you think you reacted so much against it when for most children it was a normal part of growing up in Scotland?

Two reasons. One was that I'm very susceptible to boredom; I can't stand being bored, and I bore very easily. I regard it as the greatest penance in life. I've done a great deal to enquire into what makes a bore, because I find it a very interesting and underdeveloped study. The other reason was that what the minister said in his sermon was such rubbish, and he said it with such unction and with such certainty that I found it deeply offensive. But I couldn't tell him. I just had to sit there and take it.

Your atheism caused quite a stir in the family. Have you ever had doubts about your atheism, if I can put it that way?

Never, no. It's the foundation of my belief and thought. One of the great regrets for mankind is the delusion of religion; it's done so much harm, it's caused so many wars, so much hardship, so much intolerance. Even today one of the greatest threats is Islam. Many of the religions are running out of steam, which is good, and of course even though people get married in church and bury their fathers in the church graveyard, their actual faith is very weak. They pretend, but there is a lot of hypocrisy.

Do you think as you grow older you might change your mind about religion?

No, I don't. I'm completely comfortable with the thought of dying, although one always hopes for a fairly peaceful and orderly exit. I mean, I have seen rabbits die, I have seen horses die, and I've seen men die; I think they cease to exist, and that's it. It is a very deep human instinct to try and pretend there's an afterlife, because it's consoling and people don't like to think they're going to be rubbed out. But they will; they will be rubbed out completely.

Was your lack of belief just another kind of challenge to your parents or was it a separate thing?

I think it was self-generated. I used to count all these messiahs who preceded Jesus Christ – there were seventeen of them – and I used to look at the incidence of virgin birth in other religions, and also crucifixion – the rarest of the lot – but nevertheless it was there. All the great phenomena of the Christian religion which are treated with such enormous respect are duplicated in other religions. People want it that way, therefore they believe in it. I've never been able to understand, for example, why people think God is good, but people want God to be good and so they believe in the goodness of God.

The effect of your lack of faith was quite traumatic for your parents, especially your mother. Did you come to regret that you hadn't pretended to have faith, for her sake?

At the time I was deeply upset, but I felt it was inevitable. Sooner or later you have to come clean on issues that you really don't feel it's right to conceal, and I don't think I regretted telling my parents what I did. Perhaps the way I did it was not very elegant; it certainly took them a long time to come back to having an affection for me. It really wasn't until I was in my early twenties and was wounded that I rediscovered a warmth between my parents and myself. It took ten years.

Is there any way that the Presbyterian ethic has endured, albeit against your will, or have you managed comprehensively to reject it?

Many of the Presbyterian habits have afflicted or assisted me through life. For example, it took me a long time to throw the sexual taboos off. I felt guilty when indulging in any form of sex, and that was due to an upbringing which was extremely prudish, indeed to a degree you simply wouldn't believe. On the positive side, the Presbyterian upbringing gave me a certain degree of stamina in thought. In the Scots kirk you have to argue a thing through, even though it's a ridiculous argument. That probably did assist me in later life to stick to a point of argument. The Presbyterian work ethic has bugged me all my life too; I find it very difficult not to work.

You say that by the age of nine you had reacted against the smugness of pure faith. Are you still reacting against that today?

Well, of course that smug attitude has diminished. It was prevalent in the Church of England, and also in the Church of Scotland – the idea that we ministers are superior people, we are God's chosen people, we are here to tell you how to behave. Today the Church of England is grovelling around to curry favour with pop stars, so it has rather lost its smugness, not to mention its dignity. In my view, it is a little despicable the way they try to snatch whatever public fashion will make them seem up to date.

Do you think that smugness can ever attach itself to agnosticism or atheism?

Yes, it certainly can. You can be very self-righteous as an atheist or an agnostic. I would say that of all the Christian religions, Catholicism is obviously the most intellectually respectable, because a very sound thesis has been built and, provided you have the belief, it can be defended at all points since they've spent centuries working it out. But atheists haven't spent centuries working things out; indeed, every atheist has his own argument and his own beliefs. What I tried to do for several years was to find fellow spirits who could be put together a decent funeral service for non-believers, but it couldn't be done, because there is no basis, there's no common ethic, no common ground. It would be possible to write a funeral service for myself, but no one else is going to use it, or only very few.

You said you got on well with the farm workers – you liked their directness, their strength, their endurance … did you really want to be one of them?

I suppose the short answer is yes, I did. They had a canniness, a sense of humour, a sense of perspective; they were the sort of people I wanted to be. Then I went away to school, which was a very disagreeable wrench, we sold this particular estate, but it was my ambition to buy it back, and until I was wounded I was determined to do so and to reorganise the farm and make it so much better than my father had it. I only gave up the idea because I thought – perhaps wrongly – that I ought to be able to do physically what the other men would be doing. Little did I think that farmers would come to sit in front of a computer for three weeks and then go and shoot partridges in Spain, which is what they do nowadays.

You knew you were different from the upper-class boys but you were also different from the workers – your accent marked you out if nothing else. Where did you feel you belonged exactly?

I was bilingual in so far as I could speak Lallans Scots as well as any of the farm workers – it was a completely different language. When I was with the farm workers I could speak well enough not to be identified as an upper-class person, though sometimes it went wrong. Once when I was with them cutting down a tree by the side of the drive, a car drew up and a chap jumped out and asked me if I could tell him where my father was. I replied in English: 'He's gone to Edinburgh to see an osteopath,' and the farm workers all collapsed with laughter. They started imitating me and thought it the funniest thing. I was so ashamed, but I knew I couldn't have spoken Scots to this guy because he had a bowler hat on.

You talk about the cynicism you developed perhaps as a defence against your upbringing, the idea that you would believe the worst of everyone, not the best. Did you manage to rid yourself of cynicism in later life?

In certain areas I have never been cynical – in the arts, for example. There I've been a total enthusiast, not one of those picky people who've tried to find something wrong all the time. I think my cynicism diminished with adolescence, and as I grew older I began to be an enthusiast about many things, a cynic about some, but only those concerned with class, religion and literature. I've always been leery of pompous people in literature. My cynicism was tempered finally by the army in which I was a wholehearted soldier. I thought, rightly or wrongly, that the war was of critical importance to us, that we really were fighting for our lives and our freedom. That was my motivation, not any affection for military affairs, but once I was in the army I realised there was so much wrong with it that I had to buckle down and try to change it.

In your family there were various euphemisms for bodily functions, and mention of sex was absolutely taboo. Do you think that influenced your attitude later on? What I mean is, if there had been greater openness and honesty, would you have become a different person?

I *know* that I would have become a different person. I was inhibited until I was a mature man by this terrible legacy of prudery. I can't explain why, but they managed to induce shame in anything to do with physical sex, and that association was so powerful and so deeply felt that I found I couldn't shake it off for a very long time, not until I was thirty or forty. With religion one could shake it off quite easily, because it was cerebral, but the idea of sex was absolutely taboo.

Are you saying that until the age of thirty or so you were unable to have a sexual relationship?

Well, one had experiments but one was deeply ashamed of them, which sounds ridiculous now and almost unbelievable, but it's true. One always started to feel uncomfortable, morally uncomfortable. I resented that. I didn't see why I should have the hang-up when a lot of people around me didn't.

You describe the process of divesting yourself of a myth and superstition as a very lonely business. Did you ever lose heart?

No, it wasn't like that. It was a long business and very difficult and complex, but my interest and enthusiasm grew with knowledge. I never felt for one moment downhearted or that it was an impossible task. Sometimes I realised I'd been following the wrong line and that could be frustrating, but the actual fascination of the study itself didn't impose any kind of feeling of irritation. In fact, it was wonderful. This sounds a silly thing, but I felt so proud actually to have done this, with all the people around me not doing it; I had confidence that this was right and never had a shadow of a doubt.

You joined the Argyll and Sutherland Highlanders. In your book about the war you say that an infantry officer had only two options in the Second World War – death or being wounded. Did you know that at the outset?

Not so precisely, but it was a pretty good guess. When you were actually in action, you saw your cadre of officers turn over. It just stared you in the face.

You were wounded at Cassino and lost a leg, something you make light of in your book. Did you actually consider yourself lucky to come out of it alive?

Yes, I did. I got off lightly. In a way there wasn't a worry about death at the time; in fact, one felt almost that death was relief. Blindness was the worst, two limbs pretty bad, one limb, damn lucky.

You had some very complicated feelings about the business of war. Did you ever consider not fighting for your country, or did you see yourself as part of the effort to defeat evil, or what?

Absolutely unequivocally I saw a threat to our way of life. I feared the Nazi regime, and it was real fear. When you saw the power of the Wehrmacht, their organisation, their backup, their efficiency, and compared it to our amateur bunch who were still fighting the 1914–18 war, as it were, it was truly terrifying. I wanted to get in there to do everything I could to reform and rebel against the High Command and try and get some sense into infantry training. That was my main mission.

Did you find it difficult after the war to adapt to civilian life?

No, not a bit. I was sad not to be a farmer, but that didn't last because I enjoyed other things so much. I enjoy nearly everything, and I sometimes wonder whether it's a terrible fault. I had a wonderful time after the war.

What attitude did you adopt to disability?

Well, it sounds silly, but it didn't bother me. It was awkward to get mobile enough to do what I wanted to do, but I instantly realised that certain things were out and I just shut them out of my mind. I was an athlete at Cambridge before the war and that had to go. Also, I could no longer fish in waders or do highland dancing. But you immediately make your equation, decide what you can and can't do.

The gramophone was very influential in your life and encouraged you to study music seriously. Was there something more to music than enjoyment? Did it seem to contain a truth that was lacking in everything else?

Music was always music. I've always regarded music as its own thing, in its own compartment, and I've never drawn any deductions from music to life. I mean, I think of music as an absolute. I know that operas have librettos and stories, but they are of secondary importance. I know that Kurt Weill was a communist, but that is quite separate. Music is enormously important in my life. I can't tell anyone how important it is; it's something I can't put into words.

Why did you pick Mozart to write on? What is it about Mozart that fascinates you?

Music is very hard to talk about, but I regard Mozart as simply the best. In other composers I find great qualities and also considerable flaws, but Mozart's top-class works are for me pretty well perfection, as near perfection as you can get in this world. Mozart was so quick to learn, not like Beethoven, who was slow to learn and very often clumsy. Beethoven stumbled around and is sometimes a bit of a bore, but powerful, immensely powerful.

Are you keen on Wagner?

I have an enormous respect and liking for Wagner, but the minus side of Wagner is so enormous that to do an equation is almost impossible. His political and sexual kinkiness are definitely on the debit side. The basis of his political theory in the *Ring* is simply ghastly, as is the cheap stuff in *Tannhäuser*. The only decent plots are the *Dutchman* and *Meistersinger* which bring out a Wagner acceptable in words and music, but when you get to the *Ring*, what he is saying in words is pretty horrible and also extremely boring. The plus is the most amazing score ever produced, the greatest feat of imagination in the nineteenth century. It's got that power to move which very few possess. There was a performance of *Götterdämmerung* at the Proms in the 1960s and when they finished, the whole of the Albert Hall applauded for twenty minutes. They just didn't stop, so eventually the orchestra left, the conductor left, but the audience went outside and applauded for half an hour in the rain. That's Wagner's power.

You have been a director and deputy chairman of the Royal Opera House, Covent Garden. Are you dismayed by the chaotic state of affairs at the moment?

Yes, I am. I think that the actual financial management is very poor. I don't understand how they could have got into this particularly bad mess. When I was there we had our problems, and you could see ahead the possibility of having fewer assets than outgoings, but we took adequate action and we never had a cash crisis. If you can't pay the wages, you're in bad nick.

Are you optimistic about the future of the Royal Opera House?

Absolutely. Good institutions always survive. We are the most musical country in Europe bar none, and we must have a major opera house. There are enough people who have the influence, the power and the desire to see a great opera house here, and they will see that it happens.

Your latest book, Persona Granada, *charts the history of Granada Television, of which you were a founding member. Would you say that Granada has remained true to its founding principles?*

I don't think anything remains true to its founding principles, including the Catholic Church. All institutions change with time and the idea that there are principles which are immutable is one of those follies of mankind. Once Mrs Thatcher came on the scene, a lot of principles went out of the window. Until her philosophy encroached upon it, television was set up in a way that it was your duty to provide public service programmes, and if you didn't do it you had your licence taken away. When that disappears it becomes a free for all and everything becomes dictated by market forces. I have no regrets as far as Granada goes; it's part of the general sea of change that's taken place over the whole community.

But do you think these changes are for the good?

I don't really believe in better or worse when it comes to changes. I believe that changes are inexorable and you adjust to them. They are absolutely inevitable … the tide comes in and then it goes out.

Well, do you think Mrs Thatcher was right to do what she did?

It was very much against what I would have liked, but it was a tide in human affairs, and she caught that tide. Whether it's Napoleon, or the Pope, what they're doing is riding a movement of what people are thinking, how humanity is changing. Thatcher caught that, and she jumped in the saddle just at the moment when the horse was going to run. I'd like to put a lot down to her, but she was only a pawn really in a much greater movement which I think was inevitable. How many of us now believe in the principles of the Labour government of 1945? I remember passionately believing in them, but pretty well every one of those principles has disappeared. Better or worse, I don't know … principles are as mutable as opinions.

Granada had a reputation for first-class drama programmes right from the start. Why do you think that talented writers and programme makers were particularly drawn to Granada?

The people who ran the company understood writers, we were writers ourselves, or people who were musical, and artists respond to that, they know when they're getting a sympathetic response. They know when the front office are bastards and when they're friends, and we were friends. Simple as that.

Granada made its mark with outside broadcasts. You say at one point in the book that these outside broadcasts would now seem to us grotesquely primitive, and even then they were exceedingly boring. Would you say that today a great deal of news coverage, in its endless repetition and search for new angles, is also very boring, perhaps dangerously so, in the sense of numbing the mind?

Yes, I would. I'm very critical of the present standard of news, which is very low and very poor. There are elements in news that should not be there. Very often the news is simply a list of murders, accidents and rarely, very rarely is there any point beyond a general portfolio of crime and disaster. Crime is popular, but what the hell does it matter if someone is murdered, except to the police and the people directly involved? We make the mistake of regarding rape and murder as news, whereas in fact they are a form of rather salacious entertainment. There's also an awful lot of people's insides, and new genes that have been discovered. I wouldn't say it was unhealthy, but it is again not news. The presentation is also very tedious, two newscasters who have been doing it for fifteen years. Sky News is better than BBC and ITN because they have fresh people, but otherwise it is terribly boring at the moment. They handle big stories fairly well, but all in the same sort of sermonising voice, which is quite wrong now.

Isn't the emphasis sometimes wrong, the coverage disproportionate?

Oh, crazy. But when the country has a fit of hysteria as it did over Diana, or minor hysteria as it had over Louise Woodward, it's very difficult for the news editor to know how far to run with that hysteria. If he doesn't run, he's going to lose ratings, so there's always a professional equation. The equation I favour is that you don't get ratings by talking about people's stomachs the whole time, or by reading a police gazette. News should be fun when it's not serious. The present attitude by those rather boring people who run the news is to give a sort of mock Elgarian trumpet horn arrangement to introduce it. Who the hell wants a fanfare before the news?

Do people have an endless capacity for being bored? And should television recognise that and cater for it?

Boredom is really a fascinating topic. You can suck people into an exceedingly repetitious line of thought which deprives them of the capacity to reject it; that's what boredom is, the couch potato variety. People are deprived of the power to say, oh Christ, let's switch this off. They have somehow been brainwashed and conditioned into keeping that glazed look when something is happening on the screen which they don't really care about at all. That sort of subconscious magnetic attraction doesn't get a lot of ratings, but it will give you a fundament of ratings. People will sit watching without really knowing what the hell they're watching.

Broadcasting, like publishing, used to be headed by giants, larger than life people who were supremely individual and often autocratic. For example, as you say in your book, Sidney Bernstein was extremely litigious, and given to rages, so that people were afraid to go against him. Is there room for a Sidney Bernstein or a Lew Grade in today's very different industry?

No, it's changed. Now you have enormous giants out of sight. Rupert Murdoch or Conrad Black – they're not hands-on giants, they are giants who work in the background secretly and manipulate their staff and pull the strings. Another reason is that broadcasting and publishing are now businesses, and they are run by people who are more accountants than impresarios. I was brought up in the impresario age, but the age of the impresario is over. What you get now is a committee looking at a proposal and a businessman saying, 'It's only going to deliver 4 per cent of profit.' Once again, I don't challenge change; it happens.

Your relationship with Sidney Bernstein did not always run smoothly. You had different origins and backgrounds – Sidney being the son of a Jewish immigrant tailor. Did that ever get in the way?

Absolutely not. I liked that Jewish, continental culture to which he belonged. Lew Grande had it too. I found them wonderfully quick people to work for, down to earth and very often funny. The Jewish sense of humour is wonderful. The differences between Sidney and me were those of two stags on the same hill; I was doing something that he had done before, and he did not really like to see the younger generation taking over. I think it was as simple as that; I felt that at the time, and I still feel that. If Sidney and I had not been working in the same company we would have been very close friends, as we were before I started working, and as we were at the end. But we had our problems in the middle, because he resented what I did very much, and I resented his interference. He was a perfect pain in the arse.

Your comments about John Birt have received quite a bit of attention. After giving an account of how he squandered money on programmes which were never made, you rather damn him with faint praise … you seem very unimpressed by him.

Yes, I'm not impressed by John Birt. I think he is a nice man, and he has a certain ability, but both he and his employers have enormously overestimated that ability. The BBC is not a happy place, and it's no good defending the license fee and having all these wonderful new schemes if the place is unhappy and if the basis for making programmes is not a good one. The whole purpose of administration is to give the programme people a chance and to hell with everything else. They have to have enough money, they have to have a firm base, but this idea of accountability right, left and centre in everything is hopeless. Hugh Greene was a great director general and he kept that sort of thing down by force of personality and strength of character. If a minister or an MP criticised Hugh he would put him down by what he said and who he was; he didn't need to keep working away, making friends with people in high places and producing new schemes and so on.

If I can quote from your book: 'Even then John Birt had such a passionate belief in his own intellectual process that he could persuade others he was as clever as he believed himself to be, which was a matter open to some doubt.' Do you think Birt is dangerous as well as deluded?

Not dangerous. I think he's doing absolutely his best by his own lights, but his beliefs are misguided. In an institution like the BBC people are more important than anything else. People should look after other people, and those at the top will pick others as good as themselves so that the pyramid goes down, and at the bottom of the pyramid you have the producers working in a helpful climate. John Birt does not rate that as highly as I would. He wants the system to be right, to be efficient, he will spend hours, days, years trying to make it so, but he will not build the pyramid of people, he will concentrate only on the structures and the forms.

If, as you suggest, he has no talent for the management of people, how does it happen that such a man can be in charge of a creative organisation?

It was a matter of fashion in a way. The BBC had a number of really outstanding personalities as its director general, and then there was a feeling, quite justified, that the spending got out of hand and there was money being wasted on a rather disgraceful scale. It needed tightening up and it needed a director general who would look at the economics. They got one. Meanwhile the poor buggers who struggle away making programmes are desperately unhappy, no question of that.

Of course, John Birt is operating within a very different ethos from the one which charac-terised your days at Granada … this is an era of top-heavy management and accountants – the same has happened in publishing. Is John Birt just a product of the prevailing spirit?

He has adopted the fashion of the outside world, but the terrible thing is that there is no need to do so. You have to make a commercial profit everywhere else, but in the BBC you do not need to do so. As long as you organise your resources, your income and expenditure, you do not have to produce 25 per cent profit on capital or whatever the parameters are in business today; all you have to do is to get the housekeeping organised in such a way as to permit your programme makers to do their very best. My belief always was that if you called in a consultant it meant failure; you had failed to solve the problem which you should have been able to work out for yourself. The consultant will in the end give you something you usually don't want.

Which things, if any, would you say are better on television now?

Variety. Things are being channelled by subject – there are four sports channels, for example, and I think that's good. At almost any time of the day or night you can see first class sport. I like the canalisation of broadcasting. I think the BBC and ITV were very slow to see it come, and they still have hardly caught up with it.

If you were running television now, what would be your guiding principle?

Always to create circumstances to allow talented people to make the best possible programmes – it's as simple as that. To let talent do what it wants with the min-imum of interference.

I was rather surprised to discover that you are an admirer of Rupert Murdoch. What is the basis of this admiration?

Admirer is the wrong word. What I happen to be is a defender of Rupert Murdoch against people who totally malign him. Rupert's responsibility for publishing a lot of the rubbish is criminal, but on the other hand, he's absolutely straight, so when I hear him roundly condemned I always say this. He is reliable, he is honourable, and until recently I would have said he kept his contracts. The other thing is Wapping, which was a very brave thing to do, whether you approved or not. Even though I don't like his publishing policy, I acknowledge that Rupert has done good things.

Isn't it dangerous when too much power rests with one individual?

Yes. And so far every country who has tried to limit it has failed. To me it's a comment on the fallibility of politicians, who are blackmailed into permitting this to happen for fear their own popularity will be impaired.

A recurring theme in your book is your passion for asking awkward questions. Has that got you into a lot of trouble in your life?

It's got me into trouble with governments and sometimes with my superiors, but on the whole I would say it has been a profitable exercise. Asking awkward questions is an extremely important part of negotiating your way through life. If you put diplomatic demeanour ahead of getting results you're a goner. I would do anything not to be bullied by the politician or the editor who usually says something is against the interests of the nation, or if you publish that story the country is going to lose millions of pounds. It's invariably absolute rubbish. The last resort is the Official Secrets Act; people who want to stop a programme always cite the Official Secrets Act. I don't believe there is any security matter today that merits censorship. Northern Ireland, terrorism and the drugs scene require a degree of secrecy, but the idea of national security is total rubbish. There is nothing to be secure about – the Russians always knew more than we did anyway.

Would you say you are a contented man?

Contented with my own lot, but I thrive on discontent. To be critical and constantly searching for improvements is necessary for a fulfilling life. There are angry old men, just as there are angry young men. While I'm not so very angry, I'm still alert to a feeling of things being abused or going wrong. I'm constantly feeling I want to pick up my pen, and though I don't usually do it, there is a mental letter going on most days. I don't feel in the least serene.

BETTY FRIEDAN

Betty Friedan was an American feminist, writer and campaigner for women's rights, considered by many to be the 'mother' of the second wave of modern feminism. Born in Illinois in 1921, she was educated at Smith College. While she was a housewife in New York she wrote *The Feminine Mystique* (1963), which analysed the role of women in American society and eventually sold over three million copies throughout the world. In 1966, she was co-founder and first president of the National Organization for Women, and in 1970 she headed the nationwide Women's Strike for Equality. Her other books included *It Changed My Life* (1976), *The Second Stage* (1981) and *The Fountain of Age* (1993). She became a somewhat controversial figure towards the end of her life after claiming that the success of the American Right was a consequence of the reaction to the younger feminists of the third and fourth waves of the movement. She died in 2006, but her importance has been acknowledged by many of today's feminist writers. Lionel Shriver hailed Friedan as a 'heroine'.

I feel a certain anxiety beginning this interview because I have read that you don't like challenging questions and sometimes threaten to terminate an interview ... is that true?

You've read some obnoxious thing by that woman who came over from *Harpers and Queen* and my experience with her was enough to turn me off British journalism. I agreed to see her because my new book, *The Fountain of Age,* was coming out in England, and she started to barrage me with all these questions about things I said thirty-five years ago in *The Feminine Mystique.* I have a proud record of having helped towards the raised consciousness that led to the women's movement for equality, and I have no apologies to make on that. *The Feminine Mystique* broke through previous obsolete definitions of women that kept us from seeing our real possibilities, and the women's movement is enormously diverse as a result of that. But that woman was supposed to be interviewing me about my new book, *The Fountain of Age,* which she hadn't even read, and I show people the door when they come to interview me without having done their homework.

According to Carol Sarler in the Sunday Times, *you come with a prepared script to deliver. She writes, 'The interruptions Betty Friedan will not tolerate are questions. These are either ignored completely or dismissed with abuse.' How do you react to that?*

I react by wanting to show *you* the door, because that's irrelevant. If you're interviewing me you will get your own impression of me. If you have come expecting me to have a prepared script, then you're wasting your interview with me. That woman wanted to redo old schisms in the women's movement that are irrelevant. I wasn't interested then and I'm not interested now.

The place where you grew up in Illinois is generally regarded as the quintessential cradle of mid-west provincialism. How on earth did you manage to escape from the constraints of such a background?

Because we do, we do. Growing up as a young Jewish girl in Illinois was not a very happy experience. But it made a writer out of me in a way; it made me an observer, and a social scientist, because as a Jew I was on the outside. Then of course I was very bright and I went to a good college, and I didn't go home again.

You said recently, 'My mother was bright, but frustrated because of her limited life. I saw what that did to her husband and children.' What did you mean exactly?

My mother was born in Illinois and went to college there, and then she was the editor of the women's page of the local newspaper, which she loved. But when she married my father and became the wife of a businessman, she could not continue in her career. That was the way it was in America in that era. So she was at home, she had children, she was a perfect hostess, she was everything around the house, she was perfect at all that. But that was not enough to use up her ability and her talent, and I think she was very frustrated. She took it out on us: nothing my father did was ever good enough; nothing the children did was ever good enough. If ever I wonder what made me spend so much of my life on the whole question of women and the women's movement, I think it was because even as a child I was so sharply aware of my mother's frustration, and what it did to the rest of us.

How did your parents rate your success?

My father died when I was twenty-one, but he was very proud of me. I had a brilliant record in college, and he kept newspaper clippings in his safe of the things I wrote. He would have been enormously proud of me if he had lived. My mother buried her third husband at the age of seventy and took up a career; she became a duplicate-bridge manager. She'd always been a brilliant card player, and after her third husband died she got herself a licence and ran duplicate-bridge games in California, and she didn't die until she was ninety. She was a veritable role model for *The Fountain of Age*, though I don't know how much she identified with what I was doing. But I'm sure she was proud of me.

You took a degree in psychology during the war. Was psychology still quite an unusual subject for women to read in those days?

Psychology as we know it now was just beginning to take shape. I had the great luck of being a protégée of a brilliant gestalt psychologist, and I graduated *summa cum laude* and went on a fellowship to Berkeley where I was the first woman and the first student of psychology to win the biggest science fellowship. It would have taken me straight to my PhD but I turned it down. I was going round with a physicist at that time and when he said, 'I'm never going to win a fellowship like that, so we're through,' I was devastated. The whole Freudian psychology was beginning to take hold – what I later called the 'feminine mystique' – and I gave up. The image of feminine fulfilment only through marriage, through motherhood, through sexual fulfilment, was beginning to take shape in the popularisation of Freudian psychology, and I really bought into it, and turned down that fellowship because I didn't want to be brighter than the boys. I came to New York, got a newspaper job, figuring that it would be fun and not the sort of academic job where I would be too bright. Then I got married to a returned G.I. and I had my three kids. I got fired for being pregnant with my second child, and when I went to the union to protest, arguing that no one had ever questioned my ability as a writer, they just said it was my fault for getting pregnant. We didn't have any law then on sex discrimination – we didn't even have a word for it – and anyway I was being made to feel guilty for working in the first place. In that era of Freudian thought it was decreed that if you worked outside the home, you were losing your femininity, and you would undermine your husband's masculinity and neglect your children. So I entered the housewife years and stripped six coats of paint from the stairway banisters and went to auctions and got the house furnished for virtually no money and did car pools for the children, but I couldn't suppress the itch to do something else. So I freelanced for women's magazines, but it was like a secret drinking club in the mornings, because I was the only mommy in the suburb where we lived who was doing any work like that.

How much did your study of psychology help with The Feminine Mystique, *or would you say it was written more from your own experience of life?*

My life came together in that book in the most mysterious way. Certainly my training as a psychologist helped, but the passion of it came from my own experience. It was a combination of my being both journalist and social scientist. Once I understood the image of women that was accepted by everybody in those days had something wrong with it, I got on the trail of the story and did interviews and listened to the real experience of women. A woman was defined solely in terms of her sexual relation to man, as a man's wife, mother, sex object, housewife, server of physical needs, but not ever as a person, defined by her own actions in society. That image which came to us from all the mass media, from television commercials and from the sophisticated psychology textbooks, was so pervasive that it blotted out of consciousness the whole hundred-and-fifty-year struggle for women's rights that ended with winning the vote the year after I was born. There was a noise coming out of these suburbs where women who lived according to this image should have been blissfully happy, and it was a noise of discontent. I took the experience of women seriously when it didn't fit the previous image, and my book *The Feminine Mystique* enabled millions of women to move in new ways.

You once said that The Feminine Mystique *brought you fame but not fortune. Would you rather have had the fortune?*

Oh come, that's not a question. Of course, you would always want to have the fortune. When I consider that the book sold millions and millions of copies and that it is on every list of ten books that have changed history most in the last century, it is ironic that I didn't make a lot of money.

Would you claim to have started the women's movement?

The history books say that *The Feminine Mystique* marked the beginning of the modern women's movement, that it had the critical and catalytic breakthrough effect in consciousness, which is the first stage of any revolution. Interestingly enough, ten years earlier, Simone de Beauvoir's *The Second Sex* did not have that result. It was an enormously depressing book which did not have the galvanising effect of my book.

Are you happy to share the glory with others, such as Marie Stopes, Annie Besant and Virginia Woolf?

Virginia Woolf is a literary icon as far as feminism is concerned, but she didn't start any movement. Marie Stopes had something to do with writing about sex, and though I've heard of Annie Besant, I don't know who she is.

Your book The Second Stage *was greeted by the anti-feminist lobby, certainly in Britain, as a recantation, in so far as it appealed to women to recover their lost femininity. You seem to be angry with this reaction. Were you also surprised by it?*

Of course I was. *The Second Stage* was a necessary step in the evolution of feminism and of feminist thought. I was by no means recanting *The Feminine Mystique* or the women's movement for equality, but I saw a new generation of women using the rights we fought for, entering into careers which were still structured in terms of the lives of the men who in the past had wives to take care of the domestic details. Women were somehow misinterpreting feminism in ways that evaded what I considered part of their identity. In breaking through the feminine mystique which I had done and helped other women to do, that didn't mean and shouldn't have been interpreted to mean that we were going to say no to marriage and motherhood. In other words, don't throw the baby out with the bathwater. To equate feminism with a repudiation of marriage, family, motherhood was a distortion. I thought that needed correcting and that we needed to move on to a second stage of resurrecting work and home, not just for women, but for women and men who inhabit this planet together and who more often than not make homes together and have children together. I was outraged that reactionaries greeted this as a recantation of feminism, and I was even more hurt that some of my sisters tried to attack me as if I was betraying feminism because I said we had to pay attention to these other areas of women's existence.

You have always maintained that the women who are strong and powerful can be a liber-ating source for men. Surely there is evidence to suggest, particularly in the USA, that men often feel threatened by modern women, even to the point of impotence?

Come on, that's a canard. Women who have their own sense of self and security are much freer to love men, and do not demand or play out other destructive agendas in the sexual arena. There is interesting research I cited in *The Feminine Mystique* that showed that the experience of female orgasm increased in rough correlation over the decades of this century to the winning of women's rights. Women used to be considered innately frigid; they were meant to submit to sex but not enjoy it. But women's actual enjoyment of sexual relations with men increased as their own independence and equality in society increased. A study that came out ten years into the women's movement showed that married women and men in America were having sex more often and enjoying it more. In other words, it's simply not true what you say. A castrating woman who can scare a man into impotence is usually a woman seething with frustration.

You have never been a man-hater but have always believed that women and men need each other sexually, socially and emotionally. This must alienate you from large sections of the sisterhood who at best regard men with suspicion. Are you happy to be alienated in this way?

Nobody likes being attacked, but I think I'll go with the judgement of history. I have helped to create a consciousness that broke through the feminine mystique to the personhood of woman, and made possible the massive movement to equality in my own country and other countries. I have continued to keep faith with that larger truth and to try in my professional life, as a university professor, lecturer, teacher, writer, to continue to try to make feminist thought evolve, as my own thought has evolved. I don't think it can ever harden into a fixed doctrine. I am not politically correct. I don't see every form of sexual relationship between women and men as oppressive to women. I don't see pornography as the greatest evil on earth. I am much more concerned with the economic empowerment of women than I am with some of those sexual issues. I am very worried at the moment by the male backlash in America and by the way women are being made scapegoats for the enormous economic insecurity that men are feeling as a result of the job downsizing. I've gone on to apply the lessons I learned from helping to energise the women's movement for equality to the whole question of age, where you see a comparable thing going on. People will buy anything and everything to deny age, but they have to break through the age mystique the way thirty years ago women had to break through the feminine mystique.

What hope is there for the countless women who are still at the mercy of men economically, socially, sexually? What do you say to them?

I don't know that this is the lot any more of the majority of women. In the United States the great majority, even women and young children, are working outside the home and earning. Even if they don't earn in most cases as much as the men, that second pay check is absolutely essential to the family's wellbeing. They are not now completely at the mercy of men, and the younger generation of women doesn't intend to be either. For the women and men in utter poverty, the real underclass, it isn't men who are the enemy, it's the economic circumstances.

You've mentioned pornography ... issues like pornography, abortion, rape and battering have tended to be central to the women's movement and feminist thinking. Do you question their centrality?

Yes, I do. Sexual politics has dominated too much. The real empowerment of women has come from their ability to earn. It is through having equal opportunity and beginning to have a voice in the larger affairs of society that women have become powerful both in the political and economic sphere. A part of this empowerment is control of their own reproductive process: they must have safe legal access, not only to all forms of birth control but also to abortion. It was also a part of the empowerment that women would blow the whistle on wife beating, on assault, on rape, when before they used to be helpless victims. They've even defined the terms of sexual harassment, but what is interesting is that the law that enables women to stand up to this is the law which has to do with equal employment opportunity.

Have you ever felt disadvantaged as a woman?

Of course I have. When I was young I might have gone to law school and gotten into the whole political arena, but Harvard Law School didn't take women. There are lots of fields that I might have enjoyed, but it didn't even occur to me to try because I was a woman. I was fired for being pregnant, and you couldn't go hot for another job with your belly sticking out. Historians put my book among the ten books that have shaped history in the last century, but I'm not nominated for a Pulitzer Prize or Nobel Prize, and that has something to do with the fact that my book has been enormously important to *women*.

Why do you think you have attracted the label of lesbian basher? Do you regard this as an undeserved attack?

Absolutely undeserved. I believe that the dominant thing in the women's movement is the personhood of the woman in all its diversity. I think we should celebrate the differences between women and the differences between women and men; not deny them. But just as I object to women being defined solely in sexual relation to man, I'm certainly not going to accept as a substitute for that a definition of woman solely in terms of sexual relation to other women. That would be just as much of a distortion. I support the right of people to their own kind of sexual expression, as long as it's between consenting adults. But you shouldn't be asking me these stupid questions. They are really not relevant now. I really feel like showing you the door. I really don't want to go on with this, because you're doing the same thing as that stupid woman.

I'm not attacking you. I'm just trying to clarify your position. Let me move on. Your ability to process your own experience and market it as universal truth has invited comparison with Germaine Greer. Would you be pleased by such a comparison?

I don't know what you're talking about. *The Feminine Mystique* was based on interviews with a great many other women. I took their experiences seriously even though it didn't fit the book, and I used my training as a psychologist and a journalist to get the story, to figure out what had happened and why it had happened. In a certain sense I did the same thing with *The Fountain of Age*. Germaine Greer is a completely different type of person. She is a sort of exhibitionist of her own experience. Do you understand what I'm saying? You are trying to make out that I am assuming that my experience is universal. I wrote about the experience of other women that made a chord also with my experience, and it turned out to be universal. You don't understand anything.

I do, I do. You have often professed a need for strong bonds – children, grandchildren, friends … do you feel you are blessed with plenty of strong bonds?

The research I dug into for *The Fountain of Age* indicates that the two most important things for a vital long life are purposes and projects which use your abilities to give complex structure to your days, and bonds of intimacy. Love and work. Freud was wrong about women, but not about everything. Friendship is an enormously important variable in my life.

What about lovers … do they constitute a strong bond?

Those bonds are very precious indeed, but in recent years some men I loved very much have died.

Your marriage ended six years after the publication of The Feminine Mystique. *Was the book instrumental in the marriage break-up?*

I suppose it gave me the strength to go on by myself, which I probably had to do. To get divorced was not an easy thing for me. I was terrified of being alone. But the father of my children and I are friends now. Three or four years ago, as our children married and had children of their own we had a kind of rapprochement, and so that's a strong bond too.

You are quoted as saying, 'I couldn't go on being Joan of Arc for American women and a worm in my marriage.' Does this mean you behaved badly in your marriage?

Well, it depends on what you mean by badly. I'd certainly acquiesced in it, but I couldn't go on taking that sort of treatment in my marriage. It got to be insupportable.

The marriage lasted twenty years and you have three children. Looking back over your life how does that period rate in terms of happiness, or fulfilment?

It's a very rich period of my life. I wouldn't deny that for a minute. I realise that when I see my children now. My sons are wonderful fathers and my daughter is a wonderful mother, and as I see them all now in their nesting years, it brings back to me what a rich texture those years had.

Did you ever consider marrying again?

I thought I wanted to; in fact I still wouldn't absolutely say that I wouldn't be interested in it if something possible came along. I suppose by now I have such a persona that it would probably be a little intimidating for anyone.

Do you ever feel lonely?

Yes. I have a busy life and it's full of people. I have lots of friends and I live my life mostly in public, but I think one always feels lonely if one does not have to share the everyday thing as well as the sexual thing.

How important is sex in a relationship?

One doesn't go around feeling deprived if one isn't having an active sex life, but it is a life force. There's no question about it. Just the loving and being loved, or touching somebody in the most intimate way, and sharing moments. You don't have to love the way you loved when you were thirty but I think that some capacity for this life force is in us … and it's very enjoyable.

There is a tendency to imagine that women who write books about female destiny and who have been at the forefront of the women's movement are very secure in themselves. Is that true in your case, or are you a prey to self-doubt?

When I'm on a wavelength of truth, I don't have doubts about that. But I can have doubts personally. I'm no angel, for God's sake, and I've got a terrible, terrible temper – though people think I've got more mellow in my older years. I still flagellate myself when I've done something wrong or made a mistake or been mean to somebody.

You have had open-heart surgery – more than one operation. How did you cope with ill health and the possibility of not surviving?

I've had asthma off and on all my adult life; otherwise I've been extremely healthy. But a year and a half ago without realising it I developed a very serious infection on the aorta valve of my heart, and by the time I figured out it wasn't an asthma attack, I was in heart failure. I didn't really fear death. I'd just finished *The Fountain of Age*, and I wanted to get the operation over with and get to the book launch. So I was in complete denial, which is not always the worst thing to be.

JOHN KENNETH GALBRAITH

John Kenneth Galbraith was author of the classic work on the 1928 Wall Street Crash, *The Great Crash* (1955). He was born in Ontario in 1908 and was educated at the University of Toronto, the University of California, where he took his PhD, and later as a postgraduate at Cambridge University. He was a research fellow at California for three years until 1934 when he became a tutor at Harvard (1934–9) and then assistant professor of economics at Princeton (1939–42). He went on to be professor of economics at Harvard for over twenty-five years (1949–75), and from 1961 to 1963 he was the US ambassador for India. He has written many books, including *American Capitalism* (1952), *The Affluent Society* (1958), *Ambassador's Journal* (1969) and *The Age of Uncertainty* (1977). He was married for over fifty years and had three sons. He received fifty honorary degrees from academic institutions around the world and was awarded the US Presidential Medal of Freedom in 2000. In 1997 he was made an Officer of the Order of Canada. He died in 2006, aged ninety-seven.

As a child, who influenced you most in your life?

I suppose I was most influenced by my father, who was a public figure of strong local importance in Ontario and very much concerned with local well-being – an official of the township, official of the country, ran a co-operative insurance company, and considered himself responsible for everything that happened in the neighbourhood.

Did you ever consciously feel that you were going to make a great success of your life?

I took it one step at a time.

But you were always ambitious?

Many people think unfortunately so.

You are always referred to as a liberal. What does the term imply in American politics?

The word 'liberal' has a different meaning in the United States from that which it has in Britain or indeed Europe. There it has the connotation of the liberal preoccupation with free markets, freedom of speech and, to some extent, the limited role of the state. In the United States, the word 'liberal' recognises the need for a large, compassionate and stabilising role by government, protection of the individual from the hazards of life, including those of the work place, support to trade unions and a more generally supportive attitude towards those who suffer from personal misfortune. I suppose that the nearest counterpart in European terminology is 'social democratic', with a very large emphasis on the liberty of the citizen.

American political attitudes are often puzzling to Europeans, especially in relation to socialism. Does the word have very different connotations for Americans?

I think this is true. The word 'socialism' in Europe refers to the mixed economy, in which there is a substantial but by no means total rule by the state, and where the implication is benign. But out of long-established practice in the United States, socialism has been given a much more adverse connotation, so that some of my fellow liberals unquestionably back off from the risk of being called socialists.

I have the impression that you see yourself and your career as primarily one of economist and writer rather than of diplomat.

I regarded the diplomatic part of my life very much as a departure from the norm, and in some measure as an enjoyment. I had become interested, I think I can say fascinated, by India, as did so many others in the 1950s, and when John F. Kennedy asked me to go to India as his ambassador, I was greatly attracted by the idea of learning more of the culture and civilisation, and of contributing something to better relations between the United States and India – taking that issue away from the professional Cold War warriors for a while. But I certainly never regarded diplomacy as more than a temporary career, or perhaps, as some people would prefer to have me say, a temporary aberration. Basically, I consider myself a professional writer, yes.

When you were ambassador to India it was said of you by Krishna Menon that you behaved rather like a British resident during the Raj, guiding and influencing.

I think it fair to say that Krishna Menon's views on this, as on so many other matters, are to be taken with a grain of salt. I certainly didn't see myself in the tradition of a British mandarin. There was nothing I tried more to avoid, but I did have sharp differences with Krishna Menon over his repeated attacks on the United States, and we came to a serious parting of the ways at the time of that quite useless war in the Himalayas when Krishna was defence minister. It was impossible for me to rally support in Washington as long as Krishna was defence minister, and I think he attributed his departure from that post in some measure to me, rightly or wrongly. So perhaps he had some reason to be a little prejudiced. I made it clear to the Indian government that his presence as defence minister was a formidable problem in our coming to India's assistance.

Since you ask, it was not part of my policy to have a high profile in India, but I think it fair to say that I have only a limited talent for anonymity and that at the time the United States was a source of very large assistance to India. I was instructed by President Kennedy, to my delight, to spend a good deal of time out of New Delhi, making the acquaintance of Indian leaders and the Indian scene. I was a close political and personal friend of Jawaharlal Nehru, which served to keep me in the public eye. That was something, I have to tell you, I didn't entirely avoid. John F. Kennedy considered the relationship with India very important, and one must remember that India and Nehru were the voice of the so-called unaligned world; and I shared with Kennedy a desire to have the friendship and respect of those countries.

As for any influence that I may have had with Kennedy, I think everyone should avoid exaggerating such influence. President Truman once said of the great financier, Bernard Baruch, 'I don't see why he describes himself as an adviser to presidents. Doesn't he know that all presidents have more advice than they can use?' On the other hand, Kennedy made it clear that he enjoyed my letters and my telegrams and was pleased at the annoyance they caused some of the drearier and more orthodox members of his administration.

You advised Kennedy not to become involved militarily in Vietnam – advice he did not act on.

Well, I have to go back a bit. I have always thought that Kennedy had grave doubts about Vietnam, but he was under severe pressure at that time from the conservative establishment, the military and, I regret to say, some of my liberal friends, to show he was a man of muscle and vigour in the defence of what were conceived to be American interests. I talked to him about the problems we were going to face there – that we were replacing the French as another colonial power, that we were associated with remarkably unpopular and incompetent politicians – and right up until the time of his death I found him sympathetic and, on more than once occasion, anxious to have my views and also to urge my recommendations.

In asking whether the world might have been different had Kennedy not been assassinated, you are framing a question that invites speculation. On domestic matters, including civil rights and the war on poverty, which I greatly supported, I don't think Kennedy would have done more than, and perhaps not as much as, Lyndon Johnson. We should not for a moment minimise the important steps that Lyndon Johnson took to make the United States, and especially its race relations, more compassionate and civilised. So the question turns on what Kennedy would have done in Indo-China.

It is my feeling that, at the time of his death – and this is based on many conversations – Kennedy was resistant to the idea of any full military involvement there, although, needless to say, a great many advisers had been sent. But one has to add that, if you had pressed Lyndon Johnson at the same time, he would have expressed the same reluctance. So the question is really one that cannot be answered: could Kennedy have stood against the forces that were pressing the domino theory and the notion we had to stand firm?

Why wouldn't Kennedy have fared as well as Johnson on the domestic front?

The difference was that Johnson, in his relations with Congress, always used slightly more power than he had, and while Kennedy's intentions were the same, he always used slightly less power than he had. It was partly the produce of personality, but also of Johnson's greater experience and authority on Capitol Hill.

But wasn't Johnson much more ruthless?

That's perhaps another way of putting it.

You have never suffered fools gladly, and seem to have taken a consistently abrasive line with the State Department. Did you feel this was how bureaucracies needed to be treated?

I did not believe that in pressing the case against the conventional Cold War warriors, and those who were orientated to military solutions, a conciliatory voice would have been very useful, and I think I would have to add that, on the whole, I enjoyed the power – the effect of what I saw as the harsh truth. People in a bureaucracy do not get annoyed by error. They get annoyed by what they don't want to hear. And one should never minimise the pleasure in causing that annoyance. I never thought it necessary to avoid controversy. On the whole I enjoyed it, especially if it was with people who needed to be corrected, and at that time I was in conflict with the leadership of the State Department over matters about which, I'm happy to say, history has been rather kinder to me than it has to them.

You once said: 'Politics is not the art of the possible. It consists in choosing between the disastrous and the unpalatable.'

That's what I really believe. If a public question is between what is obviously right and popular and what is obviously wrong and unpopular, no political problem is involved. A political problem only arises when you have a choice between a wrong course of action and a right course of action that is difficult and which provokes adverse comment and action.

In 1971 you said that only an intolerable level of unemployment could arrest the inflationary process. Twenty years on, do you still hold that view?

No, I think not. I think we have now learned that we can have a substantially lower level of unemployment than was once imagined without inflation. I then felt that only a very high level of unemployment would arrest the interaction of wages and prices: trade union pressure pushing up wages with a compensating increase in prices and a self-generating cycle of that sort. The pressure of that cycle is much diminished for two reasons: the movement of some of our heavy manufacturing, where unions were strongest and where employee power was greatest, from the United States to Japan, Korea, Taiwan and other countries, and the general weakening of the trade union movement. In these last years, trade unions, more often than pressing for increased wages, have had to make concessions in order to keep their employers in business. This is a very great difference.

I still believe that one can come closer to full employment and a good and healthy rate of growth by having a prices and incomes policy in the central core of the economy, but I don't regard it now as being as absolutely essential as I once thought, for the reasons I mentioned. Prices are now much more restrained by international competition, and wage claims are much more restrained by the weakness of the employees in the traditionally highly organised industries. To be specific, the United Automobile workers recognise that in making wage claims there are limits to the pressure they can bring to bear on automobile manufacturers if the automobile manufacturers are not to suffer a loss of production to the Japanese.

I wouldn't describe the trade union movement as becoming more responsible but as becoming weaker, because of circumstances. A strong trade union movement requires strong corporations and strong employers. Employers have been weakened by the rise of external competition.

But we do now seem willing to live with levels of unemployment which, a decade ago, would have seemed impossible and scandalous. Have we become accustomed to indifference?

No. The question itself has to be revised. We have not had, these last years, high levels of unemployment in the United States. Our problem has rather been the movement of people from high-wage to low-wage employment. It is true that, in Britain and Western Europe, where there's greater rigidity in the employment structures, unemployment is more of a problem. But I still continue to think that it's a mark of a civilised society that anyone who wants a job with a good income should have it.

In the early 1970s, you were not among those who were anxious to see Britain incorporated into the Common Market, but now, on the brink of 1992, full integration with Europe surely becomes impossible to oppose.

It's true that I never made a career out of advocating British membership of the Common Market, although, on balance, I would be in favour of it. But now, with the changes in Western and Eastern Europe and the reunification of Germany, I think there is an urgent need for European unity and the quieting of old nationalist attitudes. Having said that, I don't believe that 1992 is going to be quite as dramatic in the changes it brings as some of the talk makes out it will be. There will still be different budgets, different fiscal policies, different tax systems, all of that making European monetary unity questionable. National governments will still be stronger than the non-government in Brussels, so that people will look back after 1922 and think there was more talk and less change than might have been imagined.

Yet most leading Europeans, with the exception of Mrs Thatcher, want a strong federation.

That is right, but the emphasis will be on the federal character rather than on complete unity. It's possible in the long term, but I think that 1992 is only a step in that direction. One must always remember that economics and politics regularly substitute words for deeds, and this may well be true of 1992, especially in foreign trade matters. We are always talking about great changes in prospect, and when we look back we always find it very much less of a change than we expected. I have often noted that, while great importance is attached to the EEC, and rightly so, three countries that remained outside, namely Austria, Switzerland, and Sweden, have been perhaps the most successful of the post-war economies. The reason for that is that we may exaggerate the rewards of reunification and minimise the rewards of wise and sensible administration by the individual country.

It is true that Spain is bubbling, but I wouldn't attribute all of that to Spain's membership of the EEC. Perhaps Spain was awaiting a renaissance.

A great many people in Europe look upon German unity as a mixed blessing, believing they have good reason to feel nervous about a newly powerful German state.

When one looks back over the history of German politics and economics in the past forty-five years, it has been very civilised, very successful, and a good manifestation of intelligent social democracy. I see no reason for recreating the fears of a half century ago. The steps toward the unification of Europe, in which I hope Eastern Europe will come to play a part, make for certainty in this regard. Having said that, I hope that the Germans will treat with proper contempt, even alarm, those who talk, for example, about adjusting the eastern boundary with Poland.

Yet seven years after the Berlin Wall was built, you said that the Wall was a very good thing, and that at least it had preserved the peace.

I don't recall saying that. I will not take responsibility for casual comments of an earlier time. I was very glad to see the Wall go. It was, as are all such things, an insult to civilised manners.

Wouldn't a powerful economy from Britain to the Urals have serious repercussions for the United States?

That is a long-run prospect where speculation serves no useful purpose. I would like to see a strong federated economy going from Ireland to the Urals and beyond. I think that would be an assurance of peace and tranquillity and I can't think it would be bad for the United States.

But the United States has economic problems?

Oh, no question. There has been a strong tendency in Washington, and in the American economy and American economic practice generally, to substitute short-run comfort for long-run solutions. We have run a large deficit in our domestic budget when we could have had lower interest rates and more productive investment. After the war, our corporations developed a certain self-satisfaction and a bureaucratic sclerosis, and they have been further damaged by the merger and takeover mania which has substituted heavy burdens of debt for equity; and this too has been damaging to investments and new processes. All of these problems have been coupled with large and, in many respects, unnecessary military expenditure which has kept a very large part of our stock of capital and a very large proportion of our needed civilian talent in sterile war production. One of the great advantages that the Germans and the Japanese have had since the Second World War was in using their resources for the improvement of their civilian industry. We have learned that those who lose a war can win the peace.

I wouldn't blame the Japanese for a moment for their market dominance. We should blame ourselves. We have handicapped our industry by unwise fiscal policy, unwise interest policy, the damaging effects of financial manipulation, and the undue commitment of our resources to the Pentagon. Those are the matters which have given the Japanese their advantage. Admittedly, for cultural, linguistic, and other reasons, the Japanese market is not easy to penetrate, but I would attribute less to Japanese protection than I would to the lack of initiative of our own enterprises.

If you were suddenly given the reins of the US economy, how would you cure its ills?

The likelihood of my being given a free hand I think is distinctly questionable, but I would move strongly to reduce or military expenditure. I would use the proceeds from that to strengthen our internal education system, improve our roads and, particularly, improve life in the central cities, and also to provide loans to ease the transition to democracy in Eastern Europe. And I wouldn't hesitate, if the proceeds from the reduction in military expenditure were insufficient for the purpose, to raise taxes. We live in a world of affluent and even frivolous private expenditure, but as regards public expenditure; there is a very great need.

The fear of raising taxes is a matter of political error. Power has passed to the people who are conservative and comfortable and who are able to do without the public services which are so important to those in our central cities and to the poor. This is one of the great misfortunes of our time. Maybe we're passing out of that stage, but it's slow progress. Meantime, when an urgent problem arises, our president, not wanting to spend money, makes another speech.

The populations of emergent nations and those of the former Eastern Bloc naturally want the things that America and Western Europe already have, but is it actually possible to spread the same standard of living everywhere?

I would like to see greatly improved food, clothing and the basic pleasures of life in the Third World Countries, and I think much can be done to that end. Some thirty years ago, I started the first teaching in economic development here at Harvard, which could have been among the first in the United States. There has been great disappointment for me as I've watched this problem since that time, the greatest disappointments being in Africa. But in some other parts of the world there has been great progress. So we mustn't be entirely without hope. I wouldn't say I'm optimistic about the future, because I feel very depressed about Africa, but, on the other hand, there is no question that India, Pakistan and also China, while so much remains to be done, are a more hopeful prospect than they were when I first knew those countries.

I wrote some thirty years ago in *The Affluent Society* that we must balance the consequences of consumption against its effects on the environment. And this is something that I still believe. On the other hand, I would like to see the rewards of higher consumption extended to the masses of people in the world who still don't have enough to eat and wear and lack even the minimal enjoyments which we so appreciate. That is a very difficult problem. One only has to have experience in India and elsewhere in the Third World to realise what a difficult problem it is. But again some progress has been made. When I went to India, only large imports of grain from the United States kept that country from starvation. Since I left India, the population has doubled, yet India has more than the capacity to feed itself. So we mustn't be without hope.

Do you believe that we should be more dependent on government than on private enterprises?

Absolutely. One of the things that has weakened our standard of living in the United States in recent times has been the assumption that private enterprise is somehow the answer to all that can be done. This has been a way of evading responsibility and protecting the income of the affluent from taxes.

I remember you arguing that, if the market was really market led, there would be more houses and fewer television sets. I can see that up to a point, but is there not a sort of human inevitability about wanting, if you can't afford a house, a television set you can afford?

Oh, this is a very subjective matter. What I said was that capitalism provides television sets more easily than it provides houses, and that a homeless person in our time would find society much more compassionate and companionable if he had a house rather than a television set. The market economy does not meet the needs of people in that regard.

You once spoke of the way you thought Britain was 'living out the concern for some more leisurely relationship with industrial life.' Can that ever be possible for any nation in the future?

I would like to see an industrial, economic life where there was a more rational choice between work and leisure. We've moved some distance in that direction over the last fifty or seventy-five years, but I still think that universities, where leisure and academic freedom are considered to be interchangeable, are a model for economic life in general. Somebody that has to work on an assembly line should have a choice between the money he or she earns and the leisure he or she would like to have. Maybe we should have more opportunity for paid vacations and paid sabbatical leave for people who have to do heavy manual labour. We consider both of these very desirable things for college professors.

What view do you take of Mrs Thatcher and the Britain she has created during the last ten years?

I am not a supporter of Mrs Thatcher. She has allied herself with the privileged community of her country, as did her friend, Ronald Reagan, in the United States, to the distant disadvantage of the less fortunate and with damage to the social contract which had previously given the impression, at least, that everybody had an equal chance.

But in the United States she is considered to be the Iron Lady.

Not by me. I think Mrs Thatcher might now have even more difficulty in getting elected in the United States than at home. I cannot imagine that her poll-tax system would be peacefully accepted here in the city of Cambridge, Massachusetts.

Do you think Britain will come out of its economic problems?

We have built into the capitalist system a resilience that is greater than we sometimes imagine, so that while performance is not perfect, I have hopes, and indeed some conviction, that we will avoid the kind of disaster that we experienced in the 1930s or that Britain experienced in the 1920s.

You have long drawn the contrast between 'private affluence' and 'public squalor'. Do you see any evidence of the gulf narrowing?

No. I would say, for example, in American cities, it's grown worse. We have a worsening disparity between the quality of our private existence and the quality and the needs of our public life. It's been related both in Britain and the United States to public policies that favour the affluent (including, in our case, the very rich) and penalise the services to the poor. If you're very rich, you can send your children to a private school, have your own library, and maybe your own policeman on the door. If you're middle class or poor, you need those services to be provided for you. We have had, in these last years in the United States, a preferential treatment for the very rich, including those who do not need the public services.

Liberal attitudes so often look like luxuries. Doesn't it become too easy to take the liberal view about racialism, in say, South Africa, provided one lives in Massachusetts?

No, I don't think so for a moment. I quite agree that it's easier to lecture people about their behaviour if they are at some distance, but any good liberal, and I think this is true of most of my liberal friends, is most concerned with problems that are close to home. And I would like to think that is so in my own case.

You have been an advocate of civilised politics, but what hope of civilised politics is there between, say, the Palestinians and the Israelis, or the Iranians and the Iraqis?

There's no question that religious and ethnic passion are the enemies of civilised coexistence, but I certainly don't think we should give up hope. Somebody coming to the United States fifty years ago would have been equally pessimistic about race relations here, and now, fifty years later, would agree that they have greatly improved. I'm certainly not going to give up hope of improved relations between the old cultures of the Middle East. I very much hope that we will have a new period when people of Sadat's stature will take the lead. If one predicts permanent conflict then one gives up hope of a solution.

You were writing about the problems of women's liberation and black emancipation in the 1970s. Do you feel satisfied with the progress that has been made in those areas since then?

No, certainly not. There has been progress, I don't doubt. Perhaps there's been more progress than I would have expected at that time, but we still have serious discrimination against women in industry, the academic community, many other places. We still have a sad difference between the economic prospects of a child who is white and one who is black. And there's no question that we must keep pressure, public and private, strong on both of these issues.

I have been much more fortunate than most people in regard to the support I receive in my work; I would not have been able to do the things I have done without a corps of assistants, most of whom have been women. But I still do not think that women have a chance for independence as long as they're confined to a household and family work. I make the same obeisance to the family as everyone else, but I do not doubt that the family can also be a disguise, an amiable disguise, for male dominance.

Some of your views sound old-fashioned, as, for example, when you said that fortunately there were all sorts of boarding schools 'so that children can be kept separate from their parents for a great part of the time'. Do you really think that is such a good idea?

John Kenneth Galbraith

I've always felt that children take the good qualities of their parents for granted and the bad qualities as a licence for their own misbehaviour. There's much to be said, at a certain age, for children going off to school and seeing less of their parents. Old-fashioned or otherwise, I don't consider everything that's old-fashioned to be wrong.

You said at the same time that it was a huge loss when intelligent women stayed at home. What exactly do you think is lost when intelligent women devote themselves to their families?

I should think that a great deal is lost in the field of literature, music, economic achievement, much else. And I think that, so long as we confine women to the home and the house and family in what I have called a crypto-servant role, we lose half of the intelligence and cultural resource of the community. I don't want to see any intellectually or artistically expressive woman confine her talents to her husband.

Unlike many people in public life, you have had a stable, fifty-year marriage.

I haven't any secret as far as the marriage is concerned. I simply picked out a highly intelligent, very beautiful woman. She accepted me and we lived happily ever after.

Will there ever be a time when the theories of economics are implemented fully?

Looking over some of the theories of economics of my time I have every hope that they will not be implemented. I regard economic policy as something to be governed by practical good sense and not by commitment to any corps of theoretical principles. I'm persuaded that both in the communist world and the capitalist world we have a great deal to fear from those who surrender thought to ideology.

You have made enemies as well as friends. Has that been a major source of regret?

I've taken it for granted but I've always had some impression that my friends outnumbered my enemies.

You once said that modesty is a vastly overrated virtue, but may it not help in the art of diplomacy to prevent unproductive confrontations between strong-willed people equally convinced they are right?

I think this is true. I wouldn't doubt it. But I also think there are occasions when one should have confidence in one's views and express them with considerable firmness.

Some of your critics have detected a certain arrogance in your attitudes, even to the extent of power mania. Do you plead guilty?

Unquestionably, yes, I wouldn't, of course, call it arrogance. I would call it commendable self-assurance.

The power side, though, has been a humbling thing in my life. In 1941 I was put in charge of all prices in the United States. You could lower prices without my permission, but you couldn't raise them. That was an exercise of power which would satisfy almost any power-hungry individual, and I've often said that, in terms of the exercise of power, my life has been downhill ever since.

How conscious have you been of your own charm, and to what extent have you used it as a weapon?

That's a question I am forced to leave entirely to somebody else. I've contended myself with trying to write persuasively, and I've given a good deal of attention to that, but as to charm, that is something which is entirely for the judgement of others, and I advise them to be just a little bit suspicious.

Apparently the Baptist Church of your childhood provided you with what you called 'a thoroughgoing inoculation against churchgoing'. Was this ever a drawback in your public life?

Not particularly. I never made a point of it. I was fortunate to live in a community and in a country which is very tolerant in such matters. On the matter of making peace with God, I haven't yet given the matter serious attention. I'm reminded of what H. L. Mencken said when he was in his last years. He was told, as he grew older and when he was threatened with a stroke, that he should make preparations for the future. He thought about this for some time and said, 'Well, I tell you, if I have been wrong in my agnosticism, when I die I'll walk up to God in a manly way and say, Sir I made an honest mistake'. I always thought that Mencken had a point.

Is there anything which you feel you still have to achieve?

I'm going to continue to do some writing and I would like, now that time has caught up with some of the books I've written, to do some correcting of my past errors.

Oh, yes, I have many regrets. No person who is at all thoughtful can look back on life and not see a great many lost opportunities. But I'm not going to list them. As for living my life differently if I had the chance, I'm not sure. I've had a reasonably adequate life. Life has been very good to me. Better perhaps than I deserve.

MONSIGNOR GILBEY

Born in 1901 of an English father and a Spanish mother, Alfred Newman Gilbey was educated at Beaumont and Trinity College, Cambridge. He studied at the Beda College in Rome before being ordained as a priest in 1929. He was chaplain to the Catholic undergraduates of Cambridge from 1932 to 1965 and in 1950 he was created a Domestic Prelate. In 1965 he became a Protonotary Apostolic and in 1981 he was made an honorary canon of Brentwood Cathedral. He was the author of *We Believe* (1983), in which he expounded the moral and social teaching of the Catholic Church. In 1992, following his ninetieth birthday, a second impression appeared, and in 1993 *The Commonplace Book of Monsignor Alfred Gilbey*, a book of his favourite extracts from literature, was published. In May 1995 he visited the United States to promote *We Believe* and was interviewed on Eternal Word Television by the station's nun, Mother Angelica, whose views were even more ultra-conservative than his own. He lived in the Traveller's Club for many years, moving to a nursing home in January 1998 where he died three months later, aged ninety-six.

First, about your vocation. How did you know God wanted you to be a priest?

A very difficult question to answer shortly. Plainly a vocation develops like any other living thing. I had a flying start through coming from a good Catholic home. My mother was a real Spanish Catholic, of the faith to the marrow of her bones. My father, on the other hand, came from a completely Protestant English background, but he was God's good Englishman and also a wine merchant like the rest of my family. He and two of his brothers went out to Spain and they all fell for Spanish brides; they were all – how should I say – converted at pistol point. I don't mean that literally, but there was really no alternative in those days. My Spanish grandfather, whom, alas, I never knew, was reputed to have said to my father, 'You are an entirely acceptable suitor, physically, financially, socially, but my daughter' – she was the eldest daughter and the apple of his eye – 'does not marry a man who is not Catholic.' There was nothing to discuss, no argy-bargy. It was like the sun rising tomorrow. He undertook instruction for two years.

The fashion today is to dismiss people who become Catholic to marry a Catholic, but that is to undervalue that sort of conversion. Yet this is the beginning of an answer to your question: having a wonderful, very happy Catholic home. My parents started their married life in London, then moved to what was to be my beloved home in Essex, called Mark Hall – now entirely destroyed. It was in the English countryside, eight miles from the nearest church, and this was in the days of carriages nearly a hundred years ago in 1894. My father went to see Cardinal Vaughan, Archbishop of Westminster, and asked if we might have a private chapel in the house. Cardinal Vaughan said, 'You can certainly have a chapel but I can't give you a priest. You'll have to make your own arrangements if you can.' My mother then went to Farm Street to ask if they could spare a priest, and every Saturday a Jesuit would arrive and stay until Sunday evening, having given us Mass in the morning.

In this way our background could not have been more favourable. We were five brothers, but I was the only one who, from the very beginning, felt called to the priesthood. We were brought up in an entirely Catholic atmosphere, and then we were all sent to school, again with the Jesuits, at Beaumont. The school in those happy days was run entirely by Jesuits, something that applies to very few Catholic schools now – there simply aren't enough Jesuits to go round.

Beaumont made a great impression on me, but however much I admired our teachers, I never felt at all attracted to the Jesuit way of life. It is one of their characteristics, a great source of their spirituality, to emphasise a detachment, but possibly because I was so wonderfully happy at home I felt drawn towards something slightly more rooted. It's always a matter of interest and admiration to me to find how wonderfully the Catholic Church uses all sorts of natural dispositions and temperaments. The Benedictines put immense emphasis on the stability of a place and vow permanent residence at a particular monastery. The Jesuits emphasise detachment, almost depersonalisation, and that aspect didn't appeal to me.

A book that had a great influence on me was *Hugh*, A. C. Benson's memoir of his younger brother R. H. Benson. There were three brothers, the sons of the Archbishop of Canterbury at the beginning of the century, all of whom were prolific writers, though Hugh was the only one who became a Catholic and a priest. He was an immensely dynamic character, writing and preaching ceaselessly, a great convert maker, and it fell to me as a little boy at Beaumont to read what his brother had written about him. This presentation of a priest was so different from any I had known that I asked one of the Jesuits how it was that Hugh Benson was, as a priest, able to lead the life depicted. The Jesuit explained that he was a secular, and this was the first time I ever heard of the existence of the secular clergy. At about the same time one of the school's old boys, who had been called to the secular priesthood, came back from Rome where had had been ordained and celebrated Mass at Beaumont with great jubilees.

Returning to my dear parents, however, those two strains – the Spanish and the English – gave me an immense love for England aligned with the strong Catholic tradition we had at home, and gave me a desire to be able to communicate the one with the other. As a keen fox-hunting family we were devoted to the countryside, and our friends and neighbours were nearly all rooted in that world. One was aware of how indescribably remote they were from what we Catholics considered to be the world and I was conscious of there being these two aspects of the same civilisation. I think that was the source of inspiration for me to want to be a secular priest.

I didn't wish to go straight in, as was customary in those days, but wanted, as it were, to appear in the world first. My first attempt, largely because of the Jesuit tradition and the geographical position of Beaumont on the Thames, was to try to get into Oxford in 1919. But the Jesuits sent so many priests to the war that Beaumont was at that time very short staffed. One of the great losses we suffered was having no Greek at all, and in those days Greek was an essential qualification for getting into Oxford. Therefore, I turned to Trinity College, Cambridge. Looking back, it was one of the providential things in my life that I went there, and it has been the whole of my life since. I had four very idle but very enjoyable years there which, however idle, were immensely educative. I have no academic gifts; my academic history is abysmal. I scraped past a degree after three years' idleness, then went to Rome to study for the priesthood.

Were your family enthusiastic about your entering the Church?

My mother certainly was. They all had great awe and reverence for the priesthood, but my father hoped I wasn't becoming a priest out of bravado, just because I'd been saying it for so long. It would be wrong to call him enthusiastic; but he was certainly anxious that his sons should do what they felt to be their vocations, and when it became clear that mine was the priesthood, I think he took great pleasure in it.

Your family background was not a deprived one, so do you find any conflict of perspective between your vocation and your former life?

None at all. Our family situation was fortunate indeed; not rich as people think of riches today – we didn't have racecourses or a yacht – but a large family living comfortably. The question comes from that widespread idea of Catholics who don't understand the difference between the religious life and the life of a secular priest. So many people now talk as though a Christian ought to be a pacifist, ought to be a communist. I always refer them to that wonderful passage in the three synoptic gospels when a young man comes to our Blessed Lord and says, 'Master, what must I do to attain eternal life?' Ask nine people out of ten, including Catholics, and they concertina the conversation and in doing so miss the point by quoting Our Lord as saying, 'Sell all thou hast and follow me.' This was not at all what our Blessed Lord said. He said, 'Keep the commandments,' and the young man, expecting something much more dramatic, was disappointed and said, 'This I have done all the days of my life.' Then our Blessed Lord says, 'If thou wishest to be perfect, go sell all thou hast and follow me.'

He is making there a big distinction, which the Church has always observed, between those called to make the three vows of poverty, chastity and obedience and those not so called. People are slow to appreciate this distinction and don't understand that, to start with, a secular priest literally takes no vows. He takes no vow of poverty and if he has means of his own, he can keep them. He mustn't, of course, go into business – that would be incompatible with his priestly vocation – but if he has money, or money comes to him, then he may keep it. Celibacy, in the case of a secular priest, is not made by a vow but is imposed by the law. It was only gradually imposed on the clergy over the years, and you find early on that many a bishop has a son who becomes a saint.

People always talk as though there were just two possibilities: that of the present practice of the Catholic Church, which has been imposed by law, and that which you find in all the Protestant denominations. This completely overlooks a great historic development which is neither. In all the Eastern Churches, in the Orthodox and also in the Uniates, a novitiate will, while still only a deacon, go and find a wife and then be ordained a priest. If he loses her, he is not allowed to remarry; which seems to us a rather arbitrary rule, but it is important to realise how wide and varied the practice is. I mention it as a necessary preface to poverty because if you are, for example, a married man with wife and children, then you are not free to give up all you have. You are bound, in justice as well as in charity, to do all you can to support them.

On the other hand, if you have once taken that vow of chastity, or accepted it as the secular clergy do, then you are free to ask whether Almighty God may not wish you to follow our Blessed Lord more closely by giving up all material things. For a married man to do that would be for him to commit a great sin of improvidence. Unless a vow of chastity is taken first, then you cannot ask yourself whether you're called to a vow of evangelical poverty. Nor, for similar reasons, can you turn the other cheek to the smiter, as I always emphasised when instructing young men at Cambridge. If you, as a man with no dependants, are going home one night in the dark, and an assailant leaps out of a doorway with the obvious intention of taking your life, then you do have an alternative. You make up your mind in the split second that either you knock him down and kill him if necessary to preserve your own life, or you say, 'I'll turn the other cheek to the smiter. He's a boor, a man not knowing what he is doing.' But if, as a married man, you come home to find your wife being beaten up and the children killed, then you're not justified in turning the other cheek to the smiter.

How has the ethos of the Church changed? Has there been in your time a palpable shift in the outlook and practices of the faithful?

Oh, yes, enormous, but always remember, it hasn't been sudden. People who know no history are simplistic in thinking that these vast changes are from a static to turbulent church. It is never one or the other. Every living thing grows and develops all the time, sometimes more painfully, sometimes less so. I talk to many young people and they will speak as if the Catholic Church they know didn't exist before the Second Vatican Council. The same applies equally in social and political matters, as though before the Welfare State was a period of terrible deprivation, injustice and tyranny. Both are long and complex issues with deep roots, and neither Church nor state remain the same for long. There are periods of greater and lesser change, and we have been advancing through an enormous one, yet there's all the difference in the world between how a Catholic and a non-Catholic sees these changes. A Catholic always starts with the absolute assurance that the Church cannot fail in her central purposes. Under a thousand and one external changes, her identity continues as completely as it does with a human being.

Each human being has throughout life an identity no one else can simulate or take away. The Church is just like that: she is that same body, born on the first Pentecost and set to continue till the Second Coming. I am very conscious of the fact that, although the whole turn of my mind is singularly consistent, my understanding develops and clarifies all the time. Does that mean I change? Not at all. It's my self-understanding that changes; my expression of it increases in clarity, yet the identity runs through. So with the Church. She's that same identical body, and if she changes the language of her liturgy, that is immaterial. I have my own strong views that the change there was very ill-advised, especially in the way it was done, but that doesn't mean to say I think she has failed in any essential, central thing. She has not. She cannot.

The Catholic Church being radically hierarchical, be able to continue in a world that is increasingly liberal and democratic?

It can use, or try to adapt, the machinery of democratic thought and practice, but that will never be her natural way of thinking or doing. What you're talking about is egalitarianism. I think it is rather misleading to bring in the word 'democratic' sine that is a form of government. Where does it come from? From a philosophy which is egalitarian, and egalitarianism is incompatible with two basic Christian concepts. It believes that men are born equal, but nothing could be less equal than the circumstances that attend the beginnings of all our lives. The egalitarian believes that if people are not born equal, then they must be made so. That is to fly completely in the face of Nature and the facts. Ultimately it can't succeed because it isn't true; it has no foundation; it is a figment of the imagination of the rationalists of the eighteenth century that has now impinged on the Catholic Church. Many Catholics believe in egalitarianism and are shocked when you tell them it's nonsense. The idea eats into the belief that our relationship to Almighty God is an individual one. John Henry Newman says in the *Apologia* that he could never remember a time when there were not two, and only two, self-evident beings, his Creator and himself.

To say that everyone is equal in God's sight is absolute nonsense. Everyone is unique in God's sight, as every father of a family will understand. To say that a father loves all his children equally would not be according to human nature. He mustn't express the difference or show favouritism, but each child has a unique relationship to his father. The same applies to the whole of creation, not only a man. Not only does star differ from star, but God calls them by name; every pebble on the beach is unlike any other; every leaf on a tree is a unique creation; and manifest at the heart of creation is man, not merely plainly but absolutely unique, as we all are unique in our material circumstances.

We and the parents from whom we sprang were chosen out of all eternity by Almighty God. It is this that conditions the language, the culture, the timing, the colour. Equality doesn't exist. Each of us comes to the world with a box of tools containing advantages and disadvantages in our character, and that's the equipment, not anyone else's, with which we have to hammer out our sanctification. Mine is unique, yours is unique. No one has the same box of tools.

During your years at Cambridge, how did you come to see the function of the Catholic chaplain and did your views change over the course of time?

I'll answer that last question first. No. My job was absolutely clear because it was made clear by the history of the terms of my appointment. There was a long-running division of opinion in the Catholic Church as to whether, first of all, we should try to have a university of our own; an idea much derided today, but we forget that in the nineteenth-century revival of Catholicism several flourishing universities were founded in Europe. In this country we made three rather pathetic attempts to found a university with no possibility off success. The first was at Prior Park in the early years of the last century; the second was Cardinal Newman's attempt to found a university of Dublin, and the last was Cardinal Manning's effort to found a university in Kensington. All collapsed but all were part of a consistent policy. It came to nothing and most of us are very relieved – they would have become poor Catholic ghettoes.

That controversy was finally resolved by the pressure of the laity at the end of the last century. We were allowed to return to the ancient universities of Cambridge and Oxford, but under various safeguards, most of them rather unrealistic. One was that there should be at each of the ancient universities a chaplain whose job it was – and this was quite clear – to safeguard the faith of Catholics who went there. So it was very much a protective pastoral charge, and those were the terms of my own appointment. Many people now think it should involve a more positive, outgoing approach, but when the office started, it was certainly seen entirely in those terms.

Your early days as chaplain seemed marked by disputes with the Cambridge University Catholic Association. Did they find you difficult?

Very. It stemmed from the early days, lasted all my time and continues still. By a great political error, the wonderfully devoted collection of Catholic dons who founded the Cambridge University Catholic Association were allowed to own the premises of the chaplaincy they had been responsible for acquiring. Having done that wonderful work of acquiring the premises, they were also allowed to become the trustees, thereby producing a sort of congregationalism unknown to the Catholic Church. Meanwhile the bishops charged with the responsibility of safeguarding the faith of Catholic undergraduates made no attempt to raise the funds necessary for the purpose. They were, of course, terribly handicapped by their own poverty and their difficulty in fulfilling or trying to fulfil the needs of Catholic education for the poorest classes. The whole of their efforts were, quite rightly, poured out to build Catholic schools, and they regarded going to Cambridge or Oxford as rather a rich man's luxury. It wasn't true then, and it's manifestly untrue today when every student is supported by the state, but the idea they wrongly had seventy years ago was that if rich men wanted their boys to go, then it was up to them to produce the means to support a chaplain and provide the premises. That was, and is, the position as trustees of that wonderfully devoted band of Catholic dons.

When, in your early days at Cambridge, you spent a lot of your own money on the library and furnishing the chaplaincy, was it done out of generosity or impatience with the trustees?

Neither. It was wanting to have things as I thought they should be, trying to make the chaplaincy a civilised centre. Since the bishops regarded the ancient universities as an indulgence allowed to rich parents, there was consequently a feeling, certainly on the part of successive chaplains, that a chaplaincy should be a place where they would themselves feel at home. Today, of course, the need becomes to provide a welcoming atmosphere in the chaplaincy.

By the early 1960s you were still having to meet the shortfall in the chaplaincy's budget out of your own pocket. How could that have been necessary?

The cry of poverty runs right through, doesn't it? Chaplains were generally appointed with an eye to their having some means of their own. I was there longer than anyone, so saw more of it, but the shortfall, as you call it, was something that affected every chaplain. They were sent there with a ludicrous sum. I can't remember what it was in my case, but it was grossly inadequate.

In the pre-war years you evidently took part in a number of evangelical events organised by undergraduates. Did you enjoy preaching in the streets of Saffron Walden or the fields of Wisbech?

Not in the least. I don't enjoy those things at all, but my policy was a simple one. I never tried to sell these ideas to the undergraduates as I felt strongly that a man should be able to come to Fisher House without having anything asked of him; that he ought not to be badgered to join this, that or the other activity. In those days, the Jesuit schools took up what used to be called the Catholic Evidence Guild rather strongly. It was a way of trying to get the boys to take an interest in our religion. They were encouraged to join the guild, to go in for quite stiff examinations to fit them for the purpose, and to stand on soap boxes in Egham or whatever, preaching to a rather unresponsive multitude. When some young men, mostly from my own school, Beaumont, came and said it would be a good thing if we, too, belonged to the guild, I said by all means, and I'll help you, but no one is going to be asked to do it by me.

As Catholic chaplain, did you feel under an obligation to aid in the conversion of non-Catholics who came into contact with you? Was there a conflict there between duty and social propriety?

First, it wasn't an obligation, it wasn't part of my job. That was always, I emphasise, a preservative one. A fair number of undergraduates would certainly come to me, though, and say, 'I think I ought to become a Catholic.' I would always tell them,

'You must let your parents know what you are doing, and you must tell your tutor or the dean of your college. You are to come to instruction and you won't be able to become a Catholic for at least a year.' That was my practice. As a contrast, the most distinguished of all chaplains at Oxford was Monsignor Knox, a prominent convert who refused altogether to instruct people, and so he took a different line from me. At Oxford there were Jesuit and Dominican houses to whom he could send inquirers. I had nothing like that at Cambridge.

Is there anyone in particular you are especially proud to have converted?

No. It is always a wonderful privilege to believe one can bring anyone to a knowledge of truth, but I would say I've never converted anybody. I've never set out to, I haven't the gift. I don't know how the Apostles did it. All those I've instructed have come on their own initiative and they've been a source of immense consolation and happiness. I absolutely love instructing people in belief. A number have found their own vacations to the priesthood, some to religious orders. I don't think many have made their mark in the world or the Church so that you would know their names. I can think of nothing more satisfying a priest can do than being able to tell people interested in the faith what is involved.

By the 1960s there seems to have been some resistance among Catholic undergraduates to traditional practices at the chaplaincy. Did that distress you?

Any move away from Catholic practices upsets me, but I don't allow myself to be distressed. I'm so profoundly confident, and when you have the gift of the faith, then you know that the Church can't fail in Her purpose. The Church teaches us the truth and gives us the sacraments, and we ought to offer thanks for what God has given, not for the folly of men's thoughts.

It was said of you by Peter Gregory Jones, author of The History of the Cambridge Chaplaincy, *that as a great preserver of inherited values you were a historian by temperament. What were the values you wished to preserve?*

That's an enormous question which takes us right back to the structure of society. Does one, or does one not, believe in the family? The traditional sociology of the Catholic Church is that it is the duty of parents to house, feed, shelter, and (using the word as widely as possible) educate those they beget. That, of course, is a very unacceptable concept in the socialist world of today, which regards it as the duty of the state to care for housing, education, sickness and old age. Thus, we have egalitarianism, the French Revolution factor, catching up with the Catholic Church.

Jones speaks of the sense in which you found egalitarianism after the war incompatible with your idea of man's relationship with God. Could you elaborate on this position?

The whole socialisation of the world has been immensely accelerated by two world wars, but this is not just a post-war phenomenon. I never found egalitarianism an attractive concept. I always instinctively believed in a hierarchical society. Looking back over my life, I've been extraordinarily consistent in what I believe, though I now formulate it much more fully. The family – the basis of society – is of its nature hierarchical. We come into families that are not of our own choosing and are not run by children. The first enormous impetus was the French Revolution. I always try to eschew the word 'democracy' because everyone uses it now as a term of undefined praise. They make their appeal to the democracy of the Greeks, of course, though there never was a more elitist society. The educated had a whole slave population to make their civilisation possible. It was nothing to do with egalitarianism and that's why I would wish to use the word 'democracy' accurately.

It seems an odd distinction to refer, as you have done, to women as 'students' and men as 'undergraduates'.

To begin with, women were not members of Cambridge University. Because the university did not admit women, Girton and Newnham started as women's colleges outside the university, and by stages, in one of those gradual processes of which I have seen so many, became incorporated. The first thing was to found women's colleges, then to allow them to come to lectures. First they didn't take examinations, then they could take examinations but couldn't be given degrees, only what was called the 'titles of degrees'. So there was a real distinction, not just one of my vocabulary. Women were *not* undergraduates, they were *not* members of the university.

You once explained your resignation from the chaplaincy as being over the principle of authority and its limits, but was that principle not focused on the opening of Fisher House to women?

If you like to say so, yes. As long as women were not members of the university, then there was a very strong case against allowing them in, and afterwards, because the position was constantly changing, the pressure increased. If the board, which was my authority, had ordered me to take in the women, I would have resigned anyway. They did not ask for my resignation, but passed a resolution that the chaplaincy should become mixed after I had gone. The real question became, should the nature of the chaplaincy be determined by the chaplain or by demand from below? At that point, I stood down on that principle.

If you ask why I opposed letting in women, it brings us back to fundamentals. Equality is a meaningless word and sex equality means absolutely nothing. The egalitarian believes that all people are the same. Men and women are not the same, they are complementary. A great friend of mine, Outram Evans, who was president of the Cambridge University Catholic Association for a long time, and my best ally, pointed out how immensely disparate the numbers were. There were two hundred men and twenty women. You can't combine the sexes, other than on a complementary basis, without destroying the whole harmony of their relationship. I am totally opposed to the equality of the sexes.

In retrospect I have not modified my view at all. If it now seems eccentric, as you put it, then that is because of this wave of egalitarianism. What is so funny is how short people's memories are. I went up to Cambridge in 1920 when there were still these two women's colleges that were not part of the university and the women didn't enter the life one little bit. They used to come to our lectures and sit at a separate table, but I don't think I ever spoke to a woman student the four years I was there, neither did any of my friends. It was an entirely male society, a very close and happy one. That idea, I suppose, is much more common in northern rather than southern Europe. I know that some Latins seem unable to form the sorts of societies we have here, and clubs are the perfect example. I would move heaven and earth to make my club, where we are now, an entirely masculine one again. That would doubtless be considered eccentric, but from the moment of its foundation till twenty years ago, it was the law. It isn't my eccentricity at all; people just have no sense of history. Everything, even the Houses of Parliament, used to be entirely male.

My view is wholly compatible with the God-given design of women as complementary to men. They're different, yet people won't recognise the fact. The egalitarians have this absolute *idée fixe* that they're the same. They're not. Women don't like each other's company, don't form clubs. They don't like that to be said, of course, but the fact is plain to see. It's a wonder how nuns can live together, but they do. Whether we're talking about political life, the law, the Church of England, women are doing something they've never done before, and the fact is that it isn't working out equally – they're completely ignored. It's now fifty years since women have been in the House of Commons, and with the one staggering exception of Mrs Thatcher, have any of them come to do anything? No. Women are different. I wonder why people can't see what is clear as a pikestaff.

Would you discriminate against women?

There we have to define what we mean by discrimination. It's like all this talk of the underprivileged. Who has a right to a privilege? They talk of the children of poor parents being underprivileged, presupposing that someone has taken something from them. Words are used quite indiscriminately and the vocabulary is so meaningless that when you start trying to define what they are saying it becomes very difficult. Once you're an egalitarian, you have to believe that everyone has the same rights, so called. But who has and who has not, for example, the right to vote? It's not man's right except by a convention in a particular civilisation or country.

Through nineteen Christian centuries women have never enjoyed the same political standing as men, except accidentally; there was no idea of there being some universal right. Now everyone talks as if there were some self-evident reason whereby any country that doesn't have universal suffrage is out of court. It's arguable whether it's a good or bad thing to have a universal suffrage, but there is not intrinsic or fundamental reason why it should be so. We, particularly in the West, have been racing through two world wars to a universal principle, something unknown through all preceding centuries till a hundred years ago. All of that is a staggering assumption, and there is no foundation for it in history and none in reason.

It's quite another matter to discuss whether it's a good thing or not. I haven't a closed mind there. These things can be discussed, and you must discuss them and realise that what you are talking about is a relative not an absolute. It's the same with equal opportunity. Who has equal opportunity? How can I give someone in completely other circumstances than my own the opportunities I have and have had? Only one other force can even attempt it, and that is the state, and we are back to whose duty it is to educate. Is it a matter for the state or for the parents?

What is the real theological objection to the ordination of women? Is there scriptural warrant for it or is it primarily the authority of tradition?

It is a matter of the authority of the Church, which is one single thing supported by scripture and tradition and I don't like that separation of the two. The Protestant approach to Christian revelation is to confine it effectively to scripture, whereas I always regard the Church as teaching on Her own authority, which indeed arises from scripture and tradition. She is the authority. She's not getting it from anywhere else. Catholics always see the Church as being the authority in Herself. Of the Annunciation, for example, it was not only Mary, it was I who heard the angel voice.

I am against the ordination of women because it is not the Church's practice. I was dining some time ago in Trinity, my old college, and had next to me a very distinguished Anglican theologian who turned to me and said, 'Monsignor Gilbey, what would be your reaction if the Catholic Church started ordaining women?' I said, 'If the Catholic Church said it was all right, it would be all right by me. I follow what the church says and does.'

For nineteen centuries the Church has not ordained women and I see no likelihood of Her doing so. Why? Because it's something basic to Christian life and I cannot think She's got it wrong for nineteen centuries and will begin to put it right. It would be unprecedented against the whole background of the Church's history to think She might suddenly do a sort of *volte face*. The development of doctrine is a gradual unfolding of one thing. Catholics don't believe, for instance, that Our Blessed Lady became Immaculate in 1856 or that the Pope became infallible in 1870. It's a gradual developing of one truth and the ordination of women would be something quite otherwise.

Why is the Church 'She', not 'He'?

She is the Bride of Christ. She is always 'She', in all scripture and tradition. Forgive me for saying so, but I think you are always trying to get me back into what I call the Protestant position of having a view of my own about revelation.

With certain Protestant Churches already ordaining women, will any movement of an ecumenical sort be possible without some shift in the Catholic position?

I've never had any enthusiasm for ecumenism as the word is used and understood. When you talk of equality, it's a concept I don't understand, a concept that I think has no correspondence with reality and which denies two Christian concepts: first, the uniqueness of every single created being, made uniquely by Almighty God; and secondly, the fact that equality takes away the whole incentive of excellence, which, if properly understood, aspires to sanctity. Each of us should be trying to reach that height of holiness. Each man's vocation is unique. Look at the lives of the saints. They are not made to a common pattern. They include a lot of people in the world who are considered to be eccentrics.

We have remarked how the priests of the early Church married and Orthodox priests still do. Can you foresee a time when the Church will again permit marriage for priests?

That could happen, celibacy not having been imposed uniformly on Christian priests from the beginning. There has been a constant tendency that way, but, as we know from the scriptures, Peter had a mother-in law and presumably a wife, though she's never mentioned. In the early centuries, bishops and priests did marry, so there's nothing inherently improbable about married priests. Celibacy was a gradually, increasingly widely imposed discipline that could be altered without inconsistency. For many centuries, though, over more than a millennium now, it has been thought to be the ideal for the clergy.

Outsiders would say that for priests not to marry must inevitably cut them off from a great deal of human experience. Would not a married clergy be better placed to understand and sympathise with its flock's daily problems?

I wonder. I'm not saying yes or no to it, but I do wonder whether you'd say the same about them earning their livings in work or business. Would you claim it as far better for priests not to be dedicated solely to their ministry or that they'd be better able to understand the cares and responsibilities of people living in the world if they shared them? It's perfectly arguable, but I view it all with great indifference. Of course, it was vigorously advocated in France between the wars – the idea of worker priests – but I think the authorities have now abandoned the concept altogether.

Would you have married if the Church had allowed it when you were ordained?

I don't think so, because tradition was still so very strong. I certainly wouldn't marry now, even if celibacy was lifted. I can't imagine it at any period of my life because celibacy in my day has been a requirement of priests and the position hasn't changed. If it ever should change, I would not oppose it if the Church said it was all right.

But would you be in favour of priests marrying?

I always dodge that question. It seems irrelevant, whether I would or not.

But you are an important member of the Church.

Not a bit. I couldn't be less important. I am wholly unimportant in the administrative world of the Catholic Church.

Yet if there were to be a referendum within the Church?

I'm not a democrat, you know. I would not reply. I would not return the ballot paper.

Are you saying you believe in autocracy?

That suggests there can only be autocracy or democracy. Heaven knows how many grades there are in a hierarchical society. If you ask me whether I believe in a hierarchical society, the answer is yes, with every fibre of my being, but that isn't necessarily autocracy. Hierarchical societies, of which there are many, starting with the family, all have a series of pyramids going up. Every army, every regiment, every cooperation, every club, all have their power structures. I'm not, you see, remotely egalitarian.

You have loyally stated that if it's all right with Rome then it's all right with you.

It's not a question of loyalty, but a question of what I know because of what I believe about the church. Loyalty is something you can give or withdraw.

Is it going to be possible for the Church to hold together in the future in the same way as it did in the past? In South Africa priests have defied the Pope's authority in the matter of holding political office; in the United States there has long been clear opposition to the Pope's stand on birth control: any number of Catholics are clearly using methods of contraception in direct conflict with the Pope's ruling.

The Church will hold together. Catholics of my generation – those who reached maturity before the Second Vatican Council – took it for granted that the tidiness of the Church at that period was the norm. People who have no historical sense find it hard to appreciate that what was taken for granted – the tidiness in theology, in administration, in running the Church – represented an exceptional period in contrast with the previous fifteen centuries. In the early Church, that of the Fathers, you find a much greater diversity of opinion and practice. The process of tidying has been a gradual one, dependent on all sorts of administrative reasons, communication and literacy.

The fact that people claim to be Catholics and part of the Catholic Church, and yet are out of step, is no new thing at all. You find it in the early centuries, the difference earlier on being that much more immediate and drastic action was taken against them. They may now have become too numerous; I don't know. I know nothing of what goes on in the direct mind of the Vatican, and very little of what is happening outside this country, so I can't say how far people in positions of authority in the Church have gone out of step. You tell me there are bishops in the United States who reject the Church's teaching. I should doubt it very much.

Have you ever disagreed with a pronouncement of the Church or felt at odds with any item in its teaching?

Not ever. I'd have to leave, walk out of the Church, if I didn't agree. As a Catholic you simply have to believe what the Church teaches. It is a condition of membership. A Catholic cannot reject the doctrine of the Church yet remain a Catholic.

What She teaches as right or wrong – those things are a *sine aqua non* for a believing Catholic. That does not mean to say that a believing, practising Catholic has to accept the Church's policy on matters of administration and the like. It is possible to be entirely out of sympathy with many of the things the Church is doing, as I regret the liturgical changes, for example. You can be critical of such things, out of sympathy with them, and even oppose them, but you can't withstand them. It might be better to drive on the right rather than on the left. You can advocate it all you like, but you can't just start doing it. So it is with things like liturgical changes. You may think it far better to be able to have one uniform language for the whole Western Church, and you may advocate it, but you can't in practice ignore, stand outside or oppose the existing legislation. We are committed not to policy but absolutely to dogma and morals.

Many present-day Christians would see the doctrine of Papal Infallibility as standing in the way of any sort of liberalisation of the Church. Is the Church bound to adhere for ever to doctrines defined at a particular point in history?

The Church is committed to whatever She has defined. If you are suggesting that some past pronouncement imposing acceptance as grounds for becoming a Catholic might be changed in retrospect, then the answer's no. We must distinguish strongly between those things that can be altered and those that cannot. Policy can be altered; that can be done tomorrow. Definitions of doctrine, acceptance of which is necessary to being a Catholic, cannot be altered.

I would wish, however, to deplore as strongly as I can this approach to Papal Infallibility. What we believe in is the infallibility of the Church. First, the Church is a visible body here on earth, teaching infallibly what Christ has revealed to us in all sorts of ways. Secondly, that body cannot impose upon me error as a condition of belonging. Whenever She defines something, it must be accepted by every member and therefore must be true, otherwise She would be imposing acceptance of error. People talk about Papal Infallibility as if it were something never before heard of, but the infallibility of the Church is inherent from the very beginning.

When you say 'Church', do you differentiate between 'Pope' and 'Church'?

No. Quite the contrary. He is a part of it. Papal Infallibility is just one stated example of conditions for being a Catholic.

If faith is a gift of God, is it the duty of a Catholic to maintain a pious silence when it comes to a particular dogma in which he cannot compel himself to believe, even though he may wish to?

You can compel yourself to believe. If you have made the act of faith in Jesus Christ, and believe He is God, you will have to accept what He tells you. He came to open to us a whole cycle of knowledge otherwise unattainable. A Catholic must believe the teaching of the Church in all aspects of faith and morals.

Why would you say to those who find it impossible to subscribe to the dogmas of religion, who cannot, for example, understand how a good God can permit the innocent to suffer?

That's not dogma, it's a fact. We see suffering all about us and know in ourselves that we all suffer to various degrees. But we also know that God is infinitely good, infinitely kind, infinitely just, infinitely merciful, infinitely loving. It takes us back, of course, to something that *is* a dogma: The Fall of Man. There are two plains of knowledge concerning matters of religion. The first is the plain of natural reason. We can reach, and the majority of mankind have reached, a knowledge of the existence of the Supreme Being from which there follows man's free will, his consequent responsibility and his survival of death. That is what we call natural theology, and from there we go on to consider whether there has been a revelation, whether God has opened a whole cycle of knowledge to us that our native reason will bring us to accept only on faith. These are two completely different cycles of knowledge, the first requiring an act of reason, the second an act of faith. There was at the beginning of human history a complete dislocation of human nature that we call the Fall, made not by Almighty God but by the wickedness and sins of man.

Is the Church's stand against contraception to be defined as a dogma?

Yes, since it rises out of the whole concept of the purpose of sex. Sex is an inducement to continue the human race. People are so imprecise. The pleasure of sex cannot be put first. Unlike Protestants, there are many things we Catholics believe which are not found in the scripture. The Church has been left to continue Christ's Revelation.

It may seem to the outsider that the Catholic Church grudges man sexual pleasure.

We believe that the gift of sex is given to man primarily for the continuance of the human race. It provides the greatest physical pleasure known to man, precisely to give him the inducement to beget children. Who in their senses would go through the responsibilities of bringing children into this world, undertake the enormous expense of housing, feeding, educating them, bringing them up – all the annoyances and worries that lie in that – if there were not added to it the greatest of human pleasures? Many other consequences of exercising the sexual act exist – cementing affection between husband and wife, comfort, sustenance and so on – but you can't rule out the purpose for which it is given in order to isolate the secondary consequences. A parallel is the pleasure of eating and drinking.

It's the puritan not the Catholic who thinks that the pleasure sex gives is wrong. Likewise, it's the puritan who decries the pleasure of eating and drinking. That is very great too, though infinitely less so than the pleasure of sexual activity because the object is less important. The object of attaching pleasure to eating and drinking is really so that we may have an inducement to rebuild our bodily strength. You can't go for the secondary consequences and exclude the first, as the Romans did, when they had a vomitorium and, having eaten and drunk as much as they could, went out and made themselves sick so as to come back and eat and drink some more. That is to reject the purpose for which it is given to gain the lesser consequences. The use of sex for any reason excluding the main purpose is to do exactly the same.

Plainly, every sexual aberration or sin more or less excludes the main purpose. Solitary vice rules out the possibility of conception, as does unnatural sin between two people of the same sex. Fornication and adultery rule out the possibility of bringing up the children, and you cannot, always remember, separate procreation and education: bringing children into this world and bringing them up in the love and knowledge of Almighty God is a combined operation. In fornication you are plainly ruling out the very possibility of any children born to those parents being brought up within the framework of the family. Yet that is the first duty you owe them. Likewise, with adultery, you are side-stepping the whole function of the family by begetting children outside it.

So the Church itself does not discourage the pleasure of the flesh in general?

Of course not. To exclude it would be to negate God's purpose. God gave that gift, a most wonderful thing. It's impossible to exaggerate the sacredness of sex because, if you go back to the foundation of all we believe, God is the sole creator yet man is empowered to co-operate with Almighty God in the specifically divine work of creation. We rightly say that God created you, created me. How did he choose to do it? Through the sexual activities of your parents and mine. He was the Creator, but men and women take part in the creative act, a supremely god-like thing. As soon as sex is used for lesser purposes, it's belittling the whole staggering gift, reducing it to an animal level.

Some clergy are homosexual, yet they remain clergy.

It depends on what you mean by homosexual. No one, whatever their status, is justified in committing the act of sodomy. It's as simple as that. But if by homo-sexual you mean people who find their own sex more attractive and yet control their feelings, there's nothing wrong at all. It's no different from having a temp-tation to pride, or avarice, or anything. People always talk as though we can use sex as we like because it is a gift of Almighty God. Since the heterosexual can do as he likes, it's thought to be rather rough on homosexuals that they shouldn't commit sodomy. We are surrounded by a nine-tenths non-Christian population, and they all have the idea that any sort of sex is a perfectly normal thing. There's no need to marry, you can sleep with anyone you like, so it's thought to be unfair if homosexuals can't do the same.

But if a priest is a homosexual in the sense of committing homosexual acts, should he remain in the Church or should he be expelled?

I don't know whether he should or should not. That is a question of discipline. If you are practising sodomy then you are certainly in no fit state to celebrate the Eucharist each morning. But I must again emphasise the distinction between having a temptation and giving up the struggle. You're not a Christian at all if you give up the struggle.

Do you feel an intolerance of homosexuals or do you sympathise with their plight?

I sympathise with anyone who has committed a sin, be what it may. As with a man who can't keep his hand out of the till, I have to go on telling him that he mustn't do it. We all commit sins, we must all try to avoid the sins to which we are most prone. If your sin happens to be to want to commit sodomy, then you must struggle against it very hard indeed. It can be done. People do get over their evil tendencies, by God's grace. The fatal thing is to say I'm very strongly tempted and I'm not going to resist it.

If reconciliation with the Eastern Churches is a foreseeable possibility, would the Papacy ever agree to the idea of the Pope as primus inter pares?

No, he can't step down from his position. I hope and pray that such a reconcilia-tion will come about, and it seems to me a far less unlikely prospect than in the Protestant case. Protestantism is founded on a quite different belief, and every form of Protestantism, from extremist evangelical to extremist Anglo-Catholic, always comes back to private judgement. The concept of the East is quite distinct. It's an authoritative concept and this explains how it is that a bishop in the East could, in coming over, bring all his people with him. It couldn't happen in the West. If the Archbishop of Canterbury became Catholic tomorrow, he couldn't bring a single soul with him, not even his wife.

In the East, they are what are called autocephalous churches – that is to say, the head of the Church is the head of the Church. Whatever he says goes. It's much closer to the Catholic concept. All the Protestant sects in the West, on the other hand, take a stand on private judgement and democracy is applied to religion. In the same way that democracy is the application of equality in politics, so is private judgement the application of equality to religious truth.

Can the church respond effectively to the intransigence of Islamic fundamentalism without itself becoming intransigent?

The church is intransigent. She can't change. The idea of the Church changing is as foreign to me as equality or democracy. The only thing we are interested in is the sanctity of an individual human soul. The only progress is the progress towards sanctity for the individual. It matters for all eternity what you or I do between our births and our deaths. Any progress outside that is a will-o'-the-wisp, an illusion. The great landslide was the Fall. From then on human beings have been struggling between birth and death to escape its consequence. The only moral improvement of any value is between conception and death.

The Catholic Church has placed an emphasis on private confession, but since God knows our minds and hearts, is there any theological reason why communal confession should not be equally effective in seeking forgiveness of sins?

It's necessary to distinguish between what Christ gave us through His redemption of us and the means He chose to communicate it. He has redeemed us by suffering and death has chosen to communicate His gift through the sacraments, which we believe to operate infallibly. In the sacrament of penance, God's grace is given to us, brought into our souls, and so we have the covenanted means of our forgiveness. In the sacrament of the Eucharist, we receive our blessed Lord, the Fount of Grace himself, into our hearts. Almighty God is not tied to the sacraments, except, of course, that He's tied to honour them. His own omnipotence cannot, however be tied by the gift He's made, though if you are asking whether God Almighty can work outside the sacraments, the answer is yes, of course He can. There is no limit to His power. If you are asking whether that exempts us from using the covenanted means He has given us, the answer is no, it does not. We would be very foolish to ignore them. Can He work outside them? Most certainly He can. Does He work outside them?

We hope and pray that He does. But it's not our business. There's the short answer to your question.

There have been scandals in the Church over the centuries and the recent Banco Ambrosiano affair suggests that its administrative and financial arms have become very secular. Are these things inevitable?

Yes – because of fallen human nature. You can't peg things. You may have the most wonderful and altruistic machinery for running the Church's affairs, but there's no guarantee it'll continue. We can make it a great deal better than it is, but we can also make it a great deal worse. The answer to all the events we deplore is fallen human nature. Only individuals can make any moral advance and therefore are bound to be scandals. If you shall hear of wars, or rumours of wars, see that you be not troubled. And, perhaps, scandals, and rumours of scandals – see that you be not troubled. There are always scandals. None of us, God knows, fulfils his obligation perfectly. The degree of failure may vary enormously with the individual.

There was the book by John Cornwell on the death of John Paul I that suggested he was murdered.

Well, as I say, human nature is fallen. You find fallen human beings everywhere. I have no idea of the particular case, but there is nothing inherently improbable in a Pope being murdered, any more than with anyone else. There's no end to human villainy. The fact that a man is a priest, a bishop or a Pope doesn't exempt him, or those surrounding him, from the consequences of the Fall. If you are asking whether it is possible for a Pope to be murdered by his own entourage, then the answer is yes, it is possible – though I think it wildly improbable.

You are said to be a hunting enthusiast, but killing animals for entertainment, especially fox-hunting, has come to be regarded in a poor light by very many people. Is such enthusiasm really sustainable these days?

I don't like that notion of entertainment at all. It sounds like sadism. We must start at the very beginning. God gave man complete dominion over the whole of creation. Man is the apex of creation, and his use of it is conditioned by the good or bad it does to him, not by creation itself. People often talk as if animals had rights. Only rational beings can have rights, just as only rational beings can have duties. There are no rights involved in this at all. Consequently, man has hunted from the beginning and deprived animals of their freedom – we call it domesticating them. He has made them breed and lead lives not natural to them. How can they possibly have freedom in the proper sense of the term? Freedom is the free exchange of will, and animals have no wills.

We take them into captivity, domesticate them, cause them to breed, prevent their breeding, castrate them, kill them for food, for clothing, and they have no rights to prevent it. The only question for man in his dealings with animals is what moral harm may those dealings do to him? That is why I demur at the word 'entertainment'. It does man terrible moral harm to be a sadist. To enjoy and indulge in cruelty, to torture a cat, is sinful. To torture anything for the pleasure the act gives you is sinful.

So when you allow hounds to tear up a fox, isn't that sinful?

No. Of all forms of sport, hunting arouses the most animosity, the strong, popular feeling against it being largely fuelled by social considerations. It's thought to be inegalitarian, aristocratic, but when you come to analyse it, it's the nearest to nature of all the forms of field sport. No one raises a voice against fishing, yet in terms of cruelty or pain inflicted, fishing may be the most callous sport of all. You can play a salmon for two or three hours with a hook in its mouth. I'm not saying that's wrong, I'm just pointing out how disproportionate the feeling is against hunting.

Hunting is the nearest to nature because you are perfecting what nature is doing all the time. At this very moment rabbits are being savaged by stoats, hens are having their head bitten off by foxes. The whole of nature is, as Tennyson had it, red in tooth and claw. Whatever a hunger does is quite right for him to do, unless he is getting a sadistic pleasure, and then he is certainly harming himself rather than the animals he kills. He is then making a beast of himself, doing himself moral harm. All Catholics will tell you the same. You can shoot birds, hunt foxes, fish completely freely, so long as you are not doing yourself moral harm.

Is it ever a worry to you that your lifestyle – living in a London club, giving dinner parties – might be misinterpreted by some members of the Church?

First of all. I think that worry is a sin. Worry means you don't really believe in divine providence. My favourite text in the Old Testament is, 'Be still and know that I am God.' Worry is unprofitable thinking about disagreeable things. With regard to my lifestyle, I'm not an egalitarian and I don't believe in a universally acceptable lifestyle. To return to the secular and the regular clergy, there are a lot of things that would be sinful in a member of an order who has abandoned the world and all personal money. He's housed, fed and clothed, and money is not his concern, so for him to throw a party might be considered a subject of criticism.

But as I have said, a secular priest keeps what money he has, what money he comes by honestly. If he chooses to entertain friends, then he is doing absolutely nothing wrong. There's not any uniform lifestyle which it is wrong to step outside. To think there is egalitarianism is my *bête noire*.

Have you any regrets?

One has to distinguish between regrets and contrition. I suppose we all have regrets. Precious few in my case, I've been so lucky. But if you mean sorrow for sin – yes, that's a very good thing to have. I've committed many sins in my life and I am sorry for them at the present moment. One has to live in the present moment; it's all we have. One can't touch the past. It's the work of this moment to be sorry for the sins of one's whole life.

Are you looking forward to the next life?

I'm not, because I'm properly concerned for the private judgement. I hope I shall not have offended God Almighty gravely. I can't say I am certain of going to heaven. I keep hoping and praying that I shall die in the love and mercy of Almighty God and be forgiven all my sins, but that's His business. Mine is to do the best I can. My two great temptations are idleness and vanity. I'm very tempted to do nothing, and by vanity I mean liking to give and receive human affection. Thank God I have received a great deal and given a great deal, but that tempts one to think of one as important, and one isn't, of course. So that's a general confession I will make at my last moment. If a priest comes when I am dying I shall say these have been the besetting sins of my eighty years of life and I shall ask for absolution for them and for many others.

How would you like to be remembered?

I don't expect to be remembered, frankly. I have made no mark on the world at all.

RUMER GODDEN

Rumer Godden was the author of more than sixty books, mostly novels for adults and children, but also biographies, plays and poetry. She was born in 1907 and spent most of her childhood in a remote village in East Bengal where her father worked for a steamship company. She first went to school at the age of twelve in Eastbourne, but soon returned to India. She married in 1934 and had two children, but later divorced and returned to England after the war where she devoted her time to writing. Her novels *Black Narcissus* (1939) and *The Greengage Summer* (1958) were made into films, as was her Indian epic *The River*, directed by Jean Renoir. She wrote two volumes of autobiography: *A Time to Dance, No Time to Weep* (1987) and *A House with Four Rooms* (1989). She was awarded an OBE in 1993 and won the Whitbread Award for children's literature. Her final years were spent in Scotland with her daughter. Her last book, *Cromartie vs the God Shiva Acting Through the Government of India*, was published in November 1997, and she died in 1998.

From India to Dumfriesshire is a long journey in any life. Have you been able to regard Scotland as home, or is India still where you belong in spirit?

I'm always divided. I've never regarded Scotland as home, but I'm deeply attached to England. I'm like the character in the Gilbert and Sullivan play who was a fairy up to his waist and a human above. I have India in my bones and when I'm in England I'm homesick for India and when I'm in India I'm homesick for England. It's very difficult.

When you were 19 you read Forster's A Passage to India, *which changed your life. It made you ashamed of what you call your 'blindness and ignorance' – how little you understood of the India you inhabited. Can you recall those feelings?*

When I was a child in India the old shibboleth still prevailed that the men had contact with all the Indians but the women and children were not supposed to mix. My father spoke Bengali and Hindi, but we were not allowed to in case we caught the accent and became 'chichi', as they called it. We were not allowed to play with Indian children, nor they with us, and as for the Anglo-Indians, those of mixed marriages, they were absolutely outré. We sometimes used to escape and get over our garden wall into the bazaar without anyone knowing. And so even as a child I saw perhaps more of India than my mother, but if I asked questions they were never answered. It was *A Passage to India* that suddenly made me see that we were like the Turtons. After that I astonished my father and mother by insisting that I was given lessons in Hinduism and allowed to visit Indians and speak to them.

Late on you wrote; 'in India, for many people, especially women, the pastiche was their life, and nearly was mine.' Was this pastiche a reference to the hierarchy of colonisation?

Probably, but it was unconscious. For instance, I never heard the word British Raj; that was an invention that came after independence. And my father had deep compassion and fellowship with his employees. What enabled me to avoid the pastiche was that I was a born writer and writers are very curious; they like to understand where they live and not feel shut off. Later on I broke away from my family and after training as a dancer, I outraged everybody by opening a dancing school in Calcutta, an unheard-of thing. My father was shocked and told me that I would be ostracised by my fellow English. These attitudes lasted a long time. Even when I went back to India as a married woman with my children, the Swiss Italian nanny, who was very dark, used to take the children swimming. I was soon rung up by the secretary of the club to say that my nanny had been seen swimming in the pool and since she was half-caste, that was not allowed, not even with the children. The narrowness was incredible.

Much of your writing is related to the extraordinary events of your life and, in a sense, writing was not a luxury but a necessity, a means of earning a living. Do you think there was an element of necessity being the mother of invention?

I think it brought it to fulfilment, but I believe writers are born. My sister was far more gifted than I was, but she married an extremely rich man and was very spoiled. I had no option, I had to work, and I had a very stern apprenticeship when I got back to London after the Second World War. I was practically penniless, and I wrote anything I could, articles, essays, anything that came my way, and it was a wonderful training. It was something I had to do because I had two children and no husband.

Certain books you read in your younger days seem to have had a very significant effect ... Mr Darcy from Pride and Prejudice, *for example, made such an impression that for a long time no man could measure up. Can you recall the intensity of that feeling, or does it now strike you as absurd, looking back?*

No, I have it still today. I've read *Pride and Prejudice* 13 times and every time I fall in love with Mr Darcy. Nothing has changed. There is still a lot of the child in me, and though I've been through a lot of adversity, I have retained that feeling of wonder which enables me to fall in love with Mr Darcy again.

Your own romantic path did not run smooth. How much do you think was to do with colonial life and the restrictions and expectations placed upon it?

Not much. I don't think I was in love with my first husband but I was in love with the idea of being married and he was a very charming person, though he was not all he should have been. But my second husband was wonderful to me, absolutely wonderful, the most understanding man I ever met, and totally unselfish.

You broke off your first engagement, and wrote of your fiancé: 'I hurt him abominably, but not as much as I would have done had I married him.' It must have taken tremendous courage to do what you did, especially in the face of family opposition ...

Yes, my parents were furious with me. In fact I left home for a while. They so wanted me to marry him. He was a very desirable match, and it seemed to be so perfect, because he fell in love with me when I was only 8, and he waited all the time that I was at school until I came back to India with the unwavering conviction that he was going to marry me. I was barely 18, and I just knew I couldn't.

In 1934 you married Lawrence Forster, whom you described as 'unfailingly kind'. That description seemed to condemn rather than to praise ...

Well, it wasn't meant to. I just didn't know what else to say about him. When I first wrote my autobiography I left him out, but my dear publisher said I had to include him. He was absolutely charming and like very many charming people, not to be trusted. I have a deep distrust of charm. I was never really in love with him, but I tried again and again to save the marriage, because I had the children and he was their father. He had perpetual money trouble, but by then I was earning quite well from writing. *Black Narcissus* was a real bestseller and brought in a tremendous amount of money which is why I thought I could afford a nanny and a nice house. This was before I realised that my husband had gambled on the stock exchange and was deeply, deeply in debt. I used up all my money in paying off his debts, which was perhaps the most foolish thing I ever did because it didn't save the situation.

But I was very pleased by my father's reaction when I told him what I'd done. He said, 'He's your children's father. It was the only thing you could have done.'

You were pregnant when you married … was that rather a shocking thing in the 30s?

Oh frightful … dreadful. And had I not been pregnant the marriage would not have taken place.

Sadly, that baby lived only four days, 'a piercing grief' as you describe it …

Yes, it was a sadness I have carried around for the rest of my life. And he was the only boy. I went on to have two daughters, but he was my son. I was so alone because nobody would have anything to do with me. My mother rallied to me, but my father was very shocked. What I should have done was to go back to England and have the baby and not get married; but I hadn't the courage.

Do you believe that suffering helps the creative process?

Yes, I believe in the garret. This is what makes me so sad about young writers nowadays who won't do anything till they've got a commission. Money and safety are more important to them than creativity, and of course they put themselves into a straitjacket. I never try to take a penny until I've got the book approved and finished, and I can say to myself, now there is a book.

In your autobiography you write: 'It's frightening what intensity of feeling is aroused when anyone derides or desecrates something holy or simply beautiful – I cannot stop myself burning with anger.' These words were written with reference to your first husband, but is it something which extended beyond the marriage, something you have felt all your life perhaps?

Oh yes. People spoil and desecrate things, they take away a child's innocence. When I see mothers shaking their children and telling them not to daydream, I really feel like shaking them. It outrages me, I cannot bear it. It especially grieves me with religion. In Scotland where I live there is a lot of intolerance. I am a Catholic convert, and the feeling against Popery, as they call it, is very bitter. I once had to meet a nun, a very fine woman, travelling back from London to the convent near us. When she got off the train she was very pale. I asked her if she was all right and she told me she'd been standing by the carriage door waiting to get out – because I had warned her that the train only stopped at this little station for two minutes – and two women came by, and when they saw her in her habit they called out 'Satan!', and spat all over her. Now that is a terrible thing.

Why did you convert to Roman Catholicism?

I searched for a religion for a very long time. I nearly became a Hindu. Then I tried the Anglican Church which my grandmother was a great supporter of, but it seemed to me full of hypocrisy. When I went up to the alter rail to take communion I saw that people were looking at me. I went to the vicar and asked him why, and he told me it was because I had been divorced. He then said that he would prefer me not to come to communion on any of the big feast days at Christmas or Easter when people would see me. It was then I realised that the Anglican Church was not for me. With the Catholic Church, you know where you are. It was about 16 years before I could become a Catholic, because of my divorce, and I believe that a church which lays down such rules is not a hypocritical church. It is also the only Christian church that was founded by Christ; all the others were founded by men for expediency.

You have always been captivated by beautiful places and have written very movingly of the beauty of India. That country also contains a lot of ugliness, squalor, deprivation, hunger. How did you reconcile the two aspects?

By living with both. When I had my little house in Kashmir, I became the village wise woman in the sense that they all came to me if anything went wrong. The suffering in winter was simply terrible there. Women wore just a quilted cotton garment, nothing underneath, bare legs and bare feet and straw sandals. I tried to alleviate the suffering, though I couldn't do much. And when I was running my dancing school I took the Anglo-Indian children, which shocked people of course, but I wasn't going to have that kind of discrimination. I trained a troupe of very poor Anglo-Indian girls so that they could do cabaret and earn money. So one knew all about the squalor and the filth. Quite a lot of us women who had a conscience did.

Apropos the number of broken marriages in India during the 30s, you say: 'I cannot understand now why we could have broken those vows we made, though then there seemed nothing else we could do.' There seems to be an enormous amount of pain behind those words …

Yes, that's true. A broken marriage is a very dreadful thing but I didn't know what else to do. My father said to me, 'You will never bring up your children properly while you're married to that man.' Of course, if I had the belief then that I have now, I would never have divorced; but then I would never have met James, and I had such wonderful years with him.

Both you and your sister Jon divorced. Was there a degree of stigma attached to divorce in those days?

Not in India. It became extremely common. Calcutta is a terribly corrupt city, you know. They say if you put a bag of Calcutta dust under the bed of a virtuous woman she becomes corrupt overnight. There are a tremendous lot of broken marriages and unfaithfulness and affairs going on … it's a rotten society.

After the separation there followed some difficult years in India on your own with the children. Since it was wartime and the men were in any case away, did that make your own circumstances appear more normal?

My circumstances then were absolutely abnormal. We were what they call an abandoned family, though we were much more abandoned than most, because the custom was that if the husband was taken away or volunteered to go to war, his firm paid the wife half his salary and kept his position open for him. My husband had been sacked, and I had no money, absolutely none, which is why I went and lived literally like a peasant.

Looking back on that time when there was illness and shortage of money and uncertainty about the future, do you wonder how you had the strength to come through it all?

I cannot imagine where I got it from. Everybody said to me that I must get a job, but I knew I had to get my writing established. My dear father and mother who were then living in Cornwall offered me their home, but after thinking very deeply about things, I decided to live in London and write.

The 'Four Rooms' of your second volume of autobiography divided into the physical, mental, emotional and the spiritual. Have these rooms all enjoyed equal importance?

No, the physical room is very barely inhabited, because I injured my back when I was very young and I've never played a game in my life. The mental room of course is the one I'm tempted to spend a lot of time in, but that is now balanced by the spiritual. The emotional has always been there.

Your future looked bleak when you stood on the Liverpool docks with two small children after losing nearly all your possessions … were you despairing or did you manage to remain hopeful?

I think it was determination more than anything else. I knew I had to do it for the sake of the children, quite apart from anything else.

You wrote then: 'To despair is traitorous to your gift.' Do you think that creativity requires hope?

I suppose it does. You see, I am a strange person – I don't believe in self-expression. All these young people, and particularly women say, oh we want to express ourselves, but writing is not self-expression. The writer is simply an instrument through which the wind blows and I believe it is the third part of the trinity, the spirit, the Holy Spirit, that makes the artist creative. My writing is something outside me that I've been chosen to do, and I think that is what has enabled me to go on.

It seems you had a very practical unsentimental approach towards life. Most mothers would have clung to their children in your circumstances, but you sent your daughters off to school, knowing that it would be best in the long run for both of you. Did you ever regret that?

I regret that I couldn't find a way to keep them at home. If I had been able to find a good governess or nurse, I would have sent them to day school, but just after the war domestic help was terribly difficult to sustain, and I couldn't expose them to the kind of life I led when they were at school. It would have meant hours and hours shut away from them.

Black Narcissus *was made into a film and has become a classic, but you thought it was a travesty of the book. Did there come a time when you stopped worrying about that?*

No, I've minded about it always. I won't see it. I saw it only once, but never again. It is an absolute travesty of the book, I cannot bear it. Micky Powell, the director, said he saw it as a fairy tale, whereas to me it was true. I stipulated that they should send a unit to India, which they did, but they never used a foot of what they shot there. They might as well never have been near India, and my young Rajput prince was played by some coolie boy with a snub nose and lots of charm, but no more Rajput than I'm Rajput. The whole thing was an abomination.

You vowed you would never allow another book to be made into a film, but relented in the case of Jean Renoir and The River. *Did you ever regret that decision?*

No, it was the greatest two years of my life. What I learned from Jean was absolutely extraordinary, and I could feel myself growing as I worked with him. He was a wonderful man, a real genius. In Paris the film broke all records, and now it goes on and on and has become a classic. It's also beginning to go in India now.

Before long James Haynes-Dixon came into your life, but you held out for a long time against marrying again ... why was that exactly?

Because of the experience I'd had before. I wasn't going to tie myself down.

It seems that marriage came about more through perseverance and persistent kindness on his part, rather than a passionate romance. There was certainly no coup de foudre. *Do you think perhaps that made for a stronger basis in the end?*

I think it did. After being very patient, he laid down an ultimatum when I went to Beverly Hills to do the script for *The River*, and he said that if I would not agree to marriage he would not be there when I got back. The idea of life without James was more than I could bear, so I married. I needed him. I'd been fighting so long on my own, and he was like a wall behind me, always supportive and entirely unselfish.

Do you still miss him?

Oh terribly ... and I never want to be consoled. It's not given to many women to be loved like that ... absolutely selflessly.

Marriage then seemed to weigh rather heavily for a time and you missed your freedom, but as you put it, 'we grew content'. Did this take a long time?

About three or four years, I think. I hadn't been prepared for James to take complete authority over me and the children; we weren't used to it, and the children didn't like it, so life was very difficult. They were very fond of James before I married him, but then he started feeling responsible for us and asserting his authority. My mother helped a lot and used to talk to him about this. The children eventually had to come round to him because he was so extraordinarily good to them, though I think they always had reservations, even to the very end. But they were terribly affected by his death.

Pekinese dogs have always been important to you. I was struck by the story of the two sad dogs you inherited and how you did not try to cajole them out of their sadness, but instead respected their grief. Have you applied the same philosophy to people?

Yes, when I'm with people who have had a tremendous grief I always say to them not to try and be too brave. Grief is good, but not self-pity. I can't stand people saying 'why should this happen to me?' when it's the law of life.

Twice in your life you lost all your possessions – once in India, and once when your house in Sussex burned to the ground. Do you think people who have experienced loss on this scale have a different attitude to life?

Oh yes, it changes you completely. I don't want things now ... I know they're going to be taken away. As you get older, you've got to shed your possessions as fast as you can, and I have arrived at that critical time of not wanting things. I want books of course, but those are part of living. I like my house uncluttered. I like space, I like emptiness, and I like silence.

You set great store by the power of prayer. Have you ever been troubled by wondering what kind of God it might be who is persuaded to change His mind on certain matters, as a result of people praying to Him?

I've seen wonderful things done by prayer. I think that He can be swayed. And I also think you're meant to pray, to put yourself in touch with God. Everything may be preordained, but I have actually seen the most wonderful things happen after prayer.

What is your attitude towards death?

I'm not afraid of death. My mother put it to me wonderfully when I was a little girl. I was a very sensitive child and although I wasn't afraid of dying myself, I was terribly afraid of my mother or my sister dying. One night when I was crying in bed my mother came, and said to me, 'We can't understand what is going to happen to us after death, in much the same way that if we told a little two months old baby that we were going to take it to America, the baby wouldn't have the faintest idea of what we were talking about.' And that's how I think of death – we have no idea what's going to happen to us.

Do you think that without pain and suffering it's not possible fully to appreciate the great joy in life?

Some people seem to be born with the spirit of joy, and they don't seem to have much trouble in their lives, and people always wonder why. It may be that they are what I would call very old souls, they've been here before, quite often, and they're very happy and joyous. For most people, however, the pain and suffering make them prize the joy.

SIR ERNST GOMBRICH

E. H. Gombrich was born in Austria in 1909. He studied at the University of Vienna, taking his PhD in 1933. In 1936 he emigrated to Britain, where he joined the staff of the Warburg Institute in London, becoming its director and Professor of the History of the Classical Tradition from 1959 until he retired in 1976. During the war he monitored German broadcasts for the BBC. His books, for which he has received many awards, include *The Story of Art* (1950), the world's best-selling art-history book, *Art and Illusion* (1960), a study of the psychology of pictorial representation, and *The Image and the Eye* (1982). He became a member of the Order of Merit in 1988, was awarded the Goethe Prize in 1994 and continued his work at the University of London until his death in 2001, aged ninety-two.

You were born in Vienna in 1909. How important were the place of your birth and the culture of your upbringing in determining the patterns of your life?

Immensely important. I'm still an Austrian, of course, I am a product of the Viennese middle class and culture, and I have never tried to conceal this.

Vienna has entered the public perception as the cultural and intellectual centre at the turn of the century, but you have always rather rejected this view ... why is that exactly?

Because I think it is an exaggeration. Vienna was an important centre, but so was Paris, so was Berlin, and other places too. Intellectual fashions play a certain part in putting some things into the limelight and neglecting other very important influences, and I think this happened with Vienna. One cannot say that Europe owed everything to Vienna at that time.

Although you are of Jewish extraction you were not educated in the Jewish tradition. Have you ever had reason to regret this?

No, which doesn't mean that I have no appreciation or esteem for certain aspects of Jewish education. But I have been quite happy with my own formation, which after all was the choice of my parents – and why should I criticise my parents?

You say it can only be of interest to racists that the Viennese contribution to the modern world was in large measure Jewish. Why do you think this is a racist issue and not just a matter of fact?

There is an element of fact of course, but always to ask whether an artist or a writer was Jewish or not Jewish seems to me very much beside the point. In my youth, nobody asked whether they were Jewish or not; it was only after Hitler invented the term Aryan that one began to wonder where they came from.

You belonged to the middle classes, but you knew hardship and poverty from time to time. Do you think this is the kind of experience which remains with one always, no matter how one's fortunes change?

I'm sure it does remain up to a point. For example, I was surprised that I managed to live quite comfortably on a job in which I never expected to be able to make money at all. I'm grateful, but I never expected it …

At one stage you were evacuated to Sweden, suffering from malnutrition. How much do you remember of that time … do you remember feeling hungry?

No, not actually hungry, but the fare was very drab – lots of turnips and potatoes – and certainly not what one would expect a middle-class child to have. I still remember my Swedish years with very much pleasure. I learned the language, I read children's books and certain things – the full text of the national anthem of Sweden, for example – remain with me.

Your childhood was steeped in music in the classical tradition. Was this the first sort of aesthetic response you were aware of making?

Probably, though my father also took us to the great museums of Vienna, in particular to the Art Historical Museum which was only ten minutes' walk from our house, and we also had a great many books on painting. My older sister began to look at these books and then to draw, and that also played a part in my response. But certainly classical music was and remains my central aesthetic experience, even now.

You have sometimes said that the time you spent in Austria was not a happy time, and yet your childhood and adolescence seem to have been secure and enriched by caring and intelligent and cultured parents. What was it that made you unhappy?

The general atmosphere was one of depression, the political tension was enormous, there was a lot of unemployment and terrible inflation. Vienna was largely socialist – its working population came from Bohemia and Hungary, and elsewhere – while the countryside was still very much dominated by the Catholic Church. Therefore, the tension between the partly atheist Marxist Vienna and the peasant farming communities became very acute, so that one could say there was a latent civil war even before real civil war broke out. There was certainly mutual contempt and hatred. The conservative farmers and their representatives accused the socialists of being entirely Jewish led, which was not completely true, though there was an element of truth. So, the general atmosphere and the expectations were far from happy, and one was also very much aware of the impossibility of ever leading a normal life in the future.

When did you first become aware of anti-Semitism?

When I first read anti-Semitic posters on the hoardings. They were probably put there not by the Nazi party, which did not exist in that form, but by radical nationalist groups who agitated against the Polish Jewish immigrants. I remember the headlines referring to the Jews with their sidelocks and their kaftans, and the question: where are they now? The answer was given below: they are now the bankers and the rulers of finance and they swindle us.

Was the university in those days open to everyone who qualified, or was it a question of fees and who could afford to go?

They were open to everyone who did the *matura*, which was the final exam at school. There were fees but they were minimal. The number of students was therefore very large, too large, but they crowded into fields where they hoped that they would at least find teaching jobs. By the time I went to university, which was in 1928, anti-Semitism was highly organised – this of course was long before the *Anschluss*. There was a Roman Catholic league and there was a nationalist league and gradually they saw their main job, particularly the nationalists, as hunting Jews and beating them up. Because of an old medieval privilege, universities were extra-territorial, which meant that the police were not allowed to enter, and these thugs abused this privilege by gradually introducing a reign of terror against Jews within the University. The atmosphere was very tense, and as we all know, the professors, while not exactly approving, closed more than one eye; they were cowards and they themselves had certain nationalist leanings, so they minimised the criminality of these groups.

Were you ever assaulted?

I look sufficiently Jewish to have been in some danger, and yes, I was assaulted, but I was not beaten up. However, one of my best friends was badly wounded in an attack with a steel rod while he was working in the university library.

To embark on a career in art history strikes me as a brave thing to have done at that time ... *was there no parental opposition?*

My father was very dubious. He would very much have liked me to follow him and become a solicitor, and he was certainly not happy when I told him I was very interested in the history of art, but he was much too humane and kind to oppose it. He only wondered whether I would ever be able to make a living that way, and he was quite right to wonder. No, there was no opposition, and in fact my sister studied law and she eventually took over the office.

You said that you were never very interested in mainstream art history – connoisseurship *and attribution – you preferred explanation. What sort of explanation is relevant to a* *work of art? Is it possible or desirable to reach towards the artist's psychological state?*

There is no bar on hypothesis, on anything one might try to find to explain a work of art. I don't think that we know enough about the artists of the past to make an elaborate psychological hypothesis about them. What we do know is what one might call the social context of the work of art, who commissioned it, who bought it, who the artist's teachers were and what he was trying to do.

You said once that you were dissatisfied with traditional explanations of style, those which *emphasised 'the spirit of the age', and you mentioned in opposition to that the importance* *of 'formulae' ... could you tell me something of that?*

At the time when I studied there were some very eminent art historians who treated art as an expression of the spirit of the age. So you heard about the 'spirituality' of the middle ages, and the 'sensuality' of the rococo. Now I don't want to say that all this is wrong, I only say that on the whole it is pretty vacuous and empty. It has always been true that people were occasionally sensual and occasionally spiritual – even at the time of the rococo – and the idea that medieval man as he is sometimes called was a kind of different species from us seems to me slightly ridiculous. People were always people, they had their own impulses and their own ideas. Naturally there are intellectual and religious movements which one must take into account, but one shouldn't exaggerate the differences between ages and periods. The main reason why I have opposed these stereotypes and clichés is that they are insufficient – they really tell us very little.

You have always had an urge towards the scientific, but how does that mesh with an aesthetic response to art? What part can science play in judgements of this type?

Science cannot explain, and I don't think science will ever be able to tell us why a work of art or a piece of music is so great, but science may be able to explain why a tradition is necessary in art. Every artist has to start from something, the formula you mentioned before, and this science can explain. But the aesthetic experience remains outside the region of science; in other words, if somebody hears a beautiful tune by Mozart and asks me why this is so beautiful, I can have no scientific answer.

You arrived in London in January 1936. Did you think you were leaving your country for good then?

No, but I was aware of the possibility. One never thinks of the worst and the worst would have been, as indeed happened, that Hitler would invade Austria. At that time it did not seem so likely because Austria, that little state with very bad diplomacy, was vaguely protected by Mussolini who didn't want the Germans at his frontiers. There was a very precarious balance of power, and one just hoped against hope that this might hold.

You must have felt very isolated when you first came to England, and quite soon England was at war with your native country. What did you feel in those early years?

I wasn't as isolated as perhaps others may have been because my mother, who was a piano teacher, had a number of English students, and when I went to England some of them became family friends. But it is true that the lack of knowledge of the language, and of ordinary habits and customs, isolated the little enclave of scholars who had arrived at the Warburg Institute. These were very tense years because of the constant awareness that war might break out. Hitler was making one demand after another, and one was very conscious of the possibility either of appeasement or of war, and neither was a pleasant alternative.

Did you think you had come to a safer place when you came to England?

Yes, originally when I arrived, but very soon people started talking about what would happen if London was bombed and so on. People exaggerated the power of incendiary bombs, some of which could be stamped out with the foot; they talked about them almost as they now talk about nuclear bombs.

Were you conscious of any psychological change in yourself because of the war?

Yes. During that time I was really interested in the war and had very little time or inclination to think about the history of art. I was working at the BBC, very hard, long hours, terribly intense. We probably overrated the importance of our work which was to listen to foreign broadcasts, particularly German Nazi broadcasts, and the tricks of propaganda they used. Of course, one listened with a certain detachment, one didn't believe a word of what they said, though sometimes, if one didn't believe it, it happened unfortunately to be true, as in the case of Khatyn, for instance, though even then I had my doubts. On the whole one was completely absorbed in this work and in the problems of translation. It was almost like being on a ship – there were people from all parts of the world who were members of the team because they knew Greek, or Turkish, or Albanian, or Estonian and we all just sat there listening to the wireless. After a time I became a supervisor and my job was to check the translations before they were passed on to a unit for publication. So my interests in that time certainly changed. The psychology of propaganda fascinated me. For instance, I listened very often to Goebbels' speeches. There was something definitely diabolic in him, in the way he talked, in the way he insinuated himself, in the way he could apparently control his emotions. He was able to manipulate argument, and he was certainly an educated man. In that respect he was very different from Hitler who was much more vulgar and exploited his vulgarity as a demagogue.

Your parents decided to join you in London in 1938 … was that an agonising decision for them?

Absolutely. It would not have happened if my father hadn't come to believe that he was in personal danger. They both believed they were safe, but one day my mother was summoned to the Gestapo in connection with a letter she had given to a student of hers. The letter had been intercepted at the frontier so she was called upon to explain what she had written. Nothing happened to her, but it was a real warning signal. Also, my father's passport was taken away for a time because he had been a freemason, so gradually they saw that really it was necessary to leave.

It must have been very depressing to be classified as enemy aliens. How did you cope with that?

Well, one had a certain detachment, and it was after all true up to a point. I don't think it was particularly depressing. It even had its funny side. As an enemy alien a curfew was imposed and I wasn't allowed to go out after sunset. On every normal day of the week, however, I went on my bike to engage in secret work at my listening post, but on my days off I wasn't allowed to go out. Obviously ridiculous.

Did you have ambivalent feelings towards Austria at that time?

I still have. Of course, I was perfectly aware of the situation, not that I knew all the horrors, but sufficiently aware to know something of what was happening. My feelings were torn, and still are, just as when it came to the destruction of beautiful cities by British bombers. For all of us who valued the European heritage, the destruction of Dresden or the blowing up of the bridges of the Arno in Florence were very painful events.

It must have been a strange experience to find yourself monitoring broadcasts and contributing to an effort to overcome the people you had just left. Did you find it disturbing?

Not at all, but then – though there is an element of fiction in this – Austria regarded itself as an occupied country, occupied by Hitler and the forces of expansionist Germany. Traditionally Austrians never liked the Germans very much – this was based on a slightly silly jealousy – but the Austrians like all nations considered themselves superior. For example, a German tourist was always slightly looked down upon in Austria.

Have you ever had strong political leanings?

No, never. I have a horror of mass demonstrations, and whenever I see people marching through the streets and shouting I see them as parrots who cannot think for themselves. I find all that very depressing, and therefore I've never been at all inclined to join a party. Many of my friends in Vienna leaned strongly towards the socialists, but I always stayed aloof.

After the war you returned to the Warburg Institute and wrote The Story of Art, *which was to change your life, and yet you had mixed feelings about writing it, and despaired of completing it. Had you any idea of how successful it would be?*

Not the slightest idea, no. I had written a world history in German before the war, also a surprising success, and then the publisher wanted me to do a history of art. I started tentatively, and then the war came, and I didn't do anything for a while. Then I accepted a contract, and so I wrote it, but a little *contre coeur.*

Now, some 40 years later, you seem to have mixed feelings about the success because you are always, perhaps too narrowly, associated with it. Is that a sore point with you?

It's not a sore point at all. I mean, I'm quite happy if people tell me that they've read it at school, or at polytechnic or whatever, and sometimes I get very nice fan letters. I think my mixed feelings may have been exaggerated. After all a good many people do know that I am also a historian who has done genuine research.

But you become Slade Professor of Fine Art at Oxford, you were invited to America and became extremely famous, all because of that book. Is it that you feel in a sense it sold too many copies, it appealed too much to the masses?

No, I don't think that at all. I am very happy about that – after all I wrote it for that purpose. What I feel sometimes a little dubious about is when it is used as a textbook. I prefer it to be read at leisure as a book to be enjoyed, rather than as a book to be swotted up and learned for facts.

At one point in the preface to The Story of Art *you distinguished between what you call real works of art and examples of fashionable pieces. How is that distinction made?*

That is a subjective distinction, I entirely agree, though most of us would know examples of works which are sort of nine-day wonders and suddenly disappear again as fast as they appeared. They are examples of fashion rather than any real intellectual or emotional effort. But I don't think anybody can absolutely draw the line ... I mean, Picasso became very fashionable, but he was also a real artist, and the same is true of many others. In the case of Dali, I feel that he is more a case of fashion, although he was very skilful; certainly he was not contemptible, he could really paint.

I should like to touch on what I suppose is a central difficulty for art historians, and indeed anyone interested in art: the matter of taste. Unless you allow that all artifice is art and do not distinguish the good from the not so good, are you not obliged to offer your own taste as a reliable yardstick, and to explain that what you like, everyone ought to?

No, I don't think that is true, though I think it is a very understandable attitude. Most of us who are interested in art can say this work is not to my taste but I recognise it as very respectable work of art. Taste is something which fluctuates enormously ... even in my time taste has changed radically; for instance certain artists like the Bolognese of the 17th century were considered much too theatrical, much too cheap in a way, and I had friends who helped in rehabilitating these painters and now we all see that they are really masters in their own right, even if they don't appeal to our present day taste. But one has to have a basic interest in the art for taste to be able to develop. For instance, I have no taste for ballet, so I wouldn't set myself up as a judge of ballet or be able to distinguish between various ballets. When your taste is not involved you have no discrimination, no involvement in any way. Music is another good case in point: for various reasons I have no taste for Richard Wagner, but one would be a fool not to acknowledge him as a master in his own right.

You often speak of 'great' works of art, but can that mean anything other than that they have become canonical – admired in the end just because they have been admired before?

That is certainly an important element that we learn to admire them because we learn from our parents, and from tradition, and from books. That Michelangelo is a great master I have not the slightest doubt, but it's true that we do not always sufficiently test a reputation, simply because we are conditioned to admire, and therefore we may be sufficiently critical. In fact, I recently attended a lecture on the new restoration of *The Last Judgment*, where we saw many details which they have now cleaned, and I actually think that some of it is pretty repulsive. But of course, Michelangelo was a towering master and nobody can deny this.

I have heard it said that the Chinese apparently do not distinguish between an original art work and a copy which cannot be distinguished from it ... is there any virtue in an original if the only way you can tell it is original is by testing the chemical composition of the paint?

You are right ... it is a genuine problem. I don't think that what you say about the Chinese is completely true, but certainly they have much more respect for a masterly copy than people have here. Equally if it bears the signature of a famous artist of the past and it is really authentic, they would have a great respect for it. There is, however, an element of the attitude one has towards a sacred relic, the idea that Rembrandt's hand really rested on this paper and he drew it. But even though a totally faithful copy of a large painting is very hard to get, I agree with you that a perfect reproduction on the same scale can give the same effect. A Rembrandt etching is a Rembrandt etching, and whether it turns out that it is actually a phot-electric repeat of the copperplate and it's reprinted from another edition, it hardly matters.

You have spoken of connoisseurship and attribution as the mainstream of art history, but is it not precisely that professionalism which feeds the art market and distorts value as it enhances prices?

We couldn't have a history of art if we didn't know the dates of the masters. If you go to a museum you don't want to read on every frame: 'might come from any period'. In other words, when we go to a museum we get a kind of prospectus of the history of art, we want to know who painted the works exhibited there, and any collector has the right to information about a painting. I think the connoisseur has a very real function – he is really at the foundation of what one calls the history of art. We must first have the knowledge of what actually happened, and the hypothesis of who painted what is extremely valuable – except when it becomes authoritarian.

You speak at one point of 'the artist's probable intention' as a starting point, but what would or indeed could count as evidence for that?

Only the context and what one knows about the time and judgement. We would know for instance that in a religious painting the artist's intention would have been to evoke a feeling of devotion, and that he would have wanted his Holy Virgin and Child to be a moving experience. We would know that because that was part of the period in which he lived, and the same is true of many other decorations ... the wish perhaps to shock, or to entertain, or to paint an erotic picture are all pretty clear in the context of their time.

Something that interests me particularly, because I suppose I have never understood it, is the idea of 'artistic aim'. You used a phrase once, 'a master's artistic aim' ... is that a definite thing? It suggests a target, some definite end-point, but I would not have supposed an artist works like that. Can he really know beforehand what he will produce?

Not always. Certainly there is an element of what in engineering is called feedback, what he produces suggests to him other possibilities of which he may not have thought before. There are enormous differences in the various media. If you carve, for example, you have to have a good idea of what you want to get out of a block, while if you model you can at any moment respond to the clay and change it. In watercolour, accidents can very easily happen if the paint runs, though Turner told his students never to use an accident. The medieval master who built up his paintings very carefully to the last moment of varnishing certainly had a much stricter idea of what he was doing than the Impressionists had. Similarly, in ancient Egypt an artist probably intended his statue or relief to be very much like that of his predecessor, and the icon painter in the East also had a very clear aim of what he was doing; the 20th century artist often much less, if at all, so there is an interesting spectrum between these various media. But I think one can still speak of an artistic aim because every artist is also free to say, 'No, this isn't what I wanted', and to throw his work into the wastepaper basket.

You emphasise two possibilities for the individual artist, to continue a tradition or to oppose it, and you say that we must understand something of his sense of newness. But how can we do such a thing except in our own time? We can't feel as someone felt in 1550 or 1720, can we?

Up to a point I hope we can. That is to say, if you are reasonably well versed in the history of painting and quattrocento in Florence, for example, you can understand that when people saw the paintings of Perugino, they thought nothing better could ever be done. Of course they were proved wrong when they saw the paintings of Leonardo da Vinci, but I think one can appreciate that there are quite a number of such utterances in the past which show how the novelty struck. There is a very nice remark by a contemporary of Rembrandt who said that when *The Night Watch* was hung alongside other portraits, the others began to look like flat playing cards compared to the vividness and depth of *The Night Watch*. One can up to a point recapture that feeling of novelty, the thrill of innovation, what Giotto must have meant to people who only knew the earlier manner. But I agree with you that this is slightly the preserve of a historian.

It is an old question, but one fashionable at present: why have there been so few women artists? After all, some women became novelists precisely because they had leisure ...

Yes, but to paint, you needed a workshop, you needed apprentices, and it would not have been very easy for a woman to set up a workshop and to hire apprentices, nor indeed to become a painter of murals – it was hardly within the role expected of women, it was outside the range of possibility. It is therefore all the more impressive that a few managed to overcome this barrier, but on the whole, just as woman didn't become soldiers they didn't become painters, or architects. I don't say that women have less talent for painting; perhaps Michelangelo had a sister who was as gifted as he was, but we shall never know.

Speaking of Dürer's drawing of his mother, you propose sincerity as the mark of a great work of art. But what can sincerity be? After all, any number of artists have been commissioned to paint portraits, some have even worked from photographs. What sort of sincerity can be involved in such cases?

I entirely agree with you that sincerity is a very elusive term because we shall never actually know. There are many things we shall never know, but that doesn't stop us having the feeling that Dürer in this case was sincere. Why otherwise should he have done it? Equally it is possible that a work could impress us very much, and not be sincere. For example, there is a beautiful portrait of an art dealer by Titian, but in a letter Titian makes fun of the man and expresses contempt for him, though that didn't prevent him from painting a very good portrait. So I agree with you that sincerity, though it is often used in criticism and perhaps I shouldn't have used it, is not something we can ever demonstrate.

How does it help to understand a picture like Memling's Angel, *to be told that it is infinitely loveable, and then invited to agree … ?*

It doesn't. But we are all suggestible and therefore if somebody tells me, 'I am very fond of this picture – isn't it very loveable?', unless I am very distrustful I will make an effort to see it that way.

You once used an analogy with language when you explained that learning an artist's method of drawing would help us to understand his feelings, but I do not altogether see the analogy. Language depends on system, so the choice the writer makes of vocabulary will suggest his feelings, but in what case can a drawing be thought of as a system with alternatives?

Drawing is actually a system of alternatives, because various artists of the same period use different strokes and different formulae. But I agree with you that language is very special because it has a fixed range of repertoire, while in the language of painting and music – though there certainly are alternatives – they are always metaphors. They may be revealing metaphors, but they are metaphors nevertheless.

In Topics of Our Time *you publish a fine photograph by Henri Cartier-Bresson, 'Le Palais Royal', but its very quality does seem to suggest that the time may have come for representational art to be handed over to photography. I can see the great practicality of painting before the early 19th century, but must painters now look towards something else?*

You are absolutely right. I agree with you totally that the perfection of photography was a trauma for the artist; some would like to minimalise it, but I'm not one of them. The trauma was decisive in creating 20th century art, the looking for alternatives and things the photograph could not do. It remains a real challenge.

You have employed an analogy with tea drinkers to suggest something about taste in the arts, but does it follow that our greatest enjoyment derives from the finest blends? Is enjoyment not rather dependent on occasion and context?

It is also dependent on occasion and context, I have not the slightest doubt, in that you may enjoy tea when you are very thirsty, or offered tea by a nice person. But there is still discrimination in tea drinking, and the same is true of works of art.

You have deplored the notion of cultured relativism, but is not that the future, the inevitable outcome of the world as global village? Why do you think it a bad thing?

It all depends what you call cultural relativism. I think it is a very bad thing if it leads to a levelling of human achievement, or the appreciation of human achievement. There is a tendency in teaching, particularly in the United States, to say that Michelangelo is not better than any folk art which you find it Ukraine or anywhere else. I deplore this kind of cheap relativism. Of course it doesn't mean that we should despise the simple Madonna painted by a Ukrainian peasant, but there is still a difference in achievement. It is the same in music. It is an objective fact that Bach could write incredible fugues … there is nothing one can relativise in this.

In an essay called 'The Embattled Humanities' you speak of the 'Moloch of society' on whose alter academic research is to be sacrificed. Your plea is eloquent but why should research in the humanities not be subject to the same sort of restrictions as other public spending?

They can restrict it and they do restrict it, but they may regret it very soon, because the quality and the stature of British universities will suddenly suffer and gradually they will become just glorified schools instead of having there people who through their research and discoveries show the young how to advance. Research like everything else is also partly a question of attitude and tradition. A young man who enters, let us say, the Warburg Institute, or any other research institution, does not know how to proceed; his future will depend very much on the example of his elders. It is vitally important that research is supported, and if it is not inertia will set in.

You quote one public institution saying that it is not enough that we be a rich society, we must also be a civilised one. Everyone would agree with that, but it is not really self-evident that those who attend art galleries or the opera are more civilised than those who don't. In Yugoslavia poets and artists are waging a brutal civil war. What part do the arts play in civilising us?

Very little. I entirely agree with you that there might be a person with very fine tastes who is also a brute. Goebbels may have been appreciative of poetry, just as Goering may have been. There is no reason to think that the arts in that sense are good for you, that they civilise you. They may divert certain impulses into better channels, but I'm not sure. Some optimists make too much of the link between art and civilisation. The Chinese have a marvellous civilisation but they were also terribly cruel.

Don't you think it likely that the scholar will also be confronted with the suspicion that behind the talk of cultural values is the urge to private satisfaction, the wish to be well supported by public money while he does what he likes?

Yes, if people want to suspect that, you cannot prevent them from doing it, but it's very rarely true. The life of the scholar or the vision of the artist on the whole do not depend on material rewards. They are most interested in what they feel they have to do, the book they have to write, the picture they have to paint. Very few are rewarded in any comparable way to businessmen, although I don't object to that.

This is perhaps a bit provocative ... but if cultural values are what is at stake, might it not be more sensible to spend public money on artists rather than historians of art?

It is not provocative, you are quite right, but who is to say who the artists are? I am afraid that the record of the last few years – think of the Turner Prize – is not very encouraging. Anybody can say, 'I am an artist', because there are fewer tangible standards, but in contemporary art it is sometimes very hard to tell whether he is actually a poseur or not.

You have a very clear idea of what sort of education a university should provide in the humanities, but it does seem based on your own experience in Vienna before the war – the mastery of foreign languages, the destruction of any barrier between undergraduate and postgraduate, a high failure rate, and a very advantageous staff/student ratio. It seems a very elitist system and would no doubt make for high standards, but is it right to tax people to support a system from which their own children would be excluded? The alternative would seem to be private finance and another (and surely worse) sort of elitism.

You are right. I am of course partly influenced by my own experience in Vienna, though I wouldn't say that the universities I attended corresponded exactly to the model I sketched in the particular lecture you refer to. But the question of whether children are excluded is the wrong question, for it depends on the children: if they are gifted they should certainly not be excluded. There was an exchange in parliament not long ago when the question was asked why should a bus driver support anybody who becomes a lawyer? The correct answer is of course because his son might become a lawyer. There are no longer the same barriers. In questions of excellence, there must be elitism in the sense that some are better and some are less so, but not everybody is an Einstein, and that stands to reason.

I understand your distaste for what you call 'cultural relativism', but if the business of the scholar is 'truth', what counts as evidence? Is not every judgement an interpretation, every conclusion one way of seeing?

Absolutely. Every interpretation is a dominant factor in what we call truth, but if somebody finds the Terracotta Army it is not a question of interpretation. If you find a document which happens to fit a certain picture, there may be a leeway of doubt, but there may not be, and you may not disregard proper evidence. I'm certainly of the side of Popper who always claims, and rightly so, that our theories are interpretations, but Popper wouldn't have wanted this to count against individual facts.

I remember you saying that it was a commonplace observation that the principal subject of art in the 20th century was art itself. Do you think that sort of introspection is healthy, the endless concern with methodology?

I think your answer implies quite rightly that it may not be healthy, and I agree with you. If you look at the end of my *Story of Art,* or at the last chapter before the postscript, you will find that I have postulated that what would be important for artists is to get commissions so that they really would have to prove their mettle, rather than contemplating their own navels, as it were. And the same is true of methodology. I am not a believer in discussions of method: go out and do it, and then we will see what you can do.

You have an immensely distinguished and successful career ... how much has that success owed to the happiness and stability of your private life?

Very little, I think. On the contrary it can sometimes be a nuisance.

You have always rather avoided talking about yourself. Does that come from a basic shyness, or is there some other reason?

The reason why I don't really want to talk about myself is that I don't think I'm very interesting, there's very little to say. What I try to do is in my books, so my private life is not of great interest to others, not even to me.

I read somewhere that you have had a prolonged battle against anxiety for most of your life. Does this have its origin in the political turbulence of your childhood?

I don't think that's quite true. I'm perhaps a slightly anxious person, I'm not a hero, I'm not courageous, but I'm not aware of any battle against anxiety as such.

What part, if any, has religion played in your life?

That's an interesting question, but I cannot answer it simply. I have a certain respect for religion because of the way it inspired great art. The same is true of music – Haydn's Masses, Bach's Passions. If one has absolutely no sense of religious awe, one may find it very hard to enter into the feelings which great music and art inspire. At the same time I must confess that I have very little patience for religion as it is practised today because of the intolerance it preaches; it is a great misfortune that religion so often instils in people the conviction that they are right and that all others must be wrong.

Do you believe in the existence of God?

I don't believe in the existence of God in any traditional sense, and I do not belong to any established religion. I can look at the universe and the workings of nature, and experience a sense of awe and have a feeling for the mystery in everything, but that does not make me believe that there is a man with a white a beard who regulates our lives.

Are you afraid of death?

No. If you tell me I will be shot in an hour's time, I should not be very pleased, but I'm not afraid of what will happen to me after I'm dead, because I'm convinced nothing will happen. Death is simply when life is over, and in a way it will be a good thing since there are too many people anyhow and if we all went on living life would be intolerable. It may be a bad thing for one's friends and relations, but it is in itself something to be desired. One doesn't want to live forever.

LORD GOODMAN

Arnold Goodman was senior partner in Goodman Derrick & Co., Solicitors. He was born in 1913 and educated at University College London. He served as a gunner in the Royal Artillery during the war and retired as major in 1945. Between 1965 and 1972 he was chairman of the Arts Council of Great Britain. He was chairman of British Lion Films from 1965 to 1972 and master of University College, Oxford from 1976 to 1986. He was director of the Royal Opera House, Covent Garden from 1972 to 1983 and was deputy chairman of the British Council and a governor of the Royal Shakespeare Theatre when interviewed. He was the only man to have received a peerage from a Labour prime minister (Harold Wilson – he was Wilson's solicitor) and to have been made a Companion of Honour by a Conservative prime minster (Edward Heath). He died on 12 May 1995, and Harold Wilson died twelve days later.

Your mother seems to have been the dominating influence in your childhood. Was your father a shadowy figure by comparison?

He wasn't a shadowy figure, but he was the less positive figure of the two. He was a very gentle, mild man, and I think he was a bit diffident about intruding, but we were as devoted to him as to my mother. My mother was enormously encouraging. She had all the pride of the Jewish mothers put together. I don't think she had great ambition for us, but she was a woman with a good sense of values and she obviously wanted us to be happy and successful, because if you're not successful you're rarely happy. She was always there for us, and if we ever had any kind of problem or trouble, she solved it without fuss. She was a very remarkable woman. She had been a schoolteacher originally, and a competent pianist. She taught Mrs Gaitskell Hebrew. She saw me beginning to become successful. I hadn't been ennobled and hadn't even become the chairman of the Arts Council before she died, but I had had modest success and it gave her great pleasure.

I don't look back on my childhood as the happiest time of my life, because I hadn't really found a balanced situation there. There were uncertainties about relationships with people, about the extent to which one promoted one's own activities and so forth. Anything that isn't positive causes doubt and doubt causes unhappiness. I certainly wasn't an unhappy child. I loved being a child; I enjoyed being at school. I was particularly fond of cricket, and I became an adept tennis player – I even got a tennis colour at University College London. I had a passion for reading, and I loved music. My father used to take us off to concerts on Sunday afternoons, and all of this conduced to happiness. Anyone looking at me would have said I was a happy boy.

I was educated at a grammar school established by one of the great trading companies, and it was a very good school. We had everything: a good swimming bath, the river on which we could row, an excellent sports ground. It didn't ape the public schools, but it tried to extract what was best in them. I was particularly influenced by the English master because, for some reason, I was his favourite pupil. He played a great part in my life, and persuaded me of the glories of English literature.

If I had a son, I would not myself send him to a boarding school. I think that's a folly. It separates a boy from his family altogether and in a sense it agonises him, because a young child has to determine for himself why he's been exiled. I'm not at all in favour of boarding schools, but I would send a son to a good day school. There are several, like St Paul's, or University College School, or Mill Hill. Children require a certain amount of understanding, humane discipline, and a good school provides it.

My parents were always tight for money. My father was not a good business-man, but he contrived to get enough to give us a comfortable childhood. I didn't have a luxurious childhood, but I managed to travel a bit. I remember I wanted to go to Paris, and when I spoke to my father he said, 'Well, what you can manage on?' So I replied rather optimistically 'I could do a week on £5.' He produced a five-pound note and off I went. I found myself very strained for money after about four days, but it was very enjoyable. Then I wanted to go to Rome, because I've always had a particular interest in Roman affairs and Roman law and Latin, which was a language I had a great affection for. So when I said I wanted to go to Rome, he asked for how long, and I replied a fortnight. So he produced £10. I stayed at a little pension called the Pension Bus, where I had a semi-pension rate, which meant that I got breakfast and dinner but not lunch. Without any great hardship, I dispensed with lunch for a fortnight, and then had a piece of good fortune when, wandering through the Coliseum on almost my last day, an elderly American gentleman, seeing me carrying an English guide book, approached me and asked if I spoke English. When I confirmed that I did, he asked if I would mind showing him around the city, and we struck up quite a friendship. He turned out to be an American ex-judge who had come over on the melancholy errand of bringing his wife's ashes, which he had promised to bury in Rome. He became very friendly indeed and took me out every day for another fortnight. I was therefore able to stay for four weeks.

I always knew that I probably wanted to be a lawyer. There's a conventional range of occupations for middle-class Jewish boys: you become either a lawyer, a doctor or an accountant, and I certainly never wanted to have anything to do with figures and I didn't want to be a doctor. Therefore, being a lawyer seemed a reasonable alternative, and I've always had a great affection for words.

You had a successful if comparatively modest career in the army. What were the values that emerged from this for you?

I'd been very spoilt as a boy. My parents' influence was protective to the point of mollycoddling, and the army was a revelation. It introduced me to the human race and showed me what excellent qualities existed there. I never met any unkindness. I was in the ranks for a while, then I was commissioned and went up to a command headquarters, where I got some modest promotion and that was that. But I enjoyed it very much. I learned how important it was to get on with your fellow men.

The idea I was living on borrowed time during the war would have been a philosophical meditation in which I didn't indulge. I never felt at all apprehensive, although I was a member of a very active anti-aircraft battery and we operated throughout the blitz on London, then in various other parts of the country, and were out during the bombing night after night. It never entered my head that I might be killed. I suppose, in a way, that I regarded myself as too precious a person for anyone to kill me. It was a form of vanity. I'm not heroic, but I don't think I'm particularly cowardly either, and although I had several quite narrow escapes when, on various occasions, bombs fell too close to be comfortable, I can't remember being worried.

You have been honoured by both Labour and Conservative governments, which seems a very unusual thing indeed.

If I had been a determined Marxist or a passionate Conservative, I don't think the other party would have employed me. I was evidently a neutral in these matters, and not really interested in politics. The reputation I had, for what it's worth, was that I was apolitical and that, on the whole, I didn't have violent prejudices one way or the other. My sympathy was towards liberal causes. For instance, I always took a strong line about South Africa and made several critical speeches. A liberal cause usually had only to heave into sight to find me supporting it, but not every liberal cause. I didn't believe in some of the more argumentative ones.

I don't feel that I have strong political convictions. I believe we should have a world where there is, on the whole, little interference with personal freedom. We should live in a world where everyone is entitled to be educated, in which everyone is entitled to be looked after health-wise. I do believe, to that extent, in what many people would call a socialist society, but not to the point of submerging other beliefs. It's true that I have a distaste for politicians, largely because I've met too many not to. I almost worshipped Jennie Lee, but she was an exception. And Nye Bevan was an extraordinary man, as was Hugh Gaitskell: and, in a strange sort of way, Ted Heath is extraordinary. These are all people who have qualities which rise above narrow political dogmas.

Where honesty in politicians is concerned, I don't think it's possible to be totally honest in any human context, but it's even more difficult if you're trying to persuade hundreds of thousands of people to adopt your views and vote for you. It would be imposing a tremendous moral strain never to exaggerate in the slightest degree, and exaggeration is a departure from honesty. Someone with a distaste for duplicity might well be as honest a politician, or indeed anything else, as you could hope to find. In fact, it might be a great encouragement to people to vote for him. This was certainly the basis of Mrs Thatcher's support at the start of her regime. People were persuaded that she was a change in the political scene, and that she was an honourable woman.

I have come to feel that our present democratic electoral system could be improved by ensuring that a greater number of people influence the elections. Certainly, it could be improved by a system of proportional representation. One can be very dogmatic about this, because there are considerable dangers in a proportional representation which might, in the end, produce no government at all. But on the whole, I think we ought to have experimented with it. One of the things that can happen the way things are is that you can get such an overwhelming majority that no institution is safe, and that, of course is a dangerous trend. We have seen the abolition of the Greater London Council, which clearly did very good work although it was open to objection, because, in certain areas, people with extreme views got into power and did rather silly things. But they didn't do silly things enough to justify its demolition, and its destruction was a result of a system which allows one party to hold a majority of a size the Conservatives have today.

The cardinal point about Conservatism is that it binds the Conservatives together with one simple precept, which is a respect for property. And one reason why the Labour party doesn't command that respect is because, by and large, it hasn't got the property. The respect that the Conservatives have for the initiative of the individual all turns on wealth, and there's no harm in that, but since it's a respect for a man who can amass wealth, it overrides any respect for intelligence, health or any other consideration. The Labour party is meanwhile a very disorganised, disunited group, but it seems to be getting better. They have been able to shed their more extreme element, and that gives them a better chance of recognition. I think they will come back into power, but when I don't know. It's not possible it'll be at the next election.

At one point you undertook the task of trying to reconcile the difficulties in Rhodesia, and it looked as though you had managed to get an agreement.

I did get an agreement. What really happened was that the British government sent me out to negotiate with the Smith government, which meant, in effect, Ian Smith himself. I negotiated with him and we were able to evolve a constitution acceptable to him, tolerably acceptable to the more powerful voices in his government and not wholly rejected by anyone. Then, when it came to it, one of the imperatives was that it should be acceptable to the entire population, black and white. Well that was a rather silly requirement. There was no hope, when one came to think of it, of an agreement negotiated wholly between two white men being acceptable to the blacks. Smith was a wholly honest man, may I say. I never found him at all devious. He was obstinate, but the moment you had worn down his obstinacy and he agreed something, that was the end of it. He never went back on his word. The reason why the initiative failed was that the British government had defined a negotiation as something between two whites. They couldn't, in their wildest moments, have expected that that sort of negotiation was going to be either welcome or tolerable to the black population, which represented more than ten times the white population. When it came to it, Mr Smith assured us that it would be acceptable to the blacks, his reason for believing being, as he said, that his chiefs knew and respected him, would not betray him and would certainly vote in favour.

Now, Smith had lived in Rhodesia all his life and the Foreign Office had sent me out with a Rhodesian expert who had never before been to Rhodesia. As a result, no one warned me that the idea that chiefs could control the tribes was completely wrong. The tribes controlled the chiefs. When the chiefs went back to the tribal lands, they were told to vote no, and to a man they did. The first mistake was to have employed someone, like me, who had never been to the country. My parents were born in South Africa, and I had been in South Africa many times, but never in Rhodesia. I knew nothing about the country. The second mistake was not to have sent me out with a genuine expert, because there were means of establishing that the proposed agreement was unacceptable to a great number of blacks.

The imposition of sanctions certainly worked in Rhodesia. That was a major reason for their seeking a settlement. When I arrived out there, people I'd never met before came up to me and tugged at my coat and said, 'Please, please, get an agreement.' The shops were almost empty of consumer goods. And sanctions are working in South Africa today. Very much so. I was in South Africa last October and the one thing perfectly clear was that they were obsessed with the fear of sanctions, and were producing literature and arguments, all specious and all designed to show that sanctions didn't work and ought to be dropped. It was clear evidence that the sanctions were working.

I don't think that Mrs Thatcher is right at all to ease sanctions. There has been no relative improvement at all, they've hardly changed anything. Apartheid is as intact as ever, with only a few minor changes. It would be folly, having got this far, to cease the one thing that is having an obvious effect on them.

What is wrong with South Africa is that, in terms of demography, it's an idiocy. There are something like thirty million blacks being governed by three to four million whites. In demographic terms, it's an outrage, and whites have used their power in the most disgraceful way. South Africa is a heartbreaking place. There are various housing estates, including one called Crossbow which houses three quarters of a million to a million blacks. It's thick with mud, and they live in the most impoverished and rudimentary constructions made up principally of bits of iron, bits of tin, bits of cardboard. There is a water tap for every four houses, and no sanitation, just a bucket system. They manage somehow to keep these places relatively clean, but as conditions for human beings to live in, they are intolerable. The irony is that most people in Cape Town have never seen the place, even though you pass it on the way from the airport. There's a callous indifference to human suffering that makes the present regime an outrage and makes reform an urgent necessity.

If you were to argue that the one man, one vote principle cannot work because the blacks are not educated enough, then I don't know that one can say with complete confidence that there isn't a large percentage of the electorate in this country who are similarly unequipped to have a vote. The requirement to justify a vote is that a man would understand what is good for him. One saw it in Rhodesia. When they came to taking a vote on the proposed settlement, the blacks to a man turned it down. Their instinct told them that anything warmly approved by Mr Smith was not to their benefit.

As for making South Africa safe for democracy, who are you asking that it should be safe for – the three to four million or the thirty to forty million? I tend to think a secure solution is possible. Nigeria, for instance, is quite competently governed. You've got to remember that the difference is this: it is one thing to be governed by people of your own race, quite another to be governed by people of another race who you have justifiably come to regard over the years as hostile. That is the basic consideration.

There is no reason to suppose that introducing democracy will stop the violence of black against black, but equally there's strong reason to think it won't stop unless democracy is introduced. My own feeling is that the black outrages against black are quite a different thing from white outrages against black, and that they won't cause the same resentment. The black population of South Africa is very large, and it has been kept in a depressed position by the whites. Years ago there was a minister of education who said something to the effect that they would give them such education as they needed to carry out the simple humble functions they performed. That was a calculated insult.

Do you find that being the focal point of enormous pressure, as you were in Rhodesia, is something you were able to cope with easily?

I don't think I've ever felt under an intolerable pressure from other people's opinions. Perhaps I have an excessive and rather conceited faith in my own opinions, but I was never tortured by doubts. You couldn't achieve anything if you were tortured by doubt. On negotiation, I'm immensely patient. In personal relations, I'm not so sure, but negotiation should be a continuous process until you have reached a conclusion. You should listen very carefully to what the other side have to say, and make quite sure that they realise that you do understand their point of view and that, if you are rejecting it, it must be for valid reasons.

I would consider myself to be a good listener in negotiation, and in normal life I'm not an impatient listener. Of course, in this world one has to listen to a great deal of nonsense, but I'm very tolerant of nonsense because I'm tolerant of the fallibility of human beings. I wouldn't say that estimating your opponent is a very profitable activity. What you have to do is estimate the strength of your case and the strength of a case which comes midway between the two cases, and ultimately it's your job to propound a tolerable solution acceptable to both sides, or all three sides. But you arrive there by instinct. It's not a calculated process.

The legal profession in England seems in turmoil at present, with one group trying to preserve its privileges and the other to trespass on them. Is it a matter of principle more than the scramble for money and power it appears to be?

It's not a scramble for money. I once said that the strange feature of the English legal system was that, although lawyers didn't enrich themselves, they could succeed in beggaring their clients, and this was an anomaly. I don't think it's a struggle for power either. It is really a struggle for prestige. It's as simple as that. The Bar have a built-in conviction that they have a superior status, but they fail to recognise, first of all, how numerically inferior they are. In actual practice, there are between 3,000 and 4,000 barristers – and that's probably an exaggeration – as against 60,000 solicitors, so it is obvious that if they are going to have a conviction of superiority then it must be a strong one because numerically they would be in difficulty. In fact, the traditions of the Bar are really no longer appropriate for the twentieth-century situation, even less for the twenty-first. By this I mean their wigs and gowns, and their use of Latin, which very few of them understand or can construe. The whole edifice is built on a fraudulent tradition of custom – a firm conviction that a custom has retained privileges for them and has maintained them in a superior position in relation to the rest of the legal profession exists by order of the Almighty. To some extent it stems from the class system in this country, but the strange thing is that a great number of solicitors and a great number of barristers all come from the same class, the upper middle class. They've been educated at public or independent schools, and most of them have been to Oxford or Cambridge, so there isn't a great divergence of class. Nevertheless, the Bar believe that their practices or traditions are better and finer. It's largely based on the Inns of Court, for which they have a sort of masonic affection.

Meanwhile there's very little doubt that our legal system is weighted against the poor man if he's engaged in a battle. We like to pretend there's no advantage in retaining a better lawyer, but of course, there is a great advantage, and I don't know how that is going to be changed. There will have to be a more expansive legal aid system, and the reform now taking place, whereby you will be able to use a single advocate, will greatly cheapen the matter. Although the Bar deny it, it's a matter of simple arithmetic. It is bound to be cheaper to employ one man rather than four.

But won't it be very difficult to make the people who have money less privileged than those who don't?

There are some things in which, by the decree of the Almighty, the rich are less privileged. They've no privileges in relation to fresh air; they've no privileges in relation to sea-bathing. Shortly they'll have to discover they have no real privilege in relation to justice.

But if you're rich, you can go where there is fresh air. If you're poor, you're stuck where you are.

I'm not so sure. If you're born on the seashore, you get fresh air; however rich you may be, you won't be able to get more. I think the extent to which money and justice are related is a bad thing, but it is much less so here than in the United States, although France is better than we are. They have something I have a special preference for, which is what is called a civilian system, that is to say, a Roman law system. I was trained as a Roman lawyer, and I lectured on Roman Dutch law at Cambridge. It is a system which doesn't depend on precedent. The English system means that you can go back on every case decided since the year dot to see what cases have been decided in your favour. The Roman law system doesn't depend on precedent at all, but on principle, and if the principle is with you, then you win the case. This, of course, is much, much cheaper than a precedent system. I would say there is quite a lot of reform that needs to be done in relation to the English legal system.

Why is our legal establishment so against introducing the American system of contingency fees in this country?

They're against it because they think it's *infra dig*. They consider it undignified for lawyers to work under circumstances where they're paid only if they win, but there are other objections that are raised. One is that it is unfair to the losing party because he can't get any costs. Once you start a litigation on a contingency basis, at the end of the day, if the assisted person wins the case, the defendant has no means of recovering the costs. It's well controlled in America, more so than you would think from the impression that is being conveyed here by the people opposed to it. For instance, there are strict rules that the lawyer may not take more than a percentage of the win – 15 or 20 per cent. And there is a rule in some states that the court must feel that there is a prima facie chance of success. A man cannot undertake a completely hopeless cause for the purpose of advertising himself, or perhaps forcing a settlement from someone who isn't very sure. It is, like every human institution, open to objections but I would say the objections fall down by the side of the alternative, which is that a poor man can't sue at all.

When you dismissed as 'poppycock' the Bar's fears for the independence of the judiciary under the Lord Chancellor, Lord Mackay's plans for reform, yours seemed almost a lone voice, and the general reaction was one of closing ranks.

It was only the Bar. The Bar, as I said, is a tiny profession of about 4,000 active members. There was no closing ranks among the 64,000 lawyers. What it came down to was the vehemence of the Bar's opposition and the pretensions they give to themselves, despite their small numbers. If you have an agreeable monopoly, it isn't difficult to evolve a highfalutin principle to maintain it. There is no principle that enables the Bar to maintain a position which is ruinous to every litigant.

Yet they maintain that the cost will not be reduced.

That is to maintain that Mount Everest isn't there. As I say, it's a question of arithmetic. It is manifestly cheaper to employ one person than to employ at least three and possibly four doing the same job. If the problem were approached with determination and integrity it would become enormously cheaper. As for the notion that standards will go down, what standards? They have sold the myth that they are superlative advocates, but if you go to the Law Courts on any morning and pass from court to court, the thing that will horrify you is the bumbling nature of the advocacy. There are half a dozen superlative advocates, Robert Alexander being one. There are a few others. Jeremy Hutchinson was a superlative. But the number can be counted on the fingers of one hand, and to keep to this pretence as the means of maintaining a disastrously expensive monopoly makes no sense.

Doesn't it remain iniquitous that most people will be deterred from suing because of the horrendous costs?

That is not so much a reflection on the law of libel as a reflection on our legal system. I quite agree that the costs involved are prohibitive but there are ameliorations now under consideration, a very important one being that the action could be brought in the County Court, where the case could be conducted by a solicitor alone. This could have a dramatic effect on reducing the costs.

I haven't myself represented many people in libel actions. I doubt if I've been involved in twenty libel actions that went to court in the whole of my career. I've always deterred people from becoming involved. A client is perfectly entitled to ignore my advice, of course, but if I thought the conduct of the action was in some way a persecution or an impropriety, I just wouldn't do it. There'd be no reason why I should. I've refused to act for a client many times. I am under no obligation to do things I don't approve of.

When, in 1957, I undertook to represent Aneurin Bevan, Richard Crossman and Morgan Phillips after *The Spectator* accused them of being drunk on a British delegation to Venice, I agreed because the clients, and particularly Nye Bevan, who was quite a close friend, regarded it as very serious. He said, 'I was sent abroad to represent the Labour Party at an international conference, and now I am told that while I was there I conducted myself like a drunkard.' He took a very serious view of it, and he was entitled to.

Isn't it a mistake to pick twelve people from the public at random to decide in a technically complicated case, such as the Guinness one now?

You underrate them. First of all, if you have twelve people, statistically there are bound to be two or three of average, if not above average, intelligence. If they don't understand the case it's because the counsel who are explaining it to them are inadequate. My own belief is there is almost no case that a jury, given proper advice and instruction, cannot deal with better than a judge alone. There is something about a jury that inspires confidence. They will arrive at perverse verdicts, but never at insane verdicts.

Oddly enough, a judge's going over the top in his summing up is often the reason why the jury takes the other side, especially if they feel that the judge is loading the case too much. They are twelve people, not twelve fools.

Lawyers never seem very popular as a group.

I would say the general dislike is justified for the very simple reason that you go in search of a lawyer only when you're in trouble, and that is why lawyers are not loved. You won't find that doctors who specialise in cancer are the best-loved members of the community, and there's more reason for loving them than a lawyer who is going to try and extricate you from an unhealthy marital situation where your wife intends to take half your property. That's why they're not liked. It's not because they are rich. If you look at the 1,000 richest men in England, or even at the 10,000 richest, you won't find a lawyer among them. Lawyers do not make money. That is a simple fact. Certain barristers make huge income because they're in great demand, but that is a rarity. It's for the same reason that Placido Domingo gets higher fees than any other tenor. A highly accomplished barrister, like Robert Alexander, gets very large fees, which is only fair. On an average, lawyers are by no means extravagantly paid. I took three law degrees and obtained first-class honours in all of them, and I wouldn't say that the rewards that have come my way are even comparable with what I'd have got if I'd become a merchant banker. I never wanted them to be.

When Lord Mackay was disciplined recently by his Church in Scotland for having attended a requiem mass for a deceased colleague, did that make you wonder whether there was a case for saying that someone like Lord Mackay, who holds high office, should not belong to such a narrow, restrictive Church in the first place, that the latter is incompatible with the duties and requirements of the former?

The church one belongs to must be a subjective consideration. No one can know what arguments propel me to remain Jewish. These are decisions that one makes for oneself, and they are decided inside you. I understand that Lord Mackay has now left that particular Church, and I must say I heard the news with great relief, but I wouldn't seek to impose my own view about what are the right religious precepts for a man of skill and judgement. In many ways, the fact that he remained a member of the Church of his fathers was a very creditable thing. It's true that it's a Church which appears to me to be redolent of prejudice, bias and rather absurd notions, but even so, you can't condemn the entire Moslem peoples for believing some of the idiocies they believe; you can't condemn all Jews for believing some of the idiocies we are supposed to believe. These are matters of personal opinion, and so long as he is doing no damage to anyone else, no one has any right to interfere. You must remember that one of the great requirements of our present society is that people should have a faith, and I think that many of the difficulties and tragedies we encounter today are due to the absence of faith. Almost any faith is better than none. I wouldn't go so far as to say that, if you believe in cannibalism, that is a desirable thing, but whatever notions you may hold about religious precepts, to have some that are firmly held in your mind must be a good thing.

You are widely regarded as the best chairman the Arts Council ever had. Have its aims improved or declined since your time there?

As you know, at the moment there is a rumpus going on because it's proposed by the minister of arts, who is not a very experienced person, that the Arts Council should have a very reduced function and that regional arts associations should take on the major task of subsidising the majority of companies. I think this is wholly mistaken. To introduce local associations into the matter will be to introduce politics with both feet. I had quite a lot of experience in dealing with local authorities. Some were very good but a great many of them were awful, and the extent to which politics were brought in has, I'm afraid, had considerable support from this government. They view everything from a political viewpoint and don't think anyone should be promoted to any office of importance unless he is a member of their party. Things haven't improved; they've got worse.

A Labour government would have appointed a Tory to the Arts Council. Jennie Lee certainly would. You see, I've never been a member of the Labour party. When I said that what was wrong was the government policy of not countenancing non-Conservatives, someone remarked, 'Ah, but what about you? Is it not true that they appointed a person of liberal sentiments?' The answer to that was given by someone else, who said there was no party that wouldn't have appointed me.

On the subject of art for the people, especially opera, is there not a case for saying that most of the people who are contributing to the subsidies are providing an agreeable entertainment for a fortunate minority in London?

Well, that is an unavoidable consequence. If you were to say that no minority interest is to be subsidised because it isn't enjoyed by everyone in the country, then culture disappears. It is perfectly true, as I remarked many years ago, that one of the essential liberties of a free Englishman is freedom from culture, and if he doesn't want culture, he needn't have it. but that's no reason for depriving anyone else of it. The number of people who want to go to the opera is greatly exaggerated. A lot of people would like to go, and a lot do, very cheaply. You can get, if not a seat, a position from where you can hear an opera for £2. At Covent Garden it's extremely uncomfortable, but if you're a young enthusiast, you don't have to pay £100.

My feeling is that, if you provide cultural material only on the footing that the whole world can afford it, there are innumerable things that won't be there. Education would disappear. You have to accept that a large part of desirable human activity is wanted only by a few special people. But those special people are very special. They dictate the shape and form of the country's culture and education, and I don't think there's any terrible injustice. The injustice is for the state not to provide the money. When you think of the cost of a single battleship or nuclear weapon, it's absurd to say we couldn't afford a few hundred thousand or even a few million for cultural activities. Yet there is a bitter resistance to this, and it comes from very rich people. That is because most of them would rather go to jail than sit through a performance of *The Ring*.

The boycotting of Wagner by many Jews after the war was, incidentally, an absurdity. It's ridiculous to regard music as untouchable because it was composed by a man who was an anti-Semite because he believed his illegitimate father was Jewish. The important thing to remember is that music has a quality and a standing of its own.

You once said: 'It is an article of faith with this government that anything remotely progressive in politics should be stamped out. It would have been too much to expect them to keep the Arts Council immune from this.' A great deal of anger seems to lie behind this statement.

It's something about which I do feel strongly. The Arts Council was founded on two principles, one being that, although it accepts money, it accepts no political direction or dictation as to how to use the money. The corresponding and comparable principle is that, in giving its money to its various beneficiaries, it imposes no degree of political control. In fact, it has subsidised many very left-wing adventures since there are not a great many right-wing adventures because intellectuals are rarely right-wing. And what the Arts Council has to do is protect the integrity of intellectual and cultural thought, and if it proceeds to stamp on everything that it or Mrs Thatcher thinks has any appearance of culture, then it destroys an institution of international value. I do believe that, in the main, intellectuals veer towards left-wing opinions. By left-wing opinions one means opinions that are not maintained by anyone who has a bit of money.

One of the complaints made by the orthodox supporters of the arts on the right is that right-wing plays are never put on. The answer is simple. There aren't any right-wing plays. Go and search for them. You might trace a tendency towards right-wing drama in, say, John Galsworthy, but he was essentially a liberal, and if you see one of his most famous plays, *The Silver Box*, it was a cry for the dispossessed.

As for working to persuade the unconvinced of the validity of the importance of art and artists, I don't know that I would persuade them. My father used to say that one of the principles of life is that a young donkey grows into an old donkey. I would make no effort. It's quite impossible to inculcate a belief by argument. You can only do it by providing culture that the young can absorb and come to love.

In the area of education and the mounting failure of the educational system, more money should be provided and less introduced. We could then be as well educated as the French, for example. We're a long way behind them at the moment. Happily, we were never as badly educated as the Germans, because they were educated to tolerate enormities and outrages that would not be tolerated in England. There's a lot to be said for our system. It's one that encourages liberal ideas and makes it possible to live with liberal thoughts in a world where most people are illiberal. On that score, I'm a great admirer, and I can think of no other country in the world where I would wish to live, except perhaps one or two of the original British dominions, like Australia or Canada.

But what can be our grounds for optimism when we haven't enough teachers in the schools, university funds are constantly cut, students are saddled with debt before they even begin their careers, some of our fellow citizens live in cardboard boxes on the streets …

I think that is an exaggerated statement of certain outrages that are very limited in number. You see, the number of people living in cardboard boxes is tiny, and they are nearly always drug dependent, and it is impossible to eradicate the drug desire. They are people who find it impossible to organise a sane life and provide themselves with a roof, but I don't think that is a prevailing mood in any substantial number of people. England is more humane, more civilised than almost anywhere else. I won't say that the Jews are universally popular, but they are not persecuted, and the only man who tried to mount a campaign of anti-Semitism was brought to a sharp halt.

Did you ever encounter anti-Semitism yourself?

As a Jew I've had rich rewards, and I don't believe that being a Jew has interfered with them in any way. I've had appointments, I've had honours, and I can regard myself as having been very fortunate indeed. I can't attribute any misfortune of mine to anti-Semitism. It's impossible to say that there weren't people who, when they came to review the situation, didn't feel they'd rather appoint a Roman Catholic or a Presbyterian than a Jew, but I've not encountered it.

We seem a lot more restrictive than the Americans on accessibility to information. Do you think freedom is divisible in some way?

Freedom is indivisible. I think the rules should be applied with common sense. If a man divulges the time at which he takes tea and that he takes three cups and he's given two pieces of sugar, that is not a secret. On the other hand, if he proceeds to divulge the reasons why a particular civil servant wasn't promoted and things of that sort, then that can be very injurious to someone's career and is something in which there can be no public interest – or shouldn't be, unless there's some scandal associated with it.

The government's latest piece of legislation does not provide public interest as a ground for defence. I think this is very difficult, because any civil servant who feels that there is a profit in divulging the secret would be able to present a case that it's in the public interest. I'm not at all sure that you should be able to betray your trust because you believe there's a public interest. It is for the government to determine what is the public interest, not an individual civil servant. It can't be determined by anyone else. The trouble is there's a great deal of hypocrisy about these claims, especially by the press. The claim to freedom is really the claim by the newspapers to publish titillating information that will sell more copies. That's what the claim for freedom derives from, not from any lofty motivation. I think one has to have that in mind when considering the strength and nature of the claim.

You have known many national leaders of different political persuasions and all sorts of people in positions of authority and influence. Is that a world you find attractive?

I don't find people of influence more attractive because they have influence. It is usually that they have attained influence because there is some rather arresting quality about them, and, of course, that is bound to be an important consideration in assessing your interest in them.

I have not admired very much people who are evidently self-seeking, but it would be wrong for me to indicate who such people are. I admired Hugh Gaitskell very much. I also had a considerable admiration for Ted Heath, although of recent years he has been much influenced by a sense of pique. The politician I admired most was Lloyd George. He was a man who made his own way from the most humble background by employing quite exceptional persuasive and oratorical talent. He was one of the great orators of the day. And it's a source of great satisfaction to me that he was a solicitor.

To ask if he was a womaniser has nothing to do with anything. You might as well ask did he like curry? That a man likes women is so idiosyncratic a consideration that it doesn't bear examination. I don't think he did his career any harm, because the investigatory journalism of our day didn't then exist. Had it existed, Lloyd George would have been ruined within hours.

No, I don't think the British are more hypocritical about sex than other nations. I don't think they're more hypocritical than the Americans, and the Europeans are also hypocritical in the sense that they have decided to conceal their feelings about it. The French are liberal to the extent that it would be unlikely that a Frenchman would be ruined because he had a mistress, but it would now be equally unlikely that an Englishman would be ruined for the same reason. There's a general loosening of moral standards that is very welcome.

You knew Harold Wilson.

Yes, as well as anyone could.

He now appears to be a rather discredited politician, with the whole political establishment seeming to have deserted him.

I think that's because he was an unsuccessful politician in the sense that he lost the ultimate election, and he is not the easiest man to support. He was an extremely kindly man, but he also had some massive faults, and one of those was that, before he did anything, he got into the habit of looking over his shoulder to see what the effect might be before he decided. That is a very grave defect in a politician, who should go boldly ahead and do what he thinks right. I liked him very much. He was very kind to me, and I'm not sure that he's wholly discredited.

If he now seems not to be respected, that is because the organs of respectability are Tory organs. *The Times*, the *Daily Telegraph*, the *Daily Mail* are all Tory papers, the assessment of these people is a Tory assessment, and Harold Wilson was the most hated one of all because he provided the greatest risk to their beliefs and policies. I would say that has a lot to do with his present assessment.

Any desertion by his own party was on purely pragmatic grounds, because the public wouldn't support him. I'm not even sure that his own party have deserted him. It's easily said, but if Harold Wilson returned to leadership, he'd have a much greater chance of success at winning the election than Mr Kinnock. Harold Wilson was absolutely hated by the Tory press. The Conservative party has one inflexible principle which distinguishes it from the Labour party. Whereas the Labour party has all sorts of notions which add up to a policy or don't, the Conservative party has one notion only, which is to preserve private property. They saw in Harold Wilson a really dangerous threat to their well-being.

What view did you take of the alleged MI5 plot to oust Wilson?

It wasn't an MI5 plot, but it was a plot by a few cowboys in MI5, and it certainly took place. My own offices were raided twice and I hadn't any notion why until much later, when I discovered that they had been searching for documents that might in some way incriminate Harold Wilson. We had no such documents. I don't think any such documents existed. But there certainly was this disgraceful activity on the part of a few hot-headed fanatics, who saw in Harold Wilson a danger to their whole scheme of life. Of course, we didn't know of this until long afterwards.

What advice would you have given, had you been asked, on Harold Wilson's so-called 'Lavender List' of honours?

I did in fact offer some advice, I won't say to whom. It was an extremely unwise and reckless list, and my advice would have been not to go ahead with it. It couldn't have mattered twopence to Harold Wilson whether some unworthy businessman was going to get a knighthood or a peerage, so he had no great personal advantage to get out of it. He had a certain weakness towards particular influences, and he didn't have the strength of character to resist them. I think the 'Lavender List' did him great harm, but I'm equally sure that there was no element of corruption in it and that he was doing it because he thought he was obliging someone or other. He should have had a stiffer resistance to obliging people.

Ted Heath, too, is not highly thought of at present.

If Ted Heath is not highly thought of at the moment, it's because he has attacked the existing Conservative front. I've known Ted Heath since he was a schoolboy, and I met him in a rather unusual situation. I was a very junior partner in a firm in which my senior partner had a passion for rose-growing. His ambition in life was to become the president of the National Rose Society, now the Royal National Rose Society – everything being royal these days. He achieved his ambition in the last year of his life, but before that, while I was still in partnership with him, he used to go regularly down to Broadstairs where he had a patch of ground where he grew his roses. Being rather a thrifty man, he said to me one day, 'You know, it's too expensive to keep coming down here. I'm going to build a little cottage.'

He got his plot of ground and he had the cottage built by Mr William Heath, Ted's father, and that's how I got to know him, and we've been, I won't say close friends, but very good friends ever since. My impression of Ted was that you didn't have to know him long to know what was in him. He's not a complicated character. He's good natured, honourable, sympathetic and kindly. Obviously, he has the usual vanity of a man who has been prime minister and wants to be prime minister again, and he has a number of massive faults, but they're more than counteracted by a great number of massive virtues.

Aneurin Bevan was a great hero of mine when I was a student. Do you think that, had he lived, he might have mellowed and perhaps even risen to be prime minister?

One of the great tragedies of the post-war story was the deaths of two people who would have made a significant impression on the Labour party. The first was Hugh Gaitskell, the second Nye Bevan. Had Nye lived, he might easily have become the leader.

Gaitskell was a man of moderate comment but absolutely rigid principle, and he compares very fairly with the rest of the Labour party leadership. In my view, he was an outstanding figure. First of all, he was an extremely nice man, secondly, he was very articulate, and thirdly he was a man of firm purpose but moderate speech. He would have made a very good prime minister.

Michael Foot, though a great admirer of your powers, once spoke of what he regarded as your 'stunning political naïvety'. Do you think of yourself as politically naïve?

I think of myself as politically disinterested. That may amount to naïvety. Michael Foot himself is a man of great naïvety, and his greatest naïvety was to believe that he could possibly become the leader of the Labour party. He is a scholar and a man of great integrity, but he was mildly corrupted politically by a feeling that a great prize was within his grasp.

You describe yourself as a subscribing Jew, comfortable with the Jewish faith and race, but not formally practising. Do you ever feel uncomfortable about Israel or the Israeli position vis-à-vis the Palestinians?

Mine is one of the loudest voices of protest. I paid various visits to Israel recently and sought every opportunity to tell the government how wrong I thought their policy was in relation to young Arabs. And I do feel very uncomfortable about it. I think it is very wrong that a community and a race, if you like, that claims to be fully civilised has been shooting young Arabs by the hundreds. I have no doubts at all that the policy of the Shamirs and Sharons is a reactionary policy that should have no support from liberal Jews.

As a former soldier, did you feel indignant when the Jewish underground, in their fight against the British Mandate, killed British soldiers in Palestine immediately after the war?

No, I didn't feel indignant. It was one of those unhappy inevitabilities. One very much wished that it hadn't happened, and particularly the episode of the sergeant. All of that was very horrible to a British Jew.

Would you say that the Middle East problem is just too intractable to find a solution?

Oh, it's easy to identify intractable problems. You'll find one in Cyprus, one in Northern Ireland, one in Nigeria. There are intractable problems, and one just has to wait and do the best one can to oil the machinery. There is perhaps more likelihood of a solution in the Middle East than elsewhere, because the Arab world is quite practical. What they have never been able to recognise is the enormous benefits that a civilised Israel would bring to the Middle East, but I think that is the sort of recognition which one can hope will come about.

The Israelis, however, have now adopted a policy which I think is thoroughly unfortunate, and that is apparently to accept that they have an empire-building function. The worst position you can have between two conflicting nations is when one of them believes they have God's support for empire building.

You said in a recent interview that you have always had a sense of being an onlooker, which sounds strange, coming from someone who has been so thoroughly engaged in so many things.

I've always had a sense that I'm not as seriously committed to any course of conduct as other people. I know in my own mind that I'm ready to find a solution that isn't necessarily the orthodox one. In that way I regard myself as being more of an onlooker than many other people.

As for my reaction to emotional upheaval, I would be very ashamed of panic or loss of control. There are a great many things that induce irritation in me, and I think they're the orthodox things. I have a deep sense of justice and thorough intolerance of injustice, especially when it is to the weak and in particular in relation to children. This is a catalogue of rather obvious virtues, but I don't think I'm given to the more sensational emotions. I don't boil with fury and go out and attack people with axes. I'd require a lot of provocation before I attacked anyone with an axe.

I'm certainly not intolerant of mediocrity, since you ask, or one would have to be intolerant of ninety-nine per cent of the human race. Nor would I arrogate to myself the right to judge everyone. I'm intolerant of inadequacy where someone is doing a job that requires a special talent which he hasn't got, and then, like most people, I get a little irritated, but I certainly wouldn't arrogate to myself the right to determine whether someone is mediocre or not.

Do you ever feel loneliness?

I don't need people all the time. I'm perfectly happy to spend the afternoon reading a book, or watching a television programme, or going to the cinema or to the theatre. Last night I heard a wonderful performance of Verdi's *Requiem*. That gives me delight. I don't need other people there holding my hand. But that is one of the great advantages of the arts: they are a consolation for loneliness.

Do you ever regret not having married?

I can't say I regret not having married, because I could have married. I had some interesting opportunities. There have been women who have been influential in my life. I don't intend to particularise them, but certainly I can think of three. It would be impossible for me to mention them. That would be breaching their privacy, not mine. I do regret not having children. I have a great affection for children, and would have enjoyed very much playing some part in bringing them up, but you can't have everything in this world.

On a television interview you said you did not want to reveal to a million viewers your reasons for not marrying. Isn't this creating a needless mystery?

It's not a needless mystery. It is a belief that, in certain aspects of one's life, one is entitled to privacy. I do not owe the world an explanation of my personal and private life, and I don't intend to give it one. If it's a mystery, it's quite a healthy mystery, and scholars can investigate it for the next hundred years. I certainly don't intend to elaborate on it. It's not a sinister mystery, I assure you.

Have you felt more drawn to religion with advancing years?

No, I haven't. I regard most religions as superstitions, and I certainly haven't been drawn to any particularly active superstition as I get older.

You have led an exemplary life, have defended and championed the underdog, yet you must have been, like everyone else, exposed to all kinds of temptations. Did you ever succumb?

Succumbed to temptation? I don't think consciously. If a temptation rose up in front of me, I would walk around it. I'm sure there are many areas of my behaviour which I now regret, and many decisions I've made that I think were wrong. It would be a very strange human being who didn't believe that, but I don't think I've consciously succumbed to temptation. I don't think I had many wild oats to sow. Some people sow enough wild oats to make it an agricultural problem, but I had no great interest. I wasn't addicted to drink or drugs. I smoked heavily at one time, but gave that up. I'm probably beginning to sound altogether too virtuous. I had encounters with women which gave me great comfort and pleasure, but that's all I can say about it. I've not been devoid of human feelings.

There are certainly things I've regretted, but not burning issues, not things that wake me in the middle of the night, shrieking in my bed. I have a high degree of complacency. On the whole, I think I'm reasonably satisfied with myself. That is not a virtuous thing to be, but it does make life easier.

LORD HEALEY

Denis Healey was born in Yorkshire in 1917. He was educated at Bradford Grammar School and Balliol College, Oxford, where he took a double first degree. He served with the Royal Engineers in North Africa and Italy (1940–45), attaining the rank of major. After the war he was secretary of the Labour Party's International Department for seven years before becoming MP for Leeds in 1952. He was a member of the shadow cabinet for five years, after which he became Secretary for Defence in the Wilson government of 1964, a post he held for six years. From 1974 to 1979 he was Chancellor of the Exchequer, a period marked by a sterling crisis. In 1980 he was elected deputy leader of the Labour Party. His autobiography, *The Time of My Life*, was published in 1989. In 1992 he entered the House of Lords as Baron Healey of Riddlesden. A keen photographer, he published three collections of images. He appeared on the *Morecambe and Wise Show*, was made a Companion of Honour, a Privy Counsellor and a Fellow of the Royal Society of Literature. He died, aged ninety-eight, in 2015.

In your autobiography, The Time of My Life, *you are wary of over-romanticising your childhood or – like Thomas Traherne – casting too rosy a glow over it. But if we accept your own definition of childhood, 'the capacity for wonder and joy', yours seems to have been wondrous and joyful ...*

Yes, it was a very happy time. There is of course a tendency to look through rose-tinted spectacles, and not just at your own childhood: I see the children playing in the gardens outside our flat as moving jewels, but I know they're little bastards as well. But mine really was a very happy time, although I had a black dog at that period in adolescence when I was trying to come to terms with a total change in physical and psychological make-up, but that only lasted about a year.

You were closer to your mother than to your father. Did this largely have to do with the fact that your mother was much more of a physical presence than your father, or did the affinity amount to much more than that?

It was largely determined by the fact that she was always there and he was rarely there. The other thing was that Mother had interests in literature and the arts and music which I shared and which she communicated to me. In later life I think I have a great deal in common with my father, particularly a sort of sentimental romanticism which mother didn't have at all. She was extremely pragmatic.

Did your parents get on well?

My father and mother's relationship was not a perfect one, partly because she never responded to his romantic side. She wasn't capable of it. They had a satisfactory sex life but she wasn't an emotional person, and in a way he was too emotional, with the result that he found it very difficult to have a friendly human relationship with his own children, though very easy to have it with his students. The first time he ever talked to me about himself was the day I got married in London, and he told me he had been terrified on his wedding day. He masked this excessive feeling with a sort of rueful facetiousness, which I now have too.

You say that it is impossible for a child to see his parents as they really are, or even as they appear to his contemporaries, but whatever takes the place of 'reality' surely makes an indelible impression on us, perhaps in a way that even 'reality' could not, and this has a lasting effect on us. Would you not agree?

I do agree. The trouble is when you use a word like reality you beg every conceivable question. The American cartoonist Steig has a wonderful cartoon of a child's view of his father, in which there is a naked man with a very large sexual organ and an enormous amount of hair on his face.

As a child you found your father 'curiously sentimental', as you put it – that criticism comes over as a rather adult construction of something which you presumably perceived rather differently at the time. Was it embarrassment you felt, or what?

No, I wasn't embarrassed really, and I did feel it at the time. One of his great ejaculations was, 'Ah, the wistful years … ', and there was indeed a wistfulness about him which he always put on for a photograph. I have pictures of him when he was a boy, and when he was a young man, and I was very conscious of that, even at the time.

You say that your father's literary romanticism made it difficult for him to communicate directly with you …

It was basically that he was frightened of too direct an emotional relationship with his children, so he tended to avoid conversations of that nature, to a degree that mother didn't, but then she didn't risk anything in having these conversations. My father remained difficult in his relationship with my mother right to the very end, and he was appallingly rude to her when he was in hospital, just before he died at the age of 92 … and what wholly lay behind that it's very difficult to say. An interesting thing is that when he was cremated, and we had 'Pie Jesu' from Fauré's *Requiem* played, she burst into tears afterwards. It was the first time we'd ever seen her weep.

Your parents in some ways were very much ahead of their time. To have a trial marriage in those days, unless you were part of the Bloomsbury Set which flouted convention, must have been very unusual … where do you think this independence of mind came from?

It wasn't Bloomsbury – their trials were usually homosexual. Mother always reminded me of one of the heroines of H. G. Wells, and the idea of a trial marriage was very much in keeping with the feminist movement and suffragette struggle in the early pre-war years.

You say your mother was filled with enthusiasm for the Bloomsbury Group. I would have thought that she might have found their elitism rather off-putting … was it chiefly their intellectual rigour which appealed?

Oh no, not intellectual rigour; she herself wasn't in that sense intellectually rigorous. She didn't go to university, she went to a teachers' training college, and nobody would have regarded her as a great brain, but she had a very enquiring mind, and she was led to the Bloomsburys by the talks given by Harold Nicolson on the wireless in the early 30s. Nigel Nicolson was my friend at Balliol and he was also with me in the House until he was sacked by the Tory Party for opposing the Suez campaign, and deselected by his constituency. I once took mother to Nigel's house in Sissinghurst, and for her to meet the son of Harold Nicolson was one of the things she most enjoyed in her old age.

It seemed astonishing that what you describe as your first real contact with your father came on the morning of your wedding. Did you regard that as a breakthrough, or were you saddened that it had taken so long?

I was surprised and pleased, not saddened. I did a radio interview with Anthony Clare recently and he kept trying to get me to admit that I was unhappy or sad or something. I never was very much; I tended always to look forwards rather than backwards, and of course at that time my interest was in my new life with Edna.

In many ways your childhood seems to have been a perfectly ordinary one, except for the way the arts – music, painting, literature – dominated your early life. That must surely have singled you out as being rather unusual among your peers at Bradford Grammar School?

It was actually a very good school, and Bradford was buzzing with intellectual energy. We had the Hallé orchestra playing every month there, and we got cheap seats as schoolboys. We had a very good civic theatre in which Fyodor Komisarjevsky from the Moscow Arts Theatre used to produce Chekhov. And, of course, boys who were at school with me had the same pleasure as I had. It's true that people didn't go for the visual arts much at Bradford, nor indeed at Oxford when I first went there. Nobody was interested in painting, until with a couple of friends with whom I'd nothing else in common we formed the New Oxford Arts Society. We got some Picasso etchings over and held one of his early Surrealist exhibitions. But Britain is a country even less interested in the visual arts than in music.

Your scholarship to Balliol form Bradford Grammar School was an enormous achievement at that time. How far were you yourself aware of that?

Balliol was regarded as the best Oxford college, as indeed it was, and I don't think we'd had anybody at Balliol in my period. Alan Bullock whom I greatly admired would like to have gone to Balliol but went to Wadham, and so I was conscious of achievement. Mind you, I only got an exhibition; I didn't get a full scholarship.

Your political awareness developed in 1936 during a cycling trip to Germany and Austria ... were you immediately opposed to Hitler, did you sense the dangers, or did you have some appreciation of his charisma and the spell which he cast?

Both. But I was mainly conscious of the dangers. Germany was a war society when I cycled through, and there were air raid adverts in every village green. *Der Stürmer,* that filthy anti-Semitic paper of Streicher's, was posted up on every town hall and of course a lot of the youngsters I met in the youth hostels were Hitler Jugend; so I was conscious both of the danger and of the charismatic appeal Hitler had for Germans. But at the same time quite a lot of the youngsters I met were anti-Hitler, and they told me that most working people in Germany were what they called beefsteaks – outside brown and inside red. So the interesting thing is I left Germany after this wonderful holiday deeply conscious of the threat to our peace and to our values, but not disliking the Germans. Even those who were Nazi weren't of the aggressively jackboot stamping style and I've always been able to draw a distinction between the opinions people hold politically and their personality. It was a good background for evaluating some of the things that are happening now. Weimar Germany was an appalling mess, morally as well as economically and politically, and you could see why many Germans saw Hitler as a chap who was taking Germany, if I can use a phrase, 'back to basics', restoring core values – *Kraft durch Freude, Kraft durch Arbeit*, and so on. There's no doubt this gave a lot of Germans renewed confidence in themselves and in their country. I could see that, but I didn't admire it.

With the unification of Germany today, could it ever happen again?

Oh yes, of course it could, but the particular experience of Nazism in Germany in the 30s won't happen in quite the same way. The big characteristic of the post-Cold War world is the revival of nationalism, and not only in the ex-communist countries. The constant theme in my political activity has been the need to find some way of preventing war and of controlling the enormous unique power of nationalism and directing it into constructive areas. When nationalism is allied with religion, it is an even greater danger, as in Yugoslavia and in India today. Every country is vulnerable to this, and when the political situation is bad, we hear slogans like 'back to basics' and 'core values' and the cry: 'what does a nation really stand for?' Yet the people who destroy all the nation's institutions are the loudest in praising them; like Mr Portillo today, the great Spanish prophet of the British institutions.

It must have been a considerable culture shock for someone from the respectable working class in the North to enter the Oxford cloisters. You say that Balliol was above all a meritocracy – the snobbery was intellectual rather than social – but there must surely have been class snobbery in some measure?

The first term I was there I would cringe internally when I heard the easy conversation of Etonians in the quad below my rooms. Britain in the 30s was very class-conscious, and for that reason a lot of my friends tended to be Americans, Canadians or Indians, but that only lasted a term or two, because after that people judged one another not according to class standards at all. The class thing was strongest among the Etonians, who tended to stick very closely together. Julian Amery, Maurice Macmillan, Harold Macmillan's son, and Stephen Tennant, son of the then Postmaster General, tended to see more of one another than of anybody else. The Wykehamists were very different; they were meritocrats and they mixed very easily into this new society.

You were persuaded to join the communists in 1937 because, as you said, the communists were the only people unambiguously opposed to Hitler. Was there also a degree of idealism involved the brotherhood of man?

Oh yes, there was a lot of that. Post-war communism, even pre-war communism, shouldn't obscure the genuine idealism which took a lot of people into the Communist Party, not just to fight Hitler but to fight for a better world. It was anti-Hitler but it was also belief in the brotherhood of man. We totally refused to accept that there were concentration camps in the Soviet Union, or that a lot of these trials which were taking place in the 30s were totally phoney; and the analogy I make with that is the enormous power of Mrs Thatcher in the ex-communist world. Nobody has a good word to say for her in Britain, except in obscure recesses of her old party, but she is still by far the most popular politician in what used to be the Soviet Union, and in Japan, and that's because people tend to react to the other extreme from the thing they see. The young Wordsworth, with whom I find I have more and more in common, was swept away by the French Revolution – 'Bliss was it in that dawn to be alive ... ', and then he had the shock of seeing Napoleon crowned emperor by the Pope, and seeing all the things he most disliked in politics arising out of the French Revolution.

Was your move away from communism painless or was there an element of disillusionment?

I never went for the ideological element in communism, especially the dialectical materialism. It was really the stupidity of the Russians in imagining that they could make a deal with Hitler that would stick, and continuing to do so after the fall of France, which made it very easy for me to leave. But my sympathy for the communists was increased by my experience in Italy where the communist party was the backbone of the resistance movement under fascism, especially during the war. However, what killed any lingering sympathy was my experience as international secretary for the Labour Party, trying to keep the socialists in Eastern Europe alive under the communist regimes. I became very anti-communist at that time; indeed, I was the chap who persuaded Morgan Phillips to make the affiliation of the communists to the Labour Party unconstitutional. The amazing thing is that right up to 1946 the communists were applying to affiliate to the Labour Party, although they were putting up candidates against Labour all over the country.

You say you are not proud of your political activities at Oxford. How would you rather have conducted yourself?

I was far too uncritical, as most youngsters were. At that time the undergraduate body was only 4500 at Oxford and 1500 were in the Labour Club which was run by communists – over 250 people were Communist Party members.

Almost anybody on the left became communist, including people who later became prominent Tories, like Biggs-Davison, and I only mention him because I asked him before he died if he minded being named – whereas the others I don't mention. The only democratic socialists who stood up to the communists were a Catholic called Michael Fogarty, who teaches economics in Glasgow, Chris Mayhew, and people like Roy Jenkins and Tony Crosland. Tony could easily have joined the CP, for his views were very much the CP views, but Roy was never tempted; and of course his father was Attlee's parliamentary private secretary. And there was the same CP domination of the literary world; all the young poets were members of the CP or flirting with it, except Louis MacNeice. Spender and Auden flirted with it, and half of the young painters were communists, both in France and in Britain.

One imagines that despite what was happening in Germany there was still the residual conviction, from less than twenty years before, that the Great War had been the war to end all wars. When did you stop believing that?

Oh, I never believed that. My generation in England became conscious of these issues in the early 30s when we took the school certificate at fourteen. We were swept away, my lot, by the poetry and novels against the First World War, which said it was a racket, a view held very strongly by Kipling, who wrote that wonderful couplet: 'If someone asks you why we died / Tell them because our fathers lied.' So we didn't regard the First World War as making the world safe for democracy, and indeed, as we were growing up to political consciousness Mussolini was already in power. Before I went to Oxford we had the invasion of Abyssinia, and then the civil war in Spain during the holiday when I was cycling round Germany. My generation, after we'd fought in the Second World War, were determined not to make the same mess of it as they had after the first, and it was this feeling which was responsible for the tremendous Labour victory in '45. And to be fair, the Labour government of that time did carry out the policies on which it was elected. Trouble is, it's not found very many new policies since.

When war was declared you did not hesitate to volunteer. Did you ever consider any alternative to fighting?

Oh no, not at all, although it's true I had been a pacifist and resigned from the OTC at school when I was sixteen. But at twenty-one, when war was declared, I rang up immediately to ask to volunteer. And so did all my friends, even though we were severely upbraided by our CP mentors and told that it had suddenly turned into an imperialist war instead of an anti-fascist war. We told them to sod off.

Did you consider the case for pacifism to be an honourable one?

Not at that time, no, because it was a question of fighting a patent evil, and those of us who were at Oxford at that time had met refugees from Nazi Germany. My generation knew there was a terrible evil which must be stopped, and we had no doubt about that. Even when the bomb was exploded in Japan – we had no details of course – all I said was, thank God I don't have to go out to Asia now.

After the war you decided to forgo the academic career you had planned and you went into politics because, as you say, there seemed no other way of helping directly to prevent a third world war. Was this resolve shaped largely by your experience of war?

The war and the failure to prevent the war with Hitler. My youth was dominated by the inevitability of war with Hitler unless people stood up to him, and then because they didn't, we had the war. We felt it was an unnecessary war, and I still feel that about every war in my lifetime; the Falklands, the Gulf War – none of them would have happened if the people who finally stood up to aggression had made it clear to the aggressor in advance that they'd do so; but they didn't.

Did writing your planned work on aesthetics suddenly seem too trivial an activity to engage in after the war?

I didn't regard it as trivial, nor do I now; in fact, I may still write, not a major work, but a trifling essay on the relationship between art and life. There is an argument which is perfectly respectable, that governments make very little difference to what happens socially and economically in a country. All the countries of Western Europe have developed social democracies, using those words in the most general sense, whether they've had right-wing governments or left-wing governments, or no government at all like Italy. But wars are made only by governments, and it's only by engaging in an activity which directly impacts on governments, i.e. politics, that you can hope to prevent them. And I still feel that very strongly.

You met Edna in 1940 …

Oh no, I met Edna as soon as I went to Oxford, because she used to go to the Ruskin dances, the only permitted contact between male and female of a social nature. I remember her as an attractive girl whom I called 'tomato face' because of her very red cheeks, but most of her friends called her 'the Zuleika Dobson of St Hugh's'. However, it was in 1940 that we really started courting.

Did you know then that she was the one for you?

Not at the beginning. She was my girl and we liked one another very much, but we didn't really think about marriage. I didn't want to make that kind of commitment at that time, partly because I thought I would probably be killed in the war. I lost five years' marriage allowance by forgoing popping the question until I got back from Italy.

There is often a kind of Anglo Saxon awkwardness which men, particularly Oxbridge men, feel with women ...

That was never so with me. I always felt comfortable in the presence of women, and I had had girlfriends from the age of 16, though I'm bound to say I don't think I went to bed with a girl until almost the last year at Oxford. That was one of the many enormous differences between the 30s and today, that boys and girls didn't go to bed with one another; that was absolutely not the case in the 30s, and I don't think one suffered particularly because of it. I'm not against people going to bed when they want to, but I don't think the present situation is more desirable than the earlier one. And we didn't have the pill in those days. If you were wealthy and well informed you could – like Mary McCarthy – get a Dutch cap, but otherwise you relied on your male partner being prepared to wash his feet with his socks on; which not many were.

Politics is a high-risk occupation for marriages and families ... you have been very fortunate in yours. Do you think this was good luck, or good judgement?

It was good luck that I had good judgement. [laughs] We've had a happy marriage, Edna and I, with very little upset, but we were lucky. I think it's very difficult for a politician's wife, particularly if he's in London all week and she's in the provinces, which is the case with many. An enormous number of MPs have affairs with their secretaries, and the poor wife's social life is confined to weekly visits to Sainsbury's.

What view do you take of the current interest in the private lives of politicians and what might be called their moral frailty?

I think it's grossly overdone. The French cannot understand the way we go on about this, but of course people wouldn't go on about it so much if the government didn't say it was returning to core values, and Barbara Cartland wasn't able to claim authorship of the Tory attitude to life. That, I think, is what has made them excessively exposed. But if we take specific examples, such as the astounding press coverage of the actress in the oral sex case, I can't think of anywhere in the world where that would be so except Britain. Sex is still a dirty thing to be sniggered at; what D. H. Lawrence called 'the dirty little secret' is still more prevalent here than in most countries.

But do you think it's reasonable to expect higher moral standards of behaviour from politicians?

Not unless they *preach* higher moral standards. A clergyman caught out in adultery or pederasty is always going to be especially vulnerable, but in this context I recall a glorious remark by Schelling, the German moral philosopher, who was discovered to be sleeping with his girl students, and when he was asked how he reconciled that with his lectures, he replied, 'Have you ever heard of a signpost walking the way that it's pointing?'

When you entered the House of Commons in 1952, it was still regarded as something of a gentlemen's club ... I imagine that was an aspect of political life which you fundamentally disapproved of ...

To be fair, it was only the Tory side that was a gentlemen's club. When I arrived in 1952 you could tell which party an MP belonged to by looking at him. The Labour people tended to have badly cut suits or, if they were public school boys, to wear tweed jackets and scruffy trousers. Most Labour Party members were people who had worked as trade unionists in manufacturing unions. Now that's totally changed, and you cannot identify the party of an MP if you go into the central lobby. The dress and behaviour of the classes have moved together very much in the last 40 years since I came in, and the manual working class is now scarcely represented. Ernie Bevin who was, I think, the greatest British foreign secretary this century, was an illegitimate child of a girl who worked on a farm; his education stopped when he was 11 years old, and he worked with his hands until he became a trade union leader. People like him have disappeared from the House.

Didn't Bevin fail to handle the problem of Palestine by handing it over to the UN? Michael Foot, for example, regards him as being responsible for what he has called 'the Labour government's act of eternal dishonour with painful consequences for our world today'. Isn't that something you gloss over in your memoirs?

No, I think I deal with that very directly because I had to defend Bevin's policy in front of Golda Meir in Zurich at the socialist international meeting. History will tell us whether Zionist nationalism in the end has been a good or bad thing, but a lot of my Jewish friends after the war belonged to a small party in Poland called the Polish Jewish Bund, which was very anti-Zionist because it regarded Zionism as a form of imperialism. So I could see the argument against taking land away from the Arabs and against the ethnic cleansing which the Jews carried out in Palestine during the first war. I saw that it would create enormous problems for Britain and the United States in the Arab world, which it has, and not only the Arab world, but in much of the Third World also. So I don't feel as Michael Foot does about that; but then I don't think Michael has much sense of reality, and this is one reason why he wasn't a very useful leader of the Labour Party. The Foreign Office was almost universally hostile to the creation of a state of Israel and gave up because we came under such intolerable American pressure; but most of my friends in the Labour Party were Zionists, like Laski, Hugh Dalton, and some of the most remarkable Tories, like Winston. I had friends in the Zionist leadership in Israel – Shimon Perez is still a good friend – and a lot of them, particularly Abba Eban, who was a don at Cambridge before the war, always knew that the moral position of Israel in the Middle East would undermine its political position, as it has. Equally, you have to come to terms with reality, and of course the state of Israel is a reality, though it's also done things which one can't possibly approve, such as some of the activities of Mossad, and the nuclear cooperation with South Africa, and so on.

In your autobiography you say that your first ten years in parliament were dominated by the internal divisions of the Labour Party, which prevented it from mounting an effective attack on the Tories till Harold Wilson became leader. Hasn't the Labour Party continued to be dogged by internal divisions?

Once Wilson became leader there were divisions over his leadership, but they weren't fundamental policy divisions, and the same was really true of Callaghan. But I always regret that out of my nearly 50 years now as an active national politician in the Labour Party, both as an official and as an MP, we've lost two decades through internal arguments about dogma basically – the Bevanite ten years and the Bennite ten years of the 80s – and it takes a long time for a party to recover public trust. As for the Tories' struggles now, the tension between the dogmatists and the pragmatists is just like the home life of our own dear queen.

You became defence secretary in 1964 in Wilson's government, a post you held for six years. Looking back, were those the best years of your political life?

Yes. First of all, it was the first time I'd had power which is an indispensable condition of influencing policy at government level, so I enjoyed that very much.

Secondly, perhaps to my surprise, I very much liked the people I worked with, and I was intimately involved in foreign policy, which is my main interest. We were fighting wars in South America and Borneo, and it was the period when we had to decide, in order to cut our coat according to the cloth, to give up our role east of Suez, apart from Hong Kong which we were committed to by history. I also had a major role in trying to reconcile the German and American positions on nuclear weapons in Europe. I enjoyed it very much, and on the whole I think I did a pretty good job.

You have described Wilson as 'essentially frivolous'. In view of the recent biographies of Wilson, in which he has been largely rehabilitated, have you modified your critical view at all?

No, not really. He had very few political principles. He had no sense of direction, and he was an awful Walter Mitty. None of the people who worked for Wilson in the government – whether it was Barbara Castle or Dick Crossman – really had much good to say about him. One of his weaknesses, which wasted a lot of time, is that he didn't like to use his authority as prime minister to go against a majority of the Cabinet, and so to get round the problem he packed the Cabinet with yes men and yes women, just so that he'd have a majority.

Your five years as chancellor from 1974 to 1979 were rather stormy – the period was marred by a sterling crisis and then intervention by the IMF. How did that period compare in terms of job satisfaction with your time as defence secretary?

It was intellectually very much more testing, and it was physically much more demanding. I never had any spare time at all, but I think it was worth doing, and I've been relieved to find that a lot of my foreign friends who are still around think I did a very good job. Controlling spending is appallingly difficult, as all governments and chancellors have found, but the real problem is that you are at the mercy of external events. We've now got a single global financial market in which a thousand billion dollars a day can cross the exchanges in search of speculative profit, so no country can control its own exchange rate and therefore its own interest rates. We've also got a single global investment market, and people now will put a new factory wherever the relevant labour is cheapest or where it's closer to the ultimate market. The power of the chancellor is terribly limited; things can come out of nowhere and hit you.

In the general election campaign of 1983, you did battle with Michael Heseltine, then defence secretary, but it was commonly believed that you despised Labour defence policy just as much as Heseltine. Isn't that the unacceptable face of politics, to advocate something you don't believe in?

Yes, but if you're going to have choice and democracy, you've got to have parties, and you have to go along with the party unless you leave it. Some of my friends left the Labour Party, but nothing came of it, and I never thought it would. You say it's unacceptable, but I'm afraid it's the real world.

You became, as it were, the Greatest Leader Labour Never Had, and your fight against Tony Benn and the Bennites is given credit for turning the Labour Party away from almost certain self-destruction. Do you acknowledge that?

Yes. If I look back on myself as a politician, I think I should have worked harder for the leadership which I never really wanted, because, as I've always said, I'd rather do something than be something. Because I didn't fight harder we've had 15 years now of what I regard as very bad government. Of course, once I'd lost that battle I felt I had an absolute obligation to fight Tony Benn hard for the deputy leadership, even though as the Americans say of the vice president's job, 'it's not worth a barrel of warm spit' as a job in itself. If I'd not won that battle which, because of our weird constitution, I won by a hair of my eyebrow, I think there would have been a haemorrhage of people out of the Labour party. I always believed that, if we stuck to it so that the sensible people finally had control of the National Executive, we'd be all right, and I warned my friends in the Gang of Four, like Shirley Williams and David Owen, that it would take two years, and if they weren't prepared to wait two years, too bad, but outside the party they wouldn't come to anything; and they haven't.

If you had won the leadership contest you would probably have become prime minister … what are your feelings about that?

Well, in a way I would have liked to have been prime minister, but I've only really wanted leadership to prevent baddies getting in, whether it was in the party or in the government. The premiership was never my objective. The thing I most regret about my life is that I never had a chance to be foreign secretary at a time when we had influence in the world. We don't have influence now. Hurd can spend ten days in the Middle East and nobody knows he's been or come back.

You have been described as the Labour heavyweight who never made it. Does that description wound?

I'm not wounded by what people say about me. I've always upset people by saying that as long as my wife loves me I don't care about what the rest of the British people think. Besides, I get better treatment from the press than many people, although that's partly because I'm not competing; I'm a clapped-out old fart.

One analysis of your political career is that you've been more highly regarded out of office than in office, almost like a great painter who is suddenly discovered after he is dead. Presumably you see things rather differently?

To be fair, I was very highly regarded by people interested in defence when I was defence secretary, and I still am. Views about my record as chancellor are much more mixed, but I still think I got us through the most difficult period without the tragedies we've had since '86 when everything went very badly wrong under Thatcher.

Charles Laurence, writing in the Daily Telegraph *in 1989, said: 'When Healey's moment to strike for the leadership came, he had too few friends left, and the left had too many. He had spent too much time in the hinterland and not enough on the single-minded pursuit of high office.' Would you agree with that assessment?*

No, I wouldn't entirely, because the reason I was quite popular with the public is that I had a hinterland and people didn't feel I was a career politician interested in nothing but his own advancement. My misfortune was that I had to run for leadership just after having to inflict misery on the party as chancellor, but if you make politics the be-all and end-all of your life you will be incredibly miserable, like Mrs Thatcher and Gorbachev.

You are fond of Kipling's lines, 'If you can meet with triumph and disaster / And treat those two impostors just the same ... ' Is that a principle you have put into practice in your time in politics?

Yes, on the whole, although that was one of my father's favourite poems rather than my own. I prefer Kipling when he's not being so didactic but reflecting on the lessons of life, and one of my favourite passages from him is where he says: 'The dog returns to its vomit, the sow returns to her mire, and the burnt fool's bandaged finger goes wobbling back to the fire.' He was a wonderful writer, greatly underestimated, and although he was a great believer in the British role in the world, he was not a triumphalist imperialist at all.

Your wife once famously remarked that Mrs Thatcher had no 'hinterland', by which she meant, to put it bluntly, she had read very few books and had no sense of history. You suggest that the same might be true of John Major, Trollope notwithstanding, and you conclude that public life is the poorer for it ...

Well, there is a big question mark over Major's devotion to Trollope. The point is you've got to have your real values outside the political world, so an interest in music and painting and literature is very valuable. The other important thing is – and I feel this particularly since the end of the Cold War – it's very important to know history. I did a course in economics as a mature student when I was chancellor, and I've read books of political science, which is an oxymoron like public privy, but the one thing you *can* learn from is history. Human situations recur again and again in history, and you cannot begin to understand what is happening in the Balkans or Eastern Europe, or even more Russia, without knowing a bit about the history of those countries. If you know about Nicholas II, Yeltsin is very easy to explain ... another man who produces the first democratic elections and then dissolves the Duma because it votes against him.

Your own interest in Virginia Woolf and Yeats and Emily Dickinson suggests that you do not think there is any sort of gulf fixed between poetry and prose. Are they just alternative uses of the imagination?

No, not entirely, because first of all poetry is very much more concentrated. The ambiguities which Empson discussed are much more complex in poetry than in prose, and in poetry the sound is also important.

When you read Virginia Woolf and Emily Dickinson, do you feel yourself in contact with something specifically feminine, or are they rather two sensitive minds among others?

I think Virginia Woolf was self-consciously feminine and up to a point she was feminist. In *A Room of One's Own*, you do feel you're in touch with a woman's mind, but a woman of extraordinary intellectual range and sensitivity. On the whole I prefer her diaries and letters to her novels. Dickinson is absolutely unique – no man can write like that – and she clearly is very conscious of being a woman in what she writes, but without being in any sense feminist. I've no time for the claptrap of that charlatan Camille Paglia suggesting she is a sadist – people will say anything for money.

I have the impression from reading My Secret Planet *that you take a Romantic view of literature ... Shelley calls literature the record of the best and happiest moments and Wordsworth believed that it might improve our moral sensitivity. Is that a view you share?*

I half share it. You can only approach problems of the spirit in my view through the arts, and poetry is one of the main arts. But the greatest poet in our language was, if not gay, bisexual, and he was deeply realistic. That was why it was comic for this poor headteacher in north London to describe *Romeo and Juliet* as being infested with heterosexuality. [laughs] Shakespeare's view wasn't Romantic in the Shelley sense at all, and Wordsworth I put in a totally different group from Shelley because Shelley was an upper-class young man who wrote a typical public-school Romantic leftism. But Wordsworth came from a provincial professional family; his father was a solicitor, and he felt very much out of the centre. His big experience was being excited and carried away by the French Revolution and then being terribly disillusioned by it. I admire Wordsworth enormously and I know why he's called Romantic, because he happened to write in that period along with Byron and Keats and Shelley, but I would put him in a way slightly ahead of the other so-called Romantics. Again, you can't conceivably call Aeschylus, Euripides and Sophocles Romantic in that sense and yet I admire them more than any of the others, including Wordsworth; and Shakespeare lived in this violent, brutal, cruel world and wrote about it totally honestly, without any spirituality. He had no feeling for that at all, just as he was very confused about sex – 'the expense of spirit in a waste of shame'; yet on almost any page you read, you find something stupefyingly good.

Modern critical views tend to be dismissive about the meanings to be found in literature, saying it is all a matter of context ... have you any sympathy with that way of thinking?

Not really. There's a book by the Bishop of Oxford, Harris, who is rather a Tory on religion and beauty, in which he argues that religion is enormously enhanced by the arts, which I would hold; except that my view is terribly heretical in the literal sense in that I do not believe that any theology is worth the paper it's written on. You cannot use the sort of logic you use in examining the phenomenal world, or in producing the microwave or the atom bomb, to consider questions of value. Questions of value relate to the spirit or the soul which you can best explore in my view through the arts. Religious experience I believe in strongly, but I don't believe in a personal God.

You are also very interested in music and painting and photography. Does literature offer us something that the other arts do not, do you think?

Oh yes, of course it does. Music is the purest art form with no phenomenal references in the Kantian sense; poetry has to use words which are all referential, but it also uses sound, and the sound of poetry can be sweet: 'daffodils, / That come before the swallow dares, and take / The winds of March with beauty ... ' There is a music in Shakespeare's lines which you cannot relate very directly to phenomena.

In My Secret Planet you quote Emily Dickinson saying, 'It is an honourable thought to suppose that we are immortal', but also when she says: 'They went to God's Right Hand / That hand is amputated now / And God cannot be found.' Can poetry offer us some viable alternative to what used to be called the comforts of religion?

Yes, but it can also provide the same comforts in a way. I don't regard these as strict alternatives, because we're now talking about an area which is not susceptible to logical analysis. I was told that Jonathan Miller described it as sentimental tosh when I said that the '*Heiliger Dankgesang*' from Beethoven's Opus 132 in A Minor, the song of 'Thanksgiving to the Deity' on recovery from an illness, or indeed the 'Cavatina' from his Opus 130, that these took me to the heights, or perhaps the depths, of religious feeling; but they do.

You write in your anthology that it was T. S. Eliot who made you realise that it was possible for an intelligent man to be a Christian. But if you reject the theology and dogma of the Church, in what sense would you argue that an intelligent man could be Christian?

Well, it's difficult. If you belong to a church then you either have to accept one of the Protestant theologies, or the Catholic theology, yet Protestants and Catholics have actually killed one another for believing different theologies, and they're doing so today in bloody Bosnia; so I regard theology as a mistaken endeavour, as Kant did. Once you erect an institution to promote a theology you're moving in the worst political direction, because you are creating an institution which is supposed to teach a partisan view and to maintain that all other views are wrong, or even sinful.

If Donne and Vaughan, Marvel and Milton owe their power as poets to a religious conviction you can't share, how can you regard them as other than interesting museum pieces?

Because they appeal to some of the deepest instincts I have in my spirit. But I don't have to take their religion seriously, and of course Blake, whom I greatly admire, believed that Milton was of the Devil's party but didn't know it, and that the real hero of *Paradise Lost* is Satan.

In your book you raise what you call the most difficult question which confronted you at Oxford – the relationship between art and life. Have you been able to approach an answer since Oxford?

I hadn't really thought about these things very systematically until I wrote *My Secret Planet,* and I don't despair of producing a useful little contribution in this field during the second half of my life.

Like Kathleen Raine whom I interviewed last year, you are very dismissive of Iris Murdoch. Raine called her 'a mere journalist'; you say she is 'unreadable'. Doesn't this smack of intellectual elitism?

No. I liked Iris very much when she was a friend of mine as a student and I introduced her to Beckett's *Murphy*, which I've always regarded as the pebble which dislodged her avalanche. But the problem is that I find her novels are basically games with characters who have characteristics you recognise but who don't make up believable people; that's my worry with her. About the only book of hers which I found compelling to read right through was *A Severed Head*, but I haven't really tried very much recently because she seems to me to be doing an up-market intellectual Alan Ayckbourn. She is a serious thinker, of course, and though I haven't read the new book she's done about morality, my impression from the reviews is that she really rather agrees with me about all that.

Throughout our cultural history poets have sought to defend poetry against the prejudices of those inexperienced in it. What are the grounds now for a defence against the philistines, those with no sense of history or literary heritage ... ?

If people can't appreciate poetry, too bad for them, but I don't feel a need to justify or defend it. There's always a risk when you get into that sort of argument that you'll end up defending bad cases. It always struck me when I was a boy and I started taking an interest in painting, that there was a scandal every year about something being rejected by the Royal Academy, because it was too modern; but actually the paintings that were rejected were never very good. In any case there's so much poor poetry at the moment. It's rather like feminism: the great writers who want a square deal for women, like George Eliot and Virginia Woolf, they speak for themselves, but if I'm asked to defend Camille Paglia or one of these pretty new feminists like Roiphe or Naomi Woolf, I'm not going to waste my time.

You have earned yourself the reputation for being something of a political thug with remarks such as 'virago intacta' about Mrs Thatcher and 'savaged by a dead sheep' with reference to Geoffrey Howe. Is the political thug tag something you regard as a badge of honour?

Not particularly. The trouble with journalists is that one of them will use a phrase and the others rather like it, so they all use it from that moment on. The remarks you quote are not thuggish; they're rather witty, which is why they've survived. The thuggery comes much more from those occasions when I have shouted at people or had to deal with those who voted against us on public spending in the House. But I'll tell you of one exchange which hasn't appeared in print before. After the '92 election the Speaker held a party for all the retiring MPs, including me and Maggie. Maggie came over to me and said, 'Oh Denis, I've just come across a phrase you used about me when we first were fighting across the floor of the House. You called me a "Pasionara of privilege".' I said, 'Yes, but the best remark I ever made about you was only last year, when I said you combined the economics of Arthur Daley with the diplomacy of Alf Garnett.' She looked terribly puzzled because she had never heard of either. But that's not thuggery ...

You have always reserved large quantities of vitriol for David Owen, whom you likened to the Upas tree – poisoning the ground for miles around. Have you modified your opinion at all in recent years?

David's tried to do a good job in Bosnia but he was put in when the chance of success had already disappeared. Once we'd recognised Bosnia as a state on the basis of a referendum in which the largest minority refused to take part, we were on a hiding to nothing. But I think he's worked hard. He can be very offensive, but perhaps that was the one situation in which, as he was dealing with bastards, it was a good thing that he was a bastard too.

Your wife has never forgiven you for expressing in a speech in the House of Commons a personal affection for Mrs Thatcher, whom she regarded as 'lacking in common humanity'. Did you yourself come to regret what you call this moment of 'careless charity'?

No, not really, though I can add something of interest to that. Edna and I both watched the four television programmes about Thatcher – *The Downing Street Years* – in which she looked exactly like her *Spitting Image* puppet, and I said to Edna at the end that it was the most frightening thing I had ever seen on television; to think that we were run by a raving hag who was surrounded by ministers who were fighting one another like weasels in a sack, that we had this for 14 years and nobody did anything about it. But Edna said, 'No, I have quite a different feeling. I really felt the human and personal tragedy of this bright prefect from a grammar school in the provinces, who got to the top and then everything crumbled.'

You have sometimes said that you have lived in the most interesting time imaginable. That is the mark of a happy man ... are there any shadows on that happiness?

The shadow is the fact that the end of the Cold War has meant a return to the worst aspects of history; we're entering a period that will be as cataclysmic in its effect on the world as the period that came after the French Revolution. That was followed by the Napoleonic Wars and then total uncertainty and the revolutions of '48. I think we're in for a very difficult century, but it won't be a European century; it will be dominated by the powers in the Far East.

As you grow older ... do you ever contemplate your own death? Are you afraid?

There was a book written shortly after the war by a young Hungarian about his experiences when the Russians came in, and the title was, *I Am 17 and I Do Not Want to Die*. At that sort of age, the thought of death is profoundly repellent, but I find it much less so now. As people get older they don't rage so much against the dying of the light.

Patricia Highsmith

Patricia Highsmith was born in Texas in 1921. After attending Columbia University in New York, she worked as a freelance journalist until the publication of her first novel, *Strangers on a Train* (1950), which was filmed by Alfred Hitchcock. Her numerous psychological thrillers include *The Blunderer* (1954), *This Sweet Sickness* (1960, filmed 1977), *Those Who Walk Away* (1967), *A Dog's Ransom* (1972) and *People Who Knock on the Door* (1983). *The Talented Mr Ripley* (1955), the first of the Ripley series, was awarded the Edgar Allan Poe Scroll. The world she created was described by Graham Greene as claustrophobic and irrational, 'one we enter each time with a sense of personal danger'. Patricia Highsmith lived in Switzerland. She died in 1995.

Your parents separated before you were born, at a time when separation and divorce were not as common as they are now. Did you feel different from other children?

Frankly, no. I was born in my grandmother's house in Texas. It was a very warm, friendly atmosphere, and I was very happy until I was six years old when I was taken up to New York, but even there it wasn't bad. It was suddenly different to be amidst all those people, but I remember getting along very well with the blacks in my school because they seemed to have the same accent. And New York is always interesting.

You seem to have had a highly unusual childhood ... do you remember it as an unhappy time, or did you just accept your circumstances?

I had to accept them. My mother remarried when I was three or four, and she was rather a neurotic type to say the least, always picking quarrels with my stepfather, so life was a little bit difficult.

Do you believe that childhood influences and environment shape and mould our adult lives?

I believe very much what the Roman Catholics say about a child up to the age of seven. Moral training has taken place by then, and my grandmother was rather strict on those things. She was not severe, but she knew what was right and wrong, and nobody ever tried to cross her. I'm quite sure that left its mark on me.

Did you ever regret being an only child?

No. I never missed having brothers and sisters. Even now, although I very much like people, I am happy to live alone. The main point is that I can't work with anybody else in the house, so if I lived with somebody I'd have to give up my work, or else somehow create a small house on the lawn and just take myself off there.

You didn't meet your real father until you were twelve years old. Can you recall your feelings at that time?

I was shy and also curious. It was in my grandmother's house and I saw him for only five or ten minutes – we didn't even sit down. He took a look at my hand, as if to say, yes, you're my child, but he was almost a stranger, rather brusque and formal.

Did you see him later in life?

Yes. After the first encounter, he walked me to school and back a couple of times. Later between high school and college I went to Texas again to visit my grandmother, and I saw a great deal of him then. We went out to dinner and I met a lot of his friends.

And did you like him?

In my opinion, there was nothing to dislike about him.

Your novels are often concerned with anxiety, confused relationships and loss of identity, which would seem to be the outstanding features of your own childhood ... would you agree?

I don't see the loss of identity. I took the name Highsmith which was my step-father's name, but that is not a loss of identity. In any case, fiction writers tend to write about problems, not about happy families. I wrote about murders, but I never want to murder anybody.

How would you describe your relationship with your stepfather? Was he to all intents and purposes your father, or were there barriers?

He was not what you would call a strong father figure, or indeed a strong anything. He was a man of very good character, a mild man whom my mother bossed around. I was about sixteen when I began to realise it was my mother who was causing the difficulties. But I don't feel his influence. I had to make my own character.

It seems that your mother explained family circumstances to you when you were ten years old, but that you had worked things out for yourself before then. Did you feel betrayed by that, or angry that she hadn't told you before?

No. I did not feel angry at all. She had simply been evading the issue, putting it off.

I read somewhere about your mother losing one of your manuscripts which you interpreted as an act of terrible indifference. You must have felt very hurt and disappointed.

Not really. By then I was already thirty-four years old – I know because it was the time of my grandmother's death. My mother did not take care of things and she lost the manuscript along with a lot of other papers, my letters to my grandmother, my college exam results, and so on. But I did not think it malicious. She was simply disorganised.

Do you think that your experience, or perhaps lack of experience of men during your formative years – absent father, stepfather, etc. – led to a mistrust of men in later life?

No, because I had boyfriends from the age of sixteen. And, as a matter of fact, I regarded my stepfather as being very trustworthy.

The heroes of your book are invariably men. The women are less interesting – they are often sluttish or have disagreeable habits. Do you have a kind of contempt for your own gender?

No. *Edith's Diary*, for instance, is entirely about a woman and her struggles, a woman who tried to do her best. She failed in the end, but I think I wrote about her with considerable respect.

Your Little Tales of Misogyny, *in the words of the blurb, shows 'the generic awfulness of the female sex'. Were they written tongue-in-cheek, or with an underlying conviction?*

With a conviction about certain aspects of women, such as a kind of phoniness and trying to be oh-so-correct, but one could do the same kind of book about men, a similar exaggeration of masculine traits.

Do you feel a sense of solidarity with your fellow women?

No. I've never been in that position. I can be in favour of women's causes, but I don't join them. If it's a matter of donating a little money, or signing something, I might, but not extra work.

You have been independent all your life, you are successful and you are your own woman, all of which would seem to make you a shining example of the feminist movement. Have you ever felt strongly about women's liberation?

Not strongly, no, but I'm not in a job that discriminates against women. I might have become angry if I'd been working in an office all my life.

Your book Carol, *published under a pseudonym, describes the love which develops between two women. Why did the subject interest you?*

Because society was more against love between women in those days, and I thought it was a good story, especially with the ex-husband in pursuit, making things as difficult as possible. I wasn't consciously trying to convey a particular message, but I wanted to give it a happy ending.

Why did you write it under a pseudonym?

I was already labelled as a mystery writer, even though *Strangers on a Train* was not a mystery, and I didn't want to be labelled as a gay writer. My publishers wanted another book like *Strangers on a Train*, but as usual I wrote what I wanted to.

It was unusual in those days to give a positive portrayal of homosexuality. Were you trying to shock, or make people examine their prejudices, or what?

Neither. I was trying to tell a story which I thought was interesting.

Your heroine Carol has to face the choice of losing her daughter or losing her lover, but there is no attempt to portray the situation from the child's point of view, or to engage the reader's sympathy with the child. I wonder if you perhaps lack a natural sympathy with children …

The child is only ten and I don't think a ten-year-old would have been able to understand the situation then, or the feelings of society towards lesbianism. Besides, I don't know much about children because I haven't been around children since I was a child myself. Frankly I'm not particularly interested in children.

Have you ever wanted to have children?

No. Absolutely not. I think it's very difficult to raise children properly, and I cannot live with people round me.

You live quite a reclusive existence. Is that how you planned it, or did it just happen that way?

To say I am a recluse is journalistic nonsense, as though I made an effort to stay alone, which is not the case. I like talking to people on the phone, I like people to drop by for a coffee. I do not consider myself a recluse.

You have always avoided literary circles or discussion with other writers. Do you think they might be too incestuous or is it perhaps a fear of boredom?

I'm not inclined to talk about my work before it is finished – I think it is very dangerous to do so – and then when a book is finished, why talk about it? To me another writer is not enough of a challenge mentally. I very much prefer painters and sculptors and photographers; they have a different way of seeing life.

In your books violence seems to take place almost as much in the head as in any overt way. Do you think this is a true reflection of the way it is, that most violence is cerebral, and seldom actually manifests itself?

I'm not interested in brute force, which is what prevails in the world today. The kind of people I write about debate with themselves beforehand – should they do it or not? This makes for more thinking about violence in my books than doing it.

You have said that you find the public passion for justice boring and artificial because 'neither life nor nature cares if justice is done or not'. What exactly do you mean by that?

It's a rather extreme remark, but even justice frequently goes wrong. There are cases of men and women falsely accused of murder. Also, only eleven per cent of murders are discovered now. Some people don't count for very much so the police don't try very hard to find out who killed them. In the majority of cases nobody cares enough to catch the murderer, especially in America where the jails are full and the police are very busy.

The world you portray is a very cynical one, full of emotional cripples. Is this for you a totally imaginary world, or does it reflect your experience of life?

The world is certainly full of very strange people. It's a matter of degree. Sometimes people are just quirky which makes them interesting and funny and sometimes their quirks are terribly serious.

In 1965 you said that you were sick of violence and butchery and psychopaths ... yet psychopaths have followed you into the 90s.

Well, I made a mistake in 1965 then.

Graham Greene once described you as 'the poet of apprehension rather than fear'. Is that a description you're pleased with?

Yes, I regard that as a compliment. Apprehension implies that my books leave something to the imagination. The reader is made curious about what is going to happen.

He also said that your world is one 'without moral endings', in other words justice is often not done and the villains are free to carry on with their evil doings. Do you see yourself as seriously challenging the normal moral scheme of things, or is it purely a game, an entertainment?

It's more of a game. I'm principally interested in telling a good story.

But your novels often invite discussions of morality, fuelled by characters like Ripley who murder without conscience and get away with it. What message are you aiming to give people?

None. I'm simply trying to create an interesting story. Some people might say Ripley's attitude is impossible but I think his lack of conscience is entirely believable. My books are written to entertain. I don't consider myself a deep thinker; I'm much more an intuitive kind of person.

Your book People Who Knock on the Door *was dedicated to, 'The courage of the Palestinian people and their leaders in the struggle to regain a part of their homeland.' Why did you make that political gesture?*

Because I thought it was right that I should. I blame my own country to some extent for what is going on now. I know people blame England for the mandate which led to all this, but America finances it now to a great degree. They also have the press under control and people are more or less told to shut up. Well, I don't feel like shutting up. I think statements about injustice should be made. It's shocking the way people sit in Long Island saying that the Palestinians should get their act together. When Hitler used the gun and the boots on the Jews nobody told them to get their act together. Nobody is able to face up to the gun. The Palestinians can't even form small collectives to grow vegetables in poor soil on their own West Bank and Gaza without the Israelis breaking them up.

But what first brought the Palestinian cause to your attention?

The atrocity of it, the absolute injustice of the situation.

I understand you won't allow your books to be published in Israel. Do you think gestures like that have any effect?

No, only in a very small way. I'm sure the world couldn't care less, but it shows that not every American refuses to see what's happening. That is what the Israelis want, and that's frankly what they get round the New York area. From a humane point of view America turns too much of a blind eye to what Israel is doing there.

Do you feel as you grow older that your writing gets better and better?

That's very tough. Unfortunately, I feel a tremendous slowing up; everybody does at my age, I think. Also, life becomes more complicated as one grows older. There's more paperwork, income-tax returns for two countries – all this has become burdensome somehow.

You have described the criminal as a free spirit. Can you tell me what you mean by that?

It's not very flattering to the criminal because he just does anything he wants. It's not something that I admire, but he's definitely free in that respect. The rest of us have certain constraints, which is normal. For example, there are one or two people in my life whom I absolutely detest, but to murder them is out of the question.

Your heroes are usually unscrupulous, amoral and sometimes schizoid. Is it simply that they are more dramatically interesting figures to write about, or does your attention to them run deeper than that?

It's not so much attraction. I find them interesting, puzzling. Nobody questions why somebody is good, but most people are curious about a murderer – they want to know why. Also, there is entertainment value in somebody getting away with something. One may disapprove, but it's still fascinating.

Ripley differs from your other heroes in that he appears to have no conscience. Other characters are much more concerned with their own guilt. Is Ripley the exception … in art as in life?

Ripley is abnormal in the sense that he doesn't feel the same amount of guilt as other people. He feels guilty for the first murder and then is reconciled to others. I have to say that he's exceptional.

It has sometimes been said that you are in love with Ripley, the rather likable psychopath. Does this strike you as an absurd suggestion?

It's just an exaggeration. I like to write about him, yes, but that's all. It's a silly phrase, 'in love'.

Have you ever been in love with a man?

In a way, yes. When I was around twenty-one …

What happened?

Nothing happened. It turned into friendship, and we were friends until he died.

Have you ever regretted not marrying?

No.

Lucretia Stewart who interviewed you for The Telegraph *wrote as follows: 'Her manner, which is at once diffident and disdainful, precludes intrusive questioning. It is not a secret that she is or has been a lesbian, but it would have been impossible to ask her about her private life.' How do you react to that?*

It's better than some things I've read. If she wants to put that, it's OK by me.

What about the suggestion that you are a lesbian?

OK. Fine. But I don't talk about it.

Have you been a lesbian?

Yes.

One concludes from reading your books that happiness is a frail commodity, touched by anxiety and often guilt. Has that been your own experience perhaps?

Very often with regard to people, yes, but it does not apply to happiness in general. Many people of course want to say that I'm unhappy, that I'm reclusive, but I'm not going to be unhappy just because somebody tells me I am.

In all the attention given to death in your books, do you ever contemplate your own?

No, although I would really like to be sure about my will. I have made a will, actually written it in holograph which is what the Swiss want, but I have a feeling it isn't finalised yet. The most important thing is to have everything well organised before one's death; that is more important than the phenomenon of dying.

Do you see the world as a friendly place?

In principle, yes. I have an optimistic attitude. When I get up in the morning, I first of all make the coffee and then I say to my cat, we're going to have a great day …

ELIZABETH JANE HOWARD

Elizabeth Jane Howard was born in 1923 and educated at home. From 1939 to 1946 she trained at the London Mask Theatre and went on to perform at Stratford-upon-Avon and in a repertory in Devon. From 1947 onwards she dedicated herself to writing, and in 1951 she won the John Llewellyn Rhys Memorial Prize for her book *The Beautiful Visit* (1950). Her subsequent novels include *The Long View* (1956), *The Sea Change* (1959) and *Odd Girl Out* (1972). *After Julius* (1965) and *Something in Disguise* (1969) she later adapted for television. Her most famous work – a family chronicle which went on to sell millions of copies worldwide, *The Cazalet Chronicles* – saw the fourth volume, *Casting Off,* published in 1995 and the final title, *All Change,* published shortly before her death in 2014.

The one thing I know about your childhood is that you had a terribly difficult relationship with your mother. Looking back, is that the feature which stands out most in your mind?

I'm interested that you know that. It has taken me nearly all my life to get over it. I feel I am over it now but it was a long business. She just didn't like me very much. I always wanted her to, of course, and that makes a difference to how you approach other relationships.

Did you ever discover why she disliked you?

A year before me she had a daughter who died, and I suspect that she simply didn't want to have another baby so quickly. She also preferred boys. She adored my brothers, both younger than me, and it was very clear to me that she did. I just came at a bad time and I was the wrong sex. Later on she became very jealous of my combining marriage with a career. She had been a very gifted dancer and she had given up on her career when she married, partly because my father's family insisted on it, and partly because she recognised in those days that's what you had to do. She was a very intelligent, gifted lady who just didn't have enough to do. Women of her generation were allowed to do charity work, or they could tell their servants what to do, but they really didn't have enough to occupy their minds. She was bored and frustrated and although she felt it was all right for the boys to do anything, it was not all right for girls. She resented the fact that I was apparently able to do things which she couldn't.

Do you believe that such a crushing early experience sets the pattern for adult life?

It did for a long time. I have had to do an awful lot of therapeutic work on myself to come out on the other side of it, it made an enormous difference to my early life and gave me a very bad role model for my own parenting. It was also the case that for a long time in all my novels the mothers behaved very badly – that was my way of getting my own back a bit.

Your mother had also been her own parent's least favourite child, which would suggest that we perpetrate unhappy experiences and visit them on our own children. Do you think that this process is one which can be reversed, or is the genetic imprinting too deep?

I don't think that it's genetic; it's psychological, and those chains of misfortune can always be reversed provided the last link of the chain, as it were, wants it enough. For example, my daughter is a very good parent even though I wasn't, so she's broken that link. I also think I managed not to perpetrate on to her the feelings that my mother made me have, but that's taken an enormous amount of work. And it is not the norm. Nearly all abusers have been abused; cruelty is what they know. It is also a kind of attention, sometimes it is the only kind of attention a child has had, so it will be cruel in its turn as a form of attention-seeking. Often when children are victims, they become persecutor, or they may become addicted to being victims, in which case they'll find somebody who'll beat them up. It is quite usual for women whose fathers beat them up to find husbands who do the same. There is something similar going on when fathers talk about their public-school experience and say how frightful it was, and then send their sons to the same school. They've had an awful time, so their sons must have an awful time. They see nothing wrong with that.

Your parents did not have a very happy marriage ... how aware of this were you at the time, and what effect did it have?

I was aware of it from the age of eleven or twelve. My brothers were away at school, but I lived at home, so I was acutely aware of the tensions between my parents. I spent such a lot of time observing grown-up behaviour, and although I didn't always understand precisely what was going on, the feeling underneath was very clear. I knew my father was discontented, that he was unfaithful to my mother for years before it came out, and it was sometimes very uncomfortable. But I just thought that was how grown-up people behaved.

Eventually your father left and married someone else … can you remember the effect it had on your mother, or perhaps on you?

Yes, absolutely. By that time I was married myself. My mother was more angry than unhappy. She didn't like being left alone of course, but I doubt if she was in love with him; she wanted him more because he was handsome and attractive and a good catch for her. I could never believe that her feelings for my father were sincere – I didn't trust them at all. I came to believe that in some curious way she had not ever had an emotional life. I looked after her for the last six years of her life, and during that time she simply didn't have any real feelings about anything. The sexual life between my parents was probably disastrous. Although my mother was not unfaithful to him she didn't enjoy sex at all, and my father did, so she wasn't a very satisfactory partner.

You have sometimes said that couples should not stay together for the sake of children. Did you have a different opinion when your own parents separated?

No, I didn't. My younger brother did suffer badly, but that was because my father more or less abandoned him. The only children I know who seem to be really secure are those whose parents really are fond of each other, really do care about each other. I have known so many parents who didn't get on and whose children knew that all their lives. Children always pick up on the atmosphere between their parents. As a child you never see the resolution; you see the quarrels start-ing, the tensions mounting, but the reconciliation, if there is one, takes place in the bedroom or another place, so to the child it's all very mysterious and quite frightening.

As a child you described yourself as being 'neurotically inclined to homesickness'. Where did this feeling spring from, do you think?

It must have come from some kind of insecurity. It absolutely blighted my child-hood. By the time I was fourteen I could just about manage to stay with my best friend and her parents for a weekend; I dreaded it but I steeled myself to do it. I suppose I felt I didn't know what would happen if I wasn't in my own place. And I didn't have enough friends.

When did you finally get free of your mother?

Oh, I think about two years ago probably, long after she died. I had an awful lot of therapy. I had to find out how it was possible to have been so disliked by her so that it affected everything else about my life. That meant also trying to see it from her point of view, seeing that she had had a rotten life. But essentially, I wanted to disinfect the rest of my life from not having been liked by her, and I think I have managed to do that now.

You were educated by a governess. Did you ever feel the lack of a more formal education?

Yes, I still do. It's resulted in me knowing certain things that people who have been to school don't know, but not knowing a very great deal that people who have been to school and university know. I would have liked to have gone to university, but my parents, that generation, simply didn't consider the possibility. Educating a girl was not considered a very serious matter. My mind is very amateur and erratic. I probably had quite a good mind which could have been sharpened by a better education. As a child I read an awful lot, of which I understood only about a third. I would have liked to develop the discipline for work which I now have, but instead I found all kinds of excuses, like falling in love.

But you've done very well without it …

I haven't done very well. I'm very uneducated. My governess was a remarkable lady; she wrote books on philosophy and mathematics and taught me Greek and Latin, but I didn't learn enough from her. Later in my life, whenever any man fell in love with me he always made me a list of books to read. I never caught up with the lists.

Did you envy your brothers being sent away to school?

Both my brothers are younger but when the older of the two went to prep school I was absolutely distraught. When we came back from taking him, I was desperate. I spent about a year hoping I'd turn into a boy so I could join him. I couldn't bear to sleep in the room we'd shared. We are friends now, and we know each other well because we're old, but prep school marked the end of our relationship as children.

But before he went away, were you close?

We were very close, yes and I was extremely fond of him. We did everything together, and so it was awful when he went. When he came back in the holidays it wasn't the same because by then he didn't want to play with girls. That's what happens when boys go away to school. Medieval England was much better organised: a boy was sent as a page to another castle, and educated in how to behave with women, and how to behave generally. He was taught many things by the men of the household as well, and that in many ways was a far better education. Incarcerating a whole lot of boys with no women, except possibly a matron, is madness because they don't know how to behave, and they suffer all their lives. They feel that women are a bit of a threat, or very stupid, and they don't know how to be friends with them.

Yours was a very middle-class upbringing, complete with chauffeur and nanny and parlour-maid and so on. Were you aware at the time of the deep class divisions in the country, or did that awareness come only later?

I was very much aware of them, but I don't think I understood a great deal about what they entailed – poverty, for example. The prevailing attitude was very much that servants were servants. People were not necessarily nasty to them, it was thought that they led different lives. It didn't occur to me to think that nanny could be the same as my mother. Every country, it seems to me, has class distinctions, and that includes America where they go on saying they don't have them; the distinctions are very much money oriented, but they are all the same. People are more dishonest about class distinctions now. In my day they were very straight about them. I don't say it was a good thing, but they were. I also think a lot of working-class people's lives are nastier now than they were when I was a child. I think they have a worse time, worse living conditions and more impoverished lives, despite the welfare state. If I had to choose between living in a high-rise flat or living in a semi-detached back-to-back with a privy at the end of the garden, give me the semi every time. At least in those days you had a street life with your friends, and you knew who your neighbours were. In the modern blocks you don't know, you're just frightened of them.

You were only sixteen when war broke out. One imagines that people were less politically aware then than now. To what extent did you understand the reasons for war?

Very little, I would say. I was terrified of war, partly because I had read all my father's war books, and knew that he himself had gone to France when he was seventeen and had been quite badly gassed, but would never talk about it. He had a photograph on his dressing table of whole rows of men in baggy uniforms, and one day I asked him who they were. 'They're my friends,' he said. And when I asked him where they were, he said, 'They're all dead except me.' That gave me the most tremendous shock. I thought if we had another war it would be simply terrifying. When Mr Chamberlain came back from Munich with the 'peace and honour' stuff,

I really believed it was going to be alright, and then it wasn't at all, I imagined the whole of London would be bombed in the night, everybody would be dead, and that would be the end. People were politically naïve partly because at that time this country had an innate sense of superiority, which it has quite properly lost now. There was a sort of Kipling view that Britain was always right about things, so we were bound to win. But I myself felt very frightened.

You married for the first time at the age of nineteen. Was the war a contributory factor to that young marriage, in the sense that life was very uncertain and to marry was to make some statement about the future?

Yes. If there had not been a war we almost certainly would not have married. A lot of men had an instinct to marry, to have a child, because they thought they might be killed. That was certainly the case with my husband. He was fourteen years older than I was, and his mother terribly wanted him to marry, but we didn't have enough time together beforehand to get to know each other very well. I thought I was in love, of course, and I imagine he did too, but it's very hard to tell now. I spent the first two years of marriage agonising every time he went off; that was what life was like then. Every time I thought I might not see him again, and that was extremely difficult to deal with.

Your only child was born during your marriage to Peter Scott. Did you also think of yourself as being too young to be fully prepared for the experience of motherhood?

Yes, I did. I would have preferred to have become used to the idea of being married before I had a child, but he and his family were very pressing about it. I felt terribly inadequate that I didn't know how to cope. I was extremely homesick; the first year I was married I really wanted to go home, because I wasn't living a life that was remotely normal. I'd never stayed in a hotel in my life, and then suddenly after I was married I had to live in them all the time. They were entirely filled with men; there were no women at all, and there was nothing to do. Of course, I read an enormous amount, but I was very lonely, and if I went out everybody whistled at me, which embarrassed me terribly. There was a great shortage of women in the places I stayed – at one port on the Isle of Wight there were half a million men, and not even any Wrens, so it was difficult to go out without attracting attention.

Were you never flattered by that kind of attention?

I always found it very difficult. A lot of people were attracted to me because of what I looked like, without having the slightest interest in finding out what I was like as a person. In fact, I think the reason I married a second time was because I had become exhausted by people wanting to go to bed with me after just half an hour. I just couldn't deal with it all, and I longed for 'the deep, deep peace of the double bed after the hurly-burly of the chaise longue'.

Were you very careful with your own daughter, to approve and love unconditionally because of your own experience?

I don't think I was a good mother. She would say I was a very bad one, but I was vaguely frightened of her and felt I wasn't old enough to deal with her. We get on very well now, but I think that's very much more due to her than me. She had a difficult childhood, not just because of me but because her father took very little interest. He was profoundly interested in all other forms of natural life, but people no. It was difficult to be closely associated with him, because he was absolutely indifferent to people, and that included his children.

Your first marriage lasted five years, and then you were on your own for twelve years. That is a long time for a young woman not to love or be loved. How did you cope?

Well, I had lovers in that time, and people asked me to marry them, but I didn't think any of them was the right person. I regard that period of my life as a very wasted time, although when I think of the people I didn't marry I'm always grateful that I didn't. I did fall in love with people, but for a long time after my first marriage I didn't ever want to get married again. Then I suddenly felt I did want to, and I wanted children. I married a man who was not right at all, and who didn't want to have children. That lasted five years, but it was a disaster; we were hardly ever together.

Can you recall why you married him in the first place?

I married him because – and this is all to do with being very insecure – he was charming, he was clever, and he was a con man. People always asked me why I didn't see through him, but you don't see through con men until it's too late. I realised he didn't love me very shortly after we got married, and that was a terrible shock, because I still had the romantic notion that people didn't tell lies about love (or about writing – the two things I minded about). He had married me because he thought I had some money – I had a bestseller that year – and also because he thought I had connections which would get him a job. But I don't think it was just me. I doubt if he was capable of loving anyone properly.

The marriage was a loveless liaison … you have said that your husband did not even make love to you. What effect did that have – did it lower your self-esteem, or did it simply make you determined to get out, or both?

It lowered my self-esteem; lowering my self-esteem was one of the things he was good at. I'm not sure how much I want you to write about him because I try absolutely not to mention him. He still goes about saying he used to be married to me. He enjoys all that, and I feel all I can do is keep reference to him to the barest minimum. I prefer to draw a veil over it all. It was a great mistake on my part not to have seen through him, but if you have lowered self-esteem you're not very good at that; you're rather grateful for attention.

You were undoubtedly very happy for a while with Kingsley Amis … presumably it was very important and reassuring that happiness was indeed attainable after your early experiences …

Yes. One of the things about Kingsley that I found most deeply attractive was that he could make me laugh so much. It's one of the most turning-on things that there is, and he was immensely funny.

When the marriage ended, was it also very important to know that there had been happy years? Was that something you tried not to lose sight of?

I do remember the happy times, and with gratitude. We had very bad luck really. One lives in the slipstream of one's own experience, and I would know now much more how to deal with a middle-aged marriage than I did then. We needed privacy, but we didn't have it. We had the stepchildren living with us, and they were very hostile. We managed very well to begin with because we had long holidays abroad together. We used to go to Greece a great deal, and we had our grown-up time alone, but then he stopped wanting to go abroad because he was a very anxious person and didn't like travelling. Then we were not alone, and I don't think any serious relationship survives without time alone; you absolutely have to have it. Even friendship requires it – you can't develop friendships with people if you never see them alone.

Some people who knew Kingsley well suggest that deep inside he doesn't like women.

No, and that's why I had to leave. You can live with somebody who doesn't love you, but you can't possibly live with somebody who actually doesn't like you. That became palpable. He simply doesn't like women. He turns them into his mother, and he's frightened of them.

That third marriage was hailed as the perfect literary partnership. Was the pressure of this perfection one of the factors which contributed to the failure?

We were both used to a certain amount of publicity, so I don't really think that made a difference. I doubt if Kingsley knew any more than I did about the pitfalls of middle-aged marriage.

Would you say you understood him?

I understood a lot about him, but he is a very complicated person. It's difficult to say that one understands somebody completely. I was always aware that he had a very high level of anxiety, something which poets often have. In fact, I've never known a poet without it. It takes different forms, but generally they are afraid of death, afraid of accidents, of terrible things happening to them, of losing people they love. They seem to be menaced more by possibilities than actualities. Kingsley had these areas of uncertainty, and he needed bolstering up too, and we simply didn't do it for each other.

Although you haven't seen Kingsley Amis since you left, you have said you would like to be friends. Do you see that as a possibility one day?

No, I don't now, and I'm not even sure I feel that any longer. I think it would be hopeless.

In 1978 you published a collection of fragments about love entitled The Pleasures, Joys and Anguish of Loving. *Do you think these emotions are distributed fairly evenly in the business of loving, or is there generally a surfeit of anguish?*

People probably do have more anguish and suffering than ecstasy or contentment. You have to be rather an artist to get the good things out of loving, because the traps and pitfalls and the miseries are there for everybody. I am no exception. I've loved people and I've been happy with them, but I've also been very miserable about them.

Do you ever feel lonely?

Oh yes, often. If you live alone, it happens. I don't particularly like living on my own, but I'm getting much better at it. I have friends of all ages, and people come to stay here a lot, but I do spend days and days on my own. The times when one is happy are when one lives in the present, and that's something I'm trying to learn to do more. There are whole patches of my life I can't remember at all, because I was either thirsting after the past or anxious about the future. I would have liked very much to have ended my life married to somebody whom I'd known a very long time. That would have been marvellous, but I've made a mess of it, so that's what I don't get. You always pay for everything.

You were widely thought to be one of the most articulate analysts of family relationships in contemporary fiction. Do you think you have paid dearly in personal terms to arrive at that position?

I don't think I've paid unduly, but you do always pay. You may not pay at once, and you may not pay all at once, but you always pay. I paid very heavily for marrying a con man, for marrying so young and having a child when I didn't feel old enough. That's something between me and my own actions; it's nothing to do with somebody being horrible to me, or being against me. I very much don't agree with or believe in people like Cyril Connolly and his passion for guilt, which became a great fashion after the war and which somehow absolved you from any kind of future behaviour. You're never going to wipe out what you've done wrong, but you can at least not continue it. I do believe in change.

Do you think you have changed?

I've changed an enormous amount. A lot of people do change; the people who don't are the people who don't really want to, those of the fly-in-amber syndrome. While you're alive you're moving, and relationships move and they change, and if you're not prepared to move with them, there can be awful trouble. I think people who set themselves against change are fairly unhappy people.

How important do you regard sex in the scheme of things?

Like friendship or amusement or pleasure, sex is a facet of relationships. It is one of the most important elements, but of course it has been deeply misused. People who are absolutely ruled by their sexual interests and requirements do tend to repeat themselves. You have the choice between doing the same thing with a lot of different people or different things with the same person. And I would rather do different things with the same person, because you find out the other factors of intimacy, and intimacy is a very important and valuable life force. I remember meeting a man three years ago who told me he'd been to bed with eight hundred women that year. I don't know whether that was a boast or whether he was just being silly, but he couldn't possibly have known any of them, and that seems to me rather depressing. He had no concept of intimacy at all. I can honestly say I've had very little unalloyed happy sex in my life, although there was one incident that really was like that for me, and it's been very warming, very lasting, and I remember it with great pleasure and gratitude.

Family-saga books have generally been received with some contempt on the review pages of the serious press, but your Cazalet chronicles have demanded that we re-examine our prejudices. Has that given you particular satisfaction?

It's given me great pleasure to be taken seriously on my own. It's always satisfying if your peers like your books, particularly those writers whom you admire. I don't think the subject matter matters a damn; it's how you do it. There are no new ideas in the world after all, and if a painter chooses to paint frying pans from morning till night, and he does it very well, he's probably just as interesting as somebody who is painting the Resurrection all the time. One can write about a family saga in a hundred different ways.

I have the impression you are rather contemptuous of the literary world, the world of Booker Prizes and incestuous reviewing. Am I right?

I'm not contemptuous of it. I just feel, particularly with novel reviewing, that it is rather male-dominated and that there is a certain amount of back-scratching. I'm not against literary prizes or anything which draws attention to literature in this country. Writers are underrated here, unlike in France, for example. Englishmen are the only people in the world who boast that they never read novels – they actually boast about it! You'd never get a Frenchman saying that. The cab drivers in Paris all know who Camus was.

I read somewhere that you wanted very much to have children with Kingsley Amis. Was it a terrible disappointment that the marriage was childless?

It certainly was a disappointment, yes.

You worked very hard in your role as a stepmother. Were there rewards for doing that?

Well, Martin goes on saying that I helped him; he's very gracious about that in public and usually says that if it hadn't been for me he wouldn't have got to Oxford. That is true, but it's very nice that he says so, and that's a reward. I don't think there were rewards apart from that.

Are you still close to your stepchildren?

I don't see any of them ... at all ...

Not even Martin?

I haven't seen Martin for three years. I used to ring him up, make an effort to see him, and in the end I said, 'Look, you know I really love seeing you and I would love to see you regularly, but this time I'm going to leave it to you to ring me.' He never has.

Women traditionally hang on to marriages, even dead marriages, trying to shore them up. Women are also traditionally the ones who are rejected, abandoned by their husbands. You have walked out of three marriages, which is a striking role reversal. What gave you the courage to do this?

I don't believe in staying with people if you really don't feel good about it. I haven't taken money from any of my husbands; I want to make that clear. I just went each time and started afresh on my own. With Kingsley it was a case of not feeling able to stay with someone who disliked me. With Peter I was much younger and I knew he wanted a kind of life that I simply wouldn't be able to fit into. We remained friends over the rest of our lives – he died about two years ago – and we were quite amiable always. There was never great acrimony, never anything bad. It took a lot of courage to leave Kingsley because of my age in a way, and because of starting again. I went and stayed with an incredibly kind friend, and in the first six months I think I earned only a hundred pounds.

You have never filed for huge divorce settlements. Has this been a point of honour with you?

It's a point of principle, I think. I don't approve of women living on men. If you are healthy and able, it's up to you to cope with your life. I must make it clear that when I left Kingsley, although I didn't take any alimony, I did eventually get half the price of the house in which we lived together, but we bought our houses with my money to start with. On the first occasion I didn't take any of the house because Peter had bought it all. I didn't have any money when I married, so I had to start again from scratch. When I left my second husband he didn't have any money anyway, so I just stopped having to pay for things, which was very nice. If the circumstances had been different, if for example Kingsley had left me at the age of fifty-six or whatever, and I had had five of his children, and I'd brought them all up and I hadn't been able to do another job as a result, then I think it would have been fair to take alimony. I don't want to judge other people, but in my case it hasn't happened to be right to do it.

How do you stand on feminism?

I think it has a very long way to go. One of the things we are constantly being told by men is that things have become fair for women, but I don't think they have yet. Some things have changed, of course. For example, when I left Peter I could not get a mortgage on any house because I was a woman, quite simply, and nobody would have considered it. Politics probably suffers from a tremendous lack of women. No provision is made for a woman to be a wife and mother as well as a cabinet minister. Men don't have to choose between being prime minister or being fathers and husbands; it doesn't come into it for a moment.

Mrs Thatcher was the exception to the rule, I suppose …

Mrs Thatcher didn't really get into a very powerful position until her children were practically grown up, and she was married to quite a rich man, so she didn't have the pressures which an awful lot of women have.

But did you admire her as a woman?

Not as a woman. I admired her as a leader because although I didn't agree with her she did seem to me to stick to her guns, and people who keep sidestepping the whole time are very depressing. I don't think she cared very much about whether people liked her or not, and one of the great dangers of leaders today is that they mind far too much about that. It makes them unable to stick to things or have a clear line about what they regard as right or wrong. I didn't find Mrs Thatcher at all easy as a person; she's a woman who doesn't like women, and they are the only women I find hard to get on with.

Do you feel now that you have more in common with women than with men?

Yes, but that is maybe because I spend more time with them. It's true that I do have far more women friends, but partly that is because when you get to my age you know a lot of widows, inevitably.

Do you still aspire to having a great love affair?

I don't aspire to it, but I certainly would not spurn it. If it came along, I would say, how wonderful, and I would recognise it now. I think it extremely unlikely, but I am not against it in principle.

I have the impression that principles are very important to you. Have these principles been worked out according to your life experience, or did you inherit them?

I regard principles as very expensive things to have, so I think one has to be rather selective about how many one can support. I do believe in everybody having a moral structure or belief system, and that it is important to think about what that is, because if you're not very clear about it you haven't a hope of living it. I'm not a religious person at all, but I do believe that people are able to change things and themselves and we learn from the good examples of other people. In my life the things which have most impressed me and which have lasted for me have been other people's behaviour in certain circumstances. That is tremendously important, and once you recognise that, you don't want to be a bad example for others.

Isn't it true to say that the more principled one is the more one is likely to suffer?

That's always a hazard. One can't possibly live one's life on the basis of trying to avoid suffering, like avoiding being run over, but one can take reasonable precautions not to be run over. The thing about suffering is it depends whether you allow it to overwhelm you and dominate your life, or whether you allow anything else in. You might have to die for your principles, so you have to be very clear about what they are and whether you think they are worth that.

I read somewhere that your memory is now very selective and there are whole areas of unhappiness which you have simply erased. Have you found it easier to try to bury the pain rather than to try to conquer it by confronting it?

I don't think I planned to forget anything – that's just what has happened sometimes. It's not so much violent happenings I've buried; I always remember them. It's the long periods of depression or unhappiness which become a kind of fog. But on the whole I think confronting things is always better. If you hear a sound in the house at night and you're frightened, it's much better to go down and see what it is or isn't than to stay upstairs imagining all the things it might be.

How important has psychotherapy been to you? What has it enabled you to do or understand which you couldn't have done by yourself?

It's made me understand the importance of listening to people, which I don't think I understood before. People very seldom listen to each other, and as a result people don't tell each other things in a serious enough way. I've learned to tell people things, and it's cleared up a lot of unfinished business. It's not a self-indulgence; some of it is very painful.

You said you were not religious, but do you find a similarity between that kind of thing and confession for the Catholic?

No, because it's for quite a different purpose. When you go to confession, which I did briefly when I was an Anglican, what you're doing is unloading a whole lot of behaviour that you're not particularly proud of, and getting somebody to say, 'Well that's all right, you've told me now', and it's all washed away. That doesn't stop you from doing it again and again and again. The point of *talking* about your behaviour is to sort out the bits of it that you really don't want to go on being loaded with, and finding out why you behave like that and then, very often, when you do know, it's easy just to stop if you want to.

With advancing years, are you likely to seek solace in religion?

I don't think so. Faith is like love; they're both gifts, and you can't reason yourself into either of them. You can't acquire them by being wise or rich or thoughtful; they are things which come to you. I don't have faith in that sense.

Are you anxious about death?

No. Dying is the last great adventure. There are times when I feel this is the most amazing world and I can't bear to leave it, but there are also times when I can see that I will have had a lot of life and I will be prepared to let it go. I don't know whether things happen to you after you're dead or not; it may well be that we do have other lives, but I find it very hard to believe in the Catholic conception of heaven and hell. Our lifespan in that case has been organised by a particularly wicked fairy godmother: it's long enough for you to learn things, and then not long enough for you to practise them. It doesn't make sense that you should suffer unspeakable purgatory forever because you haven't done very well in your allotted time span.

When you look back on your life, is there anything you really regret?

I really regret not having had more children. I would have liked more children, very much, and when I reached the point of being mature, I feel I would have been good at it.

You once said: 'Pain, like arsenic, accumulates in the body; but while it is difficult to get rid of arsenic, it is possible to get rid of pain.' How have you got rid of your pain?

By talking about it. I think pain flourishes in solitude and silence. It was an Indian who said to me once that most people's response to physical pain is to flinch and try to get away from it, but if you actually try to explore where it's coming from and what exactly it feels like, you can diminish it very considerably. I have found that to be true.

What, if any, are the compensations of growing older?

That's a very difficult one. People talk a lot of sentimental nonsense about growing old. What I think happens is that you become more of whatever it was you were. Irascible people become more irascible when they're old, and sentimental people become more sentimental. I want to be more aware of other people and what they need. I should like to be of some use in that way. At my age you haven't got the immediate investment which you have when you are young, and quite properly selfish, when you are trying to carve out your own life. Most of my life is over and there is no longer a need for me to do that; so I might now do something for others. We all decay, and we can either be submerged in self-pity because we can't do the things we did when we were thirty, or we can find other things to do. I have found other things to do.

P. D. JAMES

Phyllis Dorothy James was born in Oxford in 1920 and educated at Cambridge High School for Girls. During the war she was a Red Cross nurse and later she was employed in hospital administration before working in the Home Office, first with the forensic science service and then in the criminal law department. Her first novel, *Cover Her Face,* was published in 1962 and in 1979 she retired from the Home Office to concentrate on her writing. Many of her novels featured the detective Adam Dalgliesh, most popularly in *A Taste for Death* (1986), which enjoyed an international vogue. In 1987 she was awarded the Crime Writers' Association Diamond Dagger. She served on the Arts Council, was a governor of the BBC, and in 1991 was made a life peer, Baroness James of Holland Park, and took the Conservative whip. She wrote fourteen Adam Dalgliesh mysteries and published 'a fragment' of autobiography in 1999. She died in 2014.

You describe your childhood as having been a time of considerable anxiety. Do you think this was primarily nature or nurture?

Probably a little of both. My parents were not very well matched, so I think it was a house where there was considerable tension. I was quite frightened of my father. I loved him very much, and I remember him with great respect and affection, but the qualities that I admired in him – his fortitude, intelligence and a certain sardonic humour – are aspects you come to appreciate only when you're older. A child wants a father to be loving and kind and rather more affectionate than mine was able to be.

It is often said that to have a great deal of trauma in childhood is an excellent preparation for the creative writer. In that sense would you say that you served a good apprenticeship?

I have to be very careful here because, although this may seem platitudinous, I'm always aware of the fact that three quarters of the human race go hungry. I didn't go hungry, so it's very difficult to feel I had a less happy childhood than I should have done when in fact I had a roof over my head, I had enough to eat, I had an education. But it was a time of some trauma; that is certainly true. It is good for a creative artist to have this, but I'm not so sure it's good for a human being. Perhaps that is why some creative artists aren't very easy people.

You seem always to have regretted the fact that you did not go to university. Is this a straightforward sadness at missed opportunity, or is it overlaid with resentment towards your parents for not making it possible?

It would have been very difficult for them to have made it possible, although if I had been a boy my father would have made a greater effort. As it was I was born in 1920, and there were no grants before the war. You had to be clever enough to get a scholarship, and you didn't get an awful lot of money even then. I wasn't bright enough for a scholarship so I didn't get the chance. I don't think I can altogether blame my father who was only a middle-grade civil servant, but I would have loved to have gone to university instead of leaving school at sixteen. It had been my childhood dream – I had always thought of university as being a very beautiful place, somewhere full of learning and books and conversation and intelligent people, much brighter than myself. Whether it would have made me a better writer, I don't know; it may have been lucky for me not to go.

Are you one of those people who believe that all our adult virtues and failings can be explained in terms of childhood influences, or can this delving into the past be overdone, do you think?

It can be overdone. I tend to think heredity is more important. The first Queen Elizabeth said, 'I am endued with such qualities that if I were turned out of the Realm in my petticoat I were able to live in any place in Christome.' And one feels she would; she would have survived. Certain people are born with such qualities of character and intellect that they are survivors, and even if they're born into bad environments or deprived families, they're going to make their way all right because it's in them to do it. Having said that, I do accept that early environment and childhood experiences are immensely important.

You yourself have made the connection between your literary interest in death and your childhood experience of seeing a drowned boy retrieved from a river. That seems to have been a psychologically significant moment …

I didn't actually see the body, though I do remember being immensely interested in it, and I wouldn't have minded seeing him. As it was, the children were herded together on one side and then taken away, but just *knowing* a body had been found was fascinating. I didn't really understand this interest, but from early childhood I certainly was aware of the fact of death in a very strange way. For example, if we were talking about what we were going to do in the summer, even as a small child I would think, 'Well, if we are still alive that's what we'll do.' Of course I do that now all the time, I always have at the back of my mind the thought 'if I'm still here' – that is because I recognise the inevitability of death and the knowledge that it can come at any time; but it's odd for a child to think in those terms.

Your mother seems to have provided the warmth and security in your life, and although later you came to respect and admire your father's qualities, you have often said that you feared your father. Was this a rational fear? What exactly were you afraid of?

Just afraid of his displeasure; of him as an authority figure. My parents were mismatched. He was very intelligent, very musical, but he didn't have many opportunities in life. He had to earn his living from the age of sixteen, so I think in many ways he was a disappointed man. My mother was sentimental and warm and not very bright. She would have been a good wife for a country parson with eight children. My mother was slightly afraid of him and that communicated itself to me.

When you became a mother yourself, were you conscious of trying to reverse this rather unhappy experience of childhood for your own children? Was it very important to convey a sense of love and approval to your children?

Oh yes. All that is tremendously important, especially a sense of approval. It was difficult of course because my husband was very ill, and obviously I had to support the family by myself. The children lived with their grandparents, so they didn't see me as much as children normally do, but certainly I was a very affectionate mother. Whether I would have been as good a mother had they been difficult children, I don't know. I'm not very fond of children as children, but I did like my own. They were very easy to love; they were themselves loving and bright, and our interests coincided, so we always had something to talk about as they grew up. But I might have been a poor mother of a stupid, irritating child.

Many people who married during the war have described how the fact of war gave their marriage a sense of urgency or fatalism – it was a defiantly optimistic act in a time of uncertainty. Was it so for you?

It was. In some ways it was such a happy time, which is a curious thing to say, but I think there was a great sense of comradeship; and during the bombing there was a great sense of excitement. It was a romantic time really, and one didn't think about things so very deeply.

You were to have three happy years before your husband's tragic illness. Are you still able to recall those years, how they felt, or was that something that was lost in the stressful times which followed?

Oh, I can recall them … I can recall them. They haven't been really lost. I was so young then, and when you're young, you've got all that optimism, that enthusiasm for life.

It seems that you coped with the difficulties of supporting two children and your sick husband in an entirely pragmatic and unself-pitying way. Were your strength and resourcefulness innate qualities, do you think, or were they born of your immensely difficult situation?

They were probably innate. Throughout life my attitude to problems has been to find a solution and to survive, and I was helped by the fact that by nature I am more suited to having a career and a job than I would have been to being a doctor's wife and staying at home. On the whole I enjoyed the jobs I did; not all of them and not all of the time, but I had no reason to feel terribly aggrieved that I was having to work. Once I realised my husband was unlikely to get well, I went to evening classes and qualified in hospital administration so that I could get a reasonably senior job. After he died I took an examination for a senior post in the civil service; so there was a lot of ambition there really.

Was your husband your first love?

More or less. There were various experimentations … but yes, he was my first real love. I still miss him. We were well suited; I was the dominant partner, but that didn't worry him; he was quite happy for me to be the one who arranged things in his life. He was eccentric, clever, Anglo-Irish; a strange race, the Protestant Anglo-Irish. He loved books and pictures, he had a wonderful sense of humour, and a very great charm. He adored his daughters, and he would have loved his grandchildren. And since he was totally without envy, he would not have minded a wife who was more successful in worldly terms than himself. I miss him very much. We were very happy.

And after he died you never fell in love again?

No, never. I didn't meet a man whom I could really love, and the men who proposed marriage to me after Connor died, I didn't want to marry. I would also have been wary of falling in love. I do believe that as one gets older one looks at marriage in a rather different light. When you're young you are forced by sexual desire and youth and romance, while underneath it all the genes are wanting to perpetuate themselves, but when you get past childbearing you begin to think, do I really want to wake up every morning and see this face at breakfast? I would have been happy to marry again if I'd met someone for whom I had a great respect and affection, but it's very easy to get quite selfish after a bit when you live alone, especially if you're a writer; you do things in your own time and in your own way.

You have an impressive record of public appointments – you were on the board of the Arts Council, you chair the literature panel, and you are a governor of the BBC. Being a woman seems to have been no impediment in this area ...

Not at all. When I was appointed to the BBC there weren't enough women on the board, so a woman can have a slight advantage in that way. Not always of course, and there are still not enough women in public life. In the Health Service I had to be much better than the men if I was going to get a job over their heads, but otherwise I've never felt disadvantaged as a woman, and I never felt that I was sexually harassed. Perhaps I've been lucky.

Is it attributable to luck, or do you think sexual harassment is a bit exaggerated?

It's been overdone. Men have always flirted, and why shouldn't they? I'm quite prepared to flirt with a man if he's attractive. And a woman always knows the difference between a man who is flirting with her because she is a woman, and a man who is sexually unpleasant. If women have lost the art of knowing that, I'm very sorry for them. If a man opens a door for you nowadays it's regarded as an insult, and I think that's dreadful and also rather sad.

You have done a great deal in your own career to advance the cause of women, but am I right in thinking you might share Doris Lessing's view on feminism – you support its aims but you dislike its shrill voice?

I share her view entirely. I also suspect that many of the extreme feminists are so because they envy men and dislike being women. I don't dislike being a woman. I have many men friends, and I admire men, but I've never wanted to be one, and I sometimes suspect that the shrillness comes from a huge resentment that they haven't been born male. I very much dislike the suggestion that all men are by nature rapists. It just is not true. There are some very unpleasant men about, one knows, but to look at the entire male population and castigate them as anti-female, uncaring, sexually harassing and potential rapists, is nonsense, complete nonsense.

In your public life you are very much an Establishment figure, an Anglican, a conservative, a former magistrate and high-ranking civil servant. So you see any link between the Establishment and the rather murky lower depths you explore in your novels?

No, I don't think so. I suppose I am an Establishment figure – I'm certainly an Anglican, though not a very good one in the sense that I'm not a regular churchgoer. I am also on the liturgical commission of the Church of England, but I think I sit there more because of my interest in the language of the liturgy. I'm not a member of the Conservative Party but that's the way I vote; I am a natural conservative, no doubt about that. And I am an ex-magistrate, so yes, I do qualify as an Establishment figure. There is in my character a natural love of order, and a real fear of violence and disorder, which may account for the kind of fiction I write. I'm very frightened of emotional and psychological violence as well as physical violence, and I think good order is important to any country. All the old certainties are just being swept away, that's the trouble nowadays. I think one needs the central certainties, just as most people need a religion, whatever form it takes. In the modern detective story, order may be restored in the sense that the crime is solved but the crime is so contaminating that all the characters are in some way touched by it. In the 1930s when the detective stories were set in a village, the crime was solved and the little village went back to what it was before. We don't write like that now, but it is still about restoring order. It is also about affirming the belief that we live in a moral universe and one that we're capable of understanding. All this is very reassuring, yet with part of my mind I wonder if we're not living in a universe that is not moral, a universe with chaos underneath.

As a governor of the BBC where do you stand on the business of violence on television? Do you have any sympathy with the Mary Whitehouse view that violence on our screens is corrupting and ought to be censored?

There is no proof that it does harm but I do think from the common-sense point of view, for young people to be perpetually exposed to images of violence cannot be good. Of course people are apt to say there is nothing but violence on our screens, but when you ask for some examples it's not so easy. I don't honestly think it's the BBC we have to worry about, it's the videos which children can buy nowadays. These videos are really quite appallingly violent, and that, I think, has to be bad.

P. D. James

What about violence in books?

In books I hate scenes of torture, but I don't worry so much about violence in the detective story, because it is such a moral form. The villain always gets found out. What worries me more is that books are becoming increasingly pornographic, and when that happens they cease to be erotic. It's the same with films. I saw *Basic Instinct*, which is supposed to be a thriller, on video and every time the main characters were near a bed we had another ten minutes of reeling and writhing. All this heaving and loud breathing and acrobatics … oh dear, oh dear … it's just not subtle enough to be erotic. Perhaps it's my age, but I do believe that some of the most erotic things are the most subtle; you can have the most erotic scenes where the couple don't in fact touch each other, you can have a huge sexual charge without having people rolling around naked on beds.

You have sometimes said that you're not a professional writer in the sense that you never have actually had to earn your living from writing. Is that something you have regarded as a liberation or a constraint?

A liberation. This is part of my innate caution. Without the writing I would have been quite poor, but we wouldn't have starved. When I worked in the Home Office it was a good wage and it paid the mortgage. I didn't expect the writing to make me rich, although it has; I had ambitions to be highly regarded, and I set out to be a good and serious writer. I certainly don't despise the money – it's totally dishonest to pretend that you're not happier if you've got money, by and large. But I've never taken a penny in advance for any book until it was completed. Some people work better if they're given a huge advance to write the next book, but I can't stand that anxiety, I never wanted that. Don't misunderstand me; I'm not making any judgement here or any moral point – it just happens to be right for me. I do remember the depression of the 1920s and being constantly told by my mother how lucky I was that my father was a civil servant. People were hungry then and I grew up with this great need for security.

I wonder if you are conscious of your readership as you write. Do you feel the need to justify the particular moral scheme within which you operate, or is it something you take very much for granted?

I don't think about the readership. I think about what is going to satisfy me. If I have an idea for a book I do the very best I can with that idea. It's a matter of total artistic pride, not to publish a book until it's as good as I can make it, and I suppose I feel that if I can satisfy myself then I shall satisfy my readers. There is a moral climate in which I write, but my characters don't always share it. My characters can make powerful arguments in favour of a world in which there is no God, for example, and I understand those arguments absolutely, so in that sense I'm not a didactic writer.

Would you increase the sexual interest in order to sell more books?

I've never done that, and I've never been tempted. But I can't imagine a book without sex, because love, including sexual love, is such an important part of human life and it controls so much of what men and women do. In detective novels where you have motives, where you have people driven by compulsions, where there is moral conflict, almost certainly you are going to have strong sexual motives. It would seem a very bloodless book if it had no sex in it, whether it's heterosexual or homosexual sex, and I've had both. In one of my books Dalgliesh remembers a constable saying to him, 'People will tell you that the most dangerous emotion in the world is love.'

Are there any passages in your books which you would mind your daughters reading?

No. I've never written anything of which I'm ashamed, or that I'd mind them reading. With regard to my descriptions of dead bodies I sometimes think they will say, 'Oh Mummy, really, this is a bit much,' but I've never written anything which I feel I couldn't justify artistically. When a body is found I want the description to be absolutely realistic, what it would look like and smell like. That's important.

Do you believe novelists have a moral responsibility towards their readers?

They have a moral responsibility to do the very best they can with their talent, without considering what is going to earn the most money, without twisting it to suit a particular market, without inserting gratuitous sex or pornography in order to increase sales. It's artistic honesty that counts.

Your books are as remote from the comfortable middle-class world of Agatha Christie as it is possible to be. It seems to me that your concern is more with the ethical problems of murder and the consequences of crime, something which allows you to probe deeper into the complexities of human nature. Is this the real area of interest to you?

Yes, it is. What I'm interested in are the people, their motives, the characters' compulsions and the moral choices. That's why there are no psychopaths in my detective stories. A psychopath murders because he just happens to enjoy murder; he has no moral choice, and therefore he is of no interest to me.

Do you perhaps rather disapprove of Agatha Christie and her Poirot and Miss Marple? Has part of your purpose been to explode the cosy class-ridden snobbish world she portrays?

Sometimes people say that I am Agatha Christie's crown princess and successor, and that always seems to me to be nonsense because I think we're very different writers. I don't think she's a good novelist; I have to say that, although I feel it's very unbecoming of any writer to deride her because she has given immense pleasure to millions of people all over the world. Some people say she's done harm to the crime novel, but I don't see that. She's a kind of literary conjurer. Every time most of us are surprised – I'm not because I now see through the trick – but if we think about it afterwards we realise it could not have happened in real life. She puts down a character as pasteboard, and we get the same ones in each book; she shifts them around, and we think ah, that's the murderer; it never is. I wouldn't be too unkind about her, but I don't think I am at all like her. The accusation of snobbery in connection with a classical detective story arises from the fact that you are really hoping to provide an intelligent murderer who knows the difference between right and wrong, makes the moral choice, and is out to commit a very clever murder; and that being so, he is very unlikely to be a stupid, professional villain. The horror of the deed is greatly enhanced if there is contrast, as W. H. Auden knew when in an essay called 'The Guilty Vicarage' he said that the single body on the drawing-room floor is a great deal more horrible than the dozen bullet-ridden bodies down Raymond Chandler's mean streets. You need contrast, and it's a good thing to have it in a fairly prosperous, orderly society. If I were to set a detective story among professional criminals in the worst areas of inner-city violence, it would not be very interesting. Murder has to be set among people to whom murder really is an appalling crime if you're going to get that contrast, and I suppose Agatha Christie felt that to an extent, even though she produced prosperous middle-class books set in cosy little villages.

You have described the detective novel as essentially an unsentimental form. Does sentiment hold many terrors for you?

I'm very wary of sentimentality and I don't think it's the same as compassion. Sentimentality is a very easy and agreeable emotion which doesn't often find its outlet in effective action; compassion does.

I imagine you are wary of conclusions about art imitating life, but at the same time your hero Dalgliesh is intelligent, self-sufficient, unsentimental, wary of relationships – is he not created in your own image?

Yes, he is a bit. If you have one character who goes through a succession of books this tends to happen.

You have used Graham Greene's words of Dalgliesh, saying that there is a splinter of ice in his heart. Is there also a splinter in yours?

Yes, there is. It's difficult to explain why because it involves something which happened to me, and telling it could be much too painful for my children. Let me just say that even when appalling things have been happening to me, part of my mind has been observing my own reaction to them; I have known myself to do that in many quite terrible situations. I know I couldn't do it if one of my children had died. If that happened I wouldn't be able to watch my own grief or record it or watch myself grieving; it would consume me, absolutely. But in most other situations, when I've been in a condition of great trauma, and sometimes if I've been comforting friends in great distress, I'm still observing the manifestations of the distress.

You have a fascination with the bridges we construct over the chaos of personal and psychological disorder, the bridges of law and order and religion. Murder, the ultimate crime, blows away these bridges and reveals how people behave under stress. Are you attracted to writing about the chaos in the knowledge that you are able to put it right?

Yes, I'm sure that's so. In life you aren't able to, but in books you are. Of course you don't put it totally right. In *A Taste for Death* in which the bodies are found in the church vestry by poor Miss Wharton and the little boy she befriends, we know at the end how the murder was done and we know who's guilty, but nearly all the characters in that book had their lives changed because in some way they came in contact with the two butchered bodies in that church. And yet it is controlled, and this profound sense of imposing order on disorder is highly agreeable to me. It's psychologically satisfying, especially in a world where there is so much disorder.

Albert Camus believed that the evil in the world almost always comes from ignorance and that 'good intentions may do as much harm as malevolence if they lack understanding'. Is that something you agree with?

I could agree with it in certain circumstances, but I don't think evil is just the absence of education and the absence of knowledge. It's true that good intentions on their own are not enough; well-intentioned people who lack wisdom and knowledge and intelligence can do a great deal of harm, but it doesn't follow that these qualities when present make for an absence of evil.

But do you think that without evil there can be no goodness?

I don't think goodness depends on evil, but it depends on the possibility of evil.

Despite the fixation on death in your books there emerges a distinct sense of the sanctity of life. Is that an intended effect, one you're pleased with?

Yes, it is intended and I am pleased with it.

Do you ever apply your mind to the abortion issue?

Yes. It's extremely difficult because here my reason is at war with my instinct. If the child is going to be grossly deformed, mentally or physically, then abortion is justified, but I find it abhorrent when abortion is used as a method of birth control or for the convenience of the mother. Of course one can argue logically that if the woman is to have a choice, then the choice includes abortion, and who am I to judge whether her motives are selfish or not. Yet it is abhorrent, it is abhorrent.

Are you saying that the sanctity of life depends on the quality of life?

Yes, I am, though I don't think that's very logical. The easy answer is to take the extreme view that abortion is never justified; or to say that it is always justified, and no child should come into the world unwanted. It is far more difficult for human beings to have to apply their minds to this essentially moral question: are there circumstances in which the destruction of an embryo is justifiable? I would say there are, when it's a question of preserving the life of a mother, or if the foetus is so abnormal that its chances of having any kind of life worth living are virtually none. But it's a very slippery slope.

You are fond of quoting the psychologist Anthony Storr who said, 'All creativity is the successful resolution of internal conflict.' How would you describe your own internal conflict?

What he said is profoundly true for me. My fear of violence and disorder reveals a basic insecurity which likes this ordered form, because in the end, although I can't put it right in the real world, I can put it right between the covers of my books.

You are generally dismissive of psychological theorising about yourself, and tend to promote the image of a respectable, sensible grandmother figure. Is this to keep intruders at bay, to keep yourself private, or is it perhaps an unwillingness to delve too deeply into your own psyche?

It's a bit of all three. I do delve quite deeply into my psyche, as deeply as I would want to delve, but I don't like other people doing it, and I don't feel much good comes of it. The old idea that if you can understand things then somehow you put them right is not necessarily so. I can see that my insecurity might well have come from a childhood trauma, that my need for religion, my belief in God is perhaps the need to have a better father figure than I had; but I don't think I gain much by knowing, or by somebody else expecting me to lie on a couch and pay a great deal of good money in order to reach that same conclusion.

You fear violence a great deal, which is perhaps a natural condition of women. But in your case it seems a rather heightened, almost irrational fear – keys always kept round your neck, doors locked, truncheon under the pillow, and so on. Would you agree it borders on the pathological?

Borders perhaps. But it's very difficult in this modern world not to feel that it's really quite sensible. The keys round the neck are simply because I have a fairly big house and if I require to open the door, if only for the postman, it's just maddening chasing up and down for keys. I am meticulous about locking up, but I think that is no more than common sense. The house was never locked throughout my childhood, and people who had cars could leave them unlocked in the street, but it's a different world now.

Do you believe that we are all potential murderers?

I believe we're all capable of homicide but I don't think we're all capable of murder. I would make a distinction between killing to save people, to protect one's children or grandchildren, to protect oneself if assaulted, but the legal definition of murder involves premeditation: 'causing the death of a living creature under the Queen's Peace with malice aforethought, death occurring within a year and a day'. And I don't think we're all capable of that. I would not plan to kill someone, but if I woke up in the middle of the night and found a rapist in my bedroom, I wouldn't give much for his chances; and it wouldn't worry me, not in the slightest.

Would it be overstating it to say that your novels perhaps offer a catharsis of the natural state of guilt, your own included?

I think the detective story does that, for my own guilt and the reader's. If people don't look back on their life and feel guilty there's something wrong with them. Guilt is almost inseparable from being a human being. I certainly think I could have been a better daughter, a better wife to my husband, a better mother to my children, and there are those to whom I could have been a better friend. At the same time we shouldn't let guilt master us. If we don't learn to forgive ourselves we never learn to forgive other people, so guilt can be very destructive, and that's why religions make a provision for coping with it.

The subtext of much of your writing seems to be a deep disapproval of the present world and its moral climate. Is there something of the old morality play in your fiction, do you think?

Not intentionally, but it tends to be so. Auden certainly thought that a detective story was the equivalent of the old morality play. Its moral stance is unambiguous: murder is wrong, and it should be discovered and punished. There should be an attempt to understand the murderer and what the temptation was, but my books would never say that what was done was right.

Do you believe in punishment as a deterrent to crime?

Yes, I'm sure it is. I remember a conference where people were saying that punishment was never a deterrent, and the speaker stood up and said, 'If the penalty for illegal parking was a public flogging very few would have left their cars where they are standing now.' And she was absolutely right. It's a common-sense thing – it would deter me. I don't know how far, if we had the death penalty, it would deter potential murderers, but by and large human beings are deterred by the thought of punishment.

Do you agree with Muriel Spark that although novels are fiction, there emerges from them a kind of truth, a moral or metaphorical truth perhaps, but none the less truth?

Yes, she is right. The truth which emerges is the truth about human beings. I don't think that one can make a universal application from a particular novel; one can say this tells us something about how human beings would behave in certain circumstances, and the consequences of that behaviour.

467

I have noticed that in your earlier books there is almost a complete absence of cruelty, or description of pain; the reader was protected in a sense. In later books, such as A Taste for Death *and* Devices and Desires, *this is not so. Why do you think your writing developed in this way?*

I think it had to do with becoming increasingly aware of the pain and the violence of life. If only our moral progress could match our scientific progress. I remain an optimist, but that is a state which is very difficult to justify intellectually.

Your latest book The Children of Men *describes a futuristic world stricken by universal infertility. Your hero Theodore recounts the fact that people's interest in sex is waning, and that 'romantic and idealised love' has replaced 'crude carnal satisfaction'. Do you think sex is dangerous when it is separated from love?*

Dangerous is perhaps rather a strong word. It can lead to the dangers of being promiscuous and that in the end is not satisfactory to human beings. When sex is divorced from love it's a sterile business. Women find it extremely difficult; men find it much easier.

Is it something you would be able to do?

I think I could. I can quite see that I could have a sexual relationship simply because the man was very attractive and I was sexually drawn to him, but I don't think I'd find it very satisfying. The highest satisfaction from sex is through love.

Your detective books are concerned with the judgement of men, but your new book is more to do with the judgement of God. This is surely difficult ground for any writer ...

Very difficult, yes. The idea for this book came to me from reading about the extraordinary reduction in fertility of Western man. The sperm rate is down by about forty per cent in thirty years, and there seems to be no reason why the same thing shouldn't happen to homo sapiens as has happened to virtually every one of the millions of living forms that have inherited our planet. In the nature of things we should die out, and dying out in one year spectacularly is not impossible, but a bit unlikely, so to that extent the book is a fable. It was a slightly worrying book to write, rather traumatic.

The book tells us that much of the sinister, bleak picture you paint can be traced back to the preoccupations of the early 1990s – 'Pornography and sexual violence on film, on television, in books, in life, had increased and become more explicit, but less and less in the

West we made love and bred children.' That sounds like a terrible indictment of modern times and morals. Is it meant to be?

There's quite a lot of truth in it, but that's what Theo says – it isn't necessarily what I believe, although I can see some evidence for his views. For example, he says somewhere that we know more and more about sex and less and less about love, and I think that's probably true. Even St Valentine's Day has been reduced to commercial nonsense about sex rather than a celebration of love.

The fact that you describe The Children of Men *as a moral fable rather than science fiction seems to place it within the possibility of human experience ...*

Once infertility had taken hold, it would not be reversed in the way I describe, but the rest of it is well within human experience. We would start storing sperm, and then there would be all sorts of interesting questions, such as, from whom do you get the sperm, and who has access to it? People would be screened for their suitability to breed, and a great many ethical and philosophical issues would arise.

Isn't the nightmare scenario you depict in which sex, in so far as it takes place at all, has become 'meaninglessly acrobatic' and woman experience what they describe as 'painful orgasms – the spasm achieved without the pleasure' – isn't this getting dangerously close to the wrath of God being unleashed, the extremist view of the Aids epidemic?

Yes. In this new world people discover that if there is not the possibility of breeding children, sex loses its point and therefore more and more they're striving after a sensation which isn't coming to them naturally. I don't know whether that would happen or not, but it seems to me it's very possible it could.

Happy sexual relationships tend not to be a feature of your novels. Is that because you regard them as a rare feature of real life?

It's rather the result of the kind of fiction I write. The detective story is an artificial form, and though all fiction is a rearrangement of the artist's view of reality, a detective story is highly stylised in its conventions in order to form a coherent entity: there is a central mysterious death, a number of clues and a close circle of suspects who are all – the reader must believe – capable of this particular murder. One of the strongest motives is the sexual motive, so the novel is not likely to be full of very happily married, jolly people, but rather people whose lives are full of tension and unhappiness and misery of some kind. As my dear mother, God rest her, used to say, why can't you write a nice book about nice people? But you're not likely to get an awful lot of nice people in a detective story; it's inherent in the situation that people aren't living very happy or stable lives.

The ending of The Children of Men, *although ambivalent, suggests that the future of mankind is not entirely beyond redemption, and that ultimately the power of good can overcome moral depravity and corruption. Do you see this as essentially a Christian message, the triumph of good over evil ... ?*

The triumph of good over evil and the triumph of love over hatred is essentially a Christian message; and it is central probably to the great religions of the world. There is a lovely story which has always amused me about a man who appeared in court for some kind of public disorder, and when asked how he pleaded, he said, 'I plead for hope against despair, I plead for good against evil, I plead for peace against war, for sympathy against unkindness,' and the judge said, 'That will be recorded as not guilty, and if we hear any more from you I shall order a psychiatric report [laughs].'

But do you yourself believe that good triumphs over evil?

Yes, I think I do. I have a fairly simple view of these things. I think of life in terms of a mountain with God at the top, and those of us who are religious or have any aspirations are slowly working our way up. I am a practising Christian because that's the tradition in which I was brought up. We start life according to where we're born – I know if I had been born in a Roman Catholic I wouldn't have changed; I would have remained in the religion of my fathers and my people. I'm a very strong traditionalist, although that does not mean that I assent intellectually to all the articles of the Church of England, with which I am sometimes disenchanted. For example, I can't accept the idea of a God whose notion of justice was to send his only son to be tortured on earth to atone for the sins of the world. I believe that death on the cross had a universal significance, but I can't quite see it in those crude terms. I don't conceive of God as being less merciful than an earthly father would be, and an earthly father wouldn't do that. So certainly aspects of the Christian religion present me with some problems, but within that basic view of religion, I am certainly a deist. If one thinks of God as being the Father, the Son and the Holy Spirit, I like the idea of the Holy Spirit moving through the whole of creation, but it is to the Father I actually pray, God as Father is my concept.

Another possibility which you might be reluctant to consider about the ending of The Children of Men *is that there is an element of romanticism in the denouement, the idea that the world can be saved through an act of love ...*

The Christian religion said the world could be saved through an act of love; what I was saying was that Theo could find his salvation by learning to love, and at the end of the book he has learned that only through love will he find redemption. I don't think that's romantic; I think it's true. E. M. Forster wrote that we must learn to love or we will destroy ourselves.

Isn't there an element of tendentiousness in The Children of Men, *the idea of divine punishment and retribution hanging over the world, and our agnostic hero ending up making the sign of the cross?*

I don't think the book ever specifically says that what happens is divine justice. God is not saying, 'I'll teach this lot, I've lost my patience with them.' The God of the Old Testament might have felt that, but I didn't see it in those terms. Theo makes the sign of the cross as a kind of impulse. He is not saying that the world is thereby redeemed; it's more a natural instinct for him to do it, an affirmation of love, the sign of redemptive love on the child.

Last year you preached the university sermon in Oxford. What was the subject of your sermon?

Faith in the modern world, and people's attitude to God and to faith. It was also a sermon about doubt, how one copes with doubt. I talked about different kinds of faith: the faith of people who, like the poet Gerard Manley Hopkins, strive with God and argue with him; the very simple faith of people who, however sophisticated they may be in other aspects of their life, have absolute certainty from the day they're born till the day they die. I talked about people who have never felt the need of faith, people who believe that man is born of the absolute chance fusion of one sperm with one ovum; that when they die they will go into annihilation and they face that without particular fear, believing that it is not among the most ignoble ways to live or die. And then I spoke about others who work towards faith, for whom life is a kind of pilgrimage, of which group I consider myself to be one.

You once said, 'When people are maimed, or sad, or die for no reason, it isn't anything you can cure by means of justice in this world, so it's important to hope there might be justice in the next.' Is that hope a tentative one, or is it central to your faith?

If you believe that God is just, and I do believe that God is just, it's rather more than tentative. There must surely be an eternal justice. Men and women have a huge need for justice; it's born in us to hate injustice, so there is a natural wish to believe that if things are terribly unjust in this world, if God exists at all, they'll certainly be put right in the next. There's a little poem about a disabled man who lives all his life in pain, who has nothing but misery and pain from the day he's born, and it ends: 'God of Heaven, God of Hell, see you recompense him well.' And I think there's a need to feel that.

You have been scrupulously careful never to use your husband's illness or the more traumatic parts of your own life in your fiction. One senses, however, that your characters are infused with your pain and suffering. Would you perhaps allow that this is the case?

I would allow that if the writer hasn't actually suffered it must be very difficult to write about suffering. No doubt some of the pain gets into the fiction; I think that's inevitable.

You have sometimes remarked that the passage of time has not helped ease the pain of loss and bereavement. Has this surprised you?

Yes it has, although you do somehow come to terms with it. You either lie down and die, or you adapt, so after a few years somehow you're coping. But time doesn't heal everything.

Do you believe in an afterlife? Do you expect to see your husband again?

I don't know, I really don't. I don't believe in the traditional old-fashioned Christian view of heaven, that's for certain. I don't think we're all going to go up there into eternal bliss with pearly gates and everlasting feasting, but I think something does survive. I suppose one would call it the soul, but in what form, I have no idea.

Do you ever feel a sense of loneliness?

No. I don't feel lonely. But I can see the possibility of feeling it. And I don't think I'd like it at all.

You are anxious not to be a burden on others. Is that partly because you yourself have borne great burdens in life?

It's not a very noble thing; it's more a matter of pride. Partly it's just not wanting to be a nuisance to one's dearly loved children, but it's also that one doesn't want to be poor old gran who has to be visited and supported, poor old gran who's got to be found a nice place in the nursing home. I don't much like old age …

LORD LAMBTON

Lord Lambton was born the son of the fifth Earl of Durham in 1922. He first stood for Parliament when he was twenty-two years old, and six years later he won Berwick-upon-Tweed for the Conservatives. He disclaimed his peerage but was allowed to sit in Parliament using a courtesy title. He served from 1951 until 1973, when he applied for the Chiltern Hundreds. From 1970 he had been Parliamentary Under-Secretary of State for Defence. In 1942 he married Belinda Blew-Jones and they had six children. After tabloid revelations involving prostitutes and drug abuse, he left political life, separated from his wife and bought a villa in Tuscany, where he lived with Claire Ward until his death in 2006. He was the author of several books, including *Snow and Other Stories* (1983), *Elizabeth and Alexandra* (1985), *The Abbey in the Wood* (1986) and *The Mountbattens* (1989).

You come from a family with ancient roots. Did the legend of the Lambton Worm figure prominently in your childhood?

No. It was a sort of fairy story and I don't think anyone took it very seriously. Two books on it have been published, and there was an opera which played in Oxfordshire. But it was a classic story about how the first Lambton broke his word. The witch who told him how to kill the Worm insisted that afterwards he must kill the first living thing he saw, so he told his father to let the dog go the moment the Worm was dead. His father was so excited, however, that he forgot to let go of the dog and instead came running up himself. Lambton failed to kill his father, and although he killed the dog afterwards, the family was still cursed. No Lambton was to die in his bed for nine generations.

The last one had the worst time of it. For eight generations the heads of the family did die in their beds, but when the ninth was ill and his servants thought he was going to depart, they kept trying to throw him on to the floor so he wouldn't die in his bed. Then one day he got better, went for a drive in the park and died on the bridge. So it did turn out to be true in a way, but before that he was so nervous he used to keep pistols by the bed to stop his servants throwing him on the floor whenever they thought he was dying. It was always rather a comic story.

The family history is certainly interesting. There was a major setback in the seventeenth century when one of the Lambtons was a Cavalier. In reprisal for him being on the King's side all the coal mines, which we always depended on for money, were flooded. But worse than that – or more expensive – was the fact that he had two wives, and by the time he died at the age of fifty-six there were twenty-seven children, and that was ruinous. He had needed to extend the house and educate all twenty-seven, a considerable undertaking even in those days.

What really changed the family was marrying into the Villiers family – a very remarkable one which had a great impact on English history. The Villiers connection produced my family's greatest member, a governor-general of Canada and the man who created the Reform Bill. He was much more a Villiers than a Lambton. Most Lambtons were rather staid and uninteresting I should think from their portraits.

Does being born into the aristocracy give a special viewpoint on the rest of society and the contemporary world?

People who are well born and brought up, go to public schools and are surrounded by people who look after them, do have a sense of security. That's partly due to the fact that you mix with all classes from an early age. The keepers, the groom, people like that. One always got to know them, so there was never any feeling of class antagonism, which is what makes for uncertainty. One realised they were just as good as oneself, if not better, so there was no sense of superiority, which is the sort of bogus thing a lot of *nouveaux riches* try and achieve. When you are fortunate enough to be born and brought up with members of all classes, you don't have that sense, and you think and know everyone is the same as you are and treat them accordingly.

Being born into the aristocracy certainly gives one confidence. I was brought up to think that you always said what you thought. My family always did that. I suppose the classic example of that came about when my first cousin, Alec Douglas-Home, was made prime minister. When his mother was asked what she thought of it, she said well, quite frankly, she'd have preferred Mr Butler – which was straight speaking. For the most part people were delighted, but she was really rather disappointed, and his brothers only said he was a good shot or something of the kind.

As an aristocrat you have a certain position in society which is not shaken much by what you do, and that is the great strength. So many people are terrified they will be dropped by society if they open their mouths and tell the truth. In my political life I always tried to be quite straightforward. I couldn't stand Harold Macmillan when he was prime minister and was always speaking out against him.

I was criticised a lot for it at the time, but now the wheel has come full circle and I think a lot of the things I said would have happened. Macmillan didn't know the meaning of truth. He was an actor, moved by emotion, and that is a bad thing for a prime minster to be.

Was Macmillan an eccentric? I think he was a conscious eccentric. At the end of his life he tried to accentuate his eccentricity and started telling stories about himself which others had told but which had never occurred. For instance, the book about him by Alastair Horne has a farcical bit where Macmillan was talking to Kennedy who supposedly said, 'I don't know about you, Harold, but I get a headache if I don't go to bed with a woman for three days.' It was just a story, but Macmillan began to believe it, as he did with a number of others told about him. He started retelling them himself as though they were the gospel truth.

As for eccentrics generally, there are certainly nothing like the ones about that there used to be – in the countryside, anyway. When I was a boy, parsons were often eccentric because the countryside was so cut off from towns that people there were able to develop their own little kingdoms, in the church, in the law, or as landlords. They became little kings on their own and did and said what they wanted, and so they became noted figures, almost caricatures of themselves.

There have recently been disadvantages attached to being an aristocrat because, after the war, the upper classes were rather looked down on. They were blamed for the war and thought to have been behind the pre-war governments, and many of them were in those governments. I think the return of the gossip column has given them a new lease of life as glamorous figures. The man more responsible than anyone for that, is, I suppose, Nigel Dempster – a remarkable columnist in his way, though he's said some very unpleasant things about me. He's a remarkably readable writer and he's made the whole class much more interesting than they were before he started on it.

The often rather bad publicity in the past had sometimes made it hard for people from an aristocratic background to get into the House of Commons. Before the war, if you had a name, you could get into the House of Commons, and a lot of very unsuitable people got in just because of their title. That doesn't happen now. Those who do succeed in being elected do extraordinarily well, and today we have the example of William Waldegrave, who is an aristocrat, and I think young people like him are surmounting the prejudice. One of Mrs Thatcher's chief assets is that she regards merit as the criterion, and if you have merit, it doesn't matter who you are. If you don't have merit, it doesn't matter who you are either. She looks for merit in any level of society she can find it.

Speaking of the charm of the aristocracy, don't make any mistake about it, a great number of the British aristocracy are not charming. Some of them are absolutely minus charm. Charm is quite distinct from breeding. The Irish peasant has enormous charm, but you wouldn't call him an aristocratic. There is hardly an Irishman who can't charm the birds off a tree, the old blarney, as they call it. In fact, the Irish lower class are probably more charming than the upper. Charm is found in every stratum of society, and it can be quite a dangerous thing because it influences people and makes them like whoever has it. Even villains can be charming.

Yes, I did know Sir Oswald Mosley, and he had charm without any doubt. He also had a gift of mesmerism, which was the strength of his political standing. I liked him very much, actually. He was fascinating to talk to, had an extraordinarily clear mind and knew exactly what he wanted. He proposed a scheme in the early 1930s which, had the Labour or Conservative party accepted it, would probably have done away with unemployment years before it happened. But he was turned down. He had left the conservative party because he found them so old-fashioned and tried the Labour party but found that they were in their way just as conservative. So he was driven out by his own talents.

It was a pity. He was a most remarkable speaker. I went to hear him after the war, and you could see people listening to him, really drinking in what he said. Of course, what he was saying by then sounded so old-fashioned that he was out of tune with the generation of Gaitskell and Butlerism. It was a hopeless uphill battle, though he did foresee the survival of Germany, the revival of Germany, and the reunification which is likely to come now as well as the necessity for a strong Europe to balance it. In fact, he foresaw many of the situations which now exist.

People are inclined to dismiss Mosley as a fascist. He wasn't a fascist in many senses of the word. He was basically a radical, though of course he did go too far towards Hitler. I think he would have made a radical leader of the country, but he was too gifted not to be in a hurry. Had he waited his time, he would probably have been prime minister in the 1930s, but one of the troubles with people who are given to a belief in their own leadership is that they are seldom prepared to wait. Therefore they make mistakes.

The classic example of a man born with all the gifts of leadership in his generation is Sir James Goldsmith. He is a man who can talk to people and mesmerise them into believing what he believes, because he believes it so strongly. He is the most Napoleonic figure of this generation. Goldsmith has built up a stupendous fortune out of bravado and a belief in himself, and has the power of leadership, but whether that power is dangerous is another matter. It's a great pity that he wasn't made a member of the House of Lords, and although he might have been in too much of a hurry to achieve a great deal himself, the very fact of him being in the House would have meant there was a constant flow of ideas and impressions. He is the most iconoclastic person I have ever met. He makes one understand great men in the past who overcome extraordinary obstacles by sheer force of personality.

How in a democratic state can we justify having an unelected house of peers as part of the governmental system?

I think the House of Lords really works rather well now, because when you say unelected house of peers, that is true in some senses, but in another, not that the government can make life peers, you are getting a good number of people brought in from outside. I wouldn't say the hereditary peers were showing up very well at the moment. A large number of the efficient ones are the life peers, especially in the Labour and Liberal parties. The hereditary House of Lords is a fairly harmless anachronism, but the more life peers of the right sort you get into it – and by that I don't mean the sort Wilson elected – the better it will be.

You always have to reward your supporters, but I think Mrs Thatcher has made one or two bad appointments to the House of Lords. On the other hand, the most extreme, the most violent of her supporters, who chanted a song about Heath after he had been defeated, was never rewarded at all. So she hasn't rewarded all of her followers, not the most extreme ones, and she's always had a lot of so-called 'Wets' in her government. She still has. Whitelaw was for years one of her stand-bys, and he was certainly not as right-wing as she was, but he always supported her in the long run. To return to Wilson's honours list, I think it was very strange and rather regrettable because they kept going to prison. A very funny lot.

Was your own entry into politics the fulfilment of an early ambition?

I always wanted to be in politics and I fought the 1945 election when I was twenty-two. I think I was the youngest candidate in England. Of course, I was overwhelmingly beaten. Then I fought the 1950 election from bed – I had pneumonia. But I got in for Berwick in 1951 when I was just twenty-nine. I have to say that although I did regard political life as a ruling passion, when it came to it I minded being out of it much less than I had expected. To begin with, I don't think I really ever had good enough health to be a politician. One of the great requisites, certainly for the modern politician, is health. I had incipient jaundice for years which made me feel very ill nearly all the time I was in politics. I really don't miss anything about politics very much, though I'm still quite interested. I always read the political articles in the papers and make up my own mind about a subject.

You ask, concerning my own experience, whether there should be restrictions on the private lives of public figures. Well, I don't see how you can have them, but there are dangers attached to the rather quaint state of affairs that exists at the moment. Before the war, politicians knew exactly what private life they wanted, and everybody knew about it. Dozens of members of parliament of all parties went to bed with their secretaries, had love affairs and indulged what are called sexual foibles, but it was never in the papers. Everybody knew, but it was always considered a joke.

Suddenly every little thing is in the papers and these things become public property because the American system of reporting, which didn't exist here before the war, now does exist and goes after exposing people. In the United States, before the war, a large number of very decent people would not go into politics for fear of being exposed as this or that. The same thing is happening here today.

The reason comes out of both public hypocrisy and the press emphasis on circulation figures. The papers do it because they know how it sells copies, but they also do it because they know people like it. Morality always has been a red rag to a bull. I remember Macaulay's famous statement that nothing was so ridiculous as the British public in one of its fits of morality. There always was a terrific degree of hypocrisy about it all.

It is rather a curious contradiction that just when the greater part of the people of this country are far more immoral than ever before, these same people want to impose immorality on others. Sexual drive very often goes with political drive. If you look at Lloyd George, he was almost manic in his pursuit of women. I once had a secretary who was said to be Lloyd George's illegitimate daughter. She told me how her father would advertise in the papers for so-called assistants, women who used to come from abroad. He would try to seduce them, and very often succeed. This daughter told me how his wife became so desperate at his peccadilloes that she eventually hired from Ireland a one-armed woman with a squint, and even then Lloyd George seduced her after a week. None of it ever came out in the papers. I think you do constrict talent if you suddenly constrict morals.

I'm not sure it's really in any way that the British public want their politicians to behave like saints. They do enjoy the scandals enormously, they love reading about them, but I don't think it matters to them. I don't want to talk about myself here, but I recall that when Profumo resigned in 1960, there was a poll taken in his constituency and an overwhelming number of his constituents said they would vote for him again. If Profumo had not resigned he could have been re-elected with a very large majority in Stratford-upon-Avon and have stayed on in Parliament. He could have said, 'I told a lie. That was the mistake I made, though I don't think it is a resigning matter.' His resignation arose out of trying to contain the thing so that other people would not be dragged into the imbroglio. The great majority of my constituents said they would support me, too, but I had also resigned by then. There was really no alternative the way things are. I received a great number of letters of sympathy and one of the papers had a poll of three or four hundred people, and they said that what had happened had nothing to do with my politics.

As for the so-called security aspects, when Profumo left I made a speech in the House of Commons saying it would have been much more dangerous if he had not been to bed with Miss Keeler. By going to bed with her it was made perfectly plain what he was doing with her, and nobody should have minded because he was probably only doing what 80 percent of the members of the House of Commons had done. If he had not gone to bed with her, he would have been talking about God knows what and it would have been very suspicious. But everything was turned upside down, and the fact he had been to bed with her was made the reason for his resignation.

Morally speaking, I haven't changed my view that most men would expect their wives to be tolerant about what are essentially unimportant episodes. If every wife left her husband because he had been unfaithful to her, there would be very few marriages going. When I said at my resignation that there's a world of difference between doing something and being found out, I think it was just the truth. It always has been the truth. A lot of leading Conservatives were having wild love affairs, had long-standing mistresses, so long as it didn't become too public. Look at Kennedy. Everybody knew roughly what he was up to and nothing about it ever came out. The American press was so much quieter then than it is now, and he was a hero to the press as well as to the public, especially to the rather left-wing press, so everything was covered up.

Interviewed by Robin Day in 1975, you said you had sometimes, when abroad, taken such drugs as hashish and opium on the basis of autres pays, autres moeurs. *Where should legalisation stand in combating the serious drug problem today?*

I think it's a terrible problem now. There's all the difference between things like opium and cannabis and the hard drugs. Heroin really is a killer, as is cocaine, but the terrifying fact we have to remember is that alcohol was also a huge killer in the 1930s in the United States after Prohibition. I don't know what the answer is. Nobody seems to have any difficulty getting drugs. People who want to have them have them, and if they don't get them they seem to murder or steal to get them.

It would certainly be quite interesting if some country did try the legalisation of drugs to see what the effect would be, but here you come up against practical politics. The fact is that if any party in Britain tried to legalise drugs, all the inborn hypocrisy of the English character would cry out against it, and legitimately in some ways, because the risk might be considerable. I don't think it's a risk that any politician will ever be able to take because the opposition party would climb on a moral bandwagon.

We once had a generation of giants in politics – giants in rhetoric and personality. Now the species seems quite extinct, the level of debate reduced to slanging and point scoring.

One of the reasons is that the right people aren't going into politics. It is now a hell of a life. I don't know quite what the divorce rate for politicians is today, but it is enormously high. You have this terrifically intense constituency life these days, where you have to go every weekend and make speeches and think not about the state of the country but about the state of your own constituents. When constituents demand more and more attention, it's not good for politicians. Constituents ought to elect a man and then leave him alone, not insist on his coming to tea once a week or once a month.

Rhetoric aside, I think Mrs Thatcher will be remembered as a very remarkable prime minister who achieved more than Churchill did in his peacetime days, though she certainly wouldn't have been as good a war prime minister as he was. Churchill was too old once the war was over. After he had a stroke the country was ruled in reality, though nobody knew it, by three men, Sir Jock Colville, Sir Burke Trend and Christopher Soames. They really kept the front up. For many months Churchill wasn't fit to be prime minister. I don't think the men of that generation were always quite the giants they were made out to be. Butler may have been a giant, but he had clay feet. And Macmillan's achievement in this country was to leave it in the most appalling state for Wilson or anyone who succeeded him.

I certainly would have been a Thatcherite today. I find the present demeaning of Mrs Thatcher rather low-spirited because she has achieved really extraordinary things for this country. The fact is that when she came in the trade unions had defeated Callaghan and were ready to take over. Her battle with Scargill was a historic battle and very few people would have been able to go into it with the strength she showed or to have succeeded as she did. That was really crossing the Rubicon for this country. If we hadn't been led across, I don't know how we would have managed, because the country was getting into a worse and worse economic mess and she has created a sort of economic miracle. We're having a bad hiccup at the moment, but fundamentally our economic position is still strong despite the so-called crisis.

Wilson is said to be discredited now, but I think it's a little hard on him because he's not very well. The trouble with Wilson was that he was too good-natured and he found it very difficult to sack anybody. Then, of course, he thought the way to placate the unions was to feed them, get them to Downing Street, give them drinks, lay on parties for them, and in that way he bribed them to follow him. And, of course, they just took more and more and ratted on the Labour Party. It was Wilson who created the third estate: the trade unionists who were really directing the government. Once they had defeated Callaghan in 1978, they then tried to defeat Mrs Thatcher. Callaghan was a much more considerable man than he's made out to be, but he never had a chance as prime minister and it was actually Mrs Thatcher who took the bull by the horns and pulled the country out of a sort of bog where restrictive practices were bringing everything to a standstill.

In the Times *of 20 January 1975, you said that not only were Sir Keith Joseph and Mrs Thatcher discredited as contenders for the party leadership, they were also discredited as leading conservatives ...*

What I meant then was that those who were called the 'Wets' regarded Mrs Thatcher and Sir Keith Joseph as dangerous lunatics, and when it looked as though she was putting herself forward as a candidate, there was a tremendous movement to discredit her. It didn't succeed because of the strength of her personality and the very shrewd campaign carried out by Airey Neave on her behalf in the House of Commons. She beat Heath to the amazement of everybody. The Tory party couldn't believe what had happened; it seemed impossible. I did not know her very well and had no idea she had all these qualities underneath her slightly genteel surface.

I can understand Heath's lasting bitterness. He is a remarkable man with great talents, but he does find it difficult to communicate and he has been his own worst enemy. He is a shy man, a very shy man, who has lived for himself and for politics, putting politics before private life most markedly. He is basically a kind man, who has good instincts, but he doesn't quite understand how to deal with people. One of the jobs of the prime minister is to see the chairman of the 1922 committee every week to get the feeling of the back benches, and I remember, shortly after Heath became prime minister, that Vere Harvey, the then chairman, went to see him. Now, Vere Harvey had been in the RAF and was a man who liked a drink, one who would settle down with a whisky and soda and talk twice as well if he had one. Heath didn't understand this at all, and Harvey wasn't offered a drink of any kind. The next time Harvey went to see Heath, he asked for a drink, and Heath rang the bell and said, 'Bring a cup of tea for the Air Commodore Harvey.'

This incident showed a misunderstanding caused by Heath's total concentration on the mechanics of politics to the exclusion of the human beings who ran them. That was his fault: he lived for politics, and when he became prime minister it was his dream come true. He thought he would transform Britain, but then he was hit by two very unfortunate things. The first was the price of oil suddenly going up from $3 to $15 a barrel, which totally upset the whole British economy and made everything he had planned impossible. The second was the miners' strike, which led to him being very badly advised, in my view, about the date of the election. Who was responsible, I do not know, but I do know Lord Corrington was against the date for which the election was called. It should either have been for two weeks earlier or two weeks later, and to have called it just after giving in to the trade unions was a disaster.

Heath minded what happened terribly, and I think he considered it was fortune and not his own mistakes that was responsible for him no longer being prime minister. He saw, as he thought, success being dashed from his lips just when he had the answer, for he passionately believed in himself as a conciliator, someone who could draw all Britain together. He was always a member of the one-nation group, as I had been years before, and that made him mind dreadfully about his failure. But he minded especially because it was a woman who unseated him; he felt that made him look stupid. I wouldn't say it did at all, but it was a great pity because the country needed Heath and, had he held his ground and been able to overcome his bitterness, he could certainly have served Mrs Thatcher and built up a power base in the party which might have made her style of government much more difficult.

Whether it was all for good or ill, I don't know, but Heath minded beyond how a prime minister should mind, the reason being that he was so totally engrossed with politics that he didn't have anything except his music- which is a minor consolation – to fall back on. He wasn't married, he didn't have children and he didn't have a family life at all. It was a tragedy – really very sad. One only wishes he could take a new lease of life because he is still a man of remarkable quality.

In 1976 you said you were afraid that if the Conservatives lost the election there would be few conservative beliefs left to conserve after another five years of socialism. After ten years of Thatcherism, many would claim we see the yuppies reigning supreme and ruthlessness and single-mindedness dominant at the expense of compassion. What is your view?

You have to be brash to make money, and so there is bound to be a lot of attention concentrated on the yuppies, but I don't think they're any worse than people who made money in the Victorian age, who talked about brass, who built hideous houses and churches. The money we're spending on the National Health service has never been greater, and it's never been a more inefficient service. Meanwhile nobody knows exactly how to tackle the problem. You could say that Mrs Thatcher has tackled it in quite the wrong way. It should be tackled by concentrating the public's attention on the number of people in the NHS who are actually nurses or doctors, or assistants to doctors or contributors to medicine. These numbers should then be published alongside what I would call the number or fellow travellers who hang about hospitals filling in forms, wasting time, red tapers and so on.

What I don't think you can say is that someone who spends the money she spends on the NHS can be without compassion. It seems to me that she cares passionately about things. She wants to get a country which is self-supporting as far as possible, where people can work hard and make money if they can. The NHS should be efficiently run with nurses doing the job and not this enormous wastage of money on those who are not actually employed in nursing. I cannot understand why the arguments have been so badly presented, and I think there is still time before the next general election to look at the whole matter of presentation and the refiguring of the structures of those engaged directly in medicine and those who are red-tape hangers-on.

Another question on which Mrs Thatcher has played it all wrong concerns the sort of federation we are to have in a United Europe. The majority of countries want, as much as she does, not a tight but a loose federation. They want to be able to continue making their laws in their own way. Mrs Thatcher, by leading with her chin, has made it possible for other countries to hide behind her and not come out with their opinions, and therefore she has miscalculated her tactics. Had she played it more skilfully and kept more in the background, others would have done what she has done and she need never have been labelled a bad European.

Whether Mrs Thatcher would win an election tomorrow is almost impossible to tell. When an election comes, it's like Dr Johnson said: When a man is going to be hung tomorrow it concentrates his mind wonderfully. When you're going to elect a government tomorrow, it concentrates your mind in the same way. I don't consider Kinnock is a very impressive personality, and I'm sure the Labour Party would be house of Babel if it were in power again, because there are left-wingers and right-wingers and there are ambitionists. I don't think they quite know what they would do.

Are they really going to renationalise? If so, where's the money coming from? Who's going to pay for it? Whether Mrs Thatcher can be unseated would depend on whether the economy was right by the time the election was fought. People vote for their own pockets as much as for anything. And if things are good, they're not going to risk it by having the Labour party back again and a lot of meaningless policies and unknown expenditure.

Do I find Mrs Thatcher colourful or attractive? No, I don't find her colourful and I don't find her a very attractive woman. I don't think she has many womanly graces, but I do think she has courage and convictions. Basically, what she wants is to create a prosperous country which can pay for itself, pay for its health and social services of all kinds, and not to go bankrupt in the process. She has made great steps in that direction despite this momentary hiccup.

A lot of young journalists claim to find her sexually attractive.

Is that so? Well, come years ago there was an association of prostitutes in Italy who were known as the Grandmothers of Milan, and I think the youngest was seventy and the eldest bedridden and eighty-seven, and they did roaring trade with very young people. So perhaps she does have this peculiar fascination for the young.

Journalists have sometimes commented to me – especially if they come from the Daily Telegraph *– that they take exception to having to address you as Lord Lambton when you have in fact relinquished your peerage. Can you clarify this?*

I don't think there has really been any confusion. What I had was a courtesy title which is borne by the eldest son of a peer. It is not a lawful title but a courtesy title. I sat in the House of Commons when my father was still alive as Antony Claud Frederick Lambton, Esquire, commonly called Lord Lambton, and that is really all there is to it. In the Peerage Bill it is absolutely stressed that courtesy titles do not exist in law. I continued to sit in the House of Commons after my father died. No change was made in the register of the House of Commons because it wasn't a legal name.

What is your attitude to the monarchy as it exists today?

I see it as a very sensible institution. Franco brought back the monarchy in Spain, and when he was asked why, he said for the simple reason that it saved so much time. If you haven't got a king you have to spend a terrible lot of time at receptions and such-like events. You either have to have a president or you have to have a king. The Queen is immensely popular and she has really done a rather wonderful job. She's been a queen for thirty-eight years and she has never made a really serious mistake in all that time. Now that is a remarkable thing. You don't want a very brilliant, dynamic queen, or a queen who interferes in affairs of state. She hasn't interfered and the whole royal family continues to be a source of enormous interest to people.

The only danger I see about Prince Charles is that he might start interfering in politics and it's something a king can't do. Neither Edward VII nor George V nor George VI nor the Queen have done so. But I think that when Prince Charles does become King he will find that he has so much to do, such varied responsibilities, that he will probably not branch out into opinions too much. It really wouldn't be his function.

I know he has said some things that made people think him eccentric, about talking to flowers and bushes, for instance, but for hundreds of years people have been talking to flowers, to bees and trees; all countrymen do it. And Prince Charles is much more of a countryman than people realise. There is no reason why he shouldn't make a good king so long he doesn't mix himself up with the politics of the country. He's obviously got charm, ability and love of art, which no member of the Hanoverian family has had since Prince Regent. And he can express himself quite well. But it's an impossible position, being Prince of Wales. It must be immensely frustrating. I think one has to forgive anyone who is Prince of Wales a great deal. He must be bursting all the time to express his own real opinion.

When you wrote your recent controversial book about Mountbatten, was it simply to put the record straight or were there other factors?

I wrote a novel some years ago, published by you, called *Elizabeth and Alexandra*, about the last Tsarina and her sister. They were Mountbatten's aunts, and I had to go through a lot of the Mountbatten papers to research the book. To my extreme annoyance I found that practically everything he said was lies. He was a myth-maker – he lived in the land of myth. I don't know what the things were that I brought out that anyone is said to have objected to, because the most damaging thing had already come out in Zeigler's book: the business of his trying to get the name of the Royal family changed to Mountbatten-Windsor. It does seem rather ridiculous that Mountbatten, who was pure German, was trying to foist a German name on to the British royal family. He didn't succeed, of course.

No doubt my book wasn't welcomed in royal circles, but a lot of the royal family aren't great readers, and if they had been they would have found all the same undesirable things coming to light in Zeigler or Mountbatten's own books. He said the most extraordinary things, and when I quoted them I was said to be wrong, though when Mountbatten himself said them, they were supposedly all right. He could not tell the truth; he simply couldn't. He didn't know how to.

Mountbatten, you see, had an agonising youth as a German boy among four or five hundred English boys. He was mercilessly bullied and in my view retreated into mythland for ever afterwards. But my book, you know, hardly dealt with Mountbatten himself; it really dealt with his family. He was as untruthful about that as he was about himself. For example, he always claimed to be royal. He wasn't royal in any way. His father was known to be the illegitimate son of a German baron, his mother the daughter of an impecunious Pole whose father had a very strange career which I could have brought out but didn't. In fact, I wasn't nearly as unpleasant as I might have been about the Mountbattens.

His books about his family are absolutely packed with imagination. He had this curious love of grandeur that he couldn't get away from, and in his memoirs one is shown how he was never wrong, never made a mistake in his life, and so on and so forth. I don't know how one would feel about him if one had been one of the people sent by him on the disaster of the Dieppe raid, but he was a very interesting man because of his remarkable personality. He was a remarkable leader of men, with the charisma to make those who served under him adore him and minimise his faults. If you met him, and he wanted you to like him, you would, but although he had the great qualities of leadership, he wasn't a considerable man otherwise. He wasn't a clever man, he was almost illiterate, and the books he advised his daughters to read you might suggest to a ten-year-old boy. But although I wrote political journalism for about thirty years, I never once attacked him. What finally really annoyed me was discovering a man gradually creating a whole school of history which was an absolute myth, all to glorify his own family.

I didn't really go into the rumours about his sexuality, though a lot of people sent me some of the most grotesque things relating to him. One was a picture of a man with a fox and hounds tattooed on his back, the fox going up his behind. I asked two of his friends who had known him very well and often seen him bathing, and they said such a tattoo simply didn't exist. But I wasn't looking for any evidence of that sort because, to begin with, his children are still alive, and secondly, it is quite wrong to go into a person's sexual habits unless they have had a profound influence on his life. Whatever habits Mountbatten may have had, they didn't change his character one iota. He was a man entirely devoted to ambition and to righting the wrong he thought had been done to his father by becoming First Sea Lord. His sexual life wasn't really sex. It was just exercise, that was all. Going to bed with a woman was no more important to him than going for a mile run.

I know nothing whatsoever about the Queen's feelings over any influence he may have had on Prince Charles, but he was probably very kind and Prince Charles is known to have been very fond of him. He was kind because he was in love with royalty, longed to be royal himself, always used the royal door at Knights of the Garter meetings when he had no real right to. He adored royalty, and his diaries after 1920 reveal how incredibly ingratiating and obsequious he was to the then Prince of Wales, Edward VIII, as a young man. Prince Edward had been best man at Mountbatten's wedding and afterwards stuck by him. Mountbatten always did everything he could with him, would travel to India with him, use him in every sense he possibly could, and then, after the abdication had happened, he didn't even go to his wedding but gave the excuse that he hadn't been asked.

Well, he usually went to everything without being asked, anyhow, and the former Prince of Wales was very upset indeed. Afterwards Mountbatten did try to go and see the Windsors and get things out of them, but there was such antagonism that the butler or footman was eventually asked to stay in any room where he was in case he put something in his pocket. He behaved in a very odd way to the Windsors, though when one says he liked Prince Charles, I'm sure he did. Whether he would have gone on liking Prince Charles if Prince Charles had stepped down as heir to the throne is hard to say. He certainly didn't like the Duke of Windsor after he abdicated – until he died, when he was his best friend again.

About your literary career: what are you working on at the moment?

I'm writing six short stories about the Holocaust. I wanted to write fiction again because it seems to me that one of the troubles with making people realise about the evil of the German reaction is that so many books about the Holocaust are presented as statistics. It is quite impossible to comprehend a book that says 350 were taken and gassed in Auschwitz, next day 400 went to Belsen and had nothing to eat. What I'm trying to do is fictionalise and put flesh on some of the things that actually happened and make them happen to real people, and to show that those who carried out many of the atrocities were not necessarily extreme Nazis but quite ordinary people who were sucked into the Nazi machine. I think the Germans have a habit, a national habit, of needing orders, wanting to obey orders. I don't know what the position is today, but as long ago as about 1800 Goethe said the trouble with Germany was that Germans prefer order to justice. I think that is quite true, and it is alarming what is happening now with the deaths of so many millions being reduced to statistics.

One of the tragic things in the world today is that Israel has begun to behave in a manner in some ways not dissimilar to how the Germans behaved in the war. You have virtually a state of war in Israel, and they are treating the Arabs like enemies. Remember the pictures on television of Israeli soldiers breaking bones. Power degenerates into cruelty. I've always sympathised with the retention of Israel as a state, but I very much doubt the Israelis will be able to hold world opinion if they go on as they are at the moment. I think they will have to withdraw from the territories, certainly from a large portion of the territories, because they can't continue to rule people who don't want to be ruled without using methods reminiscent of what happened in the war.

But to get back to fiction, what I'm interested in is telling a story, because the whole of life is a story. I was rather annoyed when I wrote a book called *Snow and Other Stories* and a critic said it was a fault that the stories were open-ended. An open-ended story is much better. All Chekhov's stories were open-ended, such stories being just glimpses of someone's life in which the author tries to portray what they were like. Story-telling is the same sort of art as painting. Berenson, the noted art critic, used the word 'tactility', which he said was one of the great virtues of painting. You had to feel that the person in a portrait was so real you could touch him. Well, I think fiction wants to be the same, wants to create real people whom you feel you know and could touch.

I remember that the late Duff Cooper – the first Lord of the Admiralty during the war, probably forgotten by the younger generation – once told me how, when he was at school, one of the masters read them a Sherlock Holmes story and said, 'Now I've read you this story I want you to remember one thing – Sherlock Holmes is a far more living personality than I am or any of you, or probably than anyone you'll ever meet.' And I believe that this is the aim of all short-story and fiction writers. If you look at the Russians, again and again there are so many people you feel you know, who might come into the room. Anna Karenina and Natasha in *War and Peace* are two of the greatest characters I suppose anyone has ever known. What I am trying to do in this Holocaust series is bring to reality events which have been lost in detail. Make something real.

Certainly, fiction does have an effect on the way people think and behave. You only need to look back at Goethe's *Young Werther*. The book completely transformed a whole generation of upper and middle-class young Germans. Literally hundreds of them killed themselves as a result of trying to be this tragic German figure. You see, the Germans haven't much sensibility, and as soon as they were suddenly told they did have sensibility, they persuaded themselves they could love, and when they found out they couldn't they simply killed themselves, which was an extraordinary syndrome. Salinger was someone else who affected a whole generation. With *The Catcher in the Rye* he made a whole generation of American boyhood comprehensible.

Do I approve of censorship? Not really. I don't think it does any good. However, in a way censorship very often helps an author. The Victorian novelists, for example, were greatly helped by not being able to write about sex. It's always said that Thackeray in *Vanity Fair* could not portray Becky Sharp as the little prostitute she was, and that that caused a novel to be written which describes her absolutely perfectly. It means you have to dwell on the details which bring the person to life. Curiously enough, the sexiest book I've ever read is probably *The Mill on the Floss*. *Adam Bede* and *The Mill on the Floss* are books of the sort of intense female frustration that could never possibly have been conveyed when there weren't morals to be kept, laws to be kept, and restraint on authors. It did pose an author great problems, but when these were overcome the result has been masterly. People's thoughts are far more interesting than the physical jerking which pervades modern literature.

Yes, I was quite waspish in my review of John Mortimer's book on Tuscany. John Mortimer's a very good writer, but I think rather a contemptible man. He believes it's absolutely fine for him to be a left-wing socialist and to drink champagne at night. When a writer descends to the level of his book about Tuscany, full of the most embarrassing things and written at the lowest common denominator tourist level, I think one wants to be as waspish as possible. I wish I had been a hornettish.

Baroness Falkender made a comment to me about your great charisma.

I don't think I've got very much charisma.

Do you hold any religious convictions?

Not very strong ones. I have a vague sort of hope that there may be an after-life, but I see no logic to prove it and every sort of logic to disprove it. There lingers something in me, however, from beliefs imbued in my subconscious in the past, the idea of there being some world beyond to which people one loved have gone and where one can meet them, though where it can be and how it can be set up is something quite beyond me. I only wish I had the faith of a good Catholic.

I find it very difficult to believe in God. It's quite easy to believe in the devil. If there is a God, what has He been doing in the world? Why has He created one and a half billion Chinese mostly living in starvation? There are millions of people being born and dying in India. Every day the dead are pitchforked into cars by men going round the streets and throwing them in like bundles of hay. Why is God doing all this? Is he punishing mankind as he did in the Old Testament?

You have to have the grace of belief, yes, but you have to believe a lot of damn silly things as well, especially if you're an old-fashioned Roman Catholic. Then, of course, one of the main reasons why religion is dying is nobody believes in Hell any more. Hell was a very salutary weapon in the hands of governments and priests. It kept a lot of people under control. In Italy, where I spend a lot of my time, the priests used to rule with a rod of iron and the wretched people believed that, if they sinned, they would go to Hell and it would be everlasting. Practically every church had a picture of Hell, flames, devils pulling people away from Heaven by the legs and sticking things inside them, killing them.

I can't understand what God is doing. I mean, if you look at the world now, what has Aids to do with the Africans – with poor people? Then you get the old arse Runcie whom I can't understand at all. He seems one of the most inadequate Archbishops of Canterbury there ever has been, a rather pathetic old man who doesn't want to upset anybody, but only wants to please every-body, yet doesn't know how to. He seems a disaster for the Church of England because he appoints people who deny a number of its tenets, like the Bishop of Durham.

I don't know what's happened to Christianity. People no longer believe in God, really, but in some sort of instinct. I myself have never been able to understand what form He takes. As for the Trinity, what's the point of the Trinity when One will do? Why should God want to shelve off his responsibilities on to the Holy Ghost and the Son, and why put his wretched Son on the Cross? Why portray it for the rest of the world to gloat at in every church in Christendom? The Christian religion is the only one I know which portrays cruelty as its symbol. The Moslems are nothing like so cruel.

But everyone has an inherent cowardliness, and as you grow older you either consciously or unconsciously try to persuade yourself there is an after-life, because the idea of leaving everybody you know and all your family behind is not appealing. You have to just face the fact that's it, really. I feel so sorry for old people who live thinking that the reward of life is going to be in Heaven. When you're nearly dead it gives you a compensation to think that there's someone who's going to look after you beyond the nursing-home bed, that there's a beneficent man who's going to take you up to Heaven. It gives you a certain satisfaction as you lie there, whereas if you think you are going to be stubbed out like a cigarette and thrown out of the window, then it depresses you. So naturally you try and see the pleasant alternatives. One does it all through life.

Looking back, do you ever wonder how you might have fared if you had stayed in politics?

I always thought after I left politics that the most important thing was to make another life. The most pointless thing in life is regret. It's the biggest waste of time in the world. One's life is a train on a one-way journey, and once you've past a particular point, there's no way you're going to get back. The only thing is to go on and enjoy the other places where the train arrives. I wouldn't say I'm a very happy person, but I don't think I'm very unhappy either. I'm not bitter and I'm very interested in people. There's no such thing as a happy life. I always rather despise those who complain of an unhappy childhood, especially once they have reached the age of twenty-five. Everybody has difficulties as a child at one stage or another. In fact, children who are too happy often lead disastrous lives because they're not prepared for the buffets and blows of fate.

As to my marriage, I have been married for over forty years and my wife and I live apart for most of the time. It is an arrangement that of course has its difficulties, though it is probably the best compromise there is. The whole of life is a compromise. Nothing is black, nothing is white. No, I don't really believe in divorce, though that, I should think, is probably a result of convention. As a child I never knew anyone who had been divorced. Childish impressions have an unpleasant way of fixing themselves in your mind.

For friendship, my greatest friends have nearly all been women. I find women more sympathetic than men. I also find them more logical. Men are so illogical because ambition is always distorting their logic. They're channelled and much more selfish. Women are watchers of life, observers in life, manipulators behind the scenes in life. I find their views much more interesting than those of men, who are always walking down their own road, not looking this way or that, just talking about the things they meet on the road – usually very boring.

Have you an unfulfilled ambition?

No. at my age – I'm sixty-seven – you can't really hope to do anything immense. One of the consolations of age is that you see the pettiness of material success, how it doesn't very often bring happiness. Also, when you're young, you mind whether people like you, you mind if you've said something stupid, you mind if you're not asked to some occasion or other, but when you get older you look on these matters with slightly detached eyes. You mind much less and things are much simpler. I don't think I could bear to be young again.

JAMES LEES-MILNE

James Lees-Milne was a conservationist and architectural historian, having written extensively on the baroque, the Tudor renaissance, Inigo Jones and the city of Rome. He was born in 1908 and educated at Eton and Magdalen College, Oxford. From 1933 to 1973 he worked for the National Trust and from 1951 to 1966 he was their advisor on historic buildings. He was also the founding secretary of the National Trust's Country Houses Committee. He wrote a biography of the sixth Duke of Devonshire, *The Bachelor Duke* (1991), and his two-volume biography of Harold Nicolson won the Heinemann Award of the Royal Society of Literature in 1982. His four volumes of diaries placed him among the foremost diarists of the century. He died in 1997.

You seem to have a dislike of being labelled – whether it be 'doyen of conservationists' or 'biographer' or 'architectural historian'. Would you have any objection to being described as a man of parts?

I imagine a man of parts is someone who is very versatile and good at lots of things. But I'm not good at anything, not even one particular thing.

Your diaries are littered with famous names from the past – Mitford, Pope-Hennessy, Sackville-West, John Betjeman, and so on. Do people nowadays seem very dull by comparison?

Alas, I belong to the past. I wish I could claim to know interesting young people. I do know a few but they can't be bothered with somebody like me. It's not that I think young people dull at all but they're rather different. I've got nothing against them, and they are very nice to me and very tolerant, much nicer than my generation were to old people.

You survived an extraordinary childhood, and like most children you seemed to accept your circumstances. Did you sometimes long for normality?

I didn't think there was anything abnormal about my upbringing, and I don't think so now. My parents weren't cruel to me at all; indeed, they were very nice to me.

My father was rather distant, that's all, but in those days children were kept in the background. I only saw them at 5 o'clock. I was made to change into a tidy pair of shorts, clean shirt, and then I was pushed by my nurse into the drawing room, where I had to make myself agreeable for half an hour. It was very boring for my parents, and it wasn't much fun for me.

Although you write entertainingly of your childhood, it seems to have been a rather unhappy time, characterised by fear. You seem to have spent more time with the servants than with your parents – in fact it comes over as a rather loveless environment. Would you agree with that?

No, not wholly, because my mother loved me very much and she was very amusing and unconventional. As I got older and she got older I suppose in a beastly way I became aware of her limitations, and we drifted apart rather. But I always remained very fond of her.

Saying goodbye to your mother when you left for Eton you describe as 'heartrending' … Can you recall that feeling?

Oh yes, but then you see, all boys of my generation wept for days beforehand because school was so horrible. It wasn't so much that home was so nice, it was because school was so beastly that we wept.

You say that Eton fostered in you intellectual and aristocratic tastes, despite your circum- stances which you describe as lowbrow and lower upper class. Have you felt that as a tension, a dichotomy throughout your life?

My background was a philistine one, that's to say my father only thought of hunt- ing and shooting and racing and gambling. He wasn't a rich man, just a sort of ordinary squire, but he lived in a small manor house, so I suppose we were what one calls gentry, but you've no idea how limited they were in those days. They despised learning, they never went to art exhibitions, they didn't go to concerts, their friends were all exactly the same, and I never felt easy with them when I grew up. I did want to get away from them, that's quite true.

In your autobiography you say, 'I'm actually conscious of, and amused by, class distinctions. I love them and hope they endure forever.' What lay behind that remark?

I think class distinctions are fascinating. All the great novels are about class … just think of the Russian classics of Tolstoy and Dostoevsky. There's a sort of leadenness about life when there are no class distinctions.

Does the political idea of a classless society fill you with horror?

It fills me with gloom. It's not that I like people *because* they belong to the aristocracy, but on the whole there's a sort of illumination, a casualness about the aristocratic view of life which I find rather appealing. They don't take themselves very seriously – think of Nancy Mitford, for whom everything was a joke up to a point – and they're sophisticated and amusing. Then of course they have lovely country houses to stay in, and the English country house is something very special.

You say you were a terrible disappointment to your father. Was that difficult to deal with?

Yes it was, because he made me feel that I was a total failure because I didn't have a good seat on a horse. And I didn't care for shooting. It bored me, and anyway I didn't like killing things. So he thought I was cissy. He didn't bother about whether I was doing well in my schoolwork, but he would have liked me to have been sporting and thereby accepted by his friends as a good old chip off the block. As it was, I think they thought very little of me.

After Eton you stayed briefly at the home of Lord Redesdale. How did your family compare with the Mitfords in terms of eccentricity?

My parents weren't eccentric at all, so there was no comparison to be made. Tom, my friend, was my link with the Mitfords, and it was through him that I went to stay there. I found that Diana, the one who was nearest to me in age after Tom, was mad about poetry and literature, and that was marvellous to me. I realised that there was a world which was completely different from boring Worcestershire, the manor house with its horses and guns, and I thought, this is too wonderful.

Tom Mitford remained your friend until he was killed in the war. You rather gloss over his death in your book … was it shattering to you?

I was very upset, and so were all his friends. We all were devoted to Tom. I saw him the evening before he left England. He didn't want to fight against the Germans, so he went to Burma and was killed at once by the Japanese. I remember being told of his death by Nancy who rang me up and said in a sort of offhand way, 'Oh, by the way, you know Tomford's dead.' They all had nicknames for each other, and she used to call him Tomford. I thought that was too much of a stiff upper lip, but that was the way they were brought up, not to show their feelings.

You were rebuked by James Pope-Hennessy for what he calls your 'collapse from pacifism', which paved the way to your joining the Irish Guards in 1940. Can you tell me how you came to adopt pacifism, and what made you relinquish it?

In between the wars I had convinced myself that the First War was totally unnecessary and was the most appalling calamity, and that no war was ever justified. I don't think that in the late 1930s I was so aware of the iniquities of Hitler as I was when the war was over, and that applied to a lot of English people. But one of my great friends, Robert Byron, a traveller and writer, was passionately anti-Hitler. I was feeling very ambivalent when the war came, and he convinced me that I should join up and be prepared to fight. So I did.

There were a number of notable pacifists at the time, including Frances and Ralph Partridge. Were you influenced by them at all?

I didn't know Frances Partridge until after the war. She remains an absolute confirmed pacifist, but the awful thing I learned is that it's no good being a pacifist unless everyone else is. You've got to stand up to evil. And how can you do it except by fighting?

Oxford seems to have been a profound disappointment to you ... why was that?

I had the idea that it was going to be a quiet secluded beautiful city, which of course it is, and that there I would lead a cloistered existence, and study, and that dons would take an interest in me, because I was young and earnest. But they didn't because I wasn't clever enough, unlike all my Eton friends. They also all seemed to have money and I had none at all. It was very difficult for me, because they used to entertain and give luncheon parties, and there was lots of drink and they were raffish and exciting and thrilling. I couldn't compete; so I minded.

But did you sow your wild oats in Oxford?

Not very much. I led a quiet life really. I was always very romantic about women and frightened of them when I was young. The idea of casually sleeping with a woman before I was about twenty-five would never have entered my head. Women were people to be courted, and they were romantic. Diana Mitford, for example, was always up there on a celestial cloud, somebody to be worshipped. I suppose I felt sexy, but that was something quite different, and you went to a brothel for that, though I never did. I was terrified of that too. But the idea of meeting a girl at a party and then going to bed with her, it never occurred to me ...

Your father had a profound contempt for intellectuals. Did you allow that to influence you at all?

It made me rather secretive in the sense that I would read books under the bed-clothes with a torch so that my father wouldn't see the electric light thorough the crack between the door and the floorboards. And I had to hide my books because when I went back to school my father would throw them away. He thought reading was something rather decadent.

You fell under the spell of Keats, Shelley and Byron, and later Gerard Manley Hopkins. Was Hopkins instrumental in your conversion to Roman Catholicism?

I think he may have been, yes. I thought I was going to write a life of Hopkins. In fact, whenever Peter Quennell gave me a book he would say, 'To the future biographer of Father Gerard.' Of course I never got down to it; I wasn't capable of it.

When you were a young man, your faith was uncomplicated, and it took you years to work out that it was because you never associated morals with God. Was it shattering to discover that the two might be related?

Yes, it was rather, because I found going to confession very distasteful. When I no longer belonged to the Church of Rome, I went back to my old church. I've always been rather religiously minded. As a child I was mad about God, and still am, and I love talking about Him, but people get embarrassed by God, don't they? I mean, most of my friends are agnostics, but I'm certainly not. I am a fervent believer, but of course I don't have to worry about morals now very much, because I have no temptations to steal or go to bed with anybody.

You appear to have lost your faith for a time when, as you put it, 'morals began to rear their beastly hydra heads'. Was that a difficult time?

It was an embarrassing time. I thought, I can't go back to the same priest, or any priest, and say, 'I've done it again, father' – I just can't. It's totally off-putting, and I think it's all nonsense too.

I'm wondering what religion could have meant to you, how it could have been experienced by you as something distinct from moral behaviour …

I think it's all to do with the afterlife and the purpose of life. I would have found it very difficult to get to the age of eighty-six if I hadn't believed in God.

In Another Self you describe the period when you were in love with three people at the same time saying: 'I reached heights of ecstasy wherein I came closer to God than ever before or since.' That's quite a significant statement ... can you enlarge on it?

It was true. I was in love with two people whom I knew, and one whom I'd never seen, but whom I adored. This was during the war and we simply spoke on the telephone. It is quite easy to be in love with more than one person, very easy indeed. It's only really embarrassing when they meet.

Sex and God do seem to have been recurrent themes with you. In 1942 you recorded in your diary: 'The lusts of the flesh, instead of alienating me from God, seem to draw me closer to Him in a perverse way.' Was that perhaps just wishful thinking?

No, because somehow love or lust did bring me closer to God. I had lustful feelings, but in fact the objects of my desire were nearly always people that I was in love with. I think one can identify the loved one with God, as perhaps nuns and monks do. The sex I had then was not squalid; it seemed to me a fulfilment of myself, almost a sort of union with God. But I think my views of God perhaps are unorthodox. I think of God as the spirit of light and of goodness and understanding ... perhaps one shouldn't really.

After your conversion to Rome you returned to the Church of England. Was your experience of Roman Catholicism a brief flirtation, or was it more like a painful love affair?

I treated it in a rather offhand way. Had I been born a Roman Catholic I should still have been one, I think, but what I liked about being a Roman Catholic was the universality of it, and what always gave me satisfaction was realising that the mass was being said all the way round the clock – every moment of the day it was being said somewhere, the same liturgy; but when the Vatican Council changed that, I turned against it. I thought it a tragedy.

As a young man you say that the idea of sex without love shocked you. Did it continue to shock you throughout your life?

Oh yes, I was shocked by myself very much when I had sex without love. I thought it was squalid, and of course now that I'm the age I am, sex means nothing to me at all; it's either a joke or it's really rather disgusting, besides being a frightful bore.

There is a very poignant account of a brief but intense friendship with a young man –
Theodore, I think – which ends in tears. It also seemed to strain the limit of heterosexual-
ity ... was that a worry for you?

No, not a bit, because I've never discriminated between hetero- and homosexuality
really. I think you can be in love with both, you know ... I've always found that.

Your first employment was a private secretary to Lord Lloyd from 1931 to 1935. Did that
suit you or did you have the feeling that you were in the wrong job?

I felt that I was not in the right job, that I had my way to make in the world, that
it was only an interim job, and he realised that too. But looking back on it, it was
a very good experience for me because he was a task master and I learned how
to work hard.

You then held the post of adviser to the National Trust, which seemed tailor-made for you.
In terms of satisfaction and job fulfilment, how would you compare that part of your life
with your literary activities?

Although I had secret literary ambitions I never thought I was going to write books
until the war. So during the 1930s there was no conflict at all. I dedicated myself
to the National Trust work and didn't even think of writing books.

Do you see yourself as having being engaged in a war with the philistines, preserving
wonderful buildings from acts of vandalism, and so on ... ?

Oh yes, very much so. I was one of the founder members of the Georgian Group in
the 1930s, and it was a fight to get the public to recognise that classical buildings in
this country were of any importance at all. The Ministry of Works, the government
department which had care of the ancient monuments, said that architecture in
England ceased in 1714, the year that Queen Anne died, and therefore no Georgian
building was even worth looking at.

You are a distinguished biographer, most notably of Harold Nicolson and the 6th Duke
of Devonshire. On the face of it biography would seem to be an art form distinct from
novel writing or autobiography, but do you perhaps think that the distinction is sometimes
blurred, that biography is often closer to fiction than we imagine?

I think you have to control yourself. You mustn't fictionalise or allow your imagination to take flight when you're dealing with another man's life. You have to be

careful not to let your prejudices run away with you, and you probably can't write a very good biography if you dislike your subject.

You have sometimes said that you prefer writing about rogues. What is it that attracts you to rogues?

It is easier to write about rogues than about virtuous men. To write the life of a saint would be frightfully difficult unless it was a funny saint. One of the reasons why newspapers are so wicked and have such an appalling effect on people's lives is because they deal with bad news and bad people. Good people's doings are very boring.

Your novel Heretics in Love *deals with the themes of Roman Catholicism and incest. Was it meant primarily as an entertainment, or were you intending it as a serious expose of moral and religious problems?*

I was trying to see whether one could make a tale of that sort seem plausible. It is about twins of the opposite sex who had grown up in the country as Catholics and had not known or consorted much with the outside world. I wanted to test whether it was possible for two people brought up in those circumstances to fall in love; and whether it was pardonable.

In your third novel, The Fool of Love, *the squire Joshua says, 'So long as one is madly in love one is living in a fool's paradise.' Was that remark based on your own experience perhaps?*

Yes. Because I think when people are passionately in love they are mad and very unreliable. I think that if one knew that the prime minister was carrying on a passionate affair with someone, one would feel extremely nervous in a crisis.

You were in your forties when you married ... were there times before that when you contemplated marriage?

The people I would like to have married were either already married or turned me down, so then I didn't bother very much for a while. And then suddenly I met Alvilde and I fell in love with her. That was difficult because I was still a Catholic and she had been married before and had a child. She had had a very unsatisfactory married life, in fact she often used to say she couldn't think how her daughter was ever born at all. Her husband was in love with somebody else, so she had a rotten life. We tried very hard to get an annulment for her, but it turned out to be quite impossible. If it had happened today we probably wouldn't have cared tuppence whether we were married, but it did seem to matter then, and we were very conventional.

You never had children of your own, and relations with your stepdaughter seem to have been strained. Did you, or do you dislike children?

I don't care for children very much. When they're responsive and affectionate I think they're sweet and nice, but on the whole I find them awfully boring until they've become adults.

One review wrote of your latest volume of diaries: 'Some of Lees-Milne's opinions are now so wildly outdated and unfashionable that one has to remind oneself that these diaries were written before anyone had thought of political correctness.' Do you have a view on political correctness?

I think it is deceitful. I'm often accused of being a snob, but really I'm not. What I am is an unashamed elitist; it's not reprehensible to want to know people who are cleverer than oneself or more amusing.

After hearing a communist express the view that the needs of poor people should take precedence over those of the upper class, you decided that left-wingers were evil and wrote in your diary, 'I have no sympathy for them at all. Let them burn.' Is that not an indefensible remark, then as now?

Oh, the left-wingers, well, I don't fancy them. I'm very impatient with them.

Is it difficult not to regard some passages in your diaries as impossibly right-wing and racist. For example, a television programmes about Bangladeshis led you to write: 'Such people ought not to exist ... these ghastly people are a sort of standing or seething pollution of the western world's perimeter, of the civilisation we have known. I can't stand the Orientals, their deceit and abominable cruelty.' Would you still stand by such comments today?

Very often I would. There are altogether too many of us, and the danger in what is called the third world is absolutely terrifying. Until they can be stopped breeding I really do think the future is very bleak indeed. But I agree, it is a very offensive remark.

In your autobiography you wrote, 'I prefer to be in the running without ever winning than never to run at all.' Is this modesty, or lack of ambition?

I don't think I am ambitious but I do like successful and interesting people, and I'm grateful that they've wanted to see me because I get more out of their company than they do from me probably. My life has not been full of achievements. I have yet to write a book that I think is much good. I'm not at all satisfied with myself.

DORIS LESSING

Doris Lessing was born of British parents in Persia (now Iran) in 1919 and was taken to Southern Rhodesia (now Zimbabwe) when she was five. She first came to England in 1949, and the following year saw the publication of her first novel, *The Grass is Singing*. In 1954 she received the Somerset Maugham Award for her collection of short novels, *Five* (1953). Her celebrated novels include *The Golden Notebook* (1962), *The Summer Before the Dark* (1973) and *Memoirs of a Survivor* (1974). In 1986 she won the WH Smith Literary Award and also the 1987 Mondello Prize in Italy for her novel *The Good Terrorist* (1985). In 1994 *Under My Skin*, the first volume of her autobiography, was published, followed by the second volume, *Walking in the Shade*, in 1997. She was awarded the Nobel Prize in Literature in 2007. She died in 2013.

During your life you have never allowed yourself to settle too long or too comfortably in any particular creed, even though you have never lacked conviction. Would you say, looking back, that you have constantly invented and reinvented yourself?

I don't agree that I am a person of conviction. The only time in my life when I had real conviction was the time when I was a Communist, but that didn't last very long. I am without fixed opinions generally, because I always find it very difficult to make up my mind about anything. When I was young I was very aggressive and antagonistic and abrasive, but then I was fighting on all fronts against a society which at that time couldn't see any reason why the tiny white minority shouldn't hold down an enormous black majority. It could be said that those were strong beliefs which I defended, but for a long time now I've been a wishy-washy liberal.

Even though you have been in London for most of your life, do you think you have always had the perspective of an exile, and this has perhaps allowed you to look at the familiar in a different way?

Yes, I have a double view all the time. My parents were so archetypally British, and yet I am absolutely outside this culture. This is very valuable for a writer.

You found the colonialism in Rhodesia suffocating and provincial and terribly unjust – and this has informed several of your novels. Was it purely an adult recognition of the iniquity of white superiority, or were you aware of it as a child and simply gave your childish reaction adult expression?

That's a very good question. You see, I was a natural rebel so it could be said that in rebelling against my parents and what they stood for it was natural of me to use the inequalities of white supremacy against them. But I don't think it was really as simple as that. I remember being shocked very early at what I was seeing around me, genuinely shocked. But of course if you are standing out against your parents you pick up any stick to hand to beat them with, and it's true they supported the British Empire as if it were a religion. No one understands this now, it's gone so completely.

Have you been aware of racist attitudes since you came to London?

Oh yes, a great deal, all the time. It's very subtle. In the circles I move among the people are probably not even aware that they have them. But I have a very privileged life, I don't live in the parts of the country where racism is violent.

You are known to be uneasy about the genre of autobiography. Indeed, you once said, 'There is no doubt that fiction makes a better job of the truth.' Can you explain what you mean by that?

Not easily. It is the simple case that a scene in which perhaps only half of the characters are real and the other half invented can be more truthful than the absolute facts; and I don't understand it at all. When I was writing my autobiography, I was actually comparing it with scenes in *A Golden Notebook*. The strange thing was that the one was absolutely full of life and yet it was only half the truth, whereas when I was writing the truth it lacked life and vividness in comparison.

Your autobiography was written as a kind of defence against the biographies and profiles written about you. What is it you fear principally?

Inaccuracy. They always get their facts wrong, they just don't care. But I always meant to write my autobiography at some point, and since I'm now seventy-six I can't keep putting it off.

Do you believe that what can perhaps be explained and resolved in fiction often remains inexplicable and unresolvable in life, in oneself?

Yes, but all the time you see your life differently. The way I see my life now is completely different from ten or twenty years ago. Maybe by the time I come to die it will all be clear to me, who knows. It's also a completely different creative process if you're writing imaginatively. Your whole self goes into it in a way it can't when you're writing an autobiography.

Under My Skin was published last year and covers the first thirty years of your life. What difference did it make that it was written by a woman in her seventies with all the knowledge and uncertainty which old age brings?

The interesting thing is that if I am spared, as they say, and if God wishes me to be alive in ten years' time, I'm prepared to bet I would see everything differently. I used to think that if I took an autobiography down off a shelf I would know what the writer thinks about life. Now I know that it is only what he or she thinks about life *at the time of writing*, like an interim report.

In your childhood the absence of love from your mother was a bitter deprivation. Do you believe that we ever really get over wounds inflicted in our early years?

No, I don't think we really do. You can compensate for them and understand them but you never really get over them. In me there's a certain bleakness of view I will never lose, a kind of wariness, a lack of trust.

How did you know there was a lack of love?

It's something as simple as how you are held by someone. I remember how my father would hold me on his knee, and the way my mother would handle me, as if I were something she had to manage. And when I met my brother in old age I saw the effect of it all. He was the much-loved boy and consequently had an amazing emotional response to everything. And I thought how strange it was that I understood more about him than he did about himself, because I could see in him an immediate physical affection which I've had to learn later in life. I would say I'm naturally a very affectionate person, but I had a blight on me when I was young, and I had to lose that.

The legacy of the First World War brutalised a whole generation and cast a shadow over your childhood. Do you think that the First World War was uniquely horrible in this respect, or do all wars exact a similar price?

I think the First World War was the worst. It wounded Europe deeply, and we haven't got over it. It was such a holocaust, such a murderous war, unnecessarily so, such a contempt for life. I don't think we've recovered from it.

There was a sense of betrayal felt by people like your father – who lost a leg and was shell-shocked – and contempt for the British government. To what extent did this shape your own attitude to Britain and the British?

A great deal. I was brought up breathing contempt for authority, which came directly from my father. It applied not only to the British, because the Germans and French had it too – you've only got to read the books of that time. The First World War left a legacy of contempt for authority all over Europe, and it's a terrible legacy.

You tried very hard not to be like your parents, not to be held together and trapped in the way they were, almost – as you say yourself – as if you were trying to stand outside the human condition. Do you think you have succeeded in standing on the outside?

No, certainly not. Who can? I don't want to go into why, but I very much regard all that, the thoughts I had then, as the most romantic nonsense.

Do you actually believe this unhappiness in childhood, this struggle and the pain of it all, actually helped the writer in you? If you had a happy carefree childhood do you think things might have turned out differently?

I don't think it's unhappiness so much. A child who's had a very stressed childhood becomes an observer, and it's very good preparation for being a writer.

You describe your mother as a tragic figure 'living out her disappointing years with courage and dignity'. Did that insight include forgiveness?

Forgiveness is a very funny word, you know. It seems to me that forgiveness is understanding. Since I understand exactly why she was the way she was, I forgive her. When I was a little girl I was full of pity for her, which isn't at all the same, but it took me almost until the age of seventy to understand her, to see just how terrible her life was. And that's forgiveness, I think.

Do you believe that we necessarily repeat the patterns of our parents, or can we simply decide to break the link in the chain?

I think we can break it, yes, but often you find it's almost as if a script is there and you have to repeat the words.

Do you think the fact that you left your own two small children had anything to do with the feeling that you in turn might inflict similar damage on them?

You have no idea of what life was like, the life of the white minority in Southern Rhodesia. It was a nightmare of stupidity and intolerance and narrow-mindedness. I wouldn't have survived it, I just couldn't have lived it. When I left my children I was thinking, at least I'm not going to inflict this terrible legacy on them, a legacy which causes women to turn into disappointed, trapped people. These women have ceased to exist in this culture, thank God – those who have talent and energy but nothing to use it on, so they take it out on their children. I would have done it to mine if I hadn't left.

But did you ever regret that decision?

No, I didn't, because I did the right thing. I'm amazed that I had the clear-minded-ness to see what I should do, because it was awful of course in one way.

That part of your story is very scantily told. Even adding together your political crusade, your urge to improve the world, your need to get away, to have a different life, they scarcely explain the enormity of what you did. Can it be explained, do you think?

It can be explained, but I don't know if people can see. I knew I would not survive that life, which is why I left. Don't forget I had my mother on my back day and night, and I was obsessed with not being like her. I was not the only woman to feel that way; all the women I knew of my age group had mothers who drove them round the bend by all the time trying to live their lives for them. When I left those children, it was not the children I was leaving, it was the way of life. Of course I should have done it; if I had not done it I would have been finished.

Did you experience the ravages of guilt?

Of course I did, it's very clear. What a lot of people miss in the autobiography is several pages of, 'Oh my God, how could I have done such a dreadful thing!' Surely it must be taken for granted that I was likely to have found it a painful experience without my spelling it out.

There are other parts of your life which might also have fascinated the reader, which you have glossed over, almost defiantly avoiding explanation or elucidation. Your marriages, for example, are presented as incidental. Is this because they are too private, or now too remote perhaps?

I think I said quite a lot about the first marriage. I walked into a role in that society where there were certain things I had to do, and I did them. I have to say I did them all rather well – I was a good wife while I was a wife. It was a classic and conventional and not very emotional marriage. What more is there to be said about this kind of marriage? The second was also a very common marriage at the time. People married refugees to give them a nationality and a status, and it was a normal thing to do. It was a political act – Lessing would have been put back in an internment camp if I hadn't married him.

Was there any room for love?

When I first married I hadn't really grown up emotionally; I was just a girl with an undeveloped heart – a competent, cheerful, affectionate woman who had never really loved anyone. There was nothing wrong with this – a lot of people got married in just this way. And he was not desperately in love with me. Everyone was getting married because of the war. The second one was completely different, in that we knew we wouldn't stay married. There was never at any point any suggestion of that. It was completely political. From my point of view I was marrying an anti-fascist, an anti-Nazi, a hero from Europe, but as far as my parents were concerned, I was marrying a bloody German in the middle of a war against Germany. It was terrible for them.

When you touch on your marriages, there is no sense of happiness or romance conveyed. Is that because there was no happiness, or is it because the happiness has been erased from your memory?

There was nothing romantic about my first marriage; it was more comradely and friendly.

But was it happy?

Apart from the fact that I hated every minute of my life, yes.

Do you think you were just unsuited to marriage itself?

Well, later on it was a different matter altogether. I don't think I grew up emotionally until my thirties. I think I was suited to marriage then, but by that time it was quite difficult for any man to marry a woman like me.

Were your political affiliations principally a way of dealing with the injustice and the unsatisfactoriness of life, or was it more that they offered an escape?

Neither. What people forget is that everybody became a Communist then. I find this the most astonishing thing, that a whole epoch has disappeared and no one understands. My editor at HarperCollins asked how it was possible for me to become a Communist a few pages after I wrote that I was socially concerned. I do not have to explain to anyone of my generation in the West why I became a Communist. Everybody did. Indeed, there was a time when I never met anyone who wasn't a Communist.

But was it a kind of a fashion, or was it because you felt deeply about the injustices in the world?

Of course I felt deeply about the injustices of the world, but the reason why everybody became Communist then was because they saw Communism as a cure for everything.

In your autobiography you write of your Communist period saying, 'We were young and foolish then ... ' But you were so sucked in, so much part of the high-minded idealism ... was the pain of disillusionment not completely overwhelming?

No, but it took quite a long time to recover. Don't forget I wasn't one of those who were a thousand per cent Communist. For them it was terrible when Communism turned out badly; it ruined their lives, they committed suicide, God knows what they didn't do. But for me when it proved not to be what we thought it was, it was not a major blow.

You have said that you are no longer political. What do you think it would take to sustain belief in a political movement?

I take the view that we kid ourselves when we think we're in charge of our affairs; we just adapt and trot along like little dogs. It's different when there is a war or something terrible like that, but most of the time nothing happens in the way it was planned; everyone simply adjusts to events after they happen. I care very much that we make such a mess of things, but it doesn't matter a damn who I vote for. We always think that somebody is going to get in and change everything; well they can't, they're netted, they're surrounded by events they have to submit to. We're not at all masters of our destiny; we just make small adjustments here and there as we go along.

I was fascinated by your description of burgeoning sexuality in a young girl, the power of desire and so on, and also by your suggestion that a fourteen-year-old girl could benefit from initiation by an older man. Did you perhaps have this experience yourself?

No, but I wish I had had it. I should have been taken on by a man of about twenty-five, and I personally think it would have been very good for me, and probably for him, but of course our society is not set up for that. What happens is that all this raging sexuality of teenagers goes into ridiculous behaviour. We make a joke of it and say that adolescents are sex crazed; well, they *are* sex crazed, nearly all of them, but it's the most terrible suffering and waste of energy. And they do ridiculous things like getting pregnant or getting married too young, all this kind of thing.

You are very much aware of the way women are in the grip of powerful forces, the various natural cycles, as well as the need to have babies, the biological imperative … are you pleased to be free of all that?

I'm very glad I don't have to menstruate any more, for example, or that I don't have to think about whether or not I should have another baby. I take the view that women, from the time they have their first period until they are middle-aged, are powerfully in the grip of nature's desire that they should have babies. I don't think young women are taught enough about this. The best you can do is to be aware of it, and most women are, of course, but it's such a powerful thing. Young people are taught they are free, they can have choices, do what they like, and they're in control; well, they're not, particularly not if they are women.

Do you think that all can be explained in terms of biological imperative?

Not quite all. My latest novel looks for an explanation for falling in love when you're old, when it can have no possible biological use. I addressed the question, but I just don't know the answer. When you're young you think that you fall in love because it's time you got married or had another baby, but I'm wondering if we don't fall in love because of a terrible lack in ourselves, a yearning for something else completely. And the yearning for another human being isn't necessarily to do with that person; it could also be for another dimension in life.

You have made some very scathing remarks about feminism … is it doubly irritating that feminists often claim you as one of their own?

I don't mind that so much. It's more that they could have achieved so much and they haven't. That great burst of energy in the 1960s was so extraordinary, but most of it was completely wasted, frittered away, mostly in slanging each other. I find it extremely painful.

You have been quite preoccupied with the problem of evil which found expression in two of your most recent novels, The Fifth Child *and* The Good Terrorist. *Do you believe that evil is innate in human nature?*

Other people saw *The Fifth Child* as evil, I didn't. This creature was a genetic throwback and I was interested in him as someone who would be perfectly valid in the wrong context. About *The Good Terrorist*, I thought I was simply describing a certain kind of political animal of whom there are far too many, but it wasn't evil, it was just a terrible waste of everything. I don't like the word evil.

Your multiplicity of styles and genres has perplexed, sometimes enraged, your faithful readership. Is that something that you understand? For example, someone who is hooked on The Golden Notebook *is going to be somewhat fazed by five volumes of space fiction …*

I'm glad to say that some of my readers like both. There are of course people who like only the science fiction, and some who only like realism, but both seem to me to be very narrow minded actually.

Where do you stand now on the question of religion? Do you subscribe to any particular faith?

I don't like the organised religions much. I try to study Sufism, but of course the Sufis are not bound to any particular religion.

Do you believe in God?

That's a very interesting question … what god? The word god is loaded. I was listening to someone on the radio this morning saying that God is a very wicked person. Well, I think we could helpfully leave this word out for a while because it is so debased.

Reading your autobiography there are many important events, such as marriage, which are attributed to the Fates or to Mother Nature or to some uncontrollable power. This is difficult to reconcile with the young girl who chanted, 'I will not, I will not', against her parents … the girl who left school, left home, went to Salisbury to become a secretary and so on. How are they reconciled in your own mind?

That seems to me to be the great irony of the book. The young girl was always saying, 'I will not do this, I will not do that,' when in actual fact she was continually doing things that she didn't want to do. When I was a girl I said to myself I would not get married until I was much older. In fact, I married when I was not quite nineteen. Why? Because war was coming, and everyone was getting married. I was a little fish in a pond with a wave.

Much of your writing has been to do with different perspectives on insanity and mental breakdown. Is writing itself, the creative process, a form of madness?

It can trip over into madness, but mostly I don't think it's any more mad than anything else we do. I take the view that we are a pretty mad race, at least not very sane. Writing is a kind of way we have evolved to examine ourselves. I always say we never pay enough respect to literature for what it is, which is an extraordinary way of describing our lives. Without it we would know so much less about ourselves.

Many writers consider their art to be a way of dealing with the mad bad world, a way of imposing order on the chaos of living … does the same go for you, and have you been successful in your own terms?

I agree it is a way of trying to impose order, but whether I've been successful is another question. I'm always aware of how little I've done of what I wanted to do. But all writers are like that. They always say, oh my God, I could have done so much better. I am no different.

LADY MENUHIN

Born in Belgravia in 1912, Diana Gould joined Marie Rambert's ballet at the age of nine, and studied with her for ten years. When she was four-teen, she partnered Frederick Ashton, dancing the premiere of his first ballet, *Leda and the Swan*. Diaghilev invited her to join his company, but he died before that was possible and she was to dance with Pavlova's troupe, but Pavlova died before it got off the ground. She took leading roles with George Balanchine's company in London and Paris, but would not join him in New York in what was to become the New York City Ballet. When the Arts Theatre Ballet was formed in 1940, she became its leading dancer, and she performed in London throughout World War II. She met Yehudi Menuhin in 1944, though they did not marry till 1947. She died in 2003.

Lady Menuhin, it is sometimes difficult to remember that there must have been life before Yehudi. Do you see your life very much in terms of Before and After?

Very much, because first of all I was a born believer. It sounds rather conceited to say this, but I was very much a metaphysical child, and I used to hear voices. I'm perfectly sure that I was born before, somewhere in central Europe, perhaps in Tashkent. I've certainly got a Byzantine face. One of the things Yehudi and I have in common is that we both were born knowing exactly what we wanted to do. It wasn't ambition; it was aspiration, which is something quite different. His was the talent of a genius, but mine was not a bad talent considering that out of all the dancers in England I was chosen by Diaghilev when I was fourteen years old, and by Pavlova when I was nearly sixteen.

Unfortunately, I had a black fairy at my baptism, and they both died, Diaghilev one month before I was to join him and Pavlova ten days before I was to dance with her. Thank goodness that fairy doesn't follow me when I'm working for Yehudi, which I've done for the last 45 years.

As a child I used to be able to get outside myself. The only place of privacy for an English child in a household with nannies is the loo, and so when I had the longing to escape I used to go there, close the door and lock it. The loo, like all those in England in the 1920s, had a black and white chequerboard floor, and as

I sat there and concentrated, the floor would rise up, and I would swing round with a terrible feeling in my heart, and I could see myself sitting there. And then I would have this shock, and come back again as myself.

At that age one hadn't heard anything about meditation; on the other hand, my mother was a Christian Scientist, and we were all brought up in that religion, which gives you an enduring disposition at the price of a ruined constitution. If you're born into it as I was, you know exactly how to switch off, but you do grow up without any sense of reality. The concrete, as one might call it, simply isn't there. When people used to wonder how I could tour with Yehudi all the time I was pregnant and drop the baby wherever the violin was on the ninth month, I used to tell them that was the way I was brought up, never allowed to complain about anything physical. It gives you an extraordinary way of being able to separate yourself from what seems actual. On the other hand, it separates you from what is actual and you always feel slightly apart, which if you're going to go into a career like the ballet isn't very helpful.

I was brought up with three disciplines: my mother's Edwardianism, which meant only the servants got toothache, the Christian Science religion in which toothache didn't exist, and the Russian ballet where if you dared admit to illness your role went to another girl. These three solid disciplines have been very serviceable for life with darling Yehudi, who prefers to live on cloud nine, which he seems to have rented for the whole of his life.

Your childhood seems to have been characterised by a struggle against difficulties and disappointments. Do you remember it as a time you survived rather than enjoyed?

This is what I ask myself. All my life I've talked to myself, actually not to myself, but to God with whom I have been furious most of the time. I was quite a different child from my brother and sister. They were the intellectuals, both blond and blue eyed; my brother called me 'battling Gould, the wild half-caste', because I rushed around the whole time while they were cool and clever. I was a romantic, passionate, wild creature who was slowly beaten into English diffidence. It was the only way to keep out of trouble from nanny and from my mother, who was not cruel, just gloriously indifferent. Like my mother I'm an absolute professional, only I haven't acted or danced since I married Yehudi, whereas my mother remained centre stage all her life. When you marry somebody like Yehudi, there's no question of being centre stage; in fact, I don't think anybody even recognises me. When he was still conducting a great deal, I was always in a corner of the dressing room putting the cap back on the thermos, and picking up his damp clothes. But I haven't answered your question, have I? Michael Redgrave used to say of me that I had a mind like a crab; it always goes sideways, and it's perfectly true.

We were talking about your childhood ... whether it was happy or not ...

What is a happy childhood? You can always complain, you can always blame your own mistakes and shortcomings on the rocking horse which frightened you when you were two, but what's the point? We were brought up in the most marvellous way. The English mother of that period was still someone who came to the night nursery dressed beautifully to go out in the evening and just said 'Goodbye darling'. When my father died we were left with practically no money, but we had a lovely house with beautiful furniture and £800 a year. It was the most wonderful upbringing, because we had beautiful things around us, and although there was not a penny of pocket money and we lived on bananas off the barrows, it was with style. I think this is what I miss very much these days – style and grace hardly exist anymore, and wit has become bitchiness and spite. Style is now called snobbism, and grace has dissolved. I feel quite alien to this world, and it is a feeling I passed on to my children. For example, I remember when my third child survived for only an hour or two because of all the touring when I was pregnant, and nanny brought Yehudi and the children to my bedroom. We told the boys that there wouldn't after all be another baby and my elder son, Gerald, who was six at the time, suddenly said: 'I don't believe in death, I believe in a circle of lives.' Yehudi asked him if he thought this was his first life and he said, 'Oh no, I used to think that I would come back in the next world, or had been in the last one – I was a tree, an animal, anything – but now I know that I always have been and always will be a humour being' – 'humour' being the nearest he got at six to 'human'. So he had, even in those days, the same faculties I had as a child.

Presumably you have very little memory of your father, who died when you were very young. Do you have any recollection of the impact his death made on your mother?

Yes. It had the effect of making her withdraw even further. I don't know that she would ever have been a very warm woman. She was enchanting, and I know that she helped dozens of young musicians with their careers, but in the home, you couldn't say that she was an affectionate mother. I remember the exact time when I stopped kissing her. I was always very spontaneous, unlike Grizelda and Gerard who were self-contained, and I would rush into the room and fling my arms round mother. Once when I did this she said, 'Oh, Diana, really, you've broken my watch chain.' I was eight years old and I never ran and hugged her again.

There is usually a special bond between fathers and daughters. Was your stepfather ever able to fill that role?

I was very fond of him. Grizelda and Gerard were not, because he was very navy blue, a real sailor. He was away all the time at sea, but I always got on with him because I didn't categorise people. When you grow up in the ballet world from the time you're eight years old, you meet every kind of person. My stepfather was a simple straightforward utterly good man, and worshiped my mother absolutely. She had that extraordinary and enviable capacity to make men worship her, although my stepfather apparently said to Harold Nicolson, 'Sexually, my little wife is an umbrella rolled up.'

You describe the 'total dislocation' you felt when your mother died in 1950 – this is in spite of the fact that you had never been particularly close. Do you think you were in part grieving for something you had never experienced in her lifetime?

I had so many awful things happen in my life, like Diaghilev and Pavlova dying, and a cruel ballet mistress who picked me out as a special victim, that I seemed to grow up with very little love, and had this strange fatalistic attitude that I couldn't expect love. You may be right about my mother, but I didn't analyse until it was too late.

In the context of your mother's death you described the huge gulf which had opened up between your total commitment to Yehudi and the previous life which you had abjured on marriage. Were you able to reconcile the two in your own mind, or were you forever going to find it difficult to look back and come to terms with your past life?

I've always looked upon love as service. To me the two have been together ever since I can remember. Secondly, everything in my life has been a challenge. When I met Yehudi, my metaphysical attitude to life made me realise that he was my destiny. He fell in love with me, and I was in love with him, but as he was married with two small children I never told him. It took two and a half really terrible years for him to get his divorce, because he is so angelic that he can't hurt anybody, even if he knows he was not to blame for his first mistake. I may have been his second mistake, but he hasn't found out yet.

The ballet conjures up images of beauty, elegance and glamour and one forgets that it can be a gruelling, almost masochistic world of hard slog and bleeding feet. What attracted you in the first place to the world of dance and what made you determined to stick it out?

Because I never give up anything, and because I had to do something about the music inside me. I went to the Ballet Rambert for ten awful years. I came back, cried into my pillow every night, but accepted my fate, because there was a kind of terrible endurance taught in the religion I was brought up in, and the feeling of always being separate.

When you look back, were the rewards commensurate with the effort and applications required?

Always the rewards came and then fizzled out. I was chosen by Diaghilev, so what greater compliment could there have been? It was absolutely wonderful, I can see it to this day. He stood in the doorway watching us dance, and I didn't even realise after an hour and a half that I was the only one in the class still dancing, the others had all gone. And then he turned to Rambert and said, 'la belle jeune fille ... ', and he was angelic to me for those ten days in which the ballet was there. I had seats every night and went with either Rambert or mummy to see the show, and he would come out of the pass door and take me by the hand and lead me backstage and introduce me to all the great dancers of that period. He designated someone to look after me and be my guide, in exactly the same way as happened to Markova about two or three years before me, but Markova didn't have a black fairy at her back.

Were you very popular with men generally?

I was known as 'the goddess' but it wasn't until I was in my mid-twenties that I suddenly woke up sexually. I was the oldest virgin on the stage in London, because I couldn't possibly have gone to bed for anything but love.

Was your first love affair with Yehudi?

Oh Lord no. He was the twelfth aspirant that year. I used to call myself a Foreign Office moll, because I had six proposals from young secretaries in the Foreign office. I don't know to this day whether if I were born again I would be the same, but I simply couldn't bring myself to go to bed with Alexander Korda, with Gilbert Miller, with Charles Cochrane, or even with attractive men like Massine and Balanchine. When you're brought up as asexually and primly as I was, when you live in a period where the contraceptive is very uncertain, and when you're an incurable romantic, it's easy to be revolted by having your dress torn off by Mr. Korda, as he was then, or by the others; but even with men like Massine or Balanchine, it would have been the wrong thing. I would only go to bed with a man I loved, and I fell hook, line, and sinker for a man who was a total monster but a wonderful lover, and of course when it was over I suffered all the agonies of a mature woman plus the silliness of somebody completely unpractised. He was a stallion who had to seduce every beautiful woman – it sounds conceited, but I did win beauty prizes. Everybody said they'd never known him stay with a woman as long as he stayed with me, but in the end he just threw me out, which is a terrible blow to one's pride, especially if you go into the relationship as a virgin.

Your account of the war years in London sounds impossibly romantic. You continued to dance, and the bomb which fell on your house during the blitz is described as 'an irritation'. You must surely have experienced things differently at the time?

What I'm going to say is going to sound utterly callous, but I am intensely dramatic, and I was known by my sister as 'the tragic fuse'. I was nearly killed in the bombing three times, and each time I was only furious, not in the least frightened. I couldn't call myself brave, but I actually enjoyed drama. I'm not saying I enjoyed the war, but I didn't suffer from fear.

In 1944 you went to Cairo and Alexandria which you described as 'blissful'. Was it possible to forget the war when you were there?

No, because the place was full of soldiers on leave, and although the war was almost over, nonetheless it was still going on. What I meant by bliss was getting away from dried eggs and not having to queue up for one orange. I had a Zulkeika Dobson time. I did Frou Frou in *The Merry Widow*, rewriting the whole script in gutter French, and because the other language of the Egyptians is French, it literally stopped the house. I was sent for by Farouk in the royal box after the first night, and he asked me out for supper, but I backed away and said, 'Je m'excuse', and disappeared.

When you left Egypt you say you wept for the lover you left behind …

Yes, I had my *coup de foudre* in Egypt. He was an English poet. There were a lot of poets there, because they were either not serviceable as soldiers or they were conscientious objectors. This particular one had gone to the Quaker ambulance service in Syria. He was asked to stay on at the embassy in Athens because he wrote the ambassador's speeches, but he wouldn't dream of it, and said he would not get out of killing people to have an easy life, so he went to drive ambulances instead. The *coup de foudre* is something you don't know anything about; it comes right out of the blue.

You have described your love for Yehudi as 'service in the highest sense', and have said many times how very lucky you are to have married someone you could serve. The notion of service seems to include the idea of one person being subservient or subordinate to the other, rather than the idea of a partnership, but perhaps you don't see it that way …

I think that's a good point, but my infinite capacity for turning away from any kind of analysis of myself would make that difficult to answer. Sometimes when Yehudi was playing in the theatre, I would go backstage to the dressing room and when I saw the fourth wall, as we call it, the blackened theatre, then my heart would give a turn. There I was, no longer coming out centre stage, no longer embracing the public, no longer giving what I had to give; but then I would remember the bleeding toes, the glass in my powder and the tin tacks in my shoes, the intrigues and horrors, the disappointments, the exhaustion, the lack of pay, and all of that was enough to stop me being sentimental. I have a capacity to undertake whatever the job is, and that's why diplomats fell in love with me. But I never really analysed. Harold Nicolson said that what kept the English from succeeding in anything other than literature were all those upper-class shibboleths such as don't advertise yourself, don't boast, die with your boots on, stiff upper lip, and so on. They are so automatic in my generation that you immediately close up when other thoughts occur to you. I've always been a worker: my sister Grizelda used to say that whenever Diana has nothing to do she spills soup down her clothes and cleans them. I'm an incurable, incorrigible worker. I think that's what Yehudi liked so much, and he recognised with great relief that we had a tremendous amount in common, that we'd both had aspirations since we were born; that I had enormous experience because I hadn't been protected by wonderful parents who had given up everything for me. He remains to this day the most incredibly modest man, and I think that's what the audience feels. Yehudi's a medium … the music comes through him; he feels a responsibility to the composer, dead or alive. He was very sad and very lonely when I met him, because his marriage had really broken up, and Yehudi wouldn't admit it; and if he had admitted it he would have blamed himself. Yehudi never blames anybody else, ever, for anything. But he told me that when he first saw me at my mother's house, he went away to sit on a pouffe at the end of the drawing room and thought, 'I am going to have her.' I said, 'Don't be ridiculous, it was your daughter's fifth birthday.' For I didn't know then that the marriage was already no good, but Yehudi has a way of knowing what he wants, and he gets it.

You married on October 1947, a day on which you said 'the dark years finally fell away' – a reference to the difficulties of the break-up of Yehudi's first marriage. Did those years continue to haunt you after you were married?

I didn't let them. Now, in old age, however, it comes back more and I wonder how in the world I stood those two and a half ghastly years; I won't talk about all I went through, but it was total agony. One of the men who was in love with me at one time said, 'You will always be badly used by men; we will always fall in love with you, and we will always use you.' I was then about 23.

Did you feel used by Yehudi?

I wanted to be used by him. I can't feel that one has any right not to help. I'd love him to have more rest, I'd love him not to become an institution, but it is Yehudi, so what can I do? All I can do is to help, to have very little life of my own, no social life whatsoever. I even read the newspapers in order to be able to regurgitate like a mother eagle for Yehudi. Any energy I have left I use for resting, and I would like him now not to do everything at high speed.

In your autobiography you say: 'the blackness and bleakness of stolen love are private pain, and were to be transmuted into a love the more sensitive and valuable for its near loss.' You must have agonised a great deal before your marriage. Did you ever doubt it was the right thing to do?

No. I knew, just as I knew that whatever it cost I was going to dance. I never lost faith, however many terrible disappointments and cruelties I had to endure. I never raised a finger to help him get rid of his first wife. I never told him I was in love with him, because I didn't want him to feel any obligation towards me. Of course, he knew, but I never said it, and when he told his wife about me and mentioned the word marriage, she just said no, although she had god knows how many lovers herself. And Yehudi, who is utterly good and sweet, but can also lack a certain will, blamed himself for everything.

In an interview, your husband spoke of his 'reprehensible behaviour ... bordering on the criminal' during these two years when he was separating from his first wife. It seemed as if he carried a terrible burden of guilt. Did you share in that guilt?

No. Yehudi had two visits here, one in the spring when he was doing a film. That was when he fell in love with me, and we had these marvellous talks together about what it was like to be born with an aspiration; what it was like to know that you simply had no other life but that. Then the first fine careless rapture suddenly becomes a conscious one. He came back in the winter of '45 and rang me up suddenly and said, 'Will you marry me?' I said, 'You're mad, Yehudi, never let me hear you use that word again – you're already married, and you have two small children.' But I was in love with him, the way I'd hoped to be in love ever since I can remember. I hadn't met his wife, though I had heard rumours about her behaviour and of course I'd seen the results in him. He was completely broken by it and had even decided he would give up playing the violin. I agonised about what to do. I remember saying to him – we spoke mostly in French those days – 'Yahudi, j'ai peur'. Finally his wife told him that he had to stay with her and the children. It trailed on and on with her promising divorce and then breaking her promise over and over again. Then, thank God, one day she realised that from a practical point of view it would be better for her to marry whichever lover she had at that time, and so after two years she let Yehudi go.

Yehudi was attacked in the Jewish press for marrying outside the faith … was that an added pressure on you at the time?

Oh no, I didn't bother about that. In any case the whole of that cabal was not because he'd married a gentile, but because he had insisted upon going to Germany. He has incredible courage, Yehudi, immense courage. He went to Germany and played night and day for every cause, Jewish and German. When we were there we heard that Furtwängler had had to run away in the middle of the night because the Gestapo had come for him. He had done nothing except get on with his job and stay in the country. I knew Furtwängler because my mother had a musical salon to which every musician in the world came, and Furtwängler would have lunch with mummy when he was over to conduct the opera, but Yehudi had never even met him. Furtwängler was decent and had helped Jewish members of the orchestra to get to America. He also wrote very dangerous letters to my sister from Denmark. He was mad about her, adored blondes, and he wrote: 'When I think I am writing from this country, occupied by my people, it makes me ill.' One night his friends came to him and said, 'Run, because the Gestapo is coming for you,' and he escaped at night with his second wife, the lovely Lizavet. Yehudi was told that the Americans wouldn't give Furtwängler his purification trial, so Yehudi sent off a two-page telegram to America – Yehudi's telegrams are full of notwithstandings and neverthelesses – saying it was a disgrace to the Americans that they hadn't at least given him the chance to clear his name. Furtwängler got his purification trial, he passed 100% clean, but of course you can imagine what the cabal in New York did about it: the ones who were jealous of Yehudi were heard to say, 'At least we've got Menuhin.' So the press attacks were not really because he had married a gentile but because he had defended a German.

What has been your attitude over the years to the vexed Jewish question and the complexities of Yehudi being a famous son of Israel? Have you influenced his own attitude in this regard?

Influence is a word I don't like. I have counselled. I've lived in a far broader world than he has. Before Hitler one didn't analyse Jewishness or non-Jewishness. For example, I realised only afterwards that many of the musicians who came to my mother's house were Jews, but to me they were Russian, or Hungarian, or German, or Austrian. Until the time of the Hitler incitement, one wasn't Jewish conscious. On Mummy's Sundays when sometimes 100 people would be there, I remember once an Englishman putting a small Union Jack in the middle of the drawing-room floor, just to remind people that this was England, because every language could be heard there. I had a very broad spectrum, but it was different for Yehudi. His father had sensibly taken him away from Europe when Hitler came to power, but his American experience was very limited because his parents simply didn't go out anywhere.

Your father-in-law was an outspoken critic of Israel, a man who extolled his universalism and humanity rather than his Jewishness. Did this ever make for tension between father and son, or create difficulties in Yehudi's public life?

That's a complex question. When I first married Yehudi he was more or less estranged from his family because they very foolishly condemned his first wife, the last thing to do to a man who refuses to condemn anybody. So when I first went out to California I told Yehudi that no Jew was ever separated or estranged from his family, above all from his mother, and I persuaded him that we should go and visit them. Abba loved America because he felt he could trust the people; everywhere else in the world he thought everyone was cheating him. Mamina is a completely emancipated Jewess, totally and absolutely Russian, though she speaks six languages beautifully. When Yehudi made his incredible debut at the age of 9 and 10, all the Jewish community in New York naturally wanted to claim him as their star. She held them off, which led to the feeling among the Jewish community that she didn't want to have anything to do with them. Abba was an inspector of Hebrew schools, but they didn't often go to synagogues, and Yehudi was brought up with no sense of what is kosher; there was nothing kosher at home at all. So there was no question of their being ritual Jews. She would never touch Yiddish, and in fact spoke good German, which laid the foundation for Yehudi's assertion that his entire culture came from Germany and Austria.

After that the Jews saw their opportunity to murder him. Yehudi's father was only anti-Israel because he had divided loyalties. He was very proud to be American, yet he was of course a Jew, the grandson of a rabbi. When they first went to look for rooms in New Jersey when their baby was about to be born, they found a very nice landlady who must have found them an attractive pair – Abba was extremely handsome, blue eyes, blond hair, and Mamina was quite incredibly beautiful with golden hair she could sit on and Tartar blue eyes. As they left, the landlady said, 'Well, I'm very glad to have you two young things, because I simply hate Jews, and I won't have them here,' whereupon Mamina turned and said, 'Well, you won't be having us because we are both Jews.' And as they walked away, she tapped her tummy where Yehudi was prenatally stored and said, 'This child is going to be called Yehudi, the Jew.' And yet that was the last Jewish gesture she made.

For Abba, the greatest thing on earth was his American passport; it made him feel that he was somebody, because Mamina certainly didn't make him feel that. Zionism threatened to break apart the feeling of being an American; it was going to demand a dual loyalty, so he joined the Philadelphia lot, a group of very distinguished Jews. It was called the American Council of Judaism, and it was made up of all those first and second-generation Americans who felt that it was terrible to be asked to be less than 100% loyal to their American naturalisation; and this was the basis of his anti-Zionism. Secondly, the Menuhins were Jews who had never suffered. Abba didn't know how important it was for the Jews to have a homeland. I talked to them and explained what it must have been like to have been a Jew in Europe. I had lived amongst it all. The Menuhins didn't know how necessary it was for the Jews to try to escape the pogroms; they had never been through a pogrom.

It's true, isn't it, that Yehudi was very pro-Israel in the sense that he couldn't see anything wrong with whatever the Israelis did ...

Yehudi was not really pro-Israel. He hated militant Zionism, yet he realised the necessity for a land for the Jews, while at the same time refused to talk about it. Yehudi was not one of your pro-Israelis at all, and that is why they tried to kill us when we first went to Israel. With a certain amount of counselling from me he realised that something had to be done about the Jews, what was left of them, but he never wanted to be a militant Zionist. He played at concerts to raise money for the Jewish fund of course ... that was the least he could do. But because we had already been to Germany, there followed a period of Jews being told to boycott his concerts. His concerts were always sold out, but only gentiles were sitting in Carnegie Hall. The Jews were told by all the Jewish newspapers to send their tickets back too late to have them resold, and that Menuhin was anti-Israel. It wasn't true. He was only anti the militancy which was being shouted from the rooftops.

He went everywhere where the Jews had really suffered, where they had been taken out and burned. He even gave a concert in Berlin for the displaced persons camp. Unless you've seen what had befallen those wretched Jews who had survived, what was done to them by the Germans, you wouldn't believe it. They came crowding round the car in a wave of hate such as you've never seen. The military police accompanied us into the hall where people were literally hanging on to the pillars, and the howl of rage was really quite terrifying. But Yehudi has a radiance that makes people suddenly understand what he is trying to be. He got up on to the platform, with a huge policeman each side. There was an *agent provocateur* with a club foot, and he was trying to incite the crowd even more. Yehudi said, 'Let me speak, let me speak.' And he spoke to them in excellent German, telling them that Jews did not go begging to others because they had been maltreated – 'We are a great race and nothing can extinguish us.' Then they clapped, they applauded, they said, 'Yehudi, Yehudi, you are wonderful … ' He changed the whole mood of the crowd and when the *agent provocateur* got up, he was booed. When we left people were crowding round the car, saying, 'Yehudi, please come and play to us again, please.' It was the most moving thing you can imagine. Yehudi hates talking about this and he may be angry with me if this comes out, but it was a wonderful moment in his life.

Did you get on well with Moshe Menuhin? I couldn't help noticing that in his book of some 250 pages, you are mentioned by name only twice, and in your own book he does not feature very prominently.

I'll tell you why that is. Firstly, in my own book I was allowed only 200 pages to write this palimpsest of a life. Secondly, the reason for my not featuring in Abba's book is that I didn't realise that by marrying Yehudi I had displaced Abba. I didn't even take it in, because I don't think of myself particularly. Abba did everything for Yehudi, went through all his bank accounts, and so on, but when we married I told Yehudi that he had to be independent, he had to have his own lawyer, his own financial advisers. Yehudi didn't even have stocks and shares; all the money was put into bonds, and although I don't know much about finances, I felt it was better if he managed his own. I didn't realise that this was doing Abba out of the one job he passionately loved; all his energy had gone into being Yehudi's chartered accountant, Yehudi's lawyer, Yehudi's everything.

Your childbearing years were fraught with difficulties … two live children out of five pregnancies. How did you cope with the cumulative grief of the miscarriages and the baby who died?

Again, I coped for Yehudi's sake, because I didn't want to make him feel guilty for having let me stay with him under all circumstances. Yehudi doesn't analyse at all, and with my upbringing it never occurred to me not to accept illness, even death, as long as you were doing what was right, which was to keep by Yehudi's side. As time went on it was difficult with the children too. They resented my being so much with their father and so comparatively little with them. Every time I came back from a tour, I spent every day with them, never taking a rest; I read to them, took them for walks, but I did have to put up with being a scapegoat, the aunt sally at the fair whenever there was a coconut to be shied. I used to ask the children if they would rather have a father who put his bowler hat on in the morning and took his umbrella and went off to the office at 9 and came back at 6 and read the evening paper; or would they rather have their father, an extraordinary and complex man. I also told them, 'This man does not belong to me either, darlings … he belongs to the world.'

Do the children consider themselves Jewish?

I don't think they consider themselves anything. You know what children are like nowadays … they're secular, and of course, when children are in trouble these days, they turn to the psychiatrist.

People are naturally suspicious of perfection and undiluted harmony within marriage. Has that been difficult to deal with?

As I told you, I've always kept in the background. No one knows I am Yehudi's wife. I know my place, as the English servant says. We have practically no social life. We work very hard. I help with Yehudi's huge correspondence, help edit his articles because Yehudi never went to school and never got the blue pencil through his schoolwork. We think alike although we have, thank God, enormous arguments, usually about certain things that he either is going to write or has written. Sometimes I win, and sometimes I don't, but I couldn't bear a sort of sugary marriage.

Yehudi is a genius; he's adored and worshipped by his followers almost like a pop star. Have you ever been jealous? A man like Yehudi must attract women …

First of all, Yehudi is of such an extraordinary quality that the attraction to him is semi-religious. He doesn't present himself as a sexual object, and that is the difference between a pop idol and Yehudi. I myself have had many lovers – I'm not saying that I've slept with them all – but he's had nothing other than one collapsed marriage. I must be ready to take it if it happens to him late in life, if he falls for someone. He won't seek it at all, because we have such a full life, and we have so much in common. In the past there have been one or two – not that he had affairs with them – but they were all extremely gifted women who were not in any way trashy, to whom, in his wonderful way, Yehudi did respond. And it gave him something. They were what the French call *amitiés amoureuses*. And I did my best to be understanding; if I felt at all displaced, I reasoned with myself that it could have happened in a really horrid way and didn't; and that Yehudi was getting something out of this relationship. And why shouldn't he have it? Why should I be mean? I've never been mean in my life.

When I spoke to you ten years ago, on the subject of fidelity in marriage, you said, 'I think infidelity can be carried out with great love and sweetness, that it often refreshes a marriage when one or the other has some little affair, and feels just enough guilt and shame to love the other more.' Was that a generalisation, or was it something you had both worked out in terms of your own relationship?

What I said, I still stand by, but since I married Yehudi, there's been no time or place for me to have an *amitié amoureuses*, and I'm not likely to have one now.

The sacrifice you have made for the sake of Yehudi in terms of career, family life, privacy and so on, has been enormous, and although it has been willingly and lovingly made, without a doubt, I somehow have the impression that you maintain this in part because you dare not contemplate anything which would destroy your image of perfect harmony nurtured over the years. Is there any element of that, do you think?

If you do it *chemin faisant*, as the French say, then you don't suddenly have to make a great effort in later life. Yehudi just goes blindly on his flight, playing too much, conducting too much, working too much or undertaking too much, while I constantly, like a good yachtsman, change the sails to catch the wind so that the boat doesn't capsize. The question of harmony is something I've put a certain amount into all the way along, when, for example, it was necessary for him to enjoy the homage of some woman. I wanted to give up my life because to me being with Yehudi is the natural prolongation of what my ballet career meant to me. I don't mean to say that marriage is a career in that common sense, but it is in a way.

If I may pursue this question of sacrifice … when I interviewed your husband in 1989 he said of you that you had an extreme Protestant sense of not giving yourself pleasure, a feeling that you could never indulge yourself. He described it as a kind of self-denial and said, 'As soon as anything can be turned into obligation or duty, she'll do it straight away.' Have you ever tried to analyse these impulses in yourself?

Yes. My darling stepdaughter who ran away from her mother to me when she was 12, said to me, 'Diney, you've simply got to lose a little pride and a little control. It's inhuman.' And I said, 'No, I daren't, I simply daren't … and anyway it's too late.' I sometimes think of my crazy side, the dotty side, when everything was ghastly and we were underfed and underpaid; I was 16, 17, and Freddie Ashton was 22, and we would do a comic act between the two shows, the matinée and the evening. I would be the male partner and he would put on my shoes and be Anna Pavlova, and I was known as the funniest dancer when I did that … I have sometimes blamed Yehudi for not giving me the opportunity to be my old wild self. And that I do miss.

Looking back on your life now, are there any unresolved difficulties or regrets?

Regrets that I wasn't the dancer that I hoped to be when Diaghilev chose me, and Pavlova chose me … that, yes, of course. The original expression of my own self was denied. That's why, when Weidenfeld asked me to write a book, I thought, I must take care, because I think I'm feeling dried out, and I'm determined never to be bitter. I was once very much a person, I was somebody in my own right; and I gave up every talent I had to looking after Yehudi, tidying up the awful mess I found him in, poor lamb …

Sir Yehudi Menuhin

Yehudi Menuhin was born in New York in 1916 of Russian Jewish parents. He and his musically gifted sisters were educated by private tutors. He made his debut in San Francisco at the age of seven, in Paris aged ten, in New York aged eleven and in Berlin aged thirteen. Following his early successes, he played with most of the world's orchestras and conductors and received numerous awards and honours, including peace prizes. During the war he played nearly 500 benefit concerts for the Red Cross. His first marriage was dissolved in 1938 and two years after the war he married Diana Gould. In 1963 he founded the Menuhin School of Music in Surrey. In 1965 he became a KBE and in 1985 he adopted British nationality, two years before he received the Order of Merit. He was awarded the Wolf Prize in Arts by Israel in 1991, and became a life peer in 1993. His recording contract with EMI is the longest in the history of the music industry, his final recording having been made aged eighty-two, in 1999, the year he died.

Albert Einstein said when he heard you play as a young boy, 'Now I know there is a God in heaven.' Where you aware of the extraordinary nature of your talent?

I'm still not aware of it, and I become less and less aware of it as I listen to very remarkable talented children who play beautifully, and then hear of others who rob banks at the age of eleven, others who tap into computers at the age of twelve and learn the secrets of the Pentagon, and others who storm into Tiananmen Square and are ready to be immolated for their peaceful purposes. I feel more and more that I'm one of a great many people, almost one of a great many young people, and at the age of seventy-three that is probably a permissible illusion. When I was a child I felt absolutely normal and resented any allusion to wunderkinder and prodigies. I hated it and I think I was right then and am right now. No doubt I played beautifully and had deep feeling, but Einstein was a man who was very impulsive, very emotional, and he could have said the same thing about his own remarkable intuitive discovery of the oneness of the universe. Anyone who looks on an insect or a flower could say there is a God within us and we are a part of that God.

I am indebted to the quality of my parents and my teachers, and their high-mindedness. There was never any talk of money in the house, no vulgarity; always high purpose, good literature and poetry and a great deal of fun. I was spared all the preoccupations with violence, or with sex, or with the unhealthy worries and frustrations that many people have to live under; the bad air, the sidewalks they have to walk on, the ugliness they are surrounded by. I feel therefore fortunate and grateful. I believe firmly that children bring a great deal into the world that they then forget. Learning is a process of forgetting. It sounds a paradox, but none the less, as we learn to live in the world, we forget that intangible quality we brought with us when we were born. People are conditioned by their prenatal stage.

I know that my mother was looking forward to having me and was very happy, and very much in love with my father, during the time she carried me. I was therefore surrounded by love, appreciation, warmth, health and trust, as well as encouragement to follow in the good ideals of unity. I remember, as a child, being disturbed when I saw the exhaust coming out of cars, because I knew instinctively that there was a unity in the world, that whatever came had to go, that whatever was burnt was transformed into something else. All these philosophical questions preoccupied me. One of my earliest dreams was to bring peace to the world; I imagined that if I played well enough it would happen. I will probably play in the Sistine Chapel next year some time, but it won't bring peace to the world.

The real demands that were made on me in my childhood were qualitative and organised. My mother impressed upon me that, if I were serious about the violin, I would have to work a certain number of hours each day. I worked early so that I could go out in the late-morning sun and walk, run and play tennis. After lunch and sleep, I worked again. The public did not see the demands. What they saw were the fruits of the demands, which were the joy of making progress and playing, of expressing oneself. There is nothing like music to give a person overall coordination. It asks everything from the mind and from the coordination of the body from the fingers to the eyes. Everything is involved, and when you use everything, everything falls into place. It's when you use only a part of yourself, like sitting in the office and concentrating on one thing, that you have to compensate with other activities, but playing an instrument or conducting is, in fact, as near a complete activity – physical, mental, emotional and spiritual – as you can have, and in that respect it keeps one in good condition, unless one abuses it.

I was also lucky since children who pursue a career often leave the parental nest early and have to fend for themselves, but I don't think any child in the world can have seen more of both parents than my sisters and I did. Of course, they had their frictions because they were totally different characters. My father was very emotional and deeply moral and felt for the whole of humanity. My mother was very maternal and felt for her own children first, then for others. She was highly disciplined and a remarkably strong character. So they had their differences from time to time, which resulted in sadness, for you always want your parents to be happy together – as they mostly were.

When we went to France in 1927, my father took a leave of absence from his school and had to decide, after three months, whether or not he'd go back. It was a major decision: either he cut himself off from any further income, and could be with the family, or he abandoned his wife and three children in Paris and went back to earning his $300 a month. He took the right decision, which was to remain with the family. On our return to San Francisco we were self-supporting. In those days there was no income tax in America and prices were reasonable, and when we returned I gave a concert at the Civic Auditorium that earned enough to keep us all for a year and a half.

There are, it follows, always penalties to pay. The sort of life I have been describing has its own inbuilt penalty, which is that the children don't have experience of the outer world. We travelled so much that of course the outer world did penetrate quite a lot, but it was always kept at a certain distance from the family, which meanwhile maintained its routine. When we were seven, eight and nine years old or thereabouts, we would go every day at eleven o'clock to the park in San Francisco. Later on, when we were in Sydney or Melbourne for a month, we would go to the Botanical Gardens every day at the same time and feed the swans and walk or run around. But that was when I was nineteen, so the routine had gone on unbroken for twelve to fourteen years.

The concerts were always in the evening, so they didn't interrupt the day. Any tribute or adulation from the public was also kept at arm's length, although I would be aware that the concerts were sold out. My father looked after the business interests and the rest of the family life on tour. Later it took me a long time to get accustomed to dealing independently with people on a one-to-one basis, for we had never been to school to receive a formal education, though my mother saw to it that we had wonderful tutors. And when you spend your life with Mozart and Beethoven, Bach and Schumann and Brahms, you are living with great minds. It is a privilege given to very few people, for the great composers are those whose works convince the interpreter of the great and good truths, eternal and immutable, recognised in the proportion and structure of their works.

When you hear your first recording of the Elgar Violin Concerto, conducted by the composer himself, do you see it as the definitive performance?

No, I don't. Rarely, if ever, do I consider any musical performance a definitive one. It can never be nearer or farther from the absolute truth, but music is a live substance, and even today performances in the recording studio can still be 'live' if you play the whole work, or a whole movement, through, for even today retouching is not always feasible in many cases. When I listen to that recording of the Elgar, I enjoy it, and I have listened to it perhaps twice or three times since I made it. I always feel it is a beautiful recording. It has the ardour of youth; it has deep feeling; it has the authority of the composer himself; and it has the historical uniqueness of the fact it was done with the composer. Therefore I am very moved by it. Naturally I can imagine certain things I could do better or differently. But it doesn't matter; it's beautiful.

It is true that, when I came to my early thirties, I had to rebuild consciously the techniques which up till then had been unconscious. It happens with everybody. For instance, you can speak a language that you know well without thinking of the grammar, and you can grow up speaking it well depending on who you've heard speak it. It's what Suzuki, the Japanese violin teacher, calls the 'mother-tongue method': imitation and repetition, by ear and by sight. Then, as soon as your mind is awake, you fall from grace, you leave the Garden of Eden, you begin to be responsible for your own actions. What you first knew you later have to understand, and you must find the path to natural knowing, and it may take years. I've traversed every minute section of that path. I could play beautifully as a child, then I had to learn what it was I was doing, and sometimes, at certain periods of my life, I lost some of that original spontaneity. Now I have it absolutely, because I just feel a piece of music. I know it, can judge it, can seize it much more quickly, and one of the great things is that I can teach, which I maybe wouldn't have been able to do had I gone on as an instinctive violinist.

It often seems difficult to relate music to moral, social or even symbolic values.

It depends on the music. There are as many different kinds of music as there are kinds of literature. You can have moral music. For instance, I have just done the Brahms *Requiem* in Hamburg where it has been done every year for ninety-two years in the church where Brahms was baptised. It was a real service and one of the most moving things. No applause. People know the words, know the music and are cleansed after it. It is like an emotional purge.

Then you have music which is entertaining, music which is brilliant, music which is music to dance to or eat to, and music which is more intellectual. Certain of the last works of Beethoven are very intellectual. All the different types of music each speak of the life of a people, or of a period. Through music we can relive the very same feelings and thoughts that the composer had wherever he was living, and we can know his society. We know the courtesies of the court in Mozart's days from his music, and we can feel with him how even tragic things were presented in a way that wouldn't shock the perfection of the elegance and so on. Music is remarkable in that respect because it's an art of time, and during the time it takes to play, it's like a life. You live through it.

There has never been a people, a society, without music. Music is the organisation of vibrations, palpable, oral, audible vibrations. As such it keeps us in touch with the universe. It allows us to express ourselves. The other night one of the friends of the Menuhin School decided he'd try to get us some support, which of course we need very badly. The government pays for the tuition, but not for repairs, or for scholarships for our overseas students. This man invited ten very important Japanese businessmen, and I produced three charming Japanese girls from my school. One played the violin and two played the piano. They played beautifully and the evening was a great success. The Japanese woman, as we know, has never been liberated, but our music gives the Japanese woman a chance to become totally liberated. What these little girls expressed in their music were some of the most touching feelings you could imagine. Who would have thought seventy years ago that Japanese women would be liberated by Western music? But it was the fact. They played with such emotion and such beauty and sensitivity, it was overwhelming.

Why does Britain show such general reluctance to support the arts by comparison with America and Europe?

It's a different background. In Germany, the state supports music and is a very great source of security to musicians. There are literally hundreds of opera houses in Germany. In America, support has come traditionally from the private pocket. In Britain there has been traditionally relatively little support, although it has grown enormously compared to what it used to be. It's a matter of collective tradition. England can't imitate others. It can only grow in its own way. I have to say that I have always loved and felt at home in England and London, so that when the British government offered me British citizenship, I accepted with joy, though on the understanding that I did not lose my American nationality.

Which contemporary violinist do you most admire?

Gidon Kremer, a wonderful violinist and interpreter.

What prompted you to record with musicians outside your own sphere, like Ravi Shankar and Stéphane Grappelli?

There are no boundaries where such superb musicians are concerned. They are simply the masters of their art, and enlarge one's mind.

What is your assessment of Furtwängler, whom many have criticised for remaining in Germany under the Nazis?

A very great conductor and an absolutely clean man, no question of that. He stood up for Hindemith, he protected a great many Jews, helped many out of Germany, and himself had to escape towards the end of the war. He happened to conduct the orchestra when some of the German leaders were there, but we can't expect everyone to behave in the same way. Sometimes it takes more courage to remain in your country than to leave it. Those who stayed suffered a pretty bad fate, and those who came out, after all, escaped. Yet there was this feeling of superiority among those who escaped, thinking that they showed great determination in leaving it behind. I would say, Jew or gentile, you can't blame those who stayed, you can't blame those who escaped. It's just the way things went. But Furtwängler himself was a man of integrity.

The anti-Semitism I have seen in my own lifetime has had a psychological impact on me only to the extent that I know it is important to maintain the dignity of the Jew and to avoid a kind of behaviour that might prompt a response. The caricature of the Jew is the businessman with the big cigar, who does exist sometimes. They can be charming and interesting people. What bothers me sometimes is that they are a little bit like the desert flowers. When they have only a drop of water they blossom. They make the most of the opportunity, as they did in Germany before the Nazi days, when they occupied extremely powerful positions. That must have created a certain amount of resentment. Of course, it gives no excuse for anti-Semitism, but you can understand it. The Jew does not stand out in Italy or Greece, nor would he in China, since the Chinese are far cleverer at business than the Jew. There are so many different types of Jew, but traditionally people have fastened on the Jew who is obviously different from them. But there are so many who are in no way different. It's like the problem of the black in the United States. There are almost a majority of blacks that are nearly white, and no one bothers about them.

It is true that the Jews are far too sensitive, though they have perhaps been sensitised by history. They are too ready to imagine an insult; they are not prepared to give enough leeway, even to allow for a certain misbehaviour; they do carry a chip on their shoulders. They have to compensate, and it is a part of the psychology. One can understand that too, and one must understand it. They have to compensate for certain established assumptions. If it's not one thing it's another. If it's not religion, it's jealousy or it's race. Yet it's none of these things actually. It's simply that people are nasty and want to condemn anything if they can find a little difference; can say that hair is frizzed instead of straight or there's a detectable accent. Then they pounce on it.

Unfortunately, the Jews have come to Israel with the narrow aim of making themselves an independent nation, to a large extent disregarding the environment and the rest of the world. They didn't come to establish a nation with the Palestinians and a wonderful federation (though now they realise that perhaps they should have done). They came instead with the pure desire to establish a Jewish state to the exclusion of everything else. They did it very successfully, but they did it ruthlessly, and probably the sense of fear is equal on both sides. I feel that the only solution lies in a federation, totally equal, as in Switzerland. If both have an equal title to the land, what else can you do? Meanwhile there is something cruel about all of us. We are capable of the most horrid things, especially if we have suffered them ourselves.

Why have so many leading musicians been Jewish? I think it's ascribable simply to the fact that there were so many Jews who emigrated from Russia to the United States. The Jew in Russia, having been oppressed, found expression through the violin, because he was living in the same world where gypsy music was prevalent – in the Ukraine and the south of Russia. The violin was simply a Jewish instrument. A rabbi in New York told me that he was in Palestine, as it then was, in the early 1900s when the Russian pogroms were going on, and that hardly a Jewish refugee family arrived without a violin case. And I don't think that, in those days, the violin cases were filled with watches and stockings; they held genuine violins. The Russian Jews who arrived in New York brought with them a tremendous intensity of music making, much like the Negro in the United States whose first step to emancipation was singing the spiritual or playing the piano. There have been a great many musical traditions, only one of which was that of the Russian Jews, and today the Russian schools are producing as many non-Jewish violinists.

Your former marriage to Nola Nicholas apparently provoked a lot of adverse criticism from the Jewish press at the time.

I wasn't aware of it. If they had criticised me for other reasons, I would have accepted that certainly, and as it turned out it was not a successful marriage. That was as much my fault as hers, but I didn't realise there was that criticism. Any number of Jews marry out of their religion, and I wouldn't either applaud it or condemn it. It is just one of the things that happens or doesn't happen.

Has the adulation you have received ever tempted you to abuse the rewards of fame?

No, because I had to play the violin. The violin is relentless, and all the adulation in the world won't enable you to play in tune unless you play in tune. When you measure yourself not by trivial adulation but by the work you have to do, then your measure is quite different. You can't be spoilt. Besides, I have a marvellous wife, and she is so wonderfully loving and loyal and, at the same time, very critical. That's the most wonderful kind of marriage. Marriages where the two flatter each other and reinforce each other are very dangerous in a way, especially if they have no children. People must have other people to criticise them.

Your wife has called you long on vision and short on imagination – a deficiency, she says, which makes you infuriatingly impractical.

Diana has a marvellous capacity to visualise things as they actually are. For instance, she will be in an empty room and be able to imagine it decorated long before it is. I see the goal, but I don't necessarily anticipate the details, although I'm willing to put up with the process as long as the goal is kept in mind. Women are possessed by the process and men see the goal. They're both essential. Sometimes the goal proves more short-sighted than the process, and sometimes the process proves more long-sighted than the goal. We balance each other that way.

I am only too aware of Diana abandoning her own talents in our marriage, and I have often felt guilty about her self-denial. I have tried to compensate and have worked very hard to persuade her to do things she wants to do. But it takes a lot of persuasion. Even when she is here alone for a week or two, she will never lift the telephone to ask a friend round. It's this feeling that she can't indulge herself – a kind of extreme Protestant sense of not giving yourself pleasure. As soon as anything can be turned into an obligation or a duty, she'll do it right away. It's very curious. It is a kind of self-denial, yet no one shines in company more than she does.

Whereas your father rejoiced in your public performances, your mother longed for you to belong more to yourself, as she put it. Did their contrasting attitudes create an ambivalence for you?

You can call it ambivalence. You can also call it balance. I love my privacy and studying my score, but I also love meeting people and going out. I love playing the violin and I love conducting – two totally different occupations, one private, the other dealing with many voices. I can make the best of different situations. If you put me with political people, I am quite at home and interested, or if you put me with people on the street, I am fascinated by their mentality and way of life. I must say, however, that there is a great deal today that revolts me in the vulgarity and noise and the lack of depth all around.

As a young man you wrote: 'Our ancestors were more honourable in that they did not trouble to conceal their feelings, they simply fought it out. In this sense the greatest hypocrisy goes hand in hand with the highest civilisation.' You seemed to think then that hypocrisy was not an acceptable price to pay for civilised values. What do you think now?

I would now be a little hesitant about using the word hypocrisy because there can be various ways of clothing one's thoughts and emotions, some of them extremely good. For instance, is it a hypocrisy to walk around clothed in warm weather when we could go naked? It's a form of hypocrisy, but it's a very useful and acceptable form, though many people who go to nude beaches show that there is a longing to be without clothes. In the same way, we clothe our thoughts, depending on the person we are with. That is a form of courtesy, not necessarily hypocritical but sincere in itself. If I know a person has lost a dear friend, I am not going to speak myself about a loss I may have had, because it wouldn't be right, even as the Chinese feign gaiety in these circumstances in order to make you feel happy and not to burden you with their sorrow.

I think I am more aware today of everything that goes to create good in the world, and therefore I am more concerned with the building blocks of good than I am with the abstract idea. The abstract idea is important, but after a while you realise that it is more important to do things. It is very important to have goals, otherwise you don't know what you're working for. In a way, I had a naughty sense of delight when the politicians were taken completely by surprise by the events that Gorbachev encouraged in Eastern Europe. All they could say was that it was going too fast. This was because they were comfortable in knowing where the enemy was, where the guns were – their mind didn't have to exercise itself; they knew what to expect. But as soon as the barriers were broken, they didn't know where they were, and they still don't. Nor do they know where they're going. But I know where they're going. I know what's happening in Europe.

I have a feeling that the next great struggle of the twenty-first century will be that of the federate principle – the principle of interdependence – against the backlog of the old nationalist thing. We'll still have to fight that, but the new road is the interdependence of peoples and cultures, and that is the road we must travel. Anyone who stands against it is in the rearguard, and that's why the creation of all these new nations since the Second World War is such an anomaly. It is out of step with the end of the twentieth century. Meanwhile it is still too early to pronounce factually on the vast changes the liberation of Eastern Europe has wrought, but it is obvious that it will enrich all the arts – music, literature, painting and sculpture.

On the question of where my own musical talent came from, I would say that heredity plays a big part in talent, but so does environment. That is one of those questions that goes on for ever in the sense that you can't have only environment and no heredity, because you might be a dog, a cat, a human being or a fish; and you can't have only heredity and no environment, because then you might be a plant that withers in the wrong kind of earth or in the sun without any water. You have to have both, and I had both. I have no doubt that I'm strong and, although I couldn't live the life of the businessman or commuter, in my own way, for my purposes, I have plenty of vitality and a natural sense of what I need to feel well in terms of exercise and diet. I am not one hundred per cent vegetarian, nor would I care to proselytise, but I have simply found that I dislike being carnivorous and that my instinct has proved right for me.

I have a very keen sense of the use of time, and I begrudge time spent that is not invested, just as some people feel about money. They don't want to give money away, they'd rather see it grow. I'm not quite like that with time, because I always have time for people whom I feel I can be of use to and I generally find time for young musicians who call. But what I always like to do is to set a score, or give a concert, for a particular purpose. Everything I am doing now fits more and more into the scheme of things. Whereas previously I would go on tour for three months just to earn money, today I try to make each concert and each tour a contribution to and a step towards a future, whether mine or somebody else's. I only wish that there were forty-eight hours in each day, in that life has presented me with so many more interests than I have had the time to follow and so many crafts I would have liked to learn.

I have been very fortunate. I have no axe to grind, I haven't suffered humiliation. I haven't ever suffered the unnatural death of any close friend. When I speak, I always speak with the thought in mind that I am perhaps speaking to people who haven't had that blessed sort of good luck or privilege. My fulfilment lies in interpreting the works of composers, because even interpretation holds a certain measure of creation. I only do what I love and feel I need to do, and if this does amount to a great deal, it comes from an independent choice.

I don't have any right to a feeling of superiority or to pass judgement. On the contrary, I feel that I have been spared by a kind destiny. My life is a constant sense of repayment for what I have had and a desire to protect the future. It goes without saying that there are still things I would wish to achieve in life. There is no horizon.

SIR JOHN MORTIMER QC

John Mortimer was born in 1923 and educated at Harrow and Brasenose College, Oxford. He was called to the Bar in 1948 and participated in several celebrated civil cases such as the *Oz* trial, defending *Gay News* against charges of blasphemy and Virgin Records for printing 'Bollocks' on a record sleeve. His series of novels featuring an amiable defence barrister were adapted for television as *Rumpole of the Bailey*. His other novels included *Paradise Postponed* (1985) and *Summer's Lease* (1988). His acclaimed autobiographical play *A Voyage Round My Father* (1971) was filmed for television in 1982, winning an Emmy. He was awarded the CBE in 1986 and knighted in 1998. He died in 2009.

Yours was the sort of childhood that, had you grown up into a complete neurotic or developed almost any other kind of psychosis, it would have been entirely explicable in terms of your early years. How on earth did you turn out to be so normal?

It's a question whether I am normal at all. In many ways, however, I had a very happy childhood because I had a father and mother who treated me very well and always as though I was a grown-up; and I was an only child, which has its advantages in that you grow up very quickly. I was treated like a good friend, especially by my father. He flew into terrible rages with other people but never with me, and my mother was long-suffering and loving. So, although I was very lonely because my father never wanted visitors who would see he was blind and feel sorry for him, I didn't have an unhappy childhood. I went to ridiculous English schools which I didn't like, but on the other hand I was able to adjust to them and survive them because I had a very secure relationship with my parents.

Both your parents were adept at not acknowledging reality. Your father did not admit to his blindness and your mother, long after his death, continued to behave as if he had not died. This phenomenon of making light of sorrow and grief, if that's what it is, is something quintessentially English. Is it something you perpetuate in your own life?

You're right – it is quintessentially English. There is a wonderful story about Lord Uxbridge, whose leg was shot off at the Battle of Waterloo, and when the Duke of Wellington said, 'By God, Uxbridge, you've lost your leg,' Lord Uxbridge looked down and said, 'By God, sir, so I have!' And nothing else was said on the subject. But that isn't altogether a failure to accept reality; it's more a stoical attitude to life which I think is quite admirable. Whether it's stoic courage or whether it's a refusal to face facts, I'm not quite sure, but that's how I prefer to live. I can quite easily put unpleasant facts out of my head – I don't think about death for instance.

Are you confident that you can look back now and remember your father as he really was, or has the act of extensive writing about him to some extent fictionalised him and put him beyond reach?

I find it very difficult to separate fact from fiction. A writer is constantly taking life and turning it into fiction, regurgitating it, and sending it out to the world, altered or not. Certainly, when I wrote the play about my father, I wrote many lines for him which he never said in his life, and now it's quite difficult for me to remember which ones were his and which were mine. He's become a sort of fictional character and not like other people's fathers who are contained entirely in themselves and their memories.

Was it partly your intention when you wrote A Voyage Round My Father *to lose your father?*

Not at all. I wanted to write a play about my father and also to celebrate the peculiarly English middle-class attitude to life of that period. That was my intention, but the effect of it has been perhaps that my father has vanished or turned into a different character from what he really was.

Woody Allen once said of Jesus that he was very well adjusted for an only child. Do you think the same could be said of you?

I don't know whether I'm very well adjusted. I've had a very easy life compared with anyone who has lived in Europe or in other parts of the world, and the period I've lived in has been very safe. Only children are fortunate really, in that they very quickly have to learn to live a grown-up life and they have terrific resources within themselves. I led a very strong imaginative life when I was a child, and was able to adjust well to most things in life.

Despite your professed loathing for public schools, you seem not to have been too unhappy at Harrow, or was that an attempt to make the best of a bad experience?

Apart from being very homesick, I had a good experience at my prep school, the Dragon School in Oxford, which was a very good school indeed. I was treated very well, and it was a progressive school for the time and even had a few girls. Instead of having to play games which I hated, I was given a bar of chocolate and sent off to the Oxford Rep Theatre, which was very agreeable. Then I went to Harrow where I was just indescribably bored. It was full of vaguely upper-class people whom I learned to dislike. I wasn't bullied or beaten – none of those dramatic things; I was just bored and being educated slightly above my station.

Is it the idea of sending a young child away at so early an age which is the basis of your objection?

Yes. It's a most extraordinary English habit, and I never quite forgave my mother. Strangely enough, I could understand my father wanting to get rid of me, and I sympathised with him, but I couldn't quite understand why my mother did. I didn't know what I'd done wrong to be dismissed to some draughty distant building. Not that I haven't had children at boarding school myself, but that was when I was young and busy and less thoughtful, less considerate perhaps. But the idea of handing over the upbringing of your child to strangers is very weird, and I think people who run English prep schools also tend to be extremely weird. My son went to Bedales, a coeducational boarding school, which I suppose is rather different. He liked it there and met a girl who is now his wife, and they've been together ever since. And I myself owe a debt to the public-school system, since it gave me an immense amount to write about it. Making fun of public-school attitudes and English upper- and middle-class attitudes, has been my stock in trade over the years, so if I hadn't been there I don't know what I would have to write about.

You have often said that you believe in middle-class virtues. Can you explain to me what these are?

They are really the virtues I saw in my mother and father, those virtues I was trying to celebrate in *A Voyage Round My Father*. To begin with, it wasn't anything to do with money, for they felt money was quite ridiculous and certainly not the most important thing. They were both liberal, my mother a sort of Shavian new woman, my father an old-fashioned Lloyd George Liberal. They were professional people, my father especially in the sense that he gave very good service to the clients he was acting for. He didn't think about doing it for money, though he liked being paid. In those days barristers often did cases for nothing, and I certainly started that way. There was a kind of tradition of middle-class professionalism, of tolerance, liberalism, all of those things, which I admire. The middle classes have been the source of most of the strength of England, and most writers have come from the middle class. With the exception of Byron and Shelley, the aristocracy hasn't produced many writers, and working-class traditions have tended to keep people in rather stereotyped conditions of mind. Political change also has come mainly from the middle classes, and all the best revolutionaries have been middle class.

Your books and plays have evoked, often savagely, the moral decline of the middle class. Do you consider yourself to be a part of that decline?

The moral decline in England came really in the Thatcher years, when all of those values I admire were derided. The idea that making money was important and everything had its price and had to be sold at the best price, all of those things marked the decline, in my view. And no, I don't consider myself any part of that. I consider myself to be an old-fashioned liberal middle-class person.

There is a character in Paradise Postponed *who is in favour of the working classes running the country while at the same time doubting if these were the kind of people she would have to tea. Does that perhaps epitomise the dichotomy in your own attitude towards the working class?*

In *Paradise Postponed* I wanted to be as rude about my side as I was about the other side. I was getting at a type of mandarin left-wing person, particularly of that era of the Webbs, Virginia Woolf, Leonard Woolf and those sorts of people, who managed to combine the view that the working classes should take over the world, with the feeling that they themselves, being extremely privileged Bloomsbury persons, wouldn't have them to tea. But I don't think that that's my own attitude. I'm as sceptical about liberal left-wing policies as I am about everything else. The radio quarrel with Julie Burchill when she accused me of being a snob made me think very closely about whether I am one, but I honestly don't think so.

You have sometimes described yourself as a 'committed leftie'. What does that mean in fact?

A committed leftie is how I would be described by other people, but it's quite a difficult thing to explain. When I was at the Dragon School the Spanish Civil War was on, and I read – perhaps quite ill-advisedly – a lot of Auden and Spender and T. S. Eliot when I was really quite young, so those attitudes of the 1930s, the Republican side of the Civil War, and so on, all of that was very immediate to me. Then when I went to Harrow which was upper class and full of rich people I became a one-boy Communist cell. There was an English public-school Communist Party and I used to get messages from King Street but I stopped being interested at the time of the Hitler-Stalin pact. Then I went into something called the Crown Film Unit, making documentary films during the war, and it was there, for the first time in my life, I met the working class, the workers so to speak. I became a member of the union and I felt extremely left-wing, and then came the great Labour victory of 1945. All those events throughout my life have encouraged me to believe in essential equality and in some version of socialism. But there are all sorts of leftie things which I'm not in favour of, like eating muesli or being against fox-hunting. I don't really accept the entire left ticket, but I would always vote Labour, though with increasing scepticism.

Do you think your views have changed dramatically since the early days of 1945?

No, but perhaps if that government had never existed, then it would have been difficult to remain faithful to the Labour Party. Those memories and those ideals have kept me going.

Isn't that a very English attitude in the sense that those who vote Conservative do so all their lives, and those who vote Labour continue to follow the Party line? Do you think that's a good thing?

I think it's a good thing not to vote Conservative, for whatever reason.

Your fellow barrister Geoffrey Robertson said of you: 'There is a legal part of John Mortimer's work which is deeply conservative, deeply rooted in the law.' Do you think that was the case when you practised?

It is absolutely true to say there is a part of me which is deeply conservative: I want the countryside to be kept as it is, I don't want the English landscape to change, and I want English country life to be kept as it is. I'm also very conservative about the British Constitution which I think works very well, and about the British system of justice. My whole attitude towards being a barrister is that the law is a kind of disease and you should try and cure your clients of it as quickly as possible. I always regarded the law as something which was getting in the way of a client's life, liberty and pursuit of happiness, and that my business was to extricate him from the law as mercifully as possible. When I started as a barrister the divorce law was absolutely ridiculous, in that you had to try and establish who was guilty and who was innocent, whereas there's really no such thing as guilt or innocence in marital breakdown. So what you had to do was to try and solve people's problems, and get them out of the clutches of the law. That's how I always regarded my work as a barrister.

When you say you believe in the British Constitution, does that apply to the monarchy?

My theory about the monarchy is that it's much better to have a head of state who isn't political. The mistake of America is to have the head of state who is the prime minister, so to speak, which gives an American president a quite undeserved patriotic glow because you can't really criticise the president without criticising America. It's an excellent thing to have a head of state who does not have any political powers and for that reason I've always thought the monarchy a good idea, though I'm becoming increasingly unsure about whether it can survive, even though it has good constitutional uses. The ridiculous thing is that people expect the monarchy to mirror decent family life or moral standards, but any hereditary line is going to have people who behave extremely foolishly from time to time. We have to evolve our own moral standards and not look to the monarchy to do it for us.

You married for the first time when you were twenty-six and inherited a ready-made family of four children. After the solitude of your own childhood, did the prospect of a large family attract you, as it might have terrified others?

I think it did. I was really entranced by the idea of a lot of children and since then I've never lived without children around. I have children now of all possible ages, from forty-two to eight years old. I think it did have to do with the loneliness of my childhood.

Since your wife had first to secure a divorce before you could be married, you went to considerable lengths to be cited as co-respondent. One imagines that in those days it was a rather sordid business with a great deal of stigma attaching to it …

It was particularly difficult for me because my father was the doyen of the divorce Bar, and it was difficult for him too, although his colleagues behaved very well about it. We used to go to endless numbers of hotels and try and make people remember we'd been there. No one ever did, but in the end a private detective called Mr Smith came to the house and found our clothes in the same bedroom, and then I made a confession. Mr Smith later gave evidence in court that we were living together. The following week I was conducting my first case as a barrister and I had to call this same Mr Smith as a witness to the adultery of the people whose case I was handling. For the next thirty years I called Mr Smith to testify about once a week. We sometimes had coffee together but we'd never refer to the time when he came and inspected my bedroom. One day Mr Smith was walking across a pedestrian crossing and a police car came buzzing along and nearly ran him over, so he hit the police car on the roof in a fit of anger, whereupon the policeman arrested him. Mr Smith sued the police for false arrest. As he needed a witness to say he was a thoroughly reliable and decent chap, I went to court and said I'd known Mr Smith for thirty years and he was an absolutely truthful, honest character. He got substantial damages.

Your marriage to the first Penelope was legendary in its tempestuousness. Most people would find perpetual fighting draining and debilitating, yet you continued to work hard and write hard. Did you perhaps find a certain exhilaration or energy in the conflict?

Not really. I had £5 a week from my father, four children to feed, a very large house in Hampstead, and another house somebody gave us in the countryside. So I really had to work. I not only earned money by divorcing people, but I wrote anything – stories for women's magazines, anything. Two writers married to each other is an impossible situation, because you're using the same material and using each other's lives. It was certainly tempestuous, but it gave us both a lot of material, and it wasn't without moments of happiness. When I look back on it now, however, I can't think how I survived it, not only because the marriage was at times stormy, but because I was working flat out as a barrister and a writer, and also enjoying myself quite a lot. I must have had enormous stamina. The funny thing about that time is that I would often leave the house in the morning battered after some long argument or angry scene, and then I'd go down to my chambers in the Temple and give advice to elderly company directors on exactly how they should conduct their married lives. Everybody else's life was absolutely easy to put right.

Your father was much given to angry outbursts. Did you inherit his predisposition to anger?

No. His anger made me very calm, and I have very few angry outbursts. What I have in common with my father is a well-developed sense of the ridiculous. He had a long succession of jokes about his life, which he told very well, and he would laugh until the tears ran down his face. We shared a sense of the absurdity of life, coupled with rather a sentimental attitude to it also. My father would weep in the theatre, yet he would make an attempt to deal stoically with his life, which is what I liked about him. I actually miss him all the time and I'm terribly overshadowed by him. When I came to live in his house I found it difficult to do anything to it, to change anything about it for a long time, and I do find myself with the feeling that I'm repeating his life.

In Clinging to the Wreckage *you describe your married life as a feverish round of longing for lucrative divorce briefs to defray 'the family's extraordinary demands for Farex, Ribena,*

Johnson's Baby Powder and knicker linings'. Were there compensations to offset this heavy load, or do you remember it as unmitigated wretchedness?

Not at all as unmitigated wretchedness. The children were a great pleasure, and it's very nice that I still see them a lot. And there came a time when the desperation to buy the knicker linings calmed down; Penelope had a contract with the *New Yorker*, and I was beginning to make money by writing plays and doing bigger divorce cases. So it didn't go on forever.

One of the things you learned from being a divorce lawyer is that people on the whole don't rush into divorce as they do into marriage, and that – as you put it – 'any human relationship, however painful and absurd, can seem better than the uncharted desert of divorce'. Was that the sentiment which kept your own stormy marriage going for about twenty-five years?

I think it was the children really, and it certainly wasn't stormy all the time. What a lot of my clients feared was being alone; they would rather have the quarrels, or they'd even rather live with people they never spoke to, than be alone. I don't think I thought that. I didn't think I'd be alone if I was divorced, so it was really the children, and also there was a lot of affection.

Did you see Penelope Mortimer's The Pumpkin Eater *as a sort of revenge?*

I honestly didn't. I thought it was a very good book, and I don't really feel that I'm like the person in *The Pumpkin Eater*. You've got to write about what's happened to you; that's what I do too, and it's not revenge.

Your play The Wrong Side of the Park *contains thinly disguised elements of your first marriage. Did writing that make you feel better about the painful aspects of marital breakdown?*

Yes, I think it did, but again I don't think it should be seen as a deliberate personal act within a relationship. It is an example of the writer's solitary way of trying to translate his experiences into some form of art.

In much of your writing the distinction between fact and fiction is rather blurred. Are there any dangers in this, do you think?

Of course there are, and it's a very interesting subject. Nothing is the literal truth, or the whole truth. That goes for journalism, documentaries and novels. In a sense the most truth comes from fiction. Tolstoy is the writer who comes nearest to telling the truth about life; you get much nearer the truth by reading Tolstoy than you do if you see some documentary or read a book which is meant to be a discussion of history. History is all written from somebody's point of view; it's a question of choice. Fiction is telling a story to make people want to know what is going to happen next, but it is really the writer's attempt to make some statement about life. The facts of the story need not be true, but the statement should be true, it should be a statement of the truth.

After the breakdown of your first marriage you had two promiscuous years. Were those the years you should have had before you married perhaps?

Absolutely. I became middle aged quite early on, and then I had to go back to being young again. I didn't go totally mad, but I was always on the lookout. I think I'm naturally somebody who wants to live with a family and children, and I wouldn't now like to have to embark at my age on a promiscuous period. I think it would be very exhausting – all that planning and wondering and making telephone calls …

Your father thought that sex, like love, had been greatly overestimated by the poets. Did you have any sympathy with this view?

I disagreed with it at the time. He derived tremendous fun from pricking any pre-conceived ideas and making them look absurd. For example, he would always say that travel narrowed the mind, and you learned much more by staying at home. So he would dismiss any kind of large idea that sex or love was the greatest thing in the world. Yet he was very much in love with his wife, and she with him.

Are you romantic at heart?

Yes, I would say so. I like romanticism mixed with – not exactly cynicism – but common sense, as in Stendhal, or Byron.

You wrote in your autobiography: 'The basic morality on which law is founded has always seemed to me inferior to those moral values which everyone must work out for themselves.' That would seem to suggest that our legal system is very crude and unsophisticated …

Yes, I think that's right. The legal system is like some sort of public utility: cleaning the drains, washing the streets, stopping people knocking each other on the head, or taking each other's wallets … but not much else. The subtler points of life will not be decided by law. That's why, for instance, I'm against all censorship laws, because I don't think the law should tell people what they should read or what they should not read, or intrude into their private morality. Those are things they must discover for themselves. The law can do simple things, like stopping robberies, and compensating if you're run over, but when it gets into the intricate realms of morality it makes a fool of itself.

Would you agree that our adversarial system is not necessarily conducive to the truth and that success is often due to powerful rhetoric?

I'm in favour of the adversarial system. An English trial isn't an exercise to discover the truth, it's an exercise to discover whether in a criminal trial the prosecution has proved its case beyond reasonable doubt. It's absolutely right that people should not be sent to prison unless their guilt is proved beyond reasonable doubt. That doesn't mean that at the end of a criminal trial the truth has been discovered; the person might be guilty but there might not be enough evidence to satisfy a jury. That's a much better system than having a judge as a kind of Hercule Poirot trying to ferret out the truth which he may be wrong about. I have grave doubts about how much rhetoric alters the adversarial system. You can lose cases by making mistakes, but I think it's quite difficult to win unwinnable cases with rhetoric.

You used to say when you grew up you would decide between being a writer and a barrister. Since you have left the Bar, does that mean you have finally grown up?

A good question. I didn't decide for years and years to leave the Bar, and I think I left it about ten years too late. The great advantage of old age is that you can behave quite childishly, whereas when you're young you're very anxious to appear grown up. I always was a writer who did a bit of barristering, like a girl who wants to be an actress does a bit of waitressing as a day job. But I still don't know whether I've finally grown up ...

You claim always to have felt somewhat out of place at the Bar. Why was that?

When I started everybody was frightfully correct and conservative, and called each other by their surnames, as though they were at English prep schools, and generally behaved in a sort of English public-school manner; and there was I, rather left-wing, writing plays, going off at the end of a court to go to rehearsals and take actresses out. So I was slightly out of place, though not completely, because I had of course been a child round the Temple. When I first went to the law courts, the ushers used to call me Master John. It was rather like the young squire taking possession of the house.

You defended some famous cases, including Oz and Gay News. Were you aware at the time the significance they would have for years to come?

No. I got into all that because I was a QC and also a writer. The first book I defended was *Last Exit to Brooklyn* and I got that off on the appeal, on the basis that the description of sex was so disgusting that it put the British population off sex for about a week. It was a frightfully moral argument which the Court of Appeal liked. The *Oz* trial just came upon me; like most things in my life, somebody asked me to do it, and I did it. It turned out to be absolutely typical of that strange flower-power generation, which seems to me much more distantly in the past than the 1930s or the 1920s. However, I'm not sure now it did change the face of England.

You grew up in an agnostic household and have never been able to bring yourself to believe in God. Have you ever felt that as a particular loss? Have you envied other people their faith?

I wasn't ever christened or confirmed, so I grew up with no religion, but I never missed it at all. And I always admired my father, because although he went blind and had awful things happen to him, he never turned to God. But I am very interested in religion; I think sometimes atheists become obsessed with religion, and I certainly love talking to bishops, or arguing with cardinals. My problem with religion, or with an omnipotent deity, is to see why he puts up with all the evil in the world and why he allowed eight million Jews to be massacred and why he lets Bosnia go on, if he is all powerful. I can't quite work out whether I would like God if he existed; that's a kind of intellectual argument which I'm always trying to get the answer to, but I never succeeded. There have been more horrible deeds perpetrated in the name of religion than for anything else, and it's difficult not to believe that the religions of the world have done more harm than good. As a writer, however, I am aware that Catholicism has provided a wonderful kind of starting-off point for novelists. If you're Graham Greene or Evelyn Waugh you can have a kind of framework for your life and your writing which I don't have, and which I suppose I might envy. I also do think that a totally materialistic view of life can be a kind of stunted philosophy; you do want to attach some kind of almost mystical importance to something, otherwise your life becomes rather Stalinist.

But as you get older, don't you hanker after some sort of faith?

No, I don't, honestly. And I certainly don't hanker after immortality. My father used to say that immortality of the soul would be like living in some kind of transcendental hotel with nothing to do in the evenings; and I don't really look forward to that. It is important to believe in something outside yourself, more important than yourself, but having some political beliefs and also believing in the importance of literature is enough for me.

In your autobiography you quote from Wordsworth's Tintern Abbey, *as if it gave expression to some scarcely acknowledged religious impulse. Have you yourself felt that 'sense sublime of something far more deeply interfused, whose dwelling is the light of setting suns ... '*

Yes. What you have to find is the mystic importance of the moment of time, that moment when you're experiencing the country, or solitude, or whatever. And I suppose the nearest I can get to religion is a sort of Wordsworthian reaction to the countryside and pantheism and the importance of nature. I can understand the mystic qualities but not the intellectual qualities of religion.

You once said, 'Loyalty is a stultifying emotion.' Can you develop that idea?

I think that anything which is uncritical is stultifying. You should be able to crit-icise everything and so if you're devoted to somebody totally uncritically, it is stultifying. But in saying that, I really meant loyalty to groups, or parties, or the old school, or whatever.

Does loyalty extend to fidelity? Is fidelity also stultifying?

No. I think it's probably liberating in a way because it removes a lot of complica-tions from your life. It's something people have to deal with for themselves, but I think on the whole fidelity is rather freeing.

You dislike Mrs Thatcher and all that she stood for, feeling she epitomised what was worst about the 1980s. Is her legacy likely to darken the 1990s equally?

Yes. It was her legacy that destroyed basic industries in Britain; we're producing service industries and computers, but nothing basic is being made in the country any longer, and I dislike the whole morality of everything having its price and the idea that nothing was important unless it was making money. Political idealism died in the 1980s and became an object of derision. We're still living in that shadow.

You made no secret of your loathing for the SDP. Does that extend to the present Liberal Democrats?

Yes, I can't stand the Liberal Democrats. They're just there to spoil everything. We've had Conservative governments for so long because the opposition has been split, and when they could have voted against Maastricht and against the government – quite legitimately because they weren't having a referendum – they kept the government going for no reason whatsoever. I dislike them intensely.

You have often been criticised for being 'a champagne socialist' and have defended yourself by claiming your role was to infiltrate the Establishment in order to change it. Do you think you can claim success in that respect?

I just believe champagne should be freely available to all. Nye Bevan was forever drinking champagne, and that was a very good sign. I also don't think attacking the Establishment from the outside has much effect. The best form of attack is humour, to laugh at the trappings. If you get the jury laughing in court, you know you've won the case. But I don't think I've succeeded very much in changing anything. The great thing about the British Establishment is that it is totally impervious. All a writer can do is to try and promote people's understanding of each other and their sympathy with each other, and to make established institutions look ridiculous.

Beneath your own cheerfulness and bonhomie, *I suspect there is a grim pessimism, and* malaise ...

Pessimism is a very good basis for a cheerful outlook on life. If you don't expect too much you don't get disappointed. I always used to tell my clients that they could go to prison for six years, and when they ended up by being fined £2 they were frightfully relieved. But if you'd told them they were going to be fined 10 shillings and they were fined £2, they would have been very cross. So I think it is better to expect the worst. I do have a fundamentally pessimistic attitude to life, but I hope I don't have too much *malaise,* except in the afternoons when I often get depressed.

Your preferred genre for writing is comedy. Do you think that is the best way of saying important things, or is there perhaps a danger that important issues will be seen as trivialised?

That's a very good question. Comedy is the most important and the most difficult form of writing. Anybody can be tragic, but to be funny is really hard and requires great skill. It's a great English tradition from the comedies of Shakespeare like *Twelfth Night* and *As You Like It*, which are quite sad plays really, through to the novels of Dickens which can be tragic and comic and savage at the same time. Comedy is also the most truthful thing; if you rule out comedy you rule out half of the truth. Does it trivialise the truth? I don't think it does. Just the reverse.

You are very sensitive to criticism and unfavourable reviews. Haven't you reached a stage where you can afford to ignore adverse comments?

I've now stopped reading reviews. They are just quite irritating, and it can be bad for the confidence. Dickens never read reviews, then suddenly he read a bad review of *Little Dorrit* by mistake and got into a terrible depression. Writers are very uncertain about what they've written, and if it gets very well received, that's a wonderful relief and surprise; if it is badly received, it's depressing.

There are many contradictions in your character which I am sure you are aware of. You are an upholder of traditional values, but a defender of liberalism; you are both worldly wise and apparently starry-eyed, and so on. Have these contradictions ever worried you? Have you ever tried to resolve them?

Oh no, I wouldn't like to resolve them. I would cease to exist if I resolved them. The contradictions are essential, and if you're writing, you have to have the tensions in your writing which are the different parts of your character.

I have the impression that the fact that you were never able to get close to your mother, even at the end of her life, was one of the hardest and saddest things for you ...

Yes, it is one of my greatest regrets. I think because I had a very strong relationship with my father, she was rather left out. Also, she came from the English tradition of – not coldness, because she was not in the least bit cold – but of not being demonstrative. Her father committed suicide while she was in South Africa and her family just sent her the local paper with a note saying, 'This story will probably interest you.' As a family they didn't talk about things like that. And although we weren't quite so remote, it was never as close as I should have liked.

I believe you are infuriated by the thought of dying. Wouldn't you be comforted by the thought of an afterlife?

No. My father's immortality is that I remember him and that my children are like him. The only sort of immortality I believe in is when people remember you, or people's lives have been shaped by you to some extent. I don't want some sort of strange and detached existence floating about the universe.

Looking back on your life, what are you proudest of?

Of the good things I have written, *Clinging to the Wreckage, A Voyage Round My Father,* and I'm also rather proud of *Rumpole.* It's quite difficult for a writer to keep going in a lot of different generations, and I'm pleased to have done that. I'm proud of my children, and happy to have kept my parents' house in the condition it's been accustomed to. I don't think my achievements have been really great. I hope I've been on the side of tolerance, liberalism, letting people alone, and social justice, but millions of other people have said all those things, so it's not anything I feel particularly responsible for.

You have sometimes said that to conduct an interview is much more difficult than to be interviewed ... do you still take that view?

This has been such a good interview that it's made me think very deeply. I was never quite so well prepared as you, and it is always nerve-racking until the interviewee suddenly says something extraordinary and then you can relax in the knowledge you've got the bloody thing wrapped up. I remember interviewing Hailsham and asking him what he did when he sat on the woolsack looking bored. And he said, 'Well, what I do is whisper bollocks to the bench of bishops.' And I knew that since I had got him to say that, everything would be alright.

DIANA, LADY MOSLEY

Born in 1910, Diana Mosley was one of the celebrated Mitford girls, daughters of the eccentric Lord Redesdale who was to feature prominently in Nancy Mitford's novels. At the age of eighteen Diana married Bryan Guinness, later Lord Moyne, by whom she had two sons. In 1932 she met Oswald Mosley, leader of the British Union of Fascists, and fell instantly under his spell. Four years later they were married secretly in Dr Goebbels' house in Berlin. She bore two more sons before she and her husband were detained during the war under the defence regulations. Her publications included a book on the Duchess of Windsor and two volumes of auto-biography, *A Life of Contrasts* (1977) and *Loved Ones* (1985). She regularly wrote book reviews for the *Evening Standard* when A. N. Wilson was literary editor, though Max Hastings, on becoming the newspaper's editor in 1996, dispensed with her services. She was reinstated on Hastings' retirement in 2002 and continued to write book reviews for the paper until her death in Paris in 2003.

Diana, when we spoke about this interview you rather suggested that there was nothing new to say. My own impression from doing research is that you have given a very uneven picture of yourself. It seems to me that you are perhaps misjudged, certainly misunderstood. You say in your book, A Life of Contrasts: *'Indifference to public opinion is an essential aristocratic virtue. It is rarer than one might imagine.' Looking in from the outside, it is a quality, however rare, that you seem to have in abundance. Is it really so? Are you not tempted to open up?*

I don't quite know what you mean by 'open up'. I don't think I've ever con-sciously dodged answers to questions. By saying that indifference to public opinion is an aristocratic virtue, I did not mean to imply that I consider myself aristocratic, I certainly do not. Of course, I mind very much about the opinion of people I love or esteem, but not of journalists or acquaintances who – quite rightly – look upon me as not 'politically correct' or whatever the fashionable phrase may be.

You have been known to say that you don't understand all the fuss about the Mitford girls. By any standards family life was strange and eccentric and it has been well documented in Nancy and Jessica's books. Was it the case that the oddness seemed perfectly normal to you, or were you conscious that yours was a very singular milieu, unlike that of others, even in your social circle?

I think there's a misunderstanding here. Our life as children was exactly like that of hundreds of other children in the same walk of life. If you lived in the country in those days you probably didn't go to school if you were a girl, you probably had a governess, you had animals, you went out hunting, you went to neighbours' parties. I honestly don't believe there was anything in our childhood which was unlike that of a great many other people. There was really nothing odd about it. Some fathers were stricter and more violent than others. Although our father was sometimes rather violent, we loved him and were amused by him. He's been a bit exaggerated by Nancy, though not very much, since he is really more or less Uncle Matthew, but I think even in her novels she says we loved him. There was never a dull moment.

I realise that the memory of your brother Tom must still be painful for you, but can you tell me what it was about him that formed so strong a bond between you?

I suppose it was that we were very close in age, not even eighteen months between us. We were very fond of one another. He was a musical boy, and I loved music, so that was a bond. It's hard to say really, but until he was killed we just were very close. I miss him even now, for many things. I can't imagine him as an old man.

When one studies the Mitford girls it's difficult not to be astonished by the sheer brilliance and individuality of all of them. It is not usual in large families for these qualities to be dealt out in such large measure across the board. Would you say that such things are decided, as it were, genetically, i.e. in advance of upbringing, or would you attribute it more to family life and parental influence?

I think it's completely genetic. I don't think that upbringing has a great deal to do with what one becomes later on. We're products of our grandparents and great-grandparents much more. That's been proved scientifically, I think. For example, if you take identical twins who are brought up in two different ways, they turn out the same in the end. It's just a curious fact.

In your early life at least, your father seems to figure much more prominently than your mother. Was he the decisive influence on you, do you think?

No, I really do not think so. We just took him for granted. In a way the person who meant most to me when I was a child was my nanny. I loved her far more than I did my parents and I often felt guilty about that. One should love one's mother more than one's nurse, but in fact I loved nanny best. My mother was a great character; she had wonderful courage and was so honest that you couldn't even imagine a dishonest thought or act coming from her. But again, she was somebody we took completely for granted; she was just our mother, always there.

If you had a problem, would you have confided in her?

I wouldn't have dreamed of confiding anything in either of my parents. Possibly one of my sisters or my brother, but nobody else. It simply wouldn't have occurred to any of us to confide in them, I'm sure.

You and your sisters seem in retrospect all to have been quite fixated on a particular man. In your own case it was Mosley, in Unity's it was Hitler, in Debo's it was her duke, and so on. In your own ways you all seemed to have been besotted by powerful men. This is not something you touch on in your autobiography. Is it not something that has occurred to you?

Yes, it has occurred to me. Strangely enough, even Nancy, who was devoted to her colonel, went over the top of the colonel, so to speak, in her tremendous feeling for de Gaulle. You see, she loved France, and she thought he was the ideal dictator. It was far more than the usual rather cool approval that one might feel about a president or a prime minister; it went much more deeply with her. You might say we all had that characteristic which must have come through our genes.

Your father does seem to have been a very eccentric man – he chased the children with a bloodhound, for example.

I don't think he was nearly as eccentric as people imagine. You see, he had a bloodhound, and it was rather fun to hunt with him, and we children were there, available. Most men love hunting after all. He didn't hunt us very often with his bloodhound, and in any case the bloodhound died. He didn't have what you might call a kennelful of bloodhounds; there was just one dear old one and he thought, well, let's give him a run.

But did there come a time when you realised that he was not like other men?

Well, he was actually very much like my uncles. It's true he had great hates which were rather unusual. There were people he disliked intensely for no particular reason, even children. Most people usually dismiss children and say to themselves, 'What a tiresome little girl or boy', but he managed to work up quite a passion of hatred for some child he didn't like. It didn't evidence itself in any way; one just realised he could hardly bear the child. The same applied to grown-ups, of course. He wasn't what you might call a very sociable man. He preferred walking with his dogs and chatting to the keeper.

I have heard it said that he was something of a philistine. Is that something you were aware of?

I suppose he was a philistine. He never went to an art gallery, he never cared the least about sightseeing, and he liked only a very simple kind of music – Puccini's arias, for example; apart from that I cannot say that he had any sort of artistic interest.

In a sense you seem to have had quite a Spartan childhood, plenty of space, but not much warmth, no fires in the bedrooms, and really rather strict 'rules'. I'm thinking of your Paris diary and its aftermath. Was that the usual patterns among the families you knew?

A good many girls of my age, who were friends of mine, had exactly the same experience, perhaps not quite so strict, but they were not allowed out except with a governess or a maid. This was by no means unique to us. When I got to Paris at the age of sixteen it seemed such a wonderful chance for freedom that I'm afraid I did one or two things which were strictly forbidden, like going to the cinema with a young man in the afternoon when I pretended to the old governess that I was going to a violin lesson. I put it all in my dairy and then of course there was the most fearful row when it was discovered. It's rather sad that my diary went west. Mother and father put it in the boiler.

You married Bryan Guinness when you were eighteen. And he was also very young, twenty-three, I think. Do you think in retrospect that to marry at such a tender age may have been a mistake?

Not really. I don't think age makes much difference. I was nineteen when my eldest son was born and when I was twenty I had another son. About a year after that my husband and I parted. It was not because I married too young, but because I fell in love with Oswald Mosley and decided that I should prefer living on my own and being able to see him occasionally, to being married to Bryan Guinness. He wanted a wife who would always be there, and that's what he got afterwards. He married a wonderful person and they were terribly happy, so I was absolutely right.

You paint a very different picture of the nightclubs of Berlin from that usually portrayed in novels and memoirs. Were they really all as dull as that? You called them 'grim places'?

Yes, you imagined you were going to find Marlene Dietrich, and then you didn't. Nightclubs are for people who are searching for something. My husband and I weren't, and we just did think them very dull – awful noise, second-rate jazz, hideous people, and lights going on and off. One's idea really was to get away to bed.

How did people you knew react to your divorce and your attachment to Mosley? I imagine not everyone was sympathetic.

Everyone was unsympathetic, without exception I should say. It seemed very unusual for somebody as young as I was to leave her husband, to live alone, particularly after having had such an amusing, entertaining and interesting life as I had had. To want to cut oneself off seemed very curious to most people. First they thought I was too young to be married, then they thought I was too young not to be married.

Were you looked upon as rebellious?

I didn't *feel* the least bit rebellious. I just followed my instinct. It's very difficult to look back sixty years, but I never regretted it for one instant, and by degrees everyone came round to my point of view. It seemed the normal thing for me and Mosley to be together.

The relationship between yourself and the Mosleys after your divorce is rather baffling. For example, you speak of the death of Mosley's wife, Cimmie, as a 'devastating blow' for him. It was also, however, the turn of events that allowed you to be together and marry. Did you have a strong sense of fate intervening? Did you know Mosley's first wife?

I knew her, not very well, but she was charming and people were very fond of her. It was a devastating blow for me as well as him. She was a young woman and the last thing either of us ever expected was what happened. It might easily have meant a complete break with Mosley because it was terribly tragic for him. It might easily have worked the opposite way, but in fact it was only three years later that we did get married.

But what were your expectations when you fell in love with Mosley?

That I would live on my own with my children and that I would see him from time to time. I was interested in his politics, and I hoped to be able to play some part perhaps. Otherwise it was to be a life alone.

When you met Mosley he seems to have had the support of a great many men who were later prominent in public affairs – John Strachey, Aneurin Bevan, Arthur Cooke – and much later Richard Crossman spoke of the way in which he was a generation ahead of labour thinking. What went wrong? Was he unwilling to serve if he could not lead?

No. As you know he was first elected as a conservative, and when he crossed the floor he became an independent and then went the whole way and joined labour. But he never felt that labour would be an instrument of action; he always thought that the Labour Party would break in your hand if you tried to do anything with it. It was dominated then (and I suppose up to a point it still is) by two such disparate elements – the trade unions and the intellectuals; and they did not want the same thing. I don't belong to the school of thought which makes out that one party is perfect and the other is devilish. By and large all politicians want the best for their country, but they go about it in different ways. England was at that time in a very poor way with enormous and growing unemployment, terrific suffering and hunger. That must never be forgotten, because to be unemployed then was far worse than it is now, awful though it must always be. Mosley therefore thought that the only thing to do was to make a grass-roots movement of his own. Some of the men you mentioned came with him, but there was a tremendous crisis in England after the Wall Street Crash in 1929. In 1931 there was an election and rather predictably the Tories won a sweeping victory and the New Party, as his party was called, was wiped out at the polls; even he was not elected. It was then that he thought he had better call things by their name and so he called his new movement the British Union of Fascists, later modified to the British Union, as you know.

Why do you think he went to such an extreme?

It wasn't considered an extreme then. In those days, for instance, a great many Tories were admirers of Mussolini. Hitler had not yet come to power. It was a different picture. The reason he called it fascism was because it was in a sense a world movement and he thought it was more honest. With the benefit of hindsight, I think perhaps it may have been a mistake, but on the other hand he didn't in the least want people to imagine it was anything it was not.

Historically speaking, it is not difficult to have some understanding of Hitler's charisma and the spell which he cast. Even your own brother, who was later killed fighting on the other side, seems to have found his politics attractive initially. How did it strike you at the time?

It struck me as perfectly normal and natural. Tom used to say that it would be either the Nazis or the Communists, and that if he were a German he would be a Nazi. It wasn't only when he was a student in Berlin; he went on thinking that he would have been a Nazi – in fact, practically every decent German was. We must remember that nothing succeeds like success. Hitler not only had what people now call charisma, he was also – unheard of in the thirties – completely successful. He made promises at the polls and he kept them. In England both Labour and Tories said they could cure unemployment, put the economy straight, make an earthly paradise, they each had a chance and neither of them was able to do it. Under Hitler, unemployment dwindled to nothing and within two or three years a despairing country had been transformed into an extraordinarily prosperous one where people were happy and worked hard. Hitler always said he would give the people *Arbeit und Brot,* Work and Bread, but the interesting thing is that he put work before bread, whereas in England, they put bread first and then work a long way afterwards. Everyone was interested in Hitler. Churchill himself wrote at the time that Hitler was the person everybody would like to get to know, because he seemed to have a political secret which was hidden from others.

You speak in your book of your conviction that fascism in Britain would have been a different sort of thing from that which overtook the Continent. It is difficult for many people now, after the horrors of the camps and so on, to understand how it could have been different. What was your own vision?

That is such an impossibly large question; to answer it properly one would have to go into every fact of life. Briefly, the British parliament would have had a great deal of power which of course the Reichstag did not have. Another point which is very important is that my husband was always against imprisonment without trial. He said concentration camps were a horror which should never have been allowed anywhere. And as to cruelty, it just wasn't in his nature.

What impression do you retain of that first Nuremberg rally? It must have been very different from the huge stage-managed affairs of later years.

Even so they managed to gather a million people for that first rally. The Germans are of course quite extraordinary when it comes to organisation, and perhaps no other country could have done it, or done it so smoothly. It was an amazing achievement, and very interesting for a foreigner to see.

Were you mesmerised by it?

I wouldn't say one was mesmerised, but it was very striking and even very moving. You saw a country which had been reduced to despair pulling itself up by its own bootstraps.

With hindsight virtually everyone thinks of Hitler as a monster, but that is a public rather than a private judgement. He clearly commanded the allegiance of his fellow countrymen. You have never denounced him, and have continued to reiterate your admiration for him … were you ever able to see things from a different perspective?

No. I saw a man whom I got to know through a very strange chance because he was a friend of my sister Unity. Unity loved and adored him, thought him utter perfection. I never felt like that about him, but I did admire him very much for what he had done. I thought it quite amazing that of all the politicians in charge of big industrial nations at the time, whether France, the United States, England, he stood alone in having been able to solve the appalling problems of poverty and unemployment. That is never admitted now because it is said that no monster could possibly have done anything as clever as that. But in fact he did, and one day history will be written in a truthful way. That was the man I knew, the public man. As for the private person, I didn't know him all that well, but I was determined after the war that I would at least say what I'd seen, because by then he had become a monster, as you say. Of course the crimes in the war were utterly terrible and unforgiveable, but I believe that THE great crime was the war itself, which engendered all the horrors, and not only all on one side, I may say. I have felt it not only a duty but almost a pleasure to describe the man I knew, because it's so monstrously unfair when people deny something which they felt very strongly at the time.

Have you regretted anything?

No, absolutely not. Why should I? A woman writer published something the other day about me being impenitent. I've never really understood what I have to be penitent about. I just speak the truth as I remember it, as I know it, as I believe it.

But obviously you didn't know some of the things that had happened. Since the war there have been horrific revelations about Hitler …

Yes, horrific. But I can't change my mind about the man I knew long before all that happened. Like everyone else, I deplore the crimes and the horrors and the miseries, but I still think the basic reason that made them possible was the fact that we had a war, and for the war I blame Hitler and I also blame Churchill.

In your autobiography you suggest that the Jewish question was one which Jews rather brought on themselves and that it could have been solved by emigration. This is surely a somewhat naïve view, if only because there must have been millions of Jews, then as now, who thought of themselves as Germans. They were people who had fought as Germans in the First World War. Why should they have felt the need to leave?

I do see that very much, but at the same time, I'm quite sure that Jews who had fought for Germany in the First World War need never have left. Unfortunately, there was this tremendous feeling of anti-Semitism not only in Germany, but all over central Europe. I've always felt that it would have been far wiser, and also far more humane, to have had a round-table conference with, say, the League of Nations, and discuss how best to separate people who were not living happily together. I still feel that. That's what was attempted in Ireland, but because there were so many Republicans who remained in the Ulster, the fighting just goes on and on. If you force people who dislike each other to live together, it doesn't make for a very happy life for anyone.

But what was the cause of anti-Semitism?

After the First World War there was an enormous influx of Jews from Eastern Europe. As we know one of their great strengths is that they always hang together, and, rightly or wrongly, they became more and more unpopular because people coming back from the front found their businesses had been taken over. This engendered an enormous amount of anti-Jewish feeling in Germany as a whole, not just in Hitler. I've always felt it could have been solved simply by separating them. Most of them would have loved to go to America, just as they do now. After all, most Jews coming out of Russia go to New York, not Israel.

In your book you recount that Professor Lindemann, a regular visitor to Chartwell, said to you of your friend Brian Howard, 'Oh you can't like him, he's a Jew'. Were you aware of much casual anti-Semitism in those days?

No, I wasn't. He gave me quite a surprise by saying that. But there are double standards here. My father, for example, was very anti-German and was quite capable of saying the only good German is a dead German, but of course if anybody said that about the Jews they'd be for the high jump, although it's supposed to be quite all right to say it about other people. English people often say they hate the Scotch, but of course when they meet the Scotch they don't hate them at all. It's rather the same thing with the Jews. Collectively, so to speak, they may be deprecated by certain people but individually they're considered brilliant, charming, clever.

How do you feel about the Jews yourself?

I feel they behaved very badly towards my husband who was not anti-Semitic. They attacked him not only in newspaper articles and newsreels at the cinema, but physically at his meetings, until in the end they practically made him into an anti-Semite. He never was one, it just wasn't in his nature, but he did think they were a perfect pest. They used to disrupt his meetings, jump up and down and shout, very often without knowing English and therefore not even able to under-stand what he was saying. We now know they behaved in this way because they were having a really bad time in Germany, but having said that, it doesn't alter the fact that they were anti-Mosley long before he was anti them.

You were very friendly with Goebbels' wife. In Leni Riefenstahl's autobiography she claimed that Magda only married Goebbels to be closer to Hitler with whom she was actually in love. Was there any evidence for that in your view?

No. She did adore Hitler, but I'm certain she was in love with the Doctor, at least when I first knew her. I think she got very fed up with him later. As minister of propaganda he had so many starlets around, and that probably annoyed her quite a lot. Nevertheless, she was very fond of him, and devoted to her children.

Leni Riefenstahl also describes a conversation she had with Hitler on the subject of Unity. According to Riefenstahl, Hitler said: 'Unity is a very attractive girl, but I could never have an intimate relationship with a foreigner, no matter how beautiful she might be.' Does this accord with your own impression?

I don't think Unity ever thought of him in that way. She adored him, of course, and the great attraction for him was that she made him laugh so much. She was so unlike German women; she just always said what she thought, did as she wished. I remember him telling me one day he had been driving in Munich when he saw somebody coming straight at him the wrong way down a one-way street. His driver had to brake and Hitler saw it was Unity. She merely laughed and said she had been trying to catch up with him. She had no idea of keeping any rules, and that in itself is very unGerman. She was lawless, completely.

You have said many times that Hitler adored Unity and was devoted to her. I'm sure you are tired to death of being asked if Unity was in love with Hitler, but if she was not, why did she try to kill herself when war broke out? Was there a chance that they could have been lovers?

No. There was a much nobler reason behind her suicide attempt. She had always told me she would kill herself if England and Germany went to war. She was always an extremely patriotic Englishwoman as well as being so in love with Germany.

But she was in love with Hitler, wasn't she?

Well, there are so many different ways of being in love. I don't think she was sexually in love with Hitler, at least not in my opinion. She was devoted to him, admired him, but he represented for her something quite different from a lover or a husband. That's my own view. She was appalled by the global tragedy of her two beloved countries going to war. When she heard Chamberlain say that war had been declared on Germany, she didn't really wish to live and see any more happen.

Unity was the one who chose consciously to adopt a national-socialist creed. Did she ever change her mind when the consequences became apparent in the revelations after the war?

She wasn't really with us after the war, her mind had gone away. The bullet went through her brain and Professor Cairns, the brain specialist, told my father that it was not possible to remove it safely. It was therefore a kind of freak that she lived at all. The Germans had been afraid that she might do something and were therefore watching her. They knew she had a gun and on 3 September 1939 she went to Gauleiter Wagner in a great state and gave him a letter to send to my father, and also one for Hitler. She then went to the English Garden in Munich and shot herself. Wagner had her followed because he had a feeling that she was going to do herself a mischief. No sooner had she fallen off the bench than two men ran up and took her to hospital straightaway. She was unconscious for several weeks and was looked after with extraordinary devotion by nuns. Hitler had been informed, of course, and he was constantly telephoning to find out how she was. On 9 November he came to Munich for the anniversary of the 1923 *putsch* and it was on that day she emerged from the coma. Naturally her brain had suffered terribly. Hitler offered her the choice between having a house in Germany where no one would pester her, or, if she preferred, safe passage to her family in England. She chose the latter. Hitler arranged the whole thing with a Hungarian friend of my brother Tom who was, in fact, a lover of Unity. He was perfect. He took her in a special train with nurses and doctors to the Swiss frontier and there handed her over to Swiss doctors. She was taken to a clinic in Zurich, and my mother travelled across France with my sister Debo and together they brought her back to England. This was in January 1940, long before France fell. Before that, my father had seen Oliver Stanley at the War Office and made him promise that Unity would not be arrested. Stanley gave his word and he kept to it. To begin with Unity was paralysed, but by degrees she got the use of her limbs again. But her mind was completely different; it was never again normal. To what extent she realised what had happened at the end of the war I don't know, and I'm sure my mother kept newspapers away from her. She knew Hitler was dead, but whether she knew anything about the horrors of the camps, I doubt it. She never spoke to me of them and of course it was the sort of subject one never would have dreamed of raising with her. She was pathetic really.

In 1944 Adam von Trott was executed for his part in the failed attempt on Hitler's life. Instead of being shot he was hanged from a butcher's hook as Hitler looked on. His death was filmed for all to see, so there was no question of this being anti-Hitler propaganda. Was there anything about Hitler and the others that suggested this sort of potential ruthlessness?

First of all, I completely disbelieve that Hitler would have wished to see any person hanged in any way; that's just the figment of some foul person's imagination. You see, he was accused of terrible atrocities and cruelties because he was in charge, but that's a very different thing from doing it himself. I'm quite sure your story is untrue, nothing would ever make me believe it. As for Adam von Trott, he was a traitor to his country. He tried to kill the person who was fighting the war and losing it – I don't suppose there would have been very much sympathy in England for somebody who had tried to assassinate Churchill. His friend von Stauffenberg was one of the dirtiest fighters imaginable. He did what is always so much denounced when the IRA does it; he left a bomb so that it would go off and kill any number of people around, but not himself. If he had wished to rid the world of Hitler, all he had to do as a serving officer was to take his revolver, shoot him and take the consequences; that would have been the act of a man. What he did was the act of a perfect common or garden terrorist. There would have been no pity for such a man in England either ...

Yes, but they wouldn't have hanged him on a hook.

Well, I don't suppose they did. But if it was done in a cruel way, Hitler would never have demeaned himself by going to watch, never. I simply don't believe it.

Why are you so sure that Hitler wouldn't have done it?

Because I knew Hitler well enough to be sure. I knew his character, he may have been cruel but he wasn't mean.

You speak of Churchill as someone who was really in love with war. In your book you write: 'The difference between M. and Churchill was that M. wanted Britain to be strong in order to keep the peace unless any part of our possessions was threatened, while Churchill genuinely hoped for war.' And you quote in support of this statement Lloyd George who said: 'Winston likes war; I don't'. But if that was the case, why did Churchill disarm after the First World War and render the country quite unprepared for war?

He disarmed after the First War because quite rightly nobody thought there would be a war for ten years; this is what they call the ten-year rule. England became more and more poor (partly owing to Churchill's muddling as chancellor of the exchequer) so the ten-year rule was forever being extended, or reimposed. But in the early thirties he did begin to want to rearm, and he never stopped speaking about it in parliament. Mosley thought it fatal to have the very tiny air force which we had, and he always maintained that a strong air force and navy together could have kept an invader out. That's why he said that as long as England was not attacked we could make peace, or at least it would have had to be such a pathetic peace that it would hardly have counted. All the same, several cabinet members were for it, but Churchill was against it. I don't myself go along with the idea of the finest hour; it seems to me that if you declare war on a very strong country and have as your ally a rather weak country and the weak country is overrun, and your army has to escape through Dunkirk as best it can, throwing away all its armaments such as they were, there's nothing very much you can do except have a finest hour. What was so utterly foolish was to declare war in the beginning, pretending it was to help Poland; as Mosley said at the time, it was simply writing Poland a blank cheque which then bounced.

It must have puzzled you enormously, as it does me, why you were arrested and imprisoned. I suppose it's arguable that your husband might have been thought potentially disruptive, but what were the authorities afraid you would do? What could you have done?

Nothing. I had absolutely no idea why they imprisoned me. I was told recently by a professor that the Japanese who were arrested and put in camps in the west of America brought a successful action against the government and won their case. I thought that was wonderful, and wondered about bringing one myself until he told me that they hadn't got their compensation, so then the idea rather died on me. To return to your question, I think it was an extraordinary thing to have done to my husband too, especially since our people were extremely patriotic. They all joined the army when they could, and long before he was arrested. Fortunately, it's in black and white in his little paper which came out nearly a fortnight before he was arrested. He said there would be no question of where members of the British Union would stand; they would die to the last man in order to drive the invader from our shores. You can't say more than that. All he had argued beforehand was that until something happened, we should try to have a negotiated peace over Poland. But France fell so quickly, and then there was the terrible tragic farce of Norway, which was entirely Churchill's idea. And after he had made such an absolute fool of himself there, the next thing they did was make him prime minister.

What did you feel about Churchill's complicity in your imprisonment? After all, you knew him quite well, and he was your father's cousin, yet he separated you from your husband and your children and imprisoned you for years without charge. Do you feel bitterness towards him?

No, none at all for that. I feel bitterness towards him for the war itself. He was one of the people responsible for it, determined to have it. Sadly, I think the same of Hitler. I think that was their great crime, because it very nearly ruined Europe, and England was ruined completely. Not only have we lost our empire, which was supposed to be so strong but turned out to be so very weak, but also England itself changed very much as a result of the war, not all for the good.

Rumour has it that Churchill was prepared to allow you a bath and running water, but you refused it. Is there any truth in that?

Yes, it's completely true. I was sent for by the governor and he said: 'There's a message from the cabinet. Lady Mosley's to have a bath every day'. Of course, it wasn't possible, so I just laughed and so did he. All we had was a horrible foul little bathroom with a very old-fashioned geyser which did only three baths twice a day. There were about sixty of us, so we had a rota, and I could no more have gone in front of the others than … well, they were all my dear friends.

What did prison life teach you?

Nothing, except to hate discomfort, which I always have hated.

Did you leave feeling bitter?

No, I just despised the government so much really. If you don't respect people, it doesn't engender bitterness.

Were you ever offered any sort of explanation afterwards? Large numbers of those arrested with you were eventually freed, but you had to wait many years. Even after the war ended the authorities tried to prevent you travelling. Why do you think this was?

I just do wonder really. It is very extraordinary. One reason is that the Foreign office, as Enoch Powell so truly said, was a nest of spies and traitors; it really was, right up to 1951 when Burgess and Maclean very sensibly went off to Russia, which was where they belonged. And if you have a Foreign Office which is a nest of spies and traitors they don't want decent people travelling.

You say in your book: 'The paramount crime was the war itself. None of the atrocities could have happened in time of peace.' But we know now of course that both Dachau and Buchenwald were in operation by the end of 1933 ...

Not in the sense that you mean. There were several concentration camps which my husband greatly deplored, but they had floating populations, so to speak. People would be told they were going to Dachau for three months, and out they'd come again. I remember an edition of an illustrated Berlin weekly just before the war which had pictures of people in concentration camps; there were very few, a couple of dozen perhaps, and they were all mentally deficient, or people who might have annoyed the government. They were neither criminal nor were they our beloved liberals or anything of the sort, they were just ordinary common or garden misfits.

Did you ever meet Eva Braun?

Yes. She was very pretty. She was also extremely loyal and brave, as we know by what she did when she flew into Berlin. She was flying to her death and she knew it.

You once said: 'Men who wage war give cruel orders which are executed with violence and provoke tragedy. This applies to them all, Hitler, Stalin, Roosevelt and even Churchill, in so far as he had the power.' Many people regard it as breathtaking cynicism that you make no distinction between the first two, Hitler and Stalin, and the last two, not even a distinction of scale.

But I said 'in so far as it was in their power'; I call that a distinction. If Churchill had had absolute power, which thank God he did not, then who knows what he might have done? When you think of the lies that have been told about Hitler since the war I should think Roosevelt and Churchill would have been *capables de tout.*

566

I realise how dreadful it must have been to be imprisoned for years without even a shadow of a charge, but in view of the fact that there were crowds protesting at your release even as late at 1943, do you think that perhaps you would have been safe had you been released earlier?

That was the most terrific canard there has ever been. I know Clementine Churchill said to my mother that she thought we were probably much safer in prison, but my mother replied that she thought it was for us to judge. There was never a breath of any trouble after we got out. The *Daily Worker* even went round Shipton asking all the villagers to demonstrate against the Mosleys and not one of them would. We also discovered from an old man who lived in a villa about half a mile away that he had been approached by the *Daily Mirror* who told him that the Mosleys were going to be his new neighbours, and he said, 'Oh, how interesting', which wasn't at all the reaction they'd hoped for. You see, English people are not like that really. You might get communists demonstrating outside the underground if they think enough people are watching, but they are not going to do the slightest harm. No, that aspect never bothered us. What we minded was not having passports. We had to buy a little yacht to get away from England.

Presumably you were not a political animal until you met Mosley. Did you actually share his vision intellectually or was it something you took on board as part of your profound love for him?

It's not quite true to say that I wasn't interested in politics; I was. The first time I had a vote was in the 1931 election and if in our constituency there had been a Lloyd George liberal standing, I would have voted for him because Lloyd George had very clear ideas about unemployment and all sorts of things. I often thought afterwards that was why he and Hitler got on so very well. They liked each other enormously when they met, and Lloyd George wrote wonderful articles in the English papers praising him. There's a beautiful story about when he was on the *Berg* with Hitler. He was in bed one morning and he rang for his secretary Sylvester and told him he wanted to lay a wreath on the war memorial. Sylvester brought him a wreath, and gave him a card to inscribe. Lloyd George wrote on the card: 'To the brave men who died for the Fatherland'. Sylvester asked, 'Don't you think it might be better to put *their* Fatherland?' and Lloyd George thought perhaps it would, so he added the two little letters. It's terribly nice isn't it?

It is often said that you were the driving force behind Mosley. Would you agree with that?

No. He had the driving force within himself. He didn't need me for that. I suppose I must have influenced him a little bit, but not very much. He was much more of an influence on me. He was so clever, so brilliant.

It is also alleged that Mosley was something of a philanderer. Was this a problem which loomed large in your marriage or were you so devoted to him that you accepted and forgave his transgressions?

Well, I suppose one never completely accepts. Jealousy is a very real emotion which nearly everybody who has been in love must feel and know about, but he was an exceptional person, and therefore very attractive to women. He himself adored women, and that's just a fact. I never blamed him for that.

But did you suffer?

Only marginally really, because it was so taken for granted. It's very hard to say looking back; I'm sure there were moments when I was jealous, but not unduly, not enough to matter.

You were upset and angered by the publication of your stepson Nicholas Mosley's book, Beyond the Pale. *I was told that you were shown the book in draft form and decided to make no changes and that it was only afterwards that you had second thoughts about what he had written being made public.*

It's completely untrue to say that I was shown it in draft. He sent it when it was already too late to make any alterations, which is an old trick, as we know. I didn't mind him saying that Mosley was a philanderer, because it was just the truth. What I minded was that he tried to make him such a trivial person, whereas in fact he had been a tremendous worker all his life and had had brilliant ideas. None of that is dealt with at all in the book.

You mean the balance was not right?

Not only not right, it was simply ridiculous. The other point is that as he was his son, he'd been told he could have the papers, and I didn't bother to look through anything. There were very intimate things, such as letters between him and his first wife, which I didn't think it was right for Nicholas to publish. I implored him to take them out and the answer was that it was already too late. He has a complete obsession about his father, which may not be entirely his fault, because the truth is that the most interesting thing about him is that he's the son of an extraordinary man. Journalists know that too, so they always get off the subject of his probably not very interesting novels, and ask him instead about his father. The book about Mosley is fundamentally such a dishonest book, because nowhere is it suggested that he was a brilliant thinker or that he could have made a difference to the world had his ideas been accepted. Instead he is portrayed as some kind of playboy, which is too absurd when you think of what the man was. That's why I object to it.

How did he get on with his father?

Very well. My husband was very fond of him and very good to him always. But of course it turns out that Nicholas must have been fearfully jealous; it can't be explained any other way. The dishonesty and the obsession must be the fruits of tremendous jealousy.

Is there any truth in his suggestion that during your marriage to Mosley you suffered from appalling migraines which disappeared after his death?

It's quite true that I did suffer from appalling migraines, but what I had was a brain tumour. It was operated on and removed, and I'm alive to tell the tale. Mercifully, it turned out to be benign, but it had been pressing on the nerve for years. However wicked Mosley may be considered by his rather dreadful son, I don't think he could have given me a brain tumour.

With the imminent arrival of a united Europe, and apprehension about immigration and its troubles, you must feel that both your husband's goal of an integrated Europe and his fears about widespread immigration have become part of mainstream politics. Do you feel that many of his views have been shown to be right?

I think his views were quite extraordinarily right. When you look back at what he wrote, you realise that he had amazing powers of seeing what might happen. It's been a wonderful joy for me to see what's happened in the last two years, to see the utter and complete failure of Socialism and the reuniting of Germany, which is something I'd always known would happen but imagined might be long after my death. As to immigration, what happened in the 1950s was a great tragedy, and it still is. The proof is the number of laws which had to be made to force it down the throats of the unfortunate English, who really should have been asked, either in an election or in a referendum, whether they wished to be the hosts of an enormous population with a completely different culture from their own. They might have said yes, but I doubt it. Luckily there was a referendum for

Europe and there was a large majority in favour. And every time the English try and put a spoke in the wheel of Europe, as Mrs Thatcher tried to do, I mind less and less, because as time goes on, if you have twelve countries and one of them is always the one that is bloody minded, it doesn't really matter very much; the other eleven have their way and the twelfth comes hobbling alone afterwards. Of course I should love to see Europe with England at the very heart of it, as Mr Major promised, but if we're not to have that, we still have Europe. I'm a complete European. I love England, but I could be as happy living in Spain or Germany or Portugal or Italy as I am in France. The reason I live in France is that the house I've been in for so many years has so many memories I don't want to leave it.

You yourself have always had a very bad press. You said in an interview in The Times *five years ago: 'People think I'm a sort of gorgon.' Do you think there has been a deliberate campaign of vilification or is it just the usual tabloid thirst for copy?*

It's fashionable to attack me and people follow the fashion. I can't say I've minded very much or that I've done anything to stop it. I don't get hurt in the least. I'm very thick skinned. I also feel very fortunate in that I have children and grandchildren and great-grandchildren, not to mention a great many friends. The people I write to and receive letters from don't attack me, so I don't very much mind whether the papers do or not.

Have you ever had the same sort of hostile reaction in France that you have suffered for so long in England?

No. They're not a bit interested in attacking private people. In fact, they have a very good law which forbids interference in people's lives, which is an absolute boon. Nobody has ever bothered me in the forty years I've been here.

Even an apparently innocuous activity such as appearing on Desert Island Discs *can provoke an outcry after nearly fifty years. Can you in any way understand the strength of the public feeling against you?*

I don't think it's public feeling; it's really rather a small number of people. Apparently, what happened was the BBC decided to broadcast the programme when it was Yom Kippur. I'm not sure when Yom Kippur is, but it's something very important for Jewish people who immediately made a tremendous fuss and said they couldn't listen to Mozart or Beethoven and Wagner at Yom Kippur. The poor old BBC had to think of another date, but the next one turned out to be the Jewish New Year or something quite important. Again there was a tremendous outcry so they had to put it off again. In the end I wrote to them and said that if it was an embarrassment, then they should cancel. But of course they didn't want to.

Your beauty is legendary in its own time. Your looks astonish still and yet you are said to feel indifferent on the matter. Can this really be true?

I suppose I was quite glad not to be a monster, but people exaggerated quite a lot by pretending one was so beautiful.

But didn't men fall for you all the time?

I don't think they did. Men don't ever fall for someone who doesn't fall for them; that's my opinion. Women usually make the first move if there's going to be anything. In any case, there's something much more important than beauty, and that is charm, which is something you can't describe adequately. But there's no doubt it's far more powerful than just having big eyes.

You were friends of the Windsors in Paris and you even wrote a biography of the duchess. It is a very sympathetic account of a royal love story which is at odds with the widespread opinion that she behaved appallingly towards the duke who was in turn masochistic, and so on. Why did you want to paint such a romantic picture to the world? Were you really not aware of the negative side?

I was well aware of it in the sense that it is always being written about. But I tried to write what I knew about, what I'd actually seen. I just don't go along with the idea that he was masochistic or that she was beastly to him, or any of those things at all. Perhaps I did bring out the nice side, but one thing is for sure, he absolutely loved her. The reason I wrote the book was not at all because writing about royals is an amusing way of spending one's life, but the Americans had gone really beyond everything in their unfairness. It seemed to me that somebody might perhaps try and put the record straight.

You have said that one thing you regret is not having been able to do more to help Mosley to achieve his aims.

I regret most being unable to do anything towards his campaign for peace. From the beginning of the war until I was arrested I was either pregnant or nursing a tiny baby, so there was nothing I could do.

But, looking back now, do you regret anything else, or wish that things had been different?

Does it sound very smug to say no? When I have regrets in the stilly watches of the night, it's always been about having been unkind to somebody or not fair, but I suppose everyone has those sort of regrets. Otherwise in the big lines of my life I wouldn't have changed anything. I would choose the same life again, and in fact it's wonderful to be able to say that. It's like Nietzsche's idea of *die ewige Wiederkehr.*

Is there anything in life you'd still like to achieve?

Not for myself, but for the people I love. I long for everything to go right for them. Of course, everyone has to live life in his own way, and nobody knows that better than I do.

La Temple de la Gloire   91400 Orsay
19 January 1995

Dear Naim,

Thank you for your Christmas card.

I've been meaning to write to you for months. When you asked me questions you said something like, Did it make a difference to you being beautiful? And I answered: No. Well, the answer wasn't quite true, although I never considered myself particularly beautiful.

I am now punished for my lie. I have cancer in my nose, and in getting it well again the poor nose was not improved, and will never be the same again. Don't worry about me, I'm quite well (though so deaf and old), and I was very lucky to get a marvellous surgeon.

But of course it *did* make a great difference to my life being *considered* beautiful, even though I didn't much agree myself about it. Forgive this selfish letter. Just to say if you are ever in Paris do come down here, I should be so pleased.

With love,
            DIANA

John Murray

Born in 1909, John Murray was educated at Eton and at Magdalen College, Oxford, where he took a BA in history. In 1930 he joined the publishing firm of John Murray, and during the war he served with the Royal Artillery. His publications include *Byron: A Self-Portrait* (1950), and he edited the *Complete Letters and Journals of Lord Byron* (12 vols, 1973–81). In 1968 he became senior director of John Murray and in 1975 he was awarded the CBE. He died in 1993.

When I was doing the research for this interview, there was very little in the press cuttings which was revealing about John Murray the man as opposed to John Murray the publisher. Have you deliberately tried to keep out of the public eye?

Yes, for two reasons. First because any importance that I have is because of the authors I have published. Secondly, my personal life is so traditional as to be hardly believable. My main claim to fame is that I am the only publisher who has typeset in the nude, something I did when I was with Robert Gibbings, who ran the Golden Cockerel Press. As a young man I would go and help him, and unfortunately I hit the short period when he was in his nudist phase, and as I was only about fifteen or sixteen years old I found this very embarrassing. It was all right for him because his nudity seemed like a fur coat. But my own life is essentially dull, except perhaps in two regards: it is a good example of family nepotism – that's the first; and the second is that during my schooldays I had a bad spell of stammering which impeded my education. But I did get over it, and this is encouraging to anyone who has a stammer. It was a most terrible handicap, but I went to see a man called Lionel Logue, who subsequently helped King George VI with his speeches. He put me through a very interesting training and taught me something which I often now tell young stammerers; that is, with your hand in your pocket beat time with one finger in rhythm with what you are saying and this will help you get over the blockages. Other than that my life has been routine. I mean, it's boring to say that one's first memory is of sucking gooseberries; one can do without that.

How would you do a thumbnail sketch of your own character?

Ask me what I think about the characters of my authors, and I could tell you very easily, but until one gets older one doesn't really examine one's own character. Nevertheless, I have given this some thought and I would say that I have no greed, no wish to have yachts or a second home. I do have incorrigible curiosity, and I also have a terrible vice – envy, envy of other people's literary skill, for example. I try to pretend it's something else, such as admiration, but it is actually envy. On the positive side I have flexibility, which I consider a strength. Of course, as a publisher one learns to be flexible within the yardstick of truth and to give way wherever one can. This is the sort of quality which would make me a good ADC. It stems from the fact that my great childhood friend here in Albemarle Street was the butler. I so admired his handing round at table, decanting the port, serving the drinks. Barnes in his waistcoat looked like the backside of a wasp. He had a little bit of paper which was the blacklist of authors for whom there was never any spare chair at luncheon. I admired his style so much, the way he helped gentlemen on with their coats, and so on, that I asked him to teach me everything in return for being allowed to play with my train in the nursery. To my amazement he agreed. He did show me everything, and I now feel equipped to be a very good ADC. Indeed, I am afraid I embarrass American publishers when I help them on with their overcoats since I always put my hand under the coat to pull the jacket down. They look round at me with the gravest suspicion.

You were at Oxford in the 1930s and contemporary with John Betjeman and Osbert Lancaster. To an outsider it always seems as if they must have been exciting days. Is that how you remember them?

Oh yes. And they remained my greatest, most exciting friends until their deaths. That was why I published Betjeman – a fascinating occupation. You would be amused to see the typescript of *Summoned by Bells* with comments by Tom Driberg, John Sparrow (warden of All souls) and me. Betjeman was certainly one of the most inspiring people in my life. No journey with John was ever dull ... There's a charming episode I remember. He was rather extravagant and he used to take people to his club and have oysters and champagne. I remember one day his accountant, called Masterson, came in and asked if we had any more royalties for John Betjeman – 'He is terribly in the red, and I find myself going down on my knees and saying, "Oh Lord, please prevent John Betjeman from going into the Garrick Club."' I also met Osbert at Oxford, and he too was a life enhancer. He used to come in, either before or after doing the cartoons in the *Express*, for what he called a snifter, usually a gin and vermouth, and of course the amount of gossip one got from him was absolutely fascinating. Both John and Osbert were much more knowledgeable and scholarly than I was, Osbert on arts, John on poetry and architecture, and I learned a lot from them. But we had a sense of humour in common, and I think of no people with whom I've shared more laughter.

When you were at Oxford, did you sow your wild oats? Were you a womaniser at all?

Not at Oxford. I found no woman to womanise with at Oxford. Magdalen was still celibate. I did a little after Oxford, but I did it in moderation. Although I thought of women all the time, and was fascinated by them, I was frightened to get too deeply involved because I thought there might be no escape or that damage might be done. I usually found something I thought I couldn't live with permanently, so I was a very cautious lover, if that word is appropriate. I then met a girl, knew her on and off for about ten years, and married her. I'm still married to her fifty years on. We laugh sometimes to remember that we first me at a rat hunt in Buckinghamshire. We never caught a rat, but I caught a wife.

How did marriage and family responsibilities alter your life? Was that an area of great fulfilment for you?

Yes, and it increased the possibilities of my career. I'd been an active publisher for about ten years before I married, which of course confirms my view that the male should have settled what he wants to do before he gets married. My wife was very intelligent, read books, liked people, and that was a wonderful bit of luck because it enabled one to entertain authors rather more happily than it is possible to do by oneself.

As you get older, are you more sure or less sure about your ideas and opinions?

Less sure. Goethe writes somewhere: 'To be uncertain is uncomfortable, to be certain is ridiculous'; and that applies to me with one exception, which is the Net Book Agreement. I'm rather bigoted about that and I only wish that the greedy boys would look more carefully at the reasons for it being started in about 1900.

I don't know whether you're religious or not, but how do you feel about that area as you grow older?

I think if anything I've become a little less religious. I certainly go to church now less often than I did. Of course, the chains of habit are too weak to be felt until they're too strong to be broken, and though I read the lesson in the Anglican church up in Hampstead when I'm asked to do so, I feel a little ashamed that I attend the church less often. I try to analyse this and I can't, but there may be something of old Voltaire on his deathbed when he was asked by a friend to confess his sins and denounce the devil, and Voltaire said: 'Oh my dear fellow, this is no time to make enemies.' But I firmly believe that churchgoing is important for unifying the community.

Was there tremendous family pressure on you to become John Murray the sixth?

There was pressure, but not tremendous pressure. I don't think that excessive pressure was needed because I'd been brought up with authors around me. I've certainly never regretted my time in publishing or wished I had broken away from family tradition.

Your own son is set to be John Murray the seventh. Did that come about easily or was it a source of family tension?

I put no pressure on him. As in my case it seemed a natural progression of events. Looking back on family history, the great oddity to my mind is that every Murray but one had one son, and none of them revolted. One of the Murrays had two sons, my grandfather and my great uncle. They didn't agree with each other because my great uncle was artistically inclined and he wanted books to be produced with lovely gilt bindings. He was far too extravagant, whereas John Murray was a very cheerful man. So my Uncle Hal retired and became a wonderful watercolour artist. To return to your question, one of the things I always did when I knew my children were getting home was to hide the typescripts and relax back in the chair, hoping to give the impression that a publisher's life was one of lovely laziness. Whether I succeeded or not I don't know.

How well do you get on with your son? Is there a generation gap in thinking?

Our views are different on some subjects, but he has sense at the back of him. I have not come across a subject in which, even though it upset me, I didn't think he was right. I can say that perfectly truthfully, but then he's a remarkable fellow.

The publishing world which your son now inhabits is very different from the one you started out in. Are you confident about the future of publishing?

I'm not confident about the future of general publishing but this is a widely held view. Fortunately, in the last century we started educational publishing which now accounts for sixty to seventy per cent of our turnover. This is the future, a difficult future, because the government doesn't keep pace with new curriculums by providing money for teams of authors to produce new series of books. General publishing is difficult. I think I'm almost the longest serving publisher in the Publishers' Association Council, and many years ago I did a private survey. I cross-examined about fourteen of the larger publishers in order to discover how many of their books paid, and the figures were not uninteresting. More than half of all the books they published made a loss, another twenty-five percent just covered the costs, and the number that made a profit was absolutely minimal – under ten percent. Nowadays the reasons are of course perfectly clear: auction of rights, squeezing by powerful retailers, inadequate funds for public libraries and so on. But I needn't tell you all that, you must know it all.

One of the changes in publishing is that what used to be called flair has given way to market predictions, trends and committees. Do you regret the passing of the good old days, so to speak, or are you resigned to the changes?

Oh no, you can't be resigned to them. I believe that if the man who has flair has the persistence and energy to publish a book and has the stamina to follow his enthusiasm right the way down, he'll make a success of it. I don't want to be conceited myself but I remember well that my grandfather had not published any poetry for a long time, and since I knew Betjeman at Oxford I came back with a sheaf of his new poems. My grandfather said, 'My dear young fellow, we can't start publishing that sort of thing.' I told him I thought they were so good and would catch on and that some of my friends had been very excited by them. I felt so strongly that I offered to guarantee them with a hundred shares of Bovril that he had given me for my eighteenth birthday. He agreed, and I never had to sell the Bovril shares.

Have you ever discovered the secret of successfully predicting a book's sales?

That's a difficult one. This immediately raises in my mind the failures and successes for which I have been responsible. I have a perfect example of a book about which people were lukewarm turning out to be a great winner. There wasn't much hope in the office for a book called *The Story of San Michele*. We only printed about a thousand copies, so little did we think it would succeed. Then H. G. Wells reviewed it in the *Evening Standard* and said it was the most extraordinary book with plots that would keep a short-story writer happy for the rest of his writing life. From that moment it shot off, has been published in eighty-two translated foreign editions and has sold something like eight million copies.

Do you still get unsolicited books which turn out be to be winners or are they mostly commissioned now?

It's increasingly rare that typescripts coming out of the blue are any good at all. If commissioned, they are mostly by authors we already know. I remember a long time ago, however, commissioning a fascinating book, thanks to Bernard Shaw. He had just met the Benedictine nuns at Stanbrook who were writing a book about the abbess, and he advised me to go down and see Dame Felicity. The Benedictines at that time had a double grille through which one had to speak. I arrived at the abbey, rang the bell, and the lay sister opened the door and asked me to follow her. She then turned to me and asked if I were accustomed to talking through a double grille. I told her I was not and that I was petrified. She said, 'Mr Murray, you needn't worry, it's not like them Carmelites what have spikes on their grilles.' For about two years we worked on the book. The manuscript had to be put in a drawer in the double grille which she pushed to me and I then made comments and pushed it back; I never saw her face. If it was autumn when I came there was always a little basket of plums in the double drawer for me to take home and if it was spring there was a little basket of eggs. It was a marvellous book and a good financial success. It told the story of the abbess, and the correspondence between Bernard Shaw and the abbess and Sidney Cockerell in which they communicate about death and religion. It became the play *The Best of Friends* with John Gielgud as Cockerell.

How well did you know Bernard Shaw?

I knew him very well. I cured his wife of lumbago. I prescribed hot cabbage water with salt and pepper to drink, twice a day. It never fails. I used to be a martyr before I was married. I lived upstairs in the flat and I sometimes couldn't get out of bed, and had to wait till the staff from the advertisement department rolled me off and put on my clothes. Then somebody told me about hot cabbage water which I still drink now.

But Shaw, what sort of a man was he?

I was very fond of him, but ye gods, he was unpredictable. He could be more rude than anyone but Evelyn Waugh. He used to come to parties here and he was heartlessly rude. I remember we had an author called Mrs Campbell who told me her long-felt wish was to meet Bernard Shaw. So I took her up to introduce her. He pierced her with a steely, terrifying look and said, 'I only know one Mrs Campbell and you are not she,' and turned away. But If you were on the right side of him he could be very kind. Evelyn Waugh was rather similar. He had a terrible urge to shock people; he couldn't stop himself. I was never at ease with Evelyn Waugh. I was afraid he would do something unpleasant to somebody I was with. He was never nasty to me, because I probably wasn't worth being nasty to, but funnily enough when he wasn't like that I was fond of him and of course I had infinite admiration for him. I know of no one except P. G. Wodehouse who had that marvellous literary skill of economy, who could describe a situation and a scene in the fewest words.

Which authors have you felt proudest to have published in your time?

Many come to mind. Apart from John Betjeman and Osbert Lancaster, Kenneth Clark played an important part in my life. As a result of my interest in architecture, I'd read *The Gothic Revival* which was a very early book he had written while still at university. I asked if we could reprint it and, because of that, we then published most of Kenneth Clarke's other books, including *Civilisation* with the BBC. I'm keen on that example because, going back to before my time, there is a precedent with Charles Darwin. John Murray Three had read his *Voyage of the Beagle* and was so impressed by it that when he heard that the publisher was remaindering copies, he wrote to Darwin to ask if he could buy up the rest of the edition. Darwin said he would be very pleased, though he thought it would be a hazardous undertaking since the book hadn't sold very well. Murray bought the sheets, rebound them and, treating it as though it were a new book, relaunched it. The whole lot was sold in a fortnight. He reprinted it, and from then on Darwin sent Murray all his books. There's a fascinating letter years later from Darwin saying: 'You very kindly said you'd publish my next book. It's not what I thought it was going to be, and I release you from the promise to publish.' Murray replied that he didn't want to be released – fortunately, as it happens, since the book was *The Origin of Species*. The curious fact about this story is that Darwin wrote to Murray exacting a promise that he would not print more than a thousand copies. Of course it went like a bomb. Now the question is, what were Darwin's motives in trying to restrict Murray? Did he honestly, kind man that he was, not want Murray to lose on it? Or was it that, although he wasn't a churchgoer, he was reluctant to shake the religious views of other people? I think that's why he did it. Murray did finally persuade Darwin to let him reprint. And I wish I'd been there to hear the arguments that Murray gave.

I delighted in the Sherlock Holmes books, and in a way that was what first endeared me to authors. I was a schoolboy on my holiday and my grandfather was ill. He said, 'I think Sir Arthur Conan Doyle is calling today; will you be kind to him? I hope he may be bringing another typescript.' Conran Doyle brought the last volume of the Sherlock Holmes stories, and I was so staggered by this distinguished man's courtesy to a young whippersnapper like me that I thought: if this is an author, let me spend my life with authors.

People often remark that there is something very thirtiesish about you ... the dress, tweeds and bow tie, the highbrow, the longish hair and your debonair manner ...

Who says that? By God I'll ... I wish I could get hold of him ... though it was probably a lady. I don't regard myself as being of any particular period because I am convinced that I'm not yet grown up. I don't relate to any age, in fact I forget my age. My physiotherapist used to quote the following:

> Man is not old when his teeth decay,
> Man is not old when his hair turns grey,
> But Man is approaching his last long sleep
> When his mind makes appointments his body cannot keep.

I sometimes still feel like a child and I'm sure there are many who feel the same. As a consequence, one is appalled by one's own ignorance of what's going on in the wide world and, indeed, of all the literature of the past and all the things of the past. One feels an ignorant child.

But do you feel with age a kind of serenity you probably didn't have twenty years ago?

No. I don't ... perhaps after the fifth glass of claret I might possibly feel it.

Do you still find yourself excited at the sight of a very pretty woman?

Oh, yes. I dream about them. At one stage I thought it would help me to go to sleep, but I have discovered that it doesn't. One of the reasons I love going on the underground, the Northern Line to Hampstead, is because I'm fascinated by the different fashions. I'm particularly expert on the kind of bottoms that the authors have. I'm amazed that Americans always have such big bottoms and I think bottoms can reveal almost more clearly the character of a person ... well perhaps not more than the face, but the way people move their bottoms gives a strong indication. And of course sexual impulse is still there. But, alas, no competence ...

Do you have strong views about censorship?

I think censorship is right under certain circumstances, if you don't want to be unnecessarily cruel to people or their beliefs. My view is very unpopular, but I've held it all along.

Have you ever regretted being a publisher rather than an author?

No, largely because I know too well that I am not equipped to be a good author. I have tried to write, and I can't do it. I can rewrite other people, I can prune like anything, but I can't write.

Authors come with a great variety of personalities. Is there a sense in which you have to judge the man or the women as well as the work?

That's a splendid subject. In our editorial meetings, if somebody suggests a book, I always ask if the proposer has met the author. If not, I always say, 'Well, I would advise you not to put forward an agreement till you've seen him and you have talked with him, better still till you've eaten with him.' I think this is frightfully important.

Tell me about Byron.

When Byron died Hobhouse (his executor) said, 'Byron liked keeping his friends in hot water and it looks as though his remains will do much the same for his executors'. Of course this is true, but he had such a magnetic quality that John Murray Two bent over backwards to please him. His demands were excessive: when he was abroad he was always asking for Edinburgh powders, or racing dogs, indeed every kind of thing. In fact, if a new author came tomorrow and I had reason to believe that he would be as complicated as Byron, then unless his skill was very great, I think I'd turn him down. But Byron was Byron.

You have edited Byron's letters. What is it about him that attracts you above all?

His immediacy. Let me illustrate it with an anecdote. You will know that we burned Byron's memoirs in the fireplace where I used to warm myself as a child. Though I wasn't present there was imbedded in me a sense of guilt. Many years later I thought the only way to make amends for burning Byron's memoirs was to publish, collect and edit his letters. So we started. We had a great many here because of course we wrote to Murray but also got a lot from Lady Dorchester. Peter Quennell and I would meet one night a fortnight here in this room to decide if they were autobiographical enough to qualify as being memoirs, and secondly whether they were unpublished. One night, Harold Nicholson was here, sitting in the armchair, and we were reading a long unpublished letter, a fascinating account of what Byron had been up to that day – a riveting letter – and at the end, it gave the date, a Friday in March 1813. Harold Nicholson sat up in his chair, slapped his knee, and said, 'So that's where he was on Friday night!' You see, that curious immediacy, the effect of our wanting to know every detail of Byron's life is very extraordinary. And it hits anybody who approaches him. We still have Byron's boots here. They came through Lady Dorchester who had a row with the Lovelace family and consequently left Bryon's letters and many of his things to my grandfather. When the dust settles on his boots I clean them now and again and laugh at myself.

How would you most like to be remembered in the publishing world?

I suppose that I have been of some help in encouraging authors to create. I can't really think of anything else of lasting value.

If you were to live your life over again, what are the two things you would be unlikely to repeat?

I'm reasonably safe on that score. I've only done one thing that I feel any guilt about and I'm sorry I did it. From the point of view of my work, I can't think of anything that I would rather not have done; which is terribly dull. My main interest lies in the relationship between author and publisher. I was very pleased, for example, to discover a letter to Murray from an author who was a flop; he writes: 'Dear Murray. You are the only publisher at whose table an unsuccessful author can sit at ease.' Now isn't that a claim to fame?

Are you a gregarious character? I mean, is it possible for you be seduced?

Oh, I think so. Given the right circumstances, I'm eminently seducible.

Looking back, which period would you single out as being the happiest, most fulfilling, or saddest of your life?

I suppose the happiest, most exciting in a way, was from about 1930 up to the war, because that was when I was meeting new people, new authors. The saddest was when my mother, of whom I was very fond, became utterly helpless. Then there was the recent sadness of going to see Freya Stark; I published all her works and adored her, but when I went to see her last autumn in Italy, she hadn't the foggiest idea who I was. That I found most unbearable.

John Murray

People regard John Murray's almost as a dynasty. Indeed, Albemarle Street is a kind of last outpost of ivory-tower imperialism. How has this affected your life? Do you feel yourself to be in charge of something sacred?

I like the word imperialism. For a firm that's been famous but never very big the word imperialism is very curious. It is sacred to the extent that it contains so much that is personal to so many authors who provided literature in this country. I regard myself as a custodian of all these things. We have all the early manuscripts and authors' letters dating from 1768. If American publishers are being really beastly to me I like mentioning to them that we were publishing books when they were still our colony.

Most people who count as oldies would claim to have learned some important lessons in life. What are the lessons you have learned?

I hardly dare to give them to you, they're so awfully dull. Modesty, because it safeguards against disappointment. By modesty I mean keep your head down or it'll be chopped off. In so far as anyone can, try to develop a sense of humour, try and see the funny side of whatever it may be. And patience is vital, because then you don't waste whatever your endocrine glands provide. The one that infuriates my wife is thrift. She gets very upset and confuses it with meanness, which it is not. It's not wasting what you don't use, it's sending newspapers to be recycled. You can train yourself to be thrifty, yet never be mean. I turn out lights that are not being used, I try not to throw away food if it can be used. But on occasions, delicious occasions, a really good blow out is marvellous.

NIGEL NICOLSON

Nigel Nicolson was born in 1917, the younger son of Vita Sackville-West and Harold Nicolson. He was educated at Eton and Balliol College, Oxford. During the Second World War he served in the Grenadier Guards and from 1952 to 1959 he was a Conservative MP. He edited six volumes of Virginia Woolf's letters and three volumes of his father's diaries. He was a publisher and the author of many books on history, politics, architecture and literature, including the biography of his parents, *Portrait of a Marriage* (1970). He lived in Sissinghurst Castle in Kent, where his parents had made their world-famous garden. His autobiography, *Long Life*, was published in 1997. He died at Sissinghurst in 2004, aged eighty-seven.

It is difficult for those of us who had a fairly ordinary childhood and background to conceive of what it must have been like to have been born into such extraordinary circumstances. Have you always regarded it as a privilege or have you perhaps sometimes felt it as a burden?

I've never felt it as a burden, and I wouldn't call it all that extraordinary. It certainly didn't seem so to me at the time. I had two parents who have become well known, perhaps better known after their deaths than during their lifetime. Most people have one famous parent, I had two, and that has been a great advantage to me throughout life. First of all, I had a comfortable home, a very good education, and the company of extremely lively and intelligent parents and their friends. In addition, I acquired from them certain moral values which stood me in good stead throughout my life, and of course I inherited material benefits. For example, I now live at Sissinghurst which they found as a ruin and transformed into one of the most famous gardens in England. The National Trust owns it, but I am their tenant, rent free. I was given a springboard in my life, not a platform exactly, more a trampoline from which to bound upwards. Many of their friends were in a position to help me with my early career and that was an extra advantage. You're right to call it a privilege.

You describe your mother and father as 'parents such as God provides for one in a million' and you felt that you and your brother could not have had greater advantages in terms of education and money and independence. People who are born with a silver spoon often have great difficulty in accepting it. Has your attitude towards your background been a complex one, would you say?

All children react against their parents' attitude in certain ways, and I was no exception. To give you one example, there's no doubt at all that my father had a strong colour prejudice, and he also admitted that he had certain reservations about Jews. It would be too much to call him anti-Semitic, but he would rather not know if one of his friends had Jewish ancestry. He was a very strong supporter of Weizmann and Zionism, but it was mainly in compensation for his dislike of the Jewish race. I reacted against all that. After all, my business partner in life was George Weidenfeld, who gained a great deal from his Jewish ancestry. And again, although my father certainly wasn't a snob – he was more of an elitist – I found it much easier than he did to mix with people in the pub. There were other areas in which one differed from him politically. He was all for the old diplomacy, I was all for the New World and the United Nations. He felt very little sympathy for people outside certain capitals in Western Europe. London, Paris and Rome were the centres of his life and those outside were – if not exactly barbarians – trainee civilised people. My mother was very conservative. Although she had had a pretty reckless youth she was in fact immensely bound by the tradition of her own family. She believed in the aristocracy very strongly. She wasn't exactly a snob, but she did believe in lineage and in ancestry, and all of these things meant less to me than they did to her.

You write in Portrait of a Marriage *that your mother was guiltily conscious that she never managed to establish an intimacy with her sons and thought herself a failure as a mother, but you say it was as much your fault as hers. What did you mean by that exactly?*

I regret very much that I didn't make any greater effort to know her better. She didn't easily form intimacies. She was very private about the things that meant most to her which were her poetry, her garden, her friendships with women. None of these things did I ever discuss with her. She never wanted to talk about her current book, for example, whereas my father would talk about what he was writing the whole time, openly. And so I felt that I responded to her privacy with a sort of privacy of my own, and that established a gap between us which was never bridged. There were only one or two occasions in my life when we broke through that barrier. I might have been in distress about something, or she might suddenly have felt passionately keen upon some activity in my life, and those were the only occasions when for an hour or two we managed to establish any intimacy.

Were you in awe of her?

Slightly. She could be rather formidable and I was very careful not to trespass on ground where I was not allowed. For instance, I only went up to her room in the tower two or three times in thirty-two years. None of her family went up there. It was her sanctum, and only one or two friends like Virginia Woolf went there.

You say that your mother felt only a distant affection for you and your brother. That is the kind of attitude which modern psychologists would claim to be deeply scarring in later life. Have you suffered in that way at all?

I wasn't conscious of a lack of maternal love. I understood that she was different, that she couldn't be much interested in the activities of little boys, and later in life when I went into the war, into politics, into business, these were all areas with which Vita had no familiarity. Psychologically, I suppose, if one dug deep enough, one could discover that faults in my character were due to the lack of maternal love, but I'm not aware of it.

You wrote that for your mother babies were 'an interruption, a reminder of duty, a reminder of their innocence compared to her guilt' and so on. Presumably this was something you became conscious of only much later. Did you find it shocking?

No. We're talking about the 1920s and early 1930s and life was very different then. Most people of our generation and class had governesses and nannies, and we would spend 95 per cent of the day with them, and for 5 per cent of the day we were allowed down to see our parents. Often I would come down and find my mother deeply absorbed in her current book, writing poetry, something which required intense concentration, and the eruption of two little boys was a great disturbance to her, just as it was when we were at school and it was expected that parents would visit their children for sports day or half-term. Vita hated doing that. We felt perhaps a little guilty in obliging her to come, wanting her to come. Because she was a woman with far greater gifts than most mothers, we assumed we would have a different relationship from that which our friends had with their mothers. It was a special situation which we accepted and didn't mind. Vita felt guilty about not being a better mother, and she wrote to my father about it. I didn't read these letters till long after her death; at the time I didn't realise that she felt like that about us.

Was your father a good father?

Our closeness to our father was another reason for the distance between us and my mother. I don't know if it's true of other children, but my brother and I certainly chose one parent rather than the other, and in our case it was Harold, because of his greater openness with us, his interest in us, in our school work. He would read a play by Aeschylus in the original Greek, just because it was our set book at school that particular term, and he wrote us wonderful letters. And although he wasn't really a great countryman himself he taught us how to shoot and how to make a lake by diverting a stream, and so on. All these activities cumulatively made us much closer to him than to our mother.

Did Vita resent the fact that you were close to your father?

No. I know that she didn't because her life and her thoughts were so extensively documented in her letters to my father. They wrote to each other every day when they were apart, and they were apart a very great deal. There are over twelve thousand letters, six thousand from each side, and I've read every one of them. I don't think there was a single indication that she was jealous of our relationship with him. There was a slight element of self-reproach but never of envy.

During the war you served with the Grenadier Guards. Your brother was at heart a pacifist and his attitude to winning the war was described by your mother as 'deplorable'. Did you have similar doubts? Did you perhaps feel pressurised to fight because of your brother's weakness in that respect?

I never did. My brother Ben was very much under the influence of certain intellectuals like Philip Toynbee who tended to be left-wing and not exactly pacifist, but contemptuous of the idea of glory of empire. My brother was in intelligence, not in the front line. I don't think his pacifism lasted very long with him, and he came to accept the war. I was very different. The Grenadiers was a combative battalion in Africa and Italy, and I did engage in active warfare. I never killed anybody, I wasn't wounded myself, but these things could have happened to me, and I didn't feel any sense of shame. In fact, my shame came retrospectively, because I enjoyed a great deal of it, and I remember writing to my father when we were advancing up Italy saying, 'There is nothing more enjoyable than conquering a country.' He wrote back and said, 'Hitler feels exactly the same.' It was a very salutary reminder that war is a horrible experience.

Would you say you were a natural soldier?

I don't think I was because I wasn't a natural leader and I had a certain feeling of distaste for killing young men of my own age on the other side. But I had a very interesting war, and I was present at many of the most dramatic occasions, like the surrender of the Afrika Korps, Rommel's army in Tunisia, the Battle of Monte Cassino, and so on. The war for me was very exciting and at moments even a pleasurable experience, which it never was for my brother.

Victoria Glendinning wrote in her biography of your mother: 'Just as Ben had to free himself from Vita's projections, so Nigel needed to free himself from Harold's.' Was Glendinning right in this assessment, and did you free yourself?

She's certainly right about Ben. He freed himself not just from my mother but from both parents, quite early on. His chosen profession of art historian was not either of their professions, and his friends were in the world of art, very many of them were Jewish people, and certainly the great majority were not British. All this was new to Harold and Vita, particularly to Vita. I followed rather closely in my father's footsteps, by going into politics and writing books. My interests by and large were his interests, in literature and politics and history. I also took from him certain moral values. He would say that an honourable life is more enjoyable than a dishonourable life – which makes him sound rather platitudinous – but he did teach me that honesty is a desirable and beneficial quality. So on the whole I've been rather pious, not in a religious sense, but a good pagan as Harold called himself. All that came from him, and in no way did I ever feel I wanted to liberate myself from it.

Your father wanted you to go into the House of Commons as he had done, and yet you thought it would be 'too soft a life', as you put it. What was it that made you change your mind when you stood for Parliament in 1950?

I don't remember feeling that. My hesitation was much more whether I had the capacity for it, whether I could speak to large audiences, and whether I knew enough about other people's lives. I had a certain mistrust of myself which diminished as I got a little more experience. Fortunately, I was adopted for Bournemouth which was a very safe Conservative seat. But before then I didn't really have much of a political philosophy – I just followed the leader and doled out to my constituents bowls of soup from the party tureen. It was only after I became a member of parliament that I found my own position within the party, which was to the left of centre.

Was it clear from the start that you would stand as a Conservative?

Yes, and here again I was guided by my father. He himself had never been a Conservative and swore that he never would become one. But he felt that he had always been tied up with minority parties which meant very unsafe seats, and he said that one of his mistakes was never having joined one of the major parties. He advised me to join the Conservative party because, after all, my background fitted that – it hardly fitted the Labour party – so I did that without any very strong conviction that I was a Conservative, and it turned out that in many ways I wasn't. I was much more of a Liberal. I believed in the abolition of capital punishment, for example, and I was very much at variance with my party over the Suez crisis. Eventually I was de-selected, which was perfectly justified, and they chose somebody else who was more in tune with the party.

But have your politics changed over the years?

They haven't changed since then. What happened was that they changed when I was between the ages of thirty and forty. It was then that I began to feel more of a Liberal than a Conservative, and to dislike some of my Conservative colleagues in the House of Commons very much, and to like some of my Labour opponents very much. My admiration, I always found, was for the other side … Nye Bevan, Denis Healey, Roy Jenkins, people of that calibre.

Would you describe yourself today as a Conservative?

I've come back to the Conservative party. I've never voted Labour, though I've often voted Liberal, but in the last six months I have re-joined the Conservative party, partly because I think that John Major has been given such a raw deal by his own erstwhile supporters. He is a very remarkable man capable of great grace, resilience, intelligence, foresight, and I believe he has qualities which will be recognised in the future. There's no issue of Conservative policy today with which I disagree.

Was it an embarrassment to you that when you contested the election of 1950, your father was by this time in the Labour party?

Yes. He was a Labour candidate at North Croydon when I was the candidate for Leicester. His was a by-election and not a general election, so we didn't actually clash, but I had some difficulty explaining the situation to my constituents.

Did you understand his wanting to change his colours?

He disliked what he called the selfishness of the Conservative party very much. Remember that these were days long before Butler and Macmillan transformed it into what is virtually a liberal party today. It was then still rooted in the old aristocracy, which my father disliked and wanted to dissociate himself from. People call him a frightful snob, but they might remember that he became a Labour candidate specifically in order to distance himself from the Ascot set. He and I were not really too far apart. The idea that he was standing as a Labour candidate and I as a Tory candidate amused people a great deal, but didn't do either of us any harm.

You were in Leicester with your mother the day your father lost his seat in the election of 1945. What were your feelings for him then?

Oh, great sorrow, disappointment, sympathy for him. He loved being in the House of Commons, and when he lost his seat to Barney Janner he could barely walk through Westminster Square and see the light on above Big Ben signifying that the House was sitting, with him no longer there. It was really painful for him. But he had a second string with his books, and he never really made up his mind whether he was a writer who dabbled in politics, or a politician with an interest in literature. Perhaps the same could be said of me.

In 1959 you were unseated in Bournemouth, most probably because you abstained from the vote of confidence in the government during the Suez crisis. Did you ever come to regret your abstention?

Oh no, on the contrary, it's the best thing I've ever done in my life. I opposed Suez because it was based upon a lie, and because it was quite obvious that it wouldn't work. I knew, and most other members of parliament knew, that Israel and the French and ourselves had done a deal, and not only agreed that Israel should invade Egypt but encouraged them. We would join in with the excuse that we were ending the war for the Egyptians when we had actually stimulated it. I believe a democratic nation like ours should never go to war unless they have at least 90 per cent of the support of their own people, and Eden had barely 50 per cent. The whole of the opposition united against him on the grounds of the feasibility and morality of the operation. That's why I abstained, and I'm very glad that I did. Most people, even Conservatives, have come to agree that I was justified in what I did. And the fact that it meant the end of my political career added a note of semi-nobility to my action.

Some people suggested at the time that your losing the constituency poll might have had something to do with your father's friendship with Guy Burgess ... was there anything in that, do you think?

I never heard that said before. I knew Guy quite well, and disliked him very much. He was a drunkard, and when he was drunk he was extremely offensive, and he was not the sort of person that I felt able to cope with. My father was amused by him since he was a very witty man and an iconoclast, always attacking the establishment. My father sympathised with a lot of that and felt a certain loyalty towards him. He was the only person to write to Guy when he defected to Moscow, and they had quite a correspondence. Of course, as a patriot my father was shocked by treachery, but also he had a strong sense of loyalty, and he felt sorry that Guy, having made an idiot of himself, should be exiled for life to this distant hostile capital, and he wanted to give him a link with his own country.

Was the publishing of Nabokov's Lolita *a good political move, do you think?*

No, because it contributed to the loss of my seat. I don't think that many people in Bournemouth had read *Lolita*, nor were they interested in the support the book gained from leading literary critics; all that mattered to them was that here was a novel about a middle-aged man seducing a teenage girl, and this was shocking. It caused me a great deal of trouble at the time, because we were publishing a book which had been banned in America, and in England too in an earlier edition. Reading it now, it all seems very innocent, but it didn't at that time. At my suggestion we published a single copy of the book, sold it to a secretary in our office, and then sent the copy and the receipt for the sale of the book to the Attorney-General, the Director of Public Prosecutions, saying, if you want to prosecute us for an obscene publication, do so on the single copy; if we win the case, we will publish the full edition the following day; if we lose it, we will destroy the entire edition the following day. We leaked this proposal to the press, and it caused a great deal of amusement, and seemed to most people eminently fair. Apart from an acknowledgement, we heard nothing from the Attorney-General, although three months passed. And then on the eve of the publication we gave a party at the Ritz Hotel for all our friends and journalists and also Nabokov himself, and in the middle of the party I had a letter from the Attorney-General saying that he had decided to take no further action. We published the book next day and it sold eighty thousand copies in two weeks.

Has your partnership with Lord Weidenfeld been a stimulating one?

Enormously so. He was and remains quite an amazing man. When you consider that he arrived in this country from Austria on the eve of war with his own country, with no friends here, no money at all, and not even speaking English, and now he is a peer of the realm, founder of an important publishing house, and his portrait is about to be unveiled in the National Portrait Gallery. It's quite amazing what he has achieved. I often wonder what I would be doing if I had been exiled for some reason to Vienna in 1939, with no friends or money or prospects. I expect I'd be sweeping the streets.

But how did you cope with his Zionism ... because although he has mellowed and is now a man of peace, he was an extremist at one time. I certainly remember clashing with him in the past ...

Remember that I myself was in favour of the Zionists. I wasn't a Zionist because I wasn't a Jew, but it seemed to me then, and it seems to me now, a very noble cause. I admire very much what they have done. And I was only anxious in a selfish way not to lose my partner to Israel. He spent a whole year there soon after we founded the firm as the right-hand man of Weizmann, and I think it was one of the finest things he ever did, out of loyalty to me very largely, to return to England when he had a future made for him in Israel. He might not have become prime minister, but he would perhaps have become ambassador in the UN, and he would have done that job marvellously.

How can you call Zionism a noble cause when it entailed uprooting people who had been living there for hundreds of years?

Oh, you mean the Palestinians ... well, there is another side to it, I suppose. Are you Jewish yourself?

No, I'm Palestinian ...

Ah, you're Palestinian ... well, I can understand your feeling about it. But remember I was much influenced by my father's support of Zionism, his friendship with Weizmann from a very early age, so I started out that way. I never had an equivalent Arab or Palestinian influence. I recognise that, but I am still a Zionist. The Israelis have had to fight for the retention of their country and they were right to do so, because they had been given it by the Balfour Declaration which my father had helped to draft.

Except it was not something they were entitled to give ...

Well, that's how it all began ...

Yes, I know. Moving on, it must have been an extremely difficult, not to say a courageous, decision to publish Portrait of a Marriage. *Did you come to have any regrets?*

No, but I had considerable apprehension about whether it was the right thing to do or not. As I expected it did arouse criticism from some people like Bernard Levin, Rebecca West, Cyril Connolly and other leading intellectuals, but on the other hand it had support from people who knew my father very well, starting with my brother Ben who was all in favour, and people like James Lees-Milne. I did feel that if my mother's autobiography was published by itself it would cause even more controversy, and I would be accused of matricide, so I decided to write another two thirds on top of what she wrote explaining what happened, elaborating it, and telling the rest of the story, how her affair with Violet Trefusis and her autobiography stopped at the point when their affair ended. Vita behaved during those three years (1919–21) very badly indeed. She was going to desert her family, her loving husband, her children, and live the rest of her life, so she said, with a woman who was in a sense a seductress. I don't think that Violet was actually evil, but I believe that she was even more crazy than Vita in wanting to destroy their whole lives for the sake of a passion which would be ephemeral. My thesis was that the rest of Vita's life showed that she had acted in a fit of madness – her own words – and that her marriage subsequently was more successful because she and my father had jointly survived the crisis. Indeed, both Vita and Violet recovered from this dramatic affair and enjoyed very happy lives. Violet had no domestic happiness, it's quite true, but she made many friends. And Vita's domestic life was supremely happy from that moment onwards.

One of the most difficult aspects must have been the question of loyalty, but you say in the foreword that your mother trusted your judgement on that. However, Suzanne Raitt argues in her book about your mother and Virginia Woolf that the form in which you published Portrait *is differently accented from the text your mother wrote. She says that you guide the reader's attention away from her affair with Violet, and on to her marriage which, she argues, in Vita's own text comes over as a mere prelude to her affair with Violet. Do you accept that criticism in any degree?*

No, I don't. The woman is making it up. She thinks that *Portrait of a Marriage* was misinformed because I concentrated on the marriage more than the affair, but I wanted to show that Vita really spent the rest of her life making up for the cruelty that she had directed towards Harold for three years. I felt that was quite legitimate and would put the autobiography which she left in the context of her whole life; that was my purpose. I believe it was right to do it that way, though of course the critics concentrated on the affair and not on the marriage.

593

Frank Kermode called Portrait of a Marriage *an ugly story with a happy ending, and you yourself say that without the ending it would have been simply ugly. Despite that, it does seem that you go out of your way to be kind in your account, extolling your parents' virtues, playing down their faults, excusing their prejudices and snobbery on the grounds that they were natural to them. Did you feel a need not just to tell the story, but to defend your parents?*

Yes I did, particularly against the charge of snobbery. I've tried, mostly without success, to draw a distinction between snobbery and elitism. Snobbery is a vicious quality, it's cruel, but elitism is a very natural and beneficial one. Vita had a certain feeling of kinship with the aristocracy, but why not? She would select from the aristocracy those worthy of being aristocrats. She didn't give the benefit of the doubt to people simply because they held a title; they had to prove themselves worthy of that title, and as often as not, they didn't. Harold and she felt very much the same about this. Harold once wrote in his diary – I can quote it to you because it was only yesterday that I reread the passage – 'I have always been on the side of the underdog, but I've also believed in the principle of aristocracy. I have hated the rich, but I have loved learning, scholarship, intelligence and the humanities. Suddenly I'm faced with the fact that all these lovely things are supposed to be class privileges.' To call him a snob is simply a tabloid method of abusing him because he happened to be intelligent and have high standards, and required high standards of intelligence among his friends.

It is a sad irony, is it not, that despite the great love between your parents and the sexual passion outside the marriage, that there was nevertheless a singular lack of intimacy within the family?

But then it happens to everybody, as they become adults themselves, marry and have children of their own, that a distance opens between them and their parents. Their own children and ultimately grandchildren become more important to them than their parents, and so you could say the older you get the weaker the intimacy becomes.

To take the point a little further, Victoria Glendinning suggests that although the family bonding seems to have been strong there was a sense in which it was merely notional. She says: 'The platonic ideals of relationship, however dearly held in the heart, are not a substitute for reality.' Do you disagree with that?

I think she was imagining a family relationship which has never really existed. She is not only demanding the impossible, she's demanding the undesirable. You have at some point to cut the umbilical cord, you have to venture out into the world on your own, and while you are indebted to your parents for what they've given to you in the way of an education and companionship and comfort and support, after a bit you have to work life out for yourself and try to pass on some of the advantages which you have had to your own children.

I understand there was no common family sitting-room at home, everyone had his own space, and it was not an easy place for you to bring friends back to ...

That's true. But the fact that we had our own sitting-rooms meant that it was the family habit to work. Both my parents were writers, they had to earn money, they had to keep us at school and they expected their sons to work, which we did. We began writing very early on in our lives. First it was letters and diaries, and then it was short stories and essays. We were a literary family, and a literary family doesn't sit all in one room unless they are the Brontë sisters.

Do you think that all the letter writing in your family was perhaps a substitute for something else? What I mean is, in all the outpouring of feeling between your parents and their lovers, the letters themselves somehow take the place of actually living the feelings and emotions they describe?

Our family relationship, it is perfectly true, was largely made by correspondence and not conversation. We would pour into our letters all our experiences and ideas and hopes and fears and disasters and triumphs, which we would never do to the same extent when we met face to face. With letters you can think out ahead what you're going to say which you can't always do when you're talking. Virginia Woolf used to say to me that nothing has really happened until it's been described in writing. She urged me to keep a diary, and I followed that advice. I was very shy when I was young and she once said to me, 'You mustn't wonder, what is this person thinking about me?, you must ask yourself, what am I thinking about him?' That was a wonderful piece of advice which I passed on to my own children.

Would you say your relationship with your own children is much warmer than the one you had with your parents?

No, I wouldn't say that. Again, I make the distinction between Vita and Harold. The relationship I have with my daughters is much warmer than that between Vita and me, but I don't think my son Adam has quite the same feeling of intimacy with me that I had with Harold. Much earlier on in his life he saw faults in his father, in me, whereas I took time to see faults in Harold. Adam reacted pretty strongly against my political views; he was very much a more natural Labour man that I am. He's not a person who gives his admiration very easily, although he gives his affection very strongly to his wife and to his children whom he really adores. He gives them his time and his care much more than I ever did with him. That was another thing that he might feel that I lacked as a father, that I didn't take enough interest in his life. I have two daughters. Rebecca, who is a very successful journalist and a very private person, but my other daughter, Juliet, is much more open. Of my three children, she is really the closest to me. I'm a little scared of Adam. He has enormous abilities as a writer, as a father, and as an action man, and in some ways I envy his gifts, meaning I wish I'd had them, not that I'm jealous of them. I feel no resentment towards him, he's a very remarkable man, and I think that he will become an important figure in English letters and writing.

Would you prefer to have had a closer relationship with him?

Yes, I suppose so. I feel a certain deficiency as a father, that I failed to have that closeness with him, but we remedied it to some extent in an extraordinary way by writing a book together called *Two Roads to Dodge City.* In 1988 we set off on the same day for the United States in separate aeroplanes. He flew to Los Angeles and I flew to Miami, and on arrival we each hired a car, and we drove for the next three months all over the United States, I over the eastern half, Adam the western half, all the way up the two coasts to Canada, then down again to the Gulf, and at the end of the three months we met in the centre of the United States – Dodge City in Kansas. We wrote to each other every day, posting the letters collectively once a week to prepared addresses by express mail. He wrote as a young man who had never been to America before, I as a much older person who had often been there, and gradually our correspondence turned into dialogue about what sort of people we were and how we differed. It wasn't intended like that but it evolved like that, and in a curious way we got to know each other much better by this correspondence, which was a public not a private correspondence, than we ever had in conversation between the two of us.

Victoria Glendinning talks about the 'insulating effects' of your upbringing. To what extent were you aware of those?

She probably means that it was an aristocratic upbringing. But it is as well to remember that I had the whole war commanding men who came from very different backgrounds, and as a member of parliament one was constantly dealing with people who hadn't had one's advantages, and here at Sissinghurst I'm on the best of terms with our tenants, our gardeners, and so on. It is quite true that my friendships are made among people who share my tastes and interests, but then that is true of everybody.

In your thirties you wrote to your mother: 'I grew up slowly, met the real difficulties so ridiculously late, and still remain strangely immature in some ways ... '

I think that one of my immaturities was sexual, though I don't want to go into this in any detail. Having no sisters, being at a boys' school only, then in Oxford where one knew very few girls, and in the army, which was a masculine occupation, I knew very few women until I was in my late twenties, and that held me back as it would hold anybody back. I was a virgin until after the war, until I was twenty-seven years old.

Did you make up for it afterwards?

Not very vigorously. I always adored women and I'm not in any way indifferent to the charm and beauty of young girls. I still feel great tenderness towards young women, and not only young women, but I don't have affairs with them; I just like their company and the presence and the sight of them very much.

But don't you ever feel a sexual tension if a woman is attractive?

Well, no. When you're my age, and remember I am seventy-nine, I don't think that one does. Lust is something which diminishes to the point of extinction. Admiration for feminine beauty, on the other hand, does not. I have a great many women friends ...

But you haven't inherited the passion of your mother?

No, I certainly haven't. I never never had feelings of desire such as she felt. I was more like Harold in a way; although he was homosexual, I think his sex was pretty casual and intermittent and really relatively unimportant. And it's been the same with me.

Your brother Ben at one point had a man friend but your parents resented it, they didn't want the man to come to the house, and yet they were supposed to be very liberal ...

Firstly, it wasn't just at one point. Ben was in fact gay. I think my parents felt sad that he wasn't heterosexual because they wouldn't have grandchildren. Both Ben and I were married late in life – I was thirty-six and Ben was nearly forty. Ben was gay, there was no question about it, and his marriage didn't succeed, but he did have a daughter. I was never gay and all my affections were for women, but sex has never played a great part in my life as it did in Vita's. You're quite right to say that I lack Vita's passion. Thank goodness.

In Portrait of a Marriage, *you write of yourself and your brother: 'Ben and I both married and had children, but our marriages did not succeed, nature having endowed us with a greater talent for friendship than for cohabitation, for fatherhood than for wedlock.' Do you feel sure that it was* nature *rather than your experience and upbringing?*

The reason I wrote that was because both Ben and I were divorced by the time I wrote *Portrait* and since our wives were still alive, I wanted to include a single sentence in as tactful and truthful a manner as possible. (Louisa, Ben's wife, is still living, but my wife has died.) I showed them this sentence before publication, and they approved it, and so it was written with a certain guile, but at the same time it was true. I didn't have a great capacity for wedlock, even though I had had a very good example in front of me in Vita and Harold. They made a success of marriage, I made a mess of it, and the same with Ben, so it wasn't an inherited incapacity. In the case of my marriage I lacked Harold's patience with what I saw as the failings of my wife, and she was exactly the same with my failings, and so the marriage dissolved, not in acrimony but in mutual indifference. I was really quite happy to be left a bachelor again.

Was it important to you that there should be no divorce while your parents were still alive?

Yes, I think so. I didn't want to wound my parents by divorce. My wife went off with another man, but she wouldn't have done so if we had been happily married, so that was the occasion, but not the cause, of our separation. Fortunately, it was after the death of both Harold and Vita, so they never knew. They knew about Ben and his wife and were very distressed by that.

Your first real love was Shirley Morgan who went on to marry someone else. Was that a crisis in your life?

Unrequited love is probably the most painful experience which men and women undergo in their lifetimes. Not everybody has experienced it but I would say that most people have, so they will sympathise with me when I say that I was shattered by it, and felt myself unmarriageable, unlovable, useless, hopeless, weak. All the self-reproach which I'd ever felt about myself was concentrated upon this disappointment when Shirley married Henry Anglesey, and it lasted quite a long time.

But we're still very great friends. I'm godfather to one of her children and she's my oldest and my closest friend.

When you married your father cautioned you that the physical side of marriage could not be expected to last more than a year or two at most. How did you view that advice?

Harold, being a homosexual, didn't attach much importance to the physical side of his marriage to Vita. I think it was quite remarkable that he managed to produce two children – in fact three, because we had a brother who was stillborn – but after my birth I don't think he had any physical relationship with Vita. When he gave me that advice he was really thinking of his own experience and not of the generality of mankind. For most people the physical side of marriage lasts almost a lifetime, but not with me, because I was never very highly sexed. I was perfectly faithful to my wife – and I'm not going in to this in too much detail because it's really too intimate – but I really had a pretty tepid sexual life; my energies were concentrated elsewhere. So Harold's advice was really rather comical, based on his own experience, but it happened to hit mine as well.

A large part of your own literary life has been devoted to writing about your parents and editing their letters to each other …

Yes, but I have of course written on many other things – Jane Austen, Napoleon, Curzon. It is true that my best-known book is *Portrait of a Marriage*, and it's made me financially secure. It was a bestseller in America and England for months and months and had dozens of foreign editions. All my finances are really based upon the success of that book, so I can't deny that it was a very important part of my life, but I do sometimes wonder whether having been the son of such famous parents has been a handicap or not, and I think it has been a bit, because people like yourself probably associate me more with Harold and Vita than with anything else. It is a certain disadvantage to be the son of a famous father and mother. It's just like Mary Soames; she is not herself, or even the wife of Christopher Soames; she's Winston Churchill's daughter.

Your mother's reaction to the possibility of Sissinghurst going to the National Trust was passionately negative. 'Never, never, never,' she said 'il y a des choses qu'on ne peut pas supporter.' It didn't pass to the National Trust till after she died, but did you sometimes think it was a betrayal nevertheless?

No, for one very simple reason. She left a letter for me with her will, which said that although she would never have given Sissinghurst to the Trust in her lifetime, she realised that I would have no alternative after she died, because of the death duties, but to sell the place or give it to the National Trust. There was no question in my mind which of the two to choose. If I'd sold Sissinghurst the money would have gone mostly to the Treasury, and it would have ruined one's life and destroyed this place, so I had no hesitation whatsoever.

Your mother wrote of you as a young child: 'If Nigel stays as he is, he will be happy and everybody will love him.' Did that turn out to be prophetic?

I don't think any man or woman can say of themselves in old age, 'Everybody has loved me.' I do have enemies. I have Lord Aldington, against whom I gave evidence in the great Tolstoy trial. He doesn't love me. And I turned a man out of a cottage which belonged to me, because he was destroying it. He doesn't love me. I don't think I have excited among a great many people what you could call love, though I wish I had. As for being happy, I've had great failures in my life and they don't make me happy on recollection. I lost my seat in Parliament, never got another one, I've never written a book which is regarded as a work of literature, as opposed to one of sensational interest. When I read my father's essays now, as I sometimes do, I wish I could write as well as he did, I wish I had his wit. But there are other things with which I feel moderately satisfied, like my standing over the Suez crisis and publishing *Portrait of a Marriage*, both of which I think were the right things to do.

CONOR CRUISE O'BRIEN

Conor Cruise O'Brien was born in 1917 into a strongly nationalist Dublin family. He was an outstanding student at Trinity College, Dublin, where he took a BA and PhD. His doctoral dissertation, later published as *Parnell and his Party* (1957), was a remarkable mingling of political analysis and literary insight. Between 1956 and 1960 he was a member of the Irish delegation to the UN. His book *To Katanga and Back* (1962), widely considered to be his finest work, is an autobiographical narrative of the Congo crisis of 1961, when he served in Katanga as representative to UN Secretary-General Dag Hammarskjöld. Following academic office in Ghana and New York, he was elected Irish Labour TD (MP) for Dublin in 1969, became Minister for Posts and Telegraphs in 1973, and was defeated in 1977 because of his opposition to IRA violence in Northern Ireland. Between 1979 and 1981 he was editor-in-chief of *The Observer* and he was a pro-chancellor of the University of Dublin from 1973. He was appointed senior research fellow at the National Humanities Center, North Carolina (1993–4), and in 1996 published *On the Eve of the Millennium* to wide critical acclaim. He opposed the 1998 Good Friday Agreement and allowing Sinn Féin into government in Northern Ireland. O'Brien defended these harsh attitudes and actions towards Irish republicans, saying: 'We do right to condemn all violence but we have a special duty to condemn the violence which is committed in our name.' His *Memoir: My Life and Themes* was published in 1998. He died in 2008.

You have said that in your youth you were more strongly drawn to the Protestant than to the Catholic ethos. Why was that?

The second school I attended was a Catholic convent school and I have unpleasant memories of the severities practised there, not actually by the nuns, but by some of the lay teachers. My recollections of Catholic teaching are of being told this is how it is, repeat after me; it was all authoritarian. Then I went to my main school, and found that I was invited to discuss, to question, and I liked the atmosphere. What appealed to me was not Protestantism, but enlightenment, and I have related to it ever since.

This was a Protestant school?

It was a school attended in equal parts by Protestants, Jews and liberal Catholics, that is to say Catholic families who did not want their children to get a Catholic education for reasons which I later came to understand. I remember being confused on my first day there when the headmaster said that the Church of Ireland boys would stay for prayers. It never occurred to me that the Church of Ireland could be anything other than Catholicism and I knew our family were supposed to be Catholic so I stayed for prayers, and witnessed the horror of people kneeling on one knee only. But I got over that initial shock.

In 1916, the year before you were born, your uncle was killed by a British officer during the Easter Uprising. Your maternal grandfather has associations with the Irish Republican Brotherhood, forerunners of the IRA. To what extent has your family background helped shape your own attitudes?

One of my uncles, the one who was married to my mother's elder sister, was shot on the orders, as you say, of a British officer in Easter week, 1916, but another uncle, just a little older than my mother, was killed in the autumn of that year of France, wearing the same uniform as that worn by the killer of my other uncle. These two deaths are an integral part of my life. I spent a considerable part of my youth puzzling out what it meant. I'm still not sure.

Do you have a strong sense of history in your present ideological position?

Yes, I'm an historian, partly by training but more and more by inclination. I find that almost everything I read now is history in some form or other.

Is not history largely a matter of interpretation?

Yes, but you wouldn't find any historians who would deny that a world war happened between 1914 and 1918. From then on they could start interpreting, but again it is a fact that one side lost and another won, and the consequences of that are there. The historian interprets, but there are great brute facts which he can't interpret away.

Your mother was a Catholic, your first wife was a Protestant, your daughter is married to the son of a Protestant archbishop. Your second wife is a practising Catholic, niece of a cardinal. Have these different threads confused your sense of your own identity, or have they clarified it?

That's a good question. All I know is that I am happy with the results, except that my first marriage broke up, and that's always a cause of sadness to all parties. But relations with my five children and with my second wife are excellent, and I have learned a lot from my wife about Catholicism. She has taught me to be more comfortable with it, but makes no effort to induce me to believe in it. Indeed, I think if I showed signs of believing in it she would deter me.

I understand that now you do not profess any religion. Is that simply a lack of faith or were you driven from the church in some way?

I was never really near enough to the church to be driven from it. My father was an agnostic, my mother indeed during my father's lifetime would have declared herself to be an agnostic, as would other members of the family. Though I don't think I ever believed any part of it, I had my first communion, I was confirmed. This, according to the teaching of the Roman Catholic Church makes you a Catholic, whether you say you are or not ... I say I'm not, but if I were to meet a bishop, he would say, well you are. When I think back to my childhood I think of it as something dark and oppressive in the background, something of that I was supposed to be part of but didn't ever wish to be any part of. I was a very priggish little boy, an only child who had spent most of his time with elders rather than contemporaries, and when a pious aunt presented me on my eighth birthday with a missal, I looked at this thing and said, 'Thank you Aunt Mary, it will relieve the tedium of the mass.' [Laughs.] That didn't go down terribly well.

Do you think you might mellow in years to come?

I have mellowed. Until 1977 ... and that's sixty years ... I was actively hostile to religion in general and most particularly to the Roman Catholic Church. After my father's death, my mother, acting on his request, sent me to a non-denominational school, as it might now be called. I learned around that time that a contemporary of mine, who also belonged to a family of Catholic background, was taken away from the school because his mother had been warned by a priest that every day the boy stayed at the school lengthened her late husband's sufferings in purgatory. I believe my mother got similar advice, but the poor thing sweated it out, and kept me at that school though she was being mentally tortured by those people. So I didn't grow up with any feelings of kindness towards the Catholics. Then my wife in the late 1970s was involved in a very bad car accident; her right leg was broken in thirty-three places, she was in intensive care for quite a long time in a hospital in Ireland run by nuns, and their care for her and kindness to all of us was something really marvellous. When the recovery happened it was very much 'thank God', and something melted then. I ceased to have the hostility towards the religion that I had before. But that didn't incline me at all towards belief in any credo.

You have had academic appointments as well as political, administrative and diplomatic ones. What drew you to the universities?

A desire for knowledge, for instruction, for leisure in which to turn around and think, to meet other people interested in ideas; and I found all those. Most of my teaching has been done at various American universities, and I have enjoyed that. I found that American students start with absolutely nothing in the way of knowledge of the subject, but they learn prodigiously fast, and are very highly motivated and full of curiosity. Most recently I was a research fellow at the Woodrow Wilson Centre in Washington DC, and I found it delightful actually to be paid for reading books which I would be doing anyway.

The universities are currently in turmoil. What do you think their function ought to be in the late twentieth century? Has Cardinal Newman's 'idea of a university' been superseded?

All kinds of things are going on in the universities. There is, as we all know, the multi-cultural agenda which in broad outline I dislike. The idea of the politically correct is obnoxious to me, but I did have a curious experience in that regard. When I went out to the Wilson Centre I said I would like to work on the phenomenon of the multi-cultural, the politically correct, and of course race studies and gender studies are a part of that. This was during the period of the Senate hearings over Clarence Thomas and Anita Hill's accusations against him. This was a strange happening, because within that agenda, race studies and gender studies people have been allies, but here the black-rights people and the women's-rights people were opposed. A poll showed that sixty-seven per cent of blacks were for Clarence Thomas, whereas all feminists of whatever colour were for Anita Hill. This prompted me to read black feminist writings. I had expected – and I'm not proud of myself for having expected – to find a great deal that would be propagandist and attitudinising. To my surprise and delight I found a very considerable body of valid and splendid historical writing by black women thinking about the past of other black women, not to make some propaganda point, but to find out. I also found that the alliance in gender studies and race studies is essentially based on white feminists and black-rights people, males mostly, zeroing in on the white male. It is Manichean stuff and the white male is the arch enemy, but the black feminists are aware that white women can be racist and that black males can be sexist, and this gives it a richness and a maturity that the other lot don't have.

In view of the turmoil which appears to be typical of sub-Saharan Africa, do you have any sympathy at all with the South African whites and their dilemma? If they prevent majority rule they are anti-democratic ... if they permit it they may be completely overwhelmed.

I certainly have a lot of sympathy with many white people there, especially the Afrikaners. De Klerk is working on the right lines; he is not about to give in to the ANC, but is looking for a power-sharing formula in which the whites would still have considerable power. It now looks as if Mandela is prepared to go down that road, which means on his part a sizable compromise. I think the ANC as we know it is about to split, and what you will have will be a coalition of all those, white or black, who have anything to lose. It is basically the people on the outside who are going to be unemployed. This is not an exhilarating prospect, but it's better than the apartheid state. I'm politically now fairly optimistic, but the demographic and social and economic realities are absolutely horrendous. Anyone you talk to in South Africa is more likely to be talking about crime than about poverty; if you're a young black and can't get a job, crime is your only career.

I believe you visited South Africa three years ago and in Cape Town you were forced to leave the platform by anti-apartheid demonstrators. What exactly happened there?

I'll tell you exactly what happened. In 1986 the World Archaeological Congress was held in Southampton, and scholars from every country in the world were invited, including South Africa which has one of the richest schools of archaeology. Then, under pressure from the ANC and the academic left in Britain, the South African scholars were disinvited; they were told they were not wanted here, not because of any flaw in their scholarship but on account of their South African nationality, although these scholars were actually from universities like Cape Town which was desegregated. This struck me, as it struck a number of other academics, as a dreadful thing to do. So I protested against it. Then, having been invited to give a course of lectures at the University of Cape Town, I publicly announced that I was accepting, thus breaking the academic boycott of South Africa. I was to give a course of fifteen lectures. In the beginning there was no serious trouble, then I was invited to a debate on the subject of the cultural boycott. naïvely I accepted, thinking a debate was a debate. When I arrived in the hall there was nobody on the other side of the debate, and although I insisted on making an initial state-ment, the evening consisted mainly of hostile questioning. The first question was, 'Why did you come here to South Africa – was it to mock the sufferings of the oppressed people?' That was just a foretaste of what was to come the following night when I gave a public lecture about the Middle East and Israel. There was quite an audience, mainly Jews from off-campus, but the same crowd gathered outside in the corridors around the lecture hall and chanted slogans just when questions had started from the audience; I was most edified by my Jewish audience who went on as if nothing had happened. They thought, wrongly, that this was an anti-Semitic demonstration, but it was actually part of the cultural boycott. The audience remained attentive until the mob broke down the doors and surged in and drove us all out. When I met my regular class in the morning, a class of about a hundred people who were racially distributed as in the general population of the University of Cape Town – about fifteen per cent black students, the rest white – again the mob broke down the door. The vice chancellor, Stuart Saunders, rang me later that day to say that there was a danger of much more serious violence, so I had to call them off. The impression it left on my mind was that I wouldn't like to be in a South Africa that was run by the ANC. I wouldn't mind a government of which the ANC was a part, but not in control.

So there was no hostility directed against you personally – it was simply as a result of the boycott?

Yes. Of course, they subsequently claimed that I had treated them in an intolerably patronising manner, but in those circumstances you either bow down or you are accused of being insufferably patronising. On the whole I'd rather be accused of being insufferably patronising.

You were devoted to the whole concept of the United Nations. What was it that attracted you to the UN?

To enter the United Nations for the Republic of Ireland; we were admitted in 1955 and took our seats in the General Assembly in 1956. It was like returning to the world, because Ireland had been neutral in the Second World War and, understandably, rather cold-shouldered by the victors. We had been vetoed by the Soviet Union for membership of the United Nations for which we had applied as soon as it was set up, it had been a pretty claustrophobic existence before that.

Katanga was described by Brian Urquhart as 'the most frustrating, nerve racking and isolated of all the UN posts in the Congo'. Did you feel honoured to have been chosen by Hammarskjöld for the job or did you think you were being exiled?

Katanga was the great challenge to the United Nations at that time. I did feel honoured, and I knew it was a high-risk post and also that it was for that post I had been chosen. Formally the request to the Irish government was to second me for service in the political and Security Council affairs department in New York, but I always knew I would be sent to the Congo. And I had no sense of being isolated or banished or anything of the sort.

You had been selected by Hammarskjöld for your qualities of courage, independence of mind and spirit, as a radical young man who would be able to put Hammarskjöld's own ideas into practice. You for your part admired him equally. This mutual high regard must surely have made the break all the more painful when it came?

Yes, it was very painful indeed. Your summary is correct, but I'd like to add an element or two to it. This is the background to why I was appointed to go to Katanga: in January 1961, Mnongo, then minister of the interior of the so-called independent state of Katanga, announced the death of Patrice Lamumba, the prime minister of the Congo. Mnongo said that he had escaped from captivity in Elisabethville and had been killed by some villagers angered by his bad behaviour. But the whole world believed that Lamumba was actually murdered by the government of Katanga, specifically by Mnongo himself. There was outrage throughout the world, in the third world in particular, and also among American blacks. The United Nations and Hammarskjöld in particular were being blamed, with – though I didn't know at the time – a good deal of substance, because Hammarskjöld's instructions to the UN forces who controlled all the airports at the time were not to intervene between Mr Lamumba and his official pursuers. This meant that with the United Nations troops looking on he was handed over in Elisabethville to be murdered. The revulsion that followed this caused the United Nations, and Hammarskjöld in particular, to change course. My instructions were to try and bring the secession to an end. He picked me for that because the Irish delegation of which I was a part had an anti-colonialist record. Also he wanted someone who was not part of the communist bloc, or African, or Asian, and not part of the Western alliance either; and I had those qualifications. But the break with him was a very grim thing. The first I knew of it, that I had lost contact with Hammarskjöld, occurred in this way. We had moved to arrest Tshombe and his ministers (Tshombe had been helped to escape by the British) but whether Hammarskjöld knew exactly what we were going to do or not, I don't know. He certainly knew what we had done because it was reported to him, and he issued a statement in Leopoldville in which he represented Tshombe's people as having been the aggressors, which they were not; we were. But he gave the impression of the United Nations being peacefully engaged until fired on by Tshombe's lot. Of course, the meaning of that was that Tshombe could have a ceasefire at any time he wanted. The legs were cut from under us. I'll never forget the reading of that dispatch.

I know it's going back a long way, but how would you sum up what went wrong in the Congo? A lot of people say that you were going to be sacked by Hammarskjöld, had he not been killed. Is there any truth in that?

I think so. Once he nullified what I had done, he couldn't live with me. He would certainly have got rid of me.

How much did your personal affairs contribute to your resignation? There must have been enormous pressure on you from the press, given that you were living, not with your wife, but with the daughter of a cabinet minister.

That was raked up, but the decision had already been taken on political grounds because I had become identified with a policy that had not worked and had to be repudiated. It was, incidentally, a policy to which they reverted after I went, because they did use force to end the secession of Katanga, partly because they were embarrassed by what I had revealed. My wife's presence in the Congo then became a convenient way of notifying my government that I would have to be withdrawn.

What are the practical limitations of the United Nations as an organisation?

I think one has to distinguish between the United Nations when there is consensus among the permanent members, and when there isn't. For most of the existence of the United Nations there was no consensus. For example, when I was in the Congo only one of the permanent members supported the secretary general in what he was doing. The Soviet Union openly opposed, Britain and France covertly opposed, so that's the context in which I and Hammarskjöld had to work at that time. No wonder it became a bit crazy. But then of course in the late 1980s, towards the end of the Iran-Iraq war, five-power consensus emerged. The secretary general in his mission to Baghdad and Teheran was backed up by the embassies of all the five super powers, a blissful condition which I had never thought to live and to see. That five-power consensus is still there, though there is of course uncertainty as to whether it can be preserved. Nobody knows what's going to happen in Russia.

But do you think it's a good thing for the super powers to dominate the United Nations?

There is only one super power, and it dominates; that's a fact of life. But there is a qualification to it: The United States likes to get the blessing of the Security Council on what it is about to do. It was the United States who determined that a war should be fought over Kuwait … nobody else. But the fact that they need to get the agreement of other powers is welcome as a limiting factor. If for example the United States at the time of the Vietnam War had needed to get consensus in the security council, I don't think they would have got it.

You were once interested in Yeats's relation to the ideas of Nietzsche. Was Yeats in any real sense a fascist?

No, he wasn't; he was a person who in certain moods was attracted to fascism. He was attracted in the 1930s when the Blueshirts – I won't say emerged – limped out in Ireland, imitating the paraphernalia of Mussolini and Hitler. They were never really a formidable lot – they never killed anybody, for instance. In 1938, the last full year of his life, his poetry is more seriously fascist. He wrote, 'You that Mitchel's prayer have heard, Send war in our time, O Lord.' The poetry of that time is certainly attracted towards Nazi Germany; it never fully flowered, but that's where it was all tending in the last few years. Yeats felt the pull of violence, and violence attracts the imagination. He was a sort of heat-seeking missile.

A lot of politicians were also attracted to Nazi Germany at the beginning.

There was something very powerful and attractive about success after success from 1935 onwards. Everyone's eyes were riveted on what was happening there and a lot of lesser politicians hitched their wagon to that, to their later regret.

You are known in some nationalist quarters as the fascist of the left. How do you react to that?

First of all, I laugh at the said nationalists using fascist as a term of abuse, because during the Second World War the IRA was pro-Hitler. Their chief-of-staff went to Berlin and they were trying to liberate Ireland with the aid of the Nazis, so when they call me a fascist I ask them, who do they think they're kidding?

But is there anything you might have done that could label you as a fascist of the left?

Yes. And not so much of the left either. I am in favour of the introduction of internment for the parliamentary godfathers on both sides of the border in Ireland, and the IRA in opposing that would of course have liberal allies.

For a long time you have been pro-Israel and anti-Arab, and have been especially vitriolic about the Palestinians. How did you come to adopt this position?

I would like you to quote – if you can – anything vitriolic I have ever said about the Palestinians, or indeed any Arabs. I have never attacked them. What I have said is that I don't think it is possible for Israel to obtain peace with the Arabs by handing over territory. There will always be, and for quite understandable reasons, a great many Arabs who don't want peace with Israel except on the basis of the destruction of Israel. That is not true of the people who are at present negotiating with them on behalf of the Palestinians, but there are other Arabs out there who will not give Israel peace on the grounds of anything that could be negotiated by the Palestinians.

Wouldn't you acknowledge that there are people on the Israeli side who are equally extreme, if not worse?

This is part of my case. This is why territory for peace is not possible either on the Arab side or the Israeli side. If, for example, a government in Israel were to say that the Palestinians can have the West Bank and Gaza, that they can set up their state there and the settlers will be withdrawn, that would mean civil war in Israel.

But one has to acknowledge that there will be no peace ever unless there is compromise on both sides. Whereas in the old days one could have accused the Arabs of intransigence, today the intransigence seems to come more from the Israelis. The majority of Palestinians want peace, and your stand on the issue, if I may say so, does not help the cause of peace.

You're quite right that the Palestinians in negotiating on the basis of autonomy have come a long way; they have come to it in the terms of Shamir's own offer. I regret that he now seems to be backing away from what he has offered, and as you say that is an unreasonably intransigent position.

Let's talk some more about this. I have the impression from reading articles you have written that you are very pro-Israeli. Presumably you don't deny that Begin and the Irgun gang modelled themselves on the IRA of Michael Collins?

Indeed, Shamir's own clandestine name, Michael, is after Michael Collins.

Since you are opposed to the IRA, how do you reconcile the two positions in your own mind?

The IRA of 1919–21 were acting at least nominally under democratic authority; they were the armed forces of the First Dáil, which was an elected body representing in free elections the majority of the Irish people. The modern IRA since 1922 has no democratic mandate at all from anyone; they are an unlicensed body of terrorists.

But Begin and Irgun were terrorists too. In one way you seem to oppose terrorism, in another way you don't condemn it.

Essentially the Zionist movement has its roots in Europe and is an outgrowth of the European history that produced Nazism. Chaim Weizmann said of 1921: 'We must have a Palestine if we are not going to be exterminated.' That seemed a very extreme and bizarre thing to say in 1921 but by 1933 it was not. And the degree of sympathy I have for Israel is based on the realisation that Israel is the result of horrendously extreme conditions. That is why I write as I do. It's an emotional issue with me.

What about the poor Palestinians? They weren't responsible for the Nazi atrocities?

No, they were not, and they have suffered as a result of the Nazi atrocities. But they haven't suffered quite as much as the Jews. Of course, nothing that one can say or do will make amends to any of those who have suffered, either among the Jews or the Palestinians. But one has to look at the here and now and see the best that is actually available. I have a high regard for the present negotiators on the Palestinian side, I think they are very brave people, but there are high risks, especially if they succeed. I wish that Shamir would meet them halfway. Palestinians are not at present demanding territory; what they are asking at the moment is autonomy, and I would hope they get it.

Most Israelis recognise that the 1982 invasion of Lebanon was a terrible mistake, yet you defended it strongly at the time. Would you now agree you were wrong?

I didn't defend it strongly at the time. I merely went against some of the denunciations of Israel that were going on at the time. I defended it to this extent, and would still defend it; the PLO on the soil of Lebanon were claiming to be carrying on a war against Israel, and they had their vast heavily armoured encampments there for the destruction of Israel; I put the point that if in the Republic of Ireland you had a similar situation with the IRA, legal and condoned by Dublin, carrying on bombings of Britain from the Republic, British intervention in the Republic would be the probable outcome and would be rather generally accepted. That is the parallel I drew. That was regarded as outrageous.

I regard it as outrageous. Shall I tell you why?

Am I interviewing you or are you interviewing me?

You are being interviewed, but I want to pick up on your reference to the destruction of Israel. Nobody can destroy Israel today; the world would not allow it.

Under certain conditions the destruction of Israel could indeed occur. For example, if as a result of an attempt at peacemaking the people of Israel should be divided to the point of civil war; that would be the end of Israel. There are great divisions in Israeli society, there's no doubt about that.

One more question about Israel before we drop the subject. You are known as a vocal champion of Israel, perhaps an uncritical one …

Not true. You wish to *portray* me as uncritical.

Not at all. It seems almost a case of 'My country right or wrong'. Whereas there might have been a case for supporting the state of Israel to begin with, what do you say about Israel's treatment of the Palestinians – well documented by Amnesty and Israel's own human-rights organisation?

The Israelis are in occupation of a territory whose inhabitants reject them and resist them. And these things happen under these conditions. I wish that Israel could withdraw from the territories it occupies. I find it difficult to see that it can, for reasons which I have set out analytically and not emotionally. The treatment of the populations of the West Bank and Gaza is based on the laws, regulations and practices with which Britain governed all of Palestine, under the mandate. The military regulations are there; they are British ones.

But you were always anti-colonial …

Yes … all right …

I'd like to ask a question in a different area now. There is a great deal of controversy about the efforts made to suppress the freedom of information. You have been a member of government – did you feel the need to keep the public in the dark as far as possible?

I don't recall keeping the public in the dark about anything in particular. In this domain I am blamed for being the author of the legislation currently in force which prevents spokesmen for the IRA and other paramilitaries from broadcasting; and there are those who hold that this is a limitation on freedom of information. I defend it on the grounds that all broadcasting codes prohibit incitement to crime, that terrorist violence is of its nature criminal and that the spokesmen in question have no other purpose than to promote this criminal conspiracy.

During your time as Minister for Post and Telegraphs, it has been suggested by some that you will be remembered chiefly for attempts to censor and control RTE. Is that an unfair assessment?

I would accept it to this extent: that if prohibition of broadcast interviews with spokesmen for terrorist organisation is censorship, then I am a censor. Beyond that not at all, never one step beyond it. While I was minister responsible for broadcasting, the RTE regularly ran a series of satirical broadcasts about the government of which I was a part, including pieces about myself. They ran it every week, for two years I believe; it was still running when my government fell. I don't think that's censorship exactly.

Mary Holland recalls that when she went to work for RTE in the mid-1970s people were 'quite simply frightened out of their minds'. Were you aware of that at the time?

Utterly ridiculous. Nobody was ever frightened out of his mind at RTE, nobody at all. They were frightened under Mr Haughey because he intervened regularly; whenever he objected to a programme, he was on the line. We never interfered with RTE at all.

Yet Mary Holland described the atmosphere as follows: 'Self-censorship had been raised to the level of an art and a caution lay like a thick cloud over everything.' Do you accept that it was like that or at least appeared to others in that way?

I think it appeared to Mary Holland like that, but it's a ridiculous portrayal. I don't think you'd find anyone in Dublin to agree except Mary Holland and some republican sympathisers.

In an interview with Bernard Nossiter of the New York Times *you attacked the* Irish Press *and said you were collecting clippings printed in the paper with a view to having the editor, Tim Pat Coogan, arrested on the grounds that the letters supported Sinn Fein. The interview was duly published in the* Irish Press *and it was suggested that only the ensuing public outcry prevented you from putting your plan into practise. How do you defend your position on this issue?*

It's not true that I suggested that Tim Pat Coogan should be arrested; I didn't. I simply showed Bernard Nossiter certain letters that they had published which amounted to incitement to violence.

In 1978 you left politics and became editor-in-chief of The Observer. *Why did you do that?*

Because it was an attractive thing to be asked to do. I had been writing for *The Observer* on and off for a good many years. I was invited by Lord Goodman to meet with him and the new proprietors of *The Observer*, and then they offered me the post of editor-in-chief of the newspaper which I was happy to accept.

There is speculation among your opponents that you got the job at The Observer *because of a possible connection with the British Intelligence Service. Do you find this an absurd idea?*

Are my opponents the IRA? I imagine they are, since nobody except the IRA has its spokesmen talk like that. I never had any connection with the British Intelligence or any other intelligence organisation ...

But have you ever heard it mentioned before?

I've seen it chalked on walls by the IRA, but I won't dignify it by further discussion.

During your time at The Observer *there were suggestions that you used your editorial powers to censor articles on Ireland, notably from Mary Holland. What do you say to that?*

An editor *is* a kind of censor. You decide what goes in and what out, and if you don't like things you want them to go out. Mary Holland wrote a piece during one of her IRA strikes, a tear-jerking thing about the dependants of the people who were on the dirty strike, and the whole article was an IRA sympathy knee-jerk performance which appeared in the *Observer Magazine*, not something that normally engaged my attention. When I saw it I naturally complained about it to the editor, but it was too late to stop it. I certainly did create when I saw it, and Mary would of course have seen it as censorship.

Do you think any sort of reconciliation is possible between Rome and Canterbury? I recall you speaking of the Pope's missionary attitude towards Protestantism. The two positions do not seem to be hopelessly intransigent.

When the present Pope talks about the unity of the Christian churches, he means unity under him and according to his laws, and if I were an Anglican I wouldn't be too keen about being incorporated into all that; but that's their business. I'm neither Anglican, nor a Roman. I wish the Pope well.

You were one of those who was instrumental in deleting from the constitution the reference to the special position of the Catholic Church in Ireland. How powerful does the church remain in Ireland?

The results of two referenda would suggest that the church still does have a lot of authority. They defeated the referendum which would have made divorce legislation possible in Ireland, and they succeeded, most ironically, in inserting the provision which appears to make abortion illegal in all circumstances but is now found actually to have legalised abortion in certain circumstances; so they really shot themselves in the foot over that one. Their authority is now less than it used to be, even considerably less, despite the results of these referenda, for the real test of authority is on the matter of contraception. The teaching of the church is still implacably against artificial contraception, and yet it is quite clear that married Catholics are using contraceptives – the reproduction patterns are the same as those of other groups – so the teaching of the church in a centrally vital matter has gone. Also, the public reaction to the original court decision in the rape-victim case was quite negative in relation to the church. You may have seen a piece of mine in *The Times*, an open letter to the Catholic bishops. That letter in a more extended form appeared in the *Irish Independent*, the largest circulating newspaper among Irish Catholics. The fact such a letter could appear is a sign of the times.

Yet last year in an interview you described abortion as 'a great evil' …

My point about abortion is that it is an evil always, but there are a number of cases in which it is a lesser evil.

How long do you think the Catholic Church will be able to hold out against letting their clergy marry, with all the ramifications of providing for widows and children and housing and pensions and divorce and remarriage and the whole secular round? Do you think it will come eventually?

I don't know. The convention of celibacy is so long established that the rule won't go unless there is such a shortage of clergy that they make the concession. I would certainly wish to see celibacy at an end. It is a bit sick to have celibate males deciding how other people should behave in bed. In fact it's disgusting.

In an article in The Observer *written twenty years ago you said that socially you belonged to the Irish Catholic community, that you were motivated by affection for it, identification with it, and a fear that it might destroy itself and you through infatuation with its own mythology. Twenty years on do you still believe that, and is it any closer to destroying you?*

I feel more relaxed about it than I would have then because the power and authority of the Catholic Church have been eroded. It doesn't inspire the same amount of fear and therefore revulsion that it used to when I was younger.

The trouble in Ireland is always put down to the differences between Catholics and Protestants, but how true do you think that is? Some of the IRA appear to be extreme left-wing revolutionaries who have only the most tenuous connection with Catholicism.

I don't think that's true. Indeed, if you look at the times when emotions have been greatly raised, for example during the hunger strikes when men died, you wouldn't have seen too many volumes of *Das Kapital* around, but you saw the missal, the rosary beads, the holy water, all the paraphernalia of Roman Catholicism. Catholic Ireland was there; the Marxist stuff was very much top dressing. There is a story that illustrates this in the Provos. There was a time before the split in the IRA when the leadership was Marxist, and in that period, the late thirties, they were trying to detach the IRA from anything that would identify them with Catholicism. They sent a circular saying a decade of the rosary at the funeral of any given IRA volunteer was to be discontinued, but eight battalion commanders sent it back with the word that they were not going to obey. Those eight battalion commanders were later the founders of the Provisional IRA, so the good Catholic boys are the core of the Provos. For that reason, the Catholic clergy in Belfast encouraged the emergence of the Provisional IRA because they thought it meant saying goodbye to those bad communists who had been in charge. And, of course, by bringing about a purely Catholic and nationalist IRA which fitted much more naturally into the scene than the old Marxist stuff did, they produced in fact a more dangerous strain of the virus. To do them justice they didn't foresee the lengths to which the Provisional IRA would go, and I think those of them who are still around now regret what they did in 1969.

Do you think the Anglo-Irish Agreement can ever do any good? It seems obvious that whatever the political talk about guarding the rights of the majority, it does put Northern Ireland in quite a different category from the rest of the United Kingdom – because of deep-rooted historical differences.

As long as the majority of the population in Northern Ireland want to remain in the United Kingdom they should be allowed to do so, and we should leave them alone and stop trying to nudge them in the other direction. By nudging them we appear to be partners with the IRA. When I say 'we' I mean the government. The historical differences in political allegiance are there, but you can't argue the population of Northern Ireland out of existence, nor can you induce the people who fundamentally disagree, to agree. It is therefore an inherently unpleasant and enduring situation.

But do you see there ever being a solution to it?

I think it could be ameliorated. One thing that would have been a positive effect would be for the Republic of Ireland to amend articles 2 and 3 of its constitution, which lay claim to the territory of Northern Ireland. This claim is very offensive to the majority of people there. I won't say this would change everything overnight; it would just reduce the temperature a little.

In 1972 you sketched two positive models for the Irish future, the 'benign' and the 'malignant'. What you said then has turned out to be largely true. Twenty years on, are there any new models?

I'm afraid not. As long as the British stay, you'll have the IRA and in turn the Protestant parliamentary response to the IRA. But if Britain goes you'll have full-scale civil war. That's my malignant model, and I still believe in it.

Do you enjoy popularity in Ireland?

When I walk down O'Connell Street, for example, I'm likely to be stopped four or five times by somebody who wants to talk to me, and those people are invariably friendly. That's not to say there aren't other people who recognise me and cross to the side of the street. Let's say I never feel uncomfortable in the parts of Ireland I do walk around in. I wouldn't go to South Armagh or Anderson's Town, places which are IRA turf, but I would regard myself as popular with everybody except people who are pro-IRA or very traditional Catholics.

I hope you don't find this offensive, but a lot of people say you're a British stooge, and I wonder how you react to that?

For 'a lot of people', read the IRA and *their* stooges, some of whom you have clearly been talking to. Give them my regards.

People have seen a parallel between you and Paul Johnson – both intelligent journalists, and initially socialists, who have become increasingly right-wing.

I can understand that. We're also both pro-Israel. Paul would certainly be to the right of me, but otherwise there's a parallel, certainly one that I would not resent.

You are known to be a very good family man. Has the experience of adopting two half-African children been a rewarding one?

Richly rewarding. This is one thing I'm extremely happy about, because there is a close and loving relationship, not merely between my wife and myself and those two children, but also between the three children by my first marriage and the two young adopted ones. That is a great joy.

Why have you spent so much time out of Ireland? Do you prefer to live somewhere else?

Ireland is the place where I like to live, but I couldn't bear living in it if I couldn't get out of it often and for long periods. As it happens I have never spent an entire year in all my long life outside Ireland.

SIR LAURENS VAN DER POST

Laurens van der Post was born in Africa in 1906. During the thirties he farmed in England before enlisting in the army. He fought behind enemy lines in Abyssinia, the Western Desert and the Far East, where he was taken prisoner by the Japanese while commanding a small guerrilla unit. His experiences as a POW were recounted in his book *The Seed and the Sower* (1963), later made into the film *Merry Christmas, Mr Lawrence*. After the war he returned to active service in Java, where he was Lord Mountbatten's representative. From 1949 he worked for the British government on a variety of missions in little-known parts of Africa. He made an expedition to the Kalahari Desert in search of the Bushmen in order to try and save them from extinction. He was the author of many books, which include *The Lost World of the Kalahari* (1958), *Journey into Russia* (1964), *Jung and the Story of Our Time* (1975), *Yet Being Someone Other* (1982), *A Walk with a White Bushman* (1986) and *Feather Fall* (1994). Laurens van der Post was knighted in 1981. His last book, *The Admiral's Baby*, was published in 1996, just a few months before he died that December.

As a child you were steeped in the legends and myths of the African people which have become so much part of your make-up. Do you believe that without that very strong childhood influence you could have become the man you are today?

It's very difficult to say what one would have been if something else had happened. The fact is that it was a very important part of my upbringing, and I feel enriched by it. It was one of the great formative experiences in my life, and one which hasn't been diminished in importance by age.

Do you think the childhood experience was crucial – was it not something which could have been learned or acquired later?

One's whole life is a process of fulfilling the person you're born, a process of being educated and growing older without losing the child that you were in the beginning, so that one can end up as a kind of child-man, man-child. It's one of the saddest phenomena of our time that very few people seem to remain young in old age.

You were thirteenth out of fifteen children ... how far did your being just one of a large family shape your character for later life?

I'm not aware consciously of what being a member of such a large family meant to me, except that we were extraordinarily happy, and that we had diversity. Some of my older brothers may have found it more of a strain, but I personally did not. My father died when I was young, so that I was more aware of my mother's influence. We were not a family of conformers, but a family of diversities, and all our diversities were respected and encouraged by my mother. I've often talked to my sisters and brothers about the great debt we owe our mother, because of her capacity not to have favourites. When I look back I can't recall a single occasion on which my mother favoured one child against another ... yet, when she was dying, I discovered that she did have a favourite. It was one of my brothers who had died some time before. In a sense he might have been thought to be the least satisfactory of the children, almost what others might have called a failure, yet when my mother was dying, although we had always thought that she would like to be buried with my father, she said to me, 'I want to be buried with my son, because I can't bear the thought of him being out there on his own.'

Africa, the place of your birth, has come to have as much symbolic significance as actual ... am I right in this assumption?

The earth where one is born always has a symbolic significance, but Africa especially, because of its immense charge of natural life. It is the continent which contains the greatest variety and abundance of animal and plant life in the world; it is also the home of the Bushmen, the oldest living people to whom we have access. I always felt in Africa that I was very near to the original blueprint of the country, and that brings one nearer to mythology. Life comes to us consciously first as a myth; then the myth becomes a legend, and the legend becomes history. Africa in that sense has an extra root in the spiritual organisation patterns of the mind which we call mythology. In Africa the myth was the earth and the earth was the myth to a degree that you don't encounter anywhere else.

You have described the story of black Africa as a horror story. Do you ever feel a sense of guilt by association, for being part of the story?

The horror story I was referring to took place before we came on the scene, when Africa was constantly being raided by the outside world for slaves. It was a great source of slave labour both for Asia and the Mediterranean world. As Europeans we were accused of being the greatest exploiters of the slave trade, but actually we came at the end of the story. We were briefly involved in the trade, but we also played a leading role in putting an end to it. One of the unfortunate results of slavery was that by the time we came to Africa the black cultures had never been able to prove what they could have done if they had not been so grossly subjected to the horrors of the slave trade. There was also disease, life was very uncertain, and people didn't live long. The further south you go, the further you are from the point of impact with the slave-owning civilisations, and the more integrated are the black cultures. That's why I always have such great hopes for the part of Africa where I was born; in southern Africa the people were least affected by what I call this horror story, and they produced considerable black civilisations of their own.

You have often said that the 1930s in England were the unhappiest years of your life, presumably because they were lived in the shadow of war breaking out. But it was also the time when your children must have been young. Was it not a time of joy and hope for the future through them?

Not really. At the time we lived on a farm in the West Country. My son was about five when his sister was born, and when he was six or seven, I was terribly unhappy about what was happening in Europe. I felt ashamed at the way Europe had allowed the Nazi horror to grow when its Evil was so obvious to me. I had been to Japan and the Far East and I had watched the Japanese invasion of Manchuria. I love the Japanese, but I watched with horror how they walked out of the League of Nations, how Mussolini went into Abyssinia and nothing was done. I thought the war was going to come in '38, so at the end of '37 I sent my wife and children out to Africa to be looked after by my family there. But of course I was a year out. I never really enjoyed my young family because my daughter, still happily alive, was just a little giggling girl when she went out to Africa and I didn't see her again until ten years later. So I didn't have that kind of happiness you are asking me about.

Your autobiographical writing sometimes strikes the reader as fragmented and seemingly selective. For example, I could not find any account of the children you had by your first marriage, nor indeed much reference to the marriage itself.

You didn't find it because I've never written an autobiography as such. I've written about those parts of my life which seemed to me to be of objective interest to others. My own personal relationships are not there, and were never meant to be.

I never wanted to indulge in writing about my sorrows; the importance of our lives is not in the outer eventualities, but in the inner eventfulnesses, and that is what I have written about.

Do you prefer to forget about those things you have omitted to tell?

Oh no, they're very precious to me. But if I were going to write properly about my life, I would have to live it a second time, and what a waste that would be. I've done it once, I don't want to do it again in books. This would be to commit the sin of looking back over one's shoulder, and all mythologies warn us against that. To do that is to be turned to salt like Lot's wife, or, like Orpheus, to lose your Eurydice. Most autobiographies are a way of looking back, making the present a past, instead of trying to make the past a present.

What were your feelings when you came to join up?

I was very glad that the sense of compromise had suddenly gone from life, although what struck me immediately was the difference between this war in 1939 and the 1914 war which I remembered as a young boy and which was the last of the romantic wars. Indeed, my older brothers were afraid the war in Europe would be over before they could take part in it. But in 1939 we all went off rather sadly; there was no feeling of romance about it. The impact on the spirit of man was not in the war itself, as in the 1914–18 war, but in the demonstration of the depths to which the human race could sink if it neglected the challenges as it did in the '20s and '30s of this century. I had been to Germany and seen the Walpurgisnacht rally in Nuremburg, and it was a horrible sight. I was reminded recently of the Walpurgisnacht march during the demonstration by the Labour Party in Sheffield just before the election which they thought they would win. Did you see the flags flying? Did you see the holy light in their eyes? It was terrifying to watch the leaders on the platform, wearing exalted expressions as if they'd seen the eternal light. On such occasions we have to ask ourselves what will happen to the human spirit if we don't stand up and fight. You must meet the challenges of life in their right dimension, and in 1939 it was clearly a dimension which could only be suppressed by force.

You must have felt fundamentally changed by your wartime experiences. Was this what led to your divorce in 1948 – was it impossible to return to the married life you had known?

No, I don't think it was due to that at all. My first wife is still alive and she is a great friend of ours, and although she lives in South Africa we see her regularly when she comes over here. She's a wonderful person and we all love and admire her very much, but there was something that wasn't quite right. For instance, I loved living in the country, while she liked living in towns; I'd already realised that I couldn't write in Africa, but she loved Africa and didn't want to be away from it ever. I can't blame it on the war, but what the war did, particularly for those who were imprisoned, was to help me enormously in the process of getting to know oneself. My father always used to say that the most important inscription over the temple at Delphi was, 'Man, know thyself.' War is a dark healer which works when all other methods of healing the human spirit have failed. One gets a heightened perspective on values; nothing but humanity counts again. In a sense war was a tremendous experience, and also confirmation of the intuition that I had had from childhood; it showed me again what I had seen when I was in the Far East, that empires would never again be able to be empires in the old way, simply because of what the Japanese had done when they won the war against the Russians. They shattered for the whole world the assumption that white races were superior. It confirmed my feeling that, great as one country is, one belongs to all life wherever it is. When the war came to an end, I went straight from prison to take over in Indonesia. Of all the prisoners, I alone stayed behind, because I found myself involved in the great revolution in the minds of the indigenous inhabitants of Indonesia. I felt I understood it and I had to stay. When the Japanese surrendered I was weak to the point of death, but I went straight back to active service because of this insight, this new feeling of certainty that there was a job to do and I must do it, otherwise I would never live my life properly. My war went on nearly ten years before I came home, so obviously when I got back to my family, the little girl was twelve and a half, and my son had done his first year at university and was charging around on a motorbike. Divorce at that moment seemed right.

I imagine that led to feelings of profound regret and sadness.

Yes, it did … it was very sad. But it was also right. That helped.

Did you find it difficult to fall in love again?

I don't quite know what that question means. One's always in love with life, and if one lives one's life properly, love is so much a part of it that however it arises, one recognises it and welcomes it.

Religious feeling, according to you, comes from the fusion of what you call our Little Memory – what we acquire in our lifetime – and our Great Memory, the memory of all life that has ever been. How does this differ from what one might call a sense of history, that is to say something one can have without the religious dimension?

Religion is a sense of where one came from and where one's going to, so it is the ultimate inexpressible intangible of history. In one of his lovely *Quartets*, 'Little Gidding', T. S. Eliot (who was a great friend of mine) wrote: 'A people without history is not redeemed from time, because history is a pattern of timeless moments, so while the light fails on a winter's afternoon, history is now and England.' History is now, but one's sense of religion is timeless.

You said in your book A Walk with a White Bushman: *'If there is no God then there is no point in being responsible – it's just chaos and eternal night.' Are you saying that without God there would be no moral order?*

The Old Testament says that God is that which cannot be named, and that is the best negative definition of God there has ever been. But something in us knows that when we speak of God, we speak about the ultimate sense of law and order and harmony which there is in nature. Even the primitive people I knew in Kalahari, when they talk about the sun, they talk about it making a ringing sound. Goethe's *Faust* begins: '*Die Sonne tönt nach alter Weise*' – 'The sun resounds in ancient manner.' There is a sense of music, or order which comes from somewhere in creation, and one knows from experience that if you lose that sense of integrity in that form of awareness, your life has no meaning. People go to pieces, and the consequences are awful.

Would you allow that throughout history many acts of barbarism and persecution have been perpetrated in the name of religion, and continue to be perpetrated?

Yes, but that doesn't mean that they were religiously perpetrated. They have been perpetrated in terms of the dogma that people have made of religion. If you study the animal world, the animals don't murder; they kill for food but that's part of their law and order. When a lion stalks its prey, the other animals scatter, but the moment they know the lion has killed, they stop running away and go on grazing all night around the lions eating one of their fellows, because they know they won't be killed. The lion will be contained in the natural order; he doesn't kill for fun, only for survival. If you ask why wars break out, I would answer that a real war, something which is consciously fought, takes place to prevent a greater killing. But the terrible slaughter of millions of Jews, which I can't ever get out of my head, or the massacre at Nanking by the Japanese, that was madness, and certainly not nature. That was man; it was not God.

On the question of forgiveness, you experienced torture and starvation at the hands of the Japanese, and yet were still able to forgive. Do you think the ability to forgive is related to innate virtue, something noble in the soul, or is it more a self-protective measure in that vengeance and bitterness are corrosive and ultimately self-destructive?

Forgiveness in the great sense of the word is a natural thing, part of the natural order. Otherwise life wouldn't go on; it would be locked in an eternal feud of killing and destruction. If you have lived honestly and truly through the challenge that's been presented to you, and it's over, then the question doesn't arise. You don't have to forgive in a conscious way; you just don't hate anymore. There was a man with whom I spent a great deal of my time in prison, a medical officer called Dunlop who stood up many times to a particularly cruel Japanese. This Japanese singled out an officer for terribly vicious treatment. He tortured him, beat him and at times nearly killed him, and once he said to Dunlop, 'Why bother giving medical treatment to that useless man – I might as well kill him.' But Dunlop stood in front of the apparently dying prisoner, and said, 'You'll have to kill me first.' And just by his bearing he prevented many further cruelties. When the war suddenly came to an end, it was decided that the people suspected of being Japanese war criminals should be tried as such, and they were duly lined up. Dunlop was asked to walk down the line and pick out the guilty men. The cruel Japanese stood in line and was obviously bracing himself to be hanged. But Dunlop looked him straight in the eye steadily, for a minute or more, and then turned his back on him and walked away. This is the kind of extraordinary thing I'm talking about, but it's something people aren't interested in nowadays.

There is a great deal of historical evidence that those who have experienced evil are very often contaminated by it. On a national scale the persecuted often turn into persecutors, and those who have been abused and maltreated as children, later grow up to inflict abuse on others. You have certainly been acquainted with evil, but are seemingly untainted by it. I am interested in how this has come about ...

So am I, and I don't pretend to know the answer. The contamination you describe happens very often when people have been exposed to evil before they have developed the natural immunity possessed by a child. When you're in a state of helplessness and you have not experienced the love and care of parents which is natural to life, and which animals show to their young, then this does happen. It starts through having had to live from childhood with a lack of love. T. S. Eliot told me that after the Korean War, the Americans appointed a high-level committee to investigate what made some human beings braver than others. They wanted to know why some people when they were subjected to brainwashing gave way to it and others not; what was this quality in people that made them, whatever happened, resist the evil to which they were being subjected. In every case they found that the most shining examples were people who had grown up surrounded by love. There's so much evil around that unless there is some provision in the pattern of life to fortify us against that form of negotiation, there wouldn't be life on earth, it would have gone. In the final analysis there has to be something which is greater than evil.

Your appeal to preserve the Kalahari Desert for the Bushmen seems on the face of it to contain a contradiction. On the one hand it runs the risk of becoming a huge tourist attraction which would defeat the purpose, and yet if it is left completely alone then no one will benefit from the lessons to be learned. Isn't this a rather naïve approach?

Perhaps all my approaches are naïve because they do tend to be defeated. I originally thought that in a world plagued by hunger, the Kalahari, which supports such a wonderful plant and animal life, could make a contribution, that it could be put to some use. But then I discovered that you can't put it to any use without destroying it. It would have been wonderful to preserve the Kalahari as it could have been preserved in those days, and in time we would have learned what to do with it and the Bushmen. All we have done in the meantime is to destroy the desert and the Bushmen. Tourists are destroying the world; they are part of a very nasty phenomenon. To travel, to see and learn is wonderful, but when you make an 'ism' out of anything you're on the way to doing something wrong. We are now fighting the greatest physical battle, also ultimately a moral and spiritual battle, that man has ever fought. We are going to destroy the planet if we don't change our ways, and we can't change our ways unless there is a profound spiritual transformation in the human being. A Roman Catholic monk in America has written of 'the comfortable disease of progress that's killing us', and he's right. We are in great peril.

This primitive and natural state which you describe so lovingly and movingly in your books is also riven with problems and difficulties such as illness and blindness which could easily be cured by Western medicine. In fact, it is difficult to escape the conclusion from reading The Lost World of the Kalahari *that these people's lives are short and often painful. How do you reconcile these two views?*

There's no conflict in my mind at all about that. I don't want people to become Bushmen themselves – that's not the answer. I don't think they've achieved a perfect state of life any more than we have. But as I see it, they are rich in a way in which we are poor. What is the point if we cure the blind, or the sick, if in the process we give them all the spiritual ills we suffer from? You may give them hospitals, but you take away the meaning of their lives. I'd much rather stay and take my chance with life the same way they do, like salmon in the sea, just because life itself has been kinder to them than we have ever been. Our way of life at the moment is a way of death to them. It's just the same problem with the rainforest Indians. We take away what is light and eternity to them by cutting down their forests, by making it impossible for them to live there. It's a horror story. You have to understand that we're not better than they are; we're only more powerful. I advised the British government not to open up the Kalahari Desert, but to keep it the way it was, or to send some officers to live with the Bushmen for twenty or thirty years and then see what they advised. But they took no notice. Every bit of that desert is staked for our destruction, whether it be for phosphate mining, opening it up for cattle, doing this or that. And once you've got rid of the desert, which according to an expert geologist took two thousand million years to create, you can never have it back. It will be gone forever.

You have had a great deal of influence on Prince Charles, who regards you as his mentor, his guru. Would you say that the knowledge he has gained from you is something which is likely to distance him from the nation, or bring him closer to it?

I don't know, but please don't let us talk about Prince Charles. I never talk about him, not even in the most glowing terms.

But he admires you, and it would be interesting for people to know …

That's all invention. People have called me his guru, but it's a very special subject and I feel honour-bound not to talk about it. I am often asked, particularly when he's so much under attack, to speak up as a friend, but I always refuse. I'm sorry. You have to be understanding and let me off that question.

Presumably you can talk about Lady Thatcher, whom you have also influenced?

No, I'm not going to talk about her either. That is another subject I never speak about. I did once give my views in *A Walk with a White Bushman* but that was twelve or thirteen years ago and I have completely pulled out of that kind of field now.

I was only going to ask what it is about her that you so much admire.

I've told you I'd rather not talk about her. I say this to you because I say this to everybody.

Perhaps you can comment on what you say in A Walk with a White Bushman? *For instance, you describe her handling of the Falklands crisis as 'a brilliant enterprise of war', and the accusations of jingoism you describe as 'radical and liberal slush'. Do you accept that that sort of language might have been offensive to a great many thinking people who very much hoped that war could have been avoided?*

I can't understand how any reasonable person could have described it as a jingo-istic exercise. It simple doesn't make any sense to me. The Second World War started because the Japanese walked into a little part of China, and nobody did anything, so they walked into a bigger part ... Can't people see it was against all concept of a civilised moral order to invade the Falklands like that, when our backs were turned? And by a Fascist government in the Argentine? To be accused of defending it out of mere jingoism seems to me nonsense. It is slush, and I don't mind saying it again, it is slush. You must know what Galtieri and his people are like, you must have seen those thousands of mothers demonstrating every night for their lost children. Are we simply to allow a government like that to invade our territory and take it away by force? Is it jingoism to throw a burglar out of your house? I could not see any moral justification or any grounds for people saying it was jingoism. When I think of how quietly and with what little fuss this incredible military operation took place, and with what courage! The point is very simple: here was naked unprovoked aggression; unprovoked because the Falklands were no danger to the Argentine and had been in British possession for nearly two hundred years. We were wholly justified in defending the Falklands. And people call that jingoism! Let people be offended by my calling it radical and liberal slush – if they can be offended, there may be some hope for them. It's a bad rotten way of thinking.

Some people thought that Lady Thatcher favoured war above all other options ...

All she was doing was throwing burglars out of her house. Is that a celebration of war? When are we ever going to learn the lesson? Stamp on the thing when it's small. If we'd overlooked that, God knows what would have happened in the world. I don't really want to go in to the Falklands issue, but what Lady Thatcher did was the brave, responsible act of a responsible government. It became a basis and precedent to show that that kind of action is still possible in the modern world.

You've described socialism as 'a rotting corpse whose smell in our midst has tainted the political atmosphere for far too long'. This statement is based on the fact that socialists 'release expectations they can never fulfil, and that is immoral'. I wonder if we can be confident about the difference between expectation *and* hope *in this context? You approve of offering people hope, yet hope may also never be realised. Why is this not immoral also?*

Socialism betrays hope. It was a fulfilment at one time of a longing rather than a hope, a longing for a better world, but it's proved itself to be such a shambles already, so clearly not a valid means of procuring for the human species what it professed to procure, that I felt justified in making those remarks. Socialism makes shallow collective values the ultimate test of human behaviour. It has done an enormous amount of harm all over the world. Not a single culture in the world infected by socialism has come to any good at all. Give me an example of a socialist country that's done well; there isn't a single one. As a temporary tactical challenge of existing values it was very good in its time, but as an ongoing pronouncement of the ultimate good for the human race, it's been proved inadequate. That's why I call it those names.

In A Walk with a White Bushman *you say that socialism was only really valid in the nineteenth-century context when the working classes had no vote. Presumably, however, you would agree that the granting of the vote has not eradicated social injustice or deprivation, and that there is still a significant underclass in Britain and elsewhere. Isn't the idea of socialism still valid today?*

No, I don't think that follows. There will always be injustice as long as there are human beings on earth, and even when we don't mean harm the consequences of what we do can be unfair and unjust. Socialism is not the answer to the prevalence of injustice, or indeed anything else. It was all right as a stage for clearing the mind and the structures of life for better things, but it has created new forms and perhaps even worse forms of injustice. You ask if I can deny that there is still an underclass in Great Britain. I do deny it, at least in the sense you mean it, in the socialist sense. People have never been more free in the history of this country to be out of what you call class, to be themselves. I don't deny that there are poor people in the country, but it's not a result of the system; it's a result of what people are in themselves. There's never been a society before in Great Britain where people, whatever their disadvantages of birth, are so free to be themselves, and not to be subjected to the sufferings of a class. The sufferings in England at the moment have nothing to do with class because people soar out of the class system with the greatest of ease if they want to.

But is there not a difference between what we might call socialist ideals and the unacceptable fate of socialism as deployed in the former Soviet Union ... ?

No, because socialism always tries to solve human problems by creating systems. That's the difference between capitalism and socialism; capitalism is not a system, and people are mistaken if they think so. It expresses itself in certain patterns from time to time but it's much more pragmatic than socialism which starts with the concept of a system: life has to conform to the ideal system. But you can't do that. It is utterly impossible and dangerous for any human being to think he can devise an ideal social system and inflict it upon other human beings. The great error started with something which was meant to be very good, like Tom Paine's *The Rights of Man*. The great fallacy of *The Rights of Man* is that it ignores the fact that rights have to be earned, and that you have no right which is not accompanied by an equal and opposite responsibility. One of the basic implications of socialism is that the so-called working man is inherently good and the person who employs him is inherently bad. There's always a villain in socialism, and an absence of self-criticism; socialism never sees into the totality of the human scene, and its values are always collective values. It's almost as if it regards the individual as a form of egotism; it doesn't realise that an individual can be most truly and utterly and wholly himself without damaging the equal right of his neighbour to be the same. This is expressed much better in what is called a capitalist climate. Terrible things happen in that climate too but it's not a climate of ideology; it's part of the process of trial and error in life.

You also say in the same book that no ideas have come out of the Labour Party since the manifesto of 1848. Isn't that a bit harsh and dismissive? What about the establishment of everyone's right to education?

The right of people to be educated was recognised before socialism. Some of the greatest pioneers of universal education weren't socialists they were industrialists, and some of the most idealistic schemes of education were launched by individuals …

But the socialists put it into practice …

Not at all. The socialists only came to power for the first time after the last world war. All the immense pioneering work in that area was done by the Liberal Party without a socialist ethic.

What about the National Health Service?

It is a good idea that every human being who needs healthcare should be provided for, but the Health Service as it was created is a disaster; it's wasteful, extravagant and uncreative. It's obviously done some good, but medicine wasn't at all bad before the war. You mustn't ignore the enormous role that the private capitalist world played in pioneering medicine. You must also remember that any smooth-running private organisation turned bad as soon as it was nationalised; there's not a single area where this isn't true, even the Post Office. Look at the railways – we had a wonderful railway system before the war. And look at the coal mines. I can't see why the Health Service should be held to the credit of socialism particularly; it's not just a socialist concept. These wonderful hospitals we used to have in London are run entirely by charity. Charity is thought to be a dirty word, but it isn't. To receive help out of the love of your fellow human beings is not degrading.

I know you admired Bevin. Wasn't he a worthy exponent of socialism?

I don't think socialism made Bevin. There were remarkable, wonderful people who were socialists, I don't say there were not; but they were so in spite of socialism.

You have surprised people by being very critical of Nelson Mandela, saying that when he emerged from prison he was 'more myth than man', and still spouting 'the moth-eaten clichés of the spirit'. Most people will regard that as harsh criticism of someone they see as essentially dignified, unsubdued by imprisonment ... not unlike yourself in many ways.

Did you see what I wrote about Nelson Mandela?

I heard, and I'm quoting.

Well, you heard wrong. I said that Nelson Mandela, when he came out of prison, had become more of a myth in the minds of people than a man, which I think is true. When he emerged from captivity it was an immense opportunity for him to speak. I had been in prison myself, and I knew it was a terrible thing to do to a human being. But I think that prison is one of the finest schools for making the human spirit that can ever be. I myself only did a crash course, so to speak, but he went to university, having been in prison for twenty-seven years. You can imagine my disappointment when I heard him talk that Sunday, when he spouted all those moth-eaten clichés, thanking the communists and so on. I had to ask myself, has he actually been in prison? And I thought of the great examples of people who have come out of prison the right way, people like Solzhenitsyn who showed from the words he used that he had learned lessons in that prison school. What I bitterly regret is that Nelson Mandela didn't come out as Martin Luther King came out saying that he had a dream for Africa, instead of giving us a lot of moth-eaten political platitudes. I was bitterly disappointed. Nelson Mandela is a miserable figure who speaks with a double tongue. You should hear the Dalai Lama on the subject of Nelson Mandela, how after Tiananmen Square he cuddled up with the Chinese government when he was there. He's a very brave man, but he's a very great disappointment to me personally. He had twenty-seven years to think about life, and yet he still belongs to a party which hasn't renounced power and war.

Are you hopeful of South Africa's future?

In the long run, yes. It's got a long way to go, and it's on a dangerous road, but the road is not so dangerous as not taking the road would have been. No doubt they'll make mistakes, but the quality of the human beings, black and white and coloured in South Africa, is potentially so great that I think they can win through. History and life work much more slowly than do human beings. This is another part of the socialist slush that I talked about. Socialists think they can pass laws for the betterment of mankind, and men will then be better. They don't realise that evolution of life and the human spirit is not a rational thing; it is a process of growth which you can't learn at universities. You can only bring the improvements in life that you brought in your own nature and it's a long and hard job. Nelson Mandela still has power over people, and he has a right to it after twenty-seven years in prison, but he didn't rise to the responsibility laid on him by his imprisonment, which Solzhenitsyn and the other great dreamers of life, such as Martin Luther King, discharged so nobly. That's the disappointment.

You were close to Jung, whom you describe as a profoundly religious person. Do you think you were on the same journey in life, only perhaps on a different route?

I don't really know how to answer that. Religion is the most important dimension in life, and in a sense I was on the same road as Jung, but I don't pretend to have been of the same calibre. He was of enormous importance for religion without organised religion realising it. It's one of the tragedies of the world. If you listen to certain archbishops nowadays, religion is a sort of socialist ethic, not religion at all; when I hear them talk, I can never recognise the religious content of what they say, but in Jung religion is given a contemporary language, it renews itself. And it's a promotion of the whole fundamental world of the dream which the universe is destined to fulfil. Dream is a profound language of nature, particularly of nature to come. It's where we get the blueprints of life, that whole area which Shakespeare and the great artists knew. Shakespeare talked about the prophetic soul of man dreaming of things to come. In that sense, yes, I felt I was in a similar dimension to Jung.

On the subject of religion, you say in A Walk with a White Bushman *that until you had understood and absorbed the mythology of Africa, Christianity did not come alive for you. Do you regard Christianity as another branch of mythology?*

No. I don't think of mythology as having branches. I think of mythology being evidence of a divine pattern in the human species, instinctively and wherever it finds itself. Religion is a profound instinctive pattern which has very often been cheated. It has suffered a great deal from what socialism suffered from, from being turned into rigid dogmas, rigid concepts and ideas, which were not large enough or flexible enough to express the true essence of religion. The mythology of Africa is an instinctive mythology, and it opened me up to religion from which I was excluded by my education, and particularly the form of Calvinism to which I was exposed.

Do you think the main tenets of Christianity – the Virgin Birth, the Crucifixion, the Resurrection and the Life Everlasting – have a symbolic rather than actual significance, metaphorical rather than literal?

They have an immense symbolic significance, but to me no actuality is complete without the symbolic. The symbol is an expression of the most profound actuality of the human spirit; it's not, as you imply, not real. They all deal with reality in the only way in which it can be dealt with at that stage of human awareness. I wouldn't like to consider them dogmatically. One of the great dangers that press upon modern life is precisely the absence of symbolic reality. Immense impoverishment of the human spirit is going on all around us because people don't realise how incomplete life is unless it is symbolic. Religion is not religion if it isn't symbolic.

How can different religious traditions be reconciled if it is part of their essence to exclude one another?

They're not really religions if they exclude one another. Conscious religion is expressed by human beings, and everything we do is approximate. Our observance of religion is whole and ultimate and perfect perhaps, but the expression of which we are capable is approximate, and it is in being aware of what is provisional and approximate in our apprehension of religion that we find very often how much other religions can contribute. Here is the tremendous importance of the symbol again, because although people may use different symbols, they are all ultimately the same. Stone Age mythology was an early expression of Greek mythology, and the link is not only highly discernible but frightfully important.

It's our interpretations of the religious experience of mankind which vary, but the experience is the same everywhere.

But most religious faiths claim that their teachings alone are true, and that they are true for everyone. It follows that other faiths are mistaken. How does one deal with this problem?

This is the problem of human beings valuing their ideas too highly, and has nothing to do with religion. This interpretation of religion is not a religious interpretation. When I'm asked this sort of question I have to say, my dear chap, you're not talking about religion, you're talking about a church, and a church is provisional and approximate and, thank God, often wrong.

Do you think you have discovered what is true for you in a religious sense?

I have a feeling sometimes that I might be on the way to discovering it, but I do know that there is a long way to go. All human beings in all societies have a feeling of impoverishment if they're not on the way. The Stone Age people I knew in the Kalahari had two dances, one for the little hunger, for food and for survival, and the other dance for the great hunger, the hunger for religion. This hunger is real and if we don't get the food for it, we decline and diminish.

But do you think that what is true for you is necessarily true for everyone?

Oh no, not for a minute. This is as far as I can testify: I live in the hope that my concept of the truth is right, but I do know that if I'm wrong it's in a way that I'm probably not aware of. How do you distinguish between truth and error in life? The struggle goes on all the time, and that's why consciousness must be increased, not diminished.

You have said that there is a kind of 'foreverness' incorporated in everyone. What basis do you have for saying that, and what exactly do you mean by it?

I can't express it more clearly than that. The little Bushman in the desert said to me, 'There is a dream dreaming us ... ' it's what T. S. Eliot called this timeless element in every human being. All of us have something in the human soul which is beyond time; it's even recognised by scientists now. The psychic nature of the human being is to behave as if it will go on forever. It is the soul of a man.

Perhaps because we live in a sick, cynical age, there are those who regard you as less of a sage and more of a charlatan, a romancer rather than a mystic. Are you wounded by such criticism?

I don't know anybody who's ever called me a charlatan, certainly nobody who knows me would ever call me that. And of course I would be hurt if people thought I was. And why a romancer? A romancer in what way? Be specific, in what way have I been romancing? I can't deal with a vague statement – you must give me an explicit example.

Well, a number of people have suggested your books are hopelessly romanticised and divorced from reality. Your Venture to the Interior, *for example, is presented as a herculean journey but according to your critics it amounts to no more than a day's walk up and down a hill. Do you perhaps mix fantasy and truth sometimes?*

I did go up those mountains, and nobody can say I didn't. This is quite absurd … these are idiots talking. The peak of Mlanje is 12,000 feet above sea level – is that a hill? Those people who say it is a hill are liars. It's three times the height of any mountain in Great Britain. Who are these idiots, where do they say these things? I can't cope with this.

Your life experience has been so singular, so unusual, as to suggest the hand of destiny at work. Is your perception of yourself that of someone singled out for a special mission?

I've never had a perception of myself. I've never lived my life by a plan, or with any ambition. I'm somebody following the flight of the bird, I just do what life suggests and I do it as well as I can. I have actually done certain things quite well in life. For example, I won a prize for the best run small farm in Gloucestershire at a three-county show. Or is that being a charlatan and a romancer? And my record in the war – is that also romancing? I shouldn't even have to respond to these remarks; they're obviously made by singularly stupid people.

You have written that death is as natural and creative a part of life as birth. Can you develop that idea?

This is how it appears to me, and it seems to be mythologically right too. The whole of life is a metamorphosis: growth, decay, decline, fall, rebirth. Death is a natural part of the process of growth and rebirth.

Now, in old age, do you feel a particular serenity?

I'm prevented from feeling serene because at the age of eighty-six I still have so much to do. I've just finished a book, but I have about thirteen others I want to write, so I have an increased sense of hurry, a feeling that my ration is running out and I must get on with it. It's not that I feel unserene, but I'm not at all of a philosophic turn of mind. I just try to live, that's my main preoccupation. And my sense of wonder about life never leaves me.

How would you like to be remembered?

One does certainly want to be remembered. My experience of being in prison and thinking we might all be killed, and the idea that people wouldn't know how we died, or even remember us, was a profound horror. I would like to be remembered as someone who tried to perform some service for what I think is the overall value in life, and that is what is expressed by Eros and by St Paul as charity. Without Eros no human being has any hope whatsoever of having this immense capacity of spirit to learn to distinguish between truth and error. It's only with charity that one somehow has the sense of where the frontier is between the two. If I can be remembered as somebody who felt that particular emotion all his life very pro-foundly, and perhaps rendered some service to it, well, I shall rejoice …

ENOCH POWELL

Enoch Powell was born in 1912 and educated at King Edward's School, Birmingham, and at Trinity College, Cambridge. He was a fellow at Trinity from 1934 to 1938 and was then appointed Professor of Greek at the University of Sydney. In 1939 he returned to England to enlist as a private in the Royal Warwickshire Regiment, was commissioned in 1940 and rose to the rank of brigadier in 1944. He joined the Conservative Party in 1936 and entered Parliament in 1950 as MP for Wolverhampton. Because of his opposition to the Common Market he did not stand for election in 1974, but returned to Parliament in October of that year as an Ulster Unionist until he was defeated at the 1987 general election. He wrote over thirty books and pamphlets, publishing his *Collected Poems* in 1990 (a best-seller) and overseeing *Reflections of a Statesman*, a large selection of his writing and speeches, published in 1991. He died in 1998.

You were a very precocious scholar, both at school and at university. Was there a price to pay for all that solitary dedication?

I think one has to examine the term 'precocious'. I was not precocious in the sense that I was enormously in advance of the year of birth to which I belonged. It is a handicap to be too far ahead of your contemporaries, and I doubt if I actually was. I was probably put in a form of an average age a year older than mine, but no more than that. Precocity is therefore an idea to be handled very gently in this context.

You said of your early days that what drove you was the urge to 'rise'. What was it to rise in your sense?

My father used to say to me that if I were not a teacher that would be contrary to the laws of biology because both he and my mother were teachers. My father always said that the great thing in life was to write and speak good English. The nature of attainment as it presented itself to me in the first two decades of my life was therefore academic.

But was it something you wanted or were you driven to it?

I was not driven. I have no sense of having been physically or mentally pushed, but the implication of the environment was that there was no point in education unless one was academically successful.

In retrospect, who do you think was more influential in your life? Your mother or you father?

I think it was my mother, whom I remember describing, in the preface to a book published in the 1940s, as my first teacher and certainly my first Greek teacher. But it was a household in which learning was respected and the prizes in life were prizes to be won mentally.

You have often been described as a puritan, which is a word sometimes used unkindly. Is it a label that offends, or do you think of it as a badge of honour?

I think of it as a severe inaccuracy. After all, I am a high churchman in the Church of England and how a high churchman can be a Puritan I do not understand, because Puritan and Anglican are incompatible terms. A Puritan is distinct from and opposed to an Anglican, which is why the attempt was made by William III in 1689 to find a *via media* between the Church of England and the Puritans. All those characteristics which predispose a man to be comfortable and find his natural niche in the higher end of the Church of England are incompatible with Puritanism.

You are using puritan in the intellectual sense. But it is a term also commonly used to mean someone who is offended by sex.

I think the word 'squeamish' is perhaps eluding us here. I'm certainly not that, and if puritan is used in the sense of squeamish I disavow the description. There is no subject to which the human mind cannot properly be applied.

People constantly use the word 'austere' in reference to you. Would you accept their judgment as appropriate?

Here again the word is used in a narrowed sense. Presumably it's intended to describe a person who does not find life primarily and self-evidently enjoyable. Well, I enjoy life; life without enjoyment would be intolerable. Indeed, sometimes when I'm asked what I have been doing for thirty-eight years in the House of Commons, I am disposed to reply that I have been enjoying myself. I don't think that comes under the heading 'austerity'.

There seems to have been a marked reluctance on your part to take up the academic life. You said you felt a sense of enclosure when you passed in under Trinity Gate. Why did you persevere if that was the case?

I didn't persevere. I tried to escape from Cambridge and eventually succeeded. From the time that I became a fellow of Trinity I sought appointment as a professor of classics or of Greek at any university which had a vacancy and when one occurred at Sydney and I was offered the appointment I accepted it. But all through those years I was quite certain that this was a very brief temporary phase, which would be terminated by the coming of a war. This notion was derived from my observation and knowledge of what was going on in Germany and Italy. I had close connections with contemporary scholars in both those countries, so that I was aware of the rising threat which I perceived as a threat to the independence and self-government of the United Kingdom, and which I believed would have terminated sooner in hostilities than it actually did. If you're interested in one of the reflections upon life from an older person's standpoint, one of the things which has surprised me most is that events take longer to happen then one would have supposed. One can be sure that there will be war, but one thinks it will come sooner. The causes are there but the causes are not necessarily effective at the earliest possible time. I've always underestimated the speed with which things can happen and the promptitude with which the foreseeable can occur. I'll enlarge on that if you like.

Please do.

It has been one of the experiences of recent years that after eighteen years of trying to make people understand what was being done to this country by European unity, what they were losing and what they were being asked to sacrifice, I've observed that at last they have woken up to its importance. I wouldn't have thought it would have taken so long, but I was mistaken; my fellow countrymen had only one eye half open. They did know, and they show signs now of remembering that they were told. So I think if I were advising my younger self I would say: you must not suppose that because saltpetre, charcoal and sulphur cause an explosion, they will cause an explosion now. There has to be a set of special circumstances arising before that explosion occurs, so do not imagine because you can trace the causes of events, because events are predictable, that they are imminent. From this I would engage in another reflection; which is that one of the great laws of life is patience. Do not imagine that because such and such a thing is ripe to happen it's going to happen immediately. You may have to spend a long time waiting for it to happen, but if you are right the world will come to meet you. If you are wrong, then you don't matter. That might almost be written up as the favourite adage of my declining years.

Your inaugural lecture in 1938 showed you conscious even then of the difficulties which attended maintaining Greek as a central part of higher education. Do you think that the battle is still capable of being won, and does it matter all that much anyway?

All battles are capable of being won, even the most apparently hopeless battles. In the mid-1920s it was the received wisdom that classical education was on its way out, and I remember the revival of classical studies which took place in the late 1920s and 1930s. There is a natural predisposition amongst people who belong to Western culture to be inquisitive about the Greeks and when you show them what Plato said, or what Jesus said, they say, let me get at it. People will not be indefinitely content to be held at arm's length from that which is ultimately intelligible or appreciable only in Greek. So long as Greek thought is immortal, Greek studies will be immortal, because people will not submit to being estranged from the source of that thinking.

In your collected poems you recall what you call the 'compulsions' under which they were written. Did you ever think of yourself writing poetry in the consciously public classical manner or was it restricted to a more self-absorbed romanticism?

Self-absorbed romanticism is a rather cruel but not entirely inaccurate expression. I wrote poetry when I had to write it, in obedience to an emotional compulsion, as a form of self-expression. Of course I was aware that I was using form, that I was entering into a tradition. Nevertheless, the necessity to do so was internal; it was not an exercise, it was not a chosen activity. In fact, I was liable to write a poem in the most adverse circumstances, on the back of an envelope in a train.

Were you at all sympathetic to the modernist tradition which was being established while you were growing up? Were you able to share Eliot and Pound's sense of a need to break from an older tradition?

I'm afraid I was absorbed in what you describe as the older tradition, and Tennyson and Milton were the principle fountains from which I drank.

Have you ever written poems which remain unpublished?

I suppose all poets have. 'Ev'n copious Dryden wanted, or forgot, / The last and greatest art, the art to blot' – that's somewhere in Pope, isn't it? The art to blot is part of the art of writing poetry, and the knowledge that you must scrap a poem is a sign that you may be trusted, at any rate.

I have heard that you have written poems to your wife which remain unpublished. Is that correct?

I write a poem a year on our marriage anniversary and I have been guilty of jocularly saying that this is part of my wife's pension. I give her a rose for each year we have been married and a poem, sometimes referring to the number of roses, sometimes not. And I can imagine a book being published one day with a reproduction of a print of a rose on one page and on the other side the serial poem for the year.

Philosophers and even historians, like Lola Martinez, now think of poetry as a valuable source of evidence. When you write poetry do you think of it as a way of exploring or as a way of persuading? Is it cognitive in some way, do you think?

It's communicative, that is certain. A painter wishes to exhibit the landscape which he has painted because he has seen something which he thinks his fellows may not have seen. Similarly, a poet says, here, listen, that's what I felt. The perception brings with it an urge to communicate. We are after all a herd animal and communicating our perceptions is bred deeply into humanity. This has a political application. As a politician I sometimes used to be asked: How do you go about your business? And I used to say it was rather like Luther in his Reformation hymn: 'I hear the nightingale in the dark hedge, the dawn is coming ... ', that is to say, I sing in the hedge to my fellow countrymen in case the song I want to sing is a song which they also want to hear. But there is a compulsion to sing it and see if somebody else will react to it; it's part of the communication mechanism of *Homo sapiens*. Homer knew that he would have an audience – perhaps he didn't know how large it would be – but if no audience had been conceivable, he would not have sung.

Why do you find it so hard to believe that Shakespeare wrote the plays and poems attributed to him? So far no one has been able to establish that he was not the author.

I find the whole chronology from the earliest quartos right through to the publication of the First Folio in 1623 or 1624 highly suspicious. Here are works, some of the earliest of which are the most mature, which appear in unofficial editions in the 1590s, then suddenly in the 1600s this flow is interrupted, with one exception, which is *Troilus and Cressida* in 1609. Then in 1623 we have a volume which contains some of the greatest plays, which have not only never been published before but of which there is no trace of a performance. How do we reconcile this with the biography of an individual who undoubtedly existed (because we must believe the parish records in Stratford-upon-Avon)? I find the whole chronology challenging and I have seen no convincing or satisfactory explanation of the appearance of those plays before the world. In 1972, after the European Communities Bill had been forced through parliament, I thought I wouldn't remain in public life much longer. I saw no point in seeking to return to the House of Commons, and when I thought of what I was to do, the answer seemed to lie either in the authorship of the plays attributed to William Shakespeare or in the Greek New Testament. The Greek New Testament beat William Shakespeare by a long head, but it's a half-open door which always beckons me whenever I glance in that direction.

But do you think you will ever open it properly?

Probably not.

But if he didn't write them, who did?

A committee. You may laugh, but we underestimate the extent to which great art can be produced by two or more hands, and undoubtedly the furnace of court dramas under Elizabeth and in the early stages of James I was fed by a group of people, and that group was a necessarily changing group, though there is a voice and a mode of apprehension detectable in that joint product. I have not been convinced by any specific proposal to put a name to that voice, but do not under-estimate the possibility of a joint creation of great works of art.

But has it happened before?

Yes, it happened in the Old Testament, the content of which is largely a joint creation. We tend to associate works of art with individuals, but in doing so we over-individualise. It's a natural human fault to exaggerate the importance of the individual – there's a Tory statement for you.

I wonder if your own poems form in the way you describe one of Shakespeare's coming to him: that is, as a germinal phrase carried in the head until a suitable framework is gathered round it?

That was certainly my experience, and incidentally it is also the sort of experience which is described by Housman in his lecture on the name and nature of poetry. I would think it quite common among those who write poetry, that it comes in pieces, that an emotionally charged blob arises in the mind, and a framework for this must grow around it.

At Cambridge you were a fervent admirer of A.E Housman and in some ways he became a role model for you. How far do you think his homosexuality was an integral, even an inseparable, part of his creativity? And did this matter to you or deduct from his greatness in any way?

I probably was not conscious of it in the years that I attended his lectures, and I doubt the practicability of detaching one element from all the rest in an individual's character, particularly an artist's.

But a lot of great artists are homosexual … do you think that homosexuality and art complement each other?

If homosexuality is a common human characteristic then that would account for what you've drawn attention to. To say that artists have two eyes doesn't prove that they are different from other men, because having two eyes is quite common, pretty well invariable. If this strain is common in humanity then we shall find it in all manifestations of humanity, among artists, among painters, among politicians. Only if we could produce a statistical survey for the incidence in mankind at large at a particular time and in a particular society, and then show that the incidence was greatly exceeded among artists, might we be justified in coming to any such conclusion.

How do you yourself look upon homosexuality? Are you tolerant of it?

Well, I voted for its decriminalisation, for it seemed to me grotesque that male homosexuality continued to be criminal from the reign of Henry VIII when female homosexuality was not. Nor did I regard it as a proper area for the criminal law to operate in.

But why do you think homosexuality appears to be on the increase?

Ah, I notice the word 'appears', and I agree with that. That which is more discussed appears to be more common. It's not a matter to which I've applied my mind. I dare say there are those who are in a position to form some rational answer to the question, but I do think we have to beware of the impression made upon our minds by publicity. Familiarity tends to multiply, so we must beware of amateur statistics.

You were keen to join up in 1939, even passing yourself off as an Australian to do so. What was the attraction of the army, was it a sense of achieved order, or a duty fulfilled, or some more basic urge to help defend Britain, the land itself, as Wilfred Owen wanted to do in the First War?

I can remember saying to my father that it was my intention to get into uniform on the first day if I could. It was a spontaneous resolve of mine, though I didn't achieve it. It was the 20 October 1939 before I succeeded in getting enlisted. I wanted to defend my country, which is quite a natural impulse.

I was told a story that a man who had been one of your fellow privates at the beginning of the war met you years later when he had become a major and you a brigadier. When he greeted you in a familiar way you had him disciplined for not saluting a superior officer … is there any truth in that story?

No truth. That's an easily invented type of story. Indeed, it's a very interesting specimen of myth making. I did put fellow privates on disciplinary charges on the first day that I was a lance corporal, but that was for urinating in the barrack room.

You spent part of the war in India which was then part of the Empire. Did you have any feelings for the imperial idea or did you think the time had come for withdrawal?

Like most Indians, I didn't think the time had come for that phase of India's immense history to come to an end. It was as surprising to the Indians as it was to the British. And I only came to terms with it when back in this country in the late 1940s I began to apply myself to the constitutional history of my own country, and to understand that there was an insoluble contradiction in the government of a population on the authority of an assembly to which they could not be elected. The Empire of India was a huge repudiation of the lesson of the American colonies, and one with which England is still struggling: that is, that you cannot govern responsibly to parliament those who cannot be, or who choose not to be, represented in parliament. That's the underlying axiom of what is meant in English by democracy, and it was curious that it was our earliest *conquistadores* in India who understood this better than it was understood at the end of the nineteenth century. In India that principle was apparently unavoidable, but persistently and tantalisingly breached. Now this is not the me of 1943 speaking to you, who came back to politics in this country with the vague idea at the back of his head that it might somehow lead to the vice-royalty of India, and then had to work out his understanding of what happened to the United Kingdom when it ceased to be mother country for a worldwide empire. The me of 1943 has arrived at New Delhi station at two in the morning on a posting from the Middle East. He realises that it is impracticable to report to General Headquarters India until a much later hour, so he undoes his valise and he goes to sleep on the platform, and when he wakes up, what he breathes he finds intoxicating. Eventually he becomes an interpreter in Urdu and one of his unrealised ambitions is to produce a critical and literary edition of the *Rise and Fall of Islam* by the Urdu poet Hali, which is really the story of the Moslems in India. I suppose in my eightieth year I am a real oldie, and one who has to be constantly aware that he carries a lot of previous beings around in himself and that they are liable to be still vocal. Just as one's dreaming self is also one's waking self, the past individuals are asleep there somehow, and occasionally their words are remembered and repeated.

What was it that attracted you so powerfully to India? As a country it can seem so hopeless, so overburdened with a huge population, so impossible to organise, its democracy so fragile, its savagery scarcely suppressed ...

You used the word 'organise'. I suppose one of the fascinations of India for the British was its organisability. Here are immense resources, human above all; if these are harnessed together, what a wonderful organisation could one not create? – and in many ways the British did. The creation of a railway system, the drainage system of the Punjab – these must have given immense delight and satisfaction to those who organised them. But what we couldn't organise was a solution to the inherent constitutional contradictions of the British Raj. Nor could Indians, for they were mainly using material which they had obtained from us, and British material is very dangerous when used by those who are not British.

In an article you wrote about E. M. Forster's Passage to India, *you spoke very fairly about the difference between his India and yours. How far, or when, do you think it is right to ask for accuracy in novels? May a book not be a good novel even if it's a bad social history?*

The dramatisation of the novel *The Jewel in the Crown* always seemed to me grotesque, because life in India was not spent as life was spent by the protagonists in that novel; but that's not to say it's not a good novel or drama. But if you present a drama to a person who has lived in a particular place and situation and say, what do you make of it? – he will react with the contrast between his own memories, his own sensations, and the drama. I'm not apologising for my review, I'm explaining it. Although the political axiom is supposed to be, never apologise, never explain, I don't mind explaining,

And you don't mind apologising when your wrong?

As a politician I try to follow the rule I've just quoted. And I've probably explained too much in politics, more than I ought to have done.

You now adhere to the Church of England, though you were not religious as a young man, and religious faith is often thought, perhaps wrongly, to be unusual in modern intellectuals. Does your faith ever sit uneasily alongside your intellectual convictions?

No, because worship and intellectual activity are manifestations of different aspects of the person, and they serve different – God forgive me, I was going to say biological purposes – no, they correspond to different aspects of that extraordinary animal *Homo sapiens*. Religion must have been very important for his survival, because he has it everywhere. One of the remarkable things which J. G. Fraser, the great anthropologist, found so alarming, was how frequently in places between which there could have been no interconnection or intercommunication, man hit upon the device of killing God and eating him. Now this is not a rational proceeding, but it may nevertheless be a proceeding which is beneficial or necessary to humanity. I hope I have not unduly alarmed you.

No. You have said that you are deeply aware of a dilemma and a contradiction between Christianity and human life. Some observers have suggested that despite your participation in holy communion and observance of religious practice it is as if you are somehow forcing yourself to believe, if you like; that you are really struggling with agnosticism.

Well, who is to look into the heart of a man and declare what he sees there, and who is a man to say what is in his heart? I can only observe that at no stage in the last forty years can a credible political motive be assigned to what I have done and said as a member of the Church of England. Self-interest is difficult to establish – a very modest disclaimer I realise – but then we're often led by motives of which we are unaware.

It is said that those who believe have the grace of belief, and that is something that comes from God. Do you feel that you have the grace of belief or do you have a constant struggle to believe?

I feel everything comes from grace; I have everything by grace. My wife and I, for example, are celebrating our fortieth wedding anniversary but our marriage was a grace; it was something I didn't deserve, something I've been given beyond my desert. I find the concept of grace, that is to say an input of indeterminate origin, unavoidable in a whole range of experiences. To arrive at a logical conclusion from premises is in a way an act of grace. Perhaps this is to acknowledge what a wonderful thing it was that man originated.

Have you any doubt in your own mind about an afterlife?

If you had substituted immortality for an afterlife, I would not have hesitated to reply in the affirmative. The expression 'afterlife' is time-bound; immortality is not. The individual, encapsulated by time, unable to think or understand or have his being except as bounded by time, ceases to belong to that framework on death, and it's therefore a misrepresentation to treat him as though he continued to exist on the same scale. Suppose time is a man-made illusion, which it probably is ... in that case the meaning of immortality will be very different.

Presumably you have a view about the ordination of women, a matter which looks as if it might further fragment the Christian Church. Is it possible theologically in your view, and is it desirable politically?

We're going through a bad dose of feminism, aren't we? Certainly, the chattering classes are. Under the influence of a worldwide cross-infection, we are calling in question specialisations which have become necessary to the survival of humanity. It may well be that the preservative and the destructive impulses of mankind have been specialised in the sexes and that we are playing with fire when we introduce confusion into that specialisation. The specialisation can, of course, be defined and debated, but the anxiety is whether we can radically interfere without unforeseeable but damaging consequences. I would place the proposal for the ordination of women and the enthusiasm for it in the context of that movement which leads all political parties at present in the United Kingdom to say that we want to see more women sitting in the House of Commons, even though those who do the work necessary for putting the members there don't think so.

There is now and there has been for a long time a great deal of agitation about women's rights. I suspect that you are not especially sympathetic to the Women's movement. Is it that you fear the consequence of a loss of natural complementarity, or what?

I am very happy to consider with an open mind proposals for a change in the law where the law differentiates between men and women, though I am not sure that to treat the female as an independent tax band will be something welcomed by all those whom it will affect. My wife was certainly alarmed when I told her that she will be making her own tax return in future and would surely not expect any help form me.

Since you are a member of the Church of England, I assume you believe in original sin. How is the outcome of that to be combated in a society without any restraints on gain?

Covetousness, greed, are not matters which can be the subject of legislation. They belong to a category of sin rather than crime, and from sin we are saved by grace.

You acknowledged once that you are intellectually arrogant. Does that degree of self-confidence not isolate you in the political world of horse trading?

I'm also a corporate man, a person at ease in society, fulfilling the laws and obeying the conventions, just as – constitutionally – the shared responsibility for the advice tendered to the sovereign extends right through political life. I accept that the unity of that advice implies give and take between those who are responsible for it being tendered. In other words, I am a naturally compliant member of a cabinet. The intellectual arrogance leads me to perceive that the whole structure of cabinet government and of party government depends on bargaining and compromise. But I'm a good colleague, one who goes to meet his own colleagues halfway, more than halfway if necessary.

Can you tell me what it is to be a Tory?

To me a Tory is a person who believes that authority is vested in institutions – that's a carefully honed definition. We have made the law, not for extraneous reasons, not because it conforms with *a priori* specifications; it has been made by a particular institution in a particular way and can be changed by that institution in a particular way. A Tory therefore reposes the ultimate authority in institutions – he is an example of collective man.

Do you believe in the Thatcher philosophy which is sometimes characterised as advocating greed and free enterprise as a way of life, irrespective of community benefit?

It is alleged that the speeches I made on the working of the competitive market in the early 1960s influenced Mrs Thatcher, but I wouldn't attribute to her the formulation which you've just provided. There is undoubtedly a role in the functioning of a human society for progressiveness, for competition, for envy, and for many urges which live in a kind of balance and coexistence with the other urges within. For instance, if we take the question of denationalisation: do we wish our railways to be run by politicians, or do we wish them to be run by those who will lose if they are ill run? The private enterprise corporation is founded upon the assumption that the resources which it puts to work are put to work most efficiently if it is managed by those who stand to lose if the customers' demand is not anticipated and met. That seems to me a very happy and ancient device which most nations have grown up with.

You have described yourself as a man naturally sympathetic to authority and its institutions. What is to be done when authority ceases to be impressive or even trustworthy, when for example a minister insists that the economy is recovering in the face of the facts, or when unemployment statistics are patently 'managed'?

No institution is immortal, any more than any other human thing is immortal, and there is no sovereign remedy against its deterioration. Institutions are not only created and strengthened, they also weaken and disappear. We cannot deny that.

You have been the subject of a great deal of abuse for stating your views about immigration. Have you modified them at all?

The aspects and consequences of immigration as perceived now in the 1990s are not the same as those which were perceived in the 1960s. In the 1960s the level of admissions was the critical subject; this resulted in a factor of almost equal importance being underestimated and largely overlooked – the age structure of the incoming population. Age structure is now asserting itself and will result in a progressive and on-going relative increase in what are called the ethnic minorities in proportion to the total population. What we don't know and what nobody can know, is how long institutions based upon the working of majorities can continue to operate. There is an on-going change in the population of this country, and one doesn't know how far that will be compatible with the continued operation of our parliamentary institutions. If you cannot change your mind between one election and another in reaction to what has been your experience in the meantime you cannot operate a parliamentary system. If an election is a census it cannot form a basis of parliamentary self-government. These are the questions which with the passage of time are now emerging, but I do find that, so far as I can judge it, public anxiety is as lively on this subject as it was thirty years ago.

Except our worst fears have not been justified?

My projections have been verified. What I said in 1968, I would say again if it were 1968.

In a discourse on Wagner's Ring, *you say that Siegfried of course did not fully understand or intend the consequences of his actions. Did you fully understand or intend the consequences of your 'River of Blood' speech?*

Those words were never used. The phrase did not occur in the speech. I don't think one ever foresees the consequences of one's actions and certainly in politics one never knows which utterances are going to be heard and which are not.

The sting in Paul Foot's book about you was that you had exploited the race issue as an act of political opportunism and not, as you claimed, as a matter of principle. What is your comment on that?

That's what he thought when he started to write the book, but after he'd met me he thought better. In fact, I ruined his book for him. When I heard he was writing it, I sent him a letter inviting him to come and talk to me. This was fatal because one can see in the course of the book that he discovered his conception was not viable.

The story goes that when you went to Northern Ireland someone called you a Judas, to which you retorted: 'I am sacrificing my political career. Judas was paid.' Is there any truth in that story?

That interchange did in fact take place after I'd delivered the second of my Vote Labour speeches in the election campaign of February 1974, but it was nothing to do with Northern Ireland.

You once spoke of yourself as a 'Lansdowne man' in the sense that since by 1943 it was clear that the axis powers could not win, we ought to have had a negotiated peace. Does that view not place you in the strange company of Oswald Mosley who also advocated a negotiated peace?

It does not put me in the company of those who see war between civilised nations as ending with the destruction of one's opponent. The object of war is to prove to one's opponent that he cannot gain his aim by force. When that has been proved the justification for war is at an end, and that point should be sought. Unconditional surrender was the most barbaric and inhuman concept to bring into the Second World War. You do not have to destroy your opponent; you merely have to prove to him that he cannot win, and when he can be persuaded that he cannot win, then you must make peace. Otherwise you will have to rebuild him and there will be a lot of other fallout too.

Many people have drawn a comparison between you and Mosley: intellectually rigorous, patriotic, a natural leader, a powerful orator, uncompromising, destined for – but never quite achieving – high office. Is it a comparison which offends you?

It's a comparison which is quite strange to me. I've never come across it. I am of course a failed politician, if one assumes that the object of politics is to gain and keep high office. Mosley was a failed politician too, so I may be included in the same category, but there is a large category of failed politicians.

Yes, but failed politicians because they were incapable ...

All right, I can be placed in the category of failed capable politicians; they're still a sufficiently large company to contain me and Oswald Mosley and dozens and dozens of others.

You once wrote that 'no time spent reading history is misspent for a politician.' But do not circumstances change beyond all recognition and invalidate the 'lessons' of history ... may it not be an error to read the future out of the past?

It is an error in any case to read the future out of the past, because history is not repeatable. The lessons we learn about the scientifically measurable and investigable world are applicable because that world is a constant. But history is not a constant; it is an artistic presentation of change in progress, irreversible and unique change. I recently improved upon my dictum about time spent reading history, and I would now say time spent reading biography is not misspent, perhaps because the repeatable element in individual human life is more substantial than the repeatable element in social or national life.

Hailsham said of you: 'He has the best mind in politics, until it is made up.' Did you understand what he meant by this, and did you accept the implied criticism?

No to the first question, and therefore the second does not arise.

A lot of people have said in that context you're your own worst enemy.

Well, it depends what a man wants, what his standards are, what life means for him.

But if you were to live that period in your life again ...

Don't frighten me with such a horrible idea. Imagine putting all my prejudices as an octogenarian into the body of a forty-year-old man – it's such a horrible notion that I decline to entertain it.

Maurice Cowling called you 'a closet socialist.' What do you think he meant by that?

He meant what I was saying earlier about a Tory being an aspect of collective man. Society is in the end normative, and politics is about the management and governance of a society. Society is prior (in a logical sense) to the individual; the individual in the last resort is an abstraction. Nobody has ever met an individual, we didn't start as individuals, we don't live as individuals, we only know ourselves as members of a collectivity. I think it was that aspect of my Toryism that Cowling may have had in mind.

It is said that an unofficial approach was made to you with a view to your becoming a life peer, but that you made certain conditions.

That's not a question I would ever answer.

Would you like to have been in the House of Lords? Conditions or no conditions?

You mean, would I have liked to have a different father? [Laughs.]

The House of Lords would have provided you with a forum in which to express your views …

I find no difficulty in getting my views onto paper, or getting what I put on to paper printed. Nor do I find any shortage of my fellow countrymen who are anxious to lend me their ears.

The House of Lord wouldn't interest you in the least?

You're putting words into my mouth.

Would it interest you?

I do not wish to say anything disrespectful about the upper chamber.

I am puzzled by your suggestion that the greatest act man is capable of is to choose death instead of life. I assume you are not writing in praise of suicide. Are you describing the capacity to sacrifice oneself for someone or something else?

Yes. It was the only way out for mankind that God could discover. It was the only way to save mankind, to allow someone to sacrifice his life for the remission of sins. It is an idea endorsed by the strongest authority.

Are there circumstances in which you would sacrifice your own life for that idea?

I suppose my decision to enlist is the only evidence that I have to offer. And I know now that I'm not the only person who put on a uniform and took it off again who has a lurking feeling at the back of his mind that there must have been something wrong with him if he came back. When I was asked on a radio programme how I would like to be remembered, and I replied that I wished I'd been killed in the war, I received a large correspondence from people who wrote that they were glad I had said that, because until then they thought they were the only people to feel that way. A large number of people who voluntarily went into the forces in 1939 are dogged by the idea that they were left unscathed when others were taken. Those who survived concentration camps also have this feeling.

Now that you have reached a certain age, are you afraid of death?

The nearer Death comes actuarially, the more he tends to present himself in the guise of a potential friend, a hand laid upon the shoulder saying, never mind old chap, I'll come along in due course and carry you away. There's a wonderful line in Homer where the prophecy is made to Ulysses that Death will come to him from the sea, with the words (in Greek) 'gentle, ever so gentle'. And one does come to regard Death as a gentle presence.

Many people have commented on your seemingly cold exterior, yet in private you are obviously a compassionate man. Are you aware of this tension between the public and the private personae?

The surprise that I sustain is how widespread and undifferentiated is the friendliness towards me, evidently entertained by large numbers of my fellow countrymen. It constantly comes as a happy but still remarkable thing to me. Perhaps that is an act of grace.

What in essence so attracted you to the music of Wagner?

Hearing it. There's a line in Caducci: 'When Wagner breathes into the sounding metal a thousand spirits, men's hearts tremble.'

What is your view on the current debate in Israel about Wagner's music? The Israeli Philharmonic wants to play Wagner but the public continues to reject him because of the association with Hitler and the Nazis.

That is their business, and I thank them to mind their business in declining to express corresponding opinions about the affairs of the United Kingdom.

Siegfried proclaimed what you call the great moral discovery of humanity: that it is better to die than to live in fear. While it is an idea which greatly captures the imagination, is there not a case for saying that in practice it is all but worthless. Many people live in fear of life itself or in fear of God, but their life still has intrinsic value.

Well, that will turn upon the word 'intrinsic', won't it? We live because we cannot help it, and we die because we cannot help it. You remember in front of Bolingbroke Richard II says: 'Give Richard leave to live till Richard die.'

When you reflected on age you said that to your surprise it was 'a constant opening of doors.' Can you elaborate on that?

I'm surprised by how much new there still is to think and to see, and the apparent immunity of one's thinking mechanism from those ravages that are making their advance in other parts of the organism. That one continues to think and enjoy thinking, to observe and to enjoy observing, is a constant marvel.

SIMON RAVEN

Simon Raven was a writer, critic and dramatist. He was born in 1927 and educated at Charterhouse and King's College, Cambridge. From 1953 to 1957 he served in the King's Shropshire Light Infantry before embarking on a full-time writing career. He wrote over thirty novels, including *Alms for Oblivion*, a sequence of ten books written between 1967 and 1976. Among his several volumes and memoirs are *Shadows on the Grass* (1977), *The Old Gang* (1988) and *Bird of Ill Omen* (1989). He was the author of several television scripts, including *Edward and Mrs Simpson* and *The Pallisers*. His memoir, *Is There Anybody There? Said the Traveller*, was withdrawn shortly after its publication in 1990 in the face of a series of libel threats, and he planned another, *All Safely Dead*, to overcome the problems, but never completed it. He died in 2001.

Your biographer, Michael Barber, speaks of your relish for 'unacceptable truths'. What are these truths, and what is it that makes them unacceptable?

These truths are absolutely obvious to everybody. For example, wars are unpleasant, death is inevitable, men are not equal. They are undeniably true and undeniably unacceptable. In the case of wars people think that since they are disagreeable they are not inevitable, and in the case of death, men have now become so vain that they believe that before very long there will be some elixir which will make them live forever. I myself don't fear death at all; in fact, I rather look forward to it, the only worrying question being the manner of one's dying – that could be disagreeable. Those whom the gods love die young. They also avoid nasty diseases and decaying old age. That's what the Greeks believed. They feared not death, but old age.

I have the impression that your passion for the classics and your respect for the teaching of the ancients has shielded you to some extent against the realities of the modern world ... would you agree?

They have certainly shielded me against a lot of nonsense that is spoken in the modern world. Both the Greeks and the Romans were full of direct and pithily expressed common sense, much of which would be considered unacceptable today.

Also, the study of the classics is a very absorbing matter, involving quite a lot of concentration and hard work, which in itself shields one from all the follies going on outside. I hardly ever read a newspaper these days except for the racing sections. Newspapers contain so much sentimental rubbish and self-pitying whining about this and that, rape and murder, or photos of politicians in silly positions sucking up to rows of proletarian children. I just don't have time for that. The trouble is that when the modern world does break through, which it is bound to do from time to time, it is uniquely unpleasant.

Do you watch television?

Only the occasional play or racing or cricket, but even then some piece of news will be thrust on me halfway through the programme. Why we have to have so much news, I don't know.

You love cricket, don't you?

Yes, indeed. I used to be moderately good at it, playing for Charterhouse in the same eleven as Peter May who subsequently became a very eminent cricketer. And since – as George Orwell put it – all modern men dislike cricket, this is a good reason for me to like it. People think it takes up too much time, or too much space which might be turned into houses, but what they really resent is that day after day you have this steady rhythm instead of the noise of builders making money; and that's what I love. And, of course, it's such a stately game and so decorative.

You are very grateful for your classical education and the civilised values which it taught you. I think you would be the first to admit that you have not yourself always adhered to these values. Is it enough to know them and to recognise them?

If you can know them and recognise them you've obviously gone a considerable way. Apart from Socrates, the only person I've ever heard of who's actually prac- tised what he's preached is Jack Jones, a great nuisance-figure in the trade unions, but a man I've always admired, and absolutely deserving of the Companion of Honour. When everybody else was getting into the best hotels in Brighton or Blackpool there was Jack Jones staying in the bed-and-breakfast joint. But Socrates and Jack Jones aside, there are very few people who practise what they preach.

Socrates believed that if two individuals had a dialogue they might discover the truth, or something which could be called their own truth. Have you discovered anything in your life which you could reasonably call the truth?

One truth I discovered from reading Lucretius and other classical writers is that there's no point in being afraid of death. There is no afterlife, so why be afraid? Another truth, and one by which I set great store, is the need to avoid violence or unkindness, whether physical or verbal. One must neither savage an individual physically, nor be unkind verbally; it's different with groups of people, because groups don't suffer. The great thing I learned at King's quite early on, even though I didn't always regard it, was that one must not seduce people. Everyone says rape is wrong and seduction is all right, but seduction is not all right because it can actually be a form of violent unkindness. The great *locus classicus* for this is the French novel *Les Liaisons Dangereuses*, a horrible and marvellous work which makes it plain that seduction, even of the most gentle kind, can at the same time be the most extreme form of violence. And at all costs one must avoid violence, whether physical or oral, if only because one feels so guilty about it later on, though that's not the only reason.

Fifty years after you were sacked from Charterhouse, you moved to this almshouse here in London's Old Charterhouse … does it seem as if you have come full circle?

Only in the sense that I am at leisure to read and reread all the books to which I didn't pay enough attention in my hot youth. I don't do much work now, and instead I spend the time studying the better work of better men, the Latin and Greek classics very largely, but also Italian, French and English classics.

The almshouse is intended for impoverished gentlemen … do you qualify on both counts, would you say?

I'm certainly impoverished, though I've never really been a gentleman. I've always been a cad, but I admire the qualities of a gentleman and I've always liked the idea of being one.

You are known to be keen on irony. Do you regard it as an irony that you have come back to an institution after a lifetime of being thrown out of institutions – school, King's College, the army …

Yes, I do regard it as an irony, though I would make a slight correction to the business of being thrown out. I suppose it's true that I was thrown out of Charterhouse, but I was reinstated as an old boy two years or so afterwards. And with King's College, yes, I may have been thrown out, but it was more a case of just not renewing my studentship. I wasn't getting on properly with my thesis because I was trying to write novels instead. As for the army, well, yes I was compelled to leave, but at the same time it was a resignation. There was no court martial nor was I cashiered at dawn with the drums beating, my sword broken and the buttons ripped off my uniform – nothing like that. I was just told to go and lose myself while they arranged the resignation.

How would you describe your feelings about institutions? Do you respect them still, or are you perhaps contemptuous of them?

I like some institutions, because they give one a sense of security and there is a logical structure to them. If you obey the rules, which are generally not very demanding, you will enjoy nothing except consideration. Above all I enjoy institutions because I find them so amusing. This was especially true of the army. A battalion of infantry, for example, is the perfect dramatic setting. There are about a thousand men and some forty or fifty officers, occupying the same space, doing the same things, and this inevitably makes for confrontations, intrigue, rivalries, sneaking and revenge. The place where I live now is very well run and most people are very agreeable, but nevertheless there are dramatic confrontations. This is because an institution offers an excellent framework for drama. Most of my writing has been concerned with institutions of one kind or another – school, army, university. Even close groups of friends almost qualify as an institution.

Reading the details of your expulsion from Charterhouse in your biography, there is no sense of large-scale scandal or disgrace attaching to it. In fact, you talk about people laughing when they heard you'd been sacked 'for the usual thing'. Even your parents seemed to take it rather well. How do you explain this?

Well, you only need to apply a little common sense to realise that if small boys play about with each other's private parts, it's no big deal. It was largely mutual masturbation and a little in the way of fellatio. There was no question of buggery, and even if there had been, it would have perhaps been all right. Except for the committed Christian – and here we come to the great big fly buzzing in this particular ointment – it's obviously a matter of total indifference if two boys, one aged seventeen and the other aged fifteen, play about with each other, provided there is no unkindness or compulsion, provided it's for mutual pleasure by mutual consent. There can't be anything wrong with it, and nobody these days thinks that there is. But at Charterhouse in the 1940s and 1950s, Christianity prevailed – it still does, I dare say – and our headmaster, Robert Birley, a man I very much admired and loved, was handicapped by believing in Christianity. There's nothing wrong with believing in Christ as a wandering preacher, since that is supported by history, but Birley also believed that Christ was the son of God and that he rose from the dead. Now, as far as I'm concerned, if you believe anything as silly as that, then there's got to be something a bit wrong and it probably alters your sense of proportion – it certainly did in Birley's case. He was a great man, a humane man who protected us against the war, and made sure we had a civilised life as long as we could till we were old enough to be called up. He did everything he could to make Charterhouse a cultivated and agreeable place, but he insisted that the tenets of Christianity be observed. And I wasn't prepared to observe them.

Did you feel any sense of personal shame about what had happened, or did you just accept that you had broken the rules and you were being punished accordingly?

I was very angry with myself for getting caught out, but I felt no guilt over it. The outcome was inevitable, and within its own framework, i.e. the Christian framework, it was entirely just. What I did very much regret was having to leave the earthly paradise of Charterhouse for the suburbs of Sheffield.

You apparently suspect William Rees-Mogg of influencing the headmaster in your expulsion. What grounds do you have for believing that?

As a matter of fact, I no longer suspect William. I did at the time because he was an enormous intriguer, then as now. He'd been a friend of mine from the beginning, and although he was a plain boy he managed to charm all the matrons who allowed him to stay in the nice warm library while the rest of us did PE. He was a great hypochondriac and he made absolutely certain that he never did anything disagreeable. He became the most marvellous gossip in the whole school. If you wanted to know anything you went to see William. He was also cultivated, though his judgements were rather marred by the fact that he was a practising Catholic. In time William intrigued his way into being head of the school, and I rather suspected him of betraying me in order to put his new-found power to the test, but I now know this is not true. My chief suspects are a couple of masters at the school, now both long dead, both tiresome Christians, who got to hear rumours and encouraged the headmaster to conduct an inquiry.

In your book, An English Gentleman, *you say that by becoming a writer one bade farewell at once to ethical restraint and to any kind of conventional status in society. Have those two factors been the cornerstones of your writing?*

They were advantages that came with the trade. The point I was trying to make was that if one was a regular army man, or a don, or a schoolmaster, or a foreign office man, one had to observe the code, largely a Christian code – and this still applies. Writers did not have to observe a code, and I was very grateful for this.

Would it be fair to say that you had more or less abandoned ethical restraint before you took up writing, that a certain dissolution preceded your career as a writer?

That is true. I was much addicted to drink, also to casual sex, generally of a commercial kind, and I saw no reason against any of this. But I was already beginning to feel the necessity of not offering violence to anybody. It was borne in on me quite early that one must respect other people, not be violent to them, not rape them, and not seduce them. I consider this to be quite a large ethical advance, something that not everybody seems to know about. Of course, one formulates these excellent rules for oneself, but it's another thing actually to keep them.

You say that you don't expect your novels to be remembered – indeed the title of your sequence of ten novels, Alms for Oblivion *is a quotation from* Troilus and Cressida, *referring to the scraps which are 'devoured as fast as they are made, forgot as soon as done'. Is this impermanence something you regret?*

I would very much like some of my work to be remembered, but when I consider what has happened to better novelists in my own lifetime, it's extremely unlikely that my own work will last. It would be tedious to go through very many examples, but if you take a novelist such as Francis Brett Young who was very important in my parents' day, whoever hears of him now? It seems to me that in order to be remembered as a novelist you have to be of supreme merit and also to enjoy a lot of luck. I could still hope in a corner of my mind not to be forgotten, but the omens are not good.

Is there anything which endures, or is everything alms for oblivion?

As far as literature is concerned, not everything is ephemeral, but if you go outside the scope of books, then everything is in flux – something the ancients knew and understood. What they found so nice about pleasure is the fact that it's transient: it comes, it is enjoyed, and it goes. Pleasure without transience would not be pleasure. The rose is appreciated because it fades, the orgasm is appreciated because it's very short and not easily repeatable, and so on. We know from classical literature that no cities and no men survive for very long. I believe in the permanence of nothing really.

Your writing is principally entertainment, and you believe that is the best possible reason for writing. Why do you deny any higher or more serious purpose?

I believe entertainment *is* the highest possible purpose. I like to entertain, and in order to make money you must entertain. Granted this, I am also quite keen to put an occasional element of serious reflection into my writing – thoughts about the things I've been mentioning, such as the transience of pleasure, the mutability of human affairs, the passing of man, and so on. I try to get all that in as part of the entertainment, since my aim is principally to amuse a certain class of intelligent people – and even if a theme is serious, it doesn't mean it shouldn't be entertaining. The whole question of the malice of the human race, for example, is something we have to consider, and all the old themes such as envy, spite, jealousy and human aspiration.

Have you always been able to be quite clear about the boundaries between fact and fiction or do they sometimes merge one into the other in your life?

They do merge. Even when I think I am absolutely clear about something, I am often very surprised by how wrong I am in fact. I once won £200 on a bet at Warwick racecourse, and I distinctly remember the horses coming round towards me in a clockwise direction. My own horse was in the lead and going on to win. When I went to Warwick again thirty years later I discovered that the horses go round in an anti-clockwise direction and always have done. Well, if one can be wrong about which way a horse that won you £200 was going – in other words, a serious matter – one is unlikely to be strictly accurate about anything.

You told your biographer that 'late middle age is a time of bitterness and spleen, of envy, resentment and sulk'. Is that really how you see this stage in your life, or was it offered as a flippant exoneration of your behaviour?

Bit of both. I think that as one grows older one grows more bitter. I believe more or less in what the gentleman who wrote the Book of Ecclesiastes believed: as one gets older one sees into the vanity of everything, and this makes one less agreeable and less charitable in many ways. This, of course, affects one's attitude to other people and what one says about them, making one more trenchant and bitter.

Yet people maintain that serenity can come with old age …

Most certainly it can, but that is the last stage when you finally realise that nothing matters at all. Rather like my own attitude towards the content of newspapers – it's all so stupid, so imbecile, so ridiculous, so sentimental, so sloppy, and much of it completely untrue, that it just doesn't matter.

Have you yourself reached the stage of serenity, would you say?

Not quite. By constitution I'm a great warrior with a very short temper. I worry about bookings at restaurants, I get angry with people who are late for the table which I have booked, and then if somebody annoys me, I lose my temper and say something very nasty indeed, and then almost instantly regret it and start to apologise and feel dreadful. But I think I'm getting increasingly philosophical.

If late middle age is as you describe, how would you characterise the other six ages of man?

Well, infancy isn't worth bothering about. Childhood can be enjoyable, even if it's corrupted. Adolescence is all spots and horror, and youth is disagreeable, a time of ambition and lust. Love is the most damaging thing for youth, because it uses up so much time which could be better spent. After youth things start to settle down; one gets a fairly mature view, and one begins to realise the absurdity of the whole thing. Late youth or early middle age is the time for getting steadily more stable, more tolerant, more amused, less serious in many ways, even more frivolous; one begins to realise how stupid the human race is, how greedy, and at the same time one realises that stupidity and greed are probably the original sin. In the end, however, one realises that none of it matters in the least, because very soon one will be dead, and so will everyone else for that matter; and with that a kind of serenity appears.

You seem to have had a rather uneasy relationship with money all your life, running up debts, robbing Peter to pay Paul, living off your wits to get by. Have you minded this very much?

I never wanted to collect huge sums of money and have lots of shares and lots of property and a huge bank account. I just wanted there to be enough – quite a lot, but no more than what was really enough to lead a fairly pleasant life and entertain my friends, and to go abroad when I wanted to. In order to do all of that I was prepared to beg and borrow, though not seriously to cheat. All the time I was at Cambridge and in the army I had to borrow and improvise. Although I enjoyed gambling, I was a bad gambler, but I wanted both to get money and have the pleasure of gambling. That went horribly wrong, but after the army I began to make enough money to satisfy these various wants of mine. I travelled and lived quite nicely for a time, but then things began to sink, my writing began to make less money, my luck ran out, my form ran out and public opinion was no longer on my side. In the mid-1980s money began to be a serious problem again, and has stayed so ever since.

Since gambling and an inability to control spending were the chief factors in accumulating debts, it could be said that your poverty was largely self-inflicted. Do you accept that?

Absolutely, without qualification. For most of the 1970s I was making a lot of money, and had I taken my accountant's advice and invested sensibly, I would now have a small fortune. But what's the point of having a lot of money to die on? I'm just as happy here living the life of a poverty-stricken gentleman as I would be in a house I'd paid for, worrying about inflation, worrying about my investments. Although I don't believe in Christ the son of God, I certainly believe there was a prophet called Christ, and the best thing he ever said was that a rich man cannot get into heaven. I like to think he meant that a rich man cannot have any happiness at all because of the constant worry. The thing about being poor is that you don't need to worry; things can only get better.

In an article in the Listener *in 1962 you gave an account of your addiction to gambling in which you spoke of 'the treasury or terror, guilt and perversity' which it entailed. You suggested that the principal motive for gambling in your case was the desire to be punished when things went badly, and the 'almost sexual satisfaction' to be derived from an evening of disastrous losses. If it is indeed sexual, it is surely masochistic …*

Yes, I think it is. It is quite true that all those things accompanied my gambling, and there was definite sexual excitement, an erection in my case, though never orgasm. But I do know of several people who, when doing very badly, actually come in their trousers. That is partly to do with fear, I think. I can remember when I was a very young boy doing a long division sum for an exam and I couldn't get it to work out. Time went on and I had no time left for other questions and I found myself becoming distinctly sexually aroused. I also remember getting a huge erection underneath one of Aspinall's gambling tables when I was still allowed to go there. I now see that the only form of gambling which is really amusing is horse-racing. You can't hope to win at horse-racing because you don't know how the horse feels. That's why hot favourites lose to 33–1 numbers, and a wail of self-pity goes up from the crowd. It's my favourite thing, particularly if I've backed the 33–1 number. The point about horse-racing is that it is just fun, it's an exciting sporting spectacle, you don't know what is going to happen, the colours are beautiful, the band plays, there are blue hills in the background and so it becomes almost a cultural obligation to go to the horse-races. Toulouse Lautrec and Degas knew this, as did lots of fine artists. The gambling side is just fun; you know you're almost certain to lose, but you also know that every now and again you have a streak of luck. Roulette, which I used to play a lot, is stylish in its way, but it's mechanical. The odds at roulette are very fair, but with horse-racing it's different. Sometimes the horse is constipated and has had a nasty journey. That's why I always back a horse when I see it crap in the paddock.

Your attitude to sex seems to have been to regard it as something of a joke, too ridiculous to be taken seriously. Do you allow that it is a joke with sometimes serious consequences?

Indeed I do. As a boy I was constantly afraid I'd got the pox, and I was always hurrying off to the college doctor or the army MO with a slight pimple, fearing the worst. Afterwards there was the idea that one would go and sin no more, but of course one always did sin some more and one got these constant scares. That's one kind of serious consequence. In the case of girls there was the fear of pregnancy, which was one reason I preferred boys. In fact, the consequences often seem too serious and annoying to make sex worthwhile in the end. I agree with Chesterton: the pleasure is momentary, the position ridiculous and the expense damnable.

When you were at prep school you were a victim of what it is fashionable to call 'sexual abuse' at the hands of a particular master …

I enjoyed every second of it …

You obviously didn't see yourself as a victim, nor did you regard it as abuse; indeed, you felt what you called 'great erotic fascination' with what went on. Is that how you most remember it, or do you think that is how it actually felt at the time?

It's certainly how I choose to remember it and I think it actually felt that way at the time. One knew, of course, that there was something not quite right about it, but what made it feel more right than it probably was, was the fact that Colonel K, as I call him, was a very good schoolmaster, a very charming man, kind, pleasant, and representing the best of the prep-school system. He taught mathematics, English literature and geography with imagination and *esprit*. As regards sex, what he did was very pleasant, no two ways about it. Small children can be sexually excited, and certainly by the time I was nine or ten I was having a sort of orgasm, whereby the thing juddered about, and the whole business was very enjoyable. He played with the other boys too, and we all did it to each other, and also to him. And great fun it was too. Once one got used to the idea, it was all quite logical. His willie was obviously bigger and had hairs around it, and he was very tactful about how he actually came. So that one shouldn't see the spurting, he used to come into a large silk handkerchief, but I was very curious and asked him if I could watch. It was infinitely enjoyable and I was never worried by it.

And you never reported him?

Why should I have reported him? He was a nice man, and God knows who might arrive in his place if he went. It wasn't as if he was sodomising the boys – he was just playing. That dreadful woman on television – I hope she's not a friend of yours – Esther Rantzen, she will not draw a distinction between somebody who rapes a child and then slits its throat, and somebody who just goes twinky winky, thereby giving much pleasure. Well, she's a silly cow. Please do quote me on that.

Do you believe this Colonel K kindled an interest in homosexuality, or do you think it would have happened anyway?

It probably would have happened anyway, though not perhaps till a little later, till one got to Charterhouse and found some boy to start one off. Colonel K got me started quite early, and one learned it was pleasant and amusing, and slightly tiresome when it was over, because one always felt a bit fed up after orgasm. One formed this attitude that sex was a splendid occasional thing, but there were lots of things which were even more fun. Reading, for example, because reading goes on and on, whereas sex is occasional and transient and swift.

Despite the fact of having many male lovers, you've never favoured buggery. Has it just never appealed, or what?

It has never appealed to me, partly because the buggers I have known have been very disagreeable one way or another. Also, it is, quite literally, a filthy practice. You wind up with great lumps of shit on the end of your whatnot. I was only buggered once, and it's painful, very painful till you get used to it, and I never got used to it. I'm told some people find it intensely exciting after a bit, and the prostate does a lot of work for you if you're being buggered. But I myself regard it as unaesthetic and rather repugnant, a view confirmed by those I know to be habitual buggers.

I think I'm right in saying that you regarded yourself as bisexual, which, in the 1950s, was not exactly fashionable. Being homosexual was accepted in a way that being bisexual was not. Did you really not have a preference?

Every now and then I tried to work out a calculus on this. I decided that boys were marginally preferable. On the other hand, with women I often favoured mutual masturbation, cunnilingus or fellatio, instead of actual coition. The whole matter of the mechanics was rather marginal because fellatio with a man was just as agreeable. And I thought that women could get rather tiresome; except for skilful prostitutes, they were always wanting to bring love into the whole thing, and make it serious and make it last. There's a passage in Juvenal where he says, don't get married, go to bed with a little boy, he won't make constant demands for money, he won't be a bit sorry if you don't want to do it, and he won't nag during or afterwards. How right Juvenal is. Even Propertius, who was obsessed by women, urges his friends to prefer boys. He likens boys to going down a gentle river in a boat and coming to a small harbour where there'll be no trouble. As for women, he says that the trouble, the temper, the demands never cease. And I think this is right.

Did you ever wish that you were one thing or the other, so to speak?

No, I've been very happy being bisexual. It seemed to me the intelligent and civilised solution. It was the position taken up by all my favourite classical authors, and a lot of my favourite more modern authors, who, even if they themselves weren't bisexual, certainly condoned the condition and sometimes actively approved it. It's so matchlessly convenient to be able to help yourself either way if the opportunity presents.

By all accounts you had a number of homosexual encounters in the army ... did your fellow officers turn a blind eye?

Well, some of my fellow officers were of course bisexual or homosexual themselves. And I was very discreet. But the main reason why there was no trouble was that I was pleasant to anybody with whom I had sexual connections, whether he was an officer or a private soldier. It's only victims that shop a man, not people who are treated kindly. You don't get reported as a rule, unless you get some terrible puritan who suffers from guilt. You have to be very careful about that. One or two of those army boys had puritan parents, ghastly low-church people, and that can spell trouble, particularly if they're Baptists.

You have a reputation for misogyny. Does it have a rational basis? What I mean is, you obviously have quite strong feelings about the worthlessness of women, their 'inability to act sensibly', as you put it, but are these principally feelings, or are they part of a thesis, as it were?

Once again, these answers are not to be oversimplified. Like everybody else I've had a lot of experience of the foolishness of women, and the foolishness of men too. On the one hand, men tend to be sexually vain and greedy. Women, on the other hand, tend to be possessive and domestic. This is quite simply biological, since nature tells us that women are there to have babies; they are naturally possessive of men so that a family can be formed. This can make them in any number of ways very tiresome. They don't want their husbands to go out on a drunken evening or do jolly things like racing, because that uses up money which is meant for babies. I find this aspect of women particularly tedious. Also this business of wanting to be in on male things. Women have gone to endless trouble to penetrate male clubs. Well, if they want clubs, why can't they have their own? After all, it's very good for people to be able to get away from the opposite sex, for women as well as men. Why do they go to such lengths to go on ships, when they're not needed on ships, they're a perfect nuisance on ships, stirring up all kinds of trouble. It's bad enough having men trying to seduce the cabin boys, so to speak, but when you've got a whole load of women there as well, you just don't need it.

Have you yourself ever suffered from sexual jealousy?

I can put my hand on my heart and say honestly that I have never felt sexually jealous. In fact, I often have great fun with boys or with women, discussing other boys or women they have been with – it can be sexually exciting sometimes. I regard sexual jealousy as one of the meanest and most absurd of human failings. Why be jealous? It's irrational, unpleasant and causes endless trouble.

Do you have an underlying fear of women? Do you feel threatened by them in some way?

Only when they try to take friends of mine away and marry them. That is a bore, and in that sense they're great destroyers of friendship. I no longer have any fear of women because I have long since been impotent, so I'm not going to get any of them pregnant, a fear I had for a long time after the one bit of trouble I had. The only fear I have nowadays is that they will interfere with pleasant arrangements, with friendships, with days at the races.

I interviewed Barbara Skelton just before she died, and she told me that she was extremely thankful no longer to have the sexual urge, that she felt at peace with herself in a way she had not before. You say that you're impotent now, but do you still have a kind of sexual urge?

I have bisexual fantasies, but I'm very glad not to want to do anything about them, because sex takes up time that can be used for other matters. It's costly, and even dangerous these days.

While you were at King's it came as something of a shock when your girlfriends Susan Kilner announced she was pregnant. The prospect of marriage appalled you, yet you caved in under pressure 'to do the decent thing'. Was this not uncharacteristic behaviour – I mean, to do what was expected of you?

No. I was afraid that her parents might make a row and that I might as a consequence lose the studentship I'd just got, and that I would be expelled. Obviously, something had to be done, but it was very much on my own conditions. I never lived a day under the same roof with Susan after we married. It was on my own terms that I married her, and the whole thing quietened down very nicely, largely because of her great good sense and cooperation.

Do you think your son was psychologically damaged by this arrangement?

I don't see why he should have been. He always knew where I was, even if he didn't see me very often, and I've always been on friendly terms with him. He's now well over forty, and we go racing together quite often, and we travel abroad together sometimes. He's a very good driver and a good chap to have on a trip, as long as he doesn't drink too much and ask for all the most expensive things on the menu.

How do you rate yourself as a father?

Not high, because I was never there when I should have been. It wasn't a great priority with me at that time, or ever. There were always books to be written, and other things to be done, so domesticity was very low on my list. Not that I'm against being a father. I'm against domesticity; that's my real hate.

Cyril Connolly famously remarked that there was no more sombre enemy of good art than the pram in the hall, something that you were aware of quite independently of Connolly. Was your difficulty with fatherhood to do with the feeling that it was incompatible with creativity, or did it go much deeper than that?

I simply felt that it meant being in one place the whole time with two people, the child and its mother, and this entailed inconvenience and constriction. It also meant spending money, and I resent the amount of good pleasure-money which children tend to absorb. The pram in the hall also meant rows and trouble. I'd heard my own parents rowing, and I decided then that married life was not for me. Sod marriage, is what I felt.

If we can talk about love as opposed to sex, you seem to have found love a difficult business ...

The trouble with love is that once again it constricts you. I've only been in love a few times in my life, once with a woman whom I still see from time to time, and twice with boys when I was at Cambridge. I was conscious each time that it was a terrible nuisance, because it was preventing me from doing all the reading I wanted to do. With the woman it was settled fairly quickly; we both fell out of love but continued to enjoy each other's company. We used to meet very occasionally, and there's nothing like meeting once every two or three years to keep interest and sexual enthusiasm alive. It's a brilliant scheme, and I'm not sure I shan't claim to have invented it.

You told your biographer that love was a disease against which you have been immunised by classical literature and personal experience ...

This is true now and was probably true then, but whether it was true when I had these affairs, I'm not sure. During the infatuation stage it was very tiresome; in fact, you could say that all love is infatuation.

Was it your experience that sexual relations were spoilt by love in some way?

Yes, because if you really loved somebody you were terrified of disgusting them or doing anything they disliked. Love makes you very vulnerable and that's the whole trouble with it. I finally learned that love is a tiresome, messy, time-wasting, value-confusing nuisance.

You obviously favour the Greek and Roman attitude towards pleasure, namely that pleasure is transient, but you also believe it is enhanced by the envy and disapproval it arouses in others. Why does that appeal to you so much?

It amuses me when other people are envious or disapproving. The two things I really despise are disapproval and envy, so when I see that a pleasure of mine is arousing these emotions in others, it's a decoration of the whole thing, and it gives me additional pleasure.

Is pleasure distinct from happiness, would you say?

I think there is no such thing as happiness. People talk about happiness, but they really mean content. People have a particularly good patch, and things go well for a number of reasons, and they are then what is known as happy. But that's never going to last for long, because happiness is essentially something that vanishes. The thing to do is to be content. Descartes said the secret of happiness, by which he meant content, is never to hanker after something you can't have, and to make yourself appreciate what you know you can have.

Do the higher pleasures – for example, intellectual pursuits, or poetry perhaps – come closer to happiness?

Oh yes, because they're always there and you can take them up again if you want to. They're available if needed, and they don't answer back. Also, the fact that one has had to use one's brain does accord a degree of self-satisfaction, which very much qualifies one for content.

About twenty-five years ago you said: 'The English, by and large, are the last decently behaved people in the world.' Do you still believe that to be true?

I do, despite all the nonsense that goes on. The great danger is so-called political correctness which could make Nazis of us all in the end. All the informing which goes on, and all the silly judgements which interfere and undermine. I don't think it's too bad in England yet, and on the whole we're still a very decent, tolerant lot.

You also said that decency has nothing to do with morality. Can you explain what you meant by that?

One can do something which is regarded as immoral – as Colonel K did – in a decent, kindly way. Decency, after all, is a combination of kindness and tolerance and good humour. Many sexual acts are rated immoral but can be done decently.

Do you admire virtues in others which you conspicuously lack?

I admire moral courage and unselfishness, both of which I conspicuously lack. I do admire them, but I know that they're beyond me.

You never had much time for religion. How much were you influenced by your study of the classics which advocate living this life to the full because only the superstitious believe in any kind of afterlife?

The classics had a great deal to do with it, and also the people among whom I was educated. Most classical authors just accepted the pagan religion as a rather decorative and poetic thing; they didn't actually believe it, but in so far as they did, it was a fun thing. The poles were very wide, and you could do almost anything you wanted.

Are you dismissive of Christianity chiefly because you find the idea of a merciful God absurd, or is there more to it than that?

The idea of a merciful God is absurd, particularly when you consider what he has inflicted on his people. I'm a deist in that I believe in a first cause, but there my own religious belief stops. My god is really just a scientific cause. As for the rest, Swinburne was right: 'We thank with brief thanksgiving / Whatever gods may be / That no man lives forever, / That dead men rise up never; / That even the weariest river / Winds somewhere safe to sea.'

In your own obituary, which you were invited to write some years ago, you complimented yourself on your loathing for what Orwell called 'smelly little orthodoxies' and what are sometimes called 'modern sensitivities'. What would you include on your list?

The whole bother about race – that's one smelly orthodoxy. I'm perfectly prepared to accept the fact that I need to call anybody of any creed or race equal, but I see no reason why they should be subjects of special consideration. Why on earth should they be? They've got to put up with things like anybody else. The whole business of equality can be solved by decency and common sense, instead of all this going round making doctrinaire fusses and having special institutions. The Race Relations Board does nothing except make trouble. Another orthodoxy I have nothing to do with is this matter of equal opportunities for women. If women are as good as men, then let them have the job by all means, but don't make a great sort of fuss about it and say there's got to be a quota. That's a big smelly orthodoxy. And as far as I am concerned, Christianity is another. Belief in Christ is not necessarily smelly, nor is belief in God, but Christianity as it stands is most definitely smelly, from the clap-happies to the most severe Catholics. There are inquisitors in our midst; they may not use heated tongs, but they are inquisitors just the same.

One of your collections of memoirs is called Bird of Ill Omen – *a reference to the bird of your name and the way it is thought to be unlucky and bring trouble wherever it goes. Is it too psychoanalytical to suggest that subconsciously you might have tried to live up to your name?*

One might of course be the catalyst of certain unpleasant occurrences, but never intentionally, and all the instances in that book were entirely accidental.

For example, one of the main stories concerns a colonel who got shot by one of his own ambushes. My only involvement with that was proximity; I had nothing actually to do with it. I have mostly been involved in tales of ironic calamity, which I have not caused directly. No, I think I can let myself off there. *Bird of Ill Omen* was merely a convenient title.

Arthur Schlesinger Jr.

Arthur Schlesinger Jr. was Albert Schweitzer Professor of Humanities at the City University of New York from 1966 to his retirement in 1994. He was born in Ohio in 1917 and graduated *summa cum laude* from Harvard in 1938. He has held academic appointments at Harvard and Princeton and between 1961 and 1964 he was special assistant to John F. Kennedy. He is author of many books, including *The Politics of Upheaval* (1960), *The Politics of Hope* (1963), *Robert Kennedy and His Times* (1978) and *A Thousand Days* (1965), his account of the Kennedy administration, for which he won the 1966 Pulitzer Prize. He opposed the 2003 Iraq War and died in 2007.

At Harvard you were once reported to have said, 'I love teaching but I hate students.'

I don't recall ever saying anything like that, nor is that what I feel. On the whole I like students more than I like teaching. I don't mind teaching and I work hard at it and believe I have done it reasonably well, but there are some people for whom teaching is an organic part of life and for whom deprivation would be equivalent to amputation. I regard teaching as better than ditch digging as a way to support oneself, and I find students quite agreeable, but I'm essentially a writer, and if I could have figured out a way of life that would have removed the necessity for teaching, I would have done it. At present I can't retire, because if I were to bring home the books that I have in my office to a house already overflowing with books, my wife would throw me or the books or both into the street.

As a celebrated American historian, you have been special advisor to a president of the United States. How did you reconcile the two disciplines: that of distinguished politician and that of political aide?

It's only in recent times that the two professions have become distinct. For a long time the two were fused in the same person without any sense of incompatibility. After all, Thucydides was an Athenian general and Julius Caesar was a far from dispassionate observer. Gibbon wrote in his memoirs, about his military experience, that the captain of the Hampshire Grenadiers was not useless to the historian of the Roman Empire. I think the opportunity to see how worldly decisions are made is as likely to enrich the historian as much as to corrupt him.

In my own case, in the United States, my mother was collaterally descended from George Bancroft, the first American historian, who wrote a history of the United States in many volumes. George Bancroft was also Jackson's and Van Buren's political man in Massachusetts. He was Polk's secretary of the navy, minister to England and to Germany, and was also a very productive historian.

You have to avoid turning history into political partisanship. Another historian once said of Bancroft that all his volumes voted for Andrew Jackson. One must guard against that. But even in libraries historians are not devoid of prejudice. The problem is that the historian can never escape the egocentric predicament, but he must continue to seek an objectivity he can never attain. At least he should take care to declare his interests.

Advisers to presidents are not elected representatives and some might not consider such appointments to be proper in a democracy. Does that not bring special problems and difficulties to the job?

It need not. A president can't do everything himself. From the beginning of the republic, presidents have had people to help them. Andrew Jackson formed what was called his 'kitchen cabinet' – advisers who were not members of the regular Cabinet but with whom he would discuss politics and choices – and that aroused a certain amount of newspaper and partisan protest, but, as Jackson recognised, criticism was really aimed at him, not at them.

The present White House staff was established in 1939 when FDR secured the passage of the Government Reorganization Act. That created the position of the special assistant to the president, and he was given half a dozen of them. Up to that time, presidents had de facto special assistants, but they were mostly on payrolls of other agencies and were co-opted. The new special assistants were supposed by Roosevelt to be endowed, in the phrase he borrowed from Tom Jones, the friend of Lloyd George, with a passion for anonymity. That passion for anonymity has waned in recent years.

In Britain we recently witnessed the resignation of the Chancellor to the Exchequer over the issue of Mrs Thatcher's personal economic adviser. What was your reading of the situation?

I guess Nigel Lawson had reached the point where he couldn't take Mrs Thatcher any more. Mrs Thatcher was getting economic advice both from the Chancellor and from her personal economic adviser, Alan Walters, and Lawson found the situation intolerable. I suppose he would have found it tolerable if his advice had been taken more often. I assume it was the culmination of various frustrations. Working with Mrs Thatcher, I would judge, is not always the easiest thing in the world.

We have a similar situation structurally in the United States. The president has a department of the Treasury, but he also has a Council of Economic Advisers, both established by statute. The chairman of the Council of Economic Advisers and the Secretary of the Treasury often bring in conflicting advice. There is a third figure, the chairman of the Federal Reserve Board, which is an independent agency. Appointments to the Federal Reserve are made by the president with the consent of the Senate, but the agency itself is not accountable to the president. So you have a triad arguing over the economy.

Since economics is far from an exact science, I don't think it does any harm for the president to hear two or three positions. In the end the president makes the decisions. The American cabinet does not enjoy the authority that, theoretically, a British cabinet enjoys. The president has the monopoly over the decision, whereas theoretically, if not always practically, decisions in British government are collegial; all members of the cabinet are implicated. A quarter of a century or more ago, Dick Crossman pointed out that cabinet government was giving way to prime ministerial government; in effect to presidential government. Mrs Thatcher has certainly illustrated the point.

In the present administration under Bush, or the previous administration under Reagan, did the advisers have autonomy, or was the president involved in everything?

In Reagan's case, he was indifferent to most of the business of government and he let people move off on their own, so long as they conformed to his set of *laissez-faire* principles. Bush is very much interested in foreign policy and probably follows that quite closely. Roosevelt had great intellectual curiosity; so did Kennedy. But Reagan was quite passive. He had no intellectual curiosity.

Who among the presidents of recent years was the most autocratic?

All presidents are ultimately the boss in the executive branch. The most auto-cratic by temperament clearly was Nixon, but that was because he was insecure. He feared congress, hated political opposition. Nixon would like to have been an elective dictator. He did not understand that debate and opposition are the same essence of democracy; so he regarded opponents of the administration as disloyal to the country and put them on his enemies list. I am proud to say I was on it. Nixon was certainly the most autocratic by disposition. Roosevelt tended to give people a loose leash, but then to rein them in rather abruptly, and cut them off if he felt they did not justify his confidence. Eisenhower was interested in what he was interested in and indifferent to what he was indifferent to. He was actually a rather tense man within, but there were a lot of things he just didn't care about.

There's been a historical revisionism about Eisenhower, and now counter-revisionism is setting in. For a time there was a theory that Eisenhower, underneath his grin and his apparent indifference and his fractured syntax, was really a very strong president. And it is evident that he played much more of a role in foreign affairs than we understood at the time. Eisenhower was a crafty man, a good politician, a selfish man. He used Dulles in what we call a good cop/bad cop routine. Dulles would do the unpleasant things and Eisenhower would be the man of peace. On the other hand, Eisenhower's instincts were good. For example, he was very sceptical about the missile gap. Having been a general, he didn't take the Pentagon very seriously. He was constantly saying – in private – that we were building too many nuclear weapons. In his farewell address, he talked about the dangers of the military-industrial complex.

Yet he did very little about these things. He complained about over-targeting by the Pentagon, but would not stop it. The military-industrial complex was really created during his presidency. One of the worst things he did was to use the CIA as the president's private army. He was sceptical about the regular army, so he never used it, and instead started the bad presidential habit of using covert action and clandestine means to achieve ends which, in a democracy, ought to be approved by legislature, by public opinion.

Kennedy tended to get more involved in the process of decision making than most presidents. He did not hesitate to call the man at the desk in the State Department or the Agriculture Department and so on if he wanted to find out what the situation really was. He would bypass the Cabinet minister in charge, which irritated cabinet ministers but exhilarated the people at the desk who received the presidential calls. Kennedy was very accessible. We could get him quite quickly by telephone, and late in the afternoon, if the door between his office and the office of his secretary was open, it meant that his special assistants could stick their heads in. He'd be reading or talking on the phone and would say, 'Come on in.' Sometimes he would just like to chat.

I find it hard to recognise the swollen White House staffs of the present time. During the Depression, Roosevelt had a smaller staff than the wife of the president has today, and he fought the Second World War with a smaller staff that the vice-president has today. Our White House staffs now are bloated. Many presidential assistants rarely see the president and have to make appointments days or weeks in advance. The great inflation of the White House staff came with Nixon, and every president since has carried it on. They all begin by saying they are going to reduce the size of the White House staff, but they never do.

As special assistant to Kennedy, your responsibilities ranged from speech writing to general advice on major issues. To what extent was it a position of real power and influence?

It was not a position of real power at all. But for an historian it was a fascinating experience to be around when decisions were made. I don't think my presence made any difference to anything, except to me, but it was very enjoyable. Working with Kennedy was exhilarating. I learned a great deal, and perhaps I was able to play a marginal role on some matters.

Did he take your advice?

I was opposed to the Bay of Pigs. I was part of the group involved in planning it, and I thought it a bad idea. I talked to Kennedy about it, and he wasn't very enthusiastic himself, but it was an expedition he had inherited from the previous administration. He was trapped because, here he was, a naval lieutenant from the Second World War, and if he were to disband a project that the great General Eisenhower had approved, people would have been critical of him, and the word would have gone around that Eisenhower had been prepared to overthrow Castro and that Kennedy refused to follow through. Then there was what Alan Dulles of the CIA called the disposal problem: what to do with 1,200 Cuban exiles who had been trained in Guatemala. Kennedy couldn't quite see how to disband them without disturbing political consequences; so rather reluctantly he let the expedition go ahead.

He was a man of great intellectual curiosity and high intelligence. He liked to hear varying viewpoints. I suppose I was one base he liked to touch, probably just to see what a professional liberal, so to speak, would think about this or that issue. One thing on which I may have helped was the question of the centre left in Italy. The Eisenhower administration had said that the United States would not countenance the entry of the Partito Socialista Italiano (PSI) into an Italian government. The US veto struck all of us as outrageous, and at a very early point I talked to Kennedy about it. I went to Italy and, when I came back, strongly recommended that he indicate we would have no objection to the socialists entering the government, which he did when Fanfani made his visit in 1961. The State Department continued to try to preserve the Eisenhower veto, but the PSI had long since abandoned its fellow-travelling inclinations of a decade earlier. Still it wasn't really until Averell Harriman became under-secretary for political affairs that we were able to turn the State Department around.

Eventually the socialists entered the government, and nothing much changed one way or t'other.

You have often been called an American liberal. Is that with a capital L?

'Liberal' means something very different in Europe. In Italy the Liberal party is a rather conservative party, and through most of the Continent liberal is understood to mean Manchester *laissez-faire* nineteenth-century liberalism with an admixture of anticlericalism. In Britain the Liberal party has come to mean the party of good-hearted, somewhat eccentric people. American liberalism is really the liberalism which Lloyd George and Churchill embraced before the First World War and it could, I suppose, be called social liberalism rather than classic liberalism.

What it means essentially is the intervention of government to enlarge opportunity for those who are poor or handicapped one way or another in life. It means the interventionist state, provision of basic levels of welfare and so on. It does not mean the command economy, or centralised planning. It's Keynesian liberalism, the market working according to rules of the game with sufficient regulation in the public interest to prevent greed from undermining and subverting the system.

Reagan represented this reaction against all that, and greed took over in the United States in the 1980s. Greed brings out the worst impulses of capitalism. The solution in my view is to do what Roosevelt did: to rescue capitalism from the capitalists. If you're going to have individual freedom, you have to have mixed ownership. Private property is essential for freedom of speech, freedom of the press, freedom of political opposition and the like. But capitalists don't understand the virtues of their own system. If they have the money, they don't have to have political power too. I believe those capitalist states are best that are run by people who are not over-impressed by the wisdom of the business community.

In 1959, you said that the biggest issue between Democrats and Republicans was the allocation of resources between the public and private sectors. What do you see as the biggest issue today?

The biggest issue is the role of the government. The view of the Regan administration was the government is not the solution; government is the problem; if only we could get government 'off our backs', then our problems would solve themselves; or the process of the market would solve them.

I would say that is manifestly not the case. Getting government off our backs means putting business on our backs. Deregulation has largely been a disaster. One reason I was a little late for our interview is that I've been calling the telephone company to get the phone fixed. We used to have a regulated monopoly. If the phone didn't work, they would send someone to fix it. Now the monopoly is broken up in the interests of deregulation, so you can call one place and they say, 'Well, we're not responsible for that,' and you have to call another place, a separate company, and so it goes on. The idea of deregulation was to bring competition into, say, the airlines. But competition did not last long. Where is Freddie Laker now? Where is People's Airline in the United States now? Competition has resulted in much more consolidation than existed under regulation.

Deregulation produced the leveraged buy-out scandals, the savings and loan scandals, the housing scandals. Regulation in the public interest is a requirement in any advanced industrial society. So is a measure of government intervention to help the poor and the disadvantaged. Democrats stand for affirmative government as against the Republican faith in negative government.

It sometimes seems that the politician who is able to give the best performance on television wins the day. Is that a cynical view, or has the stature of presidents and politicians diminished?

Television has had considerable impact on politics, but more on the party structure than on the character of politicians. In the United States the theory was that, once television became dominant, all successful politicians would have to meet standards of historic skill and personal pulchritude. Ronald Reagan came along in apparent vindication of this view. But actually Ronald Reagan succeeded because the country was entering a conservative phase in the political cycle. He would have been as effective in the age of radio, as was Roosevelt, or in the age of newsreels, as was Warren G. Harding, or in the age of the penny press, as was Franklin Pierce. I don't think he was a unique creation of television.

Indeed, he's almost alone in meeting those anticipated standards. If you look at the rest of the people who have run for president in the television age since Kennedy, none has been any good on television. Lyndon Johnson was a disaster. So was Barry Goldwater in 1964. In 1968, Hubert Humphrey and Richard Nixon were both disasters. George McGovern and Nixon; Jimmy Carter and Gerald Ford; Carter against Regan; Mondale Dukakis and Bush – none has been any good, except for Kennedy and Reagan. The television age, in short, has produced few politicians conspicuously good at television. I think that effect has been much more overrated. Indeed, consider two people who were very effective on television, handsome, telegenic, well-spoken, and possessed in addition of substantial political records. One was John Lindsay, who used to be mayor of New York, the other was John Connolly of Texas. Both tried for presidency, and in spite of the fact that they were much better on television than their opponents, they did very badly.

Where television has had a potent effect, however, is in weakening, enfeebling and perhaps eventually destroying the political parties. Television and the public opinion polls have deprived the political party of two of its most vital functions. In the old days, politics was a three-tiered operation. You had the politician, and you had the voter, and in between you had the party. The party would interpret the voters to the politician and the politician to the voter. The party was the great mediatorial agency. When the politician wanted to find out what public opinion was like in his constituency, he would ask the head of the local party organisation. When the voter wanted to know how to vote, he'd listen to the head of the party organisation.

The electronic era has ended all that. When the politician wants to know what public opinion is, he no longer calls up the political leader; he takes a poll. When the voter wants to find out who to vote for, he doesn't listen to the local political leader; he watches the tiny screen and makes his own judgement on what he sees. The parties are left to wither on the vine. During elections there used to be bumper stickers, buttons, torchlight processions, parades, volunteers. None of that any more. It's all done on television. I think the weakening of the party structure is a much more portent effect of television than any change in the character of candidates.

Many have the impression that people of great talent tend not to enter politics and that consequently our lives are ruled and shaped by, some would say, the best of the mediocre.

That assumption would certainly seem verified by the experience of the United States in the last eight or ten years, but it's a chronic, not a permanent, condition. It's a condition we've been through before, and I think that people who are turned off politics by the fact that it's too rough or too inquisitive or too political probably wouldn't be much good in government anyway. In a democracy, to be effective in governing you have to be effective in persuading. Democracy is government by consent, and I'm always sceptical when people say so-and-so would make a great president, but he won't submit himself to the rough and tumble. Unless he submits himself to the rough and tumble, he's not going to make a great president.

It's not a new complaint. You can find it in Bryce's *The American Commonwealth*, which was written a century ago. Bryce said that he kept hearing in America how a reckless and abusive press kept 'the best people' out of parties, but, 'I could not learn the name of any able and high-minded man of whom it could be truly said that through this cause his gifts and virtues had been reserved for private life.' It's a recurrent theme, and perhaps it's more an alibi than the real cause of abstention.

I've argued elsewhere that there's a cyclical rhythm in our politics. We alternate between periods of liberalism and periods of conservatism. The conservative periods generally tend to attract rather mediocre people. In this century, for example, the Reagan years, the 1980s, were a re-enactment of the Eisenhower 1950, which were a re-enactment of the Harding/Coolidge/Hoover 1920s. In conservative periods personal gain is the dominant impulse. Similarly, at thirty-year intervals, you get periods when public purpose dominated: Theodore Roosevelt, ushering in the progressive Era of 1901; thirty years after that, Franklin Roosevelt, the New Deal, thirty years after that, Kennedy and the New Frontier. If the rhythm holds, the 1990s should be much more like the Progressive Era and the New Deal and the Kennedy/Johnson years than like the 1980s.

There's nothing mystical about the thirty-year periodicity. Thirty years is the span of a generation. People tend to be formed politically by the ideals that prevail when they come of age politically. Those who grew up during the Progressive Era – young people like Franklin and Eleanor Roosevelt and Harry Truman – carried forward thirty years later the ideas they absorbed when young. Similarly, young people who grew up when Roosevelt was setting the nation's course – people like John Kennedy, Lyndon Johnson, Hubert Humphrey, Robert Kennedy – carried forward those ideals when this generation's turn came thirty years later. In the same way, Kennedy touched and formed a generation. If the rhythm holds, the Kennedy generation's time will come in the 1990s. Government is attractive when it's innovative, when it tries to meet problems, when it's idealistic. Then good people rush to join. When it's run by a Warren G. Harding or a Reagan, you get crooks and hustlers.

Talking of Truman, was he a strong president?

Yes, he was a strong president, a man of good instincts – emphatic, more decisive probably in appearance than he was internally. He was a very attractive man, a lower-case democrat in the strongest sense. He had absolutely no front, no pretence, no pomposity. He could work with a large variety of people. He came out of the Middle West, had a limited education and so on, but from the start he was an avid reader, and he knew quite a lot of American history. He made some mistakes, but he was a good man and a good president.

Was he right to remove General MacArthur when he did?

He was absolutely right. He should have done it some weeks earlier. I believe he was right, too, in the decision to drop the atomic bomb, terrible as that decision was. I believe he was wrong, however, to enter the Korean War without the Congressional authorisation he could have gotten.

But as a liberal would you, in his shoes, have dropped the atomic bomb?

Yes. I was in the army at that period. I was in Europe, facing redeployment to the Far East. Naturally I was grateful for the end of the war. But there was a deeper reason to accept Truman's decision as a tragic necessity. Even after the second atomic bomb was dropped, opposition to Japan's leaving the war was so intense that there was an attempted *coup* against the emperor. A group of Japanese historians wrote a book a few years ago called *The Longest Day* describing the events of the day after the dropping of the bomb on Nagasaki. The emperor managed to get on radio and succeeded in quietening things down. There was always the prospect of fanatical resistance that would have resulted in the deaths of many Americans and many Japanese. God knows what would have happened to the poor British prisoners of war. I was in England once when the decision to drop the bomb was under attack, and the letter columns of *The Times* and *Telegraph* were filled with letters from men who had been in POW camps. They said that if the war hadn't come to an end, they would have certainly died. It was a tragic decision to drop the bomb, but the Japanese should have thought more carefully before they bombed Pearl Harbour.

Theodore Roosevelt once said that America should speak quietly and carry a big stick. Did Kennedy subscribe to the idea of America as global policeman?

I wouldn't say that Theodore Roosevelt implied that America should be a global policeman. He just said that in foreign policy you should be prepared for any contingency but shouldn't go around provoking trouble. Roosevelt did occasionally employ the big stick, as when, for example, he fomented a revolt in Panama in order to build the canal. But although he played an active role in the making of the Philippines, he later regretted it and felt that in that case the United States was getting involved beyond its own vital interests. He wasn't a globalist. But he was perfectly willing to use American power where he thought American vital interests were concerned.

Kennedy was definitely not a globalist. He had a very acute sense of the limitations of American power. In 1961 he said, 'We must face the fact that the United States is neither omnipotent nor omniscient – that we are only 6 per cent of the world's population – that we cannot impose our will upon the other 94 per cent of mankind – that we cannot right every wrong or reverse each adversity – and that therefore there cannot be an American solution to every world problem.' Wilson had said we must make the world safe for democracy, and in a deliberate modification of that line, Kennedy in his American University speech in 1963 said we must make the world safe for diversity. That was his abiding view. He had not illusions about a *pax Americana*.

Kennedy's great triumph was surely the Cuban Missile Crisis and there must have been tremendous pressure on him at the time. Was he surrounded by advisers, or did he really have to think it out for himself?

He listened carefully to conflicting advice. It was essentially and argument between those, on the one side, like Dean Atcheson and the Joint Chiefs of Staff, who believed that the missile bases should be taken out by surprise attack, and those on the other, like his brother Robert Kennedy, McNamara, the secretary of defence, and George Ball in the State Department, who felt that the missiles should be negotiated out. There's no question in my mind where Kennedy stood from the beginning, and that was that they should be negotiated out. In effect, that was what we did. We traded. It was not known at the time, but a deal was made by which we removed the Jupiter missiles from Turkey and the Russians removed their missiles from Cuba.

To those on the outside it looked as if we were close to a third world war. How close were we?

Well, we all thought we were close at the time. In retrospect, I wouldn't say we were. The United States had a vast superiority in nuclear striking power, and also vast local superiority in the Caribbean. Khrushchev, I think, was a gambler, but he wasn't bent on suicide, and he had no intention of pushing the issue to the point of military conflict. The great danger, as Kennedy felt most keenly, was not that Khrushchev would go to war through deliberate decision, but that something would go badly wrong down the line – something, somebody, somewhere, some crazy general on one side or the other, an accident which the other side would misinterpret. That's why he was so insistent throughout the crisis on maintaining very tight control of every ship in the blockade of Cuba and every plane near the Soviet Union. One of the crises came when and American U-2 suddenly strayed over Soviet soil. That was completely wrong, and Kennedy was very much concerned that the Russians might misinterpret it. The fear of war was not a fear of a deliberate decision but a fear of an accident spinning events out of control.

Might Kennedy have actually ordered troops into Cuba if the Russians hadn't backed down?

In the end he might have done. There were two messages that arrived from Khrushchev, one rather reasonable, the other much tougher. The first was far more personal, and it was Robert Kennedy's suggestion that they ignore the second and respond to the first, which was what they did. Following that, Robert Kennedy was sent to see Dobrynin, the Soviet ambassador, and it was then that the question of the Turkish missiles was raised. Robert Kennedy said in effect, they will be out in six months, you have my private assurance, but this is a totally separate issue. If you ever publicly say a deal was made, we will repudiate it. The reason for that was that Turkey was in NATO, and certain people, including Harold Macmillan, were very concerned that a decision involving the security of a NATO country might be taken without consultation. The deal was not known for fifteen years. I found out about it in Robert Kennedy's papers and wrote the first account in my book on him.

We now know further that Kennedy called in Dean Rusk and asked him, if this didn't work, to prepare an appeal to U Thant asking the UN to take a more active role, which U Thant was prepared to do. Dean Rusk produced the document last year. Kennedy wanted to avoid military action except as a last resort. Had there been no other way to get rid of the missiles, Kennedy would have sent the troops in, but he was prepared to exhaust every other avenue.

Was Kennedy in any significant way different from presidents before him? Others had faced crisis, but Kennedy had literally the prospect of Armageddon if he made too grave a mistake. Did he grow into that sort of authority or was it native to him?

He certainly grew into the presidency. On the other hand, I would say that among my contemporaries he was already the best qualified, the best equipped of those I knew, to be president. He had a combination of natural authority and natural detachment. He saw issues and saw himself with considerable objectivity, which is quite rare in politics. He felt very strongly the weight of the responsibility created by the invention if nuclear weapons. After the Cuban Missile Crisis, when both Kennedy and Khrushchev had looked down into the nuclear abyss, Kennedy came out absolutely determined to move as fast as he could toward some restraint in the nuclear arms race. His first objective was a test-ban treaty, and in this he was enormously encouraged by David Harlech, David Ormsby-Gore, the British ambassador in Washington, and by Harold Macmillan. Macmillan was very good on the dangers of the nuclear arms race, and Ormsby-Gore had been UK representative at the UN on disbarment commissions. He was very hot on that subject and with Macmillan he fortified Kennedy's determination to do something about it. Had Kennedy lived, I think he and Khrushchev would have proceeded beyond the test-ban treats much further down the road to *détente*.

How do you think the world would have been different had Kennedy not been assassinated?

Kennedy and Khrushchev would have pursued *détente,* and I think, too, that Khrushchev might have lasted longer. Castro thinks Kennedy helped to save Khrushchev after the Cuban Missile Crisis. Certainly, if Khrushchev had been able to show some results in the international realm, then it might have helped him a bit. However, Kennedy's intention in his second term was to concentrate much more on domestic affairs. He felt he had to spend too much time on international matters where, as he said, there was a new crisis every week. I think he felt he hadn't paid enough attention at home. He was much concerned about racial justice, about the war on poverty, about economic growth without inflation. The Great Society programme that Kennedy prepared and Johnson brought to enactment would have been centrepiece of his second term.

Would you agree that President Kennedy was more popular abroad than he was in the United States?

No, he was popular in the United States, but I think probably there was less opposition to him abroad. A lot of people in the United States disliked him, as they disliked Franklin Roosevelt. Conservatives, people in the business community, felt he was not their friend. Then his strong stance on civil right and racial justice in 1963 turned a lot of people against him, especially in the South. But even at the nadir of his popularity, after the civil rights fight in the summer of 1963, he was only down to something like 60 per cent in the polls, which wasn't bad.

After his death, it became fairly common knowledge that Kennedy had been something of a womaniser. Would it have affected his political status had it been known at the time?

I don't know. I may say that, working in the White House, I was not aware of anything undue going on. If you went to Kennedys' for dinner, there were always pretty girls, but I'm all in favour of that. So, I understand, are you. But it wasn't a conspicuous feature of the Kennedy administration. I think it is much exaggerated. No doubt things happened, but in that Kennedy was like Lloyd George, Martin Luther King and other eminent political leaders. It seems to me we've got the whole thing out of proportion. Martin Luther King was indeed an incurable womaniser and notoriously unfaithful to his wife, yet he was also a fine man who did great things for his race, and great things for his nation. Pol Pot of Cambodia, on the other hand, was splendidly faithful to his wife, never looked at another woman, and all he did was to murder a million of his countrymen. I'm not sure that the adultery test is particularly relevant to statesmanship.

   In Kennedy's case, you say it was all common knowledge, but I don't know how common common knowledge was. There had always been a lot of gossip about Kennedy, before the presidency, but during the presidency I don't think there was so much. As for those around him shielding him, I didn't see much to shield. He worked very hard at presidency.

There must surely have been a lot of nervousness about Jackie Kennedy. What would she have done had she known?

I've absolutely no idea.

In contrast with his brother, Robert Kennedy inspired perhaps as much hate as love. Why did he produce those extreme reactions?

John Kennedy was a man of reason, Robert Kennedy a man of passion. John Kennedy looked at something, such as the treatment of the black minority, and he thought it was irrational for a society to act that way. Robert Kennedy thought it intolerable. They couldn't have been closer, but they were quite different in this regard. John Kennedy was a realist disguised as a romantic, Robert Kennedy a romantic disguised as a realist. Robert Kennedy did the tough, the unpleasant things. During political campaigns, he would be his brother's son of a bitch, tell people off, fire them and that sort of stuff, but he was in a way a far more vulnerable figure than his brother. John Kennedy gave a sense of invulnerability. He was a reserved man, always in control, always poised, always filled with imperturbable self-possession. You felt he was equal to any circumstance. John Kennedy liked his friends, but Robert Kennedy *needed* his friends. This vulnerability was one reason that so many people – in the press, for example – found him so attractive; that and his humour. He was very influential with his brother, but not infallibly so. Sometimes John would listen to Robert, and disagree and not do what Robert Kennedy thought he should.

At least one reviewer of your biography of Robert Kennedy – I think it was Anthony Howard in The Observer *– talked of your transparent romanticism in your view of your subject.*

It's impossible to write with complete objectivity about anything. That's why I made it clear in the Foreword how I felt about Robert Kennedy, but subjectivity need not disqualify a biographer. You don't have to hate the subject of your biography to write it.

Robert Kennedy became attorney general for the United States without ever having appeared in a state or federal court. Shouldn't an attorney general have had more experience?

Many people felt that. The *New York Times* wrote a leader strongly criticising the appointment, as did many other newspapers. Alexander Bickel, who was a distinguished professor of law at Yale, attacked the appointment. It was a risky appointment to have made. In fact, it turned out very well, and by 1968 Bickel was a strong supporter of Robert Kennedy for president. Robert Kennedy knew the problems. He surrounded himself with first-class people in the Department of Justice and is generally agreed to have been the best attorney general we've had since Francis Biddle in the Roosevelt administration. But there was great criticism at the start, and understandably so.

It is said that, had Robert Kennedy ever become president, he would have been a disaster, because he was too tough, using very strong tactics and so on. Would you agree?

No. I think he would have been a very successful president. He combined the qualities of an idealist with those of a realist. In other words, he had that capacity which his brother had, which Roosevelt had, which Wilson had: to tap the latent idealism of the American people; and he did it very successfully. At the same time, he was an astute and practical politician, so that he could mobilise the means to attain his objectives. The liberal tide of the 1960s was still running strong and in 1968 Nixon was elected president almost accidentally. He got barely 40 per cent of the vote. Had Robert Kennedy lived, he would have been the Democratic candidate and I think he would have been elected. There was a third candidate in George Wallace, who got about 12 per cent of the vote. Many of those who voted for Wallace were white working-class people who probably would have voted for Robert Kennedy. As I say, the liberal tide was still running strong, so that many things such as the Environmental Protection Administration, the Occupational Safety and Health Act and so on were produced by Congress even in the Nixon years. The tide would have enabled Robert Kennedy to move much farther along the path of reform. And by 1968, though a lot of people hated him, he was predominantly a very popular man. I think he would have become a very effective president.

You were a bitter critic of America's policy of escalation in Vietnam and what you saw as America's obsession with political victory. Do you believe the lessons have been adequately learned?

No, I don't think so. I cite the American enthusiasm for our glorious victories in Grenada and Panama as examples. Panama would seem to me to raise three issues. I do not believe that the United States should undertake unilateral military intervention in Latin America except in cases of extreme emergency. I do not believe that an American president should go to war without congressional consent, except in cases of extreme emergency. And I do not believe that the super-powers should launch sneak attacks on small countries, except in cases of extreme emergency. Noriega was a thug and a squalid, vicious fellow, but he was not a threat to the national security of the United States and his regime did not create an extreme emergency. I regret that kind of intervention, even as I felt that the invasion of Grenada was unjustified. I believe that the long-term interests of the United States lie in the world of law – movement toward a world of law – and not in the United States imitating the old Soviet Union by becoming a law unto itself. What we did in Panama violates everything from the Rio Treaty to the Montevideo Convention and the UN Charter.

In one sense, though, we may have learned a lesson from Vietnam. We are no longer attacking people our own size. We attack countries like Grenada with no army, navy or air force. When Japan attacked the United States at Pearl Harbour, FDR called it a date that will live in infamy. Why? Because it was a sneak attack. But at least the Japanese were picking on someone their own size. We launch sneak attacks against Grenada and Panama and Libya, and most Americans seem to be proud of it. I would say there's been something of a decline in American moral sensibility in recent years. Robert Kennedy opposed the sneak attack on Cuba during the missile crisis on the ground that it would be a Pearl Harbour in reverse. For 175 years, he said, we have not been that kind of nation. We seem to have become one in recent years, and I regret it.

Is America still trying to punish Vietnam?

No. I think it would be quite popular in the United States if we restored diplomatic relations with Vietnam. American Vietnam veterans have gone to Vietnam and had amiable meetings with their Vietnamese counterparts. Just as it turned out to be popular to restore relations with China, so it would turn out to be mildly popular to restore relations with Vietnam. I don't understand – well, I do understand – why we're not doing so. The reason is that the Chinese wouldn't like it, and George Bush feels it very important not to alienate the Chinese. That is why he and previous administrations, beginning with Carter, have continued to give the Pol Pot government, the most vicious government of modern times, the Cambodian seat in the United Nations; why, to this day, we are seeming to support the inclusion of the Khmer Rouge in the new Cambodian government, whereas the sensible thing would be to make a deal with prime minister Hun Sen and promote a government around him. But the Chinese are opposed to that because of their traditional hatred of Vietnam. That, I believe, is why we have not restored relations with Vietnam, rather than any desire to punish.

One of the things that puzzles and depresses Europeans about American foreign policy is the treatment of Central and South America. No degree of violence or repression seems enough to cut off American aid. Priests are killed, nuns are raped and still money pours in. Or so it seems to the outside world.

Well, it puzzles many Americans too, I can say. At no point, according to the polls, did a majority of Americans favour aid to the Contras in Nicaragua. The majority has always been opposed to such aid. Nicaragua became a personal obsession for Reagan, and inherited concern for Bush.

Why, if most Americans did not demand aggressive policies in Central America, were presidents able to pursue such policies? Bush's obsession was Noriega of Panama. Presidents have power with Congress when they request something they claim as essential to the security of the United States. Congressmen, even though they may disagree with the request, often feel under pressure to vote affirmatively, on the ground that otherwise their opponents at the next election will call them soft on Communism, soft on the Sandinistas. Legislators permit themselves to be intimidated into going along with something of which they really disapprove.

The case of Noriega was more complicated because Noriega was a thug and involved in the drug trade. Even people like Senator Dodd of Connecticut, who has been very restrained on Central America and was himself in the Peace Corps there, knows the area and speaks excellent Spanish, supported the invasion of Panama. But why this obsession with tinhorn dictators like Noriega and Ortega? The population of Nicaragua is under three million, less than the population of Brooklyn. The notion that this country is a threat to the security of the United States is ridiculous. The Noriega intervention was very popular in Panama, but no elsewhere in Latin America, and I think Bush is going to have to mend fences. Bush is a moderate man, and I hope he will take it easy in Latin America for a while.

Will it ever be possible to control the import of drugs into the United States, bearing in mind the trouble over quite a small-scale gangster like Noriega?

Getting rid of Noriega will have no effect on the drug problem in the United States. The drug problem is essentially a demand rather than a supply problem. As long as the demand exists, it will be supplied one way or another. If we were to cut off all the import of drugs, the laboratories would spring up all over the United States to manufacture the drugs to meet demand.

Is the 'special relationship' that has been said to exist between Britain and the United States a fact or a myth today?

It's a cultural fact, and it's become a political myth, but the cultural reality remains. The common heritage means that Americans are going to feel closer to Britain than they are to anyone else. The Bush administration appears more inclined to regard Germany as its ally, and I take it that the Bush relationship with Mrs Thatcher isn't as chummy as the Reagan-Thatcher relationship. Actually, the European statesman whom Bush seems to get along with personally is Mitterrand.

As for myself, my ties with Britain are long and strong. I first went to England in 1934 when my father was giving a series of lectures at the University of London and I was sixteen years old. Then, in 1938–9 I spent a year at Peterhouse in Cambridge, where I met many people who remained close through the years, like Charles Wintour and Noel Annan, Eric Hobsbawm and Aubrey Eban. Then I was in London in the Spring of '44 and was there until November when I went on to France. There I got to know Nye Bevan well. He was an enchanting man. After the war I met a lot of people among the young socialists in that period, so my political associations were mostly on the left. I got to know Hugh Gaitskell, and in the 1950s, of course, we became firm friends. Roy Jenkins, Dick Crossman, Tony Crosland – I knew all that generation of Labour people. In the 1960s my dear friend Pamela Berry exposed me to many Tories.

What about Macmillan? Historians now tend to say he was devious, a great actor who did nothing for Britain but who ruined the economy and so on.

I would have thought that Alistair Horne's two fine volumes would have done something to restore Macmillan's reputation. I liked Macmillan very much. He was a great performer. The last time I saw him was when he came to New York, I think in 1981, shortly after Reagan became president. Jacqueline Onassis gave a small dinner for him and I said to him, making conversation before dinner, 'Very odd, isn't it, to have an actor, Ronald Reagan, as president of the United States?' I was trying to think whether there had been many others in high political office who were once actors. I said, 'After all, Madame Mao Tse-tung was an actress, but I can' think of any other actors.' Macmillan looked at me and said: 'Actors? Actors? Politicians are all actors. We're all of us actors and Roosevelt and Churchill were the best actors of the lot.' I liked him, I thought he was great fun. His instincts on several things were very good – on nuclear weapons, on colonial matters, on monetary questions. He was a monetary heretic. He believed in evolving some kind of international monetary system. And he was a Wet. I mean, he was no Thatcherite.

Mrs Thatcher has dominated the political scene in Britain for more than a decade now. How would you evaluate her?

I suppose she did do something to shake up the British economy, though it's now in trouble again. I suppose her approach may have improved British competitiveness in the world markets. She liberated the newspapers from the printers' unions, which was a good thing. She appreciated Gorbachov quickly and she deserves credit for that, as does Reagan. A lot of the alleged Soviet experts and wiseacres were warning against Gorbachov, saying he was just trying to get the West to relax its guard. Mrs Thatcher said early on that he was somebody the West could do business with, and she was right. I consider that she's made Britain a colder, crueller, nation and that it's time for someone to come in and stand, to use George Bush's phrase, for a kinder, gentler Britain. But the worst things she has done have been in the realm of freedom of information. The rewriting of the Official Secrets Act was a travesty.

Take one single example. It now appears that a group within MI5 tried to drive Harold Wilson and his government, duly elected by the British people, out of power. David Leigh has written a book about the Wilson affair that makes the most serious charges you can make in a democracy: that a group of people in the Intelligence services tried to defeat and subvert the democratic process. If something like that had happened in the United States – if charges were made that a group within the FBI or the CIA had tried to overthrow an elected president – all hell would have broken loose. There would have been congressional investigations to see whether the charges were valid or not and so on. Roy Jenkins did try to get parliamentary inquiry, but Mrs Thatcher quashed any hope of such an inquiry. Since you don't enjoy the benefits of separation of power in Britain, Parliament could do nothing. Worse than that, the press showed little curiosity.

It seemed to me that you'd want to know in Britain whether an MI5 group had in fact done these things. Are these charges fantasy, or did they really do what David Leigh and the Spycatcher man – Peter Wright – said they did? I would think people would be interested in establishing the facts and, if those were the facts, to make sure nothing like it could ever happen again. But the British Parliament and press seemed to regard it all with total indifference. Mrs Thatcher succeeded in hushing the whole thing up, as she would have hushed up Watergate.

Under your system, you can hush up any kind of political scandal. She has fortified the British tendency to sweep everything under the rug and to make information hard to get. Obviously, some things have to be kept secret, but, on the whole, most official secrets could be made public with no harm to anybody. You have to fight against a tendency to classify everything as secret, and if Mrs Thatcher has her way, no one, including Parliament, will know what the hell is going on in British government. That seems the most troubling aspect of her stewardship.

Not only from Mrs Thatcher but from politicians on both sides of the Atlantic we have heard a good deal about the need to restore the ideal of family unity as something essential to preserving the social fabric. Can such a movement succeed in modern times?

First, as an historian, I wonder whether the family was always as great an institution as it's cracked up to be. People look back to the golden age of the unitary family of the nineteenth century when divorce was very difficult. But then you read about those families and the suffocating effects on the children, the paternal tyranny, the child abuse, even in a family as noted as that of Leslie Stephen. My impression is that the family has always been an ambiguous thing. It can be a source of strength; it can also be very crippling. Moreover, the family is bound to change in a society in which divorce is easy, birth control is easy, abortion is easy. Bonds are not going to be maintained as long, and in some cases that's bad. Other times maintaining bonds may artificially prolong a marriage that is dead, maybe crippling everyone involved. So it's important not to sentimentalise or romanticise the historical family.

Still, the total collapse of the family is obviously a source of great trouble for society. We have it in the underclass in this country: families where there is not father and no stability. But, on the whole, restoring the ideal of family unity seems to me partly an exercise in fantasy because I don't think the family ever played the marvellous stabilising role which some think it once did.

From our side of the Atlantic, it often seems that American governments are excessively vulnerable to pressure groups like the gun lobby or the pro-Israeli faction. Do pressures change with presidents or are they simply pressured relentlessly?

They're pressured relentlessly, but they may or may not bend to the pressure. The National Rifle Association has had no effect on Democratic presidents, but it's very powerful with Republican presidents. It has some effect on Democratic legislators, particularly in districts where a lot of hunting goes on. The Zionist lobs had impact on both parties, and it's only recently that people have become willing even to describe the operations and pressures brought by the Zionist lobby. Pressure groups can distort our policies, as in the case of Israel. Support by the United States for Likud policies was disastrous for Israel and a disaster all around. Jewish Americans have, of course, been very generous contributors to political campaigns. It should be added that, as far as I can see, the Jewish community in this country is not monolithic, and many Jewish Americans are very much opposed to blank-cheque support of right-wing governments in Israel.

There is nothing new about foreign pressure groups. The Irish lobby had great impact before the establishment of the Irish Free state, and resolutions for Irish independence were constantly being introduced and so on. We're a polyglot nation – a nation of nations, as Walt Whitman said. That means that the Poles, the Jews, the Irish, the Italians and so on all constitute pressure groups of one sort or another. Black Americans, having long ignored Africa, have suddenly constituted themselves a pressure group for black Africa.

Pressure groups are a pain in the neck for a lot of presidents. But they have to deal with them one way or another.

If you were an advisor now in the Bush administration, what advice would you give the president with regard to the Arab-Israeli conflict?

I'm not an expert on the Middle East. We don't have much influence with either side, as far as I can see, and I'm not a great believer in meddling in the affairs of other countries. I don't think we do it very well, I don't think we have enough knowledge. We tend to become prisoners of our clients. As we did in Vietnam, and they manipulate us more than we manipulate them. Where our vital interests are involved, I'm all in favour of action to defend them, by force if necessary; but where our vital interests are not involved, I'd say let other countries solve their own problems.

America has had quite an unexpected and overwhelming triumph in the way Eastern Europe has begun to embrace democracy. What should happen next?

Once the exhilaration is over, these new governments in Eastern Europe are going to face a lot of tough problems. It's up to the Western governments to do everything they can to help them meet them. Mitterand's proposal of a development bank for Eastern Europe will take a couple of years before it can get started, and meantime the World Bank should be playing a more active role. I might add that policies should come just as much from Europe as from the United States. While I think that the United States is poverty-stricken in ideas, I'm somewhat dismayed that, except for the Mitterrand proposal, more good ideas haven't come out of West European governments as to how to help Eastern Europe. The model of the Marshall Plan might well be used, and that, as you will recall, called upon the governments of Western Europe to get together and make their own economic reconstruction.

By and large, I'm hopeful about Eastern Europe but troubled about the Soviet Union. It's very important that Gorbachov survives. I suppose his strength lies in the fact that the people to his right are afraid that, if he goes, the whole thing will swing farther to the left, while the people on his left are afraid that it will swing farther to the right. Therefore, neither has a strong interest in overthrowing him at this point. But events may overthrow him. I'm not sure that the changes he's made are totally irreversible. Look what happened to China. I can see the army feeling it has to restore order, and then people coming to power who feel that Russia need a heavy hand. A lot of the freedom of the press, the freedom of the theatre, the freedom of the movies, could easily be reversed.

With the prospect of German unification, the disappearance of the Iron Curtain and the emergence of Japan as an economic super-power, do you see American influence in the world as waning?

One certainly begins to wonder who won the last war. Japan is well on its way to attaining its Second World War objective for a Greater East Asian Prosperity Sphere. A United Germany is poised to dominate Europe. All these things are troubling. I wouldn't be surprised if, by the year 2000, a united Germany were demanding revision of its eastern frontiers, and *Anschluss* with Austria, concessions to German-speaking minorities in neighbouring countries. The Allies may retain the legal capacity to impose a treaty, but I doubt that a united Germany, the most dynamic economy and most populous state west of Russia in Europe, is going to respect any limitations we try to impose regarding the inviolability of frontiers or rearmament of nuclear weapons.

I don't suppose Germany or Japan will ever again become a military threat, because in the age of missiles they're simply too vulnerable. But they do have dynamic economies, and they have extremely ominous, portentous, mystical, humourless, chauvinistic, nationalist traditions. Both countries have new generations coming to power that feel no sense of responsibility for or guilt about the Second World War, and may well nurse a desire for vindication, even perhaps for revenge. Germany at least has had forty years of democratic experience and has produced democratic statesmen like Helmut Schmidt and Wily Brandt and Richard Von Weizacker and even, in his own way, Adenauer. Japan hasn't produced anything comparable. It's been a one-party state, and a crooked and authoritarian one-party state at that.

German historians are beginning to say Hitler wasn't so bad, that he was only imitating Stalin. Japanese historians are even worse. School text books so gloss over Japanese aggression and atrocity in the Second World War that they've provoked official protest from China. Japanese historians who try to write the truth are subject to official prosecution. Both countries are filled with a kind of hyper-nationalism and the prospects are troubling.

Is the United States in decline? Not irrevocably. After all, remember that both Japan and Germany suffered from what Paul Kennedy called imperial over-stretch – that is to say, from taking on burdens beyond the capacity of the economy to discharge – and in addition suffered devastating military defeat. Yet they've come back. If the United States can pull itself together, it can come back too.

Might the trend towards disarmament in the Soviet Union mean that America could be perceived by some cynics as much the greater threat to world peace in the near future?

I doubt it. I mean, some people may like to say it but I don't think the United States will be seriously regarded as a threat to world peace.

You once said that there is no such thing as a correct perspective in history. What then do you see as the historical biographer's primary function?

Tell the truth best you can, as best you see it. The historian is constrained by the facts, he has to respect facts, and then he arranges the facts. The mere act of selection involves interpretation, so you can't escape interpretation, and interpretation cannot escape subjectivity. You try to do the best you can and make discounts for your own predilections. For the historian, the important thing is to reconstruct the past as much as possible in its own terms rather than in terms of the present. But you can't escape the present, and that's why every generation finds new issues in the past. American historians, for example, discover new pasts as a result of new concerns about racial justice or sexual equality. That's why Benedetto Croce said all history is contemporary history, why Oscar Wilde said the one duty we owe to history is to rewrite it.

In your successful and varied career, which period do you feel you enjoyed most?

My career may be varied, but I don't think of it as particularly successful. I regard it as a study in frustration. I always envied Malcolm Muggeridge's title for his memoirs, *Chronicles of Wasted Time.* The part I enjoyed particularly, I suppose, was working with Kennedy, but I'm an historian and a writer, and my great frustration is that I've spent so little time doing that which I do best, and there's been so much time wasted in various virtuous or entertaining projects. Sometimes I feel that my life has been nibbled away by good causes. What I want to do is finish *The Age of Roosevelt.* I'd also like to write a novel. I suppose I'd best like to be remembered for my historical writing. I've enjoyed politics, politics is a great sport, but essentially I'm a historian.

Brian Sewell

Brian Sewell was born in 1931 and educated at Haberdashers' and the Courtauld Institute, where he was taught by Anthony Blunt. He spent several years working for galleries, then a decade as a valuer at Christie's, including a short time as an art dealer. For three years he was art critic with *Tatler*, before going to the *Evening Standard* in 1984, where he remained until his death in 2015. He was named Critic of the Year several times in the British Press Awards and won the Orwell Prize for his political journalism. His two volumes of autobiography, *Outsider I* (2011) and *Outsider II* (2012), were both bestsellers.

You are a distinguished art historian, but it is as an art critic that you have earned yourself a reputation – indeed you might easily be called the doyen *of art criticism. Assuming that you didn't set out to achieve this designation, is it nevertheless one from which you derive satisfaction?*

Oh dear, I think I have to argue with several of those statements. I have absolutely no distinction as an art historian. I've never written the book I want to write, and I've never been involved in a major exhibition, at least not since I was a mere boy. When I first left the Courtauld I had a very promising career. I was regarded as quite a bright boy and it all looked as though it was set fair. Then I was offered a job at Christie's and I spent the next ten years of my life there being diverted from serious scholarship. Working at Christie's is a game of swift judgement and even swifter identification, or sometimes misidentification. I became a critic by accident, and the fact that I did so seemed to me clear evidence of my river having run into sand, the end rather than the beginning. I had spent my whole life up to that point looking at pictures, going to exhibitions and experiencing the frisson of excitement as things changed in the contemporary art world. As a student of art history, I was very much aware of what David Hockney and his contemporaries tried to do, and I had considerable sympathy with them. But I now find myself very detached from those revolutionaries of the 1960s and 1970s, having grown old with them, as it were. I have come to realise how trivial and idiotic much of post-war art is; I am therefore disdainful and dismissive of it. And this has given me a certain notoriety; that's all.

Critics are of course creatures much reviled – the artistic equivalent of traffic wardens, one might say. To what extent does this bother you?

The abuse doesn't bother me because although it applies to an enormous number of critics working in this country, also in France, Germany and America, I don't think it applies to me. There are very few people who are prepared to speak out and tell the truth as they see it. Most critics are ill-informed; they have no practice either as painters or as art historians, so they come to the business of looking at pictures almost like strangers. There are other critics who can only be described as Vicars of Bray, in that whatever is stuck under their noses they feel bound to praise it. Richard Cork [art critic on *The Times*] is a very good example; it really doesn't matter what it is, as long as it has been vouched for, as long as it has a certificate of quality from the Tate Gallery or the Hayward or the Arts Council, he is prepared to say it is wonderful. There is yet another kind of critic who, thank God, is now in the decline – I'm thinking of people like Marina Vaizey. She believes in signposting; that it is her duty to say that something is there, and that that is enough. Well, it isn't enough. A critic should have some kind of bite on the subject with which his readers are not expected to agree. What he should be doing is providing an intellectual peg on which readers can hang their own arguments and their own judgements.

Flaubert said: 'A man is a critic when he cannot be an artist, in the same way that a man becomes an informer when he cannot be a soldier.' Do you think there is an uncomfortable truth in that view?

No. I don't think there is any truth in that at all. Edward Lucie-Smith, for example, did not become a critic because he couldn't paint. Edward came to criticism from poetry, from being a writer, from an interest in acquiring things, which led him naturally to the intellectual pursuit of what lies behind the things we acquire; it has absolutely nothing to do with his inability to draw or paint. The curious thing is that when you do get critics who can to some extent paint, and they are rash enough to put themselves on view, they are appalling. One simply cannot understand why they have not exercised the first principle of the critic, which is to examine what he himself does, whether as a painter or as a writer.

Oscar Wilde had a different perspective from Flaubert, believing that it is precisely because a man cannot do a thing that he is the proper judge of it. Are you any more inclined to the Wildean view of things?

I'm not, but the last Conservative government was, and this New Labour regime quite certainly is. There is a belief amongst those who have the power to make important appointments that the amateur is best. This applies particularly in the area of visual arts. There is a very good example now in the invention of this New Labour organisation called MLAG. It has to do with museums, libraries, galleries and archives, and yet it is headed by somebody who cheerfully admits that he is not interested in any of those, and his right-hand man is that celebrated cook and entertainer Loyd Grossman, a man who looks through keyholes for a living. It is the devil of the art gallery and the museum in this country that their trustees are amateurs, and it is the devil of organisations like the Museums and Galleries Commission that their commissioners are people who know absolutely nothing about the history and purpose of galleries and museums. So don't blame the critic; blame the government, because in one shape or form government is always the institution through which appointments are made. They seem to have a sense of mischief for putting the cat among the pigeons. But pigeons can get on with their business perfectly well without pussy upsetting it.

The few facts that I was able to glean about your early life suggest a not very auspicious start. Your father committed suicide before you were born and your mother by all accounts was stiflingly possessive. How does a child survive such a childhood?

That's an exceedingly difficult question to answer. I think I survived my childhood because my mother treated me from my very earliest consciousness as an adult. The consequence was that when I eventually went to school, very soon after my eleventh birthday, my abilities were absurd for a child of my age. I had a considerable command of things like Greek mythology, Roman history, and opera and I read the novels that my mother read instead of baby books. This was rather unbalanced in one way, but it gave me a head start in terms of general culture. I was taken to the National Gallery every week as a child so small that I can remember looking at the undersides of frames as they projected from the wall. I don't know what I would have done had my mother not brought me up in such a one-sided way, but her one side opened windows all the time. That is why I didn't stifle.

You have said – touchingly – of your father's suicide that he put the cat out before he gassed himself. How important was it for you to be made aware of that gentle and humane gesture before an act of such self-destructiveness?

In so far as I have any folk memory, as it were, of my father, it is the thing that means most to me. I share my father's melancholy nature and there are moments when depression becomes unbearable, but what prevents me from committing suicide is that I have dogs. And I care more for them than I do for myself.

There was presumably a temptation to romanticise the father you had never known ... did you find that you could turn him into almost anyone you wanted?

No. In the very early days his absence was really not important. My life was very full with the entertainments provided by my mother. And by the age of eleven I had acquired a stepfather who was interested in music and religion, and also in the observances of the Church of England, as opposed to the Roman Catholic Church in which I had been christened. So there were plenty of things to excite and divert me from worrying or wondering about my own father.

For the first eleven years of your life you did not mix with other children ... did you accept this as part of the natural order of things?

Yes. I had no idea of what I was missing, none whatsoever.

Do you subscribe to the Larkin view of things: 'They fuck you up, your mum and dad'?

If you had asked me that question thirty years ago I would have said, yes, I am well and truly fucked up. But now I look at the married couples who are my friends, I look at their children, and I realise that the happy marriage, the untroubled family, is a great rarity. It is the nature of parenthood to fuck up children, and that's that. We shouldn't expect anything more.

Did you consciously decide against having children of your own, and if so, was this related to your own experience as a child?

I went through a period in my early thirties when I thought that it would be wonderful if one could settle down and lead the absolutely conventional life, marriage and children, and so on. But I knew deep down that this was an impossibility – I had been solitary for so long. I also had to confront the irredeemable nature of my homosexuality, which at an early stage had come into extreme conflict with my religious life. This wasn't exactly straightforward because I had been born a Roman Catholic, and though I had been diverted into the Church of England by my stepfather, I had always wanted to go back to being a Roman. But what disturbed me was the hostility of both branches of the Christian Church to what was my essential nature. It was something with which I was born, I am convinced of that; it could not be trained or educated out of me, yet it was a barrier that all my priests demanded I should deal with. It seemed to me that the only solution the church offers a homosexual is to be a eunuch, and that, I believe, is simply not possible. Like all men I am a sexual being; it need not be very fruitfully applied, but it cannot be denied.

You have described your mother's possessiveness as 'utterly destructive'. Is that something you have found hard to forgive?

Oh, I don't think I have found anything really hard to forgive. She had a fairly tough time and she did the best she could. I sometimes joke and say I am the victim of a deprived childhood, and in many ways I am, but there were many compensations. When I started school at the age of eleven, we were required to give a little talk for five minutes to the class. The other boys talked about their pets and their school holidays, but I stood up and talked about Wagner. I rejoice that I had a mother who brought me up to be able to do that.

You were packed off to school at the insistence of your stepfather. Were you dragged scream-ing and kicking, so to speak, or was it in some ways a relief to get away?

I had no idea what school was, so I didn't know what to expect. My mother didn't want me to go to boarding school, so my stepfather lugged me round all the possibilities in London, the City of London School, St Paul's, University College, but none of them would have me because I didn't know anything that fitted the school curriculum. I couldn't add two and two, and my English was completely instinctive, not soundly based on grammar. This was a huge problem, but even-tually I was taken in at Haberdashers, and then only because they were desperate. Haberdashers was just about as low as you could go. It was exceedingly unpleasant and would have been a disaster had it not been for my innate ability to run, not only quickly but over very long distances. Cross-country running and rugby saved me, otherwise I would have been teased to death.

You say somewhere that your stepfather was treated extremely badly by your mother and also by you. Was this something you recognised only with hindsight, or were you aware of it at the time?

I recognised it when I did my national service in the army, an extraordinary experience for me. It was then for the first time I realised what a decent man my stepfather was.

Is there a feeling of self-reproach when you recall the way you treated your stepfather?

Not particularly [laughter]. My stepfather got his own back in the end because he left all his money – not that there was much of it – to his first wife and his daughter, not to my mother and me, though he had been with us much longer.

Do you believe in self-improvement, that people can recognise their faults and do something about them?

There are probably episodes in people's lives that cause change of some kind. In my own case, it happened suddenly when I found I had a fairly useless heart. I had been wonderfully fit until I had a heart attack and its consequences have been disastrous. I have looked over the edge a couple of times, and the business of looking over the edge does make one feel slightly more generous perhaps.

You spent two years in the army … was that a tough time for you?

It was tough in all the conventional ways, but it wasn't intellectually tough. It was just something one had to do. The real problem for me was whether or not I should take my violin with me. I was quite good in those days, and I didn't want to stop being good, but somehow a kind of common sense intervened and told me, no, no, you do not go to Aldershot with a violin, you do not. Of course, it was the end of serious violin playing, but it did help remove any kind of lingering vanity that one might really be a brilliant violinist.

Is that a major regret?

No. Quite frankly I don't think I would ever have been good enough, and even if I had been good enough I would have been far too emotional, because music gets to the heart of me, and I can't really control my emotional reactions to it.

You turned down a place at Oxford in favour of the Courtauld Institute. Did you ever regret not going to Oxford? Do you think things might have turned out very differently if you had?

I don't think Oxford would have been the place for me. I'm unclubbable, and Oxford is a very clubbable place – it is where people go to network as much as to learn. The Courtauld as it then was suited me very well. It's a very large body of exceedingly good teachers and a very small student body. Some of us were fortunate to be taught one to one by people like Blunt, which was wonderful. No, I don't regret it at all.

You have sometimes said that your time at the Courtauld taught you how to look properly at a picture. Do you think this is something which has to be learned, that one cannot know instinctively how to look properly?

One can look at pictures in so many different ways. You can look at a picture like a clerk: how big is it, what is it made of, what is the medium, to whom did it belong, where has it been, who has written about it? And you accumulate all that information and you never ask yourself whether it is good or great or whether it excites you; it is simply documented. There are an awful lot of art historians like that who are incapable of responding to a picture as they would to a piece of music – they have absolutely no idea. And then there are other people who just look at a picture and say, isn't it wonderful? They are sent witless in front of abstracts by Mark Rothko, trying to induce some trance-like state as a result of sitting in front of a sea of colour. That's also pretty uninformed. One definitely needs a bit more than that. For myself, I need to respond not only to the dry documentation of a picture (which nevertheless can sometimes illuminate); I want to respond to the working of the painter's hand and brush, I want to see the lifting-off point, that little tail of paint when you take a brush away, I want to see when something is in pastel, when something is in glaze, I want to involve myself in the act of painting in exactly the same way as when playing a musical instrument one is somehow involved in the mind of the composer. There's a wonderful little picture by Mantegna which is always called *The Entombment of Christ*, but I think it's the Resurrection and I think it's the Resurrection because the usual paraphernalia of the entombment are not there. Christ is being propped up on the narrow end of a sarcophagus by two angels, both of whom have one leg in the sarcophagus, and they seem to me to be heaving him out of it rather than laying him in it. His lower limbs are over the edge to the fore of the picture and the face is full of pain; it's the most agonised face you could hope to find in the whole history of art. The body is pallid and the face is ruddy, and you sense that after being three days dead the blood is flowing again – think of the excruciating pain that you experience when you've been sleeping on your arm and the blood begins to flood into it again. This is what Christ is experiencing over his whole body. If you can look at a picture like this and see those things, then I think you are seeing everything that you can. To take a different example, if you look at *The Resurrection* by Piero della Francesca, you see a wonderful triumphant Christ. There's no Mantegnesque examination of the how, but there is everything in the why and the consequence of it in that really magnificent body, triumphant as it comes out of the sarcophagus; there is no pain, just victory. It's another way of looking at it, another way of informing us.

How does this fit with your view that good art should be accessible to all and that there is something in a Donatello or a Michelangelo that can be understood by every man?

I cannot imagine that even the humblest Florentine peasant on seeing Donatello's *Habakkuk* would not immediately recognise it for what it was. Similarly, a French peasant coming into contact with Rodin's *Burghers of Calais* would immediately understand, perhaps not the historical story, but from the expressions, from the body language of those figures, he would know exactly what was happening, who was being compliant, who was being heroic – all the information is there. But you look at contemporary art now, what is to be divined from ninety-nine per cent of it? Absolutely nothing. And when lecturers in galleries like the Tate are asked, 'What does this picture mean?', the answer is invariably, 'Oh, it means what you want it to mean.' This just isn't good enough.

One of your principal complaints about modern art is that there is no place for beauty, and that beauty has become almost an irrelevance. Can we talk a little about your concept of beauty … can beauty still be found in the depiction of something ugly, for example?

It depends on the ugliness. In the Metropolitan there's a piece of sculpture by Kiki Smith of a woman emptying her bowels. I don't see anything beautiful in that, just as I don't see anything beautiful in the very late Picasso of a woman emptying her bladder. But these are graceless works, disturbing only in the sense that they are distasteful. There are, however, ugly subjects that are perfectly acceptable. Goya's *Cannibals*, for example, where a human leg is waved about, is a painting so exquisite that it lifts the subject and takes the horror out of it. Again, you have Géricault painting heads that have been sliced off by the guillotine; they aren't very beautiful, but they are beautifully recorded, the beauty being in the facture of the paint. I could live with those; I might not put them in my dining room, but I could certainly live with them.

Do you find the works of Lucian Freud or Francis Bacon beautiful?

I have problems with both. I think that Bacon was a mannerist in the sense that his way of doing things was more important than the subject itself. The easiest evidence of that is when he used to load his brush with white paint and flick it at a picture which was nearing completion. This stream of white paint tells us absolutely nothing. However, there are aspects of his work which are very beautiful in terms of subtlety of handling and modelling, for example. With Lucian Freud, I think that in some ways he is such a bad painter, such a lazy painter, someone who cannot be consistent and who gets bored with what he is doing. He is also obsessive, and there is a tremendous irregularity between the various parts of his pictures.

You deplore the breed of artist who urinates in the snow and makes bronze casts of the result, and there are many people who agree with you. Do you believe that there are objective standards by which we can judge what we might call real works of art as opposed to fashionable, gimmicky pieces?

The short answer to that is no, because if you apply objective standards you will get no advance. You might condemn new ways of doing things as nineteenth-century academic painters condemned the Impressionists. Having said that, I do have very serious problems with so-called artists like Helen Chadwick, because it seems to me that neither her *Piss Flowers*, as these snow pieces were called, nor her *Chocolate Fountain*, which was a pure reference to the emptying of the bowels, nor throwing furniture out of a first floor could possibly constitute works of art. If they are works of performance, then perhaps their place is in the theatre, but not in the art gallery.

One of the central difficulties for art historians and indeed anyone who is interested in art is what might be called the matter of taste. Can taste ever be a reliable yardstick?

No, we should never have an intellectual argument based on the stomach's response to things, though I do think you can trust your stomach, since it is often a very reliable guide as to whether something is good. I know that sounds absurd, but it's that same kind of visceral clench that you get when wonderful music is being played. It should do the same when you're looking at something.

Is it possible to say, for example, that David Hockney is not to my liking, not my taste, but I recognise that he is an important artist?

I could demonstrate to anyone who would care to listen to me that David Hockney is a rotten painter. In the late 1960s and the first half of the 1970s, he became, fairly briefly, a brilliant draughtsman, and that is all I would give him. David is somebody who does not understand the paint; he has absolutely no feeling for it other than as colour between lines, absolutely none. He talks a great deal about perspective, but he has no sense of aerial perspective, nor does he know anything about varying colour, nothing at all.

To what then do you attribute his rise to fame?

Entirely to his homosexuality. He came in as a flamboyant homosexual at just the right moment in the 1960s, when everyone for the first time ever was determined to be liberal about it. People who were not themselves homosexual would buy David's work and hang it in the drawing room as a demonstration of their own liberal attitudes, and it's just gone on from there. And once you entrench a painter in the public mind as the great painter of the day, he goes on as such. We are now turning him into a guru, a wise old man, but he's no wiser than the street cleaner, if as wise.

One problem, I suppose, is that we know that when people saw the pictures of Manet or Cézanne over a century ago, they seemed outrageously modern and people were shocked and dismayed and felt that everything that they had known and loved about art hitherto was under threat. We are traditionally very bad at dealing with the shock of the new, are we not?

No. You just have to consider the history of collecting to dispute that. I mean, Degas had an agent in Manchester, for God's sake. That doesn't suggest to me that there was no appreciation. Or if you look at the great Scottish collections, there were some far-sighted Scottish dealers selling wonderful pictures to people who built ships. Then there's that old foolishness about all the Impressionists dying in poverty. They didn't. It cost Monet just ten pictures to buy Giverny, that's all. He was turning out a picture a day, and he was a rich man. Degas was rich, and Renoir was also rich. Gauguin and Van Gogh were the odd men out; you can't apply their level of penury to all the others. I simply do not understand how this myth survives. Of course, there have always been opponents, but right across Europe there have been collectors and dealers who have supported the painters at the time – you only have to look at how early their work was being bought by major institutions. In the Neue Pinakothek in Munich there is a wonderful picture by Manet, a kind of breakfast picture – I can't remember what it is called – but it went there pretty well at once. It didn't have to hang around a studio. There were great German dealers in places like Düsseldorf – Düsseldorf, for heaven's sake, the Manchester of Germany!

Setting aside your specific objection to modern conceptual art, would you concede that art, like music or architecture or literature, does not stand still; it moves (as it has always done), and this is in itself not a bad thing, but just something that happens?

It's something that must happen, otherwise there is no change. If it didn't happen then the whole of Western art would be exactly like the wretched icon. Painting in Cyprus, produced for holidaymakers and resembling things that were painted a thousand years ago. You must allow change, and the wonderful thing about the history of art is that change is so evident. How do you get from Giotto to Donatello? How do you get from Donatello to Michelangelo, from Michelangelo to Bernini? It isn't a single line, it's a cat's cradle of a line of development, looping backwards and going up and down in terms of quality.

Conceptual art leaves you cold – there is nothing, you say, that lifts the spirit. Can you be sure, however, that there is nothing that lifts the spirit of others?

That isn't quite my view. Let's take something which is possibly a familiar example: the first set of cage pieces by Damien Hirst. These are glass containers with steel frames and when they were exhibited in the ICA some years ago, I was deeply moved by them. They were very disturbing. They were not beautiful, but they did what beauty does, which is affect the spirit. Which is why I am very defensive of Damien, because he has gone through phases which are not just flamboyant things with sharks and sheep; he has also touched on things that are essential to the darker side of human nature, and no one can take that away from him. My esteem for his work is very high.

A few years ago you said: 'It is terribly disturbing to find oneself literally loathed by people. I hardly go out at all now, except to go to galleries.' Has that situation changed at all, or are you still disturbed by the strength of people's reactions to you?

I am disturbed, yes. I have become something of a recluse, and I now very largely no longer go to the press views of exhibitions in case those who most dislike me are there. My presence seems to disturb them even more than their reaction disturbs me. There was one woman critic, for example, who had a fit of hysterics at the Royal Academy and said she couldn't bear to be in the same room. She just screamed to the company at large, 'There's that terrible man!' She tried to go to another room but found she couldn't get out because she was at the end of the sequence of rooms. So I just said, 'Oh, sod the bloody woman. I'll leave and come back when she gets herself out of the gallery.' And I left.

But isn't there a very real sense in which by holding such strong views you invite strong reactions? I mean, your writing style is, to say the least, provocative, and some would also argue that it is gratuitously insulting and also sometimes designed to hurt. My point is this: if you feel wounded and distressed by people's loathing of you, aren't you also engaged in dishing out hatred and venom to others, who presumably feel pain and distress just as you do?

I only ever write about people and exhibitions which are there as targets. I am in awe of no institution, so if an exhibition is put on at the Royal Academy or the National Gallery and it seems to me to be shoddily done, then I will say so. If there is an exhibition of, let's say, the early works of Gainsborough at the National Gallery, and they are so foolish that they can't see they've got the order wrong or they have simply not understood the material, then they deserve to be slaughtered for it, because they of all people should know how to do it. If they do it badly or foolishly, then they must put up with the criticism. I very rarely tackle a young painter. I will tackle an old one who is well established, like Lucian Freud or John Wonnacott, a British representational artist. I would normally never think about writing about him, except that he is suddenly thrust under my nose as one of the great figurative painters of the late twentieth century. Well, he is nothing of the kind. I feel challenged, so I respond. But at the same time I write quite a lot of letters to painters who are virtually unknown. I am invited to their exhibitions and if I go, then I think they deserve some comment. That way they are not exposed in the *Evening Standard*, no damage is done, and I haven't been beastly to them in public, which is what I am always accused of. If they tear the letter up in a rage and stick pins in a wax image as a consequence, so be it, but I have done my duty as a critic, albeit privately.

But do you ever worry about the effect that your attack might have on the person who is under attack?

I think it's fair game. If a man has put himself forward, or is put forward by his dealer for gain, then he must take what comes. It's absurd that he should ask for praise and then be angry if he gets something other than praise. One of the most disagreeable things that ever happened to me was going to an exhibition and bumping into Lawrence Gowing, who at one point had been my tutor. He put his arm round me and told me that he hoped I would give the painter unalloyed praise. If you knew how much Lawrence spat when he said the consonant p, you would have some idea of how unpleasant this was. But the real unpleasantness lay in his expectation of unalloyed praise for a boy who was a pupil of his, just because he was his pupil and because Gowing thought he ought to be pushed. This is not good enough. Art is much more important than the people who make it.

A few years ago, the American painter R. B. Kitaj left this country after his wife's death, which he felt was connected with the savage reviews of his work. Allowing for the fact that he was clearly disturbed by his wife's sudden death, the fact remains that you called him 'a vain painter, puffed with amour propre, unworthy of a footnote in the history of figurative art'. Did you feel any measure of regret about writing that?

None whatever, absolutely none. It's completely true. Nothing has ever been published that I have felt the need to retract, although I have occasionally written a review and wondered about it afterwards, returned to the exhibition, pondered the problem, and then rewritten the review. So I do sometimes reconsider.

Putting it another way, even if you stand by your judgement of Kitaj's work, did you have second thoughts about how it was expressed?

No.

Your Evening Standard *articles are widely read and enjoyed, but the articles clearly offend a number of readers. Indeed a few years ago a group of thirty-five prominent members of the art establishment wrote to the then editor demanding your resignation. How did you feel about that at the time?*

I was given warning of the letter by young Waddington [of Waddington galleries]. He rang me and said that it had been sent to him for his signature and he thought it was a disgrace, and he wished to read it to me so that I should know what was coming. What he read was a letter which I really wish had been published in that form, because I could have sued every one of the signatories. As it was, they had clearly been told to take a bit of legal advice, and so it was rephrased, which is a pity, because I was looking forward to a fight. It made me feel physically sick, because there were names on that list of people whom I respected, whom I did not think of as enemies. I now know that many of the signatories got there by chance. Marina Warner, for example, had not read the letter or sent it – she was just told by those who organised it that I was violently misogynist and I ought to be taken down a peg or two. She is a feminist and so her name got on to it, but I know she regretted it.

You were accused of virulent homophobia and misogyny ...

[Laughter] I plead guilty to one or the other, not both. Some of my best friends are women. I own pictures painted by women.

You have sometimes also been accused of being anti-Semitic ...

I am not anti-Semitic, I owe an enormous debt to my Jewish mentors, particularly at the Courtauld Institute. I am also indebted to the Jewish boys at school, whom I am sure I called 'bloody Jews' just as everybody else did, though I regret it. They brought a level of maturity to the school that would otherwise not have been there. A twelve-year-old Jewish boy is older than a twelve-year-old Christian boy, and I benefited from that.

In your article on Clause 28 in the Standard *you wrote that a man's sexuality is deeply determined, and that we all know what we are well before the onset of puberty. Do you think that those who appear to remain confused about their sexuality in adulthood are really homosexuals trying to come to terms with their homosexuality, or perhaps trying to fit into the heterosexual mould?*

I don't believe that everybody who is opposed to homosexuality is simply covering up some kind of homosexual drive of his own; that's just a comforting myth. 'He's kicking me because he's really queer' does seem to me to be a silly argument. I don't know what the answer is. There is a deep-seated homophobia in the English psyche, and I don't know why it's there or why it persists.

The bill to repeal Clause 28 was defeated by a sizeable majority in the House of Lords. What do you think about this and the concerns of Baroness Young that standards of decency and morality are at risk if Clause 28 is repealed?

I don't think that any boy – I can't speak for girls, I know so little about them – is ever diverted from his sexual path by the alternative. He always knows what it is. About twenty years after I left school one of the few boys I had kept in touch with decided to give a dinner party for our contemporaries. There were about forty people there, men and their wives, with me the only unmarried one there. The wives seemed to me to be largely vain and silly women who were talking boastfully about their aspirations for their children and so on. At some point homosexuality came into the general discussion and during one of those crystal moments of silence, I suddenly heard myself say, 'I think I've had enough of this debate. There isn't a single man here with whom I have not had sex. And on that note I shall bid you all farewell.' The point of that story is that I had had sex with every one of those boys, and they had all married and had children. I was the queer one. They were all normal. So whatever we did together – and they were perfectly happy to have sex with me at the time – our sexual drives were established well before we were involved in any way with each other. I am convinced that we are what we are at a very early stage.

In your article about Clause 28, you refer to the 'righteous' Cardinal Winning and his 'hysterical bigotry'. Without wishing to defend Cardinal Winning, isn't he in a sense merely expressing the traditional view of the church based on scripture and theology?

Yes. It's precisely what confronted me when I was in my late teens and early twenties, trying to reconcile what I believed to be my faith, with what I knew was my sexuality. That was a long time ago, and the church is still unchanged in its attitude to the problem.

Cardinal Winning is deeply conservative – he does not want the church to move with the times on issues such as homosexuality and abortion, and there is little reason to doubt that his views are sincerely held. When it comes to art, many people would argue that you too are deeply conservative and resist any attempt to accommodate modern practices. What distinguishes your own approach from that of Cardinal Winning?

[Laughter] I think you are too clever by half. But it's actually quite an easy question to answer in the sense that there hasn't been enough time for the dross to fall away. In the art world we make various assumptions, one of which is that it is enough for an artist to declare himself to be an artist for him to be regarded as such. Since the artist is a creature of great instinctive wisdom, it follows that everything he does and says must be taken very seriously, which is what happened with David Hockney. But with the passage of time, when most of these works of art have fallen to pieces and can't be reconstructed, people will begin to sort the wheat from the chaff. The advantage of being a critic is that one can begin that sorting process very much earlier than an institution like the Tate can. The Tate is a museum as well as a gallery and as such it has a different duty from the National Gallery. The National Gallery is small, and it has no hope of covering the whole history of art. It can therefore choose the most exquisite, the most moving, the most exciting, the best examples. The duty of the Tate Gallery, certainly as a museum of British art, is to be complete; therefore, it should have eighteenth-century rubbish in it, it should have nineteenth-century rubbish in it, and by the same token I expect it to have twentieth- and twenty-first-century rubbish in it. That's what it's there for.

The point I was trying to make is that sexual mores have undoubtedly changed over the last twenty or thirty years. Things that would have once caused outrage are now widely accepted in society, if not by the church. Could it not be said that the art world is similarly resistant to change?

No, I think the art world does accept everything; it's not a bit like the church. The art world would benefit from the odd bit of discipline, somebody of some standing to say, 'This is not art – whatever it is, it isn't art.' Take so-called video art, for example. If you were to put it in the cinema, it would be seen as crap; it wouldn't have a hope of surviving because it's professionally inept. The average video artist is simply incompetent and would not be employed by any advertising agency. So I would prefer to scrap the lot of it, for it illuminates nothing, it adds nothing to the sum of beautiful things that move the soul. But going back, to your basic point, to me being the Cardinal Winning of the art world, I don't think that's true. There are things that excite me, there are things which from time to time get through what may seem to be my carapace of prejudice.

Would you argue, as many people do, that there is moral equivalence between straight and homosexual sex?

I think that in a fair society there probably could be, but I go no further than that.

Do you think ideally sex ought to take place in the context of love, or are the two quite separate in your view?

Oh, for heaven's sake, that's a terribly old-fashioned thing. Sex, like food, works at all sorts of levels. You could go to a restaurant and have something that is exquisitely titillating to the palate, or something that simply stokes the boiler. Sex exists as a kind of constant in men's lives: it's there all the time. It varies between extremes of affection and extremes of activity, which are simply purgative.

I notice you say in men's minds. Do you think women are different?

I imagine an enormous number of women, once they've had a baby or two, would say they'd rather sex went away, that they really don't want any more.

You say somewhere of your mother: 'For the first part of her life, she was a flapper and easily bedded.' What is your feeling about that? Is it pride, or dismay, or perhaps incredulity?

I think of it as a possible explanation for my own inclination to be at her age as promiscuous as I was. I'm sure that anybody who remembers me at school will remember me as the school whore.

You say in the same article that children inherit their parents' sexual problems. Would it be too literal an interpretation to infer from that comment that you are also a flapper and easily bedded?

I was. I am now something of a monk. I can no longer believe that young men with whom I would like to go to bed would like to go to bed with me.

What place does love have in your life? Do you fall in love easily, or are you circumspect when it comes to love?

I have been deeply in love with the same man for almost thirty years. He's married, he's on his second marriage in fact, but the love isn't quite unrequited. Occasionally I leave a message on my answering machine which says, 'I am busy committing adultery. Please leave your number and I will return your call when I stop for coffee.' And it's true, because although I am not married in any sense other than to him, he is committing adultery, so I share it.

Some people have suggested that you might suffer from loneliness. Is there any truth in that?

Probably. I am a melancholy soul. I have absolutely no control over it. The melancholy comes and goes without any obvious explanation; the only consolation about it is that it goes, it always goes.

Where are you on the political spectrum, would you say? You described William Hague in an article as 'ludicrous' and 'repellent'. Are you more enamoured of Tony Blair?

No. He is ludicrous and repellent too. I hate that grin, that ready grin. It's even worse than John Major's.

But do you think Blair is a good prime minister?

No, he's all wind and waffle. What I deplore about Tony Blair is that he is prepared to run with the Thatcher legacy; it suits him because it will get him re-elected. I had great hopes when John Prescott said before the election that there was a strong possibility that they would renationalise the railways, that they would not be run for profit, that we would get our money back. If he had stuck to that, I would have voted Labour but by the time the election came it was already perfectly clear that wind and waffle were all that they had to offer, and that is all we've had since. There's only one serious politician in the Labour camp, and that's Gordon Brown.

In an article entitled 'Me and My God', I couldn't help noticing that you have a slightly tortured attitude to religion. Would that be a fair comment?

Yes [laughter].

You started off as a Roman Catholic and then had Anglicanism imposed on you by your stepfather, but gradually you began to have more and more doubts about what might be called the core beliefs of Christianity, though you also seemed to be troubled by guilt ...

The guilt is entirely associated with my homosexuality. It is the feeling of exclusion and rejection. If one could change that, I might feel differently.

Would you say perhaps that it is almost as difficult not to believe as to believe?

I think it depends entirely on your background. If I had had no background in the church, then I don't think I would have any longing to join it. It would be enormously comforting to be able to return to a belief, but I don't think I shall. My lack of faith is supported everywhere I look – Rwanda, Kosovo, Bosnia. Where is God?

From what I read you are obviously troubled by what might be called the problem of evil and suffering in a world created by a benevolent God. You say, 'I have some sympathy if he cares not a damn for the human race; it is pretty ghastly. But that he should inflict harm on the animal kingdom seems beyond acceptance.' Is that your sincere belief, or is it intended to be slightly rhetorical?

It is my sincere belief. Christ preaches about the importance of the lilies in the field, the sparrows in the air, but look at what has happened to the lilies in the field and we now have no sparrows. What is the answer? The answer is that he isn't there, because if he were, he of all people would do something about it. Every time, for example, I read about the Siberian tiger or the Pyrenean bear becoming extinct, it makes me so angry.

Your love of animals is well known. What is it about animals? Do you feel they are safer than people perhaps, more loyal, more loveable?

The care I give to a bird with a broken wing is not conditional on being rewarded with loyalty and love. But the wonderful thing about owning dogs, and to a lesser extent cats, is that you do get a response which is human in some degree, or recognisably of the same nature as a human response, but that's a bonus. If I had the opportunity to live my life again knowing what I know now, I would not be an art historian, I would be a vet.

Your stand against religion seemed to waver when you had your heart attack and then a heart-bypass operation. Indeed, you told the staff that if anything went wrong they were to send for a priest. Was this a version of Pascal's wager?

[Laughter] No, it was an entirely unconscious reaction. The nursing sister had challenged me with her brisk bright businesslike approach, and with her clipboard in hand she told me there were one or two details which had to be settled, one being that I was down as an atheist. Although one feels more dead than alive in such a situation, I said, 'No, no, I'm not an atheist. I am an agnostic, but if anything goes wrong, call a priest.' It was purely instinctive. Besides, I see absolutely nothing wrong with going through the motions of the Roman Catholic preparations for death, which can be very beautiful and moving.

Are you afraid of death?

I don't think so. It will be the nature of its coming that really gives the answer. I think I can put up with pain or physical disablement, but if my brain should become addled … of course I shall not be aware, and that is the comfort. My mother in the last year or two of her life had no idea at all that her brain was not functioning. I used to go and visit her as a regular discipline, and one particular day when I went into her room she was lying with her eyes shut and her hands doing quick finger movements, as though playing the piano. I sat there and she took no notice of me – she didn't even know I was there. Eventually I got down on the floor and touched her knee. She opened her eyes, went on making her hand movements, and just said, 'Don't interrupt! I've told you before not to interrupt me when I'm practising.' And it just went straight back to my childhood. I found it terribly disturbing because it was quite clear that she had no idea how old she was, she had no idea of the circumstances, her sense of reality had gone. But I think she was perfectly happy.

Are you resigned to oblivion when you die, or would you like to think that there might be an afterlife?

Of course I'm resigned to oblivion. The great book on Michelangelo is not written. It won't be on anybody's shelf. That is the only afterlife I should have liked, to have written that book, and I now know I shan't. I suspect I shall die in harness with the *Evening Standard*, scribbling ephemera. And the book won't be there.

NED SHERRIN

Ned Sherrin – producer, performer, writer and director – was born in Somerset in 1931. He qualified as a barrister before going into television, where he made his name on satirical programmes such as *That Was The Week That Was* and *Not So Much A Programme, More A Way Of Life*. He produced several films, including *The Virgin Soldiers*, and presented the weekly radio programme *Loose Ends* and the musical quiz *Counterpoint* on BBC Radio 4. He directed many plays, including *Jeffrey Bernard is Unwell*, co-created and directed *Side by Side by Sondheim* and got an Olivier in 1984 for his adaptation of *Iolanthe*. Among his publications were *Loose Neds* (1990), *Theatrical Anecdotes* (1991) and two volumes of autobiography. He was awarded a CBE in 1997 and died of throat cancer in 2007.

You wrote in your book Loose Neds *that you had read about twenty in-depth interviews with Ned Sherrin and they were all more or less identical. Why do you think that is? Is it perhaps because you yourself decide which areas are to be covered, or are the interviewers just no bloody good?*

The latter certainly. What they do is get the cuttings out and read everybody else's interview and then they ask the same questions. Biographical stuff is usually cast in the same mould and practically everybody's heard it every time.

People are often suspicious of professional funny men, believing that behind all the jokiness and wit there lurks a sad unhappy figure. Is there any truth in that in your own case?

No. Anyway, I'm not a natural funny man. Most of my jokes depend on people writing them for me. Your question reminds me of a wonderful remark at Willie Rushton's funeral. Auberon Waugh said that he didn't think he'd make jokes as he'd been asked to do, because death was a serious business. 'On the other hand,' he added, 'I suppose if Willy was here this morning we'd both be having a good laugh at the death of Sir Laurens van der Post.' [Laughter]

That seemed to sum up the essence of the *Private Eye* joke – very funny, very topical, very cruel.

You talk about the 'differences' you felt as a child growing up on your father's farm, not having the instinct of a country boy and planning your escape route. Have you ever wondered why you felt different?

No. I liked the country, but mooning around after cows wasn't my idea of fun. The glamour and glitter of the bright lights appealed to me more. I remember as a small child there was a cocktail party held in the big house in the village. My parents hated parties so my brother and I went alone, and I was absolutely fascinated. It was there I heard my first piece of theatrical gossip. I heard somebody say, 'Did you realise that Ivor Novello has inherited the mantle of Owen Nares?' This seemed to me to be the most priceless bit of information but there was nobody in the village I could share it with. I was happy to get away.

By cutting yourself off from your roots you inevitably created a barrier between you and your family. Is that something you have been able to live with easily?

I get on particularly well with my brother even though we're wildly different. It was very convenient that he wanted to farm and could take over from our father. I didn't want the farm so I didn't have to be there.

Did you feel you were a disappointment to your father?

I don't think so. He was a bit disappointed with *That Was The Week That Was*. He had loved it when I was doing nice safe programmes like *Tonight* with that nice Cliff Michelmore, and a nice quiz programme with that nice Franklin Engelmann, but he was a bit worried about having to explain away *TW3*.

But did you get on?

Yes. My only criticism of my father – I've probably inherited it – is that if he had one joke he would flog it to death and this could be a bit tiresome. I don't think he understood why I wanted to go away but since I never had to ask him for any more money after that he was probably quite relieved.

In your autobiography you tell the story of how you were unable to kiss your dying father. You tell it matter-of-factly without sentiment, but I thought it was the nearest you came to having a serious regret …

Yes … but in fact we invariably kissed on leaving. It was simply that on the occasion in question somebody else arrived just at that moment, and so it had to wait until after he'd died.

Back in the 1960s when you pioneered That Was The Week That Was *did you and those you worked with have the feeling that you would change the world?*

No, we had the feeling that we'd all enjoy ourselves on a Saturday night. *TW3* had grown out of the news documentary aspect of the old *Tonight* programme and that great upswing of activity from *Private Eye*, the *Beyond the Fringe* team, and all the change that came about with the angry young men. What we were doing was a distillation of a movement which had already been started. The difference was that we were peddling it to a far bigger audience – that was why it had the impact.

If there was no such lofty notion as changing the world, wasn't there something terribly trivialising and therefore trivial about what you were doing, as if nothing mattered very much?

No. I think we set out to do a more adult sort of entertainment than was generally available at the time. For true satire you do probably need to have an almost irrational passion, it needs to be wild and damaging. But we were never really trying to peddle perfect satire, we were doing a sort of communication with the audience in informal terms late on a Saturday night. The only time I got really worked up about anything was when Macmillan was succeeded by Alec Douglas-Home instead of Butler. I thought it would have been much more interesting to have Butler and I commissioned a very strong piece which apparently upset Sir Alec a great deal. But in the long run I think rational criticism is probably better than burning passion.

Do you think there was a kind of shift in society at the beginning of the 1960s which made a new kind of satire and irreverence possible?

Yes. Attitudes took a little time to change after the war, but then there was *Look Back in Anger* in 1956 which altered everything. Another terribly important time was when rock and roll came in, and the whole forelock-touching philosophy seemed to go out of the window.

Do you think the success of the show had something to do with the final loss of the empire and the old English certainties falling by the wayside?

Yes, we were all getting into a more questioning mood at that time. In the old days a BBC reporter confronting a minister at the airport would say, 'Oh, excuse me, sir, have you any interesting message to tell us?' But when the Robin Days and the Ludovic Kennedys and the Ian Trethowans of the early days of ITN got to airports they asked different questions. Once the attitude started to change it became a groundswell.

The kind of interviewing at that time was certainly different from today ...

Yes, but I sometimes think it goes too far today. I'm often quite in sympathy with politicians who feel they're getting a rough time on *Today*. Sometimes the interviewing is extremely good, but at other times it really does get terribly irritating when the interviewer jumps in before the person's uttered two sentences.

What did you think of the old-style John Freeman kind of interview?

I thought his interviews were fascinating. People seemed to have more patience to listen then but now we're in the era of the sound bite. Television producers feel that an audience cannot sustain interest for more than a minute or two. That seems to me to be very damaging. The very funny interviews that John Fortune and John Bird do so exquisitely on the *Rory Bremner Show* seem to hark back to a golden age.

Bernard Levin said that TW3 was about 'filth, sedition and blasphemy'. Did Levin just fail to get the joke, or what?

I'm sure he was being funny. That was Bernard's great rallying cry. But in fact he was an integral part of the programme and chiefly responsible for a lot of the filth, sedition and blasphemy.

In a sense you were the odd one out in TW3 – you weren't a bearded leftie in sandals but more of a Tory of the old school, as Willy Rushton called you. Did you ever feel like the odd one out?

No, I felt rather paternal towards them in fact. I was roughly ten years older than Frost and six years older than Willy Rushton, and that made a difference.

When Kennedy died you went ahead with TW3 the following evening. Malcolm Muggeridge said afterwards, 'They are probably all thoroughly ashamed of it.' Were you? Or was anyone in fact ashamed?

No, I think we had no alternative. Malcolm felt that the brief of the programme was to mock everything, but in fact the brief of the programme was to reflect our feelings on behalf of the nation at the end of each week. It was like a mini New Year's Eve every Saturday night. The whole nation, the whole world indeed, was shattered by the Kennedy business; all we could do was reflect that.

Philip Larkin, in his poem Churchgoing, *describes how people hide behind jokes and irony when in fact there is an urge to be serious, of which they are half ashamed. Have you ever been conscious of anything like that?*

Yes. I've just published a novel and I found the authorial voice which pontificates on the fates and predicaments of the characters a bit embarrassing. One felt perhaps one was revealing a naïvety in oneself which one would prefer people not to be aware of.

Do you feel that your public persona is different from your private one?

No, I think it's exactly the same. I would be surprised if people who know me well would say there's any difference at all.

When I read through your autobiography each page seems to be packed with parties and social events, an endless stream of gossip and amusing observations. But I didn't get the sense of there being any serious philosophy in your life – principles or beliefs you hold dear. Do you have any?

I don't think I do. I'm a walking definition of a wet Church of England conservatism, which some people hold to be no religion at all. I'm probably just too self-satisfied. I've enjoyed life far too much to search for any more serious purpose.

Where do you stand on religion, for example?

Well, it's seven minutes' walk to Chelsea Old Church and I do that about once a month. That's where I stand on religion.

Is that out of habit or conviction?

Out of habit. Also out of enjoyment, which is another reason for doing it. I like the idea of going to communion once a month. On the whole I feel comforted by it and I like to put in a few requests each month. I don't waste my time on trying to formulate a concept of God. I have observed far brighter people than me trying to do just that and failing.

But do you find as you get older you tend to be more religious?

Again, I haven't noticed a great change in my attitude. God may have done, but I haven't.

You have often said that you have never had any problems with being gay. To what do you attribute the lack of complications?

I don't know. I didn't ever discuss it with my parents or with any member of my family. It would have been entirely outside their imagination and comprehension. One was a little worried during the early 1950s and 1960s because one didn't want to be arrested and sent to prison – for any reason let alone for one's sexual preferences. But apart from that it has never bothered me.

Is it perhaps easier to be gay when you move in theatrical and artistic circles, as you do?

I'm sure that's true. If I'd been growing up on the farm, then I'm sure it would have been very difficult and embarrassing. That may have been one of the contributory factors to my wanting to leave.

Have you ever encountered serious prejudice?

Only on one occasion and that was recently. I had been booked to speak to a firm of stockbrokers in January and at the last minute they rang up and said that perhaps I wasn't the sort of person they would like to have speak to them.

It's thirty years since Viscount Montgomery made his famous remark about homosexuality: 'This sort of thing may be tolerated by the French, but we are British, thank God.' Although we have undoubtedly come a long way since then, do you perhaps think the underlying British attitude remains the same?

Montgomery is an interesting one because he was in fact fascinated by young men always. I imagine he didn't realise that there was a sort of subliminal homoerotic feeling there. It takes an awful long time for things to change but I would have thought that prejudice was moving backwards, albeit very slowly. Homosexuality is a very difficult thing for people to imagine, and perhaps even more difficult if they're unconsciously suppressing some impulse in themselves and are rather frightened of it.

In your latest book, Sherrin's Year, *you say that you have never been reluctant to engage a male prostitute, and you describe how you respond to adverts in the* Gay Times *and so on. Have you never longed for a more sustained relationship?*

I've attempted two more sustained relationships, and in both cases they were happy, but they ended when the other person went off. Now at the age of sixty-five it is perhaps too late to be looking for a new sustained relationship, and the idea of being irresistibly attractive to somebody at sixty-five would be a triumph of hope over experience.

Most people still think there is something a bit sad and desperate about going to a prostitute ... is that a completely mistaken view, would you say?

Some prostitutes have become my best friends – an interesting variation on the idea that some of my best friends are prostitutes. I've become friends with many men whom I've met in that way, some of whom have stopped being prostitutes, some of whom have carried on doing it.

You say that prostitution is a better idea than exploiting a young actor who might be hoping for work. What did you mean by that remark exactly, and why does there have to be exploitation at all in a relationship entered into freely?

It's the old story of the casting couch. There was a whole wave of protests in the theatre in the 1940s because one of the theatrical managements which was particularly successful was reckoned to be run by homosexuals, and young actors were getting jobs for the wrong reasons. That sort of thing is tiresome.

You are chairman of a consortium which has proposed a twenty-four-hour gay radio station for the UK. How do you rate the chances of that happening?

It's difficult to know but I think it would be very valuable. It would be a music-based station and everybody knows that the best modern music is played in gay clubs. Indeed, heterosexuals often go to gay clubs simply because of the music. It's also an opportunity for communicating with gays who are not lucky enough to be in the London mainstream and may be feeling left out in the provinces with no one to talk to or understand their problems.

How politically involved are you in the gay movement?

Hardly at all apart from charity work. The AIDS thing has been such a threat that I do as much as I can for Crusaid and the Terence Higgins Trust, but I'm not good at marching.

Have you yourself ever had cause to worry about AIDS?

Yes. My sex life is really restricted now, so there's much less chance of getting it and there's all sorts of precautions one can take if one was going to the ultimate extreme. I don't actually do that anymore, but certainly I consider myself lucky not to have got it. I stopped counting after more than fifty of my friends had died, and so in those terms it's perhaps remarkable that one hasn't got it. Certainly, several of my ex- – I hate the word *partners* – lovers have died of AIDS.

Isn't it traumatic when one of your friends dies of AIDS?

Yes, but fifty traumas is a lot, so you become a bit inured to it. It doesn't stop the sadness of course.

You refer a couple of times in your diary to Peter Tatchell's Outrage campaign to expose bishops and other prominent figures, but it's not quite clear whether you approve of this action ...

I desperately disapprove of it. I always remember Runcie's address from the pulpit in Southwark Cathedral at Mervyn Stockwood's memorial service. Mervyn had been one of the people on Tatchell's list for outing bishops. The Bishop of Bath and Wells into whose diocese Mervyn had retired thought he had better ring up Mervyn and warn him, and Mervyn to his great credit told the bishop that if the press got on to him to be sure and tell them he had had lots of women as well. [Laughter] In fact the evidence suggested that Mervyn, though naturally homosexual, was celibate, but he wasn't going to be frightened by Peter Tatchell.

Do you think you can be gay and still be the messenger of God?

Oh certainly. I don't see any reason why not.

The Old Testament would suggest otherwise ... think of Sodom and Gomorrah ...

Yes, but there were all sorts of primitive community restrictions then. I mean, it wasn't a good idea to eat pork or seafood in the desert either. There's also the fact that John was the disciple that Jesus loved, so there's the other side of the question.

Are you sensitive to criticism?

I prefer good notices to bad.

Caryl Brahms, your late writing partner, described you as a narcissist looking into a lake and saying, 'I'm perfect.' Do you plead guilty?

Yes – but I don't think it's the whole man. Caryl was very acute but she was also frustrated if she didn't get her own way, and we had lots of artistic quarrels during the nearly thirty years we worked together.

In some ways you strike me as being an English version of Gore Vidal ... sharp, acerbic, also gay. Would you be flattered or dismayed by the comparison?

Oh, I'd be flattered, but Gore would be dismayed. He's not speaking to me at the moment, but that's my regret and his loss. Gore is a volcano of natural wit and a writer of the utmost brilliance. It's like comparing the genius and the journeyman.

LADY SOAMES

Mary Soames, youngest daughter of Sir Winston Churchill, was born in 1922 and spent most of her childhood at Chartwell, where she was educated privately. From 1939 to 1941 she served with the Red Cross and WVS and later in the ATS with mixed anti-aircraft batteries. She also travelled with her father on several wartime journeys. In 1947 she married Christopher Soames and campaigned with him through six elections between 1950 and 1966 when he was Conservative MP for Bedford. In 1968 she accompanied him to Paris, where he was ambassador for four years, and in 1979 to Rhodesia, where he was the last British governor. Her publications include *The Profligate Duke* (1987) and *Winston Churchill: His Life as a Painter* (1990). Her biography of her mother, *Clementine Churchill* (1979), won the Wolfson Prize for History and the *Yorkshire Post* prize for Best First Work. She was chairman of the National Theatre from 1989 to 1995, was appointed a Lady Companion of the Order of the Garter in 2005 and published her autobiography, *A Daughter's Tale*, in 2011. She died, aged ninety-one, in 2014.

When writing about your childhood you say that although elements of anxiety, sorrow and disappointment began to appear as the years went by, in your own recollection it is the happiness which predominates. Is that in effect a tribute to your parents, who helped shield you from the darker side of life?

I wrote those lines after describing life at Chartwell and the wonderful Christmases we had there. As life went on and I became a teenager I began to know that life wasn't a Garden of Eden, and it was disquieting to me because of my idyllic childhood at Chartwell. The first time I saw my mother cry was one of the most traumatic moments of my young life. I had very rarely seen grown-ups cry and to see this beautiful woman whom I loved and admired, and also rather feared, weeping and completely disintegrated with grief was a terrible shock to me. I saw my parents a lot because we children were never kept away in the nursery wing, and also I was very much the Benjamin, so I strayed around all over the house and never felt I was excluded from my parents' life when they were at Chartwell. I went to day school; I was never sent away to boarding school, and those parts of my life that my mother didn't take personal part in she organised with perfection. I also had the most wonderful duenna figure in my life, a first cousin of my mother's who came when I was a baby to look after me and stayed right through until I went away to the war; and so when my parents were absent I still had a wonderfully secure life. I adored Chartwell, believing that it was a very large house and a beautiful house; of course now I see that it isn't a very large house and it certainly isn't a beautiful one, but I do look back at my childhood as bathed in golden sunshine.

As the youngest child you were perhaps the one to benefit most from the stability that Chartwell offered. How important do you think that was in later life?

I suppose I did have a rather different upbringing from my elder brother and sisters. I could try to count all the houses, the nannies and governesses and nurses they lived through, but that would be counter-productive. Does a very stable, almost cabbage-like existence, like a plant in the garden, with one set of influences make a great difference to a child? I suppose it does. There was Diana, Randolph, Sarah and then there was Marigold who died the year before I was born, so I was brought up almost like an only child. Sarah was already seven when I was born, Diana was thirteen, Randolph was eleven ... they were godlike Olympian figures. Sarah was really the only one with whom I had close connections; I loved the others, but really didn't know them at all. They inhabited a different landscape from me.

You describe your relationship with your mother at that time as respectful and admiring, rather than close. Was that a retrospective analysis or something you were aware of at the time?

I grew into being aware of it and can almost date it: when I was thirteen my mother realised that Cousin Moppet had a great influence on my whole outlook on life and she saw that I was growing much closer to Cousin Moppet than to her. It was then that she started taking me away to ski in the holidays and I began to be more than just respectful and admiring. I came to love her in a much more real way I suppose, and it wasn't without same painful interludes, because I was a tiresome teenager. My mother was a complex character, and could also be difficult, but I came to love her when I got to know her better.

Although your mother was devoted and conscientious there was never any doubt that Winston came first. You seem not to have any sense of grievance about this. Did you come to mind it later?

Not at all. We all felt that our parents had other very important things to do. I never felt neglected emotionally or in any other way by them. It was in my mother's nature to be dedicated, and it was true also of my father, luckily for him and perhaps the whole world as well. However, much later, when I knew my husband Christopher was going into politics, I took a vow in my heart that I would try to give my children a greater priority than perhaps we had with my mother. But I think it very important in this context to remember that when my mother was bringing up her children it wasn't a mark of bad mothering to have nurses and governesses; it was part of the way of life in that stratum of society. I certainly never regarded her as a bad mother. She had some less than happy relationships within the family but I think that happens very often. If you have a number of children you're probably not equally close to all of them.

Were you the closest to your mother?

I came to be because of my position in the family as the youngest. When the war broke out for instance, Randolph was away in the army, my sister Diana was married and had her children. Sarah was married to Vic Oliver and then went into the air force. I did go into the army eventually, but by the time I was sixteen or seventeen the others had flown the nest. My mother more and more confided in me and we became much closer, but it was an accident of timing.

Was your mother difficult in her relationships with people generally?

She was a very complex and emotionally charged character, but she wasn't difficult all the time. She had enormously high standards which she imposed with varying degrees of success on her children, but she was also very hard on herself. She adored my father, was completely absorbed in his life, and involved in his politics, and she felt it all with every fibre of her being. But she was undoubtedly a highly strung animal.

But did she clash with your father because of that?

Yes. Perhaps history would have been different if my father had married a docile yes-woman; he might have had an easier time at home. But my mother had the will and the capacity to stand up to my father, to confront him, and to argue with him, and the fact that she had that capacity is more important than whether she was always right. I don't think she was always right, but she took a passionate interest in his political life, and there's no doubt about it that sometimes her judgements about his friends were truer than his. I've always thought my father married an equal in temperament and in spirit.

Would you say that she influenced his political life as well as his private life?

She was a Liberal at heart and she never really changed, but she did have an influence on him though it's quite hard to say exactly to what extent. He didn't necessarily take her advice, but it was very important to him as a politician that she could enter into the arguments and the choices.

Did your father have time to show you affection when you were young?

Both my parents were enormously affectionate, visibly so, and he was a great hugger, my father, and loved having us around. The stiff upper lip of the British upper class had really no part in our family life; it was something I read about in books. I may have been deeply shocked the first time I saw my mother cry, because that was as a result of a great drama in the family, but I often saw my father weep and it never struck me as odd that a man should express emotion. My mother could be cold when she wished to express disapproval or to distance herself from a person, but to walk into a room where they both were was to be enfolded and embraced. We were a very noisy and extrovert family; when we were happy we laughed and hugged each other, and when we were sad we cried, and when we were angry we stamped our feet – there was never any doubt about how we were all feeling.

What kind of thing made your father cry?

He was moved by events and tragedies, by people behaving nobly, by poetry … I've seen him recite Shakespeare with his eyes brimming with tears. He wept easily and he wasn't ashamed of it.

I know you hate being asked what it was like to be the daughter of Winston Churchill, so I will ask you something rather different. Were you aware of being set apart from your peers by virtue of your father's importance, and if so, was that something you found difficult to cope with?

It came upon me gradually. Of course, as a small child I took my parents completely for granted. It never struck me as odd, for instance, that my father wrote books, made speeches, built walls, painted pictures, but the realisation of his importance and fame grew upon me. I may not have had a very profound understanding of events, but I realised that significant things were afoot. I used to listen to my parents talking, and with great events impinging on our domestic life, I came to realise that my father was an important figure who played a leading role in all this. We were all brought up with a great sense of public service. I would have thought it contemptible in me to have wished my parents to be at my school sports day; what did it matter if they saw me coming fourth in the egg-and-spoon race? When the war broke out and Papa took office, my feelings for him as his child became confused and mingled with the feelings I had as an ardent young Englishwoman. 1940 was special for us all, and my father was the hero of the hour to whom we all clung. Me too.

For much of the 1930s your father had been in the political wilderness. Then in May 1940 when power slipped away from Chamberlain, Churchill began his 'walk with destiny' for which he considered all his earlier life to have been a preparation. How great a part do you think destiny played in all this?

Destiny played a great part, because he was a young soldier-of-fortune and seeking 'reputation in the cannon's mouth', he could have lost his life on about five or six different occasions. Although my father longed to be in office in the 1930s, my mother often said to me that it was a real blessing that he never held office then, because he couldn't single-handedly have turned the tide of appeasement and slow rearmament; he would have been involved in government in a time that came to be regarded, perhaps rather unjustly, as the dark decade when we were purblind. As it was he was able to start with a clean slate.

You served for five years with the ATS. The contrast between the life you had known and life in the army must have been stark. Did you find it an ordeal, or did the conditions of war make everything acceptable?

I was thrilled to go into the army and rather gloried in the discomforts. I really did want to do my bit and felt I was part of this great enterprise going on. So I loved it and was a tremendously enthusiastic soldier, rather too much so probably.

But did you feel that because of your father you were looked upon in a different light?

Yes. I had difficult moments. It was always agony going to a new unit because I knew I wouldn't be treated in quite the same way as others. I always felt I had to overcompensate, scrub more floors than anyone else.

Churchill offered his countrymen 'blood, toil, tears and sweat', and they responded with indomitable spirit. Do you think that the strength of their response surprised him, perhaps humbled him even?

Yes. The response of the British people was something which moved him deeply. He was very conscious of all the devotion and valour and dedication, and he valued them enormously. It was a pact really, between the British people and him.

Churchill was held in near veneration during his lifetime. In more recent times the history books have not been especially kind. How do you respond to criticism of your father's wartime period?

I try not to mind too much about judgements on public events. I dislike mean judgements and those based on being wise after the event. But of course my father must stand the test of history. He didn't do everything right or make all the right judgements, but we did manage to win, despite all the mistakes, so I can only imagine the enemy made even more. One must keep these things in perspective, but of course I find it difficult to detach myself entirely, and when it's a question of personal criticism, I sometimes know his critics are actually wrong.

To be a very successful politician, particularly in time of war, you have to take decisions which might be interpreted later on, or even at the time, as ruthless, where sometimes the innocent have to pay a great price. Do you think your father ever took decisions which were perhaps good for Britain but were rather questionable on moral grounds?

My father would have done almost anything to win the war, and war is a rough business. I daresay he had to do some very rough things, but he wasn't a man who took these sorts of decisions lightly. All those things weighed with him, but they didn't unman him.

You refer in your book to what you call 'slaps at Winston's departed greatness'. What did you have in mind?

I don't remember in what context I made that particular remark, but I suppose I was thinking of how much I minded that, in quieter times, people took slaps at my father. But I've been brought up in quite a rough political school, so one accepts that that must be so. No true historian of the war is guilty of unjust or ill-informed criticism, but people who write meretricious histories are being tremendously wise after the event. They assume that we knew that we were going to win. But when you lived through it at the side of people like my father who were so deeply involved in it, the uncertainties were enormous. I feel that people very often don't understand how much the war was lived step by step and day by day.

Did your father ever despair?

A lot has been made of the depressive side of his character by psychiatrists who were never in the same room with him. Of course he himself talks of his 'black dog', and he did have times of great depression, but marriage to my mother very largely kennelled the black dog. Of course if you have a black dog it lurks somewhere in your nature and you never quite banish it; but I never saw him disarmed by depression. I'm not talking about the depression of his much later years, because surely that is a sad feature of old age which afflicts a great many people who have led a very active life.

Was he dictatorial?

No. He had a greater measure of power than any leader in democratic times in our country, but you must remember that every Tuesday when he was in this country and the House was sitting, he answered questions in the House of Commons. He always regarded himself as a servant of Parliament, and I don't think there is a recorded instance of his having gone against the decisions of the joint Chiefs of Staff. Of course he would argue his corner but it's not true to say he always got his way; he didn't, and sometimes it made him very cross. Sometimes he even acknowledged they were right. Several times during the war he pressed something to a vote of confidence which people found rather tiresome because of course he would always get the vote of confidence, but he wished to demonstrate to the world that this was a war waged by a democratic country, and that he was empowered by the democratic vote, even at the height of war.

Your introduction to Christopher Soames was reportedly love at first sight ... was he your first love?

No. I can't remember who was the very first. I was quite susceptible when I was young and I'd been in love with several people by the time I met Christopher. I was very attracted to men and fell head over heels many times. I was very high spirited and had a lovely time in a way, but when I came back from the war I found it quite difficult adjusting to my own class, funnily enough.

Were you flirtatious?

Yes; but having been brought up strictly, I was quite prim. I was also horrendously innocent. I can only say the gods look after their own and I had a guardian angel. I don't think I was very sensible.

Tell me how you first fell in love with Christopher Soames.

It wasn't love at first sight on my side, I have to say, but we met for the very first time in the British Embassy in Paris where, years and years later, he was to be ambassador … and that was rather romantic. My father and I were in Belgium and he was going to fly straight back to England, but the US Secretary of State was going to be in Paris and my father wanted to see him. We both flew to Paris for twenty-four hours, and in those twenty-four hours I met Christopher Soames. I think he fell in love straightaway, and I did quite quickly after that, but the first time, I really thought he had other fish to fry.

Did you have other fish to fry?

No, I was rather unhappy when I came out of the army. I'd had an interesting, exciting war – as the equivalent of a captain. I'd served in mixed anti-aircraft batteries and, in much as it was possible then for women in England, I'd been in action against the enemy. In some ways one felt sparkling and confident and yet in other ways not. I hadn't been in my own world for five years. The men in London whom I saw when I first came out of the army were either beardless boys who seemed to me like schoolchildren, or they were young married men very occupied with beautiful young wives; and most of my friends were either dead or still in the army or abroad. I found it quite difficult to re-establish life at home and I wasn't very happy. I don't think I woke up in the morning saying I was miserable, but looking back, it wasn't a happy time in my life and I couldn't think what I wanted to do. I didn't have a vocation, certainly not a profession, and the only way I could have earned my living would have been as a lift operator or a scrubber of floors, so I was in rather a strange position. My father, although out of office immediately after the war, was enormously famous, and I was made much of and had a lovely time wherever I went with him; but my own actual personal life wasn't very satisfactory. Then, within a year of being demobilised, suddenly wonderful Christopher Soames appeared on the horizon and, like my parents, we married and lived happily ever afterwards.

In your book about your mother, you describe a certain inhibition in Clementine which made for a barrier between her and her children, a certain formality and lack of spontaneity. Was that something you tried consciously to reserve in your relationship with your own children?

Yes. My relationship with my children was quite different. For one thing it was more knockabout and workaday. It's true, I had a nanny, a wonderful nanny, who looked after them all, but Christopher and I lived in the country and life was different. I think that all of us in that age group had a freer and cosier relationship with our children than our parents had had with us.

As PPS to your father, Christopher Soames was a key figure, particularly when your father suffered a stroke and was scarcely functioning. How was it possible to keep this from the public and keep things running smoothly?

That's really an extraordinary episode, and the more I look back on it, the more extraordinary I think it is. Again fate steps in. My father sustained the stroke in the evening at a dinner party at Downing Street; the next morning he presided at a Cabinet meeting. Harold Macmillan and Rab Butler and several others were absolutely amazed afterwards when they learned of the extent of the stroke. They all said that Winston was rather silent and looked pale but none of them at the time noticed anything seriously amiss. By the morning Lord Moran had diagnosed a stroke and my father headed for Chartwell having walked to his car from No 10. When he got to Chartwell which was an hour's drive away, he couldn't get out of the car, and had to be carried inside. So it was only then that the worse effects of the stroke became obvious, and at Chartwell he was kept absolutely incommunicado. That weekend Lord Moran told Christopher that he thought my father was going to die. Christopher didn't tell me that, but I knew he was very ill. He was there for six weeks and somehow – it couldn't happen now – Christopher and John Colville between them kept the machine turning over. Julian Amery is very naughty about it: he always says that Christopher was prime minister, but it isn't true that Christopher ever said or ever felt that he was.

Did your husband ever resent the fact that his own natural politician prowess was sometimes obscured as a result of his kinship with Churchill?

Not at all. Christopher loved my father, he loved him as he didn't love his own father with whom he had an unhappy relationship. From the first they took to each other and were great friends. Christopher had become interested in politics when he was assistant military attaché at Paris during the Peace Conference, but he knew he owed an enormous amount to my father. I never heard him express anything other than that he was grateful for the start that his relationship with my father gave him. He was actually my father's parliamentary private secretary before officially being appointed. Christopher was also able to do a great service for my father in that second period of office, first as leader of the opposition and then as prime minister in 1951. My father by that time was rather old and so very eminent people were quite frightened of approaching him, and it was through Christopher that quite a number of young MPs on both sides of the House used to gain access to him.

Did the fact that Christopher was very close to your father cement your marriage more?

It was a wonderful thing. In the first ten years of our married life we lived in the farmhouse at Chartwell, and so we saw my parents constantly. It was a very close relationship, and gradually my mother became fond of Christopher. She didn't like him at first, though she was pretty good about it. But I remember one day years later, certainly after Papa's death, when Christopher, Mama and I were all sitting round at table, having a lovely cosy talk, and Christopher said to her, 'You didn't like me, did you, when I first married Mary?', and I remember it so well, she put out her hand and covered his and said, 'No darling, but I've made up for it since.'

Although his native talents were not in doubt, it was 1960 before your husband finally got out of his father-in-law's shadow. Was that a relief to all concerned?

I don't remember feeling that. It seemed progressive. He had quite a difficult time getting a seat, despite being my father's son-in-law. He was inexperienced politically and constituencies were quite wary of him to begin with. Somebody once implied that Christopher wouldn't have been anything in politics if it hadn't been for my father. It's true that he might not have had the start my father gave him, and a wonderful start it was, but if Christopher had been no good he would have just fizzled out. In fact, he held Bedford for sixteen years and increased his majority each time.

You have sometimes referred to the golden years of Paris. What is it that makes you recall that period with such fondness?

For one thing we were both strangers to diplomatic life, so it was a joint enterprise. We also had a wonderful welcome awaiting us because the French nation was in love with my father. We already had friends there and we took the school-age children with us and the others came in their holidays. Of course it had its ups and downs – the Soames affair (when the Foreign Office blabbed top-secret information) very nearly capsized the boat before we'd been there long, but Christopher survived it although his position was precarious for a while. In our time there, things were happening that were really interesting and exciting: The General died in 1970 ... in itself the passing of an era; Pompidou became President; Ted Heath became prime minister; the summit took place in Paris where it was agreed that the French would remove their veto. It was intoxicatingly exciting politically, and all the time the life of the embassy was going on. I love France, and how could anyone not love living in Paris?

What did you think of de Gaulle?

I admired him enormously; to me he represented, as he did to my father whatever their differences and quarrels, resurgent France, the soul of France. I was also much alarmed by him, but he was very civil and kind to me. The only time I really had a conversation with him was at luncheon in the Elysée, when I sat next to him shaking with nerves. He was not an easily approachable person and we had an extraordinary conversation. He asked me 'Que faites-vous à Paris, madame?' and so I panicked and I said, 'Je promène mes chiens, Monsieur le Président.' Instead of putting me down for an absolutely asinine answer to his question, he became very interested. He wanted to know what dogs I had and where I walked them, and then suggested I take them to the Ile de Cygnes which is a little island in the middle of the Seine. He drew it for me on the menu, and thereafter I always used to walk my dogs on the Ile de Cygnes with grateful thoughts of the General.

Did you warm to him?

I never had much time to, but I think one could have done. He was very fond of my mother, ever since the time when she flew at him for making a very anti-British remark. My father had missed it because he was at the other end of the table, and anyhow Papa's French wasn't very good, but when the General insulted the British fleet, Mama retaliated in perfect French. The next day there arrived the most enormous arrangement of flowers, and thereafter he respected and liked her very much. For years after my father died he sent my mother a personal letter on the anniversary of his death.

Many people now acknowledge that without your husband's work and popularity in France, Britain might never have joined the community. Do you think he would have been saddened by the current wrangles?

Yes. I'm glad he's thought to have made a difference; I certainly think he did. Our version of Europe was formed during the early crusading days, and although you can never speak for people who are dead, I expect he would be saddened by the present misconception of what Europe is meant to be.

You must have had mixed feelings about your husband's appointment to the governorship of Rhodesia. Did you ever consider not accompanying him?

Oh no. In fact, I made it a condition that if he accepted it, I should go with him.

I wasn't going to be left behind. I didn't know what I was going into, but I certainly wasn't going to let him go alone.

Many people believe that there could not have been elections without bloodshed in Rhodesia had you not been such a brilliant husband and wife team. You must feel proud of that achievement.

I feel very proud of Christopher's part.

But you played an important part.

No, I was just there. The fact that there wasn't a complete shambles and break-down was very largely thanks to Christopher and the brilliant team from the Foreign Office and the Commonwealth Monitoring Force. It was also enormously important that he was able to forge a relationship with Robert Mugabe. In the beginning their meetings were completely confrontational, and yet they became friends. I always thought it was a wonderful recognition of this when Robert and Sally Mugabe flew from Zimbabwe for Christopher's funeral in our village church.

In 1980 you and your husband were both honoured in Mrs Thatcher's list, such a joint honour without precedent. Was that an especially proud moment?

Yes, I was staggered; it was very moving, very exciting for us. That was an extraordinary time, those winter months in Africa.

The following year Christopher Soames was dropped from Mrs Thatcher's Cabinet, having been widely blamed for the disruptive strikes in the public services and for yielding to the unions. Do you think that was fair, or was he made a scapegoat?

The civil servant strike was probably the breaking point, because he had advised Mrs Thatcher that certain terms should be met, and she ignored his advice. Then she dismissed him from the Cabinet, which she had every right to do, but without giving that as an exact reason. Two months later the strike was settled on exactly the same terms. I think he was made a scapegoat, but truthfully I never think of it. After all they were very dissimilar in outlook – he was one of the wets – and they weren't easy colleagues.

It is five years since your husband died … has time 'healed you of a grievous wound'?

I've been very lucky. I have my children and I've been very busy. The acute pain diminishes, luckily, but the sense of loss is there forever; how can it not be, if one's been very happy with somebody? It's something that's gone for good.

When you were appointed in 1989 to chair the board of the National Theatre it was rumoured that you were Mrs Thatcher's revenge. What was the truth behind that appointment?

It was the most rum appointment that there ever was. I was simply staggered to be offered the job. But I've just been reappointed for another three years so I feel that perhaps I have lived down my reputation for being Mrs Thatcher's revenge. They thought I was being sent by a Tory government to sort out pinkos on the left bank, though naturally they were too polite to voice that opinion to me, but I have to say there was never at the time of my appointment any suggestion that that would be my role, and if there had been I wouldn't have taken the job. I don't know why I was appointed. Richard Luce said he just thought it would be a good idea, and nobody was more astonished than I was. It's simply thrilling for me to have entered a marvellous new world, to work with talented, gifted people, and I've learnt such a lot.

Out of all the Churchill children, you alone managed to keep your marriage intact. To what do you attribute that?

Luck. And I married a very nice man. I find your question so terribly difficult – I was dreading being asked that. Why does one marriage succeed and another fail? I don't really know. I think we were both terribly lucky in finding each other, and we both tried very hard. A lot of commitment went into our marriage, but in the end it was just blessed good fortune.

Your elder brother and sisters had a far less settled early life than you. Do you think they paid for that with their marriages perhaps?

Who can tell? I really can't go into all that, because the answer is, I just really don't know. I don't think they had a bad childhood; they were very close to my parents when they were small, and it was only later that rifts and difficulties appeared, but even so, the door was never shut; it remained always open.

Your parents were obviously saddened by the marital problems of their children – 'they grieved over the shipwrecks', as you put in the book. Did they hold themselves in part responsible, do you think?

I don't know. I never heard them say so. I often knew them to be sad about it and try in so far as they were able to be a unifying force. In any case it isn't always the result of difficulties in childhood. Two of my own children's marriages have failed, and yet they were brought up in a united family, having the same home, the same childhood influences. It's very hard to identify the root causes. The expectations that people have of marriage can be unreal and the climate we live in is not conducive to keeping a rocky show going. Sometimes people don't try hard enough, or long enough. My parents had quite a number of disagreements and rows, and they lived through very difficult times. They weren't always well-off in a marital sense, but they loved each other very much, and they also had a great commitment to the marriage, and I think that's important above and beyond the commitment to yourself.

You suggest your mother was more comprehending than your father of the difficulties which beset unhappy relationships. You describe her as gentle and fair minded. Did you try and emulate her example when your own daughters' marriages foundered?

I hope I did. But no two generations meet the same problems in the same way, and no two problems are identical.

You don't have much sympathy with the view – most current in American feminist circles – that your mother was eclipsed by your father, still less I suspect with the view that you were to some extent eclipsed by your husband ... but isn't there a degree of truth in it, all the same?

I don't feel in the least about myself. My life was tremendously widened and enriched by sharing in Christopher's. The idea that a life is necessarily wasted because it is to a large extent devoted to promoting a husband's career is something I don't understand. I'm always amazed when people say to me that my mother's life was eclipsed. It would never have occurred to her that she had been deprived, though of course it was a different generation. I certainly never felt eclipsed; I felt enhanced.

You write of your parents' relationship. 'She was scabbard to his sword, and she kept it shining.' Do you think that sort of commitment still has a modern application, or is it hopelessly outmoded?

I think it's a little sad that husband and wife enterprises aren't any longer thought to be particularly admirable. I'm in rather a muddle about this because I do want women to have careers, yet at the same time I recognise that it is quite difficult for women to have careers and to run families. I sometimes think that women have found liberation but haven't quite found out how to manage it.

You have said many times: 'I have lived with clever, gifted people all my life', which rather ignores your own special gifts. Is this what is known as British modesty, or is there some deep-seated need to make light of your talents?

I have enjoyed the company of clever, gifted people, and of course perhaps something rubs off on one. I don't at all feel unfulfilled, or that I ought to have had a bigger role at all. I think I have been very fortunate in what has come my way. I never meant to write a book, for example, but once I started I rather warmed to the task. Although I've lived all my life with political people, I'm not in myself a political animal. There was never a point in my life when for more than five minutes I considered the idea of going into politics on my own.

I imagine you found it a very emotional experience to write your mother's biography – that is certainly something which comes through in the writing.

I said in my preface that it was quite impossible for me to write completely dispassionately or in an unpartisan way, but I tried to be fair, to stand back from it as much as I could. Inevitably, however, in writing about your own family, you do lose objectivity, but you also have knowledge that other people don't have and a sensitivity that outsiders couldn't have.

I suppose you discovered many things about your mother that you were barely conscious of during your childhood and young adulthood. Did you also discover things about yourself?

More about my mother. I tried to efface myself as much as possible. When I started to write I hadn't really understood about her very difficult early life about which she told me a great deal when she knew I was serious about the book. I also discovered that Mama lacked the capacity for happiness. By that I am referring to something beyond the circumstances in her life because I would never suggest that she and my father were not happy together. In fact, I find it very difficult to understand the hurtful things that have been written recently, that it wasn't a happy marriage, for example, and that my mother was enormously difficult. She could be difficult, but it isn't only easy people who are loveable. She was someone who felt things very deeply and she was a rather lonely person.

Did you discover things that disappointed you?

No. I found things that explained certain other things which I hadn't understood before. If I ever revise the book I'll write some parts a little differently, particularly those concerning the period in childhood when you don't think about your parents as having lives of their own; it's later that you see it.

In the love and devotion between your parents which spanned over half a century, there seem to have been only two ripples … one when your father wrote to Clementine saying that she absolutely had no need to be jealous, we know not of whom; the other when your mother at the age of fifty fell in love with Terence Philip. I had the impression that you tried to play down the possible significance of this attachment saying these five months had 'the unreality of a dream'. Did you perhaps feel some conflict at that point between your role as daughter and biographer?

By that time I was old enough to want to understand, and I wrote what I believe to be the truth about that relationship. I truly believe it had the air of unreality about it; it was a holiday romance, and she came back to base. She certainly didn't seek it, and he for his part was, I believe, quite lukewarm. How much do you tell your children about a relationship you have had with a man who isn't your father? I asked her 'Mama, were you ever in love with him?' and she said, 'Well, I was rather in love with him, for a time, and he wanted me to be.' But it wasn't a commitment, it wasn't planned and plotted, by which I mean she didn't go on the cruise to meet Terence Philip. But when she came back she brought a little dove with her; it lived for two or three years with us and when it died it was buried under the sundial in the garden at Chartwell, and round the base my mother had engraved the words: 'It does not do to wander too far from sober men, but there's an island yonder. I think of it again'

Is infidelity always damaging in marriage, do you think, or can some marriages rise above it, even benefit from it?

I'm sure marriages can rise above it, and I'm very sorry whenever I see that lack of fidelity has caused a marriage to crash to the ground. Fidelity seems to me to be a very important ingredient in marriage; it's part of the commitment, but equally I think it's in certain people not to be able to be faithful, and one must hope then that they are married to partners who can sustain that. For my own part I would have hoped not to know about it; and if I had, I would have hoped to keep it in proportion.

On the issue of Edward VIII and Mrs Simpson, your father – unwisely as it turned out – publicly supported the idea of Mrs Simpson as queen consort. Your mother was shrewder, and predicted the political fall-out. Was your father simply being naïve, do you think, or did the marriage appeal to his romantic side?

He primarily felt devotion and loyalty to Edward VIII, and felt that he was being cornered. I'm sure that he deplored his wanting to marry a divorced woman, but he so much wanted to keep the king on the throne that he did search for possible ways round the difficulty. I even remember hearing morganatic marriage talked about, which has no part in our constitution at all. Because of his loyalty to the king he didn't appreciate how much public opinion was against this situation, and of course the dominions all came in strongly against it. My father underestimated that, but my mother never did. I remember they had awful disagreements over this, and my mother was very bitter because she felt that my father's views in opposition about standing up to Germany were just beginning to be accepted by a lot of people, and suddenly this issue made it seem as if he were deliberately setting out to spike the prime minister's guns, which wasn't true at all. It was a really good example of my mother being shrewder than my father, but my father's loyalty was deeply engaged, as was his sense of romance. But there was a very moving coda to the story. My parents were at the coronation of King George VI and Queen Elizabeth, and as Queen Elizabeth, now the Queen Mother, was being crowned in her own separate ceremony, my father turned to my mother and said, 'You were quite right, Clemmie, the other one would never have done.' The beauty of the service had brought home to him what the consort of the sovereign really means.

How did he view the exile of the Windsors?

He always remained on friendly terms with them, although he had quite a difficult time during the war with the Duke of Windsor who kept making unsuitable demands; trivial requests would arrive at a moment when my father was grappling with the aftermath of Dunkirk or something, and it was by no means easy to deal with them; but he always remained his friend.

As we all know, Churchill took an instant loathing to the eightieth-birthday portrait of him by Graham Sutherland, feeling that he had been betrayed by the artist. Do you feel any sense of betrayal that you were not told of the painting's destruction till after your father's death?

That was an instance when I saw a side of my mother that did quite astonish me. She used to tell me a lot, and she simply didn't mention this. Of course, I regret that she destroyed it, but I don't believe all the claptrap that she didn't have the right to. It's all a very unhappy story. Christopher and I and Mama were on our way to Jamaica for a holiday to help my mother recover from my father's death. We were on board either the *Queen Mary* or the *Queen Elizabeth*, in the drawing room, and I can remember to this day how I nearly slid off my chair when Mama suddenly cleared her throat and said, 'Oh by the way, I think I probably ought to tell you and Christopher that I had that dreadful portrait of your father destroyed.'

You must have felt a sense of discomfort at the very least when you were forced to lie about the fate of the Sutherland portrait while your mother was alive. You say it was the correct decision – what exactly lay behind the decision not to reveal the truth till your mother's death?

We all took the view that Mama didn't realise the hornets' nest it would stir up. She was a most courageous woman, but she was quite old then, and we thought that she didn't appreciate the awful reaction it would cause in the artistic world. Christopher and I tried to tell her how strongly people would feel about it, and we begged her not to say anything. She never mentioned it again. I like to think that I'm a truthful person basically, but I did for twelve years lie through my teeth when asked about it. People were always trying to get hold of it to stretch the canvas, or clean its face, or put it on exhibition or something. It was awful. But I would do the same again.

You write very movingly of your sister Diana's suicide, saying that your parents were spared the extreme shock and grief, due to what you call 'the dulling of sensibilities' which accompanies old age. You were not spared the same extremes, I imagine. How did you come to terms with it yourself?

Suicide is such a cruel thing, because it leaves a terrible legacy that people have to live with, of questioning, of self-doubt. And I agonised for her children. It was a very sad time, and one of the worst things I've ever had to do in my life was to tell my mother and father about it. My mother was ill in hospital and she was rather sedated at the time. I remember walking all the way back from the Westminster Hospital to Hyde Park Gate, trying to think how I could tell my father. I also had to tell Sarah who was in Spain. She adored Diana and was very close to her. I remember having to shriek down a bad telephone, but there you are. Diana was a marvellous person and it was a great tragedy, but worse for her children, awful for her children. I hadn't always been close to Diana, but I was growing closer; I had always been, even as a middle-aged woman, her much younger sister, and I am afraid in her eyes I was rather 'teacher's pet' – funnily enough these attitudes sometimes last into adulthood. But we were just really beginning to overcome that, and then this awful thing. She had a very unhappy life, yet my father wrote such beautiful things about her when she was born. She was such a wanted child, and much loved by both my parents, a golden child right into her teens.

Your brother Randolph died a sad and bitter man. You write most poignantly: 'As always in sorrow Clementine had little to say.' What do you imagine her thoughts to have been?

Only when I was writing my mother's life did it hit home that she had buried all but two of her five children. It's a bitter thing for a mother. She didn't have a happy relationship with Randolph, and though she always tried to be helpful and loyal, the misunderstandings were profound. And then when somebody dies, you have to wait for eternity to put them right. My mother wasn't a self-pitying woman, but she felt it all very deeply and would love to have had a marvellous relationship with both Randolph and Diana. I hate talking about these family relations, and I certainly don't do so in any spirit of judgement. But my mother was a thinking woman, not an insensitive one, and I'm sure she felt very deep regret and grief.

You must sometimes have had the feeling, particularly when your father died, that he somehow belonged as much to the British people as to your own family. Did that help ease the loss, or did it sharpen it in poignancy?

When my father died it was a great loss, but also for him it was such a release. Life had become a burden, and it would have been a selfish person who would have wanted him to linger after all he had done in life. It was time, it was time. It's quite a different sort of sadness from that which you feel when somebody hasn't run their course. He was ill for a fortnight, and after ten days it was known publicly that he was ill, and from that moment onwards you really felt that the whole world was there at his bedside. I can only say it was the most extraordinary feeling. The funeral I shall remember always.

You have sometimes joked that you feel like the last of the Mohicans. Am I right in thinking a certain sorrow infuses the jocularity?

Yes. One's alone in the little shelf of one's generation. I miss Sarah particularly; she was the closest to me, and when she died, it was awful. We were great friends, and she was always my heroine. She had unhappy times in her life but she was a marvellous person, and we were very close in the months before her death. I miss her very much. But anybody who lives beyond seventy or so is in the foothills of old age, and you can't arrive there without suffering anything. I think I've been so fortunate because I was loved by my parents, I was loved by my husband, and I am loved by my children. My father once wrote: 'You must accept life with all its contrasts, the good and the bad, the dark and the bright.' For me the death of my husband was and is a terrible loss, but I had happiness in great measure and I consider myself enormously blessed that life has brought enrichment beyond anything I could have hoped for or deserved or expected.

LORD SOPER

Donald Oliver Soper was born in 1903 in Wandsworth, London of strict Methodist parents. He read history at Cambridge and took his PhD at the London School of Economics. As a Methodist minister he was superintendent of the West London Mission from 1936 to 1978 and was widely known for his open-air speaking on London's Tower Hill and at Speaker's Corner. He wrote many books on Christianity and social questions, particularly on international issues from a pacifist angle. He was an active member of the Campaign for Nuclear Disarmament, chairman of Shelter from 1974 to 1978, and was president of the League Against Cruel Sports. He was created a life peer in 1965, taking the Labour whip, and died aged ninety-five, in 1998.

If I were to ask you for a profession of religious faith, what would it include? And perhaps more interestingly, what would it exclude?

I am professing Christian in the sense that for me Jesus Christ is the centre of my thinking and the dynamic power for the kind of life I want to live. I find in the Christian faith centred upon Jesus the expression of that which I find inarticulate in myself. Christianity for me is therefore the endeavour to copy and fulfil in my life those elements of truth and goodness which I have found in Jesus Christ, and in the Christian church. This does not by any means exclude a devotion to the literature of Christianity but it's certainly not the same thing as an attitude of acceptance of the word of God, so to speak, because the word of God comes to us only through the very imperfect media of human beings. I'm therefore not a sabbatarian and I'm certainly not fundamentalist in the sense that I regard the Bible as the final authority. The final authority is a spiritual concept which is fragile but very real.

How orthodox do you think your religious views are? Do you think orthodoxy matters all that much?

I don't think that orthodoxy matters until you put it in its true context. Orthodoxy for the primitive church was a very important element in the continuing story of Christianity. If, however, we take orthodoxy in the sense of the various commitments in theological terms that the Christian Church has made from time to time, I find some of them disturbing, some of them impossible, and most of them fundamentally irrelevant.

Isn't there a case for saying that very liberal clergymen give scandal to the faithful? There appear, for example, to be clergymen who don't believe in God and yet they are supposed to have the fullness of the faith. You appear to think that God is a vindictive old man and to deny the divinity of Christ. Is there anything left besides a sort of kindly rationalism?

I do not deny the existence of God and I do not deny the divinity of Jesus, but I am conscious of the fragile nature of what is called the vocabulary of Christian thinking. Many of the greatest truths of the Christian faith go far beyond our capacity to put them into precise words; God is altogether too mighty and too profound. The very word conveys, or should convey, profundities which are better expressed in Pascal than in a great deal of the theological documents which I'm invited to read and subscribe to. With regard to Jesus, I have always believed that if you can be sure of his humanity, his divinity will look after itself. But if you start with some concept of divinity you may never get down to the basic reality of his common humanity with us. It is for me a fundamental fact that if Jesus is divine, it may be impossible for me to follow in his steps, but if he is circumscribed within the humanities that I have to put up with, then I can look up to him as leader as well as lord.

But do you still believe that God is a vindictive old man?

Of course I don't. I believe that God is a word we use to describe all kinds of personal attitudes which have nothing to do with the ultimate truth whatsoever. I have never tried to define God because I believe a definition is an impossibility. It's only when I find God in terms which I can understand, that is to say in the life of Jesus, that the reality of God comes home to me. Otherwise God is the ultimately mysterious entity. Pascal's final argument for God's existence was that there has to be a reason for there being anything at all, and I'm content with that. I have a very imperfect piece of machinery with which to make sense of the life all around me, but what I can do is see in a human person those qualities and elements in the nature of God which I think are real.

If your views are heterodox, what is it exactly that you preach? It can hardly be 'Christ crucified' in the traditional evangelical mode.

745

You're asking a question which depends on what we mean by evangelism. I do not believe that evangelism is the proclamation of some kind of completely faultless doctrine and offer of salvation. And therefore for me heterodoxy is the necessary care that I have to take to realise that everything that does come to me from God or through Jesus Christ comes through the very imperfect channel of human life. Jesus was not faultless but he was divine in the sense that he made a complete acceptance to God instead of what for everybody else is a partial and imperfect one.

There has been a good deal of controversy in recent years about the relationship between religion and politics. Mrs Thatcher's effort to convert the General Assembly to capitalism was one example. But should they not in some sense be distinct spheres? After all Christ said: 'My kingdom is not of this world.'

But Jesus also said: 'Seek ye first the kingdom of God and its righteousness', which is very much in this world. His acceptance of leadership when he entered Jerusalem was a plain acceptance of the fact that for him the gospel was the good news of the fulfilment of God's purposes in so far as they can be fulfilled on this planet and in human affairs. For me the distinction between piety and politics is a very imperfect one. I am quite sure – and this comes from my experience of being a parson for so many years – that in ninety-nine cases out of every hundred our personal belief has a deep and clear relationship to our economic and political environment. And therefore the kingdom of God is far more important than the seeking of some personal identity when I die. The Christian Church time and time again has not been prepared to face the pacifism that is the essence of the teaching of Jesus, with the result that Christian propagandists have very largely concerned themselves with private piety, which is a very imperfect representation of what you can read in the Sermon on the Mount.

You once described your socialism as a logical consequence of your religious faith. Has your faith in socialism ever been shaken – Maxwell was a socialist after all. Socialist rhetoric can surely sound as hollow as the capitalist sort, in that they both seem to be endemically self-serving.

The sting is in the tail. Let me deal with the substance before I get to the tail. I have very frequently lost my faith in socialists, but I can say, without undue pride, that I have never lost my faith in socialism. It's not been tried and found wanting; it's been found difficult and not tried. So much of what passes for socialism today is in fact an acceptance of compromises which I feel are unworthy, and though I don't pretend to be looking for a martyr's crown, I'm quite sure that we haven't been prepared to pay the price for the socialism we've advocated. In that sense, the programme of our Christian faith increasingly has to be knitted together with the economic and political structure of society. I have never doubted that the second strongest thing in the universe is sin. That is to say, it doesn't surprise me when I find people not living up to the standards they profess, or not accepting the consequences of what they profess. That applies to me as much as to everyone else. It is a constant struggle. I wish I knew more about Maxwell – for one reason. I've been a prison chaplain and a practising parson, which has given me an increased and deepened sense that if you get to the bottom of things you'll find that people are better than their practice.

Do you ever think the problem might be original sin?

This is the ultimate question which I feel it's impossible to answer, but if I do get to heaven by a circuitous route, as I suppose is possible, then I want to ask God why he didn't give us a bit more information as to where original sin comes from. It is a problem, and in some cases it's a dilemma, because in the inscrutable wisdom of God we've got to find a place for the process of evolution in thinking and practice which is the background out of which we can think of ourselves as better than we were, or think of ourselves as striving for an ideal.

But are you yourself certain of going to heaven?

I am certain that I fulfil certain conditions down here, heaven will be attainable and in the infinite mercy of God I think there's a chance of forgiveness on the other side. I don't claim to know much about it, however, and I'm a bit suspicious of those who seem to know more about heaven than they do about their next-door neighbours. 'in my Father's house,' said Jesus, 'there are many mansions; if it were not so I would have told you.' What I think Jesus was saying was, don't clutter up your mind with these impossible questions about the next world but believe that there is a continuity between this world and the next in which there is the same love and the same purpose and the same ultimate end.

You once said: 'I believe the principles of Toryism, enlightened self-interest, are incompatible with Christianity.'

I have never dared to say you cannot be a Christian and a Tory.

Do you nevertheless doubt that Tories can in practice be fully-fledged Christians?

I'm quite sure they can't. One can't be a fully-fledged Christian anyhow, but I think Tories are further off that attainment than other people. I get tired of denouncing other people as being unchristian, but what I'm prepared to say is this: the structure of Toryism – enlightened self-interest, market values and the concentration upon the individual – is not something that belongs to the Christian faith. Enlightened self-interest is in fact a rather kindly word for selfishness. Our involvement in the community is the essence of the Christian faith; individualistic emphasis in my judgement, are to be deprecated. The reason I have never been prepared to say that you can't be a Tory and a Christian is that it depends very much on one's definition of the terms, but I am absolutely certain that Toryism in principle is a contradiction of the Christian concept.

You reject the capitalist ethic totally. Yet you obviously believe very much in the practical application of Christianity, i.e. that the church should have relevance to modern life. Is it not unrealistic to expect to have an impact on the country at large without embracing some aspects of capitalism?

It all depends on what you mean by capitalism. I can accept the machinery of capitalism in some aspects of corporate living; I cannot accept the principle of capitalism as a worthy method whereby we conduct our public affairs. That could be regarded by some people as a bit specious, but you're asking a very difficult question. I do not believe that the capitalist is totally bereft of moral principal; it would be impudent and stupid of me to say so. One has to draw a distinction which is not easy to draw between capitalism as a working programme and capitalism as an ultimate principle. I totally reject the second but I think there are necessary ways in which in this very imperfect world we have to make use of the imperfect machinery until we can find a substitute for it.

Do you think we'll ever find a substitute for it?

Not on this planet, no. That's why I believe in eternal life.

Why is it so important for you to adhere to Methodism, to serve under the banner of Methodism, when you clearly are at odds with at least some of the Methodist tenets and are not wholly approving of its founder John Wesley?

No one who took the precaution of reading John Wesley's life could totally approve of him. At the same time, he was a dynamic leader, and since I was brought up within the framework of Methodism I see no reason to discard my background (even if I could). It doesn't seem to me to be very important which particular club you play for, providing you play the right game. In that regard there is a first-class argument for multiplicity of churches with a common faith. One reason I've taken to the open air for the last sixty years is that John Wesley established the importance of open-air preaching, and in that respect I'm his dutiful son.

You have said that all statements to the effect that Jesus was the son of God are inexact, and that if only people could accept the humanity of Jesus the divinity would look after itself. This is something which doubters and agnostics would have no difficulty with, and certain humanists have always emphasised the humanity of Jesus, but the idea seems rather strange coming from a man of God like yourself. In a different century you might have been burnt at the stake for saying such things.

I quite agree. You've only to read your history book to realise how tyrannical has been the attitude of official Christianity time and time again. Dostoevsky's *The Brothers Karamazov* is a perfect example of the way in which the official church has betrayed the gospel in the interests of the power which it was desirous of maintaining. Whenever there is an attempt to reconcile the kingdom of God with any particular regime, be it imperialism, or colonialism, or the capitalism of today, it simply doesn't work.

There was a proposal some years ago that you should be ordained as a priest in the Church of England. That was abandoned in the face of expected Anglican hostility. From your point of view could such a step have been anything other than a rather desperate attempt at Church unity, and given the divergence of beliefs, would this not have rendered the appointment purely symbolic?

The answer is conditioned by the fact that I didn't promote the enquiry. It was initiated by others, and I saw no reason to reject it in the light of what I believe to be the imperative need for church unity. I found a better way of expressing it later on in conversations we had with the Anglicans, but there was no reason why the Methodists and the Anglicans shouldn't come together in one church. After all, John Wesley was an ordained Anglican priest. It is imperative to avoid the most damaging of all criticisms of the church, that we can't make up our own minds as to what we commonly believe and that we are separated at the point where the very concept of Christianity means unity. For me this is a desperate situation.

But do you think unity with the Catholic Church will ever be possible?

As things are at the moment, if unity means signing along the dotted line, that is out of the question. The hope of unity rests upon the ability of the Roman Catholic

749

Church to abandon some of its cherished attitudes, and although there is some evidence of that already it is highly unlikely in my time. I'm not being cynical when I say that unity can be more realistically conceived within the framework of the non-Catholic churches, there being a certain intransigence that is part of the absolutist concept of Rome. It is not nearly as rigid as it was, but until they change their attitude on, for example, the ordination of women priests, there's not much hope of progress. Female menstruation has been seen by the church as the time when a woman is impure, and you cannot have an impure priest. This is absolute rubbish, of course, and on this, as on many sexual matters, the church is back in the middle ages.

From time to time you have spoken of your allegiance to the catholic church. I know that you use a small 'c' and that the word means universal, but in view of the fact that Methodists do not approve of various doctrines about the Virgin, about the intercession of saints or about the real presence in the Eucharist, how is a universal church possible?

It is possible if the unity does not depend on a vocabulary which is assumed to be infallible. I'm not interested in the vocabulary of orthodoxy. With regard to the Virgin birth, for example, Mark didn't know anything about it, nor did Paul, nor the early Church, or the primitive Church. Jesus didn't know anything about it either. It seems to me to be a waste of time to ascribe to Jesus some kind of authority and divinity which is totally unnecessary. That is the way in which I would approach these problems.

Have you never felt tempted to move up to the high church, to graduate from the church hall to the church proper?

Yes. I am high chapel, if not high church; that is to say I have a firm belief that eucharistic worship is at the heart of the Christian practice of the faith. I should not feel able to go to Hyde Park on Sunday afternoon if I didn't receive the bread and wine on Sunday morning. Someone once said to me, 'I go to mass because it is the whole of Christianity in twenty-five minutes', and there's a very great deal of truth in that. Of course, reality is far deeper than thought, far more than that which can be encapsulated within the framework of a doctrine. But I can honestly say that when I receive the bread and partake of the wine, that is a symbolic acceptance of my belief in the reality and the presence of Christ; unworthy as I am to receive it, I believe it to be the evangelical offer of salvation.

Can the Methodist Church or for that matter the Church of England survive?

They have already survived crises which would have destroyed other more rigid churches. There is an adaptability within the Anglican Church of which I very much approve. One thing I am certain of: The City of God remaineth and so long as we are in that city, there is a permanence which can defy the various vicissitudes and difficulties.

You had a crisis of faith when you were at Cambridge. Looking back, do you think the doubts presented a serious challenge in your life or were they merely a necessary path to the further consolidation of your faith?

Both. The doubts were very considerable, serious and hurtful. I had grown up within the close framework of a Methodist tradition and when I went to Cambridge I was suddenly exposed. A friend gave me something to read about communism or rationalism, and it opened up a new world which was very disturbing. But it didn't last very long and the decisive factor was that the requirement of faith was a necessary filling of a gap which couldn't be filled elsewhere.

Your faith, and specifically your Methodism, seems to be wholly a product of your parentage and background and upbringing. It was not something you came to by yourself or stumbled on by chance. In other words, it is very much an accident of birth. If you had been born a Catholic or a Moslem you might have embarked on a very different religious and moral crusade. Does that ever worry you?

It perplexes me in the sense that I can't put myself in a position of an entirely different environment. What I can say is that the changeover from the narrow Methodism of my childhood to the socialist Christianity which I began to imbibe as a student was as fundamental a change as would have happened if I had started off as a Moslem and ended up as a Catholic. It was a radical and absolute difference.

Do you think that doubt is a necessary forerunner to the fullest kinds of faith?

Of course. You cannot believe unless you resolve doubt. Doubt is the precondition of questioning and enquiring. I have often been asked why I go to Tower Hill, why I go to Hyde Park on Sunday afternoon. It is because I believe in the fellowship of controversy. It is the only way in which we can deal with questions which otherwise accumulate in our minds or our make-up and are never resolved. There's no such thing as neutrality, and doubt is the first way in which you deal with that neutral presentation of brute fact.

The logic of your faith, besides leading you to socialism, also led you to pacifism. Doesn't the refusal to defend the right by arms if need be necessarily imply subjection to those who are prepared to use arms?

I believe we have yet to discover the power of non-violent resistance and indeed the power of self-sacrificing love. This is the only meaning I see of the Cross as distinct from the gun. The Cross of Jesus was his reliance upon the power of non-violent love, even when Pontius Pilate was perplexed by it, the disciples frustrated by it, and a great many ordinary people felt that Jesus was wasting his time and was no more than a lovable failure. Nobody can tell me that the way of non-violent love would not succeed, because as yet it hasn't been tried. The essence of the Christian faith today lies in finding an alternative force to the force of guns, and unless we find it I think that the prospect of the termination of this human race is as likely as that of the creatures that have disappeared already on this planet because they couldn't adapt themselves to the paramount need of living. We are in a very desperate position and in this instance I'm by no means a cheery optimist. I believe that there is a real prospect that we shall opt out of this life by the use of an ever-increasing destructive force. The emergence of the nuclear age has emphasised this as nothing previously could have done.

Is it not the case that pacifists trade on others' willingness to sacrifice themselves for the public good? Pacifists surely have a quiet conscience, but doesn't someone else just as surely pay the price?

I don't have a quiet conscience. In the cadet corps when I was a boy I was a bayonet-fighting instructor and loved it. I agree with you that if you regard pacifism as an easy option, it's discreditable, but I hope by the grace of God I should be prepared to pay the price of the pacifist case as soldiers pay the price of going to war.

Whatever good may accrue from pacifism in the long term, is it not true that in the short-term individuals will suffer terribly for those ideals – and those individuals only have a short term?

This raises a fundamental question. I don't know very much about the long term, that is to say, I believe that the essence of the faith is that by doing things which are consonant with what is right, you release into the world forces which otherwise would be damned up. I think the man who stood in front of the tank in Tiananmen Square or those who decorate tanks with flowers and engage the tank commanders in argument are opening up in a way. I have been asked what I would do if the Germans invaded Kingsway, and I said rather facetiously that we'd offer them a Methodist tea; those who haven't appreciated the cathartic effects of a Methodist tea shouldn't underrate it. Of course, this is regarded by most people as just silly nonsense, but I do believe in one sense you can create an atmosphere of non-violence which is far more dynamic than the atmosphere of combat.

But who is to defend the old, the young, the vulnerable from the bully boy who is not open to rational argument? Are they to be sacrificed to a higher ideal?

The answer is that if you attempt to save people who are violently abused by the use of violence, the sum total of violence is not diminished. It's no good telling me that you fundamentally protect people by the use of war or violence; you don't. You can provide temporary asylum for them but sooner or later that asylum turns into a fortress.

If conscience is a reliable guide to action, as you have often stated, what about those who in conscience believe that blacks are inferior or the Pope is the Antichrist ... are their conscientious objections to be respected too?

It all depends on what you mean by the word conscience. When somebody says he believes he was justified in killing, or stealing something, I don't accept that as conscientious attitude. That sort of conscience only records your condition at the moment you consult it, whereas the whole purpose of a conscience is to educate so that when the particular environment demands a response, it's an enlightened conscience which moves with the promotion of goodness and doesn't just lie fallow until it's called upon. When it's called upon in that fallow condition it isn't conscience at all; it's prejudice.

You have stated that it is more moral to risk the evil of somebody else than to apply that evil in order to prevent it. Would you really have had Britain submit to the Nazis in 1940 with all the consequences? It is hard to see how they could have been avoided without armed resistance.

The answer is if you chop up the film of life into a number of stills, you can provide yourself with insoluble problems. We could not have done anything other than what we did in 1940; but we could have done something very different in 1940 if we'd begun to do it in 1930. We very largely promoted the Hitlerism which afterwards we had to resist. I don't believe that you can at any moment, so to speak, isolate a situation; a situation is that which has developed from something that has gone before. We now have time to prevent the next war. We hadn't time in 1940 to avoid the war that happened.

It will surely seem extraordinary, perhaps even offensive to many people, that you should blame the British for the Nazi destruction of the Jews and others. You said that after we went in to defend the Jews they were massacred – they were merely persecuted before.

That is the first time I have objected to something you have quoted me as saying. I always take great care to say that I abominate the persecution of the Jews. The Christian Church should always make that humble apology since we have behaved disgracefully towards the Jews. But what I've tried to say again and again is this: that to go to the help of a persecuted people by fighting a war that meant many more of those persecuted people were in Auschwitz than if we hadn't fought a war. As a matter of fact, war exacerbates the problem you go to try and solve. Let no one accuse me of saying the Jews were getting on fairly well under Hitler; they weren't, they were in a condition of persecution which was an abomination, but the Auschwitz camps were the result of the war in the sense that Hitler was then able to isolate the problem from his own people.

The nuclear threat is certainly very real but it's difficult to understand how matters would improve by having the Western democracies surrender their weapons while leaving others in the hands of terrorists or fanatics.

The risk of peace-making is of course tremendous but we are so accustomed to accepting the risks of war-making as to be the victims of very imperfect thinking. To me and to an increasing number of people, the emergence of a new situation in Europe demands the recognition that change is by no means limited to changes in the political field of power. There are radical changes now taking place in the culture of modern generations, and I take great comfort in watching the way in which new ideas are laying hold of communities who were previously immune from them. This isn't a complete answer, and I hope you don't think it's an evasion of the answer, but it's about time we realised that the traditional concepts of dealing with the evils in the community manifestly fail when they are linked to the requirements of violence.

But the question is, really, that if you were a man of power, would you do away with nuclear weapons at this point in time knowing that others who are much more fanatical than you are, less democratic than you are, were retaining their weapons.

Yes. If I had the power then I should have been elected, and therefore there would have been behind my decision a community which was committed to it.

So you mean others would take the risk with you?

They would take the risk with me, and if that risk were generated within a community I believe it would spread like wildfire. The resistance to the communist regimes, which is the most remarkable thing to have happened in my life time, has come about because there has been a community which has taken a new road. I believe that is the hope of our survival.

You became a peer in 1965 and made the immortal remark that the House of Lords reaffirmed your belief in life after death. Is your seat in the House of Lords one which you occupy easily and happily, or are you ill at ease with the power and privilege which undoubtedly characterises the Lords?

In some ways the House of Lords can be a very useful instrument in the propagation of ideas which otherwise wouldn't see the light of day. I've had the opportunity of expressing my views on pacifism in the House of Lords and they've treated me with kindness. There is a value in the House of Lords, which is that it can be the occasion of an enquiry into matters which can take place one afternoon and can be reported in Hansard the next day. It isn't the same as a general inquiry but it is a way of fertilising the intelligence of the other House on matters about which they may be less informed than they should be.

Although you sit in the labour benches, does it never seem to you as if you're supporting an institution which runs counter to the whole socialist ethic?

I have my temptations as of course many people do, but I must be very careful not to assume a degree of piety with which I can look down on these sinners as if they're scoundrels. I have much to be thankful, for in the steadfastness and the attitude of socialists whom I've loved and revered and who have been an example and an inspiration to me, and I'm not prepared to be cynical even if you wanted me to be. But I would say this: that sooner or later the House of Lords should be abolished. In the meantime I'm prepared to make use of instruments which sooner or later will be out of date.

On one occasion you spoke in the Lords about the way opposition to restricting homosexual propaganda had the whiff of fascism about it. Do you actually approve of sodomy?

Of course I don't. What I do approve of is the distinction between the condition of homosexuality for which you are not responsible, and the practice of homosexuality which can be bad. There is a prime case for saying that homosexuality is no more within the moral code than the colour of your hair or the size of your nose; what matters is what you do with it. The desecration of sex for the mere flippancy of enjoyment is one of the most dangerous and difficult of all issues, and at the same time I believe it's wrong. The prostitution of the body either in heterosexual or homosexual practice is to be regarded as a sin.

But where do you stand on the question of homosexuality? If we follow the argument that it is a natural human practice, because human beings do it, will we not logically have to count everything that human beings do as natural ... murder, rape, slander, etc., etc.?

The distinction between the satisfaction of an appetite and the refusal to regard that satisfaction as right or wrong is a question which has to be faced. There are handicaps to the perfection of life. If, for example, you lose a leg or an eye, these are conditions which have to be accepted because they cannot be altered. In this sense one has to have profound sympathy for the homosexual because he is condemned to a world in which what is the creative and natural function of sex is to some extent changed by the fact that he is not heterosexual. In my judgement that involves a discipline which he is required to exercise which other people don't have to exercise. Far from blaming the homosexual who indulges in sodomy, I believe we have to have a great deal of sympathy with him; to condemn the thing he does but to recognise that he has a much more difficult way of dealing with himself than those who are heterosexual. That's the sympathy. I do not believe it is impossible for a future generation to find the answer to what is now the insuperable problem of how a homosexual changes into a heterosexual if he wants to. There are of course many relationships between homosexuals which are entirely right. Indeed, in the lesbian field I can think of many women in the church who have been denied the opportunity of marriage or have lost their loved ones and who with other women have formed relationships which are of benefit to society. I can think of dozens and dozens of women who have in a very real sense loved one another but have avoided the cruder forms of sexual satisfaction. Of course, this is easier for lesbians and not possible in the same way for the homosexual male. It's a very complex issue and when I criticise the church's attitude it is because I think we have to be much more charitable and to realise that some people have enormous problems which other people don't have to face, and that those problems are ineluctable in many respects. We're in a shocking mess over this whole question, and I believe only the grace of God is sufficient to meet these otherwise intransigent issues.

What are your views about allowing homosexuals within the church to give expression to their homosexual love?

It depends what you mean by giving expression to their homosexual love. I think it would be wrong to baptise, so to speak, the perversities of physical relationships; they are to be condemned as ugly. The consummation of the sexual act between a man and his wife can be regarded as a sacrament, it's beautiful. But in this very imperfect world one has to discipline oneself against misusing one's faculties in order to provide a satisfaction which is impossible in the same sense that a married couple can find that satisfaction.

Do you believe sex is a gift from God to be enjoyed?

Yes, but to be enjoyed within the framework of a creative concept and not merely the idea of enjoyment for its own sake. It is important to remember that when, for example, it is said that the Moslem believes in that enjoyment, it results in the degradation of women. There's no doubt about that in my judgement; the woman is the instrument to provide the means of enjoyment for the man, and therefore the whole concept of the inferiority of women is part of that claim that sex is to be enjoyed.

Despite your own ardent teetotalism and belief in the monogamous purpose of marriage you are said to believe that heaven might just contain some light wines and that premarital sex might just be tolerated. What led you to this concession? Was it an attempt to take on board the reality of the times we live in or was it an unhappy recognition of falling standards of morality?

It was a further understanding of the spirit and teaching of Jesus. The evidence is increasingly obvious that Jesus had a relationship with Martha and Mary which was in part sexual. The essence of any relationship I've had with other people has always contained something of sexuality within it. The question is, at what point does the sexual behaviour pattern interfere with the creative purpose of sexual relationships? I'm a teetotaller, but not because I believe there's something necessarily wrong in the ingestion of a particular liquid. I'm a teetotaller because of the social environment of drinking which I believe inhibits a great many people from leading a good life. The same hold true of premarital sex. No one is suggesting that the couples who kiss ought to wait until they're married. We have to be a lot more healthy about this, and in my judgement it would be better, strangely enough, if we didn't think so much about it. I think there's an obsession with sex now. Sex in its right place is very important, but not too much of it. I'm eighty-nine now, so I can talk objectively about this, although I can very easily become a hypocrite unless I'm careful.

Do you still desire women at the age of eighty-nine?

Yes of course, but it's rather different. In any case I'm blessed with a marvellous wife. But I see nothing wrong in admiring a pair of good legs. Why shouldn't I?

No, I think it's a very healthy attitude, I'm not opposed to it at all. You take a very liberal view of prison reform. But is there any real evidence that one can reform prisoners in any great numbers? Should public safety not be the first consideration?

I think the prison system is basically wrong, and can never be improved to the point at which it can be acceptable in a civilised society. That raises the question of what we do with the person who misbehaves, and unless we are prepared to think about that matter honestly, we shall go on perpetrating the awful system we have at present; putting people away and forgetting about them. Very few people in my judgement are suitable for isolation.

You have suggested that prisoners should be treated well, be given holidays, and even be allowed sexual intercourse in prison. Would prison then be any deterrent? A lot of people might actually want to go to prison under these conditions ...

Whatever you do, there are likely to be people who abuse the system. But if you force me I would have to say I believe the evils of masturbation in prison to be greater than would be the dubious consequences of allowing prisoners who are married to have sexual intercourse. That on the whole would be better.

Are you totally against masturbation?

No. I think masturbation is an imperfect way of fulfilling a genuine impulse, and I'm not going to stand in judgement. It is a lack of self-discipline, but for people locked up for twenty years, I'm not going to say that masturbation is a crime or a sin.

You have practised open-air preaching for over sixty years now. It was forced on the first Methodists, but what good do you actually think it does in a television age?

It offers a fellowship of controversy, and it remains the one free forum. I've enjoyed a lot of television, but I've suffered a good deal from it. That is to say, the necessary rules that govern television programmes do impair the kind of free for all which you can enjoy in Hyde Park. Open-air preaching provides a way to develop a particular argument in a real atmosphere in which there are no artificialities as there are in television programmes.

You have always pressed the need for man to be morally superior to his circumstances. In today's world, with all the modern pressures, isn't that just too daunting a task for most people?

Yes. That is why to ask them to do it on their own is an impudence. Most people are better able to face moral problems if they find somebody else is trying to face them with them. That's the great virtue of the church, not so much the sermons preached but the comradeship of effort.

Does it ever strike you that you are in a small dwindling church in an increasingly secular society? What is the point of your mission unless it is primarily a self-fulfilling one?

I can't distinguish between a self-fulfilling ministry and a public responsibility; to me they are both sides of the same medal. I believe that we are pack animals as distinct from isolated creatures who have no desire to run with the pack; at the same time we need fellowship, a word often misused. There's nothing so dangerous as the high-rise flat, the singularity and individualism of so much of modern life. One of the few real advantages of the mediaeval village was that everybody belonged; even the village idiot was a member of society.

Do you believe ultimately that faith is a gift of God?

Yes, but then I believe that everything worthwhile is the gift of God, though not something which God hands out as presents to certain people who are entitled to receive them. Faith is the way in which you deal with questions that you ask. Faith is a leap into the dark but only in so far as you have something firm underfoot to be able to make it. You can't leap out of a bog.

If faith is a gift of God do you think it is the duty of a minister to maintain a pious silence when it comes to something in which he cannot compel himself to believe even though he may wish to?

There is great value in preachers telling their congregations what they don't know as well as what they do. The preacher who gives the impression of knowing everything is going to lose his congregation; and he isn't worthy to retain it. There is a place for ignorance as well as the assertion of truth; a place for the confession that we are all sinners, doubters. Unless the preacher is like Jesus, a man among men, and unless he recognises that there is a whole world in which we are all experimenting, I don't think he can do much good.

Do you ever consider that even the most honest, decent, and well-meaning men like yourself may be mistaken in their view of the world?

Yes. One of the great advantages of speaking in the open air is that you're soon persuaded that you're not omniscient. I have any number of doubts, but one of the values of the Christian attitude embodied in the trilogy of faith, hope and love is this; my faith can be pretty slim and my love can be pretty imperfect, but there's nothing to prevent me hoping, since hope is a matter of the will. Faith is a matter of the intellect and the disposition, and love is the gift of God, but hope is something that you and I can do if we make up our minds. If you leave your mind to make itself up it's highly unlikely to do so, but hope is that solvent which brings the various facts into a focus of opportunity.

Have you ever been wrong in the sense that you believed an idea, then changed your mind?

Oh yes, very often. For example, I was a teetotaller in the Methodist form of regarding alcohol as the devil in solution. I don't hold that view any longer. Now I believe that temperance is required as a social responsibility.

Why has it been left to people like Mary Whitehouse to speak out on obscenity and related matters, do you think?

It hasn't. There have been a great many people who have spoken out just as clearly but, by accident or achievement, they haven't had the publicity. There's a great deal of the leaven of the Christian proclamation that proceeds only to make fairly small loaves. I admire Mary Whitehouse immensely, but, if I may say so, some of us have been saying the same thing for very much longer than she has.

Do you approve of all the things she says?

Not everything. But I approve of the intention she has and the general thrust of her argument which is that there's far too much dirt in the world of the media and the practice of people. My only criticism would be that in some cases there is a danger of doing more harm than good unless you can preserve an attitude of general charity. I'm not saying she doesn't, but she is representative of some elements which are not as amenable to general understanding as others.

Now that you have reached the age of eighty-nine, are you concerned about the day of judgement?

I find it a waste of time to speculate how long I am going to last. I am more concerned with what I take with me to the next world than what my mansion in the sky or my hovel on the outskirts of the city of God will be in the next world. Most of my friends of my own generation are now dead. I'd like to see them again though I'm quite sure they've changed a good deal in the interim as probably I have. In my old age I'm beginning to learn about the virtue of living a day at a time, and believing that all things work together for good for those who love God. I hope at least that the next world will be as exciting in the sense of producing all kinds of issues and problems of which we know nothing now. I don't want to be dull ... sitting on a cloud playing a harp.

Setting modesty aside, would you consider yourself to be a saint? If not, why not?

The answer is that a saint is somebody who is on the right road with his eyes persistently fixed on the horizon of the kingdom. If that is a saint, then by the grace of God I hope to be one. But it's a sheer waste of time to accord to oneself certain categories of goodness or badness; it is much more important to aim for what by the grace of God you can be. There is nothing so boring as people who feel that they have to be everlastingly telling you how good they are and how bad you are. Piety is a word which has fallen into disrepair, because true goodness is exuberant as well as faithful, and the exuberance is a part of goodness, and if you haven't got that you're about as useful as mutton.

The last question ... have you any regrets?

An infinite number. At my age one's sense of failures in the past is an interesting and solemnising experience. You haven't much time in which to put things right, which makes me say better prayers than I used to.

FRANCIS STUART

Francis Stuart, born in 1902, is the author of over twenty novels, including *The Pillar of Cloud* (1948), *Black List, Section H* (1971) and *Redemption* (1950), which are autobiographically based. He fought with the Republicans during the Irish Civil War and he spent the Second World War years in Berlin, from where he broadcast to Ireland. In 1920 he married Maud Gonne's daughter Iseult who, like her mother, had turned down a proposal of marriage from Yeats. During the war years he lived with Roisin O'Mara, adopted daughter of General Sir Ian Hamilton, commander-in-chief at the Battle of the Dardanelles in the First World War. Hamilton was a German sympathiser and became involved with Hitler in 1936. In 1987, Francis Stuart married Finola Graham, a thirty-year-old artist. He was named an Irish Saoi (wise man) in 1996, a rare distinction in Ireland. Previous recipients of the honour include Samuel Beckett, Mary Lavin and Seán Ó Faoláin. Stuart died, aged ninety-seven, in 2000.

You are Australian by birth and Ulster Protestant by background. Did you have the feeling of being different from other people from the beginning?

I did, yes, but probably more because of a certain mystery surrounding my father, who killed himself in Australia when I was only a few weeks old. I never got to know the full circumstances, except that he had made several attempts at suicide and was in a mental clinic in Sydney when he made a final and successful attempt. This haunted and obsessed me, and I began to identify with him very much. His twin brother used to tell me how he had questioned my father, asking him if he felt lonely or persecuted, to which I understand he answered yes. But psychology was not as it is today, and that seemed a very primitive way of questioning. My mother never spoke of him, and nor did her family. I think the marriage was almost certainly unhappy. Although I thought I understood his reasons for suicide, the whole business remained mysterious.

In an article in The Observer *last year you were described as an outcast in your own country, ostracised and reviled. Would you agree with that?*

No, I wouldn't mind if it was so, but it is absolutely ridiculous. In certain circles, among cultured people, I am highly regarded. I wouldn't say I haven't encountered hostility; as you probably know, I have encountered it everywhere, and here in Ireland not least, but on the other hand it is completely untrue to say I am ostracised and reviled.

You are often described as an incorrigible romantic. Do you wear that description as a badge of honour?

Again, it's not true. I'm not a romantic, I'm a realist. The imaginative writer must make a model of reality, taking in everything. I have a great admiration for Heidegger who asked: 'Why is there anything?' We don't know a lot, but from what we do know of nature and the cosmos we might expect there to be nothing. I've always been astonished at there being anything at all, and I've written in poems that it's a miracle we're here. Our task, as I see it, is to tend that miracle of existence, experience, consciousness.

Do you think romanticism is dangerous?

As I interpret it, yes, because it's far from the real. If you make a model of all there is, as the imaginative mind must do, romanticism doesn't enter into it. Realism, yes. It's a very harsh planet on which we find ourselves.

In your autobiographical novel Black List: Section H *you write: 'Anyone whose behaviour collides with the popular faith of the time and place is automatically condemned.' As someone who has experienced widespread condemnation, do you think it has been a price worth paying for your beliefs?*

Undoubtedly so for me. I can only do my work after isolation, and it doesn't matter how I come to be in that condition of isolation. I can't imagine writing as an accepted member of society, and in so far as I write for anybody, I write for people like myself – isolated, lonely, and very close to despair at times. It's not necessary for me to have had the life I have had to experience near despair and loneliness; I would have those feelings in any case since they are conditions of living. Without being presumptuous, you very likely have them too. They're surely common to intelligent, imaginative people.

You were a Sinn Fein sympathiser in the 1920s and 1930s, and you were interned by the British. How did that come about?

I would say Republican rather than Sinn Fein. During the civil war here I was on the Republican and losing side, as I have always been. It is essential in my view to be on the losing side. I was interned for about a year, or perhaps nine months. I don't remember exactly. I've been in six different prisons, mostly abroad, but never for very long. I was never sentenced – there was nothing I could have been charged with – but I was locked up all the same.

Were conditions harsh?

Hunger was the worst. In most prisons we didn't get enough to eat, but then people on the outside were also hungry. There was overcrowding of course – at one point we had twelve to fifteen men in a cell meant for one or two. That was in Germany where I was interned by the French on the recommendation of the British. I was told that by a French intelligence officer, who said they had to do what the British told them.

What's your attitude to Sinn Fein today?

If you mean the political party, I dislike all political parties. They give themselves airs and they make not the slightest difference to our lives. Any party could be in power here, it wouldn't matter which. To my mind they are all a load of rubbish. I'm not the slightest bit interested in politics.

Your first marriage to Maud Gonne's daughter, Iseult, seems to have all the elements of pain and uncertainty associated with first love and a love that was very young ... you were only eighteen. Would you agree with that?

I would, but I should add that the marriage lasted nearly twenty years, although we had terrific rows and so on. I felt very sorry for Iseult. She was one of these innocents, if you know what I mean; she put up with me, which wasn't easy, and she also put up with her mother, who to my mind was an unpleasant woman. She suffered from both ends.

Was her mother against you?

Yes, but that was understandable. I was an unknown boy from the north, with no background, no money, nothing to recommend me. A boy of eighteen marries her daughter, whom Yeats and other people would gladly have married ... I wasn't a great catch to put it mildly.

The poet Kathleen Raine, whom I interviewed a year or two ago, talks about the purity of young love, which she describes as absolute, the sense that you can't imagine feeling this for anyone else. Do you remember that first love, the intensity of it, or has it gone completely?

It's very hard to say with hindsight. What I find is that if I write about certain memories and then try and recall them later, what I remember is what I've written about them. If I hadn't written about them I could perhaps go back to the real thing, but as it is I'm wary of many of my memories. The love we had was certainly one of great intensity, and that meant great rows and violence. We each destroyed things that the other valued. I did some sculpture in those days, and I had one of a bird which I prized very much, and Iseult took that and threw it on the floor. And I once took a pile of her dresses and poured petrol over them.

Do you regret all of that?

In one way I don't. But I have given hurt, and I do regret that and find it shocking.

In Black List *the character H is jealous of the fact that Iseult and the poet Ezra Pound have been lovers … was that something which obsessed you at the time?*

I think it did undoubtedly. Sex – sensuality is perhaps a better word – is an extraordinary driving force. And to imagine your partner in the arms of somebody else, that was part of the sensuality. I became obsessed by it.

Did the fact that Iseult had rejected Yeats' offer of marriage make for awkwardness between you and Yeats later on?

I never found it so. I got on well with him, and he was extraordinarily generous to me. He said that with some luck I would be one of our fine writers. For myself I'm not an admirer of Yeats in one way. He is of course a great poet – it would be ridiculous to say otherwise – but he's not a poet I would go to for comfort in times of stress. People thought Yeats put on a lot of airs, but he didn't. He was in fact a very lonely man who would have liked to have had close friends and didn't. Ordinary people, even intellectuals, couldn't get on with Yeats much. He had none of the normal social gifts. When we used to stay with Yeats, I'd stay awake all night racking my brains to think of some profound statement to come up with the next day. Sometimes it used to go terribly wrong.

The marriage to Iseult broke up about 1940. So many things were changing and dissolving in those days – did it perhaps seem symptomatic of the times that it should have broken up in 1940?

I suppose it did, yes, and so it was. Many more important things than my marriage broke up at that time.

Can you tell me what it was about Hitler and the Nazi movement which attracted you in the first place?

One of the things which I have always thought so unjust is the powerlessness of the poet. The creative mind shouldn't be powerless, and the only way the writer is not powerless is if he has a warlord to look up to, as Milton had Cromwell. Only then is he given that power in the world that he believes is his due. I know that to be a false belief now, but at the time I wanted a warlord to revere. If Hitler hadn't had this manic anti-Semitic obsession, there was a lot to admire in him. But another reason why I went to Germany and later even broadcast from Germany was the business of war itself, which is a terrible thing. If one side wages war because they see another, foreign regime, committing awful crimes, they should know by now that they can't possibly hope to win that war without using the same, perhaps even more horrible methods, and that was so in the last war. The Allies used similar methods in order to win it, but they went into it saying they were conducting a Christian Crusade, and to my mind that is a terrible thing. It seems to me you are polluting all moral values if you say that. They were defending Europe against a horrible regime, but they weren't conducting a Christian crusade. By claiming that they were, they were doing something very evil.

Did you ever meet Hitler?

No, but I could easily have done so because the American minister here in Ireland before the war, a man called John Cudahy, asked the Führer if he would grant me an audience. When the war broke out John left the embassy and went to Germany to work as a newspaper correspondent, for the *New York Herald Tribune*, I think. He had at least two audiences with Hitler, and on one occasion I told him about this neutral Irish writer whose books he had read and liked, and who was in Germany. Hitler apparently said to bring him along, but I never did go. I remember warning John about the dangers and telling him that the British were well aware of his meetings with the Führer and they'd be very happy to get rid of him. He rather scorned the idea, but then he went to Switzerland and within two or three days he was dead. It was reported that he'd had a heart attack or something of

Do you find it surprising that fifty years later many people have still not forgiven you for broadcasting from Germany?

Oh no, that is not surprising, that's very understandable. But I have no regrets.

Your friend Samuel Beckett joined the French resistance and received the Croix de Guerre for his work. Did you never think you might have done the same?

It was entirely convenient for the French to give a high decoration to a foreign collaborator, but I thought it was farcical.

In the afterword to the recent reissue of Redemption, *you go some way towards explaining why you spent the war in Germany, ignoring the warning from a professor at Berlin University that by doing so you would be greatly damaging your own future. You explain it in terms of certain events in history having a counterpart, and despite the fact, perhaps because of the fact, that the fight against Nazism was almost universal in the English-speaking world, you thought there was a need, perhaps even a duty, to counter that consensus. Is that a fair way of representing it, do you think?*

I don't think it's completely fair, because I have always believed that consensus is evil. A consensus of intelligent people is to my mind always wrong. I think it was Simone Weil who said if you see the scales heavily weighed down on the right side, on the moral side, put your small offering on the other side. And I believe she was right.

Do you believe in evil?

Yes I do.

Would you say that a movement, an ideology such as Nazism, could be said to embody evil, and to that extent it is our duty to resist it?

I would answer yes to the first part, that it could be said to embody evil, but that it is our duty to resist it – I wouldn't necessarily agree with that. You just have to deal with it according to the precise circumstances as they arise in your life. There is no need for a general theory.

Were the Allies right to resist Nazism in your view?

Physically in terms of arms, they were right, but they were not right to claim that they were waging a Christian crusade.

Were you ever afraid that you might actually be hanged alongside people like John Amery and William Joyce who were regarded as British traitors?

It was unlikely because I did not have a British passport. I had one in my youth when I was in the North and we were all part of Britain, but after that I had a valid Irish passport. They could have hanged me, I suppose, but it would have been such a travesty of justice.

Do you think one can be morally neutral?

You can't have a morally neutral attitude in general but in precise circumstances I think you can. In my situation in Germany it was right to be neutral.

In the afterword to Redemption *you also talk of Ireland as having 'sat out the world conflict on bacon and tea'. That would seem to contain elements of judgement and condemnation …*

I was just stating a fact. In Ireland it was called the Emergency, which is a funny way of describing the greatest war in history, and they complained about rationing. They weren't going to let the business of war interfere with their lives. I'm not condemning them. Why should I condemn them? If I'd been in Ireland I would have also been eating bacon and eggs.

You have sometimes been compared with Jean Genet. Is it a comparison you welcome without qualification?

Yes, I think highly of Genet. He was a fine person. To the world he was amoral, but I think he undoubtedly acted from a certain moral faith, which is rare.

Edmund White, Genet's biographer, said that again and again Genet was attracted to the person everyone else despised, the lowest person. Do you think that has been the case with you, either in life or in fiction?

It could be, but I think with me that's incidental. I'm more attracted to the so-called war lords, because they have the power which I think – or used to think – I should have. I believed that imaginative minds, explorers and probers into reality – they should all have power in a just society.

To what do you attribute your success with women?

I wasn't ugly, let's say, but also I was positive in my approach to them. I never regarded a woman as just a passing passion or a piece of sensuality. The woman of the moment was always for me THE woman who was going to be with me for the rest of my life. I must honestly say that I think that was to my credit.

Were you sexually driven?

Very much so, yes.

Were you considered a good lover?

It's very hard to say now. If you're with a woman in a sensual situation she's hardly going to say to you that you didn't live up to her expectations. But I don't honestly think I was especially good, no.

You seem to have been more than unusually interested in finding the truth, even if it was painful. That is the backdrop to a great deal of your fiction. Do you feel that you have found the truth – if one can put it like that – and was it worth the pain?

I found what I call reality – I prefer the word reality to truth. Truth is somehow a bit pretentious. If you find only a limited reality there is no point in it. You have to ask, what is the greater reality in which this limited reality of daily life is contained?

As a Christian do you believe in an afterlife?

I don't really believe in heaven. When I say I believe in the Christian faith, I read the Gospels and get a lot of comfort and inspiration out of them. That doesn't mean I'm bound to take their views as final about anything, but it would be very wrong, just because the Gospels report something which is more or less incredible, to reject them. As regards the afterlife, it's not a question I'm in a position to answer from the intelligence I have been granted or from the experiences I've had. It's beyond me to say yes or no to an afterlife. There is no point in doing so. In my long lifetime I have some very intense memories of far-back happenings, and I can't see them being erased completely, even after I die.

Are you afraid of death?

Yes, I would say so, although my fear of death would not take priority over all my other anxieties. If I were to die tomorrow, my greatest anxiety would be what would become of my cat.

Going back to Redemption *for a moment, one of the most striking passages reads as follows: 'There is nothing in the world that couldn't be called a few scratches, from music to love. It's a question of making the right scratches.' Is that a very significant statement for you? Would you say that you have managed to make the right scratches?*

It is a significant statement, yes. Whether on a music score or in your own situation, it is only a matter of making scratches, that's all we can do. As far as my own scratches are concerned, all I can say is that they were always positive. They were always scratches of a believer, rather than a sceptic.

One of the things that struck me when I read Redemption *was the business of the girl who was raped. She recounts to Ezra the trauma and says to Ezra that it's lucky Margaretta is dead because she wouldn't have to suffer the torment of being raped. And Ezra replies that he would rather Margaretta had been raped twenty times over than be dead. Was that your own view?*

Oh yes. Because to be raped would have been nothing to be ashamed of, for her or for me, and to have her alive was everything. I meant exactly that.

Later when Ezra describes a young girl as being raped he said, 'Violence never takes the shape you imagine it will.' What has been the impact of violence in your own life?

The impact of violence has been very considerable in my life. I've experienced many violent events, and been intimately involved with violence. I've heard executions from a prison cell, and I've been within earshot of several others.

In the same book Ezra makes a distinction between what he calls 'a real lover' and 'a real and final friend', saying that a wife is actually a third thing, coming somewhere between the two. He says that 'to be a wife is to be incapable of the final unjudging friendship'. Is that written more in sorrow than in anger? Has it been a personal disillusionment for you?

Yes, I suppose so. That remark stems from the time when I wanted a *ménage à trois* with Madeline and Iseult refused. I thought our hearts has been changed by war – my own heart had been changed, and I thought I could bring back Madeline and Iseult would accept it. But their hearts had not changed like mine. And still I thought I could change them. I told a friend, a German professor at the university and he said that was very naïve of me. And then he said a funny thing – he asked me which of them I would go for walks with. I didn't see it as a problem, but he obviously did.

But presumably there would have been problems. I mean, how would you have organised the sleeping arrangements?

I would like to have acted from impulse. As a writer it's the only way to act, naturally, as it occurs.

You also write: 'Marriage may be holy but it is also apt to be heartless as far as the rest of the world is concerned.' What was in your mind when you wrote that, I wonder? Is marriage heartless?

Oh yes. Couples are heartless, ruthless towards the rest of the world if something from outside threatens them. They don't have any understanding or compassion …

In your novel Black List *you write: 'Dishonour is what becomes a poet, not titles or acclaim.' What is the foundation of that belief?*

Experience. The creative mind can only write out of isolation which comes from dishonour largely, because if you're honoured you're not isolated.

You have – perhaps uniquely, certainly more than most writers – written books which reflect the events of your own life. One might almost say you have lived your own fiction. Do you see it that way yourself? Do reality and fiction ever blur in your own mind?

Yes, they do. It's partly the fault of my memory, but they do blur, and I believe that that is a fault of many good writers today. The life and work of a writer should not be separate; they should be completely joined.

In Black List *you describe how H, after receiving Holy Communion, kneels down by a stone column and says again and again, 'My Lord and my God'. He then asks whether, if all religion be myth, that invalidates the experience of the moment. How would you yourself answer that question?*

No, it doesn't invalidate it. Even if the Catholic or any other religion is all legend and myth, it doesn't invalidate it in the slightest. Just as a parable doesn't invalidate the truth that is represented by the parable. The myth, if it's intense enough, stands by itself.

Have you thought a great deal about religion during your life?

I've thought a lot about it, yes. And still do. I've asked the questions, but the answers are quite beyond us.

In Redemption *Ezra says to the priest: 'In general what a horrible egoism family egoism is, and your Catholic family egoism is the nastiest of all.' Do you believe that?*

Yes. I've seen it at work. Their absolute ruthlessness against anything from the outside that threatens them is quite shocking, and the Catholic church encourages that attitude.

You have a special affection for Saint Thérèse of Lisieux. Why is that?

She was brought up a very strict and pious Catholic, really maudlin – it was quite sickening to read of her early running to the church. And then she got into this convent where she had at least two sisters already, who made it very easy for her. She was a pious little creature, with that conventional piety which is so horrible. After a while, I don't know how long really, but very soon, all faith, consolation and belief were taken from her. Maybe that's not the right way to put it, but she lost her faith at any rate. She became as far as possible a sceptic, and I think that must have been a terrible experience. There she was, in the convent, more or less a prisoner. She went there out of belief that she didn't have any more. And yet of course she didn't say that she didn't have it, because she couldn't have borne it. Then she became tubercular. The Normandy climate didn't help and she didn't have enough covering on her cot. Once she woke up in the night coughing, and she could feel her mouth filling with blood. She spat it into a napkin but she didn't put on the light. In the morning she saw it was obviously arterial blood from the lung and she knew her fate was sealed. The fact that she didn't put the light on was a great act of self-flagellation.

Didn't you write about her in a novel?

Yes, it was funny – well, at least the consequences were funny. I was very attracted to Thérèse of Lisieux and I wrote that I was in bed with her that night when she coughed. When she put the napkin to her mouth, I said to her, put on the light, and she said, no I won't. She only put it on in the morning, and of course when we saw it, we knew she was doomed within a very short period. I wrote all this in a novel and some people who were admirers of my work told me that it was simply horrible of me to write such a thing and vowed that was the last book of mine they would read.

They found it offensive that I should have used this obviously very private and painful event in the life of somebody whom I was supposed to revere. I just thought, well, why not.

You have often been to Lourdes. Do you actually believe in miracles?

No. I went to Lourdes because I wanted to wheel the stick down to the grotto, and then into the basilica for the blessing in the evening. I got to know them as I would not have done normally. You enter into other people's consciousness that way. Of course, in many ways it was heart-breaking.

In your novel Memorial, *published in 1973, you quote Derek Mahon who speaks in a poem of the author living 'in obscurity and derision'. Is that how you see yourself perhaps?*

Yes, I suppose so. It was certainly the fact of the matter when I wrote it. It's perhaps changing somewhat now, but it used to be that if my name was mentioned it would arouse quite a bit of derision.

Do you believe you will be read more after your death than during your lifetime?

Yes.

Is that not a bitter thought … or is it one which comforts?

Neither one nor the other really. Historically speaking, I think I won't be forgotten. But whether that's a great comfort is another matter. Presumably I won't be there to get any satisfaction from it.

Would you say you are at peace with yourself now?

No, no. I'll never be at peace with myself.

Why is that, do you think?

Many reasons, the most obvious being that nobody of imaginative intelligence who finds himself on this very harsh planet can possibly be at peace. Our life is very cruel, and if there is a divine creator, let us say that one side of him is extremely ruthless. He has compassion, undoubtedly, but let us just say that his spirit is very complex.

You were selected recently to become an Irish Saoi, while on a previous occasion you were passed over. Has the establishment now forgiven your sins, do you think, and does it mean fuller recognition of your talent as a writer?

Yes, it does of course. I write in English, which after all is one of the languages that really counts, and as a writer in English I am highly regarded. It would be rather silly of these people in the establishment not to take that into account. They are of course British, and a stupid lot, most of them.

Aren't you pleased that you're being honoured?

Not especially, no. I don't consider it a great honour, but I will go along with it.

John Updike

John Updike was born in 1932 in Reading, Pennsylvania. He graduated from Harvard in 1954 and spent a year as a Knox Fellow at the Ruskin School of Drawing and Fine Art at the University of Oxford. From 1955 to 1957 he worked for the *New Yorker*, to which he contributed short stories, essays and poems – a habit he continued for the rest of his life. His literary criticism was extensively reprinted. From 1957 he lived in Massachusetts as a freelance writer. He was the author of many volumes of short stories and numerous novels and twice won the Pulitzer Prize for Fiction with *Rabbit is Rich* (1981) and *Rabbit at Rest* (1990). His character, Rabbit Angstrom, is a legendary American literary creation on a par with Huck Finn or Jay Gatsby. His novel *The Witches of Eastwick* (1984) was made into a major feature film. He published his memoirs under the title of *Self-Consciousness* (1989) and his novel *In the Beauty of the Lilies* (1996) is considered one of the finest American novels of the twentieth century. He was awarded the National Humanities Medal in 2003 and invited to give the prestigious Jefferson Lecture in 2008. He died in 2009.

Your distaste for the idea of someone writing your biography led you to write your autobiography. Why should the idea of someone else writing about your life be so disturbing?

I'm still trying to inhabit my life, and there's not room for two people there; I'd rather be alone. Also, I'm still using my material and my memories, still coming to grips with my own life. The biographies I've seen of living people are either libellous, in an attempt to make the life sensational and interesting, or very dull, and since I have a limited amount of energy I would rather put none of it into dealing with a biographer. I have four living children, an ex-wife and a present wife, all of whom deserve some privacy even if I don't. When I am as old as Graham Greene, and if I am as distinguished, perhaps I will invite a young man like Norman Sherry in, but I am nowhere near that stage of eminence.

I admit an outsider might be more truthful in a way, but in my autobiography I tried to put down some of the things only I could know. The things anyone can find out I will leave for somebody else to deal with. A life is a very strange thing.

My mother died last fall, and I've been reading letters I wrote to her in the 1970s, which isn't so long ago, but how much I've forgotten of the day-to-day routine! I suppose a biographer goes through all that: finds the letters, tells what was happening all those years before. I don't want to face that now. I'd rather try to be a creative writer while I still can.

It is flattering to think that a lot of people might find me interesting to read about, but I honestly don't know how many there are who want to know all about me. Perhaps six; ten at most. We begin life usually with our mothers being very interested in everything we do. They record every word we say and every bowel movement we manage, and maybe that's enough of that kind of attention. I would rather have my works interest people, but have them come out of a slightly mysterious centre. It's very hard in this day and age to maintain any privacy or any personal mystery at all, since people are interested in the real lowdown, as we say in this country. We do pick up a lot of books expecting to learn what the writer has been doing lately, which almost brings it down to a level of gossip, though maybe it's a healthy kind of interest. We read the books of Erica Jong or even Phillip Roth in part out of curiosity about them as the authors of their previous books. But one would like to think that writers do more than just divulge their recent histories, and that there is some capacity to imagine lives other than their own, or some capacity to draw larger lessons from their own lives. Without being as reclusive as Thomas Pynchon or J. D. Salinger, I have tried to stay out of at least some of the gossip columns and to avoid some of the many interviews I'm invited to give.

You become less effective as an artist the more interested you become in yourself as a person, the more you're in danger of becoming a fat-headed, lazy artist. Better to wear your hair shirt and hide in a cave than come out and try and be a beautiful person. There are so many beautiful people in the world now – so many in the New York nightclubs and the London clubs – that I don't think a writer should attempt to swell that particular throng. It's one thing to wish your books to be elegant, another to wish to be elegant yourself. I'm all for elegance in the right places, and my own concern is to try and be elegant in the books. But I'm not sure that elegance is the supreme human quality we should all aspire to. It seems to be like a pear. It goes rotten very quickly. Maybe we need some sturdier virtue, something more like a potato that will keep for months and even a year in the cellar.

Did you always want to write?

Not really, but my mother was a frustrated writer. She would send off manuscripts and get them back, and was trying to write through much of my childhood, so the notion that it was a worthy thing to do dawned upon me. But my first artistic itch was to draw. I did a lot of drawing as a child, and continued certainly through college. I was on a magazine at Harvard and did cartoons and covers, but by the time I got out of Harvard, the writing side of me had become the stronger and seemed the more saleable, the more useful side. I had some early acceptances, and by the time I was about twenty-three was committed to being a writer. And I'm lucky, because you can draw in writing – in a way, incorporate the visual art into the writing – but you can't really write in drawing. Writing is quite a broad activity in which you can use almost everything you know at some point, and I would say that my drawing skill has been useful to me.

I draw very rarely today. Occasionally an amusing birthday card to a child. The *New Yorker* have sometimes asked me for illustrations, so I have had three drawings published there, always attached to an article. It's strange how, when you sit down after years of not drawing, the art picks up right where you left it. Basically, I still draw the way I did at twenty-two. I am no better, but not much worse. It's fun to try, but I really don't have the time to draw for pleasure. When I had small children I occasionally drew them as babies. Then I bought a camera and stopped drawing.

Do you find writing easy?

Some days are easier than others, and it's never totally easy. There's always a little jump into it, like into a swimming pool. I tend to postpone and make a cup of tea, and circle the desk and answer some letters. But by and large I've been pretty good about sitting down to it finally and doing a certain amount each day. I would not class myself as one of those people who really sweat out each day's work. I think I write fairly easily as writing goes, maybe too easily, yet there is always some effort to it, and some serendipity, some surprise. You always find things you didn't know you were going to say, and that is the adventure of writing: that you can't plan it entirely but need to have faith each day that you launch yourself at this blank piece of paper, knowing in a general way what you're going to try to cover but not knowing exactly. You hope for things to happen that you can't foresee, and the life of the prose is in these unforeseeable harmonies, these characters who do something other than was planned. All those little surprises are what make it such an entertaining profession. People who can make a living writing are very lucky because not only is the day short and the labour not too difficult, but you have a kind of self-therapy. You're always, in a way, expressing yourself, which they tell us is healthy if you do it to a psychiatrist. You're constantly finding out what you know and feel which you didn't know you knew or felt before.

You're right that it is lonely. One of the reasons that I was happy to come and meet you was that I must vary the loneliness. Now that my children are grown up and my wife works, I'm alone in the house for much of the day. All day, from seven to six. But then I was an only child, and maybe my tolerance for being alone is greater than that of many. I could take several days of not talking to anyone without too much discomfort. After a while, of course, the need to make contact becomes very pressing, but on the whole I like it and I guess I talk to myself and I'm my own company. I have telephone contact with various editorial people. The mail is of great interest to me, probably more than for a painter, say, or a musician. There are these various ways of relieving the loneliness. But there's no doubt ever that you must be alone at the moment of actual work. You must face yourself to that degree, and many don't want to do that. Most people enjoy the constant company of others. It's like having the radio going in the elevator – something to chase away the silence, this awful silence at the background of our lives that we're trying to shut out. The writer in some ways tries to face the silence, at least for the three or four hours a day that he works.

Nobody can be entirely self-sufficient. I'm very dependent upon the fact of getting published. My enjoyment of writing is not so keen that I would do it if there were no rewards. Proust and Kafka would both seem to have had fairly low expectations, though both had some publication. Proust paid for his first book to be published and Kafka fought to be published, but even writers as hermetic and exquisite as these at some point welcome the actual experience of getting published. And for me, who's been published quite early, it would be very sad if my publishing house and the *New Yorker* magazine were to stop publishing me. I need that kind of stimulus. I seem to need a fair amount of attention, in fact, or I wouldn't publish so many books.

Some American authors go years without publishing. Thomas Pynchon just now published a novel after seventeen years of silence. I don't think I could ever go on so long. For all of my tolerance of solitude, I do like that annual fuss that surrounds the book and like many children of this country, especially of my generation, I have a sort of love affair with New York City. I was a small-town boy – in fact I was a farm boy for a while – and I thought that where I was going to find happiness was in New York, presented to my generation as Fred Astaire and *Top Hat*, penthouses and beautiful women in lovely long white gowns. So I always thought I'd live in New York. When I got there I found there were some of the things I had expected, but there was always a great deal of hassle and no place to raise a family. My wife had no natural social life there, and was lonely. I was working, so was not so lonely, but we didn't stay long. Yet I've been able to keep a hold of New York with the writing. I talk to it often. I have friends there.

When I go I feel at home. I've tried to be a New Yorker without paying the very real price of living there.

Can you tell me something of the relationship between the life and the fiction?

I suppose I am somewhat more autobiographical than other writers appear to be, though when you look into a writer like Tolstoy, who seems almost a God-like omniscient above it all, it turns out there is a surprisingly high degree of autobiographical material. We all need some kind of personal stimulus, some moment that we want to expose or tell about, and writers can be variously clever over how they're going to package it. But these two elements – a personal sharing and a kind of packaging – I think are true of everybody. In my case, the package may sometimes seem very thin, a little cellophane around the nugget of life, but it is in my mind always a package. Even if I tell the events of one afternoon in my life, I'm not telling every afternoon, so there has been an act of selection and a sense of shaping.

Some of my work may look more autobiographical than it is. I prefer to think it doesn't really matter. I am alive now and having a life of a kind, and while I'm alive I must share what seems to me momentous about it. To be too discreet or too cunning would be self-defeating. But I always see it as a change, a metamorphosis. There is no such thing as offering the reader your life. What you offer is a set of packaged moments that in some way you have witnessed, maybe out of the dead middle of your experience or maybe in the sense of imagining. I don't think the distinction matters terribly much. In some way you must make your life interesting, must give it a kind of relevance, an application beyond that of just telling what happened today. As long as you do that and make the ideal reader care, you've fulfilled your responsibility. Meanwhile you live your life the best you can.

People talk about being put into a book as though they can be actually lifted out of life and inserted, but we know that the two orders of existence are really very different. There are the flesh-and-blood people who have all kinds of qualities and fully occupy space and time, and there are fictional characters, who are really just a few words tossed on to a page. There's such an enormous difference between the world, on the one hand, and a book on the other, that I've felt fairly free about writing sometimes about my life fairly directly. Take one example. *Couples* was a long novel that was certainly about a kind of milieu that I felt, and I made the observation that we were all set up as couples and expected to be very happy yet weren't. Having decided that here was the sociological condition worth telling about, I felt obliged to disguise all of my friends heavily so there was almost nobody in there who could say, 'That's me,' though they could all recognise the general feeling.

There's a little novel of mine called *Of the Farm,* which is autobiographical in tone. It's first person and is about a woman very like my mother, set on a farm exactly like hers, but the situation is false. The hero has a second wife. I did not have a second wife and didn't acquire one for another ten or more years. So more often than not we write not out of what happened but out of what might have happened. We write out of tendency as much as out of fact.

Are fictional characters more interesting than real ones?

I think not. A real person has endless depths. Just the anatomical qualities of a real person are fascinating: what makes the molecules click, who makes the psyche and the mass of memories each person carries around. A real person is overwhelmingly large in terms of the potential data that could be expressed. Fictional characters are therefore interesting in part because we can stand them. They don't overwhelm us, they're often very simple. If you look at even complex-seeming characters in fiction, they're really quite simple: basically dolls with three or four moving parts so our minds can encompass them. They're interesting because they're involved in a story, and a story is a suspense of some kind which makes us care about what'll happen next. We read it in the faith that it's going to have an end, that all of our immediate questions will be answered one way or another.

So we are excited by stories, whereas life doesn't seem quite to have a story, but is many stories all interwoven. Perhaps we read fiction in part as a relief from the enormous factualness of life that seems to have no clear point. A fiction writer has assumed a certain obligation. He will somehow resolve the fate of his characters. Even fairly avant-garde works do this in a way. When we put down *Ulysses* or *Remembrance of Things Past,* we feel it's come to an end and that the author has said everything that he wants to say. In *Ulysses* Molly Bloom gives a kind of blessing to life itself, and in Proust the author arrives at the revelation that time can be made to reverse itself, or does reverse itself, and it's this which justifies a life. We always come to some point of satisfaction in fiction, and we consent to be interested in the faith that all of the anxieties and questions aroused within the microcosm of the novel will be answered and placated; that, unlike life, there is no tomorrow with its own set of questions. When the book ends, there is no tomorrow.

A fictional world must have both lightness and weight, the lightness coming from the fact that when one's mind is processing it, it will somehow add up and be entertaining and, unlike life, won't contain long dull stretches. But it must also have some weight. There must be an illusion that this is enough like life so that the process we observe in the work of art can be applied to the life we then lead. This feeling of actual instruction as to how to live is very much one of the reasons why we read fiction, in so far as we do – and most people don't. Not only do most uneducated people not read books, but a lot of intelligent people, especially men, abandon fiction. Therefore, fiction has rather a small audience, but those of us who do read it and try to write it hope for some revelation about life; that we somehow emerge from the book slightly more humane and able to cope with real-life situations.

In the past twenty or thirty years fiction has become much more sexually explicit and realistic, and this has been deplored in many quarters. But for me it often has the great moral virtue of attempting to tell us how the other sex feels about sexual transactions and, in demonstrating the sexual adventures of the characters, making us more knowing and perhaps gentler and less deluded; less egocentric in our own romantic behaviour. I often read female novels just to be illuminated as to how women think, though clearly not all women think alike. Nevertheless, it is interesting for me to read about romance from a female point of view: what the expectation is and where the disappointments lie. All of that is information, and we do read for information. A slight embarrassment is that, given two novels of equal virtue, we would rather be in one about Saudi Arabia, say, then one about the city we live in. We're interested in strange places, in other lives. We travel in a way through fiction, since we can't travel entirely by ourselves, and all this fairly humble curiosity gives the writer an opportunity to expand the consciousness of his readers, to give them experiences they won't otherwise have since life is so short.

Do you subscribe to the idea that sex is the lifeblood of our existence?

In a word, I do. You might broaden sex to something like love or Eros, and if what goes on between the mother and the infant is sex, then certainly sex would cover the whole field. A lot of what we do is apparently unsexual, but I think Freud is correct: everything really has a sexual goal. In other words, the hard-working Wall Street expert in financial mergers works all day so he will cut an impressive figure, perhaps so he can buy seductive clothes. He will certainly try to enhance his own maleness, his own plumage, as it were. The job, the work, the factory, all these are male plumage. I think a lot of what we do for the pay-off comes in erotic terms. And we're far from truly knowing how our emotional life as children blends into the erotic life of the mature adult, though surely it is a continuum in that we are at every point of our lives seeking for confirmation and approval from someone else. At a very humble level, we want our bodies approved of and accepted in the various physical ways that sex allows. Beyond that, we want in some way to be confirmed in our immaterial being as well. I suppose this to be an erotic search which can be carried on via many partners or one partner, or via a stamp collection.

There seem to me to be a lot of people who really should not be enlisted in the sexual armies, as it were. There are people who have honourable reasons for just not caring, many who in the older societies would become monks or priests or eccentric bachelors – formerly a very honourable thing to be. We're in danger now, in the late twentieth century, of forcing everyone to become a sexual hero, a sexual superstar, when there are probably a number of alternative ways of working out the basic erotic patterns of your life. But when all is said and done, novels are almost invariably about love. It's as if we were saying that we are most alive when we're in love.

A writer's experience must include other people's books. Is there a distinction between what comes from experience of the real and what comes from books?

You certainly shouldn't write out of other books. I've not taught much writing, but I have done a little, and the students by and large haven't really learned to see, to have the language for their own lives. They don't see what they're living, and all they know is what they've read in books, and so they have to process their reality through what other writers have done. It's quite rare for a young man or woman to come into their own voice, their own material, much before the age of twenty-three or twenty-four, because the books we've read control what we see and screen out so much of what is real about us. We are all creatures of literary tradition, and it is the ability to be excited enough by the world of print to wish to enlarge it, to take a piece of your perception and experience, and turn it into print and make it join on to this big Antarctica of things in print, which is the basic impulse. In other words, to take your life out of being something impermanent and trivial and purely personal and make it something that can in some way enlarge the experience of people you don't even know. It's a great act of transformation, and if you can do it, it's a great privilege to expand the world of print.

It's true there are too many books, and most are junk, but to a young person it's a sacred world and a world he is totally locked out of. To find the way into it and be on the other side of that wall, to be one of the producers of the books is, even at the age of fifty-eight, still exciting. As to influence, I think you do somehow close down and that the major reading experiences of your life occur before you are twenty-five or thirty. That is to say, the writers who really give you your voice are apt to have been encountered by that age. The more of a voice you get, the less you can start to change it and the less you are struck by other people's, but the writers whom you really value and love are the ones you think have shown you the way to what you know. In my case there is this English writer, Henry Green, who in some way opened me up to what prose could do. And there's the American writer, J. D. Salinger, whose short stories seem to belong to my world.

I thought I could write stories like that, whereas I couldn't write stories like John O'Hara or Hemingway. In some way, you need those few spirits who release you, show you the way to speak yourself.

When you're in college you tend to read what they tell you, and having a lot of catching up to do, I read mostly English classics – *Beowulf*, Chaucer, Shakespeare. But for all the admirable writers you read in college, in some way you're reading them to fill in your sense of history and prepare for examinations. Once I got out of college, I read a lot of Proust, in English, because I didn't have enough French to take him in French, and that year I spent at Oxford I read Henry Green and some more Salinger, as well as a lot of Kierkegaard for personal reasons. There's a tremendous energy and rhetorical skill in him, and he's not afraid to do something thoroughly. The gift of being able to write novels came in part, I'm sure, from Kierkegaard and Proust. I also read Kafka, but I'm not a very Kafkaesque writer. I found him exhilarating because he faces those depressing things, our entrapment and our impotence, and there's a kind of relief in just voicing them. Of course, you tend to feel somewhat superior to Kafka as you read him. You think, well, I'm not that sick, not that neurotic, so in some way you can lick the sugar off the pill and not swallow it.

That's one thing we always do in reading, of course: take what we want out of a book, and there's always more we don't take. Unlike the motion picture, which gives you itself and all of itself in a big bang, a book will only give you as much as you're ready to hear or to see. It's amazing to reread a book you read ten years ago. You realise you didn't read it at all. It's almost like a brand- new book. One of the marvellous things about books is the layered-ness and the way, all the time, they have secrets to give.

To come back to the novel as the product of expert imitation, is it more convincing when experience like marriage or parenthood can be taken direct from life?

You can fake quite a lot, and the level of realism we demand from the novel isn't extraordinarily high. Our wish to be entertained and instructed is so strong that we will forgive quite a lot of fakery, but there comes a point at which fakery invalidates a novel, and we put the book down, realising we are learning nothing. Flaubert, though unmarried, wrote well enough about marriage, and there's an American writer, Ann Beardey, who has no children but has just written a book about the problems of child rearing. So it is possible. There's also many a sex change where a male writer has more or less plausibly become a woman and vice versa. Nevertheless, what we really have to share is stuff we've experienced.

As soon as I was married my writing almost immediately became better, I think because I was somehow a step up the ladder of life. Marriage is something that most writers should not seek to avoid. I wouldn't have missed having children for anything, and when I had them around me I certainly wrote better about children then I would have if I'd never known any – better, in fact, than I can do now. In my most recent novel, which has a ten-year-old and a four-year-old, I found I knew what they were like, having had four children of my own and lived with three stepsons, but also that I had grown a little out of touch with how children of that age act and think. In general I would say use your imagination, but there are limits to what imagination can do.

It's very possible to draw upon a personal encounter so early that you don't yourself know what you're using. Some of Henry James's later novels have this quality. He was drawing from very youthful memories without quite knowing it, but in the end a character is a person, and we have to have some general knowledge of people before we can begin to write novels. I don't think that even a very superior mentality from another planet, with all kinds of statistical information about human beings, could write a novel. In a novel, we are recycling people we have met, and we may be using the nose of one or the arm of another, or it may be a nose we saw in the movies, but there's certainly some human input that has to happen before there can be any output in the form of character creation.

I don't think the craft can do these things by itself. There is craft, and more of it than the romantic conception of the artist allows, but the ability is to make a thing coherent. It's like making a birdhouse. You imagine it in your head, and then do the little fitting that needs to be done. A great deal of what you might call carpentry goes into making a satisfying book, but in making a birdhouse you still need to have the bird inside it, and the bird flies out of your experience and your own passion about your experience. For example, I went to Harvard, not far from where we sit now – an admirable institution, but I've never been moved to write very much about it; enough people have already done so.

I've met hundreds and hundreds of people in my life, but perhaps only a dozen have really gotten through to me in a way that prompts me to want to make them characters. I use the same people again and again, because only they somehow have got to me. Therefore, things have to get to you, and not all of your life will; but when you sit down to make a book or a short story or a poem, you have to have something that you want to package, something you want to present to people in some form. The craft can do the form to a degree, but an awful lot of what we call writerly craft is nothing more than authenticity. It's not putting down phoney words; it's trying to have a voice that speaks; it's really wishing to communicate. That is what makes a great deal of the style, and no amount of rules is going to give you that voice.

John Updike

What sets 'literature' apart from other fiction?

In part a willingness to forget or sacrifice readers, to push forward. You can still be quite a popular artist and do this. It's a feeling of adventure and a willingness to take risks which makes the real writer distinguishable from the unreal one. It often takes a century, of course, to discover who was real and who was not. It's not always apparent at the time, and there are many creditable writers now who probably won't matter much in a hundred years. You could even call literature a higher degree of playfulness, in that the literary writer is willing to play with the thing and is not just trying to construct an engine to process a reader's emotional patterns.

I don't read much cheap fiction, I just don't have the time, but when you watch television, you sense these machines instructed to run you through a set of emotional manoeuvres. You're supposed to care about the guy, you're supposed to want him to sleep with the girl, you're supposed to get excited when they're in a car being chased. There's a kind of mechanical working over, a little like a massage. Some kind of massage accompanies a literary masterpiece too, but somehow it's more than a massage. The writer, as he or she goes along, makes discoveries perhaps, and in some way is open to interventions from outside the mechanical pattern. I suppose you can also merely say that literary writers are brighter than the others; that their vocabularies are bigger, their willingness to play with language and their intuitive knowledge about the world greater. The quality of their writing has an adventurous experimental freedom. The great artist is more free: freer to see more and to eliminate more; to do without certain kinds of obligatory performance.

Your autobiography is often provided with footnotes on the use you made in fiction of some incident or person.

That's a rather arbitrary set of footnotes. Just what occurred to me as I was writing. Several times I've given female characters experiences based on my own. I turned a pulled tooth into an abortion for a female character, and also reversed a churchgoing situation. It doesn't much matter, you know. As the structuralists say, the opposite is often virtually the same thing, and what's important is the structure. To put it on to a woman or to make it upside down is no great trick. I thought it would make the book in general more fun to read if, in some places, I acknowledged, yes, you have seen this before, or this may ring a bell for those who are devoted Updike readers. It was fun to do. It added a little dimension.

I am interested myself when writers talk about books, especially if they're admirable books. It's interesting to read Graham Greene on the period of his life when he was writing the early novels, *The Power and the Glory* and so on, because even though he doesn't say much, it's all helpful, and in a way it humanises the books. A book in the end has to float free of the man's life, but while he's alive it's fun to see these strings and to realise how much he made of something that was little; to see the imagination in operation and realise how little it needs sometimes to take off in a big way.

You wanted your autobiography to be in some sense 'representative in its odd uniqueness of all the oddly unique lives in the world', but is it not inevitable that some lives are more interesting than others?

I suppose some are more interesting than others. What I think is irreversibly interesting, and true of all of us, is that we're trapped inside a certain body and a certain set of circumstances, even a certain moment in time. Although I suppose this could be dismissed as a metaphysical riddle saying that you had to be somebody, so why not you, my childhood perception, as I began to grapple with being alive, was the extraordinary strangeness of being me instead of somebody else. And so the philosophical emotion behind the autobiography was the feeling of being self-conscious, of being conscious of being this self instead of another self. Then you stay self-conscious, and it's probably not a good thing. The memories which are most affecting are gathered by and large when you were least self-conscious, when you were either young or intensely engaged in some life experience. I'm aware of myself as a writer now, as a man who is recognised on the street, as a man who has the costume of a writer. In a way it's like a little static in the head all the time, which I try to tune out, but there's no doubt that I am somewhat self-conscious.

But no two lives are alike and we would rather live some than others. Most lives on this planet are miserable, and one of the tragedies surely involved in the human race right now is that so many lives are wasted before they've begun, largely because of poverty. I've been very fortunate. Anybody who's fairly healthy, and was born into the United States when I was, is in a tiny minority of blessed people, living in an area that is more or less disease free. Even compared to my grandparents, how relatively little pain I've had. Think of the toothaches that people in the nineteenth century had to put up with, the infectious diseases that would lift away a whole set of children, the powerlessness of all that. To be alive in an era when so much of that particular kind of powerlessness is gone is a great privilege.

Anyway, I wasn't writing about how lucky I was to be me, but more about how strange it was to be me. It's a little like Heidegger trying to write about being, being as an entity: in a sense it's absurd and doesn't get you anywhere, but on the other hand it's something to face. There is a kind of miracle involved in anything existing, and a kind of miracle involved in being you. So I hoped that some of that sense of the miraculous would express a gratitude, a glad-to-be-here kind of feeling.

You wrote about Christmas and the way the idea of a snowy Christmas was more real to you than the bleak brown ones you actually knew. Was it that imaginative vividness that prompted you to become a novelist?

Certainly a susceptibility to that kind of imagery was what prompted me. All those snowy Christmas illustrations that appeared in children's books and old-fashioned magazines like the *Saturday Evening Post* were very real to me, more real than the muddied brown world around me. Had I not responded so strongly to those little pretend worlds, had I not wanted to enter in and get on that hearth and rug with Santa Claus in the sleigh, no doubt I would never have chosen to live by my imagination the way I have done. From early on I loved these images of another world: comic strips, illustrations, Christmas especially. The stylisation of Christmas was so far advanced in American commercial art. Artists knew how to draw it, how to make those little windows with the frost in. There was a kind of vocabulary of Christmas that had descended through generations, so it was intense as a totally imaginary experience that had nothing to do with the real Christmases I experienced. All that excited me, and it seemed a good way out of the world I was in.

The experiences that gave you much pleasure as a child, like being out of the rain, but only just out of it, you explained as pleasurable because 'the experience is irresponsible, safe ... there is nothing he can do or ought to do'. This sounds very like an analogy for the art of a novelist, who is also 'morally detached, safe and witnessing'.

That's very good, and entirely your invention. I hadn't thought of it like that, but now you mention it, writing a novel is rather like being out of the rain that you're creating there on the page, but just out, so you can smell it, feel it and hear it. Being in a little shelter out of the rain still affords me pleasure. The house I live in now has a kind of open garage, and it still gives me a thrill to stand there with the rain falling all around me but not quite on me. I guess that novelists are often people who are fascinated by the rain but don't want to get wet. It's a good point.

Edmund White once said it was the particular curse of adolescence that events were never adequate to the feelings they inspired. Do you feel something similar?

It's true that when you write about them you have to be careful somehow to make them seem in proportion to the response. It's possible to be very superior to adolescent experience. On the other hand, it is a human experience. We are as alive at thirteen as at thirty-three, and it deserves to be put into print. I think we have to try to rid ourselves of our own myths about adolescence and write about it. What is awkward from the standpoint of a novelist is that adolescents don't really have their grip on the handles of the world yet. They can't make decisions, they can't decide they will marry, they can't decide they will sell the company. They aren't quite grown up. All they can do is feel and thrash around, so in that way they're unsatisfactory. I found I could write about adolescents quite easily in short stories, but that they won't carry me through a novel. You need adults who can do grown-up things to get you through a novel.

You wrote in your memoirs that you were conscious of wanting to 'show them in Shillington', to revenge your father for the slights you and he felt had been put upon him. Did you come to feel at last that you had done so?

I wrote that when my mother was alive, and I suppose, had she been dead, I would have included her, because in a way I was trying to work out some kind of revenge for her as well. It was she who felt that Shillington was a hard place. To me it seemed enchanting. It was kind to me and I love it, but I was aware that somehow there was a level of respectability that my parents didn't quite get into. Among my motives has been a wish to show Shillington that we weren't intimidated. It was a typical small town full of people, none very rich, none very poor. Somehow I have a wish to show Shillington people that we can make more money than the factory workers from the hosiery mills. What sticks in my mind as a social insult was that my father, though he had the prestige, such as it was, of a schoolteacher, made less than the full-fashioned knitters, and there was a funny feeling about being, not exactly at the very bottom of the social scale, but certainly at the lower end. If I'd stayed in Shillington I'd probably be at the lower end of the social scale myself. I had to get out to show it.

You describe yourself in your memoirs as malicious, greedy for a quota of life's pleasures, an obnoxious show-off, rapacious and sneaky. That is certainly not how you are perceived publicly.

I think that anybody who knows me would agree with all those adjectives. I was an only child who never had to compete with a sibling, and my parents were both, in their way, very loving and indulgent. Just the fact that I had the presumption to become an artist is rather ridiculous, isn't it, with no qualifications except that I felt treasured as a child. When my mother died, among her things in the attic was a scrapbook containing many of my drawings done when I was three and four. Not every child gets that kind of attention. The good side of it is I have a certain confidence, and by and large I've acted confidently in my life and had good results. The bad side of it is that I like to be at the centre of attention.

As to being malicious, I think I am more than usually malicious. That joy, that *schadenfreude* we take in other people's misfortunes, is well developed in me, though I try to suppress it. I detect within myself a certain sadism, a certain pleasure in the misfortunes of others. I don't know whether I'm average in this or whether it's exceptional, but I'm interested to a degree in the question of sadism. People who are sadistic are very sensitive to pain, and it's a way of exorcising the demon of pain.

I'm so aware of my enviousness that I try not to review books by contemporary Americans. I'm not sure that I would really give an honest opinion, and that's sneaky. People who are cowardly and don't especially enjoy confrontation or battle tend to be sneaky. In this unflattering self-characterisation, though, I was no doubt just doing my Christian duty of confessing sins. Human nature is mightily mixed, but surely all these malicious and cruel aspects are there along with everything else.

One reviewer, talking about Couples, *called you 'the pornographer of marriage'. Did you resent that tag?*

Not too much. I wasn't trying to be pornographic. I was trying to describe sexual behaviour among people, and the effect was probably the opposite of pornographic. Pornography creates a world without consequences, where women don't get pregnant, nobody gets venereal disease and no one gets tired. In *Couples* I was trying, to the limits of my own knowledge, to describe actual sexual situations and show them with consequences. Without resenting the phrase, I don't think it describes very well what I was trying to do.

One is always sensitive to criticism to a degree. If they tell you you're the best thing since Shakespeare, you want to know what's so great about Shakespeare. I remember especially some reviews I got early. When I began to write, the big figures on the scene were Jewish, by and large: Malamud, Bellow, young Roth and so on. The literary world was Jewish, and up comes this little WASP out of the country, writing in a style influenced by Proust. I think it irritated some people, because I did receive a number of harsh reviews of books that were in their way quite innocent and well meant. I was told I had nothing to say, was told it repeatedly, so some of those darts stuck in my skin and I still remember them. On the other hand, it's part of the game. Every profession has its hazards and harsh reviews.

At least I mattered enough to get bad reviews. I was enough of a presence to deserve to be debunked, and I should have taken some comfort in that. I've never consciously tried to adjust my writing to please critics. It would be a mistake, because you're never going to please many of them. Some of the things said were no doubt fair, as I see now, but when you're a practising artist you can't afford to be too much into the critic's skin. You have to push, to keep going with your own vision and your own sense of reality, and let others make the judgements. On the other hand, I was always protected from adverse judgements by the fact that I had the *New Yorker* magazine in my corner. They liked me and took most of my things, which meant that my livelihood and my ego gratification came from the same source. I could always hide behind the fact that I was a *New Yorker* writer and the people who weren't were just jealous.

I think *Couples* was certainly of its time, just in the fact that it spans very specific years and refers to a lot of historical events. In a funny way, the book is about the Kennedy assassination. It's also about the introduction of the contraceptive pill, the fact that the danger of getting pregnant was almost entirely removed and that a certain amount of promiscuity resulted directly from this technology. It also turns out that it was the pre-Aids, pre-herpes paradise, so it was a moment that's gone, a moment of liberation which broke not upon a bunch of San Francisco hippies and young people, but upon middle-aged couples, yet was a revolution of a kind. It is very much of its historic moment. Those wives did not work, but now, in that same economic group, the wives would have jobs, or half-jobs. But these were people who married in the 1950s and thought family life was going to solve their problems, then discovered it didn't.

I hope it's not too dated. I haven't read it since I checked the last proof. No doubt some of the writing I would improve if I could get my hands on the text again, but I don't think it's dated more than any book that has some roots in a historic moment. All novels belong to a certain time, to two times in fact – the time in which they're located and the time in which they're written. That book was written a few years farther on from the moment it describes, so in a way the characters are innocent Kennedy characters, whereas I wrote it in the era of Johnson when the Vietnam commitment had deepened and widened under us and people were beginning to burn flags. In a way I was already looking back to an innocent little paradise.

In a novel like Couples, *aren't you concerning yourself with what is really an American middle class?*

I think our middle classes are pretty distinct, and because we don't admit we have a class structure, the other classes are less accessible in a way than they perhaps are in a very class-conscious society like Britain. Somehow to know that there are upper and lower classes, and even some of the traits that determine them, seems to make it easier for writers like Graham Greene or Henry Green or Evelyn Waugh to cross those lines and put before us convincing thugs and servants and what not. Whereas in this allegedly classless society, we are timid. On the other hand, the American experience places you in proximity with quite a range of class. I have no first-hand experience of city ghetto life, but I do remember what it's like to be shabby small-town and shabby country, and I've been able now to get a peek into the moneyed classes, so in a way I have a sufficient social range. But the English do seem to create multi-class novels more easily.

With an acceptance of more sexually explicit writing, much of the so-called literature of concealment has disappeared. Have more relaxed attitudes always been good for literature?

Any strategy of concealment can benefit the work of art, because it imposes certain demands. Rhyme in poetry, for example, had the advantage of forcing people to recast lines and a certain ingenuity came in. Often they were driven to find words they wouldn't ordinarily have found. And so it was with sexual concealment. In a way, when you closed the bedroom door, you conveyed something was going on, and everyone knew what. It seemed important to me in the early 1960s to write about sex explicitly, because it was a little frontier. Some had crossed it already, but always in banned books. Henry Miller crossed it, and *Lady Chatterley's Lover* had crossed it, but Joyce was the best model in this because, unlike Henry Miller or D. H. Lawrence, you can't say Joyce is sex obsessed. *Ulysses* is not about sex but about life, yet sexual words and references occur and it feels right in the sense that, on a spring day in Dublin, this is how people's energies would be flowing. With that in mind, it seemed to be important to be as realistic as I could. I don't feel the need exists in the 1990s. Now people are more or less free to write what they want. I do it less because it does seem not to be an artistic frontier at all, though I would like to think that the freedom still exists for those who want to exercise it – even freedom to be pornographic if pornography is taken to be exciting. I don't see why a piece of writing can't be sexually exciting. Certainly writing excites us romantically, after all. Why not try to excite us sexually?

You have sometimes been accused of sentimentalising your women characters.

I'd have to know the characters in question. I have tried to grow in my depiction of women without abandoning my own sense of women and my own wisdom and experience of them, but I suppose I've tried to give them more credit for being something in addition to being interesting to men as sexual opposites. The women in *Couples* might be sentimental. I'm not sure. I'd have to read the book again. But as women have become increasingly vocal about their feelings, their long-held anger and their long resentment of males' views about them, so any male writer to some extent has to look into his heart and try to make his portrayal of women as honest and fair as his portrayal of men. I wouldn't want to treat them better than I treat my men.

Women have been important in my life, from my mother on, in ways I don't even know as well as a lot of ways I do. I married young, and my first wife was exceedingly helpful, shaping not only my work but my whole outlook. My second wife too. If I had to be condemned to one sex, I would rather spend my time with women than with men.

You parted from your first wife. Are modern divorce rates prompted by modern conditions, or is it that divorce has become less difficult and more affordable?

The alternative activities to marriage that society has provided have, I think, diminished. It was quite possible to be very unhappily married in Victorian America and not exactly know it. You were off at the office, you then went to the club. The wife had her own circle and sets of entertainments. In a way, once you were past the child-making phase, your contacts could be fairly few and formal, and expectations of marriage were perhaps not quite so high. The post-war world in the West has put many of its eggs, as far as personal happiness goes, in the marriage basket. The demands on marriage have upped, which increases the stress. Also, of course, this is a Protestant country without the Catholic restraints on marriage, so that many a marriage that people would, in the old world, have lumped with the help of lovers, or doing without, or the Church, or any number of other things, now has no convenient way out except divorce.

Having been through one with children who, if not exactly babies, were a little too young to have their parents break up, I'd say it's to be avoided if possible, but it's not maybe the worst thing to happen in many circumstances and the fact that it happens to so many children now has to some extent lessened the burden on each of them. You're no longer the pariah or odd-ball if you have a split family, since at least half your friends do too. It's not that we are indifferent to marriage; it's expecting so much of it that makes people become dissatisfied.

Do you write better under stress?

I have written under stress, but I wouldn't recommend it as a steady thing. As Wordsworth said, emotion recollected in tranquillity is the optimum, so by and large I try and arrange a tranquil life around myself, and I write best in it. Of course, you have to have something to write about and that often does involve undertaking or going through some stress. I'm a compulsive writer who doesn't wait for the perfect day before he writes, so I've written on some poor days and written when I was in considerable discomfort. The one thing to be said for writing when you're unhappy is that at least you're having an experience of unhappiness. In a funny way, if you're always tranquil, always satisfied, always the orderly writer who goes and does his job, words are in danger of becoming too cheap. You write too easily. Some of my best writing has been done under stressful circumstances. Nevertheless, a simple bourgeois monotony is to be desired for a steady productive life.

Dr Johnson said that a man not married was only half a man, but Cyril Connolly added to the dictum by saying that a man who was very married was only half a writer.

It raises a ticklish issue. It's true that people are always only partially married, and that a writer writes to some extent with the unmarried, the lonely, the solitary adventuring self. My own temperament has led me twice toward marriage, maybe because I don't have Cyril Connolly's needs. He was a bit of a gadabout, I gather, as many writers have been. I have the feeling that, like many Englishmen, he needed a generous amount of bachelor freedom to feel a hundred per cent a man. Trying to think about notable twentieth-century writers who seemed thoroughly married and none the worse for it, I come across two immediately: Thomas Mann and James Joyce. I've seen too many American writers suffer in a way from not being married or being stable enough. You can easily fritter away your talent in drink, wasted energy and exhausting skirt-chasing; or, indeed, in pants chasing – why leave the women out of it? In marriage the mind is unmarried enough. The mind is a kind of bachelor, in any case. It's maybe a good mix to have the body very married.

You spoke of your memories of growing up as being 'used up and wished away in the self-serving corruptions of fiction'. Do you feel that somehow you are intruding upon the reality of those who live in memory?

I suppose so. I feel also that you are selling your life in a strange way, including the people who were standing around while you were living it, which brings something a little shabby into the transaction. When I was a little boy, I was much impressed by a fairy story about a wishing hide hanging on the wall. Every time you make a wish, a little piece flies off. Eventually there's no hide left. I think I have the same feeling about writing. Each time I turn something into a story or a novel, another piece of the hide is flying off. Fiction is self-serving in so far as the writer is ultimately in control and everything that is too embarrassing will be suppressed. The general trend of his distortions is therefore in his own favour, so in that way it's corruption. Nevertheless, it's what I do for a living; I can't be too apologetic about it. But there's something consuming about it and a typical writerly fear is that you've used up everything that you want to say. In fact, you never do. Somehow, with a little patience, there's always more. But you write very close to what feels like exhaustion, to what feels like the end of your story.

In what sense do you live *your novels as you write?*

Things sharpen as you write. On the other hand, you have to have some notion of the little scene. I saw a lot of movies as a young man, and I still go to the movies. There is some degree to which our imaginations are all cinematic. I think of the novels as scenes, but I often don't know exactly what's going to happen. Sometimes the characters say less than I had hoped, sometimes more, but in general they hold within certain bounds of what can occur. A novel is unlike a play in that there is a weave of the verbal action with the background: the room, the scenery, the kind of day has somehow to come into it. The human mind wanders constantly, picks up little bits of the past and so on. All of that has to be written too, as well as the voices. It all gets sharper, and you hope it gets sharper again when you see proofs. Sharp seems a good way to think of it; clear. There should be a kind of clarity and a certain clash of edges; little jumps whereby the reader knows we're going forward. Each sentence should be a slight shock. I once saw that as a description of style, and I've tried to remember it: that good style is a succession of small surprises. I don't think it was Cyril Connolly but it could well have been an Englishman. And so, yes, there are surprises which are surprising to the writer, and then to the reader.

Do you feel at your peak as a writer now?

It's hard to know if I'm getting worse or if my critical sense is getting better. Just looking at the life curve of most writers, in America especially, you tend to peak young when your memories are fresh and youthful. It's a rare writer in this country who gets better after thirty, and may have blown up by the time they are in their forties. So at my age you're working against the trend, but in some ways I know more than ever. I'm less naïve, and it's only a question of energy. Writing is in part an athletic feat. It's all in the head, but it's a matter of images and words, of making it all have a kind of spring and a tension.

You have written only one play, Buchanan Dying. *Was that just a matter of seeing if you could do it?*

I'd tried to write that book as a novel first and found that the historical novel posed problems in terms of fakery and bluff that I couldn't meet. I might be able to do it now when maybe I'm not so inhibited about faking, but writing it all as a play was a way of unloading the considerable amount of material I had accumulated. It was bliss to write a play, bliss to try to picture the stage and to know you were making an artificial thing and could do away with all of that scenery that the prose writer is constantly creating. If the play had been produced on Broadway and been a great success, no doubt I would have tried to write others, but since it was too long and produced only in a few truncated college versions, I received no encouragement to become a playwright. Evidently I don't feel strongly enough about the form to do it on my own. I've never enjoyed other people's plays, frankly, and I'm not a great theatregoer, so a number of things have combined to prevent me from trying another, though some day I might. I don't know the theatre very well, and I'm scared of getting involved with all those other people: the director, the actors, the agents.

You once described living in modern America as like skating on thin ice.

I don't remember saying that, but a lot of being alive is a little like thin ice. There's a sense that you must keep in motion or you'll fall through, that there's never a settled place. You look at European societies, let alone Asian societies, and there seem to be moments of rest, certain roles that people achieve whereby they are honoured by the societies. Think of how a fifty-five-year-old Italian man looks, with his grey hair and wonderfully trim suit – everything just so, everything exactly right on him. He is happy, filling his skin totally. English women of a certain social class have that same air of filling their skin. Their role, their expectations and their abilities are in exact accord, and there is a satisfaction. Here I don't think we are provided with these niches of final achievement. You always need a little more, are always running, always in motion, always having to prove something. That is I guess what I mean by skating on thin ice.

I believe Americans more than Englishmen have a sense of a void underneath, maybe because we came to a wilderness and there's so much of the land that's still wild and raw: the sense that nature is not a tame collection of fields and villages, and not a man-made thing; that we are strangers on the planet and the void is all around us. That's an American idea, a part of the bleakness Melville talks about: the American sense of reality that makes one anxious.

Do you feel pressure as a writer to reflect the times you live in?

At thirty I was on the crest of cultural developments: the songs being sung were the ones I was singing and so on. Now I'm fifty-eight, I'm aware of there having been several cultural waves since me. But in general I feel we all reflect the times we are alive in, are products of a certain set of decades and might as well admit it. Although not all of my books have specific years and dates, many of them do. We are all so calendar conscious in this day and age. The fashion designers change fashions, the news media keep producing new stories. It would be silly to try to write a timeless book about a century that is so very time conscious. Just by beginning to particularise, you're going to get into a certain time-specific feeling, no matter whether you want to. I always admired Ivy Compton-Burnett, who always wrote about families who were having their discussions around 1900, and she made it work. We're not too interested in what fifty-eight-year-olds do anymore; the interesting age for us as novel readers is the mating age, people, more or less, up to their thirties. It used to be that people or characters were all twenty, surprisingly young in fact.

The English novelist and critic Malcom Bradbury wrote of you: 'His books are uneasy celebrations of American life, troubled interplays between bright domestic interiors and dark history ... which sense like the couple themselves that Grace has gone but might be restored with aesthetic care and attention.' Do you believe that Grace has largely disappeared from the American way of life, and are you in the business of restoring it?

I've read that description and it seems just. Maybe it's not typically American, however. I was reading another English critic the other day, and she makes the point, about American writing in general, that it's all against a background of utopian expectation. The Puritans came here expecting to create a Utopia, so we Americans tend to be very hard on our own society, because it isn't perfect. No society is, but perhaps only this one expects to be perfect. My life has taken me from the Depression, of which I have selected memories, to the Second World War, which I remember quite well, from an adolescent's point of view, as a time when we and the British and some few others were fighting what seemed to be the forces of utter darkness. We emerged triumphant as well as very powerful, so obviously from the high plateau of 1945 there could only be a slide down.

I've been a witness to that long slide, but on a political level I'm probably more pro-American that most American writers, and more willing to give the government the benefit of the doubt. Nevertheless, in the texture of life around me, in the way people behave toward each other, the way the cities look, the amount of garbage of all kinds – garbage in the trash masher, garbage on the television sets – there's a lot to complain about. I suppose I have registered this is in my novels, but basically I try to describe the human condition as I happen to have seen it as an American. If I had been born in England or France, I would be writing about Englishmen or Frenchmen, but I happen to have been handed this subject and love the idea behind America and the natural landscape we were handed – or rather that we grabbed. But there's a lot wrong with the country when you compare it with the ideal we're trying to live by.

With so much talk of censorship in the air at the moment, would you say people's lives are particularly changed or affected by the fictions they read?

Well, mine has been. It's not the only thing that's affected my life, but certainly I've been affected by the books I've read, especially by a book like *Madame Bovary*. One is encouraged to fall in love by reading about people falling in love. In some sense our erotic expectations are shaped by what we read, as our notions of our responsibilities to society are also, I'd say, somewhat shaped. I'm trying to distinguish between my reactions as a citizen, as it were, and my reactions as a writer, because clearly, as a professional writer, I'm especially open to being affected by books. I'm always trying to learn how to do things or always willing to be surprised. But one very good American novel, *The Adventures of Augie March* by Saul Bellow, not only really told me about Chicago, which I'm happy to know, but also excited me and made me feel better about being American.

I think that censors are correct that books, even in this day and age, can be quite important. They're very important in societies where they're censored, and where, of course it has a reverse effect. The Soviet Union was until recently a country where writers mattered enormously because they were almost the only people who would even begin to tell the truth. They couldn't tell all of the truth, and they often got kicked out and had their books censored, but nevertheless, in both the Soviet Union and Tsarist Russia, they were caretakers of the truth. That will probably change as the pressure on them becomes less and less, and they'll eventually achieve the status of writers in the West, where what they say doesn't seem to matter much. But it does matter to a degree. Our notions of how to be human are to a considerable extent affected by what we read, and even if we don't read we go to the movies, we watch television shows prepared by people who have read, so in a way there's a trickle-down effect of significant writers in that it permeates pop culture and affects the way people act.

If my own books were censored, I'd quite mind it. I'm not used to it, of course. As an American I was raised on the Bill of Rights and so regard all attempts at censorship, even fairly mild ones, as a great affront. George Steiner kept telling us in his columns that Eastern European writers were better writers than Americans because they had to cope with censorship. This may be, but it's still not a price I want to pay. I don't like the revival of puritanical school boards and library staffs. The pernicious effects aren't so much at the front line, because there are lawyers to fight these suits and the censors often lose, but at a remove, when the publishers start to pull on their horns; they would rather not go to the trouble of seeing a controversial or too sexy text in print. So even when they apparently lose in the courts, the censors win in the publishing houses. I can't think of too many cases where I'd be for a book being censored. In wartime I might consider the right of the government to censor a book that gave away military secrets, but I certainly don't think there's anything sexual that should not be put into print now. I find censorship offensive, and every artist has an obligation to resist it.

What, indeed, about television? I would say that is a real issue. Without wanting to sound too pontifical, the United States has a fairly puritanical past. We were founded by Puritans, we participated in the great Victorian prudery, and in pop culture we have always lagged behind France and Britain with what could be shown. Bare breasts on television, for example, are highly uncommon here, not that I think that seeing the human body will harm children. Presumably they have experience in their own little lives of naked adult bodies. I would say the violence is more alarming than the sex.

I just wouldn't know where to draw the line, though neither would I trust the censors to know what's good and what's bad for us. No sooner had we suppressed violence on television than it might turn out that, psychologically, it was saving lives to have all this surrogate violence. Bruno Bettelheim wrote a very nice book about the violence in fairy stories and how they should not be bowdlerised, should not be made less violent, the violence being the point. It helps the child to exorcise its very real fears. So although I wouldn't say there never can be any censorship, in general I don't trust people who would administer it and I'd rather take my chances in a censor-free society.

Well-intentioned liberalism, some would claim, breeds ironies, such as that there have been more deaths in abortion clinics than in the whole of the Second World War. How do you, as a writer, cope with such ironies?

As a citizen you taken certain stands, like everybody else. You vote for certain candidates, have certain feelings, some strong and some weak, about positions. But almost all things worth discussing have two sides, so there is always more to be said about the paradox of liberalism. I was struck, during all the Vietnam protests, by the eagerness of American liberals to wish upon the South Vietnamese a kind of government they wouldn't want for themselves. That, to me, seemed paradoxical, but no doubt there's much to be said on the other side. As a writer of fiction, you can certainly enjoy having two opinions or more about everything, and give them each a voice. A novel is a good arena, not to vote, but to express your knowledge of the contradictions.

In writing fiction, I'm not compelled to express a view, but I am allowed to be as alert as possible to the paradox and the tension involved in all these instances. To be human, after all, is to live in a state of tension between opposites, making decisions that are the best of a series of bad choices. So many of our choices have a bad side. It's one of the things in which the Christian doctrine of original sin makes a kind of sense. We're in a position as humans where we cannot but do something wrong, no matter what we try.

At the time of the American involvement in Vietnam, you were misinterpreted and castigated as a 'hawk' and government supporter, but wouldn't a policy of non-interference have matched your sympathies more closely?

I just don't think that the United States, at least in the mid-1960s, could avoid interfering. The Vietnam involvement went back to Truman and Eisenhower, and Johnson was in a way just picking up the overdrawn cheques that other administrations had written. I suppose an all-wise government would intervene only where it could win, and stay out where it would lose, but I don't think there is any government that wise. I could understand perfectly well how we got into it. I could have wished we could get out, but I differ from many of my dovish confrères in understanding how we got there. It wasn't so different from Korea. We were trying to prevent the southern half of a country from being taken over by the northern half. I admired Truman for looking at China back in 1947 and saying we're not going to get involved with that. We didn't, and it's still running its course. I suppose an all-wise president would have looked at Vietnam and come to the same conclusion, but I did feel very sorry for the administration and for the Americans trying to make sense of this muddle, and I was shocked by the amount of hatred for our own government that seemed to be present in the young and the old in this society.

It seemed to me wrong to be enjoying the benefits of being an American and to pretend we could enjoy those benefits while always having clean hands. I don't think you can. Obviously the great power is great in part because it's willing to use force, but all peace, including our personal peace and our right to walk down the street, is based upon a threat of violence somewhere behind us. So I was happy when we got out of Vietnam and sorry we were there so long, but it seemed to me a more honourable attempt than was alleged by many.

Famous novelists are often called on to sign public petitions for good causes. Do you have any feelings about that sort of pressure being morally intrusive?

It is morally intrusive. On the other hand, if it's a cause I believe in I'm happy to sign. I've signed a number of petitions, but they may not be as common here as in England. I get a lot of requests from Britain, it's strange to say, to sign things, or to contribute to this and that. I have no quarrel with most liberal causes and I once signed a petition saying that Cassius Clay – Mohammad Ali – should be allowed to be heavyweight champion even though he had resisted going into the army. I got some theatre tickets for doing it, so I remember that particular cause with pleasure.

May I quote you something you wrote that reminded me of Blake: 'The essential self is innocent and when it tasted its own innocence, it knows that it lives forever'? Can you elaborate on that?

That's one of those feelings you don't have all the time, but there are moments when you seem to be tasting your essential self and the kind of bliss that goes with it. There's a moment near the end of *The White Hotel* by D. M. Thomas in which he describes this moment, a sense of revelation and of everlastingness that I think is a real human sensation for whatever reason. If we ever try in our imagination to delve beneath our circumstances toward our actual selfhood, as in the course of my memoir I did, I think we come upon something that tastes good rather than bad, that tastes delicious. Our basic feeling about cosmic matters is that somehow life is good, and that it is good to be alive and to be a witness to the world in its process. I suppose that's another way of talking about this essential innocence: a certain goodness at the root of things that we feel but can't prove.

You have had to contend with psoriasis, stuttering, claustrophobia, asthma. Have such problems tended to isolate you and turn you into an observer, hence a novelist?

The psoriasis was isolating to a degree where I felt insecure and didn't feel I had hundred-per-cent credentials for being human. I was embarrassed and in some way ashamed, and entered more timidly into the standard human adventures than I would have otherwise. On the other hand, psoriasis is not to be classed with having a real disease or bad eyesight or one arm. I want to keep it in proportion, but it certainly did have an isolating effect and made me feel that I was somehow singled out; and this feeling of being singled out also helped me in choosing a solitary profession. I think I'm less claustrophobic now than many people. I seem able to fly in aeroplanes and go through tunnels without much of a quiver, whereas some people really can't, so I'm not as claustrophobic, it turns out, as I thought. I've had a pretty successful life by and large, so that's eased me out of some of my neurotic feelings. Asthma was not good, but it seems to have been cat related and did go away. I still think of myself as a basically healthy person.

But you actually say that nothing, not even love and sexual contentment, has reconciled you to your psoriasis?

Certainly the psoriasis has made me doubt my humanity in the ideal way, and that kind of doubt isn't easily erased. The personality you acquire as a youthful psoriasis sufferer will stay with you all of your life. I'm really beyond being made to feel wonderful. My skin insists on having psoriasis. We've tried everything against it, with immediate success, and then a slow leakage back into failure. That's happening now, and now it's returning I realise that with it returns this sense of being unclean and unfit, which I suppose has the effect of channelling me into myself as a writer: the books don't have psoriasis, the books are clean. I've had a lot of love compared to many, but no amount of love would ease away the self-distrust that comes from having had psoriasis at such an early age as I did. I notice that my daughter, who has a little bit of it – it came on in her twenties – doesn't seem to have this really bad feeling. She just accepts it's normal. It's not her fault and it doesn't matter, whereas I feel it is my fault and does matter greatly.

Would you now see the early reviewer who said of you that you wrote very well but had nothing to say, as having passed an unintended compliment? Auden, whom you admire, once said that art cannot be a midwife to reality, so perhaps writing well is exactly what a novelist should do, and there is no real reason why he should be more right about life than anyone else, is there?

It was kind of a compliment, and Auden is to a degree right, though he is perhaps more right about poets than prose writers. The basic itch has to be the verbal itch, the wish to play with words; and content follows upon the fascination with words. It is felt of a prose writer in this country that he ought to have something to say, and it is true that you write best when you have something to say and your subject is sufficiently strong to give an energy and thrust into the writing. Therefore I was hurt to think I had nothing to say. It seemed to me I did have things to say, and that they weren't the things that had been said already. The trouble with that kind of critic is that he thinks everybody is going to write like Dreiser or James Jones, but I had my own message and my own particular slant, and I believe the fundamental desire, without which you do not have a writer, is the wish to make books and to find something to say. So I suppose it wasn't such a bad thing to have said about me, in a way.

Talking about the way a writer's work is reproduced endlessly, you called it 'a mode of self-assertion that leaves the cowardly perpetrator hidden and out of harm's way', but isn't the opposite true too – once something is in print there is no going back and you are subject to all the vagaries of taste and opinion?

On the one hand you are out of the rain, as we were saying earlier, but on the other you're getting all wet constantly because you've extended yourself, you've thrown this hostage out there. It's not you, it's cut off from you. It's like a baby, only even more remote than a baby. Once the publication has occurred, your mind is on other things and you don't really see the effects it's having on any but a few people. You read a few reviews, you get a few letters, you see the sales reports. Otherwise the book just fades away and you don't have to harvest the results. It's not like a personal act where you must be there to reap the grain, so it's an extension of you, but a relatively painless one. I've always had a distinct feeling that I am myself John Updike and have a certain history and birthdate and a certain body, but that what my books say is quite detached from that, is in a way the real me. I try to be honest, to describe what it's like to be a person, an American male, but it's not really me and I don't feel endangered by the books as they make their way in the world.

You asserted that: 'My assets as a novelist I take to be my taste for American life acquired in Shillington'. What is it that is really characteristic of American life?

Having written that, I wonder if it is true. Maybe I've had enough American life. We are certainly becoming more European as we become more civilised and the wilderness recedes. Yet Europe has learned many lessons from America in the past forty-five years, but the difference, I suppose, is that this country was based upon the notion of equality. It was there at the very start in the Puritan settlements, was reinforced by the Constitution and the Bill of Rights, and the notion we are all equal and must prove ourselves is still there. So we are not hopelessly handicapped by any conditions of class, even of race, though certainly to be black in this country isn't an easy row to hoe. Then there's the fact that so much of our culture is in the way of being lowest-common-denominator culture. On the one hand, it's vulgar and simple minded, on the other there's a kind of energy. Think of the Hollywood movies of the 1930s and the 1940s, which were mass culture with a vengeance, yet they now seem works of art in their style. We're able to see that in fact this was an art form and that it can't be done now. I like the levelling that happened in America and the fact that any structure is going to be put up from scratch. You can begin again, and every generation begins again. That's what I would say the difference is between America and Europe.

In view of some rather unsavoury aspects of Christianity through the centuries, what now remains of Christianity in your view that seems worth clinging to?

Well, it says: 'Fear not.' It tries to assuage our basic dread, to placate our fear that comes from being a death-foreseeing animal. The New Testament also holds out the idea of people being equal in the sight of God, and that is as useful a way to try to form society as any. It obviously holds up a number of other ideals, not all of which it has always lived up to, but I like the need, the empowering yes of it.

In my own life I've taken courage from a sense that I was doing something useful and relatively harmless, but to some extent the energy has all been generated by faith, and by unreasonable faith, because it's a long way from Shillington to the Ritz Carlton. And so, having lived by faith, I intend to be more indulgent of faith.

I'd say my Christianity is a way of coping with life. It regularises my week, puts something in it that is entirely voluntary. I get to see a lot of other people who've also gotten up on a Sunday morning and put on their good clothes, and it holds up a set of standards that aren't strictly worldly. It says there are other standards, and it's healthy for a writer to realise that what matters so much maybe isn't the results we get but the spirit in which we do something. Sometimes the best success comes to people who don't try too hard, and Christianity has enabled me maybe not to try too hard but to try enough.

I wouldn't say I've found that I become more religious as I get older. I was most religious when I was in my twenties and most scared. The older I get the less scared I seem to be, and in a sense the less needy. Yet I'm still a church-going Protestant, though it's been many years since I read theology with any real passion. I used to read a fair amount of it. I was so desperate to find some place where I could stand. Now I seem to think I'm standing on a place, but the rug could be pulled out from under me at any moment.

I don't think a society should enforce religion. In this country there's a lot of constitutional language saying it should not, though America does seem a little too pious. All the presidents talk about God, for example, at though he's right next door, even though some of them have not been very religious, or at least very faithful churchgoers. It seems very bad when a country professes an official religion, and I would resist that here, and resist even the tendencies towards it. Government of the society presided over should be minimal. It should be the least number of laws that can create order, and everything else should be left up to human initiative and human emotion, even human whim. A society that tries to create goodness is in danger of becoming a tyranny. The constitution, as I understand it, doesn't expect people to be good but allows for them to be bad up to a certain point and then says the rest must step in. This seems a more realistic approach than the kind of total package the ayatollahs of Iran, say, would like to enforce, or which you find, for that matter, in Mao's China, where a total lifestyle, a total set of directives is offered to you by the state.

For the last ten years or so you have displayed signs of anxiety at growing old. Are you fearful for your art, or is it more do with mortality?

One doesn't like being mortal, and one certainly doesn't like feeling one's body stiffen and age under one. I'm not in bad shape at fifty-eight, but there are things I used to be able to do that I can't. I used to be able to hold a broomstick in my two hands and jump up in the air and over it while still holding it. This is not a great accomplishment, but it was something I could do, and at a party in the late hours I would sometimes do it and astound the other party-goers. When I was little I used to wonder how these big people around me could stand being so close to death, and still walk around, smiling, being silly and cheerful, reading the newspaper. How could they hack it? Now I'm in that position, I see that you hack it in part because you have no choice.

I don't think that I'm abnormally aware of being old. My wife has a healthy and brisk attitude towards the ageing process. She doesn't deny it, but she thinks life is there to be lived and our duty, as long as we're alive, is to enjoy it in some way. A lot of writers are dead at my age, and certainly many are dead as writers, so some of that may be a pep talk to myself, saying don't give up, don't stop trying, don't get complacent, keep trying to learn. You have fewer grey cells, but maybe you can make better use of the ones you have. There are advantages to being fifty-eight. A lot of decisions have been made already, a lot is behind you. Your child-raising years are over, you've made your career choices. In a way your mind is clearer to concentrate on meaningful things. I'm aware that I tend to make my men older than myself. I put a lot of them in their sixties, for some reason. My present novel is all about getting old and useless, though I myself still feel in pretty good shape.

Do you still feel you have an unfulfilled task?

I haven't many regrets, things I'd go back and change. I've certainly behaved badly on occasions and foolishly on others, but the basic decisions of my life were the choice of profession, where to live, which women to marry, which college to go to. I've been lucky in those decisions. I think they've been the right ones, and the world has tended to confirm me in that thought.

I have hopes of writing books better than the ones I've written. I do feel I have something still to say, and to locate that thing and say it seems possible and worth doing. I'm in a position in which what I write will get published, will get some attention, so I'm well located and should try to measure up to the opportunity I still have.

I'd like to think I'm pretty adventurous still. A certain safety enshrouds me now. I can't escape safety to a degree, especially since American writers, as we've said, burn out so notoriously that if I do nothing it'll be no great disgrace; I'll merely be behaving like most of my predecessors. If I look back on my novels, they've all had an element of self-challenge. They're all stunts in a way, they all had some trick at their heart. I don't know if that's good or bad, but I was able to write them because the trick amused me.

Fiction is potentially frivolous, and since I came from a line of practical people, doing something so impractical and making a living at it makes me feel guilty in a way. My initial ambition was aimed a little under where I've actually landed. I wanted merely to be a cartoonist or a magazine writer and to make a living at it. Instead I've found myself catapulted into trying to write literature, really trying to write lasting and significant stuff. I suppose the kind of language I use is a way of protecting myself from the true awesomeness of trying to write really well. It doesn't mean I don't try to write well, but I have to frame it in some way a little lightheartedly or bashfully to make it possible to be productive, because it's quite possible to get overawed by writing. The only final response to the awesomeness of what you're trying to do is silence, and I don't want to become silent.

Appendix

The following two pieces are not written down using the interview construction of the other forty-nine. However, both were based on extensive
discussions between Naim Attallah and the two subjects and are included
here because of their interest.

MARK BIRLEY

Mark Birley, born in Sussex in 1930, was the only son of Captain Sir Oswald Birley, the portrait painter. He went to prep school in Devon and then to Eton. He spent a year at Oxford and then did his National Service in the Intelligence Corps. After six years with an advertising agency he decided to go into the nightclub business. In 1954 he married Annabel Vane-Tempest-Stewart, daughter of the eighth Marquis of Londonderry. They had three children but suffered the tragic loss of the eldest, Rupert, in Africa a few years before this interview. Mark Birley was the founder of Annabel's in Berkeley Square, named after his wife (who went on to marry Sir James Goldsmith), Harry's Bar and Mark's Club. He opened a health club, the Bath and Racquets Club, and launched a men's fragrance, Mark Birley for Men. The Walbrook Club was opened in the City of London in 2000. He died in 2007.

Any question about my relationship with my mother is rather hard to answer. It must have had some kind of lasting effect. It wasn't so much a strange relationship, more the absence of any normal relationship. To her credit she was very keen on my taking an interest in everything artistic, including music and the ballet – she had been one of the original supporters of the Diaghilev ballet – but I was not musical. I think we got on better in her later years because there was nothing left to disagree or argue over. An absence of affection, that was the point. We were rather a divided family: my sister and I, my mother and my father. It was a pretty good mess.

I suppose the fact that my father was fifty when I was born must have made for some remoteness in the relationship there. I was extremely fond of him, but he was almost like a grandfather. We were sometimes rather united about Mama. The age gap was wide between them as well. I always got on pretty well with my father, but there were too many people pulling in too many different directions in the family: my mother saying one thing, my sister another and my father trying to get on with his work and painting and wanting a bit of peace and quiet occasionally. You can hardly blame him.

I never really thought of my nanny as being a kind of surrogate mother figure, but in a sense I suppose that is what she was. She's still alive today at 96, and quite extraordinary. She has had every kind of stroke and should have gone but hasn't. She has moments of rather brief lucidity. I was devoted to her as a child. Frankly I was glad to leave that period of my childhood behind me, although I've wiped my mind pretty clear of all the bad things that happened. I expect it was Annabel who told you I detested Eaton. I didn't detest it at all. I was relatively happy there, the thing about the place being that you had your own room and felt you were a bit grown up as soon as you arrived.

I do admit to having many regrets about wastage of time. I certainly didn't work hard enough during my only year at Oxford. At that stage I lacked any sense of direction and didn't know what I was going to do afterwards. Not that many people do know, but I think I was more lacking in purpose and direction than most of my contemporaries. I had certain artistic ambitions at one point because I was born with a talent for drawing. Had I worked at it, I probably could have done something with it, but I grew bored. I didn't know what I wanted to be, but I knew I didn't want to be an artist, though that, in any case, was a time when artistic talents were being treated rather contemptuously. Had I been born in France, things would probably have been quite different.

The point where I first came into my own was, I think, when I opened a sort of advertising office, some years before Annabel's got going. At least the agency represented independence and I had it for quite a few years. Looking back, it was really great fun. Afterwards I had the Hermès shop in the corner of Piccadilly Arcade and Jermyn Street, but then I came to think that what I wanted was somewhere bigger and better, probably in Bond Street. Annabel's was just starting, however, and so I sold out, having decided I wasn't after all really interested in embarking on a larger shop which would only have taken up much more of my time.

Annabel's arose out of my friendship with John Aspinall. When gambling became legal, he was looking for suitable premises. I already had an idea for some kind of piano bar somewhere, something on a relatively modest scale. No. 44 Berkeley Square had then been empty for about 12 years, and after Aspinall saw it himself, he told me I ought to take a look. Of course, the basement to the house was very small, but we had the garden dug out and we connected up the whole building. I needed to persuade people to invest in it since I didn't have any money myself just then.

While Annabel's was being built, I was trying to gather a little team around me, and even then I realised that the key person was going to be the manager. I knew perfectly well that, unless I had the right person, I would be in every kind of trouble because I didn't really know how to do it myself. I remember calling at the Mirabelle and saying to Louis, the manager there, 'I'm looking for a manager. If you can think of anyone you think might be suitable, please let me know.' It simply didn't occur to me that he would want to come to me, but it was just at the time when the Mirabelle was being taken over and its staff were a bit unsettled. Louis said he thought he might be interested himself, and of course that was my lucky break, because he has been with me ever since and without Louis the story could have been very different. Then Mabel, whom I'd known at the old Wilton's, came to run the ladies' room, and still does, and George Hobart, whom I'd known at Jules' Bar, was barman, though he has since died.

I know there are a lot of people who think I'm very difficult about a lot of things. Who's put you up to asking? I suppose it is true, yes, because I want to get people to think the same way as I'm thinking straight away, and if I can do that, then everything's fine. With Louis, for example, we mesh well and we've hardly had a cross word in the last 27 years. The fact that I insist on my staff always addressing me formally doesn't indicate a lack of friendliness or camaraderie or anything of that kind, it's just that I feel that degree of formality should be maintained. When you're not working, it's a different matter altogether, but I don't really like the American system where everybody's Jim and Bob and goodness knows what, and everything's wonderful, except on Monday, when it's, 'Bob, you've done a great job but we need your desk.' That's all superficial.

I'm not good on committees. One of my failings is a lack of patience, and when I feel I'm right about something and that everyone else is wrong, then the whole process of listening to all the arguments makes me rather impatient. I'm used to taking my own decisions in my business without reference to anybody else, obviously within the constraints of what is possible. That rather autocratic way of running things has advantages and disadvantages, but one of the main advantages is that it makes for speed and makes your employees happier, I think. They like somebody who can say yes or no.

Speaking of management really does hit on one of the problems. I find that aspect very difficult. I suppose I've got about 200 staff now, and one of the difficulties occurs in part because my headquarters in Hays Mews is exactly the same as it was when I started 28 years ago and I can't make it any bigger. Another office, in Charles Street, deals with the accounts side of the business, but the businesses are actually managed in quite an unorthodox way. It is still all a bit of a one-man band. The latest effort of building the Baths and Racquets Club has put a great strain on the office, because it took a great deal of time and effort. The new club's been open about a year now, and I still have endless problems with water leakages, builders and staffing. It needs a hell of a lot of everyday attention.

Management is a simple reason why I remain reluctant to take Annabel's across the Atlantic, though people keep suggesting I should do so. The usual concept behind this operation is to pick it up, put some paper round it, get on Concorde and dump it on a corner of Fifth Avenue. Yet I couldn't very well stay in America for a year or so and leave everything here in London to get on with itself. It would never work out.

I'll give you an example. Harry's Bar in Venice is owned by Arrigo Cipriani, who inherited it from his father as a kind of license to print money. He wasn't content with that and he had to go to America and get involved in a great shemozzle in New York, transporting all the key staff from Venice to New York. Of course, the bar in Venice started to go downhill. Who needs these headaches? He certainly didn't need the money, so what was the point? Nobody is content nowadays to do what they do and stick to it. It was the same with Geoffrey Vennison, who was very well known as a wonderful antique dealer before he became an interior decorator and did so much for Annabel's and Mark's Club. He also became a very great friend, and was a splendid raconteur as well as a bit of a snob. Well, whenever Concorde tickets arrived from all these very rich ladies in New York who said, 'Will you come and advise us on our cushions?' Geoffrey couldn't resist it, and off he had to go. It killed him, you know.

It's not so much perfectionism I'm after in the way I run Annabel's as the way I think things ought to be. This is not necessarily the same as perfection. I just want to get everything right in the way I think to be best. Of course, it is a matter of going on and on for years and staying interested enough to try to improve things.

In some funny way, Annabel's has managed to satisfy people's needs. It's a place they really like to be in. If you asked a selection of people to define their ideal nightclub, they would all answer with different specifications, but probably none of them would answer truthfully because they will all have little secrets which they're not going to disclose. But I think I happen to know what some of these secrets are, and Annabel's incorporates a few of them. Since I launched Annabel's, quite a number of other clubs have sprung up, and every time a new one comes along there's a fresh wave of excitement. I know perfectly well that a lot of people will go rushing off there, but equally I'm pretty certain that they'll be back. I strongly believe that, if you do your utmost to look after people properly, they will remain loyal.

Contrary to what one might suppose, there haven't been many appalling scenes in Annabel's. There really haven't been any big fights, though we've had lots of drunken behaviour. Geoffrey Keating, who used to be in charge of public relations at BP and who helped to promote Montgomery's reputation when he was on his staff during the war, used to sit there as if he owned the place. Whenever things got too much, after he'd insulted whole parties of Arabs and so on, we had a procedure for getting him out. One of the doormen used to walk him home through Berkeley Square, and as he passed the J. Walter Thompson Building, he would stop, undo his flies and pee into the letterbox with great accuracy all over J. Walter Thompson's expensive stationery. After that he would be quite happy. He was like a lamb once he'd been lead home. The stories of Geoffrey in Annabel's are absolutely legion. I used to have frightful rows with him, but I adored him. He was one of my greatest friends, and was never frightened about the consequences of his behaviour, drunk or sober.

Perhaps I do have a slightly withdrawn personality, though it depends on the circumstances. I'm the opposite to extrovert, I suppose. I need to have people around me, but I don't need a lot of people. People think I'm a melancholic because I'm not forever grinning at everybody. Nowadays everybody is expected to wear a permanent grin from ear to ear.

I find it perfectly easy to have close relationships, but I also find I've reached a point in life where I'm probably not going to make, or don't particularly wish to make, many more close friends. Certainly, there are a lot of people I love to see and who are going to be friends, but I'm not going to make anymore very intimate friends. We all know hundreds and hundreds of people and it all becomes too much. The assumption of a lack of warmth on my part springs from an attitude of, oh my God, this restaurant owner really hasn't been to charm school, has he? I'm expected to remember everybody's name from either side of the Atlantic, and to say all those things people say when they're 21. That's not my style. One of my strengths at Annabel's and the clubs is that, when I'm there, I think of myself as a kind of customer and so get a detached feeling about it. This is very helpful. If you allow yourself to grow too close to it all, you can only attend to detail and you can't see the thing whole.

If Louis says that I have a wonderful sense of humour, then all I can tell you is that Louis' idea of a good sense of humour is so awful and disgusting that the girls in the office have to be trained to listen to the stories he produces. As for being happy, I think it all depends. I don't know that you can exist in a permanent state of blissful happiness, though you go through periods of happiness. If you are too happy too much of the time, it seems to imply some kind of complacency that is rather unattractive. I realise I have a reputation for being a misery. I can become unhappy for all kinds of reasons, but to call me melancholic is to aim wide of the mark. If people say I find it difficult to show affection and to trust on an emotional level, there is maybe some truth in it. You've been doing quite a lot of research, I must say.

No, I wouldn't consider that the British have good taste. If we're talking about the post-war years, I would say most definitely not, and in fact they've been swayed in the opposite direction in hundreds of different ways. Architecture is the most obvious example. I'm one hundred per cent behind Prince Charles on that one. The whinging of architects who feel they shouldn't be criticised by anybody unless it's by another architect seems quite extraordinary. It's such a pity we don't have a Lutyens around today.

My own passion for collecting is a sort of acquisitiveness, I suppose. I can get caught up in a new interest at the drop of a hat. If I had the time to go round all the salesrooms, there would be no end to the stuff I could get interested in. At Sotheby's recently they had the most beautiful old picnic baskets which I wanted to buy, but I didn't manage to go.

I once had the most frightful disaster, bidding for some drawings at Christie's. My secretary is very good at bidding – very quiet about it where I get over-excited. Here in the office that morning I told her I wanted her to bid for 10 drawings and that when I wanted her to stop bidding then I would shake my head. Simple. The trouble was that we went separately to Christie's and I couldn't find her when I reached the salesroom. When the lots came up I thought she'd disappeared off the face of the earth, so started bidding myself. Just as the items were being knocked down to me, the auctioneer said, 'Ah, a new bidder at the end of the room,' and on the bidding went again. When I got out of the salesroom, I found my secretary and asked, 'Where the hell have you been?' She replied, 'Well, I couldn't find you, but luckily I managed to buy one or two.' By bidding against me, she had managed to pay the world record price for one drawing.

I see quite a lot of Annabel, and yes, she is a most important person in my life. Getting married to her was the most important thing that happened to me, and Annabel, when all is said and done, probably shaped my life more than any other person, though without being particularly aware of what she was doing. The thing that you say she said to you, about me being the true love of her life, is reciprocated. Though if Jimmy Goldsmith walked into this room now, I'd be perfectly pleased to see him.

My God, do you have that typed out: 'Difficult to have as a lover, but, once the affair is over, the most wonderful friend?' I'm sure the first statement is absolutely true. I'm not aware of being so difficult, but I suppose whoever told you must be right. I feel very comfortable in the company of women. By today's standards, I should think I probably discovered women pretty late. It was after I left school, I suppose, when I was up at Oxford. They have been important in my life, but none more so than Annabel, you know. But if I have never remarried, it's not because I consciously avoid long-term relationships. I have been with the same person now for quite a long time, and I don't know whether we'll get married or not. We probably will.

In respect of possessing patience, I probably made a very bad father. I should have gone to my children's school more often, but I think they probably forgave me for not doing so. I remember one awful sports day, pouring with rain, when Rupert found a pavilion, and said, 'Pup, don't you worry, you stay in here. I'll go and get you a glass of brandy.' All the other parents were busy doing something constructive around the place, talking to the masters or whatever, but I hated it. The children were certainly very much closer to their mother at the beginning and, to be truthful, probably are still, but we got on with each other well now.

When you look at your children, I think you look to see whether your own worst characteristics are emerging, but Robin, for example, is much more mature at 30 than I was at his age. He has a better aptitude for business; he's extremely hard-working. He gets up very early in the morning, a thing that I have always found very difficult to do. My daughter is the only one who has really inherited my artistic ability, and now she fully understands that talent needs to be combined with a lot of hard work to produce results. She is a good artist. I sense she's going to do great things. She is enormously talented and is working hard; she paints in oils, she draws. She has always drawn since she was a child, but now she has a very disciplined pencil. Her first exhibition was a great success and she's going to have another. John Ward, whose opinion I respect, thinks highly of her.

It is rather difficult to know whether one of my children will take over from me when I retire. I think Robin would eventually be quite interested, if for no other reason than that it could be a hell of a launching pad for something else. Rupert was far more literary. He would have liked to be a writer. When I asked him what benefit he thought he had derived from Oxford, he said it was the ability to write. When he came down, he found it quite difficult to get a job. I'm all for people going to university, but I think that too many sons and daughters go up to Oxford and Cambridge and are promised by their tutors that the world is theirs if only they get a decent second in PPE – Philosophy, Politics and Economics. It's not necessarily the case. I felt that Robin could have gone up to Oxford quite easily, but part of the strength of his position today is that he did not do so, but started work instead. Things have been difficult for Robin for various reasons, mainly because of an accident he suffered in childhood, when he was only 11. He was mauled by a tiger and the injuries were very serious. The lower part of his face was crushed in the tiger's jaws and he came within an inch of death. Luckily there was a hospital which dealt with motorway accidents and urgent cases only two or three miles away. They got him there very quickly, he was operated on and they managed to save his life.

The boys absolutely adored each other, though I would say that Rupert was the closest to me. I'm sure he could have become an accomplished writer, but unfortunately he wanted first to prove to all his contemporaries that he wasn't just some vague scribbler, that he could actually make a success in business too. So he went to Togo. I don't know if you've ever been there. I hope you never have to go. All I can say about it is that it is a bloody miserable place. Even the American ambassador to Togo apologised to me for just being there. Rupert didn't exactly like it either, but he managed to make friends in a most extraordinary way. Everybody adored him. When I got out there after the accident, the warmth of feeling I found for him was quite extraordinary.

I did discuss with Rupert whether he would ever want to take over from me, but he was very sensitive and didn't want to be given anything on a plate which he felt he hadn't rightfully earned. He also felt that that would be unfair from Robin's point of view, so he was rather confused about what he should do. But quite certainly I think that he would've come into the business eventually.

On the subject of tragedies in my life, I'll tell you something. I really hate people who wear their emotions on their sleeves. I simply don't want to show how I feel sometimes, and if I can manage to conceal it, so much the better. The spectacle of a man breaking down in front of people, in public, is always rather a sad thing to witness. I'd rather it wasn't me. In Rupert's case, at least there was something I could do. I was sitting out on my balcony having a cup of coffee before going to the office when my secretary rang and said she had someone from Togo on the line. I absolutely knew at that second that the news was bad. All they could tell me was that Rupert couldn't be found.

There was no reason at that point, or even after we got out there – Robin came with me – to assume he was dead. There was certainly no time to sit and mope. The question of abduction arose and we felt we had to get to the truth of the matter. I called in a firm of investigators, which deal mostly with kidnappings, and I must say they were very good, very thorough. At all events, we satisfied ourselves that there was no question of an abduction. Rupert used to go swimming at a particularly horrible beach where the currents were strong and you could easily be dragged out. There had been quite a number of other cases where people weren't recovered, and this is what almost certainly happened with Rupert. It was a very great shock to us all. Robin was absolutely marvellous. I had to have awful phone calls with Annabel, who used to sit by the telephone in London waiting for me to ring in the evening. I went back to that bloody God-forsaken place to or three times. I think Rupert was the only white man who ever went out there through choice. I miss him terribly.

I would describe myself as being more heart than head. I am perhaps a little on the cynical side sometimes, but hard-headed, no. I am vulnerable to failure, or when I lose a friendship, and I dare say self-esteem comes in there a little bit. But I am hyper-sensitive, not thick-skinned at all, and I very easily get hurt.

We've all got regrets, mostly about things we didn't do rather than things we did. Timing is also important. I would like to have done everything a few years earlier. Probably we all feel like that. I expect I would live my life differently if I had the chance again. One often thinks, if only I was 25 years younger and knew what I know now. It would be like putting a bull who had already had one fight into the ring. I'd have been a much better student and everything else. In those days the dividend, if there was one, seemed far too remote to be worth bothering about. On top of that, schools were then very different. Boys nowadays look forward to going back to school after their holidays because they have much more fun. They have more freedom, they're more grown up and, of course, they travel. I was at school during the war years, and went abroad only in 1946 or 1947 for the first time, when I was 17. I know children nowadays who have been absolutely everywhere by the time they're 12.

I'm not unduly apprehensive about the future. In general, I feel reasonably confident and optimistic. I am not planning to take on a lot more work. I think I'd rather work a bit less fairly soon, though I don't see that I can retire. Anyway, what is it one would retire to? A kind of blank day.

MOSHE MENUHIN

In 1989 Naim Attallah interviewed Yehudi Menuhin after receiving a strong recommendation from Richard Ingrams. Several years before that he had struck up a friendship with his father, Moshe Menuhin, who was then living in California. Moshe had written to Attallah after the publication in 1979 of *The Palestinians*, with a text by Jonathan Dimbleby and photographs by Don McCullin.

The book was virtually the first of its kind to describe the Palestinian side of the conflict from the years of the British Mandate to the creation of the Zionist state and its consequences. The tone of the book was temperate, well balanced and objective. Nevertheless, the Zionist lobby attacked it mercilessly. Amid the vocal turmoil of the assault, one Jew stood apart to express the voice of reason.

This was Moshe. He sent Attallah not only a warm letter of congratulations for having published the book, but also a tape-recorded interview he had done with Colin Edwards, a British journalist, about his life as a young boy in the city of Jerusalem. It was high time, he said, that someone stuck up for the Palestinian Arabs and gave their side of the story. The tape, when Naim Attallah came to play it over, moved him totally. After that, although he never met him face to face, they kept up a regular correspondence till Moshe's death in 1983.

The tape has lost none of its significance, and is of even more topicality today when the international community is renewing attempts to find an equitable solution in the Middle East. Earlier failures to resolve 'the Palestinian question' have undoubtedly shaped the world we live in and our fears for its future to a phenomenal degree. The voice of Moshe Menuhin takes us back to a basic understanding, buried under years of Jewish and Arab rhetoric, and for that reason alone we feel it should be transcribed in full. With this goes the hope that it may move people in the way it did Naim Attallah when he first heard it more than three decades ago.

When I was taken to old Jerusalem by my mother I was a little embarrassed because I had ear locks and was wearing a kaftan, like a long nightdress, so the boys of the Jewish colonists, who were already more 'civilised', looked down on this Jewish boy with his ear locks, though no one ever harmed me. The Arabs, I always found, were friendly, decent, kind people, entertaining me, talking to me. We used to hike from Jerusalem to certain places holy to the Arabs, the Jews, the Christians, to certain non-kosher areas where Jews were not supposed to go. Every summer I went to Rehovat to eat grapes on an uncle's estate, eating them till I was sick, though it was supposed to be good for me. At the end of my stay one of the Arabs who worked for my uncle drove me to Ramallah, where in those days not a Jew ever lived. He would let me off the horse and buggy to sit around outside the railway station to wait for the train from Jaffa to take me back to Jerusalem. Nobody ever molested me, I wasn't afraid, I wasn't aware of being a foreigner. (I spoke Arabic fluently by the way.)

Under Turkish Ottoman rule, the officials, the judges, the working people were all Arabs. There were about 35,000 of us when we arrived in Palestine, just a meek, quiet Jewish bunch. There was no such thing as oppression from the Muslims. I could never apply the word 'oppression'. I cannot recall a single incident. The Arabs gave me more joy than the Jews ever did. They were nearer to life and the Jews had obstructing safeguards against mixing with the world. In those days there was no interest among the Orthodox in Dr Herzl and his Zionist movement. The insane political nationalism that would give rise to the First World War was meanwhile taking its hold in Europe and becoming the religion of the world, and the Zionists swallowed it. I would go to the House of the People in Jerusalem to hear when Zionists – non-religious Jews – gave lectures and used to arouse the people with the slogan 'Our nation, our country, our homeland' and of course people fell for the clever speaker.

Already there was the preliminary to warring from the Jews among themselves. You were told don't go to an Arab dentist, don't go to an Arab merchant, or a grocer or fruit trader, even though there weren't enough Jewish traders to go around. People had to buy from Arabs, but there was this constant programme of preaching individually. We had good teachers at the gymnasium in Jaffa, but I would say, to summarise, that underneath the teachings there was one principle premise, repeated again and again, 'Our country, our nation, our homeland'.

Yet I cannot recall one student in the entire gymnasium – and they were all nice boys and girls who'd been born in Arab Palestine. We were all immigrants who'd come from Russia to escape the pogroms, or to get a Jewish education, or a Zionist education in most cases. Day after day we heard the slogan whenever a teacher could stick it in; even in science they somehow managed it. It was to subvert us, to poison us into becoming Jewish nationalists. I never met a rabbi and there were no religious services of any kind they were all agnostics or atheists. The gymnasium became a hotbed for wild, insane political nationalism. We were taught to hate the Arabs, to despise them, and to drive them out from 'our' homeland, 'our' country, 'ours' not theirs, quoting the Bible, of course. For five years they were pumping into me the Jewish nationalism, Zionism; happily, for me as a civilised being who belongs to the world and not to any nationalist group, unsuccessfully.

There were few Jewish colonists: 35,000 Jews where there were 600,000 normal, healthy, hard-working, innocent, unknowledgeable Arabs. There were few farming cooperatives, though I always remember the kibbutzim with affection and admiration. Many a time I slept and worked on the kibbutzim in Galilee during my student days. The kibbutz was the one and only outstanding, eternal contribution that Israel might contribute to the world if it stops going back on itself, as it begins to do already now, and stressing political nationalism. There were 2,000 or 3,000 Jews among the cooperative farms of Galilee. The Arabs could have wiped us out in no time if there had been any organised scheme, but there was no group that planned to do anything among the Arab population. They were individuals. Zionist fanatics and Orthodox fanatics now kept going to Palestine, but most of the Jewish people chose to go to the United States, to Canada, to South Africa, to South America. Even ten or so years after the Balfour Declaration in 1917, Weizman had to go to Romania to plead with the Jews, 'Look, we extracted the Balfour Declaration out of the British, and now they keep asking us, "Where are your Jews?" If we are to have a Heretz Israel, come to Palestine.'

There were 9,000 Jews who came in, though 6,000 emigrated. It was only when the Jews had to run away from Germany, or from Russia to work in Palestine, that there came in any numbers the Jews who were ghetto Jews, who had a hatred for the gentiles and then had it a hundred-fold for the goy in Palestine.

As a boy I suffered terribly from bad teeth. They were uneven and some of them protruded to cut my lips. At one point the pain became so unbearable that, when I was walking through a narrow alley in the old city and saw a sign indicating an Arab dentist, I stopped and went inside. After negotiating some narrow stairs, I reached a crowded waiting room where people sat awaiting their turn to be seen by the dentist. I sat myself down in a corner and stayed there till the room had emptied and the dentist treated his last patient. As he came out of his surgery he saw me sitting there, obviously in great pain. Although he was ready to leave for home, and I had neither appointment nor the money with which to pay him, he invited me to come into the surgery. As he examined my teeth he was horrified by the rotten state in which he found them. If I came to the surgery the same time each day, he suggested, he would attend to me and not expect to be paid for his services. At the end of the treatment I said the day would perhaps come when I could repay my debt to him. He simply replied, 'Ask your people not to stir trouble so we can live side by side and share the land of our forefathers.'

Many, many decades later, when I was living in old age in California, I had occasion one day to see a dentist, and he was astounded at the good condition of my teeth. Then I told him the story of that kind and wonderful Palestinian dentist who had looked after my teeth as a boy in Palestine, and treated them with such love and dedication. That is the reason why I find it always traumatic to watch pictures on the television of scenes in the Palestinian refugee camps and the misery surrounding them, wondering whether any descendants of my noble dentist benefactor languish there with no hope of ever seeing their land again.